MIDDLE CLASS SHANGHAI

OTHER BOOKS BY CHENG LI ON SHANGHAI
AND THE CHINESE MIDDLE CLASS

The Power of Ideas (2017)

China's Emerging Middle Class (2010, ed.)

Bridging Minds across the Pacific (2005, ed.)

Rediscovering China (1997)

MIDDLE CLASS SHANGHAI

Reshaping U.S.-China Engagement

CHENG LI

BROOKINGS INSTITUTION PRESS
Washington, D.C.

The Brookings Institution is a private nonprofit organization devoted to research, education, and publication on important issues of domestic and foreign policy. Its principal purpose is to bring the highest quality independent research and analysis to bear on current and emerging policy problems. Interpretations or conclusions in Brookings publications should be understood to be solely those of the authors.

Artwork Plates: ShanghART

Library of Congress Control Number: 2021932884

ISBN 9780815739098 (hardcover)
ISBN 9780815739104 (ebook)

9 8 7 6 5 4 3 2 1

Typeset in Minion Pro

Composition by Meghan Healey

In memory of

Qu Shaoxu (1980–2018)

whose migration from Shandong to Shanghai
embodied the struggles and dreams of securing a
middle-class life in an evolving nation

CONTENTS

Artwork plates follow page 294.

LIST OF FIGURES AND TABLES

TABLES

ABBREVIATIONS

AI	artificial intelligence
APEC	Asia-Pacific Economic Cooperation
APIs	active pharmaceutical ingredients
BLM	Black Lives Matter
BRI	Belt and Road Initiative
BRICS	Brazil, Russia, India, China, and South Africa
CAS	Chinese Academy of Sciences
CASS	Chinese Academy of Social Sciences
CATI	computer-assisted telephone interviewing
CDC	Centers for Disease Control and Prevention
CCG	Center for China and Globalization
CCP	Chinese Communist Party
CCYL	Chinese Communist Youth League
CEIBS	China Europe International Business School
CELAC	Community of Latin America and Caribbean States
CGP	chemistry graduate program
CMC	Central Military Commission
CPPCC	Chinese People's Political Consultative Conference
CPS	Central Party School
CSSA	Chinese Students and Scholars Associations
CSSC	China State Shipbuilding Corporation
CUSBEA	China–United States Biochemistry Examination and Application program
CUSPEA	China–United States Physics Examination and Application program

CVRD	Companhia Vale do Rio Doce
DRAM	dynamic random-access memory
GDP	gross domestic product
AGP	Agreement on Government Procurement
FARA	Foreign Agents Registration Act
FBI	Federal Bureau of Investigation
FDI	foreign direct investment
FTZ	free-trade zone
HSBC	Hong Kong and Shanghai Banking Corporation
IMF	International Monetary Fund
IOT	Internet of Things
IPR	intellectual property rights
LGBTQ	lesbian, gay, bisexual, transgender, and queer/questioning
MNCs	multinational corporations
NBA	National Basketball Association
NDAA	National Defense Authorization Act
NDB	New Development Bank
NDRC	National Development and Reform Commission
NGO	nongovernmental organization
NIH	National Institutes of Health
NPC	National People's Congress
NYSE	New York Stock Exchange
PBOC	People's Bank of China
PLA	People's Liberation Army
PPE	personal protective equipment
PRC	People's Republic of China
PSA	Power Station of Art
PSC	Politburo Standing Committee
RMB	renminbi (Chinese currency)
S&T	science and technology
SAIC	Shanghai Automotive Industry Corporation
SARS	severe acute respiratory syndrome
SCO	Shanghai Cooperation Organization
SFTZ	Shanghai Free-Trade Zone
SOEs	state-owned enterprises
SSE	Shanghai Stock Exchange
SSTIC	Shanghai Science and Technology Innovation Center
STEM	science, technology, engineering, and mathematics
TVEs	township and village enterprises
UNCTAD	United Nations Conference on Trade and Development
UNESCO	United Nations Educational, Scientific, and Cultural Organization

VAT   value-added tax
WHO   World Health Organization
ZNIIDZ   Zhangjiang National Indigenous Innovation Demonstration
                  Zone

ACKNOWLEDGMENTS

Ernest Hemingway once wrote that "If you are lucky enough to have lived in Paris as a young man, then wherever you go for the rest of your life, it stays with you, for Paris is a moveable feast." My life has also been a movable feast, although my feast began in a city known in some quarters as the "Paris of the East." After growing up in Shanghai and being immersed in the subculture of the city, my Shanghainese identity has always remained an integral part of who I am.

Experiencing both the dark era of red terror during the Cultural Revolution as a young boy and the happier and more promising times of Deng Xiaoping's economic reform and opening up in the early 1980s as a student at East China Normal University nurtured in me lasting memories of and expectations for my native city. I was also privileged to witness the emergence of the Chinese middle class in the mid-1990s as a research fellow living in Shanghai for two years with the support of the U.S.-based Institute of Current World Affairs, the same institute that sent A. Doak Barnett, a distinguished China hand, to Shanghai to witness the Communist takeover in the late 1940s. Over the past two decades, I have traveled back to China many times, observing firsthand the growth and unmatched expansion of the city, which has paralleled my own personal growth as a college professor and a think tank scholar on the other side of the Pacific.

This book project examining Shanghai's middle class has lasted ten years and benefitted from the guidance of many scholars on and in China. Many seasoned Western scholars of Shanghai have greatly influenced and enhanced—directly or indirectly—my understanding of the distinct characteristics and paradoxes embedded in both the intriguing history and contemporary life of Shanghai. At the unavoidable risk of missing many important scholars, I want to mention a few: Sherman Cochran, Deborah Davis, Brian Hook, Emily Honig, Leo Ou-fan Lee, Lu Hanchao, Elizabeth Perry, Jeffrey Wasserstrom, Wen-Hsin Yeh, and the late Frederic Wakeman Jr., my teacher at the University of California at Berkeley.

The scholar who has had the greatest professional and personal influence on me throughout my career is my adviser at Princeton University, Lynn T. White, who is a leading expert on Shanghai in the United States. He has inspired me through his teaching and scholarship in many areas, which include his unparalleled knowledge and insights regarding the socioeconomic, political, and cultural life of Shanghai, as well as the emerging middle class in the city and beyond. Words simply cannot convey my deep gratitude for his mentorship and friendship over three decades.

This book has been greatly enhanced by feedback from two anonymous reviewers, whose intellectual critiques helped me to enhance its structure and arguments. I am particularly grateful for my scholarly exchanges over the years with distinguished leaders and China hands, including Ambassador Julia Block Chang (a fellow Shanghainese), Secretary William Cohen, Secretary Carla Hills, National Security Advisor Stephen Hadley, Ambassador Jon Huntsman, Senator Mark Kirk, Ambassador David Lane, Yale University president Richard Levin, Ambassador Gary Locke, Ambassador Winston Lord, Social Science Research Council president Alondra Nelson, Ambassador J. Stapleton Roy, and Ambassador Robert B. Zoellick.

The global leader who has had the greatest impact on me is Dr. Henry Kissinger. It has been an immense honor and privilege to meet with him regularly over the past fifteen years. Through our countless one-on-one meetings, he has imparted his legendary experience, historical perspective, vision, and strategic thinking, all of which have helped to shape this book. It's safe to say that no one has more greatly shaped America's opening to China, an effort through which he has profoundly changed millions of Chinese and American lives for the better. Without Dr. Kissinger, the opportunities opened through bilateral exchanges—including economic, financial, and trade engagements, as well as academic, educational, and scientific exchanges—could never have been realized. Not only did his efforts lead to the end of the Cold War, he also still provides inspiration and encouragement to strengthen people-to-people diplomacy between the two most powerful countries in today's world.

On the topics addressed in this book and beyond, I continue to learn from my good friends and fellow China scholars, including David Bachman, Jan Berris, Alexander Brenner, Robert Daly, Bruce Dickson, Brad Farnsworth, Scott Kennedy, Elizabeth Knup, David Mike Lampton, Jacques deLisle, Deborah Lehr, Liu Yawei, Christopher Marquis, Richard McGregor, Dewardric McNeal, Evan Medeiros, Andrew Mertha, Andrew J. Nathan, Steve Orlins, Doug Paal, Qi Ye, Joshua Cooper Ramo, David Rank, Stephen Roach, Stanley Rosen, Anthony Saich, David Shambaugh, Susan Shirk, Denis Simon, Sun Yun, Sun Zhe, Robert Sutter, Michael Swaine, Travis Tanner, Joseph Torigian, the late Ezra Vogel, Dennis Wilder, Zhang Xudong, and David Zweig.

While these Western China experts have helped translate their intimate knowledge of a foreign land for Western audiences, Chinese experts have played an equally important role in exposing the realities about Shanghai and the Chinese middle class. These experts include Lu Hanlong, Xiong Yuezhi, Yang Dongping, Yu Qiuyu, Yu Tianbai, and Zhou Wu on Shanghai and Shanghai culture; Li Chunling, Li Lulu, Li Peilin, Li Qiang, Liu Xin, Zhang Yi, and Zhou Xiaohong on the Chinese middle class; and Fu Ying, Huang Renwei, Huang Yiping, Jia Qingguo, Li Nan, Ni Shixiong, Shen Dingli, Shi Yinhong, Wu Xinbo, Yuan Peng, Zheng Yongnian, and Zhu Min on U.S.-China relations. This project would not have been possible without Yuan Yue and his Horizon Research Consultancy Group for the survey research they helped to conduct in Shanghai in 2009 and 2013–2014.

This book covers a wide range of areas, including politics, the economy, education, society, culture, architecture, legal development, and foreign relations, and it is particularly unique in sharing insights about the Shanghai art scene and avant-garde artists. While I cannot acknowledge every artist who has contributed to the Shanghai art scene, I am particularly grateful to the artists whose artwork is discussed in this book. Their influence could not have been fully realized without the amplification of other artists and curators. For their intellectual guidance and artistic inspiration, I want to convey my profound gratitude to Wu Hung (a distinguished art critic and a University of Chicago art historian who I know only through his writing), Xu Bing (a close friend and an internationally renowned artist), and Fan Di'an (professor and president of the Central Academy of Fine Arts). I am especially grateful to Lorenz Helbling, who is the founder and director of the ShanghART Gallery. Lorenz has provided great assistance over the past two decades in helping many around the world (myself included) to appreciate the vitality and creativity of Shanghai avant-garde artists. He has generously allowed me to share the works by Shanghai artists in this study, providing most of the plates that are presented in this book.

My colleagues at the Brookings Institution's John L. Thornton China Center have been important sounding boards on this project and many others over the years. I am profoundly appreciative of the collegiality, guidance, and friendship of Jeffrey Bader, Richard Bush, David Dollar, Rush Doshi, Ryan Hass, Lindsey Ford, Jamie Horsley, Kenneth Lieberthal, Jonathan Pollack, and Jonathan Stromseth, as well as nonresident scholars Thomas Christensen, Charles Freeman III, Diana Fu, Paul Gewirtz, Evan Osnos, Peter A. Petri, Pavneet Singh, Rachel Stern, Susan Thornton, Robert D. Williams, Daniel B. Wright, and Xue Lan.

The enduring support of Brookings leadership for my work and our China Center more broadly is impossible to convey adequately in words. Brookings president John R. Allen, shortly after his appointment in 2017, named the study of the middle class in the United States and around the world as a key priority of Brookings, and he has been immeasurably supportive, just as former president Strobe Talbott was before him. I am also grateful for the leadership and guidance of executive vice president Ted Gayer and vice president and director of Foreign Policy Suzanne Maloney, as well as Martin Indyk, Ted Piccone, and Bruce Jones before them. Michael E. O'Hanlon, the director of research for the Brookings Foreign Policy program, has been an intellectual force at Brookings for more than twenty-five years. His review of the manuscript was enormously helpful, and his guidance and support throughout the publication process have been exceptional. Many improvements were made to the book as a result of his constructive comments, including adjustments to the multi-dimensional perspectives presented herein.

I am most indebted to Ryan McElveen, my friend, colleague, and associate director of the John L. Thornton China Center. Over the past eight years, he has been my right hand and supported me in countless ways. Ryan is the model colleague and collaborator. Not only has he provided research assistance for this volume throughout his tenure at Brookings, he has also supported me in every other research project I have undertaken. I am so proud of the scholarly and administrative projects we have undertaken together, which have built the China Center into what it is today. Ryan is an intellectual force in his own right and a team leader for whom I hold the deepest respect and appreciation.

Over the course of a decade, many John L. Thornton China Center research assistants and interns have played a key role in research and editorial support for this book. The research assistants and junior colleagues who have contributed to this project include Zachary Balin, Diana Liang, Vincent Wang, Wang Wei, and Lucy Xu, all of whom have moved on to other important endeavors, as well as my current research assistants Kevin Dong and James Haynes. My words of appreciation for them are deceptively brief, but my gratitude for each of these very talented and capable young colleagues is profound. In the Brookings Foreign Policy program, I am thankful to Theodore Reinert for arranging the print copies of the manuscript for external review during an immensely challenging time amid the outbreak of COVID-19 and to Anna Newby for her excellent editorial guidance and promotional assistance.

I am also grateful to the China Center interns who contributed research and other assistance over the past few years, including Sarah Aver, Ding Li, William Duanmu, Elliot Ji, Ji Xinyuan, Kong Xiangrong, Hans Lei, Li Xinran, Amber Liao, Crystal Liu, Liu Yalin, Amanda Oh, Tan Xiao, Aubrey Thibaut, Marx Wang, Wang Yuqi, Lillian Weng, Bridget Wu, Gary Xie, Gracie Xie, Xue Haiyue, Yuan Shimeng, Zhang Xinyue, Zhao Du, and Zhou Shangsi. In particular, Angela Zhang provided immensely helpful research on Shanghai's avant-garde artists; Song Biyun and Charlotte Yang offered research help on higher education development in Shanghai; Carla Wang offered brilliant editorial assistance on the entire manuscript; and Ma Senqi contributed exacting proofreading and fact-checking help on both content and style with his impressive command of both English and Chinese.

The Brookings Institution Press deserves huge thanks for their efforts in publishing the book. I am especially grateful to the Press team of Bill Finan, Yelba Quinn, Elliott Beard, Cecilia González, Kristen Harrison, Fred King, Robin Ceppos, and Steve Roman for their ongoing commitment to amplifying the voices of Brookings scholars and their efforts to publish, market, publicize, and distribute this publication. The contributions of Diane Ersepke in copyediting this volume were enormous. It is extraordinarily challenging to capture the message of this book in a single image, but Dana Mendelson's creative cover design has done just that.

I acknowledge the Smith Richardson Foundation for funding this project and remaining committed to this research for more than a decade. I am especially grateful to Dr. Marin Strmecki, senior vice president and director of programs, and Allan Song, senior program officer, International Security and Foreign Policy, for their enduring and generous support, without which I was unlikely to embark on this book project. While I am deeply embarrassed by the long delay in completing this book, its publication happens to be timed just right to contribute to the intellectual and policy debate on the future direction of U.S.-China relations.

In the John L. Thornton China Center, we are blessed with a long list of supporters. First among them is our namesake and Brookings China Council co-chair John L. Thornton, whose advice and counsel have been invaluable. Our other China Council co-chair Qiu Yong, president of Tsinghua University, has also been a strong supporter of academic exchanges and mutual understanding across the Pacific. I am also grateful for the support and friendship of our other Brookings China Council members, who have remained committed to our China scholarship at an immensely challenging time in U.S.-China relations. These members have included Michael Ahearn, Anla Cheng, Jacob Carney, Deng Feng, Ding Jian, Barbara Franklin, Jiang Weiming, Ling Hai, Kevin Martin, Shen Nanpeng, Harry Shum, Vaughan Smith, Michael Sweeney, Tang Xiaodan, Jerry Weng, Yang Bin, Jerry Yang, Yang Yuanqing, and Zhang Chi. I am also very thankful to Evan Greenberg and Lee Folger for their strong support over the years. Other supporters to whom I am grateful include Paul Dyck, John Lenhart, Ben Harburg, Jenny Zeng, and Rachel Zhang.

The support of all these individuals and institutions has been instrumental in moving this project forward. They have given admirably and selflessly to sponsor independent, impartial, and objective research, no matter the findings. Of course, the arguments found within this book, including any and all remaining errors, are solely my own.

I could not have completed this book, nor any of my other projects, without the constant, unwavering, and loving support of my spouse, Yinsheng Li. My family members in Shanghai and the United States, and particularly my sisters and brothers, have provided inspiration on this project. And I remain thankful to my friends for their support, including An Ping, Sally Carman, Grace Hao, Jordan Lee, Hou Minyue, Daniel Lin, Liu Ying, Lu Yong, Wang Shi, Yu Jianxin, Zhang Guoqiang, Zhang Tao, Zhang Yuxin, and Zhu Sha.

This book is dedicated to Qu Shaoxu, or "Xiao Qu," as I called him. I met Xiao Qu in Shanghai during the 2003 SARS outbreak, and he soon became a member of my extended family. As a new Shanghainese, he embodied the struggles and dreams that so many residents (both natives and migrants) of Shanghai share. I will always regret that I did not do more to help him overcome his health problems to achieve those dreams. His memory will live on through this book.

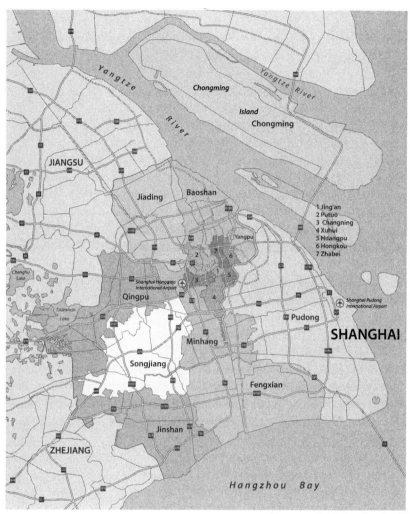

Shutterstock / Rainer Lesniewski

MIDDLE CLASS SHANGHAI

PROLOGUE

Rethinking Global Integration at a Time of Destructive Confrontation

Those who make peaceful change impossible,
make violent change inevitable.
—JOHN F. KENNEDY

At the 2000 Shanghai Biennale held in the Shanghai Art Museum, a sculpture by internationally renowned Chinese artist Huang Yongping captured a great deal of public attention. Huang had crafted a sandcastle replica of a famous building located along the Shanghai Bund that was once owned by the Hong Kong and Shanghai Banking Corporation (HSBC). This award-winning artwork was satirically entitled *Bank of Sand, Sand of Bank* (see Plate 1). The most poignant feature of the piece was its transformation over the course of the exhibition, slowly drying and disintegrating.

The collapse of this replica landmark building was highly symbolic, particularly in its allusion to both the impressive impact and the potentially catastrophic effects of globalization. Since its completion in 1923, the HSBC building (*huifeng yinhang dalou*), which was designed by the British firm Palmer and Turner, has embodied the glory days of colonial rule in the city.[1] The building's facade is a spectacular manifestation of Roman-style architecture, flaunting three granite arches at its front gate and capped by an enormous dome. The British once boasted that the building was "the finest and most imposing anywhere between the Suez Canal and the Bering Strait."[2] Many imperialist powers, including the United States, all had substantial ties to (and received loans from) this international bank throughout their engagement with the Middle Kingdom during the first half of the twentieth century. Over the four decades since the founding of the People's

1

Republic of China (PRC) in 1949, this edifice served as the headquarters of both the Shanghai Communist Party Committee and the municipal government.[3] Since 1996, the building has housed another bank—the Pudong Development Bank—a principal financial backer of the earthshaking construction in the eastern part of Shanghai across the Huangpu River, particularly in the Lujiazui district, which many consider to be China's Manhattan.

The impacts of pivotal events in recent history—whether it be the 9/11 terrorist attacks in the United States, the 2008 global financial crisis, or most significantly, the COVID-19 global pandemic—have collectively reaffirmed Huang's sentiment and fear of the cataclysmic shocks and aftereffects that stem from an increasingly interconnected world. The COVID-19 crisis caused sudden interruptions and stoppages to daily life and business routines across the entire world. International flights, cruises, and other long-haul transportation mostly ground to a halt. Schools, factories, shops, restaurants, movie theaters, stadiums, and other entertainment facilities were all closed, as were the borders of most countries. Wuhan, the initial epicenter of the coronavirus in China (a metropolis with over 11 million residents), was completely locked down through most of spring 2020. Worldwide, from the initial outbreak of the coronavirus to the end of 2020, about 83.7 million people were infected, more than 1,819,000 people died, and billions lived under quarantine in a state of isolation, anxiety, or even panic. In March 2020, for example, 3.4 billion people in 78 countries (about 43 percent of the world population) were under government orders requiring that they "shelter-at-home."[4] As of April 2020, the pandemic had forced 191 countries to close schools, preventing more than 1.5 billion students worldwide from studying in normal classroom environments.[5]

The long-term implications of this "pandemic of the century" are far from clear. Prior to the outbreak of COVID-19, economic disparities within and between countries had already given rise to antiglobalization movements across the world. The epidemic has understandably cast further doubt on the prospects of globalization. In addition to a devastating public health crisis, COVID-19 has also revealed fundamental problems in domestic governance and international order. As Henry Kissinger asserted, "Many countries' institutions will be perceived as having failed," and "the world will never be the same after the coronavirus."[6] One can reasonably expect that cynicism regarding regional and global integration, as well as radical populism, racism, and xenophobia, will likely all rise across many parts of the world, leading to a transformation of people's mindsets, behaviors, preferences, and priorities.

With these developments in mind, it seems the aforementioned Chinese artist Huang Yongping sought to use his imaginative artwork to remind observers of the dramatic changes—the unexpected twists and turns—that

China has experienced in its encounters with the outside world throughout the modern era. The nuances of his sculpture are rich with meaning. For instance, the medium of sand recalls Sun Yat-sen's infamous description of the Chinese people as "a sheet of loose sand." It also suggests China's sense of vulnerability throughout its contemporary encounters with the outside world. Huang, a Fujian-born avant-garde artist who lived in Paris for over a decade, has long been critical of China's single-minded drive for modernization and the destructive effects of globalization.[7] For him and other critics, economic and cultural globalization connote different meanings and phenomena—not all of them positive.[8] Problems such as corruption by officials, economic disparities, financial disruption, social dislocation, environmental degradation, misallocation of public health resources, cultural alienation, and international tensions are common side effects of the globalization process for many countries, and China has been no exception. According to Hou Hanru, one of the curators of the 2000 Shanghai Biennale, Huang's installation illustrates that "the dream of becoming modern and global always implies the risk of destruction and disaster."[9]

Huang's warning has deep historical roots. As the Harvard historian Tu Wei-ming has observed, "China has witnessed much destructiveness and violence in her modern transformation."[10] Notably, Huang's work gives artistic expression to simmering intellectual critiques that the path of globalization was "inevitable," "irresistible," and "irreversible."[11] In fact, many seemingly unavoidable developments during China's twentieth-century history—Western-style modernization in the first half of the century and Soviet-style socialist transformation during most of the second half—were later firmly rejected or displaced.

The real risk for China—and the overarching challenge it faces as an emerging global superpower—is not a scenario in which the government collapses or the country returns to what the Chinese deem "a couple of bad centuries," like the period following the Opium Wars. China, arguably more than any other country, has benefited enormously from economic globalization. In tandem with its domestic market reforms, the country's deepening integration with the outside world sparked the "Chinese economic miracle" of the past four decades. In the forty years since Deng launched economic reforms in 1978, approximately 800 million people have been lifted out of poverty in China—ten times the population of Germany, the most populous nation in Europe. Just a quarter-century ago, a distinct socioeconomic "middle class" was virtually nonexistent in China. But today, a growing number of Chinese citizens (currently estimated between 400 and 500 million), concentrated in Shanghai and other major cities, enjoy a middle-class lifestyle with private property, personal automobiles, improved health care, accumulation of financial assets, and the ability to afford overseas travel and foreign education for their children.[12] According to an October 2019 large-scale survey of China's urban residents conducted by People's Bank of China, 96 percent of Chinese families in cities and towns owned property, among which 31 percent owned two housing units and 11 percent had three properties or more.[13] Compared to forty years ago, China's GDP in 2019 had grown sixty times larger, and its per capita income was twenty-five times higher.[14]

The daunting challenge that now confronts China is how to reconcile its rapid ascension to the world's largest middle-class country and second-largest economy with the fears and reservations of other nations—especially those in North America, Europe, and Australia—who worry that China's rise in status and expanding outreach will come at the expense of prosperity and peace in the region and the world. Xi Jinping's Belt and Road Initiative is already reshaping the global landscape—as are other newly established financial institutions in which China plays a key role, such as the Silk Road Fund, the Asian Infrastructure Investment Bank, and the New Development Bank. While some see these Chinese-led initiatives as providing much-needed infrastructure development, capital, and more effective tools for poverty alleviation in developing countries, others consider them as undertakings in "debt-trap diplomacy." According to these critics, unsustainable loans and debt distress could allow the Chinese Communist Party leadership to wield influence and extract outsized concessions from vulnerable countries in the developing world. Similarly, China's growing influence in international institutions, such as the World Health Organization, which grew further during the COVID-19 pandemic, has induced much resentment among critics around the world, especially because they view the Chinese leadership's response at the outset of the coronavirus outbreak as slow and tainted by disinformation.

Most alarmingly, the growing tension between the United States and China has manifested into a prolonged trade war, increasingly hostile criticism of one another's political systems; highly oppositional stances over issues regarding Taiwan, Hong Kong, and Xinjiang; frequent military exercises near the East and South China Seas, and intensifying competition in 5G, artificial intelligence, cyberspace, and outer space. There is growing sentiment in Washington that the United States faces the potential for a major conflict with China on multiple fronts—strategy, diplomacy, security, military, politics, ideology, economics, finance, science, technology, health, and even education and culture. In the eyes of some political and opinion leaders in Washington, education and culture have been elevated to the arena of "high politics" and are now issues of national security. These leaders have recently claimed that Beijing is "weaponizing" the large number of Chinese students enrolled in U.S. universities, accusing these students of pilfering intellectual property and stealing advanced technology.[15] These concerns have led many within the U.S. political and intellectual establishments to conclude that the country's long-standing engagement policy toward the PRC has failed. Instead, the approach of comprehensive decoupling with China in virtually all domains has gained support in Washington.

Similarly, hostile views of the United States are also growing more prevalent in Beijing. The Chinese leadership has increasingly leveraged the PRC's economic, technological, and military power to retaliate against the United States, other Western nations, and China's neighboring countries, which have had disputes with—or have been critical of—China on various issues. Beijing has elevated state-led industrial policies to promote "national champions," and it has encouraged more direct competition with Western firms in the high-tech space. Xi Jinping's active and audacious foreign policy—characterized by its new catchword "fighting" (*douzheng*) regarding China's relations with the United States—differs profoundly from Deng Xiaoping's strategic emphasis on "peace and development." The Chinese Foreign Ministry's "tit-for-tat" approach, which has been described as "wolf warrior diplomacy" by foreign critics, has further mobilized ultranationalist sentiment among the Chinese public. To some foreign analysts, the Chinese middle class has acted more as a political ally to the authoritarian ruling party than as a political rabble-rouser.

The deterioration of U.S.-China relations has taken place at an unprecedented speed and scale, much faster and broader than almost anyone previously imagined. Urgency is building for the world's most powerful nation and the world's rapidly rising power to find a way to prevent their mutually reinforced fear and animosity from spinning out of control—a situation that could lead to a direct confrontation or even a catastrophically destructive war. This dire situation seems to echo the pessimistic sentiments held by some in China and conveyed by the art piece by the late Huang Yongping (1954–2019). Through his sculpture, Huang highlights the unpredictability of history and the vulnerability of monumental places in an ever-changing environment. But perhaps even more importantly, this art piece encourages people to rethink the significance and value of global integration and cultural exchanges in our precarious world.

At this very critical juncture of growing U.S.-China discord and looming global disorder, American policymakers must not lose sight of the expansive dynamism and diversity in present-day China. The caricature of the PRC as a Xi-dominated, burgeoning hegemon with aggressive intentions, or as a monolithic, Communist apparatus set on disseminating its ideology and development model, is simplistic and anachronistic. China today, as exemplified and led by Shanghai, is a crucible of political, socioeconomic, entrepreneurial, cultural, and civil society change resulting from the explosive growth of the middle class. There are, of course, important elements of nationalism, and there is sometimes even anti-American sentiment, among members of the middle class. But this vital group also holds open-minded, worldly views and values, a willingness to challenge central authority, demands for government accountability, and a strong desire to work with the United States—a place where many members of this group have studied. Washington should neither underestimate the role and strength of the Chinese middle class nor ostracize and alienate this force with policies that push it toward jingoistic nationalism to the detriment of both countries and the global community.

The future of Shanghai is, of course, unwritten, but there is much to learn by studying where it has been, where it stands now, and the likely ways it could change in the decades ahead. As the most Westernized Chinese city before 1949—and currently the frontier city of the country's global integration—Shanghai serves as the ideal case study for evaluating the impact of transnational forces and the interaction between culture and politics, between state and society, between the East and the West.

At the heart of the inquiry lies an open question about the role that China's middle class will play in shaping the country's future on the world stage. Will it act as a catalyst for positive political transformation at home, a stumbling block, or something else? Will a rapidly growing middle class, which tends to usher in new expectations and responsibilities for its future, promote a constructive (rather than destructive) Chinese presence in a rapidly changing global environment? Can a solid understanding of the views, values, and voices of the Chinese middle class, especially the group's similarities with its counterparts in the West, help mitigate the ongoing "China panic" and American overaction to China's growing power on the other side of the Pacific, as recently described by the renowned international affairs commentator Fareed Zakaria?[16]

The answers to these questions could not be more consequential as China continues to advance along its path of development. Understanding a core constituency—the middle class—through the prism of the country's most dynamic city of Shanghai is as promising a place as any to begin seeking answers.

I

INTRODUCTION

CHAPTER 1

Shanghai's Middle Class and China's Future Trajectory

If there is any lesson to be learned from history, it is that
the doctrines and the causes that arouse men to passion and
violence are transitory; that more often than not they fade into
irrelevance with the erosion of time and circumstance. We must
learn to conduct international relations with patience, tolerance,
openness of mind, and, most of all, with a sense of history.
—PHILIP COOMBS

To learn about the 2,000-year Chinese history, one should visit Xi'an.
To understand the 500-year Middle Kingdom, one has to see Beijing. To
grasp the past 100-year changes in China, one must look at Shanghai.
—A CHINESE SAYING

Among the many forces shaping China's domestic transformation and its role on the world stage, none may prove more significant than the rapid emergence and explosive growth of the Chinese middle class. China's ongoing economic transition from a relatively poor developing nation to a middle-income country is likely to have wide-ranging implications for every domain of society, and especially for the country's economy, environment, education, politics, internal social cohesion, and culture. On the international front, the emerging Chinese middle class has already begun changing the ways in which the People's Republic of China (PRC) interacts with the outside world, both by keeping abreast of transnational cultural currents and by expanding Chinese socioeconomic outreach and soft-power influence.

The Chinese middle class will be both the driver of change and the recipient of its costs and benefits in the decades ahead. Attaining a better understanding of the characteristics and myriad roles of the Chinese middle class amid the country's rapid transformations will help elucidate its economic and political trajectory. For the overseas community of China-watchers, the nation's middle class is also a proxy for the multidimensional changes underway in Chinese society and thus presents a useful subject of study for foreign governments—especially the United States—to identify effective policy options in their relations with Beijing. The growing tension between the United States and China—evidenced in Washington's heated debate over ending the four-decades-long engagement policy in favor of comprehensive decoupling from the PRC, and Beijing's sharp criticism of a U.S.-led "conspiracy" to contain China's rise and its tit-for-tat, aggressive approach—has extended far beyond economics and trade. Both nations have intensified naval activities and other military exercises in the Asia-Pacific region, accused one another of nefarious cyber campaigns, deported the other country's journalists and threatened ending people-to-people exchanges, and amped up their increasingly hostile political rhetoric. With the current state of relations, a military confrontation or even a full-scale war between the world's most powerful nation and the world's fastest-developing country is by no means inconceivable.

This research presents a thesis that runs contrary to some of the prevailing views in Washington regarding the failure of U.S. engagement policy toward China. By viewing China's developments and external relations over the past two decades through the lens of its most cosmopolitan city, Shanghai, it is clear that the dominant assumptions and associated policy measures in the United States about the "all-dimensional China threat" are simplistic, premature, and misguided. While American policymakers understandably never want the United States to lose its military edge and technological supremacy, which deter potential challengers, they should make greater efforts to leverage the advantages of American soft (and smart) power.[1]

Washington's recent push to decouple with China, which has involved sensationalizing the Chinese nation as a "whole-of-society threat" to the United States, not only alienates China's vast middle class, a dynamic and progressive force in the country, but also severely damages American public diplomacy and national interests, potentially paving a collision course that could lead to war.[2] An empirical and comprehensive study of China's domestic dynamics and the diversified nature of Chinese society, especially the ever-expanding middle class, can broaden the analytical horizon of—and intellectual debate on—China's future relationship with the United States and the world.

DUAL FOCUSES: THE MIDDLE CLASS AND SHANGHAI

What exactly can a study of Shanghai's middle class and its cultural values tell us about China's political trajectory and foreign relations, including the likelihood of war and peace? From Plato to Machiavelli—and from Confucius to Mao—people have long recognized the connection between cultural and political dynamics and between internal forces and external relations. As China's global influence grows, the international community—and American policymakers, in particular—are increasingly torn between two contending scenarios of how China might shoulder its role in the world and its relationship to other nations. Either outcome is deeply intertwined with the trajectory of China's rapidly emerging middle class.

In the first scenario, which is more pessimistic, China becomes a superpower buoyed by decades-long, double-digit economic growth and military modernization. China's middle class grows to an unprecedented size, and this population's strongly nationalistic views come to guide almost all state affairs. Demagogues continue to stoke this toxic, hostile strain of nationalism by taking advantage of rising tensions stemming from the aggregate demand of hundreds of millions of middle-class consumers, global resource scarcities, international consternation over China's swelling carbon footprint, and global concern about other negative externalities from the country's rapid industrialization and urbanization. To a great extent, the Chinese middle class serves as an active and influential player in the country's pursuit of state capitalism and industrial policies overseas, including in the Belt and Road Initiative. In this scenario, an ascendant China, still cognizant of the "century of humiliation" it endured at the hands of Western imperialists, may easily choose to disregard international norms, disrupt global institutions, and even consider aggressive expansionism in the East and South China Seas, along with other parts of the region.

In the second, more optimistic scenario, China's burgeoning middle class embraces more cosmopolitan values, having forged close economic and cultural bonds with countries in the West, especially the United States. The growing consumption of China's middle class helps reduce the U.S.-China trade imbalance, easing economic tensions, and China's middle-class lifestyle comes to mirror that of developed countries. Additionally, the growing number of political, economic, and cultural elites in China who have received some Western education and possess a more sophisticated understanding of the outside world act as catalysts for progressive change in China. The Chinese middle class consists of a large number of private entrepreneurs and private sector employees. Like their counterparts in other countries, they value property rights and economic freedom, which are preconditions for increased political freedom, according to both distinguished American economist Milton Friedman and political sociologist Seymour Martin Lipset.[3] In most nations, there is an important link—and an ultimate need—for close ties between economic development and regime efficiency to mediate interests. China's middle class may help create and strengthen these ties by pushing for political reform and better governance in domestic affairs. This group will also demand that China acts as a responsible stakeholder on the foreign policy front, building more constructive relations with the United States and the international community at large.

Each scenario seems to present an extreme case, but both are based on serious assessments of the possibilities. For example, the Chinese middle class has already demonstrated its strong desire and ability to purchase foreign goods. In August 2019, the U.S. wholesale chain Costco expanded into China by opening a store in Shanghai. Within hours of opening on the first day, the store had to close due to the overwhelming mass of customers that showed up.[4] More than half of its products were from overseas, and many sold out almost immediately. Thus China's rising middle class clearly wields incredible economic power and could potentially become a force that seriously undermines the interests of the United States, underscoring the real danger of the more pessimistic scenario. One could argue that the United States has partial responsibility to do whatever it can to promote the optimistic scenario, chiefly by avoiding actions that needlessly inflame Chinese nationalism, and by engaging constructively with China and incentivizing adherence and "buy-in" to the current international system. Unfortunately, the current mainstream discussion of U.S. policy toward China has largely neglected the role and impact of the country's middle class. In general, China has often been treated as a monolithic entity with no distinction between state and society.

Regardless of which scenario unfolds in the years to come, China's emerging middle class will be a driving force behind the country's domestic political evolution, which will feed directly into the PRC's external posture. In order for the United States to establish an effective China policy, the American foreign policy community must acquire a more informed and comprehensive understanding of the Chinese middle class—from its basic composition to its values, worldviews, and potential political agency in deciding the country's future trajectory. In a twenty-first-century world driven by global connectivity, we must ask whether it is desirable and sustainable for the two largest middle-class countries to be set on a confrontational course.

Shanghai was the most Westernized city in pre-1949 China, and it still spearheads the country's dynamic participation in economic globalization and cultural exchange. It is thus the ideal case study for understanding the rise of the Chinese middle class, the impact of transnational forces on China, and the complex interplay of these two trends within Chinese society, culture, and politics. In a sense, Shanghai has been both a laboratory and a trendsetter for the country's economic and sociopolitical developments in the reform era (from 1978 to the present).

Shanghai has served as the "cradle" of both the new middle class and foreign-educated returnees. According to a study conducted by the Institute of Sociology at the Chinese Academy of Social Sciences, the middle class made up roughly 40 percent of the labor force in Shanghai in 2010.[5] *The Report on China's New Middle Class* indicates that in 2018, over 5 million households in Shanghai could be counted as middle-class families.[6] Looking at the wider region, households in East China (Shanghai, Zhejiang, Jiangsu, Fujian, Shandong, and Anhui) account for 44 percent of the country's middle class.[7] This, of course, is not an entirely new development in Shanghai. As early as 2005, about 82 percent of families in the city owned a residence, and 22 percent of these families owned two properties.[8] Based on a 2019 report by the People's Bank of China, the average value of urban household assets nationwide was 3.18 million yuan (about US$454,000), with a median value of 1.63 million yuan (US$233,000). In the same year, the average value of household assets among Shanghai residents was 8.07 million yuan (US$1.15 million).[9]

In 2009, Shanghai was home to more than one-fourth of the country's foreign-educated returnees, and it was ranked first among China's thirty-one province-level administrative regions for total number of returnees.[10] About 4,000 returnees established innovation-driven business firms in the city. Additionally, a significant number of senior executives of multinational companies and international organizations in Shanghai were returnees. Furthermore, in the same year returnees constituted over 60 percent of the academicians at Chinese Academy of Sciences and the Chinese Academy of Engineering in Shanghai, with 102 of them coming from stints abroad. Among the 66 chief scientists of the National 973 Projects in Shanghai, 97 percent spent time studying overseas.[11] Overall, a higher percentage of returnees in Shanghai hold advanced academic degrees, and they are younger, on average, than their peers in other regions. For example, in 2009 approximately 64 percent of Shanghai's returnees held a master's degree or above, and 73 percent fell between the ages of 21 and 30.[12]

Shanghai's competitiveness both nationally and internationally relies heavily on its pool of human talent. As follows, a country's most important resource is arguably its higher education system and other institutions that promote cultural and knowledge-based economic activities. The concentration of prominent universities and cultural institutions (e.g., museums, art galleries, theatrical companies, and other performing groups) in

Shanghai not only makes the city one of China's two educational centers (the other being Beijing) but also helps foster a distinct Shanghai culture (*haipai wenhua*). In contrast to the mainstream Beijing culture (*jingpai*), which is sometimes characterized as aristocratic, conservative, elitist, and bureaucratic, *haipai* culture is often described as pragmatic, entrepreneurial, innovative, pluralistic, leisurely, modern, and forward looking.[13]

The *haipai* culture—whether in the domains of art, literature, music, or the public discourse—has a high tolerance for different values, views, and lifestyles. This is partly attributable to the fact that Shanghai is a relatively young, largely immigrant-friendly city with strong foreign influences, in both its colonial past and its globalized present. For instance, the host of the Jin Xing Show—the highest-rated late-night talk show in China from 2015 to 2017—is a transgender woman. Jin Xing is a new Shanghainese, an ethnic Korean, and a returnee from the United States. The recurrent theme of this Shanghai-based show was to introduce Western ideas, new social norms, progressive values, and middle-class lifestyle trends to the Chinese public.[14] The Jin Xing show ended in late 2017, but Jin Xing has continued to host other popular TV programs promoting *haipai* culture.

These dynamic and pluralistic developments in the distinct subculture of Shanghai are vitally important. As some scholars observe, present-day Shanghai "has been transformed into a city of world significance."[15] This is not only because of the city's growing economic and financial status that has resulted from the explosive growth of the middle class, but also because the city exemplifies the reemergence of a cosmopolitan culture and the dynamism of transnational forces.

SHANGHAI: "THE OTHER CHINA"?

Shanghai is, of course, not reflective of all of China. The metropolis is to China what New York City is to the United States. Notably, Shanghai's rise as a cosmopolitan city coincided with the decline and disintegration of the Middle Kingdom after the Opium Wars. This has left an indelible impact on the identity and characteristics of Shanghai. Unsurprisingly, many historians of Shanghai recognize it as a city at the crosscurrents of history, often undergoing experiences quite different from the rest of the country.[16] Stella Dong, for example, argues that for more than a century prior to the Communist victory in 1949, "China's losses were always Shanghai's gains."[17]

Thus some scholars of Shanghai history assert that the city could be a "lens through which one sees a distorted vision" of China.[18] For instance, despite the devastating dual impacts of the Japanese imperialist invasion in 1937 and the Chinese Civil War, for most of the first half of the twentieth century, Shanghai was seen as "the most urban, industrial, and cosmopolitan city in all of Asia."[19] In a sense, Shanghai's prosperity in the early decades of the twentieth century was achieved in large part as a result of its relative independence from China itself.[20] According to one analyst, "Shanghai's independence relied on China's weakness."[21] A strong central government in Beijing, especially when led by top leaders who did not come from Shanghai, could marginalize the importance of this cosmopolitan city.

"Other China," a term coined by French historian Marie-Claire Bergére, later became the defining label that described Shanghai's course of development in contrast to that of the rest of the country.[22] In spite of the city's unique cosmopolitan influence and strong local identity, Shanghai nevertheless played a central role in promoting Chinese nationalism in the first half of the twentieth century by offering a "new vision of the place of China in the world." Bergére observes that "Shanghai is at once more open to the outside world and more aware of the place which China should have in it. Nationalism and cosmopolitanism proceed in a parallel and complementary fashion."[23] In the 1930s, a large number of prominent Chinese writers, publishers, educators, and artists, including many foreign-educated returnees, resided in Shanghai. Most of them were also advocates of Chinese nationalism. As Carrie Waara notes, "It was their international orientation combined with their strong economic and cultural nationalism that gave the Shanghai style its own unique and local flavor."[24]

What was true about the multiple identities of Shanghai in the first half of the twentieth century holds true to this day. Since Shanghai serves as the exemplar of China's coming-of-age in the modern era, the city's rise to international prominence reinforces Chinese nationalistic sentiments. Shanghai's local, national, and cosmopolitan identities are all dynamic; they serve to mutually reinforce one another while also retaining independent value in different specific contexts. Shanghai's opening to the outside world is not cultural convergence, but cultural coexistence and diversity.

Some Chinese scholars argue that Shanghai's recent experiences invalidate many of the conventional approaches to Chinese cultural studies, such as the simplistic dichotomy between the West and the East, along with the model of Western impact and Chinese response.[25] These scholars assert that cultural transnationalism functions as a two-way street. The localization of transnational cultural movements in Shanghai since the 1990s demonstrates that the city's political and cultural elites feel confident in promoting foreign exchanges. It also conveys "a sense of entitlement in claiming the localized foreign culture as their own," a characterization used by Yan Yunxiang to describe the "cultural globalization" of another Chinese city.[26] However, in a way, Shanghai's pride in its cosmopolitanism and local identity has also hindered the city's pursuit of excellence in cultural and educational development.[27] The dynamism of transnational cultural forces makes it possible for Shanghai's scholars, educators, and artists to consider issues in conjunction with the international community.

Yet it would be a mistake to overlook the trailblazing role Shanghai has played both in the previous century and in more recent decades. Understanding Shanghai is vital to understanding modern China.[28] Due to its special role in cultural dissemination, Shanghai has long been called China's "window" or "gate" to the outside world, the "bridge" between the East and West, and the "key" to grasping the driving force of China's rise in our time. Shanghai often served as a bridge, for example during the Republican era, in managing the influence of the West and "leading the rest of China into the modern world."[29] To a certain extent, Shanghai is the product of the integration of two civilizations. It was Shanghai that introduced the world to China, and it was also Shanghai that brought China into the world.[30]

Thus Shanghai's designation as the "other China" can be challenged on three fronts. First, despite strong Western influence on the city, Shanghai has always remained an inherently Chinese city. Shanghai was always "China's Shanghai," and it never lost its cultural identity or feeling of "Chineseness."[31] A 2003 Chinese book on foreigners in Shanghai used the phrase "China has a Shanghai" to characterize Shanghai's contribution to the development and diversity of the country.[32] Throughout the twentieth century, Shanghai always held an important position in China's economic, political, social, and cultural life. As discussed in the prologue of this book, Shanghai was the birthplace of China's attempt at Western-style modernization *and* of Chinese Communism, the two most important forces that have shaped the country's contemporary history. Time and again, in virtually all major phases of PRC history—the socialist transformation, the Cultural Revolution, reform and opening up, and China's search for global superpower status—Shanghai has proved to be a critical ideological and political battlefield "too important to lose" to competing forces.[33]

Although Shanghai's prominence as a wellspring of Western cultural influence in China has fluctuated over the last century and a half, the rise of modern China would be inconceivable without Shanghai. According to Albert Feuerwerker, "Shanghai set the style of the foreign presence in China"—a style that other Chinese cities "sought to emulate."[34] And as Shanghai-born and U.S.-educated historian Lu Hanchao observes, the Western influence on the Shanghai lifestyle during the pre-1949 era not only endured, but also spread in many important respects to other Chinese cities over the second half of the twentieth century.[35]

Second, Shanghai has set the pace for the country's socioeconomic development since the 1990s, when China designated Shanghai as "the head of the dragon" and aimed to transform the Yangtze Delta region into an economic powerhouse. To a great extent, Shanghai is the de facto capital of all Jiangnan (consisting mainly of Zhejiang and Jiangsu provinces). The Shanghainese middle class shares close ties to the hundreds of millions of middle-class families who reside in major cities across the region, such as Suzhou, Wuxi, Changzhou, and Ningbo. Analyzing Shanghai is the key to fully understanding China, arguably now more than ever. In May 2019, Xi Jinping convened a Politburo meeting to discuss the "high-quality" and "more integrated" new development plan, which emphasizes modern manufacturing and the service sector for the Yangtze River delta—Shanghai's geographic domain.[36] The Chinese leadership proclaimed that this regional plan would have "a great demonstration role" for the country's economic growth in Xi's new era.

In fact, many important phenomena in post-Mao China—the resurgence of a commercial society, the establishment of a stock market, foreign investment, land leasing, property booms, rural–urban migration, the proliferation of e-commerce, the application of artificial intelligence in urban development, and the negative externalities of capitalist development—were either initiated in Shanghai or otherwise affected the city in a deep and direct way. Over the past quarter-century, the city has experienced a remarkable economic boom and transformation. Many of these developments rapidly spread to other parts of the country. In a profound way, the resurgence of Shanghai as a cosmopolitan city has become a metaphor for China's drive to join the "global club"—a symbol of China's coming of age in the twenty-first century.

The quick emergence and growth of the middle class have spread beyond Shanghai in recent years to other Chinese cities, including Tier-two and Tier-three cities in inland regions. According to a study conducted by Dominic Barton and his colleagues at McKinsey, in 2002, 40 percent of China's relatively small, urban, middle class resided in the four Tier-one cities—Beijing, Shanghai, Guangzhou, and Shenzhen. However, by 2022, the proportion of China's middle class that resides in those megacities is expected to drop to about 16 percent, and 76 percent of the middle class will live in Tier-two (45 percent) and Tier-three (31 percent) cities.[37] In terms of the geographic distribution of the middle class, the study forecasts that China's middle class will shift from 87 percent living in coastal regions and 13 percent in inland regions in 2002, to 61 percent and 39 percent, respectively, by 2022.[38]

Third, Shanghai is also a source of political leadership for China. Over the past two decades, many of the nation's top officials have had personal ties to the city, or they have been promoted to Beijing from political postings in Shanghai. In the third generation of leadership, examples include former secretary general of the Chinese Communist Party (CCP) Jiang Zemin and former premier Zhu Rongji; in the fourth generation, former vice president of the PRC Zeng Qinghong and former chairman of the National People's Congress Wu Bangguo; and, in the fifth generation, president of the PRC Xi Jinping, CCP propaganda chief Wang Huning, and current executive vice premier Han Zheng. The latter three currently sit at the pinnacle of power as members of the seven-member Politburo Standing Committee. With the exception of Xi Jinping, who only served as party secretary in Shanghai for eight months, most of the aforementioned top leaders were either born and raised in Shanghai or spent many years running the city. Generally, leaders who grew up in Shanghai or began their political careers there tend to have a more nuanced understanding of the globalized world. They have a better comprehension of the factors that have driven the development of middle-class Shanghai, and their unique perspectives have helped them shape China's domestic and foreign policy as the nation's top officials. In post-Deng China, there have been three important political developments: (1) the rise of the so-called Shanghai Gang in the national leadership; (2) the adoption of Jiang Zemin's theory of the "Three Represents," which instructs the CCP to recruit private entrepreneurs and capitalists into the party to broaden its power base; and (3) Xi Jinping's call to fulfill the "Chinese dream" and the "great rejuvenation of the Chinese nation." Together, these seminal developments have bolstered the reemergence of Shanghai as China's cultural capital, and they have accelerated the rapid growth of the city's middle class.

Shanghai, therefore, cannot be the "other China." Instead, one may argue that due to its distinct cosmopolitan subculture, Shanghai is a unique city within China that wields the power to *change* the country to align more with international norms and values. Robert Hormats, former U.S. State Department under secretary for Economic, Energy and Agricultural Affairs, observed that Shanghai has a much better record of respecting intellectual property rights than any other Chinese city.[39] Zhang Chuanjie, deputy director of the Center for U.S.-China Relations at Tsinghua University, conducted a public opinion survey measuring Chinese attitudes toward the United States. Zhang broke down the responses across five demographic variables: gender, age, education, income, and location. He found that *location* was the only dimension along which there were strikingly different Chinese views of the United States. Specifically, Professor Zhang found that respondents from Shanghai have a much more favorable view of the United States than do respondents from elsewhere in the country.[40]

All of these unique features of Shanghai make the city an attractive subject for academic inquiry, and also an ideal case study, as previously noted, to document the rise and expansion of the Chinese middle class and the impact of transnational forces on China. This book combines eclectic human stories with rigorous empirical analysis to reveal how Shanghai has served three essential functions throughout China's modern history: (1) introducing and absorbing foreign culture and investment; (2) highlighting the growing diversity in Chinese society and the imperative for an inclusive culture; and (3) disseminating and showcasing cosmopolitan (or "postmodern") views, ideas, and values to other parts of the country.[41]

INQUIRIES, METHODOLOGY, AND ORGANIZATION OF THE BOOK

Examining Shanghai's resurgence since the 1990s sheds light on the city's roles, which are of prime interest to the policymaking circles in the United States and China, the China studies scholarly community, and the social sciences community as a whole. This book explores the aforementioned three important inquiries by placing them in the context of two sets of major policy and intellectual debates about China's future relationship with the United States and the world: (1) How do China's unprecedented and multidimensional international exchanges—for which Shanghai serves as a nexus—influence policy debates about U.S.-China decoupling in Washington, as well as concerns in Beijing about an alleged U.S.-led conspiracy to contain China? (2) How should one assess the impacts of foreign influence and changing levels of social stratification in China? What can a conceptual and empirical analysis reveal about the main characteristics of China's middle class?

This study adopts an analytical framework appropriate for understanding the dynamic and complicated interactions among the economy, politics, culture, and education, with a focus on the cultural and educational aspects of the emerging Chinese middle class. The book adopts the generally accepted definition of culture as a set of values, practices, norms, customs, symbols, anecdotes, and myths that create specific meaning for a society. Culture also includes lifestyles, religious beliefs, artistic and scholarly works, philosophies, and historical memories. Culture is often classified into two categories—elite culture and popular culture. The former refers to literature, art, and education, and the latter includes mass entertainment, talk shows, and new media outlets, including popular bloggers that disseminate new ideas and expressions. Museums, art galleries, pubs, teahouses, and other public gathering places serve as common cultural venues.

The concept of cultural diversity in an increasingly globalized world has three main features. First, institutions and individuals are the agents or players in promoting various kinds of cross-cultural endeavors. Second, symbols and ideas are used to promote communication and understanding of beliefs and norms across national borders. Third, methods and tools are available to facilitate transnational movement.[42] Together, these three components constitute the transnational forces of culture. In a sense, "cultural globalization" is a conceptual paradox. Globalization suggests diffusion and convergence of local and national norms or ideas, while culture implies distinct features embodied in heritage historical circumstances. Cultures are necessarily diverse and inconsistent; the people of a given culture have experienced varied pasts involving different memories, symbols, myths, styles, and norms.[43]

Rather than using "cultural globalization," this work uses the terms "cultural transnationalism" and "cultural internationalism," which can be used interchangeably. The idea of cultural transnationalism involves the formation of shared norms, common knowledge, and multiple identities through transnational exchanges, resulting in greater interconnectedness among different populations and traditions.[44] This book applies four methodological approaches with original research: (1) biographical and occupational data analysis, (2) case studies of Shanghai's institutions of higher education, (3) survey questionnaires, and (4) content analysis of avant-garde artwork.

The next two chapters address the aforementioned inquiries. Chapter 2 focuses on the policy debate between continuing U.S.-China engagement versus decoupling on various fronts. Chapter 3 examines the scholarly discourse about social stratification and cultural pluralism, specifically in regard to present-day China. The chapter also reviews the Chinese scholarly literature on the main characteristics of the Chinese middle class and the impact of international exchanges.

Chapter 4 shows that the modern history of Shanghai is also the history of China's integration into the outside world. Shanghai was always, and has remained, the most westernized and cosmopolitan city in China. This chapter examines the degree to which Shanghai's culture has been subsumed by foreign influences, which has left a lasting impact on the social norms and cultural values of the city's inhabitants. About 500,000 non-PRC citizens, including Taiwanese communities, live in Shanghai and have shaped the city's social fabric by fostering a distinct middle-class culture. The chapter also highlights how some of the seemingly local and international identities formed in this process have become contentious political issues dividing segments of Chinese society. By examining both Shanghai's exceptionalism and its cultural transnationalism, the chapter argues that Shanghai's contemporary culture is simultaneously local, national, and international, and that *haipai* culture balances out the ultranationalistic sentiments expressed in other Chinese cities, such as Beijing.

Chapter 5 documents a fascinating set of transnational exchanges that have taken place in Shanghai over the past three decades, especially after Deng Xiaoping's decision to develop and open up the Pudong district to foreign investment. The discussion bolsters the argument that new market forces may function only as the *"engine* of change," whereas a new middle-class culture can determine the *"direction* of change." The middle class often serves as the agent of market efficiency, and the CCP needs to control that dynamic in the interest of its own longevity. The chapter examines the seemingly contradictory phenomena of the parallel development of private firms, state-owned enterprises, and foreign companies in the city over the past decade.

Chapter 6 reviews three important political events that took place in Shanghai within the past thirty years: the rise of the Shanghai Gang in the mid-1990s, the fall from power of Shanghai Party secretary Chen Liangyu in 2006, and the surprising ascension of many members of the Shanghai Gang at both the 2012 and 2017 party congresses. The chapter argues that something new is afoot in Chinese elite politics, largely due to the political dynamism stemming from Shanghai. This analysis showcases some of the new rules and norms embraced by the country's top leaders as they seek to manage intraparty political conflict and increasing localism in socioeconomic policy, while also maintaining rapid growth, social stability, national cohesion, and one-party rule—some of the enduring challenges of governance in the Xi Jinping era.

Chapters 7 and 8 focus on the role and impact of international educational exchange, especially with respect to Western-educated Chinese returnees. Over the past two decades, and more so in recent years, China has seen a tidal wave of these returnees coming home after studying abroad. Examining this population provides insight into the macro trends of China's study abroad movement during the reform era, and it also offers a deeper look into the microlevel impact of U.S.-China cultural and educational exchanges. Large-scale quantitative research on China's top universities reveals the status, distribution, and leadership roles of returnees working in college administration, curricular development, social science research, and other aspects of academia.

Chapter 9 presents a longitudinal survey of foreign-educated elites in Shanghai, examining how they differ from those who never studied abroad. The survey shows that U.S.-educated Chinese elites are not necessarily less nationalistic and more pro-American than other Chinese elites. However, one must not disregard how U.S.-China educational exchanges can have both short- and long-term, positive impacts on the multifaceted transformations taking place in the world's most populous country. This detailed and empirically grounded study of Chinese foreign-educated returnees elucidates how to improve future U.S. educational exchanges with China; how to positively nudge Chinese political, educational, and cultural elites; how to prevent anti-American sentiment from dominating Chinese public discourse and defining the views of China's younger generations; how to turn this emerging power from a potentially formidable authoritarian adversary into a liberal and likeminded partner; and how best to navigate a way forward that contributes to a peaceful and secure world in this era of dramatic—and often disruptive—change. This is a tall order, but a failure by foreign policy scholars and professionals to recognize and study these questions could, in hindsight, be a mistake of historic consequence.

Chapters 10 and 11 analyze avant-garde art in Shanghai, with a focus on exploring the booming contemporary art scene in the city and understanding how avant-garde artworks reflect the profound change in artistic and intellectual pursuits of some of the most forward-looking, critical minds in this influential cultural hub. Chapter 10 explores the stunning development of art galleries in Shanghai over the past decade, including some large-scale, privately owned art museums. The chapter also highlights the important role of the Shanghai Biennale and the great impact of international cultural exchanges in the reform era.

Chapter 11 offers an analytical discussion of some representative work of Shanghai's avant-garde artists, revealing that the political messages conveyed in their art tend to be subtle, culturally broad, and oftentimes restive without the brashness of some of the antiregime "shock" artists based in Beijing. Shanghai's avant-garde artists use modern media (e.g., computer programs that require audience participation, international symbols, and performance art), yet these works do not situate themselves solely in their contemporary and immediate environment. Rather, they start a more critical, international dialogue about China's—and the world's—growing obsession with consumerism and its negative effects, especially these artists' widely shared resentment of the perceived U.S. policy of containing China's rise, as well as American moral hypocrisy in world affairs. The messages these artists share tend to transcend the usual intellectual boundaries between modernity and tradition, socialism and capitalism, East and West, and politics and culture. A close inspection of these works provides a look into the rapidly changing perspective of the denizens of Shanghai and the intellectual community's critical but constructive demand for a dialogue with the West on equal footing. Through their works, Shanghai artists have sought to convey a powerful sense of common humanity, which can triumph over seemingly stark cultural differences.

Chapter 12 discusses what all of these developments related to Shanghai's middle class, especially as a reflection of the dynamic and diverse nature of Chinese society as a whole, mean for China, the United States, and the world. It offers further thoughts for U.S. policymakers about how to minimize misunderstanding and mistrust between the two countries and how to maximize the positive and constructive role of the Chinese middle class in both U.S.-China and global relations.

II

THE RISE OF
MIDDLE-CLASS CHINA:
ISSUES AND DEBATES

CHAPTER 2

A Failure of U.S.-China Engagement?
Policy Debates in Washington and Beijing

It is far more difficult to murder a phantom than a reality.
—VIRGINIA WOOLF

Civilization is not national—it is international.
—FRANKLIN D. ROOSEVELT

Having just celebrated the fortieth anniversary of diplomatic relations between the United States and China, it may seem like an odd time to analyze the factors driving the recent and rapid deterioration of this bilateral relationship. On the contrary, now is perhaps the best time to do so, as both the historical context and enormous consequences of the current moment may help chart the trajectory of arguably the most important bilateral relationship in the twenty-first century. Over the past forty years, these two countries, each with unique qualities, have become intimately intertwined. Engagement between the two nations had never been broader, deeper, and more frequent than it was at the time of the fortieth anniversary in 2019—whether it be at the government, military, subnational, commercial, cultural, educational, think tank, nongovernmental organization (NGO), tourism, or people-to-people level. Since then, the Trump administration has taken antagonistic steps against China, and there has been growing sentiment in Washington that the United States faces a major, multipronged threat from China and must "decouple" from this emerging superpower.

The recent deterioration of the bilateral relationship has reached a level similar to that of—or even worse than—the post-1989 Tiananmen period.

Yet no defining, singular event or factor has triggered this new round of tensions. This deterioration is the result of years of disputes, disappointment, and distrust between the two countries. For many analysts in the United States, the long-perceived "China threat" now extends to all dimensions of the bilateral relationship and has expanded to have both regional and global implications. Through its aggressive economic expansion, political outreach, military modernization, ideological and cultural dissemination, and technological advances, China is widely considered to be undermining American power, influence, and interests. There is a palpable sense of urgency in the United States to protect and advance American security, prosperity, and credibility on the world stage.

The conventional view at present among decisionmakers in Washington—both Republicans and Democrats—is that U.S. engagement policy toward China, which began with Nixon and Kissinger's visit to Beijing in the early 1970s and continued through eight successive administrations, has failed. American leadership now calls for a much firmer, more confrontational policy toward China. The fear is that unless the United States pivots to a new and effective approach to dealing with China, this formidable rival will surpass the United States in many important areas and gain a substantial, competitive edge in just a couple of decades, if not sooner. Although the current U.S. anxieties and criticism of China's political, economic, and security policies can be viewed as largely bipartisan in nature, it would be an overstatement to conclude that the United States has reached broad strategic and policy consensus on dealing with China.

Some initial decoupling measures have already borne substantive impact. For example, joint U.S.-China investments in the technology sector in 2018 and 2019 plummeted to almost zero in 2020. Over 100,000 fewer Chinese citizens received business, leisure, and educational visas from the U.S. between May and September 2018 compared to the prior year—a 13 percent drop.[1] Partly due to U.S. efforts to limit the number of People's Republic of China (PRC) students studying science, technology, engineering, and mathematics (known as STEM), the American government granted 54 percent fewer student visas to PRC nationals in fiscal year 2018.[2] The White House even reportedly considered a complete ban on student visas to Chinese nationals.[3] In 2020, the Trump administration made a number of drastic decisions to accelerate decoupling with China, including withdrawing its Peace Corps program from the country,[4] issuing an executive order to end the U.S. government–sponsored Fulbright program in China and Hong Kong,[5] suspending entry of PRC graduate students and researchers believed to be connected with the "military-civil fusion strategy" of the People's Liberation Army (PLA),[6] ordering China to close its consulate in Houston, and threatening a sweeping ban on travel to the United States by Chinese Communist Party (CCP) members and their families, which, if implemented, would likely affect at least 270 million Chinese people.[7]

From Beijing's perspective, Washington's political narrative and decoupling policy have reaffirmed suspicions of a U.S. conspiracy to contain China's rise. In China's eyes, "Washington now seems determined to do everything it can to hold China down."[8] President Trump's prolonged trade war, which has placed heavily punitive tariffs on Chinese products, has now probably become the least significant challenge that China confronts. The CCP leadership apparently not only decided to pursue its aggressive foreign policy but also to retaliate on various fronts, even at the risk of military confrontation with the United States. Both Chinese nationalism and anti-American sentiment have skyrocketed with alarming speed and scope.

Such hostility between two great powers and an emerging threat of a devastating war calls for serious discussion within the policy and scholarly communities in the United States. What are the costs and consequences of decoupling with China? Is it premature for the United States to abandon fifty years of engagement policy? Is it too simplistic to treat China as a monolithic entity without acknowledging its diverse and conflicting internal forces, or without drawing a distinction between the CCP leadership and CCP members, or between state and society? Is it desirable or even feasible, in a twenty-first-century world driven by connectivity, to decouple the two largest economies? Could a strategy that attempts to isolate China also isolate the United States, especially given a growing preference for unilateralism among the U.S. public, and China's embrace of multilateralism and its economic and political benefits? If America disengages from China in the areas of economic development, environmental protection, energy security, and educational exchange, what leverage and influence, if any, can the United States have on China's future evolution?

Questions should also be raised about the Chinese side of the policy discourse. Some Chinese opinion leaders argue that the CCP leadership should recognize that the country's remarkable advancement in science and technology over the past four decades is only *partially* due to internal efforts. China's success primarily stems from open educational exchanges and technology collaboration with the West, especially the United States. Many Chinese believe that the recent U.S. strategic shift from regarding China as a partner or cooperative competitor to an adversary may reflect the decline of American confidence in its global supremacy. Although there may be some truth to this perspective on evolving geopolitical power dynamics, these changes cannot justify Beijing's conduct in the economic (state capitalism and intellectual property violations), political (tight media censorship, "reeducation camps" in Xinjiang, and the national security law for Hong Kong), ideological (authoritarian overseas outreach), and military (island construction in the South China Sea) domains, of which China's neighbors and the West are highly critical.

This chapter begins by reviewing the historical context of U.S. engagement with China, including educational and cultural exchanges, and discussing the incentives and concerns on both sides, especially in regard to the "evolution" of Chinese top leaders through five generations, ranging from Mao to Xi. The chapter then analyzes the causes leading to the deterioration of the relationship in six major domains, as well as the perceived fault lines for conflict. By exploring dissenting opinions about decoupling policy, this study argues that it is premature and detrimental for the United States to discard its fifty-year engagement with China. This discussion then concludes with a focused analysis of how the increasingly volatile U.S.-China relationship has affected the Chinese middle class and how its views and reactions can provide valuable guidance for American policymakers who are creating a revised form of engagement in an evolving world.

U.S. ENGAGEMENT POLICY AND ITS OBJECTIVE OF "PEACEFUL EVOLUTION"

First articulated by John Foster Dulles in the 1950s, the American idea of using international integration to encourage the "peaceful evolution" of Communist regimes has long been a cornerstone of the U.S. strategy to engage and transform China. Based on this theory, if China continues to "evolve peacefully" toward an open economy and society, further integrating with the U.S.-led international system, there will eventually be some form of political transformation. This does not mean that the United States intends to turn China into a Western-style democracy or, an even greater fantasy for some American leaders, to make China dependent on the United States. Indeed, very few Americans would naïvely engage in such wishful thinking. Rather, for decades, Washington policymakers had hoped only that this most populous country would refrain from undermining the liberal international order. As Mary Brown Bullock, a distinguished historian of U.S.-China educational and cultural exchanges, observed in the 1980s, "Drawing China into an American orbit through education became a widespread goal."[9] Some scholars held that China might transform as a result of the time-honored and then-believable idea of the democratic peace theory.[10] In accordance with this, these scholars also argued that it was the responsibility of the United States to promote liberal democratic change within both the Chinese state and society.

As a form of cultural diplomacy, educational exchanges with non-Western countries were promoted by Washington, especially during the Cold War era, as the "fourth dimension" of foreign policy—in addition to political, economic, and military efforts.[11] The fourth dimension stressed the importance of "the human side" of foreign relations by emphasizing "peoples, ideas, and values."[12] In the words of President Dwight D. Eisenhower, "Just as war begins in the minds of men, so does peace."[13] Education, therefore, could be used as a vital channel through which to train the future leaders of foreign countries about American values and ideas.[14] This theory is a long-standing view in the American foreign policy community—that the country which educates China's youth will eventually influence China's development.[15] As Yale University historian Jonathan D. Spence observes, for many Western internationalists, China presents a "chance to influence history by the force of personality."[16] This education-based strategy "would do a far better service than guns and battleships in keeping a peaceful world."[17]

Top leaders of both countries have explicitly linked Sino-U.S. educational exchanges with broader aspirations of world peace and regional stability. When the "Agreement on Scientific and Cultural Exchanges between the United States and China" was signed in Washington, D.C., in January 1979, Deng Xiaoping told the international media, "It is my belief that extensive contacts and cooperation among nations and increased interchanges and understanding between peoples will make the world we live in more safe, more stable, and more peaceful."[18] At the same meeting, President Jimmy Carter proclaimed to Deng and other Chinese guests, "Our aim is to make this kind of exchange between our countries no longer the exception, but the norm; no longer a matter of headlines and historians, but a routine part of the everyday life of both the Chinese and the American people."[19]

During the past four decades, educational exchanges between the United States and China have become so commonplace that people tend to overlook their remarkable impact on China's political transformation, the multitude of people-to-people exchanges between the two countries, and the stability of the Asia-Pacific region. Between 1978 and 2019, a total of 5,857,100 PRC citizens studied abroad, with a significant percentage going to the United States.[20] In 2018 alone, approximately 703,500 Chinese students studied overseas, making China the primary source of international students in other countries.[21] In the 2017–18 academic year, 363,341 PRC students were enrolled in American schools, marking the ninth consecutive year that Chinese students represented the largest proportion of foreign students in the United States.[22] PRC students accounted for 33 percent of the total international students in the United States that year. By comparison, the total number of American students studying in China that year was 20,996.[23] As for tourists, prior to U.S. decoupling measures, approximately 5 million people traveled between the United States and China each year.[24]

In the past two decades, China has witnessed a tidal wave of returnees to the country. By 2018, approximately 3,651,400 Chinese students and scholars who studied abroad had returned to China, representing 85 percent of all Chinese students and scholars who had completed a program abroad.[25] In 2017 alone, approximately 480,900 Chinese students and scholars returned to their native country after finishing studies overseas.[26] Among them, 227,400 received advanced degrees (master's or doctoral degrees) or postdoctoral training. A majority of these foreign-educated returnees belong to China's emerging middle class. They now play important roles in many walks of life, including in China's educational institutions, research centers, central and local governments, state and private enterprises, foreign or joint-venture companies, law firms, hospitals and clinics, media networks, and NGOs. A new Chinese term, *haiguipai* (returnees from study abroad), has been coined to describe this rapidly growing elite group.

America's emphasis on cross-national educational exchanges is also based on the belief that, to a large extent, peaceful international relations depend on the personal relationship between the leaders of these nations.[27] Thus it is notable that a significant number of Western-educated returnees have already ascended into the Chinese leadership. Four members of the Politburo formed at the 2017 Party Congress, including one member of the Politburo Standing Committee, are Western-educated returnees. Wang Huning, who was a visiting scholar at the University of California at Berkeley, is in charge of party affairs; Liu He, who received an MPA degree from Harvard's Kennedy School of Government, is responsible for financial affairs and China's trade negotiations with the United States; Yang Jiechi, who studied at the University of Bath and the London School of Economics and Political Science in the early 1970s, went on to serve as China's ambassador to the United States and is currently serving as the chief representative of the foreign affairs bureaucracy; and Chen Xi, former top administrator of Tsinghua University and visiting scholar at Stanford University, is now in charge of personnel for the CCP. Never before in PRC history have there been this many Western-educated returnees serving in the Politburo. As this study's quantitative analysis reveals, on the 376-member central committee of the Chinese Communist Party, the percentage of foreign-educated returnees has gradually climbed from 6 percent in 2002 to 11 percent in 2007, to 15 percent in 2012, and then to 21 percent in 2017. A majority of these leaders studied in the West, particularly in the United States.[28]

Western-educated political elites in China are likely to become even more prominent in the future, as many young students, including the children of senior leaders, have studied in the West over the past couple of decades and then returned to China afterward. In addition, a few educational joint ventures between the United States and China have produced a significant number of graduates who hold important roles in all walks of life.

For example, the Hopkins-Nanjing Center, a joint program established in 1986 by the Johns Hopkins University's School of Advanced International Studies and Nanjing University, has produced over 3,000 graduates, many of whom serve as leaders in government, academia, industry, media, and NGOs in both countries.[29]

A senior Taiwanese official predicted a couple of decades ago that, by around 2030, the top leader of China would likely be a U.S.-trained returnee and perhaps even a classmate of the incumbent U.S. president. During their summit meeting, the two leaders might chat about memorable events from their school years.[30] In describing this imaginary scene, the Taiwanese official implied that military tensions over the Taiwan Strait could be mitigated, if not fully resolved, should all the top leaders of the parties involved have attended the same American university.

One may argue that these reform era developments in China align with the expected changes brought by a "peaceful evolution" toward American values and interests. Early studies of the newly affluent groups in China, including the country's nascent middle class, tend to emphasize their status quo–oriented, risk-averse nature in political views and behavior, and a large body of research suggests that this may be only a transitory phase in the development of the middle class.[31] Already, there is widespread resentment among the Chinese middle class due to the corruption of CCP officials, the state's monopoly of major industries, and the growing demands for environmental protection, property rights, food and drug safety, and government accountability in these areas. Thus, to a certain extent, China's middle class has started to display similarities to their counterparts in democratic countries.

Other recent Chinese economic and political developments, however, have made some in the American political and intellectual establishments skeptical of the U.S. engagement policy's success, especially because of the huge gap between the objectives and outcomes of "peaceful evolution." Notably, the aforementioned developments in Chinese politics and society have not weakened China's authoritarian, one-party state. In fact, other concerns and tensions have continued to fester since the two countries began engaging in broad educational and cultural exchanges.

Without a doubt, policymakers in Beijing and Washington have had different agendas when planning and engaging in far-reaching educational exchanges over the past four decades. For Deng Xiaoping, the primary goal behind sending large numbers of Chinese students to Western countries and Japan for academic training was to "make up for the years lost" during the Cultural Revolution, when China was almost completely cut off from the international academic community.[32] Through these educational exchanges with advanced Western countries, Deng intended to enhance China's economic productivity, improve people's material standard of living, increase educational competence and technological competitiveness, and strengthen China's national cohesion.[33] Today, it is clear that Deng's goal has been fulfilled: China's GDP has increased sixtyfold over the past forty years, its economy has grown to be the second largest in the world, and the PRC's international ranking based on the number of scientific papers published has shot up from 38th in 1979 to 23rd in 1982, to 15th in 1989, to 5th in 2003, and to 2nd in 2017.[34]

The dilemma for Chinese leaders, however, was that they could not promote foreign studies without taking two major risks: the "inevitable brain drain" and the "unavoidable spread of Western ideas." With respect to the brain drain problem, Deng was confident that "even if half of those sent abroad do not return, there remains one half who return to help with the four modernizations, [therefore] it is better than not sending any or sending fewer."[35] Instead, throughout much of the past four decades, Chinese leaders worried "more about China's isolation from the outside world than a 'peaceful evolution,' " in the words of a prominent scholar on international relations in China.[36]

The dilemma for U.S. policymakers is that American universities cannot teach foreign students liberal and democratic ideas without also allowing them to pursue scientific and technological research. China's increasing willingness to encourage its citizens to study abroad and the tidal wave of returnees back to the country have generated apprehension, rather than satisfaction, for Washington. China's extraordinary economic growth, its drive to achieve scientific and technological modernization, and its heightened military capability in the event of a war over the Taiwan Strait or the South China Sea are cause for concern in the United States. This unease explains why President George W. Bush perceived China as a major threat even prior to the September 11 terrorist attacks, as revealed in two best-selling books about the Bush administration.[37] The U.S. government's concern over sharing scientific and technological knowledge that could threaten national security has led to restrictive policies for foreign students—especially those from authoritarian countries like China—preventing them from studying certain "sensitive subjects."

BEIJING'S REACTION TO "PEACEFUL EVOLUTION": FROM MAO TO XI

Since the founding of the PRC in 1949, Chinese leaders have been suspicious of the West exerting undue influence on Chinese cultural values and sociopolitical norms. Mao considered John Foster Dulles's policy of "peaceful evolution" as America's strategy to impede the Chinese socialist revolution.[38] Preventing China from falling into the U.S. conspiracy was a central concern for Mao, who resolutely opposed any substantial economic and cultural contact between China and the United States. "Drawing China into an American orbit through education," the U.S. strategy outlined in previous sections, was long perceived by Maoists as an American scheme to mold the views of China's next generation of leaders to align with U.S. interests.[39]

China's polemics against the Soviet Union during the early 1960s and Mao's Cultural Revolution in the mid-1960s can also be attributed, at least partly, to Mao's paranoia that Dulles's grand strategy had already influenced the Soviet Union and could lead to a similar revisionist "change of color" in the PRC.[40] Many intellectuals, especially those who were educated overseas, were persecuted because they were considered part of the U.S. threat.

Under Deng's leadership, China largely abandoned Mao's xenophobic and isolationist policy toward the West. For example, in 1978, Deng made two milestone decisions: to attract foreign investment and to send Chinese students to study abroad. He outlined China's strategic plan to catch up with the scientific and technological development of the West, famously declaring in 1983 that "education should face modernization, the world, and the future."[41] During the Deng era, conservative political and cultural elites in China feared that the spread of Western ideas from extensive foreign educational exchanges would reshape the Chinese political system, aligning it with the interests of the West. In response to this concern, Deng adopted countermeasures such as the campaigns against "spiritual pollution" and "bourgeois liberalization," especially in the wake of the Tiananmen incident in 1989 and the collapse of the Soviet Union.[42] Nevertheless, the Deng era saw a rush of business engagement with other countries. His famous southern trip in 1992 called for the acceleration of economic reforms and greater openness with the outside world.

Deng's successor, Jiang Zemin, further broadened China's global relations. During the Jiang era, Chinese government propaganda promoted the idea that China should strive "to connect with the track of global development" (*yu shijie jiegui*), reflecting Chinese political leaders' strong desire for the country to be accepted by the "modern world" through economic and educational globalization.[43] In the words of some Chinese journalists, "China has to change itself in order to be connected with the world."[44] China's World Trade Organization accession and successful bids for both the 2008 Olympics in Beijing and the 2010 World Expo in Shanghai are often cited as the results of this effort. In contrast to Deng, who was often resistant to cultural influence from the West, Jiang unambiguously embraced Western culture. For example, Jiang allowed an Italian opera troupe to perform in the Forbidden City, invited a French architect to design a postmodern grand theater for Tiananmen Square, and urged the Chinese public to watch the American film *Titanic*. In 1999, China published some 5,000 foreign book titles, accounting for 10 percent of the total number of newly published books—a relatively high percentage compared to the share of foreign books published in other countries.[45] Jiang's endorsement of cultural pluralism and transnationalism has manifested in Shanghai's dynamic cultural activities since the mid-1990s, and later chapters will elaborate on this subject.

Hu Jintao and Wen Jiabao's interest in Western culture included economic management, cultural entertainment, and technological development, as well as political culture, social welfare systems, and political institutionalization. Under their leadership, the proceedings of the Politburo meetings, including decisionmaking sessions and group study sessions, were made available to the public for the first time in PRC history.[46] During a study session on the governance of the ruling party held in the summer of 2004, Hu urged his colleagues to be "open-minded" about the "valuable experiences and methods of other ruling parties in the world," including those in Western democracies.[47] On a number of occasions, Wen Jiabao argued that China should adhere to universal values (*pushi jiazhi*).[48] While neither Hu nor Wen ever said that China should adopt a Western-style democratic system, they both repeatedly stressed the need for checks and balances in the Chinese political system, especially within the ruling Communist party. In the foreign policy domain, Hu and his advisers at the Central Party School formulated the "theory of the peaceful rise of China" (*Zhongguo heping jueqilun*), which argued that China should strive to be a respectable and responsible member of the international community so its rise would not be perceived as a threat to world peace, especially by neighboring countries.[49]

Since reaching the pinnacle of China's leadership in 2012, Xi Jinping has become known for strengthening the CCP and cracking down on corruption. He has tightened restrictions on civil society through fierce enforcement of internet censorship at home. On the world stage, Xi has adopted a more aggressive foreign policy, promoting a "go global strategy" with far-reaching programs, such as the Belt and Road Initiative (BRI). Xi has also expressed concerns about a U.S.-led "color revolution" that toppled the Soviet Union and the regimes of other socialist countries, and his public call for "fighting" perceived U.S. containment has led both Chinese liberal intellectuals and Western China-watchers to worry about increased risks to stability in China and to peace around the world. But for a majority of people in China and elsewhere, especially Africa and South America, Xi's words and actions have made him an immensely popular leader. In their minds, Xi's undertakings—including his strong anticorruption campaign, military reform, firm commitment to eliminating domestic poverty, effective nationwide mobilization against COVID-19, bold goals for environmental protection, promotion of economic growth through infrastructure development abroad, and vision for China to become a technological superpower by 2049—all serve the best interests of China and balance out the hegemonic power of the United States.

Interestingly, these contrasting views of Xi Jinping have caused fear and anxiety among the political and intellectual establishments in the United States and many like-minded people elsewhere. Two views are particularly prevalent. The first view holds that instead of a peaceful evolution to a more liberal state, China is becoming increasingly autocratic and repressive. The second view sees Xi's party-state as gaining more support at home and more influence abroad. Some Western critics identify Xi as a powerful leader presiding over a high-tech surveillance state. George Soros, for example, recently named Xi the "most dangerous enemy" of free societies. He notes that while Xi's China is not the only authoritarian regime in the world, it is the "wealthiest, strongest, and technologically most sophisticated."[50] Growing fear and anxiety have led to a strategic shift in the narrative on China, which has become more pronounced under the Trump administration.

WASHINGTON'S CONCERNS ABOUT CHINA AND "DECOUPLING"

American policymakers' concerns about China's increasing aggression in bilateral, regional, and global relations have extended to a wide range of domains, many of which are closely related. These areas of concern have been mutually reinforcing, contributing to a deeply intertwined but troubling bilateral relationship. From Washington's perspective, all areas of U.S. interaction with China now carry strong political overtones and merit serious scrutiny. There are six areas of concern for the United States: (1) strategic and diplomatic, (2) security and military, (3) political and ideological, (4) economic and financial, (5) scientific and technological, and (6) educational and cultural. Together, these areas of concern have led some policymakers in Washington to call for a complete decoupling with China.

Strategic and Diplomatic Front

As has long been known, Chinese leaders and the Chinese foreign policy establishment are strongly inclined toward strategic planning, particularly with diplomatic policy. Over the past decade, a widely shared argument within the Chinese discourse on foreign policy is that China has been playing—or must learn to play—the "great chess game" (*xia yipan daqi*) on the world stage. China's opponent in this contest is, of course, the United States. According to some American strategists, such as Michael Pompeo and Steve Bannon, China's overall objective is not just the country's sustainable development but to surpass the United States.[51] For these analysts, China's strategic goal is most clearly articulated in Xi Jinping's "two centenary" visions, which set forth goals for the hundredth anniversary of the CCP in 2021 and the hundredth anniversary of the PRC in 2049. By 2049, according to Xi, China will have become a global leader in terms of strength and influence.

In response to these developments, U.S. government officials have made statements highlighting that China should be seen as a strategic rival or adversary. These statements can be found in several reports released by the U.S. government, such as the *National Security Strategy of the United States* and the *National Defense Strategy of the United States of America*, and in major foreign policy speeches by U.S. top leaders, including President Donald Trump's 2018 State of the Union Address, Vice President Mike Pence's 2018 speech at the Hudson Institute and 2019 speech at the Wilson Center, Vice Chair of the Senate Intelligence Committee Mark Warner's 2019 speech at the U.S. Institute of Peace, Attorney General William P. Barr's 2020 speech on China Policy at the Ford Presidential Museum, and Secretary of State Michael Pompeo's 2020 speeches at the National Governors Association meeting and at the Nixon Presidential Library. All of these reports and speeches claim that the reemergence of long-term, interstate strategic competition from revisionist powers—namely China—rather than terrorist groups and alleged rogue regimes, now constitutes "the most formidable threat to the United States."[52]

From the U.S. perspective, China's expanding global engagement reveals its strategic and diplomatic ambitions. Some of China's outreach in Latin America, Africa, and the Middle East comes at the expense of the United States. For example, when it comes to multilateral diplomacy, Beijing has chosen the Community of Latin American and Caribbean States—to which the United States is not a party—as its primary vehicle for engaging the region. In Europe, as a lengthy report by European scholars recently observed, China's strategic relationship building has not only put China " 'at Europe's gates'—it is now already well within them."[53]

Given the circumstances, U.S. policymakers have asked American allies to bolster their strategic alliances with the United States, and have also urged other countries in Latin America and Africa to take a position.[54] Meanwhile, diplomatic engagement between the United States and China has undergone significant changes in recent years. During President Obama's eight-year tenure, there were as many as 105 government-sponsored regular dialogues. The Trump administration reduced the number to 4 in the first two years, and subsequently even those dialogues were discontinued. The most significant blow to diplomatic relations came in July 2020, when the United States ordered the closure of the Chinese consulate in Houston, Texas, in response to alleged Chinese economic espionage and attempted theft of scientific research. The Chinese government, in retaliation, revoked the license of the U.S. consulate in Chengdu, which had served as an American gateway to western China since 1985.

Security and Military Front

Over the past two decades, the PLA has transformed from a third-rate military with minimal offensive power to arguably the second-most-powerful armed force on the planet, behind only that of the United States. Xi Jinping's military reforms will likely, in his words, "make the Chinese forces more lethal and more capable of projecting military power well beyond China's shores."[55]

While the U.S. military will likely remain superior to its Chinese counterpart in the years or even decades to come, China's strategic challenges in the following areas still warrant attention from the rest of the world. First, the Taiwan situation has always been the most sensitive issue in U.S.-China relations. With passage of the Taiwan Travel Act by Congress in 2018, the United States has strengthened its "commitments under the Taiwan Relations Act to provide for Taiwan's legitimate defense needs and deter coercion."[56] This action has caused—and will continue to generate—very strong reactions from Beijing, as the Chinese leadership and public's claim to sovereignty over Taiwan is a core national interest. Second, over the past decade, China has consolidated disputed territories in the South China Sea by rapidly creating and militarizing artificial islands. Third, China recently established its first overseas military base in Djibouti, signaling that China's BRI may extend beyond the economic sphere and could be used to significantly enhance Chinese strategic and military presence and capacity around the world. Finally, the PLA's current motto is unambiguous: "Be Prepared." The PLA is preparing for warfare in every domain—land, sea, air, space, and cyberspace. In recent years, China's military modernization efforts have accelerated with the adoption of advanced technology, artificial intelligence (AI), cyber warfare, and asymmetrical warfare.

According to some U.S. analysts, the long-term challenges resulting from China's military modernization and expanding military capacity will be formidable. Currently, China's military budget still amounts to only one-third of the military budget of the United States, but according to *The Economist*, China's military spending will surpass that of the United States by about 2035. In 2050, China's military spending is forecast to be around $1.75 trillion, whereas U.S. military spending will be $1.25 trillion—significantly less than that of China.[57] These projections, accurate or not, have greatly reinforced anxiety in Washington. One outcome has been U.S. Senator Marco Rubio's argument that the United States should develop strategic countermeasures on this front before it is too late.[58] In a hearing for the

Senate Select Committee on Intelligence in February 2018, Senator Rubio asserted, "I'm not sure in the 240-something-odd-year history of this nation we have ever faced a competitor and potential adversary of this scale, scope and capacity . . . [the Chinese] are carrying out a well-orchestrated, well-executed, very patient long-term strategy to replace the United States as the most powerful and influential nation on Earth."[59]

Political and Ideological Front

There is broad consensus within the U.S. political and intellectual establishments that under Xi Jinping's leadership, the Chinese authoritarian system has advanced at a more aggressive pace and scale than at any period in the post-Mao era. China's belligerence is most evident domestically, where political repression and ideological indoctrination have risen extensively. Internationally, the aggression of Chinese authorities has manifested in a propaganda campaign and "united front" approach. Critics often highlight the following four aspects of the CCP's aggressive political pursuits both at home and abroad.

First, Xi's China has implemented a series of measures to control public discourse. In 2013, just one year after Xi Jinping became the top CCP leader, Chinese authorities launched a campaign to influence domestic public discussion, with a special focus on university campuses and social media. They cracked down on the so-called seven subversive currents, referring to public discourse on constitutionalism and judicial independence, human rights, civil society, universal values, media freedom, crony capitalism, and previous mistakes made by the CCP. The Chinese leadership has consolidated its control over media and the internet, symbolized by the "great firewall," and it has also begun to pursue what Francis Fukuyama refers to as "twenty-first century authoritarian mechanisms," such as "big data" analytics of citizens' behavior, AI-based "social credit systems," and facial recognition software to monitor the populace.[60]

Second, the recent amendments to the PRC Constitution—particularly those allowing Xi Jinping to serve as president for life—have undermined Deng Xiaoping's plan for institutionalized political succession through term limits and collective leadership norms. In addition, a cult of personality and ideological indoctrination in the style of the Cultural Revolution have both returned to official Chinese media. The separation between the party and state—an important institutional reform initiated by Deng—has become increasingly blurred as Xi Jinping strengthens the role of the party in the government, in the private sector, and even in foreign joint ventures and foreign companies operating in China.

Third, the recent Nineteenth Party Congress has enshrined the concept of "Xi Jinping Thought on socialism with Chinese characteristics for a new era" in the Constitution. China's resilient authoritarianism has not only endured, it has also become increasingly influential in other countries. Beijing has exerted significant effort to create a more positive global perception of China's political system ("single-strongman authoritarianism"), economic system ("state capitalism"), and "nationwide mobilization system" (*juguo tizhi*) as viable alternatives to liberal democracy, a market economy, and federalism.

Fourth, the CCP aggressively uses its propaganda machine to promote the party line overseas. China's official newspaper is now included as a free insert in mainstream foreign newspapers, such as the *Washington Post*, and the CCP has also funded the distribution of Chinese-language dailies overseas. *Overseas Chinese Daily* (*Qiaobao*), for example, has more than 100,000 Chinese subscribers in at least fifteen major cities in the United States. Its main news sections are almost identical to those in the *People's Daily*. The online Chinese-language *College Daily* on WeChat also toes the CCP line, and its primary audience consists of Chinese students studying overseas.[61] Critics of China's ideological and political outreach have observed that Beijing is increasingly targeting four groups of people: former politicians; opinion leaders in the media, think tanks, and academia; state and local governments in the United States and elsewhere; and Chinese diaspora communities.[62]

Economic and Financial Front

The U.S. business community may not favor an all-out, prolonged trade war with China, but their frustration with the country's practices is long-standing and multifaceted. Xi Jinping's support of state capitalism and inaction over business and trade practices considered unfair by many in the United States have disappointed supporters of engagement, clearing the way for President Trump to aggressively confront Beijing. The CCP leadership's insertion of party branches into private and foreign firms is seen as a step backward, and these actions contradict the government's promise to facilitate greater opening to the outside world. Many U.S. companies resent China's aggressive industrial policies—in accordance with its "Made in China 2025" plan—that promote state-backed domestic players in the Chinese leadership's "strategically important sectors," such as aerospace, shipbuilding, biomedicine, and robotics.

Critics also point out the slow pace of market reforms and long-delayed promises on intellectual property protections and market access, which have frustrated the American business community—a group that has traditionally played a moderating role in the U.S.-China relationship. In the

United States, the most hawkish voices on China argue that the country is "taking advantage" of the international trade order and has been a bad faith actor in the World Trade Organization.

Furthermore, China's splashy, international economic initiatives have heightened U.S. concerns that China is expanding its unfair practices and political influence, incorporating economic programs into its geopolitical strategy. Large-scale programs, such as the BRI, have been criticized as "debt-trap diplomacy," in which unsustainable loans and debt distress allow China to gain influence and extract outsized concessions from indebted countries. China is also making efforts to use the Chinese yuan rather than the U.S. dollar for oil settlements with Russia, Brazil, and Venezuela. The BRI has aroused extended discussions in Washington about the risks of Chinese ascendency and its encroachment on U.S. power and global leadership.

These rising anxieties, coupled with President Trump's long-standing call for a trade rebalancing, have led Washington to markedly change its economic position on Beijing, and the resulting U.S.-China trade war has dealt a severe blow to the Chinese economy. China's stock market in 2018, for example, saw its worst performance since the global financial crisis, losing $2.4 trillion in value and making China's stock market the worst performing one that year. That same year, China's GDP growth fell to 7 percent—its slowest pace in 28 years—according to official government figures. China's investment in the United States in 2018 was only one-sixth that of the previous year and 10 percent of that in 2016, suggesting the first hints of decoupling, as U.S. and Chinese interdependencies began to weaken. In the wake of the COVID-19 pandemic's devastating impact on the U.S. economy, the White House urged companies to rearrange their global industrial supply chains to reduce dependence on Chinese manufacturers, and requested that American companies in China move elsewhere.[63]

Scientific and Technological Front

The focal point of tensions between the United States and China is centered around the increasingly intense competition in the scientific and technological domains. The digital revolution has affected human security, prosperity, and dignity faster than perhaps at any other time in human history. This unprecedented transformation frames some of the central and complex issues related to growing tensions and competition in the U.S.-China bilateral relationship.

Science and technology challenges with China are intimately linked to economic, security, and political concerns in the United States. The recent "U.S. National Security Strategy" report asserts that "data, like energy, will shape U.S. economic prosperity and our future strategic position in the world."[64] In technological areas such as 5G, AI, and quantum computing, China is catching up at an alarming speed, and in some cases has already surpassed the United States. The *National Security Strategy* report also claims that China aims to control information and data to repress civil society groups domestically, as well as expand Chinese influence overseas.[65] Some analysts argue that a lack of a robust rule of law and ethics-based regulations in China have unfairly advantaged the country's development of AI and other cutting-edge research.

Critics in the United States assert that technological theft, intellectual property rights infringement, forced technology transfers, and industrial policies have all been major drivers of China's technological domination on the world stage. These concerns, in turn, have understandably led to a rethinking and reevaluation of technology policy by the United States. Policymakers in Washington have come to believe that the United States should not only limit high-end technology transfers to China but also prevent Chinese companies from accessing the high-tech market in the United States, as well as prevent Chinese students from conducting research in the United States on sensitive subjects.[66] Recently, the Federal Bureau of Investigation (FBI) has made great efforts to investigate—and, in a number of cases, order research institutions and universities to fire—PRC nationals or ethnic Chinese scientists who have received federal funding while being engaged in research projects in both the United States and China.

The Trump administration has sought to ban Huawei, a Chinese flagship information technology company, from the United States, and it has lobbied allies to do the same. In so doing, the Trump administration looks to undercut China's science and technology goals, threatening to isolate China unless it plays by U.S. rules. To this end, Australia banned Huawei and ZTE from providing 5G technology for the country's telecommunications network. Most notably, the United States submitted an extradition request to Canada for Huawei chief financial officer Meng Wanzhou, who was arrested while transiting through Vancouver in the fall of 2018. The risk of a full-fledged tech war with China has grown larger following a decision by the U.S. government to put Huawei on its Entity List in May 2019 (although Huawei was later given a reprieve). This designation means that U.S. companies and their foreign partners would have to receive permission from the U.S. government in order to supply Huawei with their products. According to the Chinese media, this U.S. government decision will affect 13,000 of Huawei's suppliers in 170 countries, including 211 of the Fortune Global 500 firms.[67] This is likely to have an earthshaking impact on the global telecommunications market.

Educational and Cultural Front

From the perspective of educational institutions in the United States and China, educational and cultural exchanges between the two countries have been constructive and mutually beneficial since the establishment of diplomatic relations in 1979. But in recent years, policymakers in both Beijing and Washington have had second thoughts about these engagements. In Beijing, there has been increasing political control over international educational exchanges. The PRC's 2017 Foreign NGO Law has created extensive restrictions on foreign educational institutions and civil society organizations that engage in educational, cultural, and people-to-people exchanges.[68]

Critical opinions on bilateral educational and cultural exchanges seem to be even stronger in Washington. In the fall of 2018, the White House considered banning student visas for Chinese nationals, which would end forty years of educational exchanges with the PRC.[69] The proposal by hawks in the White House eventually failed because of "concerns about its economic and diplomatic impact."[70] Amid the COVID-19 pandemic in July 2020, the administration tried yet again to expel international postsecondary students engaged in a full online course load from the United States—which would have had an outsized impact on Chinese national students—only to retract the policy after a significant outcry and a challenge in court. On a number of occasions between 2018 and 2020, FBI director Christopher Wray made very strong remarks about the "China threat" on the educational and cultural exchange front, reaffirming the 2017 U.S. *National Security Strategy* report's statement that "part of China's military modernization and economic expansion is due to its access to the U.S. innovation economy, including America's world-class universities."[71]

Further, American media has widely reported on CCP influence within U.S. educational institutions. Most notable are reports that alleged CCP agents have been embedded among Chinese students and visiting scholars at some universities in the United States.[72] A number of Chinese Students and Scholars Associations have been reported for acting as extensions of Chinese embassies in the United States and other countries.[73] Confucius Institutes have become some of the most controversial entities in U.S.-China educational exchanges and are key targets of criticism. In 2017, there were altogether 512 Confucius Institutes and 1,074 Confucius Classrooms in 131 countries, of which 103 Confucius Institutes (20 percent) and 501 Confucius Classrooms (47 percent) were located in the United States.[74] Critics have levied a number of accusations against the practices of Confucius Institutes: (1) the Institutes, run by an agency of the Chinese government called the Hanban (which has been renamed the Center for Language Education and Cooperation), tend to compromise academic freedom and jeopardize the autonomy and integrity of their host American educational institutions; (2) the Institutes were described as "an important part of China's overseas propaganda set-up" by Li Changchun in 2009, who was then a member of the Politburo Standing Committee in charge of party propaganda; (3) Confucius Institute contracts are often inaccessible to the public, pledge adherence to Chinese law, and give Hanban the right to vet all curriculum and course plans; and (4) Confucius Institutes have fostered a generation of American students with "selective knowledge and imbalanced information" about China's history and present-day life.[75]

In August 2018, President Trump signed the National Defense Authorization Act, which included a provision that "required universities to choose between hosting Chinese language programs funded by the Pentagon or China's Confucius Institute."[76] By July 2020, 45 Confucius Institutes in the United States had closed or were in the process of closing.[77] Additionally, two reports by the National Endowment for Democracy and the Hoover Institution accused China of increasing its use of "sharp power" to penetrate American universities and think tanks, with the goal of influencing American attitudes toward China.[78] Former chief executive of Hong Kong C. H. Tung's China-United States Exchange Foundation, which has provided funding for foreign universities, think tanks, and NGOs, is often cited as an example of China's promotion of sharp power.

To address these perceived problems, U.S. Representative Joe Wilson, U.S Senator Marco Rubio, and U.S. Senator Tom Cotton cosponsored a bill, named the Foreign Influence Transparency Act of 2018, that would (1) amend the Foreign Agents Registration Act, a 1938 law requiring agents of foreign governments and political parties to register with the Department of Justice; (2) clarify that educational and scholastic organizations would be exempt "only if the activities do not promote the political agenda of a government of a foreign country"; and (3) amend the Higher Education Act, which currently requires colleges and universities to disclose gifts totaling $250,000 or more in a calendar year from a foreign donor, calling for lowering the threshold to $50,000.[79]

Kiron Skinner, the former director of Policy Planning at the State Department, has put forth the most extreme proposal of reconsidering—or possibly ending—cultural exchanges with China. In a public forum held in Washington, D.C., in April 2019, Skinner described tensions with China as "a fight with a really different civilization and a different ideology, and the United States hasn't had that before."[80] She continued, "It's also striking that this is the first time that we will have a great power competitor that is not Caucasian."[81] Some elements of the U.S. decoupling policy toward China— for example, the aforementioned proposed travel ban of CCP members and their families (estimated to be at least 270 million people)—will inevitably cause all PRC citizens (or even ethnic Chinese persons) to be subject to suspicion and scrutiny.

OPPOSITION TO COMPREHENSIVE DISENGAGEMENT WITH CHINA

While revisiting or resetting the fifty-year U.S. engagement policy toward China has become a prevailing stance in Washington, there are still those who oppose disengagement in many policy and intellectual establishments in the United States. Reservations and disagreements remain over every aspect of the aforementioned decoupling policy. Some believe that decoupling will fail to protect and advance American interests, and it may further undermine the potency of American power and influence. Furthermore, decoupling will enhance the risk for a war between the two countries.

In regard to China's aggression on the strategic and diplomatic front, it is certainly debatable whether all Chinese pursuits under Xi's leadership have been designed to undermine U.S. interests. Some practices can be seen as common occurrences in international affairs, or they may be measures primarily implemented for China's self-defense. As is true for any other country, China has its own legitimate national interests. Being the world's second-largest economy, China is naturally interested in seeking energy security and resources from overseas. At this critical time of rapid change in the geopolitical landscape, especially amid the deterioration of the U.S.-China bilateral relationship, Chinese leaders—like their American counterparts—must be constantly assessing and reassessing the country's strategic and diplomatic objectives. As Susan Thornton, former acting assistant secretary of state observed, it is in the vital interest of the United States to "maintain regular dialogues and working-level discussions to ensure the appropriate crisis management mechanisms are in place in the event of a crisis."[82]

Reevaluating engagement policy is no longer of interest to just the most hawkish Washington analysts; it has attracted attention from all U.S. decisionmakers. Yet the substance of this strategic revision remains hotly debated, and no consensus has crystallized.[83] Though U.S.-China policy has changed in fundamental ways, there remain important ongoing disagreements within the American political and intellectual establishments. When it comes to strategy, some believe that outside the broad statements in the *National Security Strategy* and *National Defense Strategy*, there is no strategy—at least no sound strategy based on serious thinking about priority and capacity—coming from the Trump administration. Both President Obama's "pivot to Asia" and President Trump's "Indo-Pacific" strategy have long-range visions, but they fall short on resource allocation and implementation, reflecting serious logistical inadequacies in their design. To the extent that there is a containment strategy, there are disagreements about what containment would entail. Additionally, some argue that any new containment policy would be too late and ineffective.[84] Other countries, including some U.S. allies in Asia and elsewhere, also may not wish to take sides even if they have serious concerns about China's aggressive behavior.

Similarly, on the security and military front, some American opinion leaders argue that the prevailing fear and sensationalism in Washington do not allow proper consideration of the Chinese perspective. In the words of Jeffrey Sachs, "The United States refuses to view itself through China's eyes."[85] Sachs explains further:

> If it did so, it would see a nation with: military bases in more than 70 countries, including throughout Asia (compared with China's one tiny overseas naval base in Djibouti); by far the world's largest military budget; a chronic case of warmongering and regime-change operations in Asia and elsewhere, most recently including Afghanistan, Iraq, Syria, and Yemen; . . . and deployment of ballistic-missile defenses in Korea that threaten China's nuclear retaliatory response.[86]

In a recent study published by the Rand Corporation, author Timothy R. Heath observed that, in contrast to the American military that has almost constantly been engaged in combat operations over the past half century, the PLA last fought a major conflict over forty years ago "when a seasoned Vietnamese military demolished a bungled Chinese invasion in 1979."[87] Heath concluded, "China's military has an increasingly impressive high-tech arsenal, but its ability to use these weapons and equipment remains unclear."[88] It is one thing for China to possess a number of aircraft carriers, but it is quite another thing to operate these aircraft carriers in a real conflict.

Some scholars have argued that on the security and military front, it is premature to announce that U.S. engagement policy with China under the past eight presidents has failed. According to Jeffrey Bader, who served as senior director for Asia in the Obama White House National Security Council, "East Asia has avoided major military conflicts since the 1970s. After the United States fought three wars in the preceding four decades originating in East Asia, with a quarter of a million lost American lives, this is no small achievement."[89] In Bader's view, abandoning the engagement policy will likely enhance the risk of war in the region.

On the political and ideological front, Xi Jinping and his predecessors have never explicitly claimed that China seeks to export its development model or its authoritarian political system. Beijing's persistent refrain over the past four decades has been that each country should choose its own political system in accordance with its own socioeconomic environment, historical background, and indigenous culture. Washington is divided over whether Chinese influence efforts more broadly—such as purchasing advertising supplements in international newspapers—are unique, and how similar they are to U.S. efforts to promote soft power.

Also, in contrast to the Cold War, during which ideology was one of two major areas of confrontation, today's Chinese leaders seldom claim that communist ideology will prevail. Instead, they often complain that the United States and the West tend to look at China through an overly ideological lens. As an American student of world politics recently observed, Washington's narrative about China's ideological threat to the United States is "a threat of our creation," because its foundational assumption—that "China and the U.S. truly represent two intrinsically antithetical ideologies"—is incredibly weak.[90] In fact, both countries' societies have deep, internal divisions in terms of worldviews and values. In America, these fractures are most evident in the disparity of opinions about President Trump's governance and ideology, especially in regard to demonstrations against systemic racism in the wake of George Floyd's horrific death.

On the economic and financial front, serious competition is both present and palpable between the U.S. and China. Beijing's economic power poses a real and substantial challenge to the United States. Many distinguished American economists argue that one of the top priorities of the U.S. should be to "clean up its own house" in various respects, and make the American economy more competitive and innovative. Yale University economist Stephen Roach believes that the United States and China are locked in "a codependent economic relationship."[91] As Roach points out, "American consumers need low-cost imports from China in order to make ends meet; the U.S. also needs surplus Chinese saving in order to fund a seemingly chronic federal government budget deficit."[92]

For the U.S. business community, exerting pressure on China to encourage changes to unfair economic behavior is a beneficial strategy. However, brash actions and rhetoric that heighten the risk of a decoupling from the world's second-largest economy—especially as China looks to improve economic relations with the EU and Japan—is a mistake. It should be noted that in response to foreign criticism, Xi Jinping has shown some willingness to engage and compromise on the economic front. To address American anxiety over Chinese infrastructure investments in foreign countries, the Chinese government has stated that future BRI projects will emphasize transparency, inclusiveness, and debt sustainability. Additionally, China's recent opening of economic sectors and industries—including financial services, public health, electric vehicles and driverless cars, smart cities, and green development—provide many business opportunities for U.S. companies in a country that is fast becoming the world's largest consumer market. As a result, the U.S. business community is concerned that economic decoupling may lead to the long-term effects of lost market share in China.

As for U.S.-China competition on the scientific and technological front, some American scholars believe that a U.S.-led decoupling with China in these areas will not prevent China from becoming a technological superpower. The United States is simply not ready to implement such an approach, and it is unlikely to succeed.[93] Meanwhile, although China is an unfair competitor due to intellectual property rights infringement and forced technology transfer, China has yet to surpass the United States in overall capacity in science and technology. In today's world, no country can have absolute supremacy in these fields. In a sense, China could survive or even benefit from a U.S.-led decoupling in science and technology, but it lacks the strength and influence to become the world's sole technological superpower. China possesses advantages in the areas of research and development funding, human resources (in terms of the size of its STEM workforce), scale of e-commerce, volume of scientific papers published, state-sponsored innovation, and rapid increase in patents. Nevertheless, the country's technological growth remains constrained by its lack of academic freedom, tight information control, and digital censorship.[94]

Critics of the U.S. policy of scientific and technological (S&T) decoupling accuse it of being based on a poor understanding of S&T development. The policy is tainted by troubling evidence of ethnic bias and racial profiling, as demonstrated by the FBI's public speculation that Chinese (and even Chinese American) professors, scientists, and students are spying for China. These racially charged actions undermine American interests and serve as ammunition for the Chinese government. In fact, these developments help China accelerate the country's drive toward indigenous innovation and S&T breakthroughs. Annually, China now awards degrees to 1.8 million STEM workers (scientists, technologists, engineers, and mathematicians), while the U.S. produces only about 650,000 STEM graduates.[95] Additionally, over one-third of these U.S. university graduates are foreigners, and in the field of computer science, over 50 percent are foreigners. Currently, about one-fourth of the world's STEM workers reside in China, and this technological workforce is eight times larger than that of the United States.[96] As Massachusetts Institute of Technology president Rafael Reif recently noted, "No other nation has as large a pool of first-rate scientific and technical talent as China."[97]

Accusations that a large number of PRC nationals are systemically committing espionage and other wrongdoings in American universities and research institutions have harmed U.S. interests. According to David Ho, a Taiwan-born American scientist who serves as professor and director of the Aaron Diamond AIDS Research Center at Rockefeller University, threats of unfounded FBI investigations have pushed some top scientists to return to China, which has "actually doubled China's top talents."[98] Ironically, this American-instituted policy has been much more effective at encouraging talent to return to China than any previous efforts made by the Chinese government.

While the United States can complain, it cannot stop China's economic rise or contain its aspirations to become a technological giant. As former U.S. Treasury secretary Larry Summers has said, "Trying to do so risks strengthening the most anti-American elements in Beijing."[99] Chinese authorities accuse U.S. decoupling in S&T with China as being "state-led technology policies of the very sort it seeks to deny to China." The country contends that its state-led capitalism is not deserving of the U.S. criticisms leveled against it, and China has a right to leverage its "nationwide mobilization system" and industrial policy to promote its high-tech sector.

Both China and the United States overemphasize competition and overlook cooperation in the domain of science and technology, and they increasingly view such competition as a zero-sum game. This leads to mutually reinforcing fears on both sides. While the two countries have different priorities and perspectives about cyber issues and AI, these disparities should not prevent two AI superpowers from collaborating in these areas. Both China and the United States are vulnerable and unprepared to manage increasing incidents of cyber terrorism, cybercrime, and misinformation. In today's world, cyber and AI attacks have become more rapid, undetectable, and unpredictable.[100] These two superpowers are also the most likely victims of such attacks. Some American analysts argue that the AI "arms race" between China and the United States is misguided, because both sides are missing the real enemy and shared threats.[101] In terms of public health, COVID-19 is a global threat requiring U.S.-China cooperation, particularly in the area of vaccine and drug development, in order to end this devastating pandemic.

On the cultural and education front, a large number of American university administrators fear the return of McCarthyism in the United States. In an open letter to affirm support for the international community at the University of California at Berkeley, Chancellor Carol Christ and other senior administrators addressed negative comments implying, without basis, that the university's Chinese American faculty, as well as researchers collaborating with Chinese companies and institutions, could be acting as spies. The letter pointedly affirmed, "As California's own dark history teaches us, an automatic suspicion of people based on their national origin can lead to terrible injustices."[102] Yale University president Peter Salovey recently joined administrators from the University of California school system, Massachusetts Institute of Technology, Columbia University, and other higher-education institutions in issuing an open letter to express "steadfast commitment" to international educational exchanges, even as tensions rise between the United States and China.[103] Since an increasing number of Chinese students and scholars were delayed or denied visas to pursue academic studies in the United States, Salovey urged federal agencies to clarify "concerns they have about international academic exchanges."[104]

Notably, some accusations against China on this front lack supporting evidence. For example, in a 2017 report on the problems posed by Confucius Institutes, the U.S. National Association of Scholars made the following odd and unusual claim: "There is no positive proof that the Institutes are also centers for Chinese espionage against the United States, but virtually every independent observer who has looked into them believes that to be the case."[105] This sort of witch-hunt paranoia particularly harms members of the Chinese American community, who are concerned about being perceived as a "cultural threat" and fear becoming targets in this new wave of McCarthyism.

Kiron Skinner's previously described framing of U.S. policy toward China in race-based terms has elicited strong condemnations from around the world, including Washington. Critics have derided her remarks as markedly un-American.[106] In a way, Skinner echoes the late Samuel Huntington's conceptual framework of a clash of civilizations between the West and the "non-West," and her statements are the first public, federal official endorsement of this theory. During the public event when Skinner made her remarks, the moderator, Anne-Marie Slaughter, wisely pointed out the similarities between Skinner's ideas and Huntington's theories.

Huntington, a distinguished political scientist at Harvard, laid out his thesis in a 1993 article for *Foreign Affairs*.[107] The piece defined the nature of world politics in the post–Cold War era along cultural lines, and it identified culture as the primary source of conflict. Huntington predicted that, in addition to a vast Islamic world that is hostile to the West, Confucian culture—or the Oriental civilization manifested in modern East Asian countries—will form an economic and political bloc, challenging not only Western power but also Western civilization.

Critics in Asia, the United States, and other parts of the world found many aspects of Huntington's thesis to be troubling. For one, his interpretation of East Asian values was overly simplistic. He not only unduly emphasized certain elements of the so-called Confucian civilization—with no appreciation of the yin and yang concepts—but also failed to appreciate that the Chinese cultural tradition incorporates elements of Taoism, Buddhism, and other value systems. Taoism, for example, advocates almost exactly the opposite worldview of Confucianism. It is inappropriate, therefore, to assume that people in countries belonging to "Confucian civilization" are homogeneous in their values and perspectives.

Great differences, of course, exist between China and the United States—a fact of history, geography, politics, and socioeconomics. Yet all human societies are touched by the problems and challenges of governance and technological revolution. The central question is whether the lines between different civilizations have become blurred or clearer as the world moves toward a more interconnected, digital era. In other words, is the world witnessing an integration of civilizations, or a clash of civilizations?

Interestingly, several years after Huntington published his controversial article, several governments with strong Confucian traditions—such as Taiwan and South Korea—transformed into liberal democracies, undercutting Huntington's argument. At the same time, however, almost like a self-fulfilling prophecy, the clash of civilizations thesis has fueled mutual misunderstandings among cultures and heightened the risk of conflict and war.

The recent race-based rhetoric from Skinner and other officials in Washington, which echo Huntington's outdated thesis, may alienate the vast number of people with Chinese backgrounds living both within and outside China—including ethnic Chinese people in countries like Singapore, Malaysia, Indonesia, Australia, Canada, and the United States—as well as other peoples in Asia who revere Confucius as a cultural icon. Also, a lack of cultural sensitivity among some U.S. policymakers is playing directly into the efforts of Chinese hard-liners. Recently, China has worked to unite Asian countries by emphasizing cultural exchange among "Asian civilizations," as exemplified by China's hosting of the "Conference on Dialogue of Asian Civilizations" in Beijing in May 2019.[108]

The clash of civilizations worldview and race-based rhetoric about a Chinese threat serve to hurt, rather than protect, American interests and security. These ideas and words run completely against American values. In a congressional hearing in May 2019, House Permanent Select Committee on Intelligence chair, Adam Schiff, offered the following judicious statement:

> There must be no place for racial profiling or ethnic targeting in meeting the rise of China. In America, one of our enduring strengths is welcoming and celebrating diversity. Chinese Americans have made countless contributions to our society. Chinese Americans are Grammy-winning producers, Olympic medalists, cutting-edge scientists, successful entrepreneurs, academics, acclaimed artists, and some of our most successful intelligence of-

ficers and national security professionals. We would all be wise to view Chinese Americans as one source of our great strength and not with pernicious suspicion.[109]

CHINA'S MIDDLE CLASS: A WILD CARD

If there is one recurring mistake that people in the United States make when analyzing present-day China, it is to describe the world's most populous and dynamic country in monolithic terms. Those who favor decoupling with China often fail to draw a distinction between China's ruling elite and Chinese society when they assess the country's current status and forecast future trends. Like every country, China may rightfully pursue a prosperous economy, while cultivating a distinct culture and a thriving middle class. The United States should not judge China, Chinese society, or the CCP leadership as overly ideological, ahistorical, or stagnant. China's trajectory is not predetermined, and it faces serious constraints due to both domestic and international factors. As Henry Kissinger recently noted, "China is still in the midst of searching for the nature of its place in the world."[110] The U.S. grand strategy toward China, therefore, must be holistic, forward looking, and flexible.

Unfortunately, with few exceptions, the current strategic discourse in Washington has hardly included any consideration of the role and stance of the Chinese middle class in the bilateral relationship. The ongoing tensions between Washington and Beijing—including the so-called trade war, tech war, cultural war, and new Cold War—have been analyzed largely through the lens of state-to-state relations. But any attempt to fully assess how the dispute will affect China's domestic development and foreign engagement must take into account the country's dynamic middle class, which has borne the brunt of negative consequences from rising tensions. The political clout and fickle views of the Chinese middle class are among the most intriguing—and consequential—factors affecting U.S.-Chinese relations. Without a solid grasp of the complicated and ever-changing relationship between the Chinese leadership and the country's middle class, American policymakers and analysts may have difficulty accurately gauging the efficacy of U.S. policy toward China.[111]

During Xi's first term, members of the Chinese middle class generally applauded the president for his bold anticorruption campaign, sweeping military reforms, and strong commitment to green development. But judging from public discourse on Chinese social media, middle-class enthusiasm for Xi declined precipitously following his decision to amend China's constitution and abolish presidential term limits in the spring of 2018. Xi's actions were seen as playing into Western fears about China.

From this vantage, Xi seemed to provide American hawks with further evidence to conflate China with other authoritarian regimes, such as Russia and Turkey. Fostering an environment of distrust would only strengthen U.S. support for a containment policy toward China. As U.S.-Chinese trade frictions mounted in 2018, Chinese social media gave rise to a new wave of criticism—both explicit and implicit— directed toward the party leadership. Chinese citizens logged online to air grievances over the leadership's overconfidence in China's economic leverage, misallocation of state financial resources for personal domestic "achievement projects" and ill-planned foreign aid programs, and miscalculation over the Trump administration's strategy toward China.

In the United States, some believe that this middle-class discontent threatens President Xi's position and economic vision, and it indicates that the United States holds an advantage in the trade dispute with China. But more recently, the views of the middle class—which are the foundation of Chinese public opinion more generally—may be poised to turn in favor of the Communist Party. This change in Chinese public perception is largely due to the rapid deterioration of the bilateral relationship, Washington's comprehensive decoupling policy toward China, and in particular, President Trump's ongoing use of the terms "Chinese virus" and "Kung flu." The Chinese media, which saw Trump more favorably than U.S. outlets during the initial years of his presidency, have now flipped and are attributing trade frictions to a "crazy" and "greedy" American president. U.S. trade actions against China and the Trump administration's strategic shift—from partner to rival—have led most Chinese to conclude that the primary goal of the United States is nothing more than to contain a rising China. The broader anti-China trend in U.S. politics has been an unwelcome surprise to the Chinese middle class. This development, in turn, has led many Western China watchers to regard this group as a de facto ally of the ruling Chinese Communist Party.

Chinese middle-class views of the United States, however, are neither fixed nor homogeneous. Their disappointment with the United States seems especially acute because the American middle class has long served as a model for fellow strivers in China. A large number of Chinese students and scholars who studied in the United States and returned home retain their aspirations for American middle-class lifestyles and values. But the aforementioned statements by U.S. government officials implying that professors, researchers, and students from China serve as spies for the CCP, as well as confrontational statements like FBI director Chris Wray's characterization of China as a "whole-of-society threat," have bred hostility. Implicit or explicit racially charged statements about China, like those made by U.S. policymakers such as Kiron Skinner, have stoked outrage among Chinese citizens. Where once the Chinese middle class eyed the United States with envy, it now regards it with indignation.

Xi Jinping and his team have recently adjusted economic policies to counter increasingly vigorous U.S. trade tactics, as well as economic and technological decoupling. Chinese leadership has been incentivized to adopt more economic reform measures, including accelerating domestic consumption, instituting new financial mechanisms to support small businesses, and promoting imports. In March 2019, the State Council announced new policies to support private companies through substantial tax cuts totaling $298 billion, as well as a reduction in fees and easier access to loans. The Xi administration is set to enact measures such as a 3 percent value-added tax cut for manufacturers, a higher value-added tax threshold for small technology companies, and a reduction in employer contribution rates to government pension insurance.

Whether the Chinese middle class will rally to support the hard-line reaction of the Chinese leadership to U.S. actions is not entirely clear. But many Chinese are deeply familiar with two major events in the 1990s, namely Japan's "lost decade" of economic growth and the collapse of the Soviet Union. Some official Chinese sources have implied that both episodes were products of an American conspiracy. Fear of a similar plot against China—however irrational—might ultimately be enough to tip support in favor of the CCP's hard-line response.

Ultimately, Washington's failure to distinguish the perspective of the CCP ruling elite from that of Chinese society more broadly risks undermining U.S. policy toward China. China is currently in the midst of a delicate process of transitioning its economy away from manufacturing toward domestic consumption and innovation. Its leaders view this shift as fundamental to sustaining the growth of China's middle class, and consequently, preserving support for the Communist Party. The Chinese leadership knows the tremendous and ever-growing political influence of China's middle class. U.S. policymakers would be wise to recognize this same dynamic.

CHAPTER 3

Social Stratification and Cultural Pluralism in Reform-Era China

Scholarly Debates

The middle class were invented to give the poor hope; the poor, to make the rich feel special; the rich, to humble the middle class.
—MOKOKOMA MOKHONOANA

The great events, they are not our loudest but our stillest hours. Not around the inventors of new noises, but around the inventors of new values does the world revolve. It revolves inaudibly.
—FRIEDRICH NIETZSCHE

The emerging Chinese middle class poses a challenge for the China studies community—not only because of its sociological heterogeneity but also because of its ambiguous ideological stance and relationship with the Chinese government. This new socioeconomic entity consists of many subgroups that differ profoundly in terms of family origin, occupational identity, level of education, and sociopolitical background. Despite, or perhaps because of, the conceptual and methodological difficulties inherent in studying China's middle class, scholars and public intellectuals around the globe, and especially those in China, have long engaged in serious academic research on the recent ascendance of this socioeconomic force in the world's most populous country.

To a great extent, scholarly disputes over conceptual and definitional problems and the heterogeneity of the Chinese middle class stem from earlier theoretical questions related to social mobility and social stratification in China. Hence the central inquiry of Chinese scholars is understanding whether China's socioeconomic structure is transforming from a pyramid to an oval-shaped socioeconomic structure, where the two small ends represent the rich and poor, and the larger center represents the middle class—the majority of the population.[1] Over the past decade, the research interests of Chinese scholars have expanded from questions related to the basic existence and size of the middle class to topics such as the worldviews, lifestyles, behaviors, foreign educational experiences, and potential political aspirations of its members. These new scholarly inquiries in China have drawn influence from Western scholarly works on important subjects including the middle class, dissemination of values through international education, and constructivist paradigm in cultural studies. As a result, the Chinese scholarship has enriched the global academic discourse on the nature, role, and implications of cultural transnationalism in an increasingly interconnected world, as well as the comparative analysis of countries' middle-class characteristics.

This chapter addresses these major scholarly inquiries and debates, and it consists of three parts. The first part lays out the Chinese historical and political context, and it reveals the slow recognition or even lack of interest on the part of Western scholars regarding the Chinese middle class. This part also reviews the persistent efforts to "enlarge the size of the middle-income group" by the Chinese government, and the enthusiastic initiatives from the business communities—both Chinese and foreign—to promote the "world's largest middle-class market."

With the objective of ensuring critical, comprehensive, and coherent intellectual inquiry into this nascent, hotly debated subject, the second part examines the concept, definitional criteria, and cross-country variations of the middle class. It is invaluable for overseas observers to develop a clear comprehension of social stratification in present-day China, as well as a deep understanding of how People's Republic of China (PRC) scholars assess the sociological heterogeneity of China's emerging middle class and its implications for the country's transformation.

Given the strong connection between China's active participation in economic and educational globalization and the rapid rise of the middle class during the country's reform era, the third part of the chapter highlights the breadth of literature on the impact of cultural dissemination and international education—more broadly, the debate about cultural convergence and divergence—in an era of global exchange within and between Western and Chinese scholarship.

The term "middle class" (*zhongchan jieji*) was rarely used in the PRC during its first four decades. Even in the pre-Communist era, it was largely a foreign concept. According to the late John King Fairbank, capitalism failed to flourish in China during the late nineteenth and early twentieth centuries because China's merchant class did not coalesce into an independent, entrepreneurial power outside the "control of the gentry and their representatives in the bureaucracy."[2] Thus, lacking a "middle class" of their own, the concept remained foreign to the Chinese. Additionally, Western scholars rarely applied the "middle class" concept to frame their analysis of social mobility and social stratification in China.

The few groups considered part of the middle class in pre-1949 China—namely, the private entrepreneurs and petty-bourgeois intellectuals who had emerged in preceding decades—either quickly disappeared or were severely diminished in numbers after the Communist revolution.[3] Indeed, by the mid-1950s, the four million private firms and small businesses that had existed in China before 1949 had been systematically dismantled.[4] Maoist ideology dictated that the country should consist of only three social strata (workers, peasants, and intellectuals), and the Marxist notion of intellectuals as an "intermediate stratum" bore little resemblance to the Western concept of the middle class.[5]

Only after Deng Xiaoping instituted economic reform and opening up did the term "middle class" begin to appear in Chinese academic writings. The earliest references to the concept were made occasionally in the late 1980s, when scholars started examining the sudden emergence of rural industrialists—owners of township and village enterprises in the countryside—and the arrival of private entrepreneurs in the cities. Even then, the consensus among Chinese scholars was that the concept of the middle class should not be employed to describe these groups, in large part because many of these rural industrialists and urban entrepreneurs came from underprivileged or uneducated social strata.[6]

Only since the turn of the century has research on the middle class found its way into the PRC's intellectual mainstream. In the early stages of research on this concept, Chinese scholars often used the terms "middle stratum" (*zhongjianceng*), "middle-income stratum" (*zhongjian shouru jieceng*), and "middle-income group" (*zhongdeng shouru qunti*) to refer to this new socioeconomic force. The increasing use of these new terms among PRC scholars in the reform era reflects the profound changes in domestic social mobility and social stratification that occurred.

In addition to the rapid development of rural industries and urban private enterprises, other important changes facilitated the meteoric rise of the middle class in China. These include the proliferation of foreign joint ventures, the establishment of stock markets in Shenzhen and Shanghai, urban housing reforms and large-scale urbanization, significant expansion of higher education, constitutional enshrinement of property rights, rapid growth of private enterprises, dynamic development of Chinese information technology firms and e-commerce both domestically and internationally, and increasingly cosmopolitan lifestyles driven by economic globalization and international cultural exchanges.

Business-Driven Empirical Research

The business community in China, including both domestic and foreign companies, recognized early on that popularizing the notion of a middle class in China would greatly benefit their bottom line. The prospect of a growing Chinese middle class has been a primary draw for foreign investment and other business activities in the country. It has been widely noted that China's savings rate is one of the highest in the world. In 2008, for instance, Chinese households saved approximately 40 percent of their disposable income. That same year, American households saved only 3 percent of their disposable income.[7] The latent potential for domestic consumption in China, the world's most populous country, has understandably captured the imagination of the international business community.

The emergence of the middle class in China parallels the reemergence of China on the world stage, and it also coincides with public recognition of the enormous PRC market. Since the turn of the century, large corporations (both Chinese and foreign) have obsessed over the commercial metrics for middle-class growth. One such indicator is the rapid increase in credit card use. In 2003, there were 3 million credit cards issued in China. By 2019, the total number of credit cards in the country reached 970 million, with a transaction total of 38.2 trillion yuan.[8] The number of credit cards per capita increased from 0.17 in 2008 to 0.7 in 2019.[9]

Another indicator is the stunning increase in the number of private vehicles in the country, from some 240,000 in 1990 to about 26 million in 2009.[10] In the latter year, China's auto production output and sales volume reached 13.8 million and 13.6 million, respectively, making the PRC the world's leading automobile producer and consumer for the first time.[11] By the end of 2018, China's car-owning population reached 325 million.[12] There were 187 million registered private automobiles in the country, or 40 private vehicles per every 100 households.[13] That same year, there were 3.9 million cars in Shanghai, of which 3 million were registered private automobiles.[14] At the beginning of 2020, China's private car ownership exceeded 200 million for the first time.[15] A total of 66 cities had more than 1 million vehicles, of which 30 cities had more than 2 million vehicles. Eleven cities, including Beijing, Shanghai, Tianjin, Chongqing, Shenzhen, Chengdu, Suzhou, Zhengzhou, Xi'an, Wuhan, and Dongguan, each had more than 3 million cars.[16]

According to the Credit Suisse Research Institute, in 2015, China surpassed the United States for the first time in total middle-class membership, becoming the country with the largest middle-class population in the world.[17] Two years later, the Credit Suisse Research Institute reported that, based on an income range of US$10,000–US$100,000 per capita, China accounted for 35 percent of the global middle class, and the Chinese middle class accounted for 34 percent of the country's total population (table 3-1). In comparison, the United States accounted for just seven percent of the global middle class, and the American middle class accounted for 31 percent of the U.S. population—a significantly smaller figure than the 50 percent that

TABLE 3-1. The Proportion of the Middle Class in the World, 2017 (Top 10 Countries)

Rank	Country	Country's middle class as a proportion of the global middle class (%)	Country's middle class as a proportion of the country's population (%)
1	China	35	34
2	The United States	7	31
3	India	6	7
4	Brazil	4	26
5	Japan	4	36
6	Mexico	3	43
7	Indonesia	3	17
8	Germany	2	34
9	Russia	2	17
10	Spain	2	48

Source: Rupert Hoogewerf and Lu Zhaoqing, *2018 Zhongguo xin zhongchan quan ceng baipishu* [China new middle class report] (Beijing: Jinyuan Investment Group, 2018), 9. The original data are from Credit Suisse Research Institute, *Quanqiu caifu baogao* [Global wealth report], Hong Kong, 2017, www.credit-suisse.com/corporate/sc/press-release/2017-global-wealth-report.html.

FIGURE 3-1. China's middle class in a comparative perspective (in millions), 2015

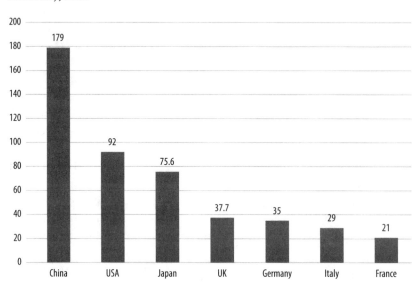

Source: Rong Yueming, *Shanghai wenhua chanye fazhan baogao, 2018* [Annual report on cultural industry development of Shanghai, 2018] (Shanghai: Shanghai renmin chubanshe, 2018), 5.

is often cited by American demographers and economists. A 2018 Chinese report, based on a British study of the size of the middle class in China and G7 countries (excluding Canada), found that in 2016, the size of China's middle class already exceeded that of any of the G7 countries (figure 3-1). According to a McKinsey forecast, by 2022 more than 75 percent of Chinese urban dwellers (over 550 million people) will join the middle class.[18]

Most of these studies were conducted by groups of economists comprising local Chinese researchers, foreign-educated PRC nationals, and expatriates based in China. Their methodologies are often quite opaque, and some might not meet the standards of rigorous academic research. Additionally, some of the more optimistic forecasts may obscure the social stratification and social tensions in present-day China. Regardless, these business-driven research projects have motivated further study of China's middle class, especially by raising public awareness of the far-reaching changes occurring in both the Chinese and the global economic landscapes. As one Chinese sociologist observes, it was business firms operating in China that initially turned the idea of a Chinese middle class from an abstract academic subject into a mainstream topic.[19]

The Ideological Shift and Policy Priorities of the Chinese Leadership

For the first half century of the PRC, social stratification was a politically sensitive subject. According to Marxist theory, the ultimate goal of the Communist state is to establish a "classless society." In the mid-1960s, Mao believed that a small number of privileged elites in the Chinese Communist Party (CCP), led by top leaders Liu Shaoqi and Deng Xiaoping, had become a new revisionist ruling class. Mao therefore called for the launch of the Great Proletarian Cultural Revolution to carry forward the "class struggle" against the exploitative classes, new and old, and to restore the "governing role of the working class."[20]

After his return to power in 1978, Deng Xiaoping profoundly changed the course of China's economic and sociopolitical development by abandoning these notions of class and class struggle. The ideological and policy changes ushered in by Deng paved the way for market reforms and the reemergence of the private sector. The post-Deng leadership also avoided class-based analytical frameworks—a deliberate departure from the communist doctrine. The year 2000 marked the beginning of a major ideological and policy shift for Chinese state leaders. Jiang Zemin, then the secretary general of the CCP, formulated his "theory of the three represents" (*sange daibiao*).[21] In contrast to the Marxist notion that the Communist Party should be the "vanguard of the working class," Jiang argued that the CCP should broaden its base of power to include entrepreneurs, intellectuals, and technocrats, all of whom occupy the "middle-income stratum"—the official euphemism for the middle class.

At the Sixteenth National Congress of the CCP in 2002, the Chinese leadership called for "enlarging the size of the middle-income group." With this pronouncement, the need to "foster a middle-income stratum in Chinese society" became a clear policy objective of the Chinese government.[22] Although Chinese leaders and official publications tend to use the term "middle-income group" rather than "middle class," the two are interchangeable and refer to the same socioeconomic stratum. This official shift in policy reflected a new line of thinking within the Chinese leadership, where the middle class was seen as an asset and political ally rather than a threat to the party's primacy. Based on this logic, the real threat to the CCP was not the middle class, which was as invested in social and political stability as the authorities, but rather the possibility of a vicious struggle between rich and poor—a scenario that grew more likely in the absence of a rapidly expanding intermediate socioeconomic group that could bridge the two extremes.

Since he became secretary general of the party in 2012, Xi Jinping has elevated the expansion of the middle class to be a top policy priority and a key component of China's "strategic blueprint."[23] In November 2012, Xi announced the concept of the "Chinese dream," which is rooted in the nationalistic image of a strong China with a noble past, before the country was invaded by the West and Japan. In Xi's words, the Chinese dream is essentially "the great rejuvenation of the Chinese nation."[24] At the same time, Xi also defines the Chinese dream in a more socially conscious sense, referencing a well-off society or "a moderately prosperous society" (xiaokang shehui). According to Xi, all levels of society should band together to collectively ensure that a majority of Chinese people live prosperously.[25]

At the central conference on economic affairs held in December 2017, CCP leadership came to the same conclusion as the aforementioned Credit Suisse Research Institute report: China is now the country with the largest middle-class population in the world.[26] During the 2018 National People's Congress annual meeting, He Lifeng, minister of the National Development and Reform Commission, stated that China's middle class now includes as many as 400 million people, accounting for 28 percent of the population.[27] PRC officials forecasted that by 2030, the middle class would likely number near 600 million (40 percent of the population). By 2049, the centenary of the founding of the PRC, the Chinese middle class is expected to grow to more than 900 million people, accounting for more than 60 percent of China's total population.[28] Chinese officials believe that when the middle class accounts for 60 to 70 percent of China's population, the country will achieve an oval-shaped socioeconomic structure, which is most favorable for economic development, social stability, and improvement of the welfare state.[29]

Western Scholarship's Slow Recognition of China's Middle Class

Most Western social scientists, including political scientists, sociologists, and academic economists, have been generally dismissive of the idea of a Chinese middle class since it emerged in the 1990s.[30] Western China watchers are nearly unanimous in recognizing the country's rapid economic growth over the past four decades, but the use of the term "Chinese middle class" remains controversial. With a few notable exceptions, for the past two decades Western scholars have been hesitant to acknowledge the existence of a Chinese middle class, let alone explore its political implications.[31]

There are several reasons for this dearth of Western scholarship on the Chinese middle class. The most notable is the difficulty that foreign researchers have in obtaining extensive empirical data on the subject, cultural differences in conceptualizing the idea of a middle class in the Chinese context, sociological heterogeneity (especially the educational and occupational diversity) of this group, and reluctance on the part of Western analysts to accept that Communist China could produce a middle class similar to those found in the West.[32] As for this last reason, a long-standing Western maxim postulates a dynamic or even a causal relationship between the expansion of the middle class on the one hand, and the growth of civil society and political democratization on the other.

Pioneering works on this topic by Barrington Moore Jr. and Seymour Martin Lipset, among many others, all emphasize the vital role of the middle class in a democracy. Moore believes that the existence of a forceful middle class—or in his words, the "bourgeois impulse"—creates a more autonomous social structure in which new elites do not depend on coercive state power in order to flourish, as is the case under an aristocracy.[33] For Lipset, a professionally educated, politically moderate, and economically self-assured middle class is an important precondition for an eventual transition to democracy in a given country.[34] In his view, mass communication media, facilitated by industrialization and urbanization, provide a broader arena in which cultural elites can disseminate middle-class views and values, thus creating a moderate, mainstream public opinion. At the same time, political socialization and the professional interests of the middle class also contribute to the growth of the legal system and civil society—key components of democracies.

These conceptions of the middle class and its perceived, inherent connection with civil society, rule of law, and democracy, have led sinologists in the West to believe that affluent Chinese have yet to develop the sense of rights consciousness, impetus for political participation, and distinct value system that characterize their counterparts in other countries.[35] This skepticism among China watchers in the West is, of course, not wholly without justification given that the rise of the Chinese middle class is admittedly a very new phenomenon.

SOCIOLOGICAL HETEROGENEITY AND POLITICAL UNCERTAINTY: CHINESE SCHOLARLY INQUIRIES

Over the last couple of decades, scholars in China have published comprehensive and data-rich studies on the emerging Chinese middle class, but in Western academic circles, there is a distinct lack of in-depth scholarly work on the subject. The research conducted by Chinese scholars employs a variety of methods, including theoretical and conceptual analyses, survey questionnaires, behavioral analyses, cross-country comparisons, assessments of national income distributions, and regional case studies.

In just the first decade of this century, over 100 Chinese scholarly books on the country's middle class were published in the PRC (some of which can be found in this volume's bibliography). According to a 2009 analysis of major PRC academic journals and periodicals by Li Chunling, a sociology professor at the Chinese Academy of Social Sciences (CASS), from 1980 to 2007 there was a surge in the number of Chinese articles that included the term "middle class" in their title. These academic writings reflect three waves of scholarly interest on the subject: the first wave in the late 1980s focused on the emergence of rural industrialists in township and village enterprises; the second wave in the mid-1990s came from an uptick of interest in the middle classes of other countries; and the third wave in the early 2000s produced a plethora of multifaceted research on various aspects of the emerging Chinese middle class—including its size, composition, rate of expansion, consumption patterns, cultural norms, and political attitudes.[36] These studies and their attendant controversies have increased in frequency year after year.

The surge in PRC scholarly studies of China's changing social structure and emerging middle class reflects the importance of these trends as well as the active and growing influence of Chinese social scientists in the country's intellectual and policy discourse. In other words, PRC sociologists' academic pursuits have become an indispensable source of information for both the Chinese government and the public. Through books, academic articles, and public intellectual discussion, Chinese scholars have engaged in three important debates regarding the middle class. The first concerns its definition, the second concerns its characteristics—especially the ways in which the Chinese middle class differs from its counterparts around the world, and the third concerns its political role and potential ideological stances.

Definitional Criteria and Size Estimates

Like many other sociological concepts, the term "middle class" is widely used but lacks a universally accepted definition. There is little scholarly consensus on the criteria for determining who belongs in the middle class. This lack of a clear, consistent, and consensus-based definition is not limited to research on China's newly emerging middle class. It also afflicts middle-class studies in general, including those that focus on the United States or other developed Western nations.

In the United States, income, particularly household income, tends to be the most essential criterion for determining middle-class status. According to Gary Burtless, the U.S. middle class encompasses the portion of the labor force earning between one-half of the country's median income and twice the median income. Based on U.S. census data from the late 1990s, Burtless reports that middle-class annual incomes in the United States range from roughly $25,000 to $100,000.[37] In their 2010 study of the middle class in the global context, Homi Kharas and Geoffrey Gertz proposed an absolute definition of the middle class that included those with expenditures surpassing $10 a day.[38] They also predicted that by 2020, China would surpass the United States to become the world's largest middle-class market. The range for middle-class incomes, however, has always been controversial. As the Harvard political scientist Alastair Iain Johnston notes, "There is no consensus over where the income cut points are to divide the population."[39]

The considerable differences in household size, inherited family wealth, geographic location, housing costs, and other factors related to a family's standard of living all contribute to the problems inherent in the income-based criterion. Although American sociologists and economists generally consider income as the central component for defining the middle class, other factors, such as an individual's educational attainment, occupational status, consumption patterns and lifestyle, values, and self-identification as a member of the middle class, are also important. This multifaceted approach to defining middle-class membership can be traced back to C. Wright Mills's classic study, *White Collar: The American Middle Classes.*[40]

The conceptual complexity and diverse definitional criteria found in Western studies of the middle class suggest that defining the Chinese middle class is also a challenge. Some sociologists who study social stratification in China strongly reject definitions of the middle class that are based solely on earnings. As Wang Jianying and Deborah Davis incisively point out, by using the income metric, "the middle class would never expand beyond the middle 20 percent."[41] As a result, like their peers elsewhere, many PRC scholars adopt a combination of criteria, or a composite index, to define middle-class membership. Li Peilin, former director of the Institute of Sociology at CASS, has formulated a comprehensive index for the classification of middle-class membership based on three characteristics: income, education, and occupation.[42] Similarly, his colleague at CASS, Li Chunling, applies four factors—occupation, income, consumption, and self-identification—to define the middle class. Based on all four criteria, she then calculates the size of the middle class in 2005 within four groups—total population (2.8 percent), metropolitan residents (8.7 percent), labor force (4.1 percent), and people ages 31 through 40 (10.5 percent). Her findings provide both general and specific assessments of the size of the middle class in China at a given time (table 3-2). For each of the four criteria listed in Li Chunling's 2005 study, most respondents met at least one metric for membership in the middle class, but only a small portion met the comprehensive criteria for membership in the middle class.

Given the diverse approaches to defining the Chinese middle class and the lack of a clear consensus, it is difficult to settle firmly on one uncontroversial standard. Since the middle class is still an inchoate concept, it is highly likely that the most acceptable definition of the Chinese middle class

TABLE 3-2. The Size of the Chinese Middle Class by Several Classifications, 2005

Classification criteria	Share of population (%)
Occupation	15.9
Income	24.6
Consumption	35.0
Self-identification (subjective identity)	46.8
Comprehensive criteria (combining all of the above four)	
Total population	2.8
Metropolitan population	8.7
Labor force (age group 16–60)	4.1
Age group 31–40	10.5

Source: Li Chunling, *Duanlie yu suipian—Dangdai Zhongguo shehuijieceng fenhua shizheng fenxi* [Cleavage and fragment: An empirical analysis of social stratification in contemporary China] (Beijing: Shehuikexue wenxian chubanshe, 2005), 485–499.

will continue to evolve alongside the vagaries of its development. Currently, perhaps the most acceptable and ecumenical approach is Li Chunling's comprehensive four-part typology, which makes a great deal of analytical sense and produces intuitive results. Hence, this study uses her criteria as a working definition for qualitative analysis, but also combines it with income distribution in the global context for more quantitative references.

Over the past fifteen years, China has witnessed a dramatic expansion of the middle class. In his 2010 book, which was based on a large-scale nationwide survey, former director of the CASS Institute of Sociology Lu Xueyi notes that, as of 2009, the middle class constituted 23 percent of China's total population, up from 15 percent in 2001.[43] Lu's study also finds that in 2009, the middle class constituted 40 percent of the population in major coastal cities, such as Beijing and Shanghai. In interviews with the Chinese media, Lu predicted that the Chinese middle class would grow at an annual rate of 1 percent over the next decade or so, meaning that of the 770 million people making up China's labor force, approximately 7.7 million would join the ranks of the middle class each year.[44] Lu also posited that in about twenty years, China would likely become a true middle-class nation, reflecting the Chinese leadership's pronounced goal of achieving a "moderately prosperous" society.[45]

The latest Chinese official estimates—as provided by National Development and Reform Commission minister He Lifeng in 2018—seem to align with the results of Lu Xueyi's influential 2009 survey. In 2018, Su Hainan, a leading Chinese expert in middle-class studies, explained that based on the absolute standard of "daily income between US$20 and US$100," more than 200 million people in China belonged to the middle class, and based on the relative standard of "three times the median per capita disposable income," that number exceeded 300 million.[46] According to Su, by the end of 2020, the size of the Chinese middle class and its share of the national population are expected to rise to more than 400 million and 28 percent, respectively. By 2030, the total membership and population percentage are predicted to grow to 600 million and 40 percent, respectively.[47]

Distinctive Characteristics and Occupational Heterogeneity

Assessing definitional criteria of the middle class also draws attention to the issues of occupation-based and socioeconomic categorizations, which can illuminate some of the more distinctive characteristics of the Chinese middle class. The most influential study on the social strata of reform-era China is detailed in the *Research Report on Social Strata in Contemporary China*, which was published in 2002 by the late Lu Xueyi. Based on three years (1999–2002) of nationwide fieldwork and survey research, Lu and his colleagues produced a framework of ten different strata to conceptualize social stratification in reform-era China (figure 3-2).

FIGURE 3-2. Breakdown of the Chinese population according to social stratum, 2002 (percent)

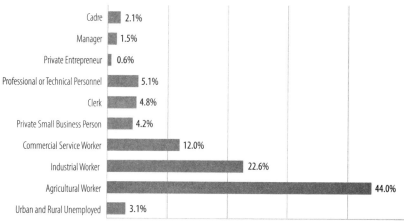

Cadre	2.1%
Manager	1.5%
Private Entrepreneur	0.6%
Professional or Technical Personnel	5.1%
Clerk	4.8%
Private Small Business Person	4.2%
Commercial Service Worker	12.0%
Industrial Worker	22.6%
Agricultural Worker	44.0%
Urban and Rural Unemployed	3.1%

Source: Lu Xueyi, *Dangdai zhongguo shehuijieceng yanjiu baogao—Zhongguo shehuijieceng congshu* [Research report on social strata in contemporary China] (Beijing: Shehui kexuewenxian chubanshe, 2002), 44.

Occupation served as the primary criterion in their analysis, but Lu and his colleagues also considered the administrative (*zuzhi*), economic, and cultural resources that members of each stratum possessed or could access.[48] In addition to occupation-based categories, Lu also employed a five-tiered ranking system based on socioeconomic status: upper, upper middle, middle, lower middle, and lower (figure 3-3). In his framework, each member of an occupation-based stratum could belong to one of several socioeconomic strata, and vice versa. For example, a private entrepreneur could be a member of the upper, upper middle, or middle strata. Similarly, a member of the upper middle stratum could have one of four occupational identities—cadre, manager, private entrepreneur, or professional/technical personnel.

Lu's 2002 study of social stratification was truly a landmark study in the PRC for two reasons. First, it was both a political and an ideological breakthrough to recognize and categorize a vast number of the working class (both industrial and agricultural workers) as part of the lower or lower-middle strata. Workers, previously considered the "masters of the PRC," now fell to the bottom of Chinese society in terms of their socioeconomic

FIGURE 3-3. Socioeconomic strata and occupation-based strata, China, 2002

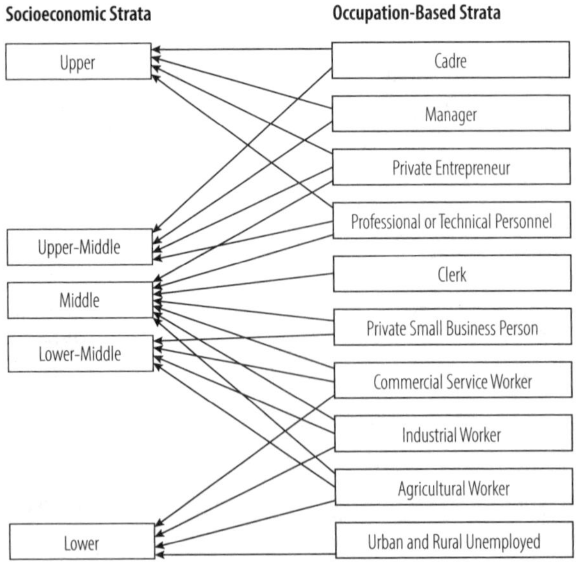

Source: Lu Xueyi, *Dangdai zhongguo shehuijieceng yanjiu baogao—Zhongguo shehuijieceng congshu* [Research report on social strata in contemporary China] (Beijing: Shehui kexuewenxian chubanshe, 2002), 9.

status, occupational standing, and access to resources. Lu's study revealed the persistence of the pyramidal, rather than oval, structure of socioeconomic and political life in China at the turn of the century.[49]

Second, the study provided a more applicable and comprehensive paradigm for conceptualizing the rapid expansion of the middle strata in China and analyzing membership in the middle class. Although Lu used the term "middle stratum" (*zhongjian jieceng*) rather than "middle class," his analytical framework highlighted the importance of this rapidly emerging group in society. For example, comparing data from 1978, 1988, and 1991, Lu found that the number of cadre members, managers, private entrepreneurs, technical clerks, and private small-business owners—key constituents of the middle or upper socioeconomic strata—all increased significantly.[50]

Studies of Chinese social stratification completed by Lu Xueyi, Li Chunling, Li Peilin, and their associates have often drawn criticism from other PRC scholars and public intellectuals. The sociological heterogeneity of the Chinese middle class, in the view of critics, makes generalizations about the group problematic. Areas of dispute generally fall into three categories: the size of the Chinese middle class, its distinctly heterogeneous composition, and its lack of a unifying core value.

The first subset of criticism centers on the group's size. Many note that the Western norm where the middle class constitutes a large proportion of a country's population, and often a majority of the workforce, does not apply to China's alleged middle class. Critics cite Lu Xueyi's studies, which find that agricultural workers and industrial workers constitute a significant portion of China's workforce (44 percent and 22.6 percent, respectively; see figure 3-2). Thus China today still consists primarily of peasants, migrant workers, and the urban poor, rather than a middle class. In a May 2020 press conference during the National People's Congress meeting, Premier Li Keqiang remarked that "600 million people in present-day China earn only 1,000 yuan a month," and critics latched on to this comment as affirming their cynicism about the large size of the Chinese middle class.[51] For them, the narrative about China becoming a middle-class country has mainly served as self-promotional propaganda for some Chinese leaders. The premier's recognition of the large number of low-income people in the Chinese population also highlights the enduring economic disparities that China confronts.[52]

The second subset of criticism centers around the claim that subgroups within contemporary China's emerging middle class differ profoundly from each other in terms of family backgrounds, occupational identities, educational credentials, and political associations. Thus the composition of this broad socioeconomic category is far too heterogeneous to be meaningful. According to Li Lulu, a professor of sociology at Renmin University in Beijing, the diversity of the Chinese middle class can be explained by the existence of three vastly different channels through which individuals can ascend to middle-class status. Li and his associates coined the terms "power-based executive-type access" (*xingzhengxing jinru*), "market-driven access" (*shichangxing jinru*), and "social network–linked access" (*shehuiwangluoxing jinru*) to characterize these three pathways.[53]

China's emerging middle class is a complex mosaic of groups and individuals, and its component subgroups differ significantly from one other. In terms of occupational and sociological factors, members fall into three major clusters:

1. An economic cluster, which includes private sector entrepreneurs, urban small businesspeople, rural industrialists and rich farmers, foreign and domestic joint-venture employees, and stock and real estate speculators

2. A political cluster, which includes government officials, office clerks, state sector managers, and lawyers

3. A cultural and educational cluster, which includes academics and educators, media personalities, public intellectuals, and think tank scholars

Critics argue that members of China's middle class hold very different values, leading to different public policy preferences. For example, private entrepreneurs tend to prefer less state interference in the market, while white collar workers employed by the government or state-owned enterprises are interested in maintaining or even increasing governmental control.[54] Additionally, two studies conducted in the 1990s show that a plurality of entrepreneurs in Shanghai (83 percent in one study and 44 percent in the other) had received only a middle-school education.[55] The heterogeneity of occupational and educational backgrounds within the middle class leads critics to doubt whether this population can be considered a unified, coherent socioeconomic force.

The third subset of criticism frequently quotes Western scholars of social structure and the middle class, such as Talcott Parsons, who posit that shared core values must play a central role in the formation of a socioeconomic stratum. A coherent value system is normally determined by members of society's most influential stratum, and it becomes the glue that holds together the middle-income group.[56] According to He Qinglian and Xu Zhiyuan, however, the so-called Chinese middle class lacks such shared values.[57] In line with other critics, they believe that without this shared normative stance, the term "middle class" simply connotes income levels and, consequently, loses much of its analytical significance. As Yuan Jian states, "The middle-income stratum, in fact, exists in any given society in the modern world. Such an identity is meaningless if its members do not have a mainstream consciousness and values that are identical with the middle-class members in other parts of the world."[58]

Proponents of a Chinese middle class reject most of these criticisms. They acknowledge that in terms of population percentage, the middle class in China is still relatively small compared to its counterparts in many Western countries. But they hasten to add that no country can bring a majority of residents into its middle class in just a few years or even a few decades. One should distinguish between the existence of a middle class in a given country and that country's status as a middle-class country. China cannot be considered a middle-class country at present, but it is difficult to deny that its middle class has already grown to an impressive size and is rapidly expanding. Some proponents argue that even in terms of percentage of total national population, China's middle class accounts for a similar proportion of the population as Japan and Germany's middle classes (as presented in table 3-1).

Scholars also assert that the middle class is an inherently flexible concept and that its definition, while imprecise, is equally imprecise for all countries. They observe that members of the middle class in Western countries are just as diverse in terms of family backgrounds, occupational identities, and educational attainment as their counterparts in China. Furthermore, the middle class in Western countries is also subdivided into many groups.[59] Some note that upward trends in higher-education attainment and social mobility in China mirror the remarkable growth of American and French universities about a century ago. In 1977, China enrolled only 270,000 college students. Four decades later, 7.61 million Chinese students attended university, a twenty-eight-fold increase.[60] When the U.S. and France underwent this type of rapid development in higher education, it led to the establishment of their middle classes.[61] In China, however, it has taken only one generation for most members of the middle class to attain the same baseline level of education.

Proponents also reject the notion that the Chinese middle class lacks shared core values. In their view, its constituent members are unified in their appreciation for the middle-class lifestyle, the development of a market economy at home and economic integration abroad, the protection of private property rights, a policy emphasis on primary education, social stability, and pride over China's rise on the international stage.[62]

Notably, the Chinese term for middle class emphasizes a sense of ownership or property rights (*chanquan*), a connotation that the English term lacks. Some scholars speculate that this shared notion of ownership or property rights may serve as a powerful glue to unify the otherwise starkly different socioeconomic groups that constitute China's middle class.[63] While these subgroups may differ from each other in occupation, socialization, or political position, they do share certain views and values. One such value is the "inviolability of the private property of citizens," which was only recently added to the PRC constitution.[64] In the words of Zhang Yiwu, a professor of Chinese literature at Peking University, this new notion may prove to be an "important beginning of group consciousness and the sense of rights protection for the Chinese middle class."[65]

While the heated debate over the validity of China's middle class may not have resulted in clear outcomes, it does suggest that this new social segment is aggressively searching for its own identity and for ways to express its values. The prevalence of public discussion about the topic indicates that the middle class's self-consciousness, group identity, and shared values are all on the rise.[66] Highlighting the popularity of the middle-class aspiration, Zhou Xiaohong's study of urban residents in five major Chinese cities finds that as many as 85.5 percent of respondents self-identify as members of the middle class.[67]

Political Roles and Social Stability

Arguably the most important debate about the Chinese middle class is related to the potential impacts it will have on the political development and social stability of the PRC. Two ancient philosophers, Aristotle in the West and Mencius in the East, are frequently quoted in Chinese scholarly writings that draw a correlation between a strong middle class and sociopolitical stability in society. Aristotle asserted over 2,000 years ago that the middle stratum is a balancing and stabilizing force. Absent such a stratum in society, dynastic crises and social upheavals are far more likely.[68] Mencius voiced roughly the same principle: "Those who have property are also inclined to preserve social stability."[69] Along these lines, Chen Yiping, a scholar at the Guangdong Academy of Social Sciences, argues that the middle class has three functional roles: a leadership role in shaping the market economy, a pioneering role in creating society's social norms, and a buffering role in reconciling political tensions and conflicts.[70]

Tang Jun, a research fellow at the Institute of Sociology at CASS, characterizes the pyramidal social structure as "static stability" and the oval structure as "dynamic stability."[71] The former appears to be stable but could suddenly collapse if faced with a formidable crisis; the latter, while constantly subject to minor bumps and bruises, is not likely to collapse overnight.[72] According to Tang's optimistic prognosis, China's rapidly expanding middle class will help to establish an oval structure.

When considering social stability, Tang emphasizes a country's socioeconomic structure over its political system. Some critics, for example, He Qinglian, believe that the prospect of a democratic China may become more distant as the middle class rises.[73] The underlying rationale is that members of the new middle class are primarily interested in economic wealth, not political power. As a result, they strike a political deal with the CCP establishment on this hidden rule (*qian guize*), which guides their relationship.[74] Zhou Xiaohong's characterization of the Chinese middle class as the "consumer avant-garde and political rear guard" (*xiaofei qianwei, zhengzhi houwei*) echoes this view.[75]

In a national survey of political attitudes and behaviors across social strata in China, however, Li Peilin and his team at CASS found that compared to other groups, the middle class is more critical of the current social and political situation and less confident in government performance.[76] The study also reveals that middle-class consciousness and values sometimes differ from mainstream consciousness (*zhuliu yishi*), or the official core values. The work of Li and his team illustrates that as a group, the middle class often expresses greater skepticism of official ideology and China's present-day power structure. In their view, the middle class would be unlikely to play a conciliatory role in major sociopolitical conflicts, were they to occur, and might very well oppose the authorities or simply "take a laissez-faire attitude" (*tingzhi renzhi*).[77]

Zhang Yi, a junior colleague of Li Peilin at CASS, finds that China's new middle class tends to be more cynical about policy promises made by authorities, more critical of government policy implementation, and more concerned about corruption among officials.[78] In his analysis, if a large portion of the middle class feel that their voices are suppressed, that their access to information is blocked, or that their space for social action is confined, a political uprising will likely take place. Zhang implies that middle-class demand for direct elections, which happened in South Korea and Brazil, could also occur in China.

Middle-class grievances directed at government policy have grown in recent years. The rising unemployment rate among recent college graduates—who usually come from middle-class families and are presumed to be future members of China's middle class—should alarm the Chinese government. The proliferation of protests initiated by the middle class reflects the complicated relationship between this group and the Chinese government. The video *Under the Dome* by Chai Jing, a former CCTV anchor who became the country's leading advocate for environmental protection, garnered approximately 200 million views in China when it aired in 2015, reflecting growing middle-class resentment about the government's failure to prevent air pollution.[79]

Three recent, highly publicized events aroused further disapproval of

CCP leadership among the middle class. The first was the collapse of the online P2P (peer-to-peer) lending markets, which wiped out about 7,000 platforms and cut off hundreds of thousands of middle-class investors from loan resources.[80] The second event was the revelation that faulty vaccines for diphtheria, tetanus, and whooping cough had been administered to nearly half a million children.[81] The third event was the nationwide public mourning in response to the tragic death of Dr. Li Wenliang, a whistleblower who exposed the coronavirus at the outset of the 2019–20 outbreak. The wave of widespread grieving reflected the public's outrage at Dr. Li's mistreatment by Chinese authorities. In all of these cases, self-identified middle-class protesters or critics succeeded in pressuring authorities to change course or acknowledge their mistakes.

In his study of community governance in Shanghai and other urban centers, Liu Xin finds that members of the middle class have a higher rate of participation in local elections and rights-protection activities than other groups. Members of the middle class are also more interested in pursuing legal action when disputes occur, and they are less tolerant of governance malfeasance than other groups.[82] This accords with the conventional view that because members of the middle class are the primary taxpayers in a given society, they have an interest in influencing how their tax contributions are being used. To a certain extent, China's nascent middle class represents the first generation of Chinese citizens with an awareness of consumer rights.

In attempting to understand the complex political questions surrounding the middle class in China, some PRC scholars have developed sophisticated theoretical frameworks for the Chinese context. Li Lulu asserts that the social function and political role of the Chinese middle class are neither stagnant nor one-dimensional.[83] He suggests that the middle class's dynamic position within China's social stratification might provide clues about its seemingly contradictory political preferences, and hint at the circumstances under which they will likely change. According to Li, three factors—the economic climate, the political system, and the social order (institutionalization)—may determine the social function of the middle class, which could be conservative, radical, or dependent on economic and sociopolitical circumstances.

Li Lulu contrasts this theoretical role for the middle class in China with that of a democratic system, where the middle class tends to be more conservative because it benefits from the prevailing social order and power structure. Li questions Samuel Huntington's well-known proposition that the middle class tends to be revolutionary in its early development but grows increasingly conservative over time.[84] Li asserts that in authoritarian regimes, the middle class depends on the political system in its early development. However, as the economy matures and the middle class gains more autonomy, the likelihood of the middle class clashing with the government increases. Eventually, it ceases to depend on the regime and might even challenge authorities. Li offers three factors that influence this process: ideology or values, the international environment, and the degree of homogeneity within the middle class. Li points out that a globally oriented, capitalist, consumer culture—and the transnational political values that often accompany it—will increasingly push the Chinese middle class to align with, rather than resist, international trends.

Li Lulu's open-ended and optimistic assessment of the political implications of China's rising middle class is by no means anomalous within the PRC scholarly community. Many PRC publications on this topic highlight the mercurial character of this group's politics, with some scholars describing the middle class as "vacillating opportunists" (*shoushu liangduan*). In the words of one Chinese writer, the "middle class will neither risk their vital interests to promote democratic changes nor refuse the benefits of democracy that a democratic system can bring to them."[85] In a similar vein, Qin Hui, a distinguished historian at Tsinghua University, argues that no class in the world is born progressive or conservative.[86] Instead, its political orientation evolves in accordance with historical context.

Hu Lianhe and Hu Angang, researchers at the Center for China Studies at the Chinese Academy of Sciences, coauthored a comprehensive article on the middle class and China's sociopolitical changes. They argue that in China, as in any other country, the political function of the middle class is multifaceted and malleable. It can be a "stabilizing device" (*wendingqi*), a "subversive device" (*dianfuqi*), or an "alienation device" (*yihuaqi*).[87] The crucial question, in their view, is for what reason and under what circumstances would the middle class shift from one role to another. The authors provide a checklist for Chinese authorities to ensure that the middle class remains an ally rather than an adversary. According to the authors, the Chinese government needs to prevent economic fluctuations, protect property rights, avoid any sense of status loss (individually or collectively) among the middle class, allow greater institutionalized political participation, and shield middle-class members from "excessive political attention."

Notably, all these scholarly writings—whether they offer guidance for Chinese authorities, assess trends from the perspective of a potentially aggrieved middle class, or present more objective analysis—suggest the changing nature of interactions between the authoritarian state and the middle class, as well as among the country's wealthiest class, middle class, and poorest class.

GLOBAL INTEGRATION AND CULTURAL PLURALISM: BEYOND THE CONSTRUCTIVIST PARADIGM

China's emerging middle class is largely the product of economic global-ization and cultural transnationalism. During the reform era, discourse in China about globalization often presented the topic as a "continuation of the grand narrative of the modernization project."[88] Some Chinese scholars have argued that the modernization of a given country is ultimately not an economic phenomenon, but a cultural phenomenon, or more precisely, a transnational process of cultural modernization.[89] This view appears to have drawn inspiration from a similar thesis by Western scholars, notably Anthony Giddens, who asserted that globalization is essentially just the mobility of modernization.[90] In other words, products, people, technol-ogy, landmarks, symbols, ideas, and information mobilize by transcending space and time, often resulting in a profound change in both social mobility and cross-cultural exposure of views and values. This mobility can be un-derstood as cross-cultural exchanges, which make the world increasingly interconnected.

These ideas of globalization and modernization present two import-ant theoretical questions. First, will international educational exchange and cultural dissemination—especially the penetration of Western soft power—lead to global cultural convergence and thus reconstruct the cul-tural identity of a peripheral country such as China? Or instead, will global integration facilitate cultural pluralism, diversity, and the coexistence of civilizations in an era of technological revolution? Second, will the trans-national forces embodied by cultural and educational exchanges lead to in-ternational understanding and thus prevent ideological and ethnic conflicts while contributing to world peace?

Cultural Convergence or Cultural Diversity?

According to the distinguished historian of American diplomacy, Akira Iriye, cultural internationalism "entails a variety of activities undertaken to link countries and peoples through the exchange of ideas and persons, through scholarly cooperation, or through efforts at facilitating cross-national understanding."[91] Iriye believes that international relations are both interpower and intercultural relations. The study of international re-lations, therefore, entails three categories of inquiry: "power-level interac-tions, cultural interchanges, and the relationship between these."[92] For Iriye, the principal subjects of analysis in international relations should not just be nations and governments, but should also include the diffusion of ideas and cross-national movements—phenomena that have been overlooked for too long. He argues that "cultural internationalist forces may prove to be a key factor in defining the world" of the twenty-first century.[93]

Along the same lines, Joseph Nye uses the term "hard power" to refer to the economic and military strength of a given country, and the term "soft power" to refer to its cultural resources and influence. According to Nye, while hard power is more essential to a country's economic well-being and security, a country cannot persist without soft power. When a country's culture embodies universal values that are accepted by other countries, that country's foreign policies are more likely to be seen as legitimate and therefore achieve desired outcomes. In contrast, "narrow values and parochial cultures are less likely to produce soft power."[94]

Iriye's argument for cultural internationalism and Nye's soft power thesis have been remarkably influential in Chinese scholarly circles over the past two decades. In addition, Chinese scholars who hold positive views of cultural convergence often cite David Harvey's concept of "time-space compression" and Roland Robertson's thesis about "growing consciousness of the one world" as evidence of the unprecedented cultural transnationalism experienced at the turn of the century.[95] For example, Ma Qingyu, a professor of public administration at China's Institute of State Administration, believes that in the era of globalization, people are conscious of cross-national comparisons and have a strong sense of cultural evaluation.[96] Ma argues that emphasizing cultural relativism could impede China's political and cultural modernization. Ma's view reflects the century-old perception in Chinese intellectual thinking that modernization by its very nature involves cultural regeneration and cross-cultural interchanges.[97] For example, at the beginning of the twentieth century, the late Qing reformer Liang Qichao argued that to rejuvenate a country, one must first reinvigorate its people through cultural and educational development.[98] The twentieth century indeed began with "educational reform as the cornerstone of an ailing effort by the imperial dynasty to save itself and the country from collapse."[99]

Some Chinese scholars believe that in an era of globalization, the cultural resources of a given country are often developed through international cultural exchange. In other words, cultural dissemination is the prerequisite for the development of any given culture. Cultural transnationalism is often viewed as the only way in which human societies can escape from savagery, ignorance, and chaos in order to become civilized, scientific, and intelligent.[100] An analysis of China's long history shows that when China has pursued more dynamic cultural exchanges with the outside world, the country has become stronger. The cultural vitality of the Tang Dynasty, often cited by Chinese scholars who favor the cultural convergence thesis, occurred at a time when China was substantially engaged in foreign exchanges on both the economic and cultural fronts. Present-day China, they argue, is in another dynamic period of international educational exchange and global engagement in Chinese history. In 2019, for example, the country had more than 600 international high schools.[101]

Arguably, the most important cultural resource of a given country is its higher-education system. These educational institutions generally reflect the mainstream or elitist cultural norms of a given country. Higher education systematizes and rationalizes culture. It advances culture through academic and scientific research, curricular development, and classroom teaching, as well as through informal exchanges on campus. With its obligation to serve society, higher education also shapes the public's cultural preferences.

Wang Ning, a prominent Chinese scholar on cultural and educational globalization, argues that a university, by definition, should not restrain its focus to a particular locality, but instead should aim to transcend space and time.[102] Rather than just a physical space, a university should be a cultural center that concerns itself with the situation of the whole world and the fate of humanity.[103] Higher education's role in cultural assimilation, including student exchanges and international academic cooperation, is fundamental. In present-day China, as David Zweig observes, higher education is one of the "most internationalized arenas in Chinese society."[104] Population mobility, including the international exchange of students and scholars, is often seen as the conduit of this critical and effective form of cultural dissemination.[105]

Like critics from other countries, some Chinese scholars believe that the term "cultural globalization" or "cultural convergence" contradicts itself. They assert that the creation of a global culture is impossible because the very concept of culture implies that people differ from each other. From this view, culture can never converge and must always be pluralistic.[106] As some Chinese scholars note, in the era of globalization, convergence occurs primarily in the economic and financial arenas, but not in the cultural and philosophical domains. The complementarity and diversity of cultural exchanges in today's world should be appreciated. While people in the non-Western world might welcome the spread of liberal and democratic ideas, they reject ideas of cultural dominance, homogeneity, and uniformity, as well as the dogmatic and stagnant view of the "end of history."

Also like their counterparts elsewhere, Chinese critics reject the main assertion of convergence theory that both globalization and modernization are identical and linear processes for all countries. They argue that theories on modernization often portray advanced industrial countries in the West as "privileged vanguards" whose path of development can be universally applied and should be an example for "traditional" and "backward" countries.[107] Chinese scholars of globalization studies often make two conceptual distinctions. First, they argue that it is one thing for China to participate in Western-led globalization and quite another thing to conceive of China's modernization as a process of Westernization. They believe that China could accept the former but must reject the latter, because it is problematic to associate all good cultural influences with the West.[108] As Wang Ning argues, in cultural studies, to "meet with the world" does not necessarily mean following the West, but rather to engage in dialogue with the West.[109] Second, this group of scholars distinguishes between cultural globalism and cultural transnationalism. A global cultural identity is either one that all people in the world share or one that all people claim simply does not exist. But cultural transnationalism, a process by which cultural commodities, people, and ideas can literally flow across national boundaries, has become increasingly prevalent in today's world.[110]

Cultural transnationalism does not necessarily entail the triumph of Western culture, but rather is a testimony to the resilience and adaptability of non-Western cultures. The resurgence of cosmopolitan Shanghai in the reform era supports the argument for the endurance of multiple identities and cultural pluralism. The time and space visualized in Huang Yongping's artwork presented in the prologue reveals, though perhaps unintentionally, the remarkable ability of this Chinese city to transcend multiple boundaries—ideological, cultural, and sociopolitical. The Hong Kong and Shanghai Banking Corporation building symbolizes radically different historical occurrences—colonial legacy, communist power, and the reemergence of Shanghai as an economic and financial center. Its multifaceted symbolism, however, does not cause much confusion in the minds of its residents. Shanghai was the birthplace of both China's Western modernization and its form of communism, two of the most influential forces on China's modern history. Shanghai has, more than any other place in the country, adapted well to dramatic changes over the last century.

Paradoxically, the site of the first National Congress of the Chinese Communist Party, which was held in 1921, has been transformed over the past two decades into a commercial complex called the New Heaven-Earth (*xintiandi*). Funded by investments from a Hong Kong tycoon and his associates, the $150 million complex was designed to resemble traditional Shanghai-style alleys with two-story houses (*shikumen*).[111] The complex is packed with elegant nightclubs, cafés, bars, art galleries, and fashionable shops, including many Western-style restaurants and an American Starbucks. Not surprisingly, the complex has evolved into a hub for the Chinese middle class, foreign and domestic tourists, and expatriates from Taiwan, Hong Kong, and overseas.

As if this symbolic triumph of capitalism over Communism is not enough, the complex has also become enmeshed with "Shanghai nostalgia"—not for its revolutionary Communist roots, but for its colonial heritage. This colonial past is conveyed through an emphasis on Shanghai's cosmopolitan glory, rather than China's humiliating encounters with foreign powers in the colonial era. "This is," as a Chinese writer observes, "a place where elders feel nostalgic, the young feel fashionable, foreigners find Chinese and traditional characteristics, and the Chinese find foreign characteristics."[112] Shanghai's cosmopolitan history seems more relevant to the future of the city than to the present. Appropriately, the motto of the complex is, "Where yesterday meets tomorrow in Shanghai today."[113]

In a highly symbolic way, the Xintiandi Complex redefines the time and space of this rapidly changing city.[114] The marvel of the Xintiandi Complex and its overtly positive message about transnational interchanges aligns with the argument made by Anthony Giddens that globalization can be understood as a switch, or relocation, between time and space.[115] The Xintiandi Complex blends Chinese and Western cultures and blurs the conventional dichotomy between tradition and modernity. In a sense, Shanghai is home to a distinct *haipai* culture, wherein "[Chinese and Western] cultures met but neither prevailed."[116] In the words of a Shanghainese scholar, the greatness of the *haipai* culture lies in the fact that, while absorbing the merits of foreign cultures, it also enhances local identity.[117] These claims echo the argument made by some Western scholars of globalization studies, who assert that contemporary cultural development is characterized by the coexistence of transnationalism and pluralism. Roland Robertson coined the term "glocalization" to describe the dynamic interaction between globalization and localization.[118]

Since Shanghai serves as the exemplar of China's coming-of-age, the city's rise to international prominence has reinforced Chinese national pride. Shanghai's local, national, and cosmopolitan identities are all dynamic; they mutually reinforce each other while retaining independent value in different specific contexts. What is most evident from Shanghai's opening to the outside world is not cultural convergence, but cultural coexistence and diversity.

Constructivism: Impact of Cultural and Educational Exchanges on International Peace?

To better understand the implications of the emergence of middle-class Shanghai on the socioeconomic development of China and peace in the Asia-Pacific region, one should consider how they affect broader intellectual debates about realism, liberalism, and constructivism in the area of world politics.[119] Mainstream international relations scholars have long overlooked the role of culture in foreign affairs. Both realists and liberals focus their concerns on security and economic issues, respectively, and neither pays much attention to cultural and educational dimensions.

Realists recognize the crucial role of knowledge in the information age, and they believe that technological advancement powered by universities and research institutions can be converted into economic and military power.[120] Realists often perceive competition for technological know-how between nations as a zero-sum game. In general, realists are more concerned with protecting national interests in the midst of international flows of technology and human resources, rather than exploring how national interests change through the spread of ideas, values, and norms across national borders. Realists are suspicious of normative changes in the political goals, attitudes, and behaviors of states, because they believe that international politics is inherently anarchical.[121]

Contemporary liberals, on the other hand, focus on the economic interdependence between countries. As Martha Finnemore and Kathryn Sikkink have observed, "neo-liberals" and "neo-realists" might more appropriately be called "econo-liberals" and "econo-realists," because "what was new in both causes was an injection of microeconomic insights."[122] Generally, liberals' belief in utilitarianism and universalism leads them to overlook the influence of culture. They tend to emphasize peace and prosperity through the dissemination of liberal democratic ideas, and liberals in the West are often insensitive to the cultural concerns of developing countries.

Constructivism, a relatively new approach to the study of international relations, attempts to fill the intellectual vacuum that realism and liberalism have largely failed to explore.[123] This scholarly approach is called constructivism because "it focuses on the socially constructed nature of international politics."[124] In contrast to neo-liberals, who have turned to economics for insight, constructivists draw heavily on sociology, especially the analysis of cultural institutions. In contrast to realists, constructivists believe that normative context influences the behavior of decisionmakers and the general public in a given state. Elite beliefs, cultural identities, and social norms all profoundly shape state behavior. While realists such as Samuel Huntington assume that the clash of civilizations is the defining framework for understanding the post–Cold War world, constructivists believe that the ever-growing diffusion of international norms can lead—and in fact, has often led—to cultural communication or reconciliation, including attitudinal and behavioral changes in elites.[125]

Martha Finnemore argues that "normative context also changes over time, and as internationally held norms and values change, they create coordinated shifts in state interests and behavior."[126] Using the International Red Cross and the Geneva Convention as examples, she argues that "states' redefinitions of interest are often not the result of external threats or demands by domestic groups. Rather, they are shaped by internationally shared norms and values."[127] Alexander Wendt further explains the two basic tenets of constructivism: first, "the structures of human association are determined primarily by shared ideas rather than material forces;" and second, "the identities and interests of purposive actors are constructed by these shared ideas rather than given by nature."[128]

Meanwhile, constructivists reject the liberal notion of the "end of history"—the ultimate triumph of liberal democratic ideas throughout the world.[129] This is because, in the view of constructivists, state preferences are perpetually influenced by social norms, culturally determined rules, and "historically contingent discourse."[130] Thus the diffusion of international norms occurs in all parts of the world, but this does not suggest that all countries will become liberal democracies, because cultural variations will transform political behavior and social norms.[131]

Constructivists' emphasis on the cultural dimension of international affairs does not mean that the influence of culture has now become more important. In fact, culture has been a strong, hidden influence in politics and scholarship throughout history. As Frank Ninkovich argues, the rediscovery of the importance of culture has "contributed to a growing sense that even power struggles like the Cold War were also cultural-ideological struggles of ideas, at least partially and perhaps even predominantly so."[132] But more importantly, as Ninkovich observes, the "turn" or "return" to cultural issues to explain political behavior has been "influenced by a new 'post-modern' intellectual climate that emphasizes the role of 'discourses' in shaping world views."[133]

Constructivists' explanation of changing elite beliefs and behaviors offers valuable insights in this study of Shanghai's pioneering role in China's peaceful evolution. To some degree, China's rise during the reform era provides empirical evidence in support of constructivist theory. In contrast to Beijing's Tiananmen Square, which often symbolizes China's authoritarian tradition and brings to mind the bloody crackdown on the 1989 protest movement, the emergence of Shanghai as China's Manhattan conveys an image of a dynamic, pluralistic, and forward-looking middle-class nation. As some Chinese scholars argue, this "Shanghai miracle" was achieved through the "reconciliation of civilizations" (*wenming de hejie*) rather than the "clash of civilizations" (*wenming de chongtu*).[134] These scholars believe that Shanghai's prominence as a city with multiple cultural identities not only signifies a detour from the Chinese revolutionary political path but also reflects a profound change in the perspectives of the middle class and public intellectuals in the PRC.

CONCLUSION

Over the past decade or so, a lively intellectual discourse about the existence and characteristics of the Chinese middle class has taken shape within China's scholarly community. This ongoing dialogue is replete with open comparisons of striking statistics, bold criticisms, insightful analyses, and theoretical propositions. The intellectual fervor it represents was spurred, in part, by both admiration for the middle-class way of life in developed countries and evaluation of the maxims and methodologies of Western social science. As a result, Chinese scholars have enriched, both conceptually and empirically, the world's academic literature on the middle class and its sociopolitical ramifications, both domestically and internationally. In doing so, they have broadened the scope of their intellectual inquiries beyond the definition, size, and characteristics of this emerging socioeconomic force, and they have also focused great attention on how the middle class relates to the ruling class, other socioeconomic players in China, and an ever-changing international environment.

The middle class has already emerged as a core constituency with its own unique needs and desires. As China's growth model shifts from an export-based model to a domestic consumption–based model, the middle class, more than any other group, holds the keys to the governance and prosperity of the country. A slowing economy due to domestic structural change and international tensions, coupled with tightening political and ideological control at home, has created challenges for the middle class. Reflecting these growing concerns, China's flagship English language television program, *Dialogue*, featured a panel discussion in 2018 titled "Age of Anxiety for the Chinese Middle Class."[135] The Chinese leadership certainly understands the link between public pessimism and the CCP's perceived legitimacy, and thus it has sought to make improvements that appease the country's middle class. China's future political trajectory, similar to the Chinese middle class's relationship with the CCP leadership, is neither stagnant nor predetermined. At the same time, the surge of Chinese nationalism in the wake of the U.S.-led decoupling with China has dampened middle-class hopes about America's acceptance of China's rise.

For foreign observers, especially policymakers in Washington, it is essential to have an accurate picture of China's social stratification, social mobility, cultural inclusion, and cultural diversity. In order to do so, one must understand how Chinese scholars and public intellectuals wrestle with the profound and ongoing changes in their country's global integration.[136] The Chinese scholarly community's careful, straightforward, and oftentimes bold discourse on the political implications of China's emerging middle class is itself testimony to these important and evolving political dynamics.

III

SHANGHAI:
THE PACESETTER IN
CHINA'S SEARCH FOR
GLOBAL POWER

CHAPTER 4

Haipai

Shanghai Exceptionalism and Cultural Transnationalism

Stones from other hills can polish the jade of our mountain.

—A CHINESE SAYING

The fad of Shanghai today is nostalgia.

—CHENG NAISHAN

The rapid rise of the middle class in the reform era, including the entrepreneurial elites known as China's nouveaux riche, has created a new entrepreneurial middle-class culture in Chinese society. Like elsewhere in the world, factors such as social acceptance of market competition, glorification of material success, an entrepreneurial work ethic, the coexistence of different lifestyles, enthusiasm for foreign ideas and innovations, and wide-ranging consumer demand reflect the prevalence of commercialism, and they also contribute to cultural pluralism in society. To a great extent, cultural pluralism can be found in all aspects of Chinese life today: fashion, diet, music, sports, dance, the fine arts, movies, television programming, advertising, social interaction, public opinion, and political attitudes.

These societal circumstances contrast sharply with the Mao era, especially the Cultural Revolution, during which the diversity of subcultures was strictly suppressed and only "monochromatic socialist culture" was accepted. Arthur Miller, a distinguished American playwright, and his photographer wife traveled to China prior to the 1978 reforms, and they saw this suppression first-hand. They noted that the Chinese all wore exactly the same clothing—the gray or dark blue Sun Yat-sen jacket (often referred to as the Mao jacket by many Westerners).[1] Conformity in clothing, color, behavior, and mindset is how totalitarian regimes destroy individuality and plurality within society. The result of conformity is uniformity. As Václav Havel, the renowned Czech Republic dissident who later served as president of the country, once observed, "Standardized life creates standardized citizens with no wills of their own."[2]

Just as individuals were pressured into wearing the same clothing during the Mao era, people in different regions were also pushed to follow the cultural standards of Beijing—the revolutionary center of the country and the embodiment of "authentic socialist culture."[3] Thus, throughout the first four decades of the People's Republic of China (PRC), Shanghai did not even publish a scholarly book documenting the history of the city.[4] The official line on Shanghai was that "Shanghai is China's Shanghai."[5] A scholar from the Chinese Academy of Social Sciences observed that both popular culture and foreign culture had been slighted—and even forbidden—in the pre-reform era.[6] Given the recent history of the PRC, the so-called Shanghai boom in cultural studies in the early 1990s was an exciting development.[7]

Since the 1990s, China has witnessed a rapid growth in the number of teahouses, coffee shops, internet cafés, karaoke bars, disco clubs, nightclubs, fitness centers, private bookstores, private salons, and private theaters. These venues first appeared in coastal towns and cities like Shanghai, then spread into China's inland regions. According to research conducted jointly by Shanghai Jiaotong University and the University of Southern California in 2019, Shanghai ranked first in terms of the number of coffee shops and teahouses among the world's fifty-one metropolitan cities.[8] Shanghai had a total of 5,567 coffee shops in the middle of 2019, which was 1.5 times more than Beijing and 2 times more than Guangzhou.[9] Starbucks has a major presence in China, and in 2019 Forbes magazine revealed the extent of the company's aggressive expansion in China, reporting that Starbucks had opened over 3,700 stores in the country.[10] Shanghai is home to the world's biggest Starbucks, with a "29,000-square-foot sanctuary staffed by 400 employees."[11] If one accepts Jürgen Habermas's well-known argument that the pubs and coffeehouses of seventeenth-century London drove the formation of British civil society, the surge in Starbucks and other places for informal association may contribute to the emergence of China's civil society.[12]

Furthermore, cultural pluralism is reflected in—and has reinforced—the resurgence of provincial and municipal identities. As Elizabeth Perry, a political scientist at Harvard, observed, "Renewed interest in local dialects, histories, customs, and cuisines is emblematic of a growing geographical differentiation with potentially momentous implications."[13] China's trend toward cultural pluralism has generated a renewed sense of locality, individuality, and diversity.[14] According to some analysts, these cultural and social changes may have an even more profound political impact than public protests or other demonstrations, which have been described by some observers as "movements of masses rather than of citizens."[15]

Arguably, during the reform era, no city or town in China has been shaped more greatly by the revival of distinct, subnational cultural identities than Shanghai. *Haipai* (Shanghai style or Shanghai school) was reborn during the post-Mao era and became a far-reaching cultural phenomenon. The term originated a century ago around the time of the May Fourth Movement, when a group of avant-garde visual and dramatic artists in Shanghai—heavily influenced by Western cultures—produced unorthodox pieces of artwork.[16] *Haipai* was also prominently associated with the emerging Shanghai style of literature exemplified by the "Mandarin Ducks and Butterflies" fiction of that period.[17] Altogether, *haipai* differed profoundly from the traditional Chinese imperial works that were prevalent in northern China, most noticeably in Beijing, known as Beijing-style (*jingpai*) culture. The difference between *haipai* and *jingpai* has often been characterized as a contest between a vibrant, cosmopolitan, liberal culture and a traditional, confined, conservative culture. While the May Fourth Movement originated in Beijing, the turbulence in China during the 1920s compelled talented people from all parts of the country to move to Shanghai, making the city the "birthplace of contemporary Chinese literature, movies, music, fine arts, and urban planning."[18] In a way, Shanghai was both the product and the accelerator of the new culture movement in China's Republican era.

From its inception, *haipai* embodies ideas of openness, diversity, entrepreneurship, cosmopolitanism, innovation, and inclusiveness. Shanghai's importance in both its interaction with the West and its cultural radiation to the rest of the country is partly attributable to its geographic location. The two Chinese characters for Shanghai literally mean "the city above the sea," a reference to the port city's location on mudflats barely above sea level.[19] Shanghainese often use the metaphor of "a sea embracing water from a hundred rivers" (*haina baichuan*) when they refer to the distinct cultural characteristics of the city. Like many other port cities, Shanghai is inherently outward looking. Located midway along the Chinese coast, Shanghai links "the north and south domestically and east and west internationally," in the words of a scholar at Shanghai's Tongji University.[20]

Shanghai's unique place in China's contemporary history has contributed to its purported exceptionalism. This characterization of Shanghai is not new, and it has persisted throughout several crucial periods of the city's development. Questions about Shanghai's distinct qualities and role in China have reemerged in the past two decades, as the city has assumed even greater prominence in China and the world. How should we reconcile contradictory perceptions of Shanghai in both its historical encounters and ongoing engagement with Western transnational forces? How can competing identities—global, national, and local—interact constructively in Shanghai's search for its place in the globalized world, rather than negatively offset each other? In what ways do the main characteristics of *haipai* culture differ from *jingpai* culture, and how have these contrasts contributed to the intellectual and policy narratives about changes in domestic governance and international relations? Today, at a time when China faces vast economic disparities between coastal and inland areas, sociopolitical tensions at home, as well as heightened public anxiety and uncertainty given rising tensions in Sino-U.S. relations, Shanghai's idiosyncratic identity and the unique and important role it plays in China's past, present, and future deserve greater attention.

SHANGHAI'S EXCEPTIONALISM: HISTORICAL LEGACY AND FOREIGN INFLUENCE

Historians widely believe that Shanghai's history can be traced back 3,000 years. During the Tang Dynasty (around A.D. 600–900), Shanghai served as a minor river port. It received its official designation as a market town (*zhen*) in 1074 and then as a market city (*shi*) in 1159.[21] The promotion of Shanghai to the level of county (*xian*) in the late 1200s reflected its elevated status as a center of commerce for both inland and maritime trade.[22] In the thirteenth century, the production and trade of cotton, a new cash crop, transformed Shanghai and the entire Yangtze River delta into one of the most prosperous areas of the country. According to Alan Balfour and Zheng Shiling, in the early fourteenth century, about 10 percent of the country's total income tax came from Suzhou and Shanghai alone.[23] By the time of the Ming Dynasty (A.D. 1368–1644), Shanghai enjoyed a reputation as the "bustling port and grand metropolis in the Southeast."[24]

As Balfour and Zheng observe, from a historical perspective, Shanghai was never "marked in any way by the grandeur of the imperial order" or "a city distorted by illusions or false promises." Instead, it was always a place dominated by commerce—"a place ordered by circumstances and reason, free from unnecessary regulation."[25] In the words of the famous Chinese writer Lu Xun, "*Haipai* is just the helper of commerce," whereas "*jingpai* is the hack of officialdom."[26] In terms of its imperial administrative function, Shanghai differed greatly from the northern capitals of Xi'an and Beijing as well as from nearby cities, such as Hangzhou, Suzhou, and Nanjing.

Shanghai was by no means a Western creation. When Lord Amherst sailed up the Huangpu River in 1832, "Shanghai was already a flourishing port, the harbor filled with the brown trapezoid sails of hundreds of junks."[27] Prior to the arrival of Westerners after the Opium Wars, Shanghai was already among the top twenty Chinese cities in terms of commerce, although it was not able to compete with more prominent cities at the time, such as Beijing, Suzhou, Guangzhou, Wuhan, Hangzhou, Chengdu, Fuzhou, Xi'an, and Nanjing.[28]

According to Zhou Wu, a distinguished scholar on Shanghai studies and fellow of the Shanghai Academy of Social Sciences, Shanghai's development was also unique from a global perspective. Shanghai differed from London and Paris; these two cities developed from their own evolutionary mechanisms, whereas Shanghai transformed quickly and abruptly throughout the concession period.[29] Although Shanghai, like New York, started as a city of immigrants, the two cities followed alternate paths. New York developed under a sovereign nation, whereas Shanghai bloomed when China lacked full sovereignty. Yet Shanghai also differed from other colonized cities, such as Calcutta (now Kolkata) and Hong Kong, because Shanghai maintained its own Chinese territories during the concession period.[30]

China's Most Westernized Metropolis

In 1843, Western colonial powers transformed Shanghai into China's most Westernized commercial city when it became an open port—one of the five "treaty ports," along with Canton (Guangzhou), Ningpo (Ningbo), Foochow (Fuzhou), and Amoy (Xiamen)—after the First Opium War. Through the late Qing Dynasty period, Imperial China was forced to grant more and more concessions (*zujie*) to foreign powers in these treaty ports and other places. Foreigners governed and occupied these concessions, which were given extraterritorial status—the state of being exempted from the jurisdiction of local law. Shanghai established its British concession in 1846, its American concession in 1848, and its French concession in 1849.[31] The British and American concessions merged in 1863 and were renamed as the Shanghai International Settlement. These concessions were not located in the old downtown area, but were instead primarily constructed in areas of uncultivated land.[32] During that period, Shanghai transformed from a regional city of domestic commerce to a metropolis of international trade.

When Shanghai became an open port in 1843, the population numbered approximately 250,000. By comparison, at that time Hangzhou had a population of almost 1 million, and Suzhou, Nanjing, and Ningbo each had 500,000 residents.[33] By 1900, Shanghai's population had skyrocketed past 1 million, replacing Hangzhou as the most populous city in the country.[34] Shanghai's population increased further to 1.3 million in 1910, 2 million in 1915, 3 million in 1930, 3.8 million in 1936, 4.5 million in 1947, and 5.5 million in 1949—about a twentyfold increase within the span of a century.[35] Table 4-1 shows the population growth in Shanghai from 1852 to 1949. By the mid-1930s, Shanghai had already become the seventh most populous

TABLE 4-1. Population Increase in Shanghai, 1852–1949

Year	Number	Annual growth (%)
1852	544,000	
1865	692,000	1.87
1876	705,000	0.17
1885	764,000	0.9
1890	825,000	1.55
1895	925,000	2.31
1900	1,087,000	3.28
1905	1,214,000	2.23
1910	1,289,000	1.21
1915	2,007,000	9.26
1920	2,255,000	2.36
1927	2,641,000	2.28
1930	3,145,000	5.99
1935	3,702,000	3.81
1942	3,920,000	0.82
1945	3,370,000	–4.91
1946	3,830,000	13.65
1947	4,494,000	17.34
1948	5,407,000	20.32
1949	5,455,000	3.55

Source: Xin Ping, *Cong Shanghai faxian lishi—Xiandaihua jinchengzhong de Shang-hairen jiqi shehui shenghuo* [Discovering history from Shanghai: Shanghainese and their social life in the process of modernization] (Shanghai: Shanghai renmin chu-banshe, 1996), 40–41.

city in the world.[36] Shanghai's resemblance to some Western metropolises at the time earned the city the nicknames Paris of the Orient and New York in the East. In his study of early 20th century Shanghai, Lu Hanchao called the city "the 'bridgehead' for foreign encroachment on China."[37]

Even before the proliferation of planes and international travel, Shanghai was already a hub for people from around the world. In the mid-1930s, a British diplomat published a famous book titled *Shanghai, The Paradise of Adventurers,* in which he described his experience walking near the Palace

Hotel (now called the Swatch Art Peace Hotel), which opened in 1909 on Nanjing Road along the Bund:

> On the way everything attracted my attention and interested me. I found myself in a very old world, new and strange to me; different and incomparable: what lay behind this kaleidoscope of people from every corner of the earth? French, Germans, Spanish, Americans, Russians, Japanese, Turks, Persians, Koreans, Malays, Javanese, Hindus, Tonkinese . . . all gathered here with their individual districts, stores, clubs, hotels, cafes, and products.[38]

During the hotel's inaugural year, the First International Opium Commission was held there, and Chiang Kai-shek and Soong Mei-ling celebrated their engagement there in 1927.

According to Xiong Yuezhi and other historians of Shanghai, in the 1940s the city's foreign residents came from fifty-eight different countries.[39] The number of foreign residents in Shanghai increased from 26 in 1843 to 2,757 in 1865, 12,328 in 1905, 37,808 in 1925, and 69,429 in 1935, and it peaked in 1942 at 150,931 people.[40] The largest increase occurred during the Second World War when many European refugees settled in Shanghai. In 1949, on the eve of the Communist takeover, the city had about 30,000 foreigners because many had left due to China's civil war in the late 1940s. Most foreigners lived in the international settlement and the French concession. Table 4-2 shows the distribution of foreigners by territory and their percentage of the total population in the international settlement, the French concession, and Chinese territories in Shanghai in 1928.

TABLE 4-2. The Distribution of Foreign Residents and Chinese Residents in Shanghai, 1928

Location	Chinese	Foreigners	% of foreigners	Total
International Concession	827,075	31,610	3.7	858,685
French Concession	348,076	10,377	2.9	358,453
Chinese Territories	1,497,587	9,383	0.6	1,506,970
Total	2,672,738	51,370	1.9	2,724,108

Source: Xiong Yuezhi, Ma Xueqiang, and Yan Kejia, *Shanghai de waiguoren, 1842–1949* [Foreigners in Shanghai 1842–1949] (Shanghai: Shanghai guji chubanshe, 2003), 155.

Despite the strong presence of foreigners in the concessions and the public image of Shanghai as a European city in China, foreign residents of Shanghai were always an insignificant proportion of the city's total population. In 1910, there were only 11,000 foreigners (0.8 percent) in the city of 1.3 million people.[41] Based on the census conducted in 1927–28, the total Shanghai population was 2,710,423, and among them, 47,760 were foreigners (about 1.8 percent).[42] Similarly, in the early 1930s, Shanghai had 2,980,000 residents, of which only 58,000 (2 percent) were foreigners.[43] Thus, in terms of ethnic composition, Shanghai was always a predominantly Chinese city.

Before 1910, the British accounted for the largest number of foreign residents in Shanghai, followed by Americans, French, Germans, Japanese, and Portuguese. After 1915, Japanese residents accounted for the largest share of foreigners in Shanghai. In the early 1930s, the Russian community in Shanghai consisted of about 25,000 people, constituting the largest foreign community after the Japanese.[44] In the mid-1930s, about one-third of the total number of Americans in China resided in Shanghai, with a population of approximately 3,700. Many of these Americans worked at electricity, oil, and telephone companies owned by Americans and other foreigners.[45] During the Japanese occupation in the late 1930s, there were about 95,000 Japanese living in Shanghai, more than all other foreign residents combined.

These foreign residents were, of course, a diverse group. Some came to Shanghai to fulfill dreams of making a fortune in this "paradise of adventure," some were missionaries, some arrived in the gateway city of Shanghai as oppressive colonial rulers, and still others came to escape persecution, conflict, and war. They differed profoundly from each other in terms of nationality, religion, sociopolitical background, and economic status, further enhancing the diversity of the city.

With people flocking to Shanghai from both international and domestic locales, Shanghai became widely recognized as a city of immigrants. These immigrants were mainly Chinese natives from other regions of China. Between 1885 and 1935, 80 percent of Shanghai residents in foreign concessions were immigrants, as were 75 percent of the residents in the Chinese territory.[46] In 1950, one year after the founding of the PRC, the proportion of Shanghai residents who were migrants from other parts of the country reached 85 percent.[47]

A Haven for Refugees and Religious Inclusivity

According to a study conducted by historians in Shanghai, the city experienced three large waves of domestic refugees from the middle of the nineteenth century to the middle of the twentieth century: (1) between 1855 and

1865, 110,000 refugees entered Shanghai to escape the chaos of the Taiping Rebellion (1850–1864); (2) from 1938 to 1941, the population of the foreign concessions surged by 780,000 due to the Japanese invasion of China; and (3) during a three-year period in the late 1940s, about 2.1 million refugees entered Shanghai due to the civil war between the Communists and the Nationalists.[48] The amalgamation of different people living in Shanghai inspired some foreign observers to call it a "city of odd juxtaposition." A bestselling travel book described pre-1949 Shanghai as a city of bums, adventurers, pimps, child prostitutes, swindlers, gamblers, sailors, socialists, dandies, drug runners, coolies, rickshaw drivers, student activists, strikers, intellectuals, and the like.[49]

The idea of Shanghai as a "paradise of adventure" drew many foreigners to the city, and it also attracted many domestic migrants who hoped to pursue entrepreneurial opportunities. For many of them, "the city was the substance out of which the dream for a better life might be spun."[50] Many of these "adventurers" found success in Shanghai, outnumbering the number of native Shanghainese people occupying prominent positions in the city. Based on a study by Lu Hanchao, in the early 1920s, 86 percent of the members of the Shanghai General Chamber of Commerce were from nearby Zhejiang. Of the thirty-five members on its board of directors, only four were natives of Shanghai. Of the fifty-nine local Chinese banks (*qianzhuang*), only seven were run by Shanghai natives.[51]

The uniqueness of Shanghai's history is also evident during the Japanese occupation period, when the city was often called a "lone islet" (*gudao*). The term holds multiple meanings and reflects what Christian Henriot and Wen-Hsin Yeh called "the singularity of Shanghai in the Chinese war experience."[52] In 1932, Shanghai was damaged heavily when Japanese troops launched large-scale and indiscriminate bombing raids of the city. According to some studies, about 10,000 civilians died in the bombing and military conflict.[53] Hundreds of thousands of Shanghai residents escaped to the international settlement and the French concession to seek protection. The first troops that entered Shanghai after the Japanese surrender were not the Nationalist Army but American soldiers, for whom the Shanghainese were very grateful, as one famous Shanghainese writer noted.[54]

One of the most remarkable historical accounts from the Second World War period was Shanghai's international reputation as "a haven for visa-less Jewish refugees." At the time, Shanghai was the only location in the world unconditionally open to Jews.[55] An estimated 30,000 Jewish refugees from Germany, Austria, and other German-occupied countries escaped to Shanghai between 1933 and 1941.[56] Among them, about 5,000 passed through Shanghai and then went elsewhere, and the other 25,000 remained in Shanghai until the end of the Second World War. They established their own synagogues, newspapers, cafés, schools, hospitals, and shops. In late 1941, under pressure from their ally Germany, the Japanese moved the Jewish population to what became known as the "Shanghai ghetto."[57] Notably, this was not the only time in Shanghai's history when the city served as a haven for foreign refugees. After the Russian Communist Revolution in 1917, many Russian refugees, including musicians, dancers, and artists, had also fled to Shanghai.[58]

Understandably, Shanghai was a metropolis in which different religions sought to exert their influence and conduct missionary work. As early as the Ming Dynasty, Xu Guangqi (Hsu Kuang-ch'I, 1562–1633), a native Shanghainese and well-respected scholar-bureaucrat who served as grand minister, met the Italian Jesuits Matteo Ricci and Sabatino de Ursis. Xu not only assisted with their translation of several Western classics into Chinese, including Euclid's *Elements*, but was also instrumental in modernizing the Chinese calendar. In 1608, Xu invited Jesuit missionaries to start a Roman Catholic congregation in Shanghai and establish several churches there.[59] Centuries later, in 1891, about 6,200 college graduates in the United States went abroad to undertake missionary activities, with one-third going to China.[60]

As some Western scholars have observed, the Chinese attitude toward religion was generally inclusive, whereas Western religious practice could be exclusive.[61] Prior to the Communist takeover in 1949, Shanghai had a total of 2,996 places of religious worship, including 2,069 Buddhist temples, 236 Daoist temples, 19 Islamic mosques, 392 Catholic churches, 277 Protestant churches, and 3 Orthodox churches. There were also 140,000 Catholics, including 1,509 fathers (among them 695 were foreigners), and 17,000 Muslims residing in Shanghai.[62] Interestingly, except for a couple of violent Chinese movements against foreigners, such as the Small Sword Rebellion (1840–1855) and the Taiping Rebellion (1850–1864), the welcoming Shanghainese attitude toward religions provided an environment conducive to missionary work in the city. As two Shanghai scholars described, "Many Western missionaries were determined to beat Confucius before they arrived in Shanghai, but later they found that 'Confucius was a friend, not an adversary.'"[63]

Shanghai was the center of Christianity in pre-Communist China. According to official Chinese sources, when the PRC was founded in 1949, fourteen of the twenty-six national Christian organizations were headquartered in Shanghai. Nine of twelve Christian institutions (churches and schools) and all eight Christian philanthropic organizations were located in Shanghai.[64] Western missionaries also established institutions that facilitated modern educational and cultural dissemination starting from the eve of the twentieth century and beyond. By the early 1900s, foreign churches had opened sixty-one schools in Shanghai, including twenty-five middle schools, which accounted for about 70 percent of the total number of middle schools in the city at that time.[65] In 1872, foreign missionaries founded the Foreign Study Preparatory School in Shanghai, the first school meant to prepare young Chinese students to study overseas, making the city the center of China's study abroad movement in the contemporary era.[66]

In 1843, British Christian missionaries established the London Missionary Society Mission Press (*mohai shuguan*) in Shanghai, the first modern print house in China.[67] In 1868, American missionaries set up the *News of the Chinese Churches*, later known as *Globe Magazine* (*wanguo gongbao*), which provided news coverage and disseminated religious sermons. Its main readers were members of the Chinese gentry class, new intellectuals, and reform-minded officials. In 1889, its readership hit 38,400, making it the most widely read newspaper in the country at that time.[68]

Several prominent missionary organizations and a major Christian church in the international settlement were all located on the same street, which was first called Priest Road or Church Road and then renamed Shima Road or Fuzhou Road. Interestingly, this street was also home to many licensed brothels. In 1871, there were about 1,500 registered sex workers in Shanghai.[69] In the 1890s, according to municipal government data, 12.5 percent of the female population living in the Shanghai foreign concessions were prostitutes. At the beginning of the twentieth century, several major bookstores also found their way onto this famous street. The presence of a large number of bookstores resulted in a new nickname for the road— "cultural street."[70] The harmonious coexistence of churches, brothels, and bookstores—priests, prostitutes, and intellectuals—on this crowded street reflected a great degree of cultural diversity and tolerance, which have been among the defining cultural norms and values of the city.

A Breeding Ground for New Intellectual and Cultural Endeavors

The strong foreign presence, unique administrative status, and geographic location of Shanghai made the city an ideal breeding ground for many new intellectual and cultural pursuits in the last few decades of the nineteenth century and the early decades of the twentieth century. The political significance of these endeavors should not be underestimated. Liang Qichao, China's leading reformer in the late Qing Dynasty, hailed from the Pearl River delta (the other large cultural mixing bowl of China) and believed that bringing about renewal in a country requires revitalizing its people through cultural changes.[71] Many such cultural changes occurred in Shanghai:

- In 1850, British auctioneer Henry Shearman founded China's first English newspaper, the *North China Herald*. Its daily edition, which began publication in 1864, lasted for almost nine decades and ended distribution in 1951.

- In the 1850s to 1860s, Western missionaries established a few all-female schools in Shanghai, earlier than in other parts of the country.[72] Between 1898 and 1911, there were seventy-six newspapers and magazines for women in the country, thirty-two (42 percent) of which were published in Shanghai.[73]

- In 1868, French missionary Pierre Marie Heude established China's first modern museum, the Xujiahui Museum, which showcased the natural history of the Yangtze River.

- In 1872, British businessman Ernest Major founded *Shenbao* (*Shun Pao* or *Shanghai News*), which was considered the most influential newspaper in the country at the time and the "encyclopedia of politics, society, economy and culture of contemporary China." Shanghai was the center of modern Chinese journalism.[74] In 1890, there were seventy-six newspapers in all of China, of which thirty-three (43 percent) were published in Shanghai.[75] In 1936, Shanghai was home to 320 magazines and newspapers.[76]

- In 1896, cinema was first introduced in China, only five years after the world's first movie house was founded in San Francisco.

- In 1905, the first Chinese film, *Dingjun Mountain*, was produced. Shanghai served as the capital of the country's movie industry, and in the late 1920s, Shanghai had a total of fifty film studios.[77]

- In 1906, Shanghai became home to the country's first Chinese-run library.

- In 1917, Huang Yanpei, a Shanghai native, established the nation's first modern vocational school in the city.

- In 1922, American journalist E. G. Osborn established the first Chinese radio broadcasting station. Its programming included violin works by the famous Czech violinist Jaroslav Kocian, as well as local, national, and international news. By 1937, China was home to seventy-six radio stations, of which forty (53 percent) were run out of Shanghai.[78]

- In 1927, Cai Yuanpei and Xiao Youmei founded the National College of Music, the country's first educational institution for modern music. It is now the Shanghai Conservatory of Music, an internationally renowned music school.

The spread of Western culture throughout the colonial period was particularly vigorous in the translation and publication of Western writings into Chinese. Without a doubt, Shanghai played a leading role on this front. Between 1850 and 1899, 556 translated books were published in China, of which 473 (85 percent) were published in Shanghai.[79] From 1902 to 1919, a total of 608 foreign novels were translated and published in China, and 515 (85 percent) of these were published in Shanghai.[80] At the beginning of the twentieth century, Shanghai had a total of seventy-nine publishing houses.[81] Among the 5,299 translated books printed in China between 1912 and 1940, around half were published in Shanghai.[82]

The famous Translation House of Jiangnan Manufacturing Bureau (also called Kiangnan Arsenal) was established in Shanghai in 1868 by the Qing government. The House was instrumental in the translation of modern science and technology textbooks in the country. It made available the intellectual resources of many modern academic disciplines in China, including chemistry, optics, and forensic medicine.[83] Over the years, this translation house hired a total of fifty-nine professional translators, including nine foreigners and fifty Chinese. John Fryer, a British scholar and missionary, joined the translation house at the time of its founding and worked there for twenty-eight years, translating sixty-six books into Chinese.[84] In 1876, Fryer established the Shanghai Polytechnic Institution (*Gezhi Shushi*), which was devoted to education in science and technology rather than missionary work. This institution, located on Fuzhou Road, was the predecessor to the Shanghai Gezhi High School, one of the top high schools in present-day Shanghai.

Another important publishing house in Shanghai was Guangxuhui (also called Tongwen Shuhui), which was founded in 1887 by the British missionary Alexander Williamson. Initially, the English name for the house was the Society of the Diffusion of Christian and General Knowledge among the Chinese. Between 1890 and 1911, this institution published 400 titles with 1 million printed copies altogether. It was reported that during the 1898 modernization reform, the Guangxu emperor ordered 129 books to help him advance his knowledge of the West. Among these books, 89 were published by Guangxuhui.[85]

In the 1920s, Shanghai's three commercial publishing houses (Shangwu, Zhonghua, and Shijie) dominated the publication market in China. These three publishing houses monopolized textbook publication in the country, occupying 60 percent, 30 percent, and 10 percent of the publishing market share, respectively.[86] According to research conducted by the late American political scientist Lucian Pye, the number of books published by the Shangwu Publishing House alone was equal to the total number of books published in the United States during that time.[87]

Studies by Shanghai scholar Chen Bohai reveal the astounding number of books on various subjects put out by the Shanghai publishing houses during the 1920s.[88] These organizations released 65 percent of all new books published in China between 1927 and 1936.[89] Shanghai's dominant role in the publication of textbooks in China was significant. Although the rest of the country was still undecided about whether to teach in classical or vernacular Chinese in schools, these houses in Shanghai had the power to actually decide, as they controlled the publication of Chinese textbooks for middle and elementary schools. As some Chinese scholars remark, "Shanghai used commercial means to pave the way for the ultimate victory of the vernacular."[90]

Shanghai was also the birthplace of the women's liberation movement in contemporary China. The country's first school for women was opened in the city in 1850. By the end of the nineteenth century, Shanghai had established itself as the first city in the nation to offer comprehensive modern education for women. The education of women in China, especially Shanghai, inspired some to push for greater women's empowerment. At the beginning of the twentieth century, Qiu Jin, a foreign-educated female activist, established the *China Women's Daily* (*Zhongguo nü bao*), a periodical that advocated for women's rights. Some Chinese scholars argue that this movement had a lasting impact on the formation of the feminist consciousness in the nation.[91]

During the Republican period (1911–1949), no city in China offered more freedom of the press, cultural diversity, and intellectual vigor than Shanghai. The city nurtured and groomed China's most prominent writers and artists, as well as the country's would-be reformers. In the late 1920s and 1930s, many leading figures in China's new cultural movement converged in Shanghai. They flocked to the city from other places, and they included those who had been persecuted by warlords in Beijing and elsewhere (e.g., Xu Zhimo, Wen Yiduo, Hu Shi); those who had returned from studying abroad in Japan (e.g., Li Chuli, Cheng Fangwu); those who had just participated in the Northern Expedition (e.g., Guo Moruo, Mao Dun, Jiang Guangci); those who had escaped from the Japanese occupation in northeast China (e.g., Xiao Jun and Xiao Hong); those who came from teaching careers in Guangzhou (e.g., Lu Xun and Yu Dafu); and those who migrated from Sichuan (e.g., Sha Ting and Ai Wu).[92]

Distinguished Chinese educators, though different in their educational philosophy and methods, also settled in Shanghai. They included the intellectual giants of the time, such as Cai Yuanpei, Shu Xincheng, Tao Xingzhi, Yan Yangchu, and Liang Shuming. This period of rapid educational and cultural development, as some foreign scholars have described, was "a time of 'cultural awakening' in China, and Shanghai was at the forefront of this change."[93] Furthermore, many prominent political figures, such as Sun Yat-sen, Huang Xing, and Chiang Kai-shek, began their political careers in Shanghai, and the Chinese Communist Party was born in the city's foreign concession. Since the late Qing Dynasty, Shanghai has played an important role in Chinese political and intellectual movements, and many consider it to be "the center of new political trends outside Beijing."[94] During the Republican period, Shanghai served as the "shadow political center outside of Nanjing."

The Center of Commerce and Innovation

In contrast to left-wing Chinese critics who view Shanghai as a "foreign enclave" (*fei di*), many consider this large cosmopolitan city to be the commercial center that shapes China's future.[95] As in the domains of culture and education, Shanghai was also quick to adopt innovations in business and technology. Shanghai started importing trains just seven years after the completion of the first transcontinental railroad in America. Additionally, Shanghai's first textile mills were built before any in the American South, and by 1930, according to some estimations, the city had the largest textile mill in the world.[96]

In 1865, a few British, American, German, and other foreign merchants who had long lived in either Shanghai or Hong Kong banded together to establish the renowned Hong Kong and Shanghai Banking Co. Ltd. In 1897, the China Commercial Bank, the first contemporary Chinese-owned bank, was established in Shanghai. From 1897 to 1911, there were altogether seventeen Chinese-owned banks in the country, ten of which began operations in Shanghai.[97] By 1935, China had a total of 164 banks, of which 58 were headquartered in Shanghai. In addition, the city hosted 182 other financial institutions (both foreign- and Chinese-owned).[98] In 1931, the total foreign capital invested in Shanghai was $1.1 billion, accounting for 34 percent of the total foreign investment in China at the time. Before Imperial Japan occupied Shanghai in November 1937, 79 percent of China's foreign financial investment was flowing in through Shanghai.[99]

The first national industrial firm, the Shanghai Fachang Machine Building Factory, was established in Shanghai in 1866. Among the 1,975 industrial firms that were established in the country between 1912 and 1930, 837 (42 percent) were located in Shanghai.[100] In 1933, 40 percent of Chinese-owned factory assets were based in Shanghai, and in 1948, over half of China's factories and factory workers were based in Shanghai.[101] As the cradle of China's contemporary industrial revolution, Shanghai was the first place in the country to commercially adopt the use of gaslights (1865), telegraphs (1871), telephones (1881), electric lights (1882), running water (1884), cars

(1901), and trams (1908).[102] Shanghai gained a reputation as the incubator of Chinese industrialization. Tellingly, Shanghai accounted for 7,932 (86 percent) of the 9,224 trademarks registered in China in 1934. Similarly, Shanghai was home to 40,000 (80 percent) of the 50,000 trademarks registered in the country through that year.[103]

The presence of Chinese industrialists and capitalists was most prevalent in Shanghai compared to other major cities like Tianjin, Guangzhou, Hangzhou, and Beijing. These business-minded individuals transformed Shanghai into the commercial, manufacturing, and banking center of modern China. They also organized a variety of entrepreneurial groups and business associations, such as the Shanghai General Chamber of Commerce and the Shanghai Bankers Association, to protect and advance their interests and rights.[104]

For seven consecutive years between 1988 and 1994, Deng Xiaoping spent the spring festival holiday in Shanghai, which helped him appreciate Shanghai's cosmopolitan legacy and distinct culture, especially its large pool of talent. During his stay in Shanghai in 1990, Deng stated that "Shanghai is China's trump card. It is a shortcut for China to catch up through Shanghai's take off. . . . One of my big mistakes was I did not include Shanghai when I launched four special economic zones [in 1980]."[105] That same year, China launched its historic plan for developing Pudong (east Shanghai) and further establishing Shanghai's prominence as the country's center of innovation and economic growth. Deng's recognition of Shanghai paved the way for Jiang and the powerful Shanghai municipal leadership to adopt decisive policies for "Shanghai's take off," which led to the city's evolution to China's Manhattan.

ARE MULTIPLE SHANGHAI IDENTITIES MUTUALLY EXCLUSIVE?

Shanghai has been recognized as having three distinct identities in contemporary history—a global, cosmopolitan image during the era of the foreign concessions, a statist uniformity and nationalism in the Mao era, and a nativist character and localism in the Jiang era. Each one highlights the remarkable differences between various periods of Shanghai's development, as well as the inherent tensions among competing forces and players within the city. Shanghai's diverse history explains why Shanghainese think of themselves in a variety of ways.

The multiple identities of Shanghai and its people have continuously evolved from the turn of the new century and beyond—arguably more dramatically than ever before—by drawing on each of the city's three self-conceptions. Shanghai's cosmopolitan identity is itself inherently multifaceted. There is no monolithic "Shanghai identity" from which to deduce residents' behavior. The perceptions Shanghainese hold of their city are simultaneously local, national, and cosmopolitan. One can only guess at the preferences and attitudes of Shanghainese people based on the given circumstances.

Identities are not constraining, but freeing, in that they offer people options. In a sense, a distinct, singular identity often emerges through conflicts among alternative, coexisting, and separate identities. For residents attempting to navigate varying circumstances, identities can provide useful flexibility, because different approaches and motifs offer advantages in various situations.[106]

To a certain degree, identity is valuable in politics and policies only when it remains flexible.[107] During the Mao era, in order to mobilize the Chinese people for revolutionary causes, the Communist regime both elevated national identity above everything else and purposefully suppressed other identities. Shanghai was ultimately pushed to become like the "rest of China," and it was largely cut off from any foreign or overseas contact.[108] The Chinese authorities—both central and local—promoted rigid and orthodox frameworks of identity that required loyalty to the nation-state. Maoists emphasized the importance of China's national pride and strength, while diminishing the value of other types of collectives, such as subnational localities or even families.

Yet, as in other periods in history, imperial or statist influence decreases with distance from central power. As the age-old Chinese saying goes, "Heaven is high, and the emperor is far away." This has been particularly evident in Shanghai, where local and coastal traits, as well as colonial and cosmopolitan heritage, are so prevalent that, while they may have been temporarily suppressed in the past, they could never be fully eliminated. Conversely, people in peripheral regions, especially in more economically and culturally developed urban centers, may forgo traditional aspects of social and prescribed norms. For Shanghai, foreign influences, invasions, and emigrations have shaped the city for over a century, making it difficult for Beijing to ignore these historical influences. Thus the limits to central control are exemplified by the impressive resurgence of diverse identities in the born-again Shanghai during the reform era, especially the distinct "Shanghai nostalgia" for the city's cosmopolitan glory in the previous century.

In his influential study of cultural identity, the distinguished Singaporean scholar Wang Gungwu presents a nuanced view of the "multiple identities" of the Chinese diaspora in Southeast Asia, who are shaped by their kinship, culture, politics, and economic class. As Wang argues, these "are not situational identities, or alternative identities which one can switch around or switch on and off, [but they show] the simultaneous presence of many kinds of identities, e.g., ethnic, national (local), cultural and class identities."[109] These traits are *primordial* because they cannot quickly be changed, *flexible* because individuals can sometimes choose to highlight one or another, *political* because such choices have purposes, and *multiple* because they always coexist. The primary takeaway is not about which of these identities is more valid, it is that their variety reflects their utility.

Similar to the multitude of identities found among Southeast Asia's Chinese diaspora, Shanghainese people also have nativist, nationalistic, and cosmopolitan identities that are by no means mutually exclusive. Their interactions are dynamic—sometimes they are in tension, but at other times they are mutually reinforcing. During the concession period, one of the more interesting interactions between Western and Chinese culture in Shanghai was the expansive development of distinct housing structures, known as two- or three-floor *shikumen* houses (stone warehouses) and *longtang* (interconnected courts).[110] Respectively, they were hybrids of northern China's *siheyuan* (quadrangle) and Western-style warehouses, and of Beijing's *hutong* (alleyways) and Western-style lanes, and they sprouted throughout the city, beginning in the 1870s.

Shanghai's urban neighborhood structure of *shikumen* and *longtang* reflect some of the city's distinct cultural traits, which are strongly reflective of commercialism. Shanghai's commerce-centric subculture lacks strong moral, religious, or hierarchical overtones. As Lu Hanchao has observed, Shanghainese are "astute, resourceful, calculating, quick-witted, adaptive, and flexible (always ready to compromise but not budging an inch unless absolutely necessary)."[111] Additionally, the *shikumen* architecture suggests that although Western influence may have served as the initial inspiration for Shanghai's development, later innovations were almost entirely Chinese. As Lu describes, "*Haipai* culture, although it became distorted, continued to exist in the decades after 1949. This is an indication of the persistence of a tradition rooted neither in the Chinese cultural superstructure, nor in an alien ethos brought by foreigners, but in the quotidian life of the city's people."[112]

Shanghai's adoption and integration of regional, national, and international influences was certainly not limited to neighborhood structure and urban development. Foreign ideas and ideologies were contested, but only those congruent with Chinese circumstances prevailed. These dynamics in Shanghai may help explain how China's May Fourth Movement led to the founding of the Chinese Communist Party there, and why Marxism rather than liberalism eventually "found fertile ground in China's cultural soil."[113]

China's more recent embrace of cultural cosmopolitanism in the reform era, however, does not erase or replace the politically nationalistic sentiments among Chinese people (Shanghainese included).

Interestingly, during the reform era, top national leaders with strong ties to Shanghai explicitly advocated the promotion of cultural cosmopolitanism and *haipai* culture. In 1998, when Jiang Zemin was party boss, he claimed to have invited the entire Politburo to a screening of the American movie *Titanic*.[114] In the annual National People's Congress meeting with the Guangdong delegation that year, Jiang said,

> We should not think that capitalism is inherently lacking ideas for public intellectual dissemination.... The film *Titanic* was brilliantly effective in exploring the relationship between money and love, the relationship between poor and rich, and reactions of individuals in a distressful crisis. Before the founding of the PRC, I saw a lot of well-made Hollywood films in Shanghai, including *Gone with the Wind*, *A Song to Remember*, and *Waterloo Bridge*.... We should not assume that only we communists can pursue ideological work effectively.[115]

Jiang's endorsement turned *Titanic* in particular, and Hollywood movies in general, into big hits among moviegoers in China.

On numerous occasions, both in domestic gatherings and during foreign visits, Jiang performed the Italian song "O Sole Mio" for the public.[116] When Jiang was Shanghai mayor, he danced with then San Francisco mayor Dianne Feinstein and sang "When We Were Young."[117] In the 1997 Asia-Pacific Economic Conference, Jiang partnered with then Philippine president Fidel Ramos for a rendition of Elvis Presley's "Love Me Tender." As a *Washington Post* reporter commented, Jiang actively worked to prove to both China and the world that he was a leader "as versatile politically as he is musically."[118]

Shanghai authorities have generally encouraged various types of cultural exchanges with the outside world. Events such as the Shanghai International Cultural Festival, the Shanghai International Film Festival, the Shanghai International Television Programs Festival, and the Shanghai International Art Biennale have been held regularly since the 1990s. Additionally, in 2004 alone, internationally renowned artists and entertainers, such as Elton John, Whitney Houston, Britney Spears, Mariah Carey, and the Backstreet Boys, performed in Shanghai. In the last few years, world-class musical artists, such as Taylor Swift, Jon Bon Jovi, Queen, Bruno Mars, Ariana Grande, and the Chainsmokers, have all performed in the city. The

National Basketball Association's (NBA's) Houston Rockets and Sacramento Kings played their first China-based NBA games in Shanghai (the birthplace of professional basketball player Yao Ming) during the 2004 preseason. China has since hosted over two dozen NBA preseason games, not only in Shanghai but also in other major cities, such as Beijing, Guangzhou, and Shenzhen.

Chen Yun, a politician whose power and influence approached those of Deng Xiaoping in the 1980s, was a native of Shanghai and thus felt partial to the city. Chen was a huge fan of *pingtan*, a form of storytelling and ballad singing in the Suzhou dialect that is popular in Shanghai. It was reported that Chen attended *pingtan* performances in Shanghai, Jiangsu, and Zhejiang as many as seventy-nine times after the Cultural Revolution.[119] Chen organized fifty-nine roundtable meetings with *pingtan* performers and producers, and he wrote 246 letters and comments calling for the promotion of *pingtan* performance and *haipai* culture.[120]

In Shanghai, the coexistence and prevalence of cosmopolitan, national, and subnational cultures are reflected in everyday life. As Yan Yunxiang has observed, newly accepted norms include the "rising demands for romantic love and sexual freedom, the escalating divorce rate and emergence of single-parent families, the triumph of consumerism and commodity fetishism, the fever for MBA degrees and English language acquisition, the popularity of American fast food chains, and the competition among urban youth to be 'cool.'"[121] In the first two decades of the reform era, this trend of American-led globalization was not seen as a threat to China, because globalism brought diversity rather than uniformity. China's national and local cultures could not only survive but also "localize foreign culture as their own, or as part of the emerging global culture in which they too play a role."[122]

For Chinese people, there is no concern over whether cultural hybrids belong to socialism or capitalism, to the West or the East, or to America or China. The Chinese populace—including the Shanghainese—claim full ownership over their revitalized and globally oriented culture. Especially in Shanghai—the city that has led China into the world and brought the world to China—there is a strong sense that the people themselves set the socioeconomic and political agenda.

CONTRASTS BETWEEN HAIPAI CULTURE AND JINGPAI CULTURE

During the reform era, the resurgence of Shanghainese subculture and the corresponding national, heated discussion of its rise illustrate that neither Chinese society nor Chinese culture are monolithic.[123] If cultural trends can influence the sociopolitical trajectory of a given country, competing subcultures reveal the possibility of alternative paths, rather than a single and predetermined outcome. Beijing and Shanghai, the two largest cities in China, have long been recognized for their contrasting historical experiences, geographical features, cultural characteristics, and national politico-economic roles. In their classic categorization of world cities published in the 1960s, Robert Redfield and Milton Singer, two anthropologists of the "Chicago School" of urban studies, classified Beijing as an "administrative-cultural city" and Shanghai as a "metropolis-city."[124] According to Redfield and Singer, an "administrative-cultural city" was dominated by the literati and the indigenous bureaucracy, concentrating within its boundaries the administrative and political functions of a large empire. Conversely, a "metropolis-city," led by a managerial and entrepreneurial class, would flourish due to its advantageous urban location and dynamic economic activities. Historically, over 80 percent of Chinese cities were political and administrative centers in their regions—Shanghai was a notable exception.[125]

Redfield and Singer's analysis can still be applied to China in the reform era, as differences between Beijing and Shanghai have become increasingly acute. As Shanghai has ascended to an even more prominent role through China's opening to the outside world, Beijing has been struggling both to throw off the weight of its 800-year history as the country's imperial capital as well as to reestablish its dominant power and influence over the Middle Kingdom.

Shanghai has not always been viewed more favorably than Beijing. As early as the 1930s, Chinese intellectuals were engaged in a debate over their assessments of—and attitudes toward—Beijing and Shanghai. Several well-known Beijing writers, such as Shen Congwen, initiated this dispute by condemning the Shanghai literary circle as too utilitarian and commercial. They even disparaged Shanghai literature as the "literature of prostitution." In response, Shanghai writers brushed off their Beijing counterparts as being out of touch with a changing world.

This exchange of insults in the 1930s between Beijing and Shanghai has played out many times since then, expanding into areas far beyond literary taste and style. The tensions between *jingpai* and *haipai* do not just concern city-to-city cultural differences. Rather, they suggest the revival of an urban cultural consciousness in China during the twentieth century and beyond, which reflects three major ideological and political conflicts in China—namely, tradition versus modernity, nationalism versus cosmopolitanism, and uniformity versus diversity.[126]

Many scholars in Shanghai have challenged the conservative view that defends mainstream culture at the expense of subcultures. For those scholars, the "capital city mentality" (*jingzhao xintai*) of Beijing reflects an imperial hierarchy and cultural arrogance. A well-known scholar of Shanghai cultural studies, Yu Qiuyu, observed that one of the most important social norms in Shanghai is reflected in the city's local idiom: "It's none of your business" (*guannong shashiti*). In other words, everyone should mind their own affairs and stay out of the lives of others.[127] Whereas this Shanghai idiom indicates acceptance of social pluralism and a high degree of tolerance for diverse views, values, and lifestyles, people in Beijing, by contrast, are seen as busybodies who intrude with their "political correctness." Additionally, contrary to Beijing, some Shanghai scholars claim that "we can perceive Shanghai in a hundred different ways" and "there are a hundred kinds of Shanghainese."[128]

In the early years of the reform era, the controversial six-part TV documentary production *River Elegy* drew public attention to the contrast between two subcultures within China. There was the traditional landlocked agricultural culture—and its accompanying moral centrism and strict bureaucratic hierarchy—centered in Beijing, and the "outward-looking, trade-oriented," and therefore competitive and commercial, culture exemplified in Shanghai and Guangdong Province.[129] The TV series, as many observed, attempted to provide a historical rationale and ideological justification for the coastal economic development strategy championed by Deng Xiaoping, Zhao Ziyang, Xi Zhongxun, and other reformers.[130] Similarly, in a 1992 book titled *Shanghai: Her Character Is Her Destiny*, the Shanghai-based author Yu Tianbai argued that the distinctiveness of Shanghai embodied in its *haipai* culture is both a cause and a consequence of the miraculous economic changes during the reform era, because, as the title of the book suggests, "her character is her destiny."[131]

Criticism of Beijing's "authentic mainstream culture" comes not only from Shanghai writers but also from writers in other cities, including Beijing. Luo Shuang's book, *A Critique of the Beijingers?!*, forms part of a series on urban cultures in China.[132] The author particularly denounces the "imperial capital complex" (*huangcheng qingjie*) of Beijingers and argues that Beijing has become incapable of handling its own problems.[133] The book's criticism of Beijingers' mentality is reminiscent of another book that was widely read in China during the reform era, *The Ugly Chinese*. This controversial critique of traditional Chinese cultural values was written in the 1970s by Bo Yang, a well-known Taiwanese writer. Luo Shuang characterizes Beijingers as "political animals" (*zhengzhi dongwu*), whereas the Shanghainese (and Cantonese) are "economic animals" (*jingji dongwu*).[134] Beijingers love to talk about "isms" and care about politics, political status, family backgrounds, and other sociopolitical credentials. In sharp contrast, the practical-minded Shanghainese and Cantonese prefer to discuss nothing but business.

Arguably the most influential Chinese book about the *haipai* and *jingpai* cultures is Yang Dongping's *City Monsoon: The Cultural Spirit of Beijing and Shanghai.*[135] Yang's research reveals that the adjectives used to characterize Beijing and Shanghai often sharply contrast, with Beijing being described as aristocratic, noble, rigorous, traditional, elitist, and bureaucratic, whereas Shanghai is referred to as popular, common, leisurely, utilitarian, practical, commercial, modern, colonial, and so on. The coexistence of and the clashes between these two subcultures carry political implications. Beijingers, as characterized by Yang, worship politics more than other Chinese. The first career choice for Beijingers is often to become government officials, because they live "at the foot of the Emperor."[136] In Yang's words, "Politics is salt for Beijingers. Without it, Beijing life would become tasteless."[137]

As Yang observes, the political influence on social life in Beijing inevitably leads its residents to devalue commerce and the middle-class comforts of life—things that are highly valued by Shanghainese. Beijingers are more interested in what people call *kanshan*—chatting about major topics, such as national affairs and elite politics. Also, in contrast to the Shanghainese, who purportedly prioritize their own best interests, Beijingers are described as having a "broad-minded attitude," and in relationships with other people they stress a kind of fraternal loyalty. Consequently, Beijingers do not have the same "contract consciousness" as Shanghainese, according to Yang. Shanghai's "middle class civil consciousness" is also stronger than that of the rest of the country. Thus, in addition to greater political and social tolerance, Shanghai culture, unlike Beijing culture, does not draw a clear division between elite and popular culture. This contributes to what Yang calls the "secularization in socio-political life" of the Shanghainese.[138]

The characteristics of Beijingers reflect the masculine aesthetics of the capital—a male-dominated city. Yang discusses in great detail the differences between Beijing and Shanghai in terms of male-female relationships, marriage, family, the role of women, and feminism. Given that Shanghai was the birthplace of the women's liberation movement in China, Yang concludes that Shanghai women have a longer history of workforce participation, professional careers, and striving for their own rights. Therefore, the "depth" of women's liberation in Shanghai has surpassed that of Beijing. Beijing women experience more obstacles than Shanghai women with regard to women's societal and family roles.[139]

In the book, Yang Dongping summarizes six distinctive characteristics of the Shanghainese:

1. "shrewdness," being capable, flexible, and clever;

2. a strong sense of "practical benefits," emphasizing concrete material interests (estimating and weighing gains and losses);

3. "rationalism," demanding that everything be as fair as possible, such as reasonable prices;

4. "standardization of etiquette," which attaches great importance to regulations, rules, and order (this is a reflection of "the contract consciousness" in daily life necessitated by commercial actions);

5. "secularization," which refers to the establishment of new standards of meritocratic achievement based on the values of a commodity economy, replacing the political and ideological authorities that once controlled society; and

6. "Westernization," which is defined to be synonymous with civilization or enlightenment. Shanghai endows its residents with a tolerant attitude toward foreign culture, an attitude different from that of many people living inland.[140]

In the first decade of the twenty-first century, two of the most important opinion leaders in Shanghai, Zhou Libo and Han Han, personified these characteristics. Zhou Libo is a popular talk show host who is known as China's Jay Leno. Han Han is a spokesperson for the post-'80s generation who once ran the most frequently visited blog in the world. In 2010, Han Han was named by both *Time* magazine in the United States and *New Statesman* in the United Kingdom as one of the 100 most influential individuals in the world.

Both Zhou and Han had very unconventional career trajectories—neither finished high school, and they both became successful largely because of their advocacy for middle-class lifestyles and worldviews. Zhou Libo is best known as a Shanghainese comedian, whose talk shows are unique for two reasons. First, he was the first talk show host in the PRC to regularly mock China's top leaders, including Deng Xiaoping, Jiang Zemin, Hu Jintao, and Wen Jiabao. Second, his target audience is primarily the middle class—both in Shanghai and in the country as a whole. His shows often focus on issues such as stock and property markets, income tax, foreign influence, and middle-class consumption.

Han Han, a rebellious young man in his thirties, has been a household name in China for almost two decades. A high school dropout, Han is also a rally driver, best-selling novelist, essayist, singer, and film director. But what made him famous is his blogging. His blog, which had as many as 330 million hits in 2010, frequently makes fun of Chinese leaders and occasionally critiques their incompetence and irresponsibility. Both Zhou and Han have called for citizens' rights and middle-class participation in political and policy discourse. But as some Chinese scholars observe, in contrast to

Beijing intellectuals who tend to be sensationalist and moralistic in their criticism of authorities, critiques by Zhou Libo and Han Han are often subtler, more humorous, rational, and practical.[141]

FINAL THOUGHTS

Yang's generalization about the characteristics of Shanghai and Shanghainese, as outlined in this chapter, is subject to debate. Nevertheless, in recent years Chinese scholars have continued to emphasize cultural and academic pluralism. In 2018, two distinguished Chinese scholars in the field of international relations, Qin Yaqing, president of China Foreign Affairs University, and Guo Shuyong, a professor at Shanghai Jiaotong University, published a pair of articles comparing different approaches to the study of world affairs in China. They argued that one must use plural names rather than singular names (e.g., Chinese schools of international relations), to refer to the field of world politics studies in China. In particular, they highlighted the difference between the Beijing school and the Shanghai school of international relations.[142]

Qin and Guo believe that while the Beijing school of international relations emphasizes general diplomacy, war and peace, and power transition in the international system, the Shanghai school is more focused on middle-level theories, symbiotic theory, public diplomacy, multilateralism, international political economy, and international political sociology. According to the authors, Shanghai scholars tend to break ideological constraints in academic and policy discourse, and they place more emphasis on introducing and translating Western scholarship—the lasting legacy of the early twentieth century.

One interesting question is how national leaders who have roots in Shanghai differ from their peers elsewhere in China, especially in terms of their governance and policy orientation. This topic is explored in chapter 6. Some national leaders have drawn connections between the essence of *haipai* culture and policy initiatives originating in Shanghai. For example, for five consecutive years between 2014 and 2018, Xi Jinping referred to the "Shanghai spirit" (*Shanghai jingshen*) during the annual meeting of the Shanghai Cooperation Organization.[143] Xi claimed that the Shanghai spirit consists of "mutual trust, mutual benefit, equality, consultation, respect for diverse civilizations, and seeking common development."[144] Thus Xi's notion of the Shanghai spirit for international affairs seemed to draw inspiration from some distinct Shanghai characteristics.

To artfully describe China's transformations over the years, there is a fitting quote from an epigraph in Yang Dongping's book, *City Monsoon*, written by one of the most famous Chinese poets during the early decades of the twentieth century, Xu Zhimo, who writes, "I don't know in which direction the monsoon is blowing." The last century certainly has proved that the "direction of the monsoon" in China has shifted numerous times in dramatic ways. Each shift has had enormous consequences, not only for the country but also for the world. A review of Shanghai's development over the past century and a half shows that the birth and growth of China's most cosmopolitan city undoubtedly draws from strong Western influences. Yet this should not cause one to overlook the fact that the city's development path has also been distinctly Chinese and, even more so, Shanghainese.[145] Chapter 5 elaborates on the interaction between economy and culture, and how this dynamic has molded Shanghai's pivotal role in China's global engagement.

CHAPTER 5

The "Magic Capital" and the "Head of the Dragon"

The Birth of China's Manhattan

To explore up to the edge of the world, there is no place better than the two banks of the Huangpu River.
—A SHANGHAINESE SAYING

Shanghai won't be a center just for China—that's too small. It will be a leader in the world.
—JING YING

In 1923, a Japanese novelist named Shōfu Muramatsu journeyed to Shanghai, where he lived in the international settlement for several months. While there, he not only embedded himself among ordinary residents—both foreign and local—of various walks of life, but also became acquainted with leading Chinese intellectuals, such as Yu Dafu, Guo Moruo, and Tian Han. Based on his experiences in the city, he wrote a travelogue entitled *Magic Capital* (Modu or Mato in Japanese).[1] In the book, he portrayed the paradoxical nature and multilayered dichotomies of Shanghai—juxtaposing a bright, open, modern, eloquent, and civilized facade with a hidden side characterized by darkness, secrecy, old-fashioned style, vulgarity, and crudity.[2]

At the time, neither Muramatsu nor his coined nickname for Shanghai received much attention beyond the literary circles of Japan and China. Both have been largely forgotten over the decades. Interestingly, however, almost a century later, "magic capital" is now a term frequently used by

Chinese people to speak about Shanghai.[3] In recent years, some well-known Chinese historians, political scientists, sociologists, and economists, as well as ordinary people, have adopted this term in their writings on and public discussion of Shanghai.[4] Shanghai party secretary Li Qiang, a member of the powerful Politburo of the Chinese Communist Party (CCP), has also used the term "magic capital" in recent public speeches. For him, the magic within "magic capital" suggests imagination and creation. Li asserts that Shanghai's reputation for innovation in urban development should be its most recognizable "name card."[5] Along the same line of thinking, a comprehensive research article recently published by the Planet Institute claims that "one simply cannot find any other words that better characterize the essence of Shanghai than 'magic capital.'"[6]

Understandably, different people may invoke different connotations—positive, neutral, or negative—when employing the term "magic capital." Their references to the term are largely based on their experiences, perceptions, and perspectives of Shanghai. Some use the term to contrast with another new term, "imperial capital" (didu), which refers to Beijing and has been frequently used on Chinese social media in recent years.[7] Others find "magic capital" particularly appropriate for encapsulating the geographic and demographic characteristics of Shanghai. With an average altitude only 4 meters above sea level and its subtropical monsoon climate, Shanghai is commonly filled with fog (and smog), which often makes the city appear blurry, concealed, and kaleidoscopic. With an area of 6,341 square kilometers, official data from 2018 report that Shanghai has a total of 24.24 million residents, including 14.48 million with permanent household registrations and 9.76 million long-term migrants.[8] In this overcrowded city, the majority of Shanghainese live in the shadow of high-rise buildings among narrow streets and hidden longtang (interconnected courts).

The term "magic capital" highlights the sharp contrast between foreigners and local Chinese, past and future, inclusion and exclusion, humility and arrogance, as well as the mysteriousness of this fast-moving and ever-changing metropolis, especially with respect to its nature as an economic and cultural melting pot.[9] For some Chinese, the city is not just magic, but surreal. However, economic disparities have remained enormous despite the birth and growth of the middle class. The various forces that have shaped the past and present—and will shape the future—of Shanghai are far less harmonious in reality. For others, Shanghai as a "magic capital" intoxicates both migrants to the city and its inhabitants with the sweet dream of a better future.[10]

Since the early 1990s, Chinese authorities have designated Shanghai as "the head of the dragon," symbolizing the leading role of Shanghai in China's quest for power and prosperity in the twenty-first century. This metaphor also suggests that Shanghai leads the Yangtze River delta region, and more broadly, the whole country, in China's efforts to play economic catch-up with more developed countries. The degree of favorable policies toward Shanghai has varied from time to time due to changes in the top leadership in Zhongnanhai, but Shanghai has set the pace for the country's socioeconomic development over much of the past four decades. Shanghai's neighbors can make rapid economic progress if they remain "well connected" (*jiegui*) with Shanghai's development.[11] The cities near Shanghai have already become attractive destinations for investors. Cities in Jiangsu Province (e.g., Suzhou, Wuxi, Kunshan, and Nanjing) and Zhejiang Province (e.g., Jiaxing, Ningbo, Yiwu, and Hangzhou) have greatly benefited from the surge in both foreign and domestic investment in the greater Shanghai area.[12]

It may be premature to predict that the spirit embodied by the "head of the dragon" will spread throughout the country, thus engendering similar changes in inland cities, especially in China's western region and northeast rust belt. There is no doubt, however, that China has emerged as a global economic powerhouse, with Shanghai as the country's exemplar of economic development, international engagement, and cultural dynamism. Shanghai party secretary Li Qiang, a protégé of Xi Jinping, previously served as a top leader in both Jiangsu and Zhejiang provinces. Li seems exceptionally well positioned to promote greater economic integration in the lower Yangtze River delta region, which centers around Shanghai. In spring 2019, he told other Shanghai officials that "Shanghai must always insist on jumping out of its own narrow interests to take a more holistic view of its role and to develop Shanghai in service to the country."[13] Li called for his colleagues to "dare to be the first in innovation" by embracing further economic reforms, greater opening to foreign firms, and good governance in the city and the region. Li also claimed that Shanghai should develop a homegrown brand name in four areas: service, manufacturing, shopping, and culture.[14]

Under the leadership of Li Qiang, one of Shanghai's "magical" endeavors took place amid rising tensions in the U.S.-China trade war during the summer of 2018, when Tesla established its largest overseas plant in the city. Tesla, a Silicon Valley automaker, built a factory in Shanghai with an annual production of 500,000 electric cars. When the plant opened, Li had a widely publicized meeting with Tesla's CEO Elon Musk. Li proclaimed that because this plant was Shanghai's largest foreign manufacturing project so far, it served as a testament to the city's capacity to transform technological achievements into commercial profits, as well as the tremendous potential for U.S.-China economic cooperation.[15] It took only ten months for this joint venture to progress from construction to full operations. Within a year of beginning car production, registrations of Tesla vehicles in China rose fourteenfold.[16] By the start of 2020, with strong sales in the car market in China, Tesla's stock market cap skyrocketed to $84.5 billion and eclipsed the combined value of General Motors and Ford.[17] In late July 2020, its stock market cap further increased to $290 billion, a surge that likely came from both the sales of electric cars and the launch of the Tesla Roadster.[18]

Shanghai has benefited significantly from both market reform and foreign engagement on the one hand, and strong government support and industrial policy on the other. As noted by Chinese authorities, the number of central government–run, state-owned enterprises (SOEs), Shanghai municipal government–run SOEs, foreign-owned companies, and private firms has been relatively equal since 2010, which contrasts sharply with Shenzhen and Guangzhou in Guangdong, as well as Hangzhou and Ningbo in Zhejiang, where private sector investment is far more prevalent.[19] In Shenzhen, private firms account for 90 percent of the total number of enterprises.[20]

Xi Jinping's strong support of what Western scholars call state capitalism is particularly evident in Shanghai. The Chinese government's top ten strategically important areas in its "Made in China 2025" plan are prominently represented in this magic capital, with projects such as the C919 aircraft, modern shipbuilding, large-scale integrated circuits, artificial intelligence (AI), new energy vehicles, the Beidou Navigation Satellite System, robots, bioengineering, and life sciences.[21] In May 2014, during a visit to the R&D Center of the China Commercial Aircraft Design Institute in Shanghai, Xi Jinping stated, "The capability of R&D and manufacturing of large passenger aircraft is an important indicator of national aviation advancement. It is also an important symbol of the overall strength of a country."[22]

The seemingly paradoxical development strategy of present-day Shanghai—a unique combination of private entrepreneurship and foreign investment with the promotion of Chinese state capitalism and industrial policy—further highlights the great need to study the magic capital of the Middle Kingdom. This chapter consists of two parts. The first reviews the transformation of Shanghai's "magic landscape," especially its rapid rise over the past three decades. The second explores Shanghai's goal of establishing itself as "five centers" (*wuge zhongxin*) of the country and of the globe—namely in the areas of economics, trade, finance, shipping, and science and technology (S&T)—to expand the city's broader economic interaction with the outside world. By exploring these elements of this magic city, this chapter reveals the dual factors of government industrial policy and market reform that have contributed to China's economic miracle.

THE SHANGHAI MIRACLE: STRIVING TO BE CHINA'S MANHATTAN

For Shanghai's urban planners, nothing more effectively demonstrates the city's reemergence on the international stage than its appearance. The physical transformation of Shanghai since the mid-1990s has been "unparalleled in urban history," as noted by Alan Balfour, a distinguished American scholar in architecture and urban studies.[23] The rise of dazzling skyscrapers across Shanghai's skyline is the most visible testimony of China's quest for power and prosperity in the twenty-first century. Perhaps nowhere is this more salient than at the waterfront area in central Shanghai. Any visitor cannot help but be impressed by the imposing view of—and the distinct historical contrasts between—the two sides of the Huangpu River: the Bund on the western side (*Puxi*) and the newer Lujiazui area on the eastern side (*Pudong*).

The Bund (*Waitan*), which starts from Waibaidu Bridge (also known as Garden Bridge or Soochow Creek Bridge in its earlier days) and stretches southward to East Jinling Road, spans only 1.5 kilometers. The Bund had been part of the British Concession (and later the International Settlement run by both British and American colonists), and it consists of dozens of Western-style historical buildings, which housed foreign banks, trading companies, and clubs at the turn of the twentieth century, including the famous Hong Kong and Shanghai Banking Corporation building described in the prologue of this book.

On the eastern side, the 468-meter-high Oriental Pearl TV Tower became a symbol of Shanghai at the turn of the twenty-first century. The tower was designed by three Chinese architects, and at the time of its completion in 1994, it was the tallest tower in Asia and the third tallest in the world. More recently, three additional landmark skyscrapers—the 420-meter-high Jin Mao Tower (completed in 1999), the 492-meter-high Shanghai World Financial Center (2008), and the 632-meter-high Shanghai Tower (2015)—have become the new symbols of Shanghai's ever faster and higher ascendance. Altogether, these three new landmark buildings have not only successively expanded the boundaries of the city skyline but have also formed what some architects called "the world's first trio of adjacent super-tall skyscrapers" (nicknamed the three musketeers).[24]

The contrast between the graceful old mansions on the Bund and the futurist, modern high-rises in Lujiazui evoke a meaningful dialogue spanning two centuries. It is both a salute from Shanghai's modern age to its remarkable history and a greeting from the past to the present.[25] At the Fortune Global Forum held in Pudong in 1999, then president Jiang Zemin delivered a speech to several hundred global business leaders and government officials, remarking that "only six years ago, in this Lujiazui District of Shanghai's Pudong area where we are gathered this evening, there were only run-down houses and farms."[26] Jiang made similar remarks about Shanghai's development two years later at the Asia-Pacific Economic Cooperation summit meeting held in Shanghai in 2001, which was attended by twenty heads of state, including then U.S. president George W. Bush and Russian president Vladimir Putin.[27]

Jiang's description of the Shanghai miracle is largely accurate. In 2009 alone, 140 skyscraper office buildings along with over 500 foreign and Chinese banks, insurance companies, and other major financial institutions were established in the Lujiazui area.[28] As both Chinese and foreign scholars in urban development have observed, "It took Manhattan more than a century to achieve its dramatic form; new Shanghai has emerged in little more than a decade."[29] During his visit to Shanghai in 2004, then president of France Jacques Chirac called the development of Pudong "another project of epic proportion like the Great Wall and the Grand Canal."[30]

Construction Fever in Shanghai since the 1990s

In the early 1990s, over a million construction workers were mobilized to build the city's key projects.[31] According to one study, the number of commercial high-rise office buildings constructed in Shanghai in just three years (1992–1995) was equal to the number of commercial high-rise office buildings constructed in Hong Kong during its four decades of rapid urban construction.[32] In 1998, Shanghai had about 21,000 building construction sites.[33] It was frequently mentioned at the turn of the century that "one-fifth of the world's construction cranes are in intensive service" in Shanghai alone.[34] A reporter for the *Wall Street Journal* was not entirely exaggerating when he wrote that "what's going on in Shanghai, and up and down the China coast, might be the biggest construction project the planet has ever seen since the coral polyps built the Great Barrier Reef after the last Ice Age."[35]

Chinese policymakers have enthusiastically promoted the nickname "China's Manhattan" for Shanghai, which advances a new image and new aspirations for the city's urban development.[36] The resurgence of Shanghai since the early 1990s is truly remarkable in both its grandiose scale and its sheer speed. Table 5-1 shows the rapid increase in the number of high-rise buildings in Shanghai resulting from the breakneck pace of construction during the reform era, especially since 2000. While there were only three buildings in the city that exceeded twenty stories in 1980, the number of such buildings increased to 137 in 1990, 1,266 in 2000, 1,556 in 2003, 2,936 in 2010, and 5,906 in 2017.

A major outcome of the construction fever in Shanghai during the reform era has been the remarkable advancements in the city's transportation system. Prior to the late 1970s, there was no bridge crossing any point

TABLE 5-1. The Increase in the Number of Buildings over Eight Stories High in Shanghai, 1980–2017

Stories	1980	1990	2000	2002	2003	2010	2015	2017
8–10	78	207	536	742	874	2,744	5,568	6,588
11–15	33	244	684	1,217	1,616	9,672	18,302	20,094
16–19	7	145	831	1,101	1,251	4,247	10,046	11,962
20–29	3	137	1,266	1,518	1,556	2,936	5,337	5,906
30 and above	0	15	212	338	374	980	1,569	1,670
Total	121	748	3,529	4,916	5,671	20,579	40,822	46,220

Sources: Shanghaishi tongjiju, *Shanghai tongji nianjian 2004* [Shanghai statistical yearbook, 2004] (Beijing: Zhongguo tongji chubanshe, 2004), 170; and Shanghaishi tongjiju, *Shanghai tongji nianjian 2018* [Shanghai statistical yearbook, 2018] (Beijing: Zhongguo tongji chubanshe, 2018), table 11-7, http://tjj.sh.gov.cn/tjnj/nj18.htm ?d1=2018tjnj/C1107.htm.

of the 113-kilometer-long Huangpu River. People had to take ferries to cross the river. But by 2020, thirteen bridges connected the banks of the Huangpu River. Of these, twelve were built after 1991, and six are in central Shanghai. These include Nanpu Bridge (completed in 1991), Yangpu Bridge (1993), Xupu Bridge (1997), and Lupu Bridge (2003). In addition, there are fourteen tunnels linking the two sides of the river. Aside from these new bridges and tunnels, Shanghai has also significantly improved its public transit infrastructure. The German-built magnetic levitation train, the Shanghai Maglev (2004), which is capable of traveling at 267 miles per hour (or 430 km per hour), cost 4.8 billion RMB to build. The maglev train began operating in 2003, making the 19-mile trip from Pudong's Long Yang subway station to the Pudong airport in just eight minutes, as opposed to forty-five minutes by car. When it was completed, it claimed to be the fastest commercial high-speed electric train in the world. In 1993, Shanghai established its first metro line. By 2020, 387 metro stations dotted across the city, with 18 metro lines crisscrossing western and eastern Shanghai, totaling 672 kilometers in length.[37] These transportation and infrastructure developments have facilitated the rapid expansion of the Pudong new district.

Revival of the "Exhibition Hall of Architecture of All Nations"

Shanghai's drive to become "China's Manhattan" has profoundly changed the architectural landscape and cultural fabric of the city. In the 46,000-plus high-rise buildings found all over Shanghai, both the external facade and the internal layout of apartments are similar to those in New York, Paris, Sydney, Tokyo, Hong Kong, Taipei, and Singapore. Thus foreign visitors to Shanghai should not be surprised that the buildings and other urban projects in Shanghai seem familiar, as many buildings are, in fact, designed by well-known foreign architects.

Arguably, the most influential marriage of Western and Chinese cultures in Shanghai during its modern history is the architecture of homes, which range in style from Western high-rises to Shanghai *longtang*, as described in chapter 4. British, French, German, Russian, Northern European, American, and Japanese styles of architecture as well as classic, Renaissance, eclectic, modern, and other genres all found their way into the city during the first half of the twentieth century. In the 1920s, more than 300 real estate developers were involved with the management and development of both the pure Western-style buildings of Shanghai, as well as the *longtang*, refining their form until they best resembled the garden apartments of Europe and America.[38] This phenomenon explains why Shanghai was deemed the "architectural exhibition hall of all nations" (*wanguo bolanhui*) between the 1920s and 1940s.[39]

Ladislaus Hudec (1893–1998), an Austrian Hungarian architect, lived in Shanghai between 1918 and 1949. His architectural portfolio includes sixty residences, churches, schools, and hospitals, including the Park Hotel, Huadong Hospital, and Daguangming cinema. He was regarded as the "man who changed Shanghai" during the first half of the twentieth century.[40] Chinese architects also began to play an important role in Shanghai's urban development beginning in the late 1920s; most were returnees who had been educated abroad, primarily in the United States.[41] Based on a study of telephone books from that period, the number of Chinese architectural firms increased from one in 1927, to seven in 1928, to forty-five in 1936, which then accounted for 49 percent of all architectural firms in the country. By the end of the 1930s, 55 percent of architectural firms were Chinese owned, and 50 percent of architects working at foreigner-owned firms were Chinese.[42] In the 1940s China had about seventy foreign-educated architects, with about 70 percent of them working in Shanghai.[43]

Shanghai's overall urban development is also unique in a historical context. Shanghai's main function as a commercial center breaks the model of the Chinese traditional city, which is generally first and foremost a political center.[44] Since the construction fever of the 1990s, Shanghai has strived to become the "newest exhibition hall of international architecture" in the world. For example, the Gothic spire of the Shanghai Grand Hyatt Hotel, located atop the eighty-eight-story Jin Mao Tower, was designed by the American architectural firm Skidmore, Owings & Merrill—the same firm behind the famous Sears Tower in Chicago and the AOL Time Warner

Center in New York.[45] The construction of the Shanghai World Financial Center, which was stalled for four years in the wake of the Asian financial crisis, restarted in 2003. The firm responsible for this postmodern edifice was New York–based Kohn Pedersen Fox Associates. This 101-story building became China's tallest building with the highest roof tip in the world at the time. The Shanghai Tower, the tallest building in Shanghai at present, was designed by Jun Xia, a native Shanghainese who was educated in both China and the United States. The Shanghai Tower has been lauded for its focus on sustainability. Its asymmetrical, spiraling profile helps it withstand typhoon winds. The tower also utilizes wind turbines, collects rainwater, and features a double-glass skin for cooling and ventilation.[46] Due to its remarkable design, this landmark building received the annual American Architecture Prize for Architectural Design of the Year in 2016. As some scholars at Shanghai's Tongji University note, the Shanghai Tower is based on the concept of a "vertical city." With its irreplaceable iconic structure, it aims to highlight futurist Shanghai's global influence.[47]

Zheng Shiling, professor and former vice president of Shanghai's Tongji University, observed that no city has "held so many international architectural and urban design competitions" in such a short period as reform-era Shanghai.[48] Many internationally renowned architects and experts, such as the late I. M. Pei, Phillip Johnson, Paul Ludolf, Richard Meier, John Portman, and Michael Graves have visited Shanghai since the 1990s, either to give lectures or to participate in projects.[49] Between 1991 and 1996, international companies placed bids on approximately 40 percent of all of the design projects in the city.[50]

For Chinese leaders, the presence of both old and new foreign architecture in Shanghai exemplifies the city's cosmopolitanism, and it highlights the city's importance as a place where East and West meet. Therefore, leaders have often favored foreign architects for building projects in Shanghai, overlooking Chinese architects when awarding international bids for projects. Wu Jiang, a professor at Tongji University, observes that "one can hardly find a single Chinese architect who did not experience a hard time competing with foreign competitors."[51] Among the Chinese architects who have won international bids in Shanghai, many have been significantly influenced by Western art and architectural ideas. For example, Zhang Haiping, a well-known sculptor in Shanghai, has said he was inspired by Western artists, such as Alexander Calder, David Smith, Antonie Caro, Eduardo Chillida, and Albert Feraud.[52] Xu Jiang, former president of the China National Academy of Fine Arts and the nephew of Jiang Zemin, observed that Shanghai-led urbanization in the country since the mid-1990s has shown a distinct preference for "upward mobility" (*qugaoxing*) and a futurist outlook.[53] Table 5-2 shows the ten tallest skyscrapers in Shanghai, of which

TABLE 5-2. Shanghai's Ten Tallest Skyscrapers, 2020

No.	Building Name	Height (meters)	Floors	Completion	Use
1	Shanghai Tower	632	128	2015	Hotel/office
2	Shanghai World Financial Center	492	101	2008	Hotel/office
3	Jin Mao Tower	421	88	1999	Hotel/office
4	Xujiahui Center Tower 1	370	70	2016	Office
5	Shimao International Plaza	333	60	2006	Hotel/office/retail
6	Sinar Mas Center 1	320	65	2017	Office
7	Zhenru Center	305	57	2021	Office
8	Greenland Bund Center Tower 1	300	64	2022*	Hotel/office
9	Plaza 66	288	66	2001	Office
10	Henderson Xuhui Tower	285	61	2020	Office

Source: The Skyscraper Center, Global Tall Building Database of the Council on Tall Buildings and Urban Habitat, www.skyscrapercenter.com/city/shanghai.

*Anticipated.

nine were built after 2000 and six were completed within the last few years or remain under construction.

In recent years, Chinese architects have made concerted efforts to apply new technology in urban design and landscape development. In 2019, for example, the world's largest 3D printed concrete bridge was erected in Shanghai's Baoshan District.[54] Critics of Shanghai's construction fever, however, have raised concerns about the dislocation of downtown inhabitants, the growing disparity between rich and poor, the hazards of a narrow-minded drive toward modernization and globalization, and the possible destruction that may come from an endless effort to reach new heights and experiment with new technologies.[55] Despite these concerns around potential socioeconomic and technological problems, top leaders in Shanghai are still obsessed with high-speed property development and have continued to embrace ideas for cutting-edge urban projects, such as Asia's biggest shopping mall, Asia's longest commercial street, the world's first levitating train, and the world's tallest building.

For Chinese leaders, ranging from Jiang Zemin and Zhu Rongji to current leaders, such as Xi Jinping and Li Qiang, the prosperity and cosmopolitan appearance of Shanghai have economic and political implications that go far beyond the city's physical landscape. The drastic changes in Shanghai over the past two decades have brought about rising sociopolitical tensions and economic disparities. However, the rise of China's Manhattan has also enhanced the country's prestige on the world stage, boosting nationalistic sentiment among the public. Thus Shanghai's cultural dynamism and continuous integration with the outside world represent a fresh image for an ages-old Chinese civilization, and they may also herald a new era of development in China.

In November 2018, at the opening ceremony of the first China International Import Expo, President Xi Jinping explicitly promoted Shanghai in front of 172 heads of state and regional and international organizations. "The reason why Shanghai has developed so well is closely linked to its open character and advantages in economic openness," Xi told the crowd.[56] Even more significantly, beginning in 2013, for five consecutive years at the National People's Congress annual session Xi Jinping joined the Shanghai delegation discussion, in which he repeatedly used the terms "pioneer" (*paitoubing*) and "frontrunner" (*xianxingzhe*) to describe Shanghai's role in the country's economic reforms and innovation.[57]

A Born-Again City after a Half Century of Slow Growth

Prior to Deng Xiaoping's decision to make the economic development of Shanghai a strategic priority, the city's growth was relatively slow. During the first four decades of the People's Republic of China (PRC), the cen-

tral government placed heavy fiscal burdens on the city. In 1980, Shanghai ranked first in the nation in terms of industrial output (accounting
for one-eighth of the national total), exports (one-quarter), and revenue
sent to the central government (one-sixth).[58] But at the same time, Shanghai received the lowest average share in national funding allocations for
housing, roads, and transportation. The disparities between Shanghai's
contributions to China and the central government's support of Shanghai were widely publicized in the article, "Shanghai's Ten Tops and Five
Bottoms in the Country," which compared the city's leading role in China's development against its astonishingly poor infrastructure and living
conditions.[59]

According to one study conducted in the early 1980s, between 1949 and
1985, the central government received RMB 350 billion from Shanghai in
revenue but invested only RMB 3.5 billion in Shanghai for municipal infrastructure development.[60] From 1949 to 1988, Shanghai paid 83.5 percent of
its fiscal revenue to the central government, retaining only 16.5 percent for
services and the development of the city.[61] This drain in resources severely
hindered the development of Shanghai. Before 1949, Shanghai was the city
with the largest number of high-rises (thirty-eight buildings of ten stories or higher) in the country, including the twenty-four-story Park Hotel,
which was completed in the early 1930s and was the tallest building in Asia
at the time.[62] The Park Hotel remained the tallest building in Shanghai for
almost five decades, and the physical appearance of the city in the 1980s
differed little from that of the 1930s or the 1940s. In 1988, James Fallows,
a correspondent for *The Atlantic*, visited Shanghai and wrote an article entitled "Shanghai Surprise."[63] What struck him was not something new in
the city, but the fact that buildings and streets had remained unchanged for
over half a century.

Throughout most of the 1980s, central government policies favored
other cities, such as Beijing, Guangzhou, and the newly built Shenzhen. In
the late 1980s, however, the Shanghai municipal leadership gained funding from the international financial market to pursue major projects known
as the "94 special projects."[64] The government raised US$3.2 billion for 94
major construction projects, such as the Nanpu Bridge, Metro Line 1, the
International Terminal of Hongqiao Airport, and Huating Hotel.

The 1990 decision to develop Pudong as China's largest economic zone
was a major strategic shift in the country's resource allocation. During his
tour of Shanghai in early 1992, Deng Xiaoping recognized the great potential of the city and allowed the municipal government to invest more in
its local economy and to attract foreign investment. During the four years
between 1992 and 1996, the city completed more municipal construction
projects than it had over the previous four decades.[65] These new projects in-

cluded the Pudong Airport, the Shanghai metro system, the elevated high-way system, a renovated railway station, a new port for container shipping, and three bridges and two tunnels across the Huangpu River.

After consolidating his power in Beijing in 1995, Jiang Zemin was even more intent on turning Shanghai into the "head of the dragon." For ex-ample, Shanghai's total investment in fixed assets in 1998 was RMB 196.6 billion, which was much higher than that of the three other municipalities directly under central government authority—Beijing (RMB 112.4 billion), Tianjin (RMB 57.1 billion), and Chongqing (RMB 49.2 billion).[66] Addition-ally, Shanghai received a large number of grants and loans from the central government between 1990 and 2002, when Jiang served as general secre-tary of the CCP. As a result, Shanghai's investment in urban infrastructure increased from RMB 4.7 billion in 1990 to RMB 45.1 billion in 2000. The amount of revenue dedicated to construction projects increased from RMB 1.4 billion to RMB 13.2 billion over the same period.[67]

The influx of state grants and loans, in turn, stimulated foreign direct investment in the city. In 1993 alone, the city attracted more foreign in-vestment than it had during the previous ten years combined.[68] At the turn of the century, Shanghai authorities launched a campaign to attract 200 major multinational corporations (MNCs) to move their Asia-Pacific headquarters and research centers to Shanghai.[69] By early 2019, Shanghai hosted some 50,000 overseas companies, the highest number of foreign firms among all cities on the Chinese mainland. A total of 677 regional headquarters of MNCs were located in Shanghai, including 88 Asia-Pacific headquarters and 444 foreign investment R&D centers.[70] Among these were the headquarters of the newly founded New Development Bank—an orga-nization that was jointly run by the BRICS countries (Brazil, Russia, India, China, and South Africa), the regional headquarters of QVC Group (the world's largest TV shopping network), UBM Group (the world's largest ex-hibition and display service provider), NTT Corporation (the world's larg-est communications operator), and Fortune 500 companies such as Volvo, L Brands, and Yamaha. In January 2019, Microsoft's largest AI and IOT (In-ternet of Things) lab was established in Shanghai.[71]

Buoyed by the growing presence of MNC regional headquarters in the city, Shanghai has experienced the largest boom in real estate development that the world has ever seen. According to Han Zheng, then mayor of Shang-hai, the city maintained a GDP growth of over 10 percent between 1992 and 2003. In 2003, about 100 countries and regions provided funding to support approximately 30,000 projects in the city.[72] Additionally, by the year 2000, land leases to foreign firms in Shanghai brought in over RMB 100 billion for the municipal government, which was used primarily for infrastructure de-velopment in the city.[73] A large number of foreign-brand hotels have found their way into Shanghai as well. For example, in 2018 Shanghai had a total of seventy-two five-star hotels—the same number as Paris that year.

The influx of foreign capital and infrastructure projects to Shanghai came with improved living conditions for the city's residents. The per capita living area in Shanghai increased significantly during the reform era, from 4.52 square meters in 1983 to 6.6 square meters in 1991, to 13.1 square meters in 2002. The percentage of homeowners in Shanghai also increased from 31 percent in 1989 to 34 percent in 1991, to 87.4 percent in 2002.[74] Although growing economic disparity has become a serious sociopolitical problem in the city, especially between residents and migrants, a large number of Shanghai families are still able to purchase apartments and other kinds of housing in the outskirts of the city. According to a study conducted by Gallup Polls of China, the percentage of Shanghai's population that owned homes reached 82 percent in 2005, with 22 percent of respondents saying they own a second home.[75] Just two decades prior, the percentage of private ownership of housing in Shanghai was almost nonexistent. This change has significantly contributed to the birth and growth of the middle class in Shanghai, and it has facilitated a new, more comfortable middle-class lifestyle.

In recent years, Shanghai has focused more on environmental sustainability and protection. The per capita green area increased from 1 square meter in 1992 to 3.5 square meters in 1999. The green coverage rate doubled from 10 percent in 1992 to 20 percent in 1999, and then increased to 36 percent in 2018.[76] However, these green initiatives have caused some disruption. The construction of the Yanzhong Green Belt in the 1990s, for example, displaced 10,000 families. The municipal government spent much financial and political capital on this project, which was controversial at the time, though now it is perceived to be a welcome addition to the city.[77] Yet it should be noted that compared with other global cities, such as New York, London, Tokyo, Hong Kong, and Singapore, Shanghai does not score well on major indicators of a green environment (table 5-3). Shanghai has the lowest ecological land ratio, forest cover rate, and green cover rate among all these cities, and the second-lowest public green space per capita.

For many decades, the Suzhou Creek was heavily polluted, and its stench was often the most salient impression for any passersby.[78] During the 1970s and 1980s, the hotels along Suzhou Creek, including the famous Shanghai Mansion, had to seal their windows to avoid the smell. To resolve the issue, the Shanghai municipal government launched the three-phase Suzhou Creek Confluence Sewage Treatment Project in 1988. It took twenty-four years to complete. By 2012, the smell of the river had been eliminated, and following a twenty-seven-year absence of fish and shrimp, the river was reported to be the new home to forty-five kinds of fish.[79]

TABLE 5-3. Comparing Green Indicators between Shanghai and Major Global Cities, 2012

City	Ecological land ratio (%)	Forest cover rate (%)	Green cover rate (%)	Public green space per capita (m2)
New York	n.a.	24	n.a.	19.2
London	63	34.8	42	24.64
Tokyo	58	33	64.5	4.5
Hong Kong	71	70	70	23.5
Singapore	50	75	58.7	28
Shanghai	30	13	38	12

Source: Shanghaishi renmin zhengfu fazhan yanjiu zhongxin, *Jianshe zhuoyue de quanqiu chengshi: 2017/2018 nian Shanghai fazhan baogao* [Annual report on development of Shanghai (2017/2018)] (Shanghai: Gezhi chubanshe, 2018), 65.

n.a. (not available).

In November 2018, during his visit to Shanghai, Xi Jinping spent time learning about the garbage sorting and recycling system in a neighborhood community in Hongkou District. A year earlier, Xi had presided over the CCP Central Financial and Economic Leading Group meeting to discuss the general implementation of China's garbage classification system. Xi's investigation of the waste management system in Shanghai's Hongkou District seemed to have left a positive impression on the Chinese public. In 2019, Shanghai became a pilot city for the country's new initiative for garbage sorting and recycling.[80] This new initiative is extremely important for the city and the country, given the scale of environmental damage stemming from the rapid growth of middle-class consumption and e-commerce. According to a 2017 Chinese study, there were at least 400 million food deliveries per week in the country, resulting in the use and disposal of 400 million packaging boxes and 400 million plastic bags per week. It was reported that China dumped 8 million tons of plastic into the ocean every year, accounting for one-third of the world's plastic pollution.[81]

In addition to the environmental degradation that has coincided with the rise of the middle class, unequal economic developments have also aggravated tensions between the rich and poor. The need for land to construct Shanghai's new skyline, along with the corresponding escalation in real estate prices, has forced ordinary working-class inhabitants out of the city into distant areas. Based on data released by the municipal government, a total of 2 million Shanghai residents were relocated between 1992 and 1997 in order to pave the way for property development, including 1 million residents who were pushed out of downtown areas.[82] Meanwhile, a large number of wealthy people, including nouveau riche from other parts of the country as well as people from places such as Hong Kong, Taiwan, South Korea, Singapore, the United States, Australia, Germany, France, and Canada, have become the new residents of downtown Shanghai. The results of this drastic urban relocation can be understood through the following local saying: People in Lujiazui District (Shanghai's financial district) speak English; residents in downtown Shanghai speak Mandarin; and only those who live on the outskirts speak the Shanghai dialect.

Shanghai's Pioneering of "National Firsts" during the Reform Era

During the reform era, and especially since the start of the development and opening up of Pudong New District in 1990, both Shanghai in general and Pudong in particular have achieved dozens of "national firsts" in PRC history:

- In September 1985, the first securities trading counter in the PRC, the Jing'an Securities Sales Office, was established. John J. Phelan Jr., then chairman of the New York Stock Exchange, witnessed this historic development for a communist country. The Shanghai Flying Happiness Acoustic Company became the first stock-shared company in the nation. Five years later, in 1990, all sixteen securities trading counters in the city merged and formed the Shanghai Stock Exchange (SSE), located in Pudong.

- In 1986, Shanghai Auto formed a joint venture with Germany's Volkswagen, becoming the first joint automaker in China. In 2017, the Shanghai Automotive Industry Corporation (SAIC) was ranked no. 41 on the Fortune Global 500, with an annual production of 7 million cars and a 23 percent share of China's domestic market.

- In August 1988, the Shanghai municipal government approved a fifty-year land lease in the Hongqiao District to Japanese Sun's Enterprise for commercial use—the first land lease in the PRC.

- In 1990, the Waigaoqiao Free-Trade Zone (FTZ), the first bonded area for free trade in China, was approved. By 2008, this FTZ already had 10,242 projects from 94 countries approved, including 111 companies listed on the Fortune Global 500.

- In 1992, the first foreign insurance company in the PRC, American AIA Shanghai Company, was established in Shanghai.

- In 1995, the first foreign bank in the PRC, the Japan Fuji Bank Shanghai Branch, was founded in Shanghai.

- In 2002, China's first joint venture fund management company, China Merchants Fund Management Co., Ltd, jointly owned by the Dutch firm ING Asset Management B.V., was established in Pudong.

- In 2013, the Shanghai Free-Trade Zone (SFTZ)—officially called the China (Shanghai) Pilot Free-Trade Zone—was established in Pudong's Waigaoqiao FTZ. The following year, the Chinese government issued a management policy negative list for foreign firms in Pudong, the first such issuance in the country, and an important practice considered to be in line with international business norms. The negative list of foreign investment was reduced from 190 in 2014 to 122 in 2015, to 95 in 2017, to 45 in 2018, and to 37 in 2019.

- In 2015, the first wholly foreign owned specialist hospital, Shanghai Forever Gynecology Hospital, run by Japanese practitioners, was founded in the Shanghai Pilot Free-Trade Zone.

- In 2015, the first foreign-owned performance brokerage agency, the Japanese Wandai Nanmeng Palace (Shanghai) Interactive Entertainment Co., Ltd., was founded in Shanghai.

- In 2016, the first wholly foreign owned vocational training institution in the PRC, PricewaterhouseCoopers Business Skills Training (Shanghai) Co., Ltd., was registered in the Shanghai Pilot Free-Trade Zone.

- In 2018, the first wholly foreign owned travel agency in the PRC, Yixin Dalv (Shanghai) International Travel Service Co., Ltd., was registered in Shanghai.

- In 2018, the first foreign-owned credit investigation and rating agency, Moody's (China) Co., Ltd., was allowed to register in China.

- In April 2019, the first foreign-controlled stock broker, Nomura Holdings Co., Ltd., from Japan, which held 51 percent of shares, began operating in Shanghai.

- In May 2019, the first securities company controlled by foreign investors, JPMorgan Chase & Co., from the United States, which planned to invest RMB 800 million, began conducting business in Shanghai.

- In May 2019, Shanghai became the first city in China to approve full implementation of the newly issued Foreign Investment Law.

- In June 2019, foreign companies were allowed to list their shares and raise funds in mainland China for the first time through the Shanghai-London stock connection scheme.[83]

- In January 2020, Shanghai issued the first business license to an enterprise funded by a Chinese individual or a "natural person" (*ziranren*) together with foreign investors.[84]

All of these examples show the pivotal and pioneering role of Shanghai in the country's economic reform and opening up. Foreign reactions to these initiatives, however, have been mixed. As some foreign critics recently observed, "While Xi might have pledged to speed up reform of the world's second largest economy, his mindset is very different from that of Deng Xiaoping" in the early years of reform and opening up.[85] China's huge trade imbalance with the United States, along with its protectionism in the service and telecommunications sectors, have become serious concerns for the international business community.

Furthermore, a significant number of the commitments China made when entering the World Trade Organization in December 2001—and other promised reforms outlined in the third plenum of the 18th National Congress of the CCP in 2013, including the objectives of the SFTZ—have noticeably gone undelivered. With regard to China's World Trade Organization commitments, for example, the country has failed to open the telecommunications market, reduce export subsidies, join the Government Procurement Agreement, abolish technology transfer as a requirement for market access, liberalize foreign film distribution, grant foreign banks national treatment, and more.[86]

Foreign companies have been generally disappointed with China's inability to deliver on its promised objective of financial opening, which was announced when the SFTZ was established in 2013. As a *Financial Times* reporter accurately observed, "Financial reform advocates touted the zone as a laboratory to test deregulation of China's interest rates, currency and cross-border fund flows. But with authorities now grappling with capital outflows and a depreciating currency, they appear reluctant to push ahead with measures that would enable even greater outflows."[87] In opposition to promised reforms, Xi has prioritized the role of state-owned firms to deliver on his long-term goals for China in sectors such as high-tech manufacturing.[88] In fact, the Chinese leadership has a long-standing interest in adopting industrial policies for international competition. This is particularly evident in the Chinese government's well-publicized initiatives to designate Shanghai as an international center in five crucial areas.

MAKING SHANGHAI THE LOCUS OF "FIVE INTERNATIONAL CENTERS"

At the 14th Party Congress in 1992, the Jiang leadership decided to designate Shanghai as "the three centers" (*yige longtou, sange zhongxin*) of China's development, referring to economic, trade, and financial centers. In 2001, the State Council under the leadership of Premier Zhu Rongji added "shipping center" as a target for Shanghai's future development. In 2017, based on comments by Xi Jinping, the Chinese leadership further expanded Shanghai's role in national development as the location for "five centers," adding "international S&T innovation center" to the list. Shanghai's designation as the locus for these centers means that the central government grants favorable policies, tax incentives, and more resources to Shanghai, giving the city more leverage in international competition.

International Economic Center

Shanghai has long acted as the economic center of the country, in part because of its tradition of foreign engagement and its geographic advantages. Before the Communist Revolution, nearly 50 percent of total foreign investment in the country was concentrated in Shanghai.[89] Since the turn of the century, Shanghai has undergone the fastest economic growth in its history. Shanghai's GDP started at RMB 3.67 billion in 1949, increased to RMB 30 billion in 1978, and then surged to RMB 3.27 trillion in 2018. The per capita GDP of registered residents in Shanghai exceeded US$20,000 in 2018, reaching the level of upper- and middle-income countries.[90] That same year, Shanghai's general public budget revenue reached RMB 1.76 trillion, of which local income made up RMB 710.81 billion. Shanghai's financial contributions made up nearly one-tenth of the country's total fiscal revenue.

Before economic liberalization in 1978, the per capita disposable income of urban residents in Shanghai was only about 3 percent of that of the United States and Japan. In 2010, the per capita disposable income of urban residents in Shanghai exceeded RMB 30,000. In 2017, the per capita disposable income of urban and rural residents in Shanghai had grown to RMB 62,596 and RMB 27,825, respectively, or 154 times and 96 times the 1978 amounts. In that time frame, the per capita disposable income of Shanghai's urban residents increased 13.8 percent annually, and the per capita disposable income of rural residents increased 12.4 percent annually. After adjusting for price factors and incomparable factors, they actually increased by 20 times and 12 times, respectively, with an average annual growth rate of 7.9 percent and 6.6 percent. Figure 5-1 shows the dramatic increase in GDP per capita and household disposable income of urban residents in

FIGURE 5-1. The rapid increase in GDP per capita and household disposable income of urban residents in Shanghai, 1978–2017 (RMB)

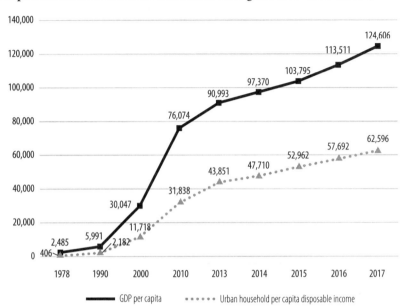

Source: Lu Hanlong, Yang Xiong, and Zhou Haiwang, eds., *Shanghai shehui fazhan baogao (2019)* [Annual report on social development of Shanghai, 2019] (Beijing: Shehui kexue wenxian chubanshe, 2019), 364.

Shanghai over the four decades from 1978 to 2017. Notably, Shanghai has slowly started to catch up with countries it used to lag behind, as the per capita disposable income of Shanghai residents now reaches about a quarter of that of the United States and about one-third of Japan's.[91]

At the end of 2017, retail sales in Shanghai reached an astounding RMB 1.18 trillion, and Shanghai surpassed Beijing as the largest consumer city in China, with a per capita annual consumption expenditure of RMB 39,800. Consumption has been the main driver of economic growth in Shanghai.[92] In conjunction with rising consumption, the average life expectancy of Shanghai residents has also increased. In 2018, the average life expectancy of residents was 83.63 years (81.25 for males, and 86.08 for females), 10 years higher than in 1978 and comparable to life expectancies in developed countries. The quality of medical and health care in Shanghai—along with the quality of life and health of residents—has improved substantially.

The economic reforms in Shanghai over the same four decades have also greatly changed the city's economic structure—shifting the distribution of various sectors and the composition of ownership types. Giving priority to the development of the tertiary or service sector is the key to Shanghai's becoming an international economic center. To this end, in the early 1990s, Chinese authorities established a strategy wherein "finance serves as the mainstay, trade as a pilot, and transportation and communication as a base for Shanghai's economic restructuring."[93]

The proportion of the tertiary sector—including information services, business services, scientific research, cultural and creative industries—in Shanghai's GDP was 18 percent in 1978, increased to 30 percent in the early 1990s, and is 70 percent today.[94] Table 5-4 shows that the labor force working in the agriculture sector dropped by half from 1991 to 2017, whereas the labor force in the service sector increased fourfold during the same period. In terms of the distribution of employees by ownership type shown in table 5-4, those who worked in the private sector increased from only 0.1 percent of the city's total workforce in 1991 to 34.4 percent in 2013, and those who worked for foreign firms increased from 0.1 percent in 1991 to 12.8 percent in 2013. During that same period, the percentage of the workforce employed by SOEs dropped from 79.8 percent to 34.7 percent.

The more than 50,000 foreign-funded enterprises located in the city have become an important force supporting Shanghai's economic development. They account for only 1 percent of the city's employment and 2 percent of enterprises, but in 2018 they made up 27 percent of GDP, one-third of tax revenue, two-thirds of foreign trade imports and exports, and two-thirds of the industrial output value of the whole city.[95]

TABLE 5-4. The Change in Number of Employees in Shanghai by Sector, 1991–2017 (thousands)

Sector	1991	1996	2001	2010	2017
Agriculture	825.3	794.0	871.8	370.9	424.4
Industry	4,648.5	4,119.8	3,099.1	4,437.4	4,305.1
Service	2,269.5	3,015.5	3,551.7	6,099.3	8,997.7

Sources: Yin Jizuo, *2003 nian Shanghai shehui baogaoshu* [Report on the society in Shanghai in 2003] (Shanghai: Shanghai shehui kexueyuan chubanshe, 2003), 3; Shanghai tongjiju, *2018 nian Shanghai tongji ninanjian* [2018 Shanghai Statistical Yearbook] (Beijing: Zhongguo tongti chubanshe, 2019), table 3-1, http://tjj.sh.gov.cn/tjnj/nj18.htm?d1=2018tjnj/C0301.htm.

TABLE 5-5. The Change in Number of Employees in Shanghai by Ownership, 1991–2013

Ownership	1991 Number	1991 Percentage	1996 Number	1996 Percentage	2001 Number	2001 Percentage	2013 Number	2013 Percentage
State-owned enterprises	4,035,000	79.8	3,125,300	71.6	2,142,400	41.2	1,625,300	34.7
Collective firms	1,013,800	20.0	769,000	17.6	405,600	7.8	405,600	8.7
Private firms	3,310	0.1	471,000	10.8	1,611,300	31.0	1,611,300	34.4
Share-holding companies	n.a.	n.a.	n.a.	n.a.	441,500	8.5	441,500	9.4
Foreign investment firms (including Taiwan, Hong Kong, and Macao)	4,800	0.1	n.a.	n.a.	602,000	11.6	602,000	12.8
Total	5,056,910	100.0	4,365,300	100.0	5,202,800	100.0	4,685,700	100.0

Sources: Yin Jizuo, *2003 nian Shanghai shehui baogaoshu* [Report on the society in Shanghai in 2003] [Shanghai: Shanghai shehui kexueyuan chubanshe, 2003), 3; Shanghai tongjiju, *2014 nian Shanghai tongji nianjian* [2014 Shanghai Statistical Yearbook] [Beijing: Zhongguo tongji chubanshe, 2015), table 3-2, http://tjj.sh.gov.cn/tjnj/nj14.htm?d1=2014tjnj/C0302.htm.

Note: n.a. (not available).

International Trade Center

For at least half a century, Shanghai has been considered the country's commercial hub. The Shanghai First Department Store, Hualian Business Mansion, Fashion Mall, and Shanghai First Food Store were among the most famous stores in the country in the early decades of the PRC. Before 1978, they were the only four stores in the city to cover more than 10,000 square meters of commercial area. In 2018, by comparison, there were 255 shopping centers in Shanghai that well surpassed a commercial area of 10,000 square meters.[96] Thirty-nine of these shopping centers are larger than 100,000 square meters each, and five of them are larger than 200,000 square meters. The largest one in Shanghai, Guomao Shopping Center in Xujiahui, has a business area of 320,000 square meters. In 2018, Shanghai's total retail sales of consumer goods exceeded RMB 1.2 trillion, more than any other city in the country.[97] In 2019, on average, Shanghai had a convenience store for every 3,278 residents, while Beijing had one for every 9,620 residents.[98]

Over the past decade, Shanghai has made significant efforts to promote its position as an international trade center. In 2017, the total import and export value of Shanghai Customs Supervision reached US$881.47 billion, a nearly 290-fold increase in the forty years since 1978.[99] According to Chinese official state media, by 2015, "the import and export of goods at the Shanghai port accounted for 27.6 percent of the country's total and 3.4 percent of the world's total, with the latter figure putting Shanghai above other international trade centers such as Hong Kong and Singapore."[100] Shanghai's service import and export volume approached US$200 billion in 2015, accounting for 28 percent of the country's total and 2 percent of the world's trade transactions. In 2017, Pudong's imports alone accounted for 60 percent of the imports to Shanghai and 10 percent of those to the country.[101]

Shanghai has also become the first stop for launching new products in the Chinese market for both international high-end brands and China's established domestic brands. Based on official statistics, in 2017 there were 1,265 brands holding national "debuts" in Shanghai, making the city number one in the country for these debuts.[102] Also, 226 flagship stores or "first stores" (*shoufa dian*) of chain establishments were set up in Shanghai, accounting for nearly 50 percent of the country's grand openings. In the same year, about 90 percent of the world's high-end name brands were carried in Shanghai's department stores or specialty shops. By 2018, Shanghai had hosted more than 90,000 foreign trade and investment projects.

The Shanghai Pilot Free-Trade Zone, which was established in 2013, promises to actively help foreign companies launch their first investment project in the city. The FTZ also aims to accelerate the construction of a global asset management center, continue the accumulation of foreign capital management institutions in the Lujiazui financial area, and promote the expansion of offshore trade and service trade. In pursuit of these goals, Shanghai hosted the first three China International Import Expositions from 2018 to 2020.

International Financial Center

As early as 1992, Deng Xiaoping made an important statement about Shanghai's role in the country's financial development: "China's international status in finance, first and foremost, depends on Shanghai."[103] By design, the financial sector in Shanghai has had a pivotal role in the city's journey toward national and international prominence since the early 1990s. The 2009 global financial crisis had an enormously detrimental impact on China's economy, and it not only fed into the narrative that the Western model is problematic, but it also gave greater impetus to Shanghai's mission of enhancing its capacity to deal with risks and challenges in the financial arena.

The decision to build Shanghai into an international financial center came from the Chinese government's desire to put the city on par with global financial centers like London, New York, Hong Kong, and Tokyo. Sun Lijian, associate dean of the Institute of Economics at Fudan University, has argued that Shanghai should strive to promote several areas of international finance—among them shipping finance, marine insurance, international settlements, fund management, foreign exchange transactions, and intermediary services. The development of these service-oriented businesses would help complete the transition of the city's industrial sector to more high-value-added industries.[104] Over the decade beginning in 2010, the city has become a major player in areas such as commodity futures, bond trading business, and finance leases. In 2019, Chinese authorities made the decision to establish six research centers (Global Asset Management Center; Cross-Border Investment and Financing Service Center; Financial Technology Center; International Insurance Center; Global RMB Asset Pricing, Payment and Clearing Center; and Financial Risk Management and Stress Testing Center) in Shanghai to support China's financial endeavors, especially the country's global financial outreach.[105]

Shanghai is well positioned to play a leadership role in China's forays into international finance. The financial sector's share in Shanghai's GDP increased from 10 percent in 2008 to 17 percent in 2017.[106] That year, the SSE was ranked fourth in the world for stock-trading volume, third in the world for total fundraising, and fourth in the world for total global market capitalization. The Shanghai Gold Exchange's gold spot trading volume has remained number one in the world for many years.[107] Shanghai is presently the world's second-largest diamond spot trading center. By the end of 2018, the total market capitalization of the SSE exceeded RMB 27 trillion. As of 2019, there are 1,450 listed companies with a total of 12,089 bonds and 296 million open accounts on the Shanghai securities market.[108]

Shanghai hosts licensed financial institutions trading in stocks, bonds, futures, currencies, notes, foreign exchange, gold, insurance, and trusts, with foreign financial institutions in the city accounting for more than 30 percent of the country's total foreign financial institutions. In 2016, Shanghai's financial industry employed more than 360,000 people representing about 1,500 licensed financial institutions. The total amount of assets under custody of the insurance asset management companies was around RMB 6 trillion, accounting for half of the national share. The securities asset management business in Shanghai had a total value of RMB 16.6 trillion, accounting for one-third of the national share.

In the area of insurance, in 2017 there were seven insurance asset management companies in Shanghai, or about one-third of the country's insurance institutions. The city had fifty-five corporate insurance agencies, which accounted for 25 percent of the country's total. In addition, there were twenty-eight foreign-invested insurance companies located in Shanghai, the most of any city in the country. These Shanghai-based insurance companies currently manage about half of the country's insurance assets. Shanghai has become one of the most concentrated centers of financial institutions in the world.

Shanghai's importance in the financial sector reflects China's growing competitiveness in the international arena. In July 2020, for example, four of the top ten banks in the world in terms of total assets were Chinese banks. These four Chinese banks occupied the top four spots on the list, with the Industrial and Commercial Bank of China ranked first (table 5-6). Two decades ago, American and European banks dominated the top ten list, and no PRC-based bank was even close to being on it. While many banks in developed countries sustained significant damage in the wake of the financial crisis, with several falling more than 20 percent in market capitalization, Chinese banks have remained relatively stable.

Based on other important criteria, however, Shanghai's financial sector still has a long way to go before it is truly comparable with the world's other financial hubs. By the end of 2018, there were 2,285 listed companies on the New York Stock Exchange (NYSE), of which 510 were foreign companies, accounting for 22.3 percent of all listings.[109] The NYSE's stock-trading volume was $19.34 trillion, ranking first among global exchanges and almost three times the amount of the SSE during the same period. Additionally, the SSE had a total market capitalization of $3.92 trillion at the end of 2018, accounting for only 4.36 percent of total market capitaliza-

TABLE 5-6. The Top Ten Banks in the World by Total Assets, 2020

Rank	Bank	Country	Total assets (US$ billion)
1	Industrial and Commercial Bank of China (ICBC)	China	4,322
2	China Construction Bank	China	3,822
3	Agricultural Bank of China	China	3,698
4	Bank of China	China	3,387
5	JPMorgan Chase	USA	3,139
6	HSBC Holdings	UK	2,918
7	Mitsubishi UFJ Financial Group	Japan	2,893
8	Bank of America	USA	2,620
9	BNP Paribas	France	2,430
10	Crédit Agricole	France	1,984

Source: "Top 20 Largest World Banks in 2020 by Total Assets," *Forbes,* July 20, 2020, https://fxssi.com/top-20-largest-world-banks-in-current-year.

tion globally. Furthermore, the average daily turnover of OTC (over-the-counter) derivatives in New York and London accounted for 80 percent of the world's 2.759 trillion transactions.

The foreign exchange transaction volume in the Chinese mainland market accounts for only 1.12 percent of the global total, lower than Japan's 6.13 percent. Although nearly 30 percent of financial institutions with a presence in China are concentrated in Shanghai, market participation is low, and it only exceeded 10 percent for the first time in 2017. In international shipping finance, Shanghai's role has remained quite marginal. Despite the lack of progress in these areas, many Chinese officials and their advisers maintain that China's strategic emphasis on Shanghai as an international financial center signifies the new phase of a finance-driven approach to China's industrial restructuring (*chanye tiaozheng*).

The prolonged protests in Hong Kong have accelerated Beijing's efforts to promote Shanghai in the global financial landscape. The tumult of the protests has dealt a blow to Hong Kong's long-standing role as a gateway for international financial exchanges into China, causing investors to seek out a different entryway. The ultimate goal, as one scholar in Shanghai notes, "is to challenge American financial hegemony."[110] From the Chinese perspective, at present and in the near future, nothing is more crucial than ensuring financial security, including the security of China's large foreign reserves. To this end, the Shanghai municipal government recently launched "100 initiatives" to enhance the openness and transparency of the Shanghai International Finance Center.[111] Thus Shanghai will likely play a crucial role in achieving national objectives of financial security in the years to come.

International Shipping Center

Shanghai is the biggest container port in the world today. It has held this title for ten consecutive years since surpassing Singapore in 2010.[112] As the world's leading container port, Shanghai is connected with 200 countries (and over 500 ports) via sea transportation, and one-fifth of the city's trade is related to the Belt and Road Initiative (BRI).[113] In 2017, the Port of Shanghai berthed 512 cruise ships, and the passenger throughput of cruise ships was 3 million people. It has become the fourth-largest cruise ship home port in the world. Shanghai's advancements in international maritime transit in terms of both cargo and passengers, especially with the establishment of the Yangshan Deepwater Port, is truly remarkable if one considers the historical context of shipping facility development in Shanghai.

In 1996, for example, the Port of Shanghai had an annual throughput of 1.5 million TEU (a TEU—20-foot equivalent unit—represents the capacity of a standard 20-foot shipping container). Thirteen years later, in 2009, the figure had jumped to 28 million TEU, an eighteenfold increase.[114] That year, Shanghai had a number of large container terminals—the Jungonglu, Zhanghuabang, and Baoshan terminals—which accounted for 35 percent of the Port of Shanghai's total throughput. At the end of 2008, Shanghai began to build a large international terminal in Wusongkou designed to accommodate several 80,000-ton cruise ships. With the addition of the Yangshan Deepwater Port, the Port of Shanghai is now able to handle 42 million TEU annually (Table 5-7), placing its throughput well ahead of that of its international competitors.[115]

Before the establishment of the Yangshan Deepwater Port, the South Korean government conducted a study of its potential impact. They found that the Yangshan Deepwater Port would have a throughput three times greater than that of Busan, one of the top ten container ports in the world and the largest in South Korea.[116] Because of its scale and proximity to the vast hinterland of China, the logistical costs associated with operating the Yangshan Deepwater Port would be 40 percent lower than the operating costs for many other major ports, such as the Port of Busan. Consequently, the report asserted that the cargo-handling volume of Busan could be ex-

TABLE 5-7. The World's Top Ten Busiest Container Ports, 2018

Rank	Million TEU*	Port City
1	42.0	Shanghai, China
2	36.6	Singapore
3	26.4	Ningbo, China
4	25.7	Shenzhen, China
5	21.9	Guangzhou, China
6	21.6	Busan, South Korea
7	19.6	Hong Kong, China
8	19.3	Qingdao, China
9	16.0	Tianjin, China
10	15.0	Jebel Ali, Dubai, United Arab Emirates

Sources: Hong Kong Marine Department; also Daniel Ren, "China Has Six of the World's 10 Busiest Container Ports, Spurred by Booming Trade and a State Coffer That Invests in Public Works," *South China Morning Post*, April 13, 2019, www.scmp .com/business/companies/article/3005945/china-has-six-worlds-10-busiest-con tainer-ports-spurred-booming.

pected to drop by 30 percent. The other major container ports in the Asia Pacific region, including Singapore and Hong Kong, would also be significantly affected by the growing shipping capacity of Shanghai. The study concluded that the construction of the Yangshan Deepwater Port would cause an "earthshaking change" (*diqiao bianhua*) in the international shipping industry. The predictions of this study, of course, later proved to be right.

Located on a small island 27.5 kilometers (17 miles) from the mainland, the Yangshan port is connected to Pudong by the East Sea Grand Bridge (*Donghai daqiao*). Construction on the Yangshan Deepwater Port began in 2002, requiring four distinct phases, and it was completed in 2017. The first phase of construction involved the building of a manmade island, the first part of the container terminal, and the East Sea Grand Bridge, all of which took more than three years to complete. The second and third phases of the project, as well as the liquefied natural gas terminal and refined oil terminal, were completed and began operation in 2006 and 2008, respectively. In 2008, Shanghai was already the world's largest cargo port and the second-largest container port.[117] With the addition of this gigantic deepwater port, the city gained a huge lead in the ongoing competition for global preeminence.[118] The third phase of the project, completed in 2008, resulted in a 5.6-kilometer coastline, sixteen container-specific berths, and sixty large red container bridges lined up along the manmade island port. A fourth phase involved constructing a fully automated terminal, which was completed and operational in December 2017. At that point, the 13-kilometer-long dock was fully complete. With that final addition, the fully automated terminal equipment expanded to include 26 bridge cranes, 120 track cranes, and 130 automatically guided vehicles. This automated terminal was expected to have an annual handling capacity of 6.3 million TEU by 2020.

When it comes to shipping and transportation, Shanghai in general, and the Yangshan Deepwater Port in particular, benefit greatly from strong economic support and state-of-the-art facilities. There are four ways by which containers can be transported to China's vast inland areas from the Yangshan Deepwater Port: railway, highway, river, and sea. Approximately 85 percent of Shanghai's export containers come from other cities in the Yangtze River delta, and most of them are transported via highway. In fact, this emphasis on highway transportation has led to significant traffic jams, with about 5,000 container trucks passing over the East Sea Grand Bridge daily.

To reduce the burden on the highways in the area, the central government adopted "the Yangtze Strategy" (*changjiang zhanlue*), aiming to increase the number of container ships that the Yangtze River cities can accommodate.[119] According to this plan, Nanjing, Wuhan, and Chongqing are to expand existing facilities to harbor 1,000, 500, and 200 container ships, respectively. Other cities in the Yangtze River delta can then transport their containers first to the Waigaoqiao port in Pudong and then have them transferred to the Yangshan Deepwater Port via waterbus.[120] As part of the Yangtze Strategy, several cities on the river, including Jiujiang and Chongqing, have built new container ports.[121] Altogether, between 2012 and 2018, China's government spent a total of RMB 1 trillion to expand the country's port facilities.[122]

Table 5-7 shows the clear dominance of Chinese ports in the global shipping industry. Of the world's top ten busiest container ports in 2018, seven are located in China. Although North America and Europe are home to international shipping hubs, such as New York, Los Angeles, Rotterdam, and Hamburg, none of their ports are on the list. Notably, just two decades ago, no PRC city made it to the top twenty list for busiest container ports. Clearly, the geographic landscape of international shipping has changed dramatically as a result of China's economic rise. Shanghai is leading the way on this front.

International S&T and Innovation Center

Compared with Beijing, where a large number of China's top universities and research institutions are located, Shanghai is lacking in R&D capacity and institutional support. Compared with Shenzhen and Hangzhou, where many private S&T firms have been actively engaged in technology and e-commerce innovation, Shanghai's private entrepreneurs have also noticeably lagged behind in the area of innovation. Nevertheless, the "magic capital" has its own comparative advantages in other aspects, and, throughout the reform era, Shanghai has always been regarded as an important player in the country's knowledge industry and S&T development.

According to Chinese official sources, in 2018 Shanghai's R&D expenditures were equivalent to 4 percent of the city's total GDP.[123] At present, Shanghai has received and accounts for one-third of the country's top scientific research achievement awards, national science and technology awards, and new drug research and development projects. When the Pudong New District was established in the early 1990s, one of its subdistricts, Zhangjiang, was designated as the area that would concentrate on S&T research and business innovation. In 2011, the State Council also approved the establishment of the Zhangjiang National Indigenous Innovation Demonstration Zone (ZNIIDZ). A number of major technology infrastructure and research projects have been carried out there, including the construction of photonic science facilities focused on hard X-rays, super-ultra-short lasers, and second-phase light sources. ZNIIDZ claims to be the largest, most diverse, and most powerful photonic science facility in the world.

The 2017 decision by central authorities to make Shanghai an international S&T and innovation center has accelerated Shanghai's drive to be a leader on this front. Zhangjiang Science City, with a total area of about 95 square kilometers, is the core functional area of the newly established Shanghai Science and Technology Innovation Center. This center is the locus of Shanghai's construction of a globally influential S&T innovation hub. Biomedicine is a key area of research in the center. Six major new drug innovations have been attributed to the center, more than sixty clinical phase 2 and phase 3 trials have been conducted for these medicines, and "nearly 30 of them are leading a new class of drugs."[124]

To advance Shanghai's new role as the country's international S&T innovation center, the municipal government has organized a number of large-scale brainstorming research task forces. A 400-page strategic report released in 2015 lists five major fields and fourteen subjects under the Shanghai government's strategic plan for S&T catch-up and innovation between 2015 and 2025.[125] The five major fields include (1) internet and new-generation information technology, (2) life sciences and public health, (3) new energy and self-driving vehicles, (4) aerospace, and (5) AI manufacturing.

The Shanghai leadership's strategic plan has greatly emphasized AI and big data. In 2013, Shanghai announced to the public a three-year action plan for promoting big data R&D in Shanghai between 2013 and 2015. The city's leadership focused on six major industry big data public platforms—health care, food safety, lifelong education, smart transportation, public safety, and technology services—and six categories of big data industry application R&D—financial security, internet, digital life, public facilities, manufacturing, and the power sector.[126] In the area of health care, Shanghai already has the world's largest medical data sharing system. The city plans to build and improve an electronic medical record archive covering 35 million patients, which can support about 2,000 doctors simultaneously treating patients online.[127]

The strategic plan for S&T development and other related reports released by the Shanghai municipal government often lay out specific objectives for certain time periods. For example, short-term plans go until 2025, mid-term plans go to 2035, and long-term plans go to 2050. The 2015 strategic report claims that Shanghai will cultivate fifty big data publicly listed companies over ten years, and the output value of the data service industry will reach RMB 100 billion within the same time frame.[128] Also according to the plan, in 2050 Shanghai will have at least 50 Fortune 500 corporate headquarters, 3,000 regional headquarters of MNCs, and 20 global top 100 innovative enterprises. The added value of high-tech industries should account for 60 percent of the total industrial output value.[129] As for driverless vehicles, the Shanghai Automotive Industry Corporation launched a driverless car for highway use in 2020, and large-scale distribution is to scheduled take place in 2030.[130]

Throughout the reform era, Shanghai's leadership has made concerted efforts to attract S&T personnel to the city, especially top scientists and technical experts. According to one Chinese source, in terms of its number of global and regional headquarters of R&D companies, Shanghai is second only to Silicon Valley and Tokyo. Based on estimates from academic researchers, Shanghai's high-tech workforce totals more than 50,000 people.[131] By 2017, Shanghai had recruited a total of 62,000 high-level professionals, including nearly 7,500 people who have been deemed by the Chinese government as "science and technology innovation and entrepreneurship talents." At present, there are more than 75,000 people designated as science and technology innovation and entrepreneurship talents in Shanghai. Additionally, the number of Shanghai invention patents increased from 4,689 in 2004 to 56,515 in 2014—more than tenfold in a decade.[132] In 2017, Shanghai had thirteen academicians newly elected to the Chinese Academy of

Sciences and the Chinese Academy of Engineering, accounting for 10 percent of all new members. The total number of Shanghai-based academicians in the two prestigious organizations was 182.

There are currently 215,000 foreigners working in Shanghai, accounting for 23.7 percent of all foreigners in China and placing Shanghai first among China's thirty-one province-level entities. Since the implementation of the work permit system for foreigners coming to China in April 2017, Shanghai has issued more than 120,000 "Work Permits for Foreigners," including more than 20,000 for foreign high-level talents. According to the Shanghai municipal government, both the number and the quality of foreign talents in Shanghai are the highest in the country. Since the implementation of the "foreign talent visa system" in 2018, Shanghai has approved the "Recognition Letter of Foreign High-end Talents" for nearly 500 foreigners, ranking Shanghai as the number one destination for such individuals in the country.[133]

In November 2018, at the first China International Import Expo held in Shanghai, Xi Jinping announced that China would establish a "Sci-Tech Innovation Board" (*kechuang ban*, SSE STAR Market) and a pilot registration system on the SSE. This new category of stocks caters to science and technology innovation enterprises that align with the national strategy, have the potential to produce breakthroughs in key core technologies, and have strong market recognition. Specifically, it aims to support new-generation information technology, high-end technology equipment, new materials, new energy, energy conservation and environmental protection, biomedical advancement, and other high-tech industries.[134] In July 2019, eight months after Xi's announcement, a total of 122 Chinese IT companies had applied for listing on the science and technology stock board, and 25 companies had passed the inquiry process and been approved.[135]

In response to recent tensions between the United States and China regarding Huawei, as well as Washington's discussion of technological decoupling with China, the Chinese leadership is planning to accelerate its indigenous technological innovation. Shanghai once again seems to be the likely center of this new drive. Shanghai is also geographically and economically well positioned in Xi Jinping's BRI. In the words of Shanghai officials, Shanghai is the bridgehead (*qiaotoubao*) of the BRI.[136] Due to its leadership role in the country's trade, commerce, finance, transportation, aerospace, and biotechnology sectors, Shanghai is critical to connectivity both within China and between China and other countries. For example, as some Chinese scholars assert, the use of the RMB as monetary settlement in BRI deals will largely be conducted through the "financial market" in Shanghai.[137]

FINAL THOUGHTS

The phenomenal change in Shanghai's skyline, along with the city's equally astonishing development in the reform era—especially with the rise of China's Manhattan in Pudong—are indisputably miraculous. A key question regarding the rapid resurgence of Shanghai as a global city, however, centers on the causes of this extraordinary development. Should it be seen as the result of market reform and opening up, along with factors such as Shanghai's distinct Western influence and entrepreneurial subculture? Or should it be attributed to the strong role of the state and Chinese industrial policy?

The answer is not an either/or dichotomy, and it could be reasonably argued that both forces are crucial contributing factors. Shanghai's pioneering experiments and full application of major economic initiatives—most notably its stock market, land leases for commercial use, acceptance of foreign joint ventures and solely foreign owned businesses, opening of banking and insurance business to private and foreign financial institutions, negative lists for foreign investment and trade, and private firm dominance of e-commerce—all reflect genuine moves toward market reforms and "opening up." They are a remarkable departure from orthodox communist or socialist economic practices.

Yet, at the same time, China's market transition and opening up in the reform era—even in this frontier city for the country's global economic integration—has retained much of what CCP leaders call "socialism with Chinese characteristics," or what critics describe as "state capitalism." To a great extent, Chinese state capitalism has not only restricted market access for foreign and domestic private firms, but it has also given state support to SOEs and other flagship companies through unfair economic practices, with the goal of dominating certain strategic important sectors. China's nepotistic industrial policy has helped elevate Shanghai to a prominent role in many of these sectors, especially in aerospace, biotechnology, AI, information technology, sustainable energy, and new energy vehicles. The Chinese central government's grand strategy of making Shanghai the locus of "five international centers" suggests that this broad-scale endeavor will likely continue for years to come. These dynamics further underline the importance of studying Shanghai, and the causes and consequences of Chinese leaders' aspirations to build it into a global city.

Shanghai's unique status may come at the expense of some of its rival cities, both in China and abroad. For over a decade, Beijing and Tianjin have competed vigorously with Shanghai to claim dominance as China's financial center. China's other major seaports—Shenzhen, Guangzhou, and Ningbo to the south of Shanghai, and Qingdao, Dalian, and Tianjin to the north—will likely suffer in terms of international shipping as Shanghai continues its major port developments. Shanghai may also exert greater competitive pressure on other major seaport cities in the Asia Pacific region, such as Singapore, Busan, Kaohsiung, and Yokohama. In a sense, Shanghai's reclamation of its status as China's head of the dragon has redistributed economic clout around the country and region, and it has also reinforced the dynamics of elite politics in China—the focus of chapter 6.

CHAPTER 6

From Jiang to Xi

The Enduring Power and Influence of the "Shanghai Gang"

The glory of yesterday is a culture; the glory of today is a power.
—A SHANGHAINESE SAYING

Shanghai is a barometer of the growth and decline of political forces in various factions.
—ZHOU WU

Since the reform era, China's national leaders have often accrued experience by working in provincial-level administrations, including those of major cities (namely, Beijing, Tianjin, Shanghai, and Chongqing), for extended tours of duty as provincial or municipal chiefs. As a result, top leadership positions in China's provinces and these four major cities have become the most important stepping-stones to political office at the national level.[1] For example, at both the 17th and 18th Central Committees, formed in 2007 and 2012, respectively, three-quarters of Politburo members (nineteen of twenty-five members) previously served as provincial or municipal chiefs (party secretaries and governors or mayors).[2] The large contingent of former or current provincial and municipal chiefs in the national leadership reveals several important trends in contemporary Chinese politics.

In general, provincial and municipal chief positions have carried much more weight since the mid-1980s compared to the first three decades of the People's Republic of China (PRC). The qualifications for leadership positions at the provincial and national levels have shifted from revolutionary credentials, such as participation in the Long March and the Anti-Japanese War, to experience in economic management and other administrative skills, such as coalition building and political networking, both vertically and horizontally. Today's leaders are far more focused on advancing the regional socioeconomic performance of their own jurisdictions than ever before.

China's provinces and four major cities are large socioeconomic entities. It is often said that a province is to China what a country is to Europe. China's provincial chiefs, similar to the top leaders of European nations, are constantly working to spur regional economic development, and they must address daunting challenges in their jurisdictions, such as economic issues, unemployment pressures, political tensions, environmental protection, public health, and social welfare needs.[3] For China's national leaders, experience in provincial and municipal administrations serves as an ideal training ground. China's provincial leaders are also a political force in their own right. Top national leaders often expand their power and influence in Beijing by leveraging their political bases and support from provincial-level administrations.

All of these dynamics are particularly evident in Shanghai—the nation's economic and commercial hub. Shanghai has enjoyed the strong political backing of powerful patrons in Zhongnanhai. At the turn of the century, an all-powerful political elite faction known as the Shanghai Gang (*shanghaibang*), informally established in the 1990s by then Chinese Communist Party (CCP) secretary general Jiang Zemin, dominated the national leadership. At the 15th CCP Central Committee formed in 1997, for example, five members of the Shanghai Gang served in the Politburo (Jiang Zemin, Zhu Rongji, Wu Bangguo, Huang Ju, and Zeng Qinghong), and two of them (President Jiang and Premier Zhu) served in the Politburo Standing Committee (PSC), the supreme decision-making body in the country. Wu Bangguo, Huang Ju, and Zeng Qinghong were also promoted to be members of the PSC in the 16th Central Committee, formed in 2002. At present, the Shanghai Gang remains as an important force within Xi Jinping's political coalition.

In March 2007, Xi Jinping was transferred from Zhejiang, where he served as party secretary, to the position of Shanghai party secretary for eight months. From there, Xi moved to Beijing to assume his membership on the PSC. From 2007 to 2012, Yu Zhengsheng also served as Shanghai party secretary before moving to Beijing to serve on the PSC, passing the party secretary post to Han Zheng. After serving in this role from 2012 to 2017, Han Zheng was also promoted to be a member of the PSC. He currently also serves as the executive vice premier of the State Council. These three former top Shanghai leaders have very strong patron-protégé ties with both Jiang and former PRC vice president Zeng Qinghong.[4]

Xi Jinping's relationship with the Shanghai Gang in general—and Jiang and Zeng in particular—is an intriguing one. Strictly speaking, Xi is not a member of the Shanghai Gang. But it has been widely acknowledged that without the strong endorsement of Jiang and Zeng, Xi might not have been able to take up the top leadership mantle in 2012.[5] All three leaders are also "princelings"—party officials who came from prominent Communist veteran families, especially Zeng and Xi, whose fathers were senior national leaders. To a great extent, Jiang and Zeng's Shanghai Gang as well as Xi and his own group of protégés have sought to broaden their power and influence by forming a political coalition to better compete with other factions and coalitions in the CCP.

After Xi became the top CCP leader, he promoted a number of Shanghai Gang leaders to the PSC, including the aforementioned Han Zheng and Wang Huning, who were confidants of both Jiang and Zeng for decades. The current Politburo also includes a few other members from the Shanghai Gang: Ding Xuexiang, who serves as Xi's chief of staff; Yang Xiaodu, who is in charge of China's anticorruption agency; Yang Jiechi, who is the top diplomat of the PRC; and Xu Qiliang, who is the highest-ranking general in the People's Liberation Army (PLA). In addition, Xi appointed his longtime protégé from his Zhejiang years, Li Qiang, to be the party secretary of Shanghai in 2017. Li Qiang also serves in the current Politburo. At present, the number of top CCP leaders who have strong ties with Shanghai account for 43 percent of the PSC and 36 percent of the Politburo, reflecting the enduring power and influence of this elite faction.

The distinct characteristics of Shanghai's cultural development and socioeconomic conditions may be a contributing factor to the prevalence of Chinese national leaders with strong Shanghai ties during the reform era. Shanghai is a unique place, and governing this city has influenced the political attitudes and behavior of its leaders, as demonstrated by the reactions of Shanghai's officials to a number of major crises since the 1980s. For example, during the 1989 protest movement, the city experienced large student demonstrations, similar to those in Beijing. But, rather than implement a bloody government crackdown like that in the capital city, Jiang Zemin and Zhu Rongji, party secretary and mayor of Shanghai at the time, defused the political crisis without bloodshed through persuasion and cooperation with workers in the city. During the Taiwan Strait crisis in 2000, in contrast to many belligerent Chinese leaders, officials in Shanghai reportedly lobbied against military hard-liners. Xu Kuangdi, then mayor of Shanghai, made significant efforts to reassure Taiwanese businesspeople working in the city. Similarly, President Jiang has been recognized by many analysts both in China and abroad for implementing a moderate approach to crises such as Taiwan's presidential elections in 1996, the Belgrade embassy bombing in 1999, and the EP-3 airplane crash in 2001. Premier Zhu also strongly and skillfully pushed for negotiations leading to China's accession to the

World Trade Organization in 2001. These "soft" actions or reactions were criticized by many Chinese at the time, but they are now widely regarded by the public as wise policies.

The political characteristics of leaders who were born or have worked in Shanghai—their strong and enduring representation in national government, intimate factional networks and vigorous political competition, well-articulated regional and policy interest, and distinct leadership style—are important subjects of inquiry for China watchers. An empirically based analysis can help reveal the crucial role of factional politics and the interaction between political forces and socioeconomic changes throughout Shanghai's rise. Such analyses can also shed light on how Chinese decision-makers may respond to daunting domestic and international challenges in the years to come, as the Shanghai Gang continues to play a central role in the national leadership.

THE SHANGHAI GANG: ORIGIN, DEFINITION, AND REPRESENTATION

From a historical perspective, the Shanghai Gang is not the first group of cadres with Shanghai origins to dominate national politics in China. During the 1940s, the "four big families" (*sidajiazu*)—the wealthiest bureaucratic-capitalist families in the Nationalist regime—were based primarily in Shanghai. Toward the end of the Cultural Revolution, the "gang of four" (*sirenbang*) leaders were also largely from Shanghai, and they wielded enormous power and influence over the country. Yet both the "four big families" and the "gang of four" were later decisively defeated by opposing political forces. These historical events show the costs and risks of power concentration in a singular faction, which could portend similar difficulties for the Shanghai Gang.

Contrary to what the name suggests, membership in the Shanghai Gang is not entirely based on geographic origin, although a significant number of members were born in Shanghai and two nearby provinces, Zhejiang and Jiangsu. Rather, leaders are considered part of the Shanghai Gang based on political association, and the group encompasses leaders whose careers have advanced mainly as a result of their political association with Jiang Zemin while he was in Shanghai. When Jiang served as mayor and party secretary in the city during the mid-1980s, he began cultivating a web of patron-protégé ties with his Shanghai associates. In a broader sense, faction members also include leaders who were promoted by Jiang's successors in Shanghai and served as Shanghai party secretaries (e.g., Zhu Rongji, Wu Bangguo, Huang Ju, Chen Liangyu, Yu Zhengsheng, and Han Zheng). In addition, some Shanghai locals or natives of Zhejiang and Jiangsu who studied or worked in Shanghai earlier in their careers and were later promoted by Jiang after he became general secretary of the CCP are also considered to be members of the Shanghai Gang. The best examples are current Politburo member Yang Jiechi and former Politburo member and former vice premier Zeng Peiyan.

Since the 1990s, Jiang and the Shanghai Gang have exercised firm control over the municipal leadership in Shanghai. A majority of the senior leadership positions in the Shanghai municipal government have been filled with candidates from the same city, which likely violates the norms of cross-region elite rotation and the law of avoidance. Party regulations require provincial party secretaries—including the party secretaries of the four major municipalities—to be transferred from another province or city, or from the central government, rather than being selected from the same province or municipality.[6] Table 6-1 shows that, over the past twenty-five years, three out of six Shanghai party secretaries (namely Huang Ju, Chen Liangyu, and Han Zheng) have been Shanghai natives, and the other two (Yu Zhengsheng and Li Qiang) were natives of nearby Zhejiang. Additionally, among the nine mayors listed in the table, five are Shanghai natives. Three were born in nearby Jiangsu and Zhejiang, including current mayor Gong Zheng, who was born in Suzhou. Between 2012 and 2017, then party secretary Han Zheng and mayor Yang Xiong were both born in Shanghai and had never worked outside the city.

Table 6-1 shows that among the nine Shanghai party secretaries since the mid-1980s, seven (78 percent) went on to serve as members of the PSC. Two held the position of CCP secretary general, one served as premier of the State Council, one as chairman of the National People's Congress (NPC), one as chairman of the Chinese People's Political Consultative Conference, and two as executive vice premier. The remaining two have served as Politburo members, including current party secretary Li Qiang, who is well positioned for membership on the next PSC in 2022. Six of the nine Shanghai party secretaries were directly promoted from positions in Shanghai, with five previously serving as mayor of Shanghai. The average tenure of Shanghai party secretaries has been roughly three years. All Shanghai mayors—except Jiang Zemin, who was transferred from a minister position in Beijing, and Gong Zheng, who was transferred from Shandong—were promoted from within the city leadership structure, and they had previously served as deputy party secretary, vice mayor, or both. The average tenure of Shanghai mayors has been roughly four years.

Table 6-2 shows the percentage of PSC members who were born in Shanghai or had prior leadership experience there starting from the 14th Central Committee formed in 1992 to the 19th Central Committee formed in 2017. Leaders with a Shanghai background have always been well represented in this supreme decisionmaking body, accounting for an astonish-

TABLE 6-1. An Overview of the Party Secretaries and Mayors of Shanghai, 1987–2020

Position	Name	Native	Tenure	Position before
Party secretary	Jiang Zemin	Jiangsu	1987–1989	Shanghai mayor
	Zhu Rongji	Hunan	1989–1991	Shanghai mayor
	Wu Bangguo	Anhui	1991–1994	Shanghai dep. party sec.
	Huang Ju	Shanghai	1994–2002	Shanghai mayor
	Chen Liangyu	Shanghai	2002–2006	Shanghai mayor
	Han Zheng*	Shanghai	2006–2007	Shanghai mayor
	Xi Jinping	Beijing	2007	Zhejiang party sec.
	Yu Zhengsheng	Zhejiang	2007–2012	Hubei party sec.
	Han Zheng	Shanghai	2012–2017	Shanghai mayor
	Li Qiang	Zhejiang	2017–date	Zhejiang party sec.
Mayor	Jiang Zemin	Jiangsu	1985–1988	Min. of electronics ind.
	Zhu Rongji	Hunan	1988–1991	Shanghai dep. party sec.
	Huang Ju	Shanghai	1991–1995	Shanghai dep. party sec.
	Xu Kuangdi	Shanghai	1995–2001	Shanghai dep. party sec.
	Chen Liangyu	Shanghai	2002–2003	Shanghai dep. party sec.
	Han Zheng	Shanghai	2003–2012	Shanghai dep. party sec.
	Yang Xiong	Shanghai	2012–2017	Shanghai vice mayor
	Ying Yong	Zhejiang	2017–2020	Shanghai vice mayor
	Gong Zheng	Jiangsu	2020–date	Shandong governor

Position after	The highest position	Membership in PSC or PM
CCP secretary general	CCP secretary general	PSC
Vice premier	Premier	PSC
Vice premier	Chairman of the NPC	PSC
Executive vice premier	Executive vice premier	PSC
Purged	Shanghai party secretary	PM
Mayor	Executive vice premier	PSC
PRC vice president	CCP secretary general	PSC
Chairman of CPPCC	Chairman of the CPPCC	PSC
Executive vice premier	Executive vice premier	PSC
n.a.	n.a.	PM
Shanghai party secretary	CCP secretary general	PSC
Shanghai party secretary	Premier	PSC
Shanghai party secretary	Executive vice premier	PSC
President of China's Academy of Engineering	Vice chairman of the CCPCC	
Shanghai party secretary	Shanghai party secretary	PM
Shanghai party secretary	Executive vice premier	PSC
Vice chairman of the NPC Financial Committee	Vice chairman of the NPC Financial Committee	
Hubei party secretary	Hubei party secretary	
n.a.	n.a.	

Source: Cheng Li's database.

*Acting.

Note: CCP (Chinese Communist Party), CPPCC (Chinese People's Political Consultative Conference), dep. (deputy), ind. (industry), Min. (minister), n.a. (not available), NPC (National People's Congress), PM (Politburo member), PRC (People's Republic of China), PSC (Politburo Standing Committee), sec. (secretary).

TABLE 6-2. Percentage of Politburo Standing Committee Members Born in and/or with Prior Leadership Experience in Shanghai, 1992–2017

Central Committee	Year	Total no. of PSC members	No. of PSC members with strong Shanghai ties	% of Shanghai	Names
14th	1992	7	3	42.9	Jiang Zemin, Zhu Rongji, Qiao Shi
15th	1997	7	2	28.6	Jiang Zemin, Zhu Rongji
16th	2002	9	3	33.3	Wu Bangguo, Huang Ju, Zeng Qinghong
17th	2007	9	2	22.2	Wu Bangguo, Xi Jinping
18th	2012	7	2	28.6	Xi Jinping, Yu Zhengsheng
19th	2017	7	3	42.9	Xi Jinping, Wang Huning, Han Zheng

Source: Cheng Li's database.

Note: PSC (Politburo Standing Committee).

ing 43 percent of members of the PSC in both the 14th and 19th Central Committees. Over these twenty-five years, leaders with a strong Shanghai connection accounted for, on average, roughly one-third of membership in the PSC. No other province or municipality has ever had such impressive representation on this supreme national leadership body. This record has made Shanghai "the cradle of top national leaders of the PRC."

For Jiang Zemin, Shanghai has served as both a power base and a show-case of China's economic progress under his rule. Like any other top leader in China, Jiang had two primary concerns when he was in power: his legacy and political security for him and his family. This explains why he fought so vigorously to maintain control over his turf, even at huge political cost. Table 6-3 lists the twelve highest-ranking leaders (i.e., party secretary, deputy secretaries, mayor, and vice mayors) in Shanghai in 2001. Ten were born in Shanghai, including then party secretary Huang Ju and then mayor Chen Liangyu. Seven completed their college education in Shanghai. Most had never served in a leadership role outside Shanghai, and they had been tied to Shanghai since their college graduation about two decades earlier. The only exception was Yang Xiaodu, then the vice mayor of Shanghai, who had substantial work experience outside the city.

But even Yang had extensive leadership experience in the city prior to ascending to more powerful positions. Yang was born in Shanghai in 1953 and grew up during the Cultural Revolution. He was "sent-down" to Anhui, where he worked as a farmer in 1970. Three years later, he returned to his birthplace, where he attended the Shanghai Traditional Medical School. After graduation, he was sent to Tibet, where he advanced from party secretary of a hospital to party secretary of a prefecture. He became vice governor of Tibet before being transferred back to Shanghai in 2001. Yang then worked in the Shanghai municipal administration for thirteen years as vice mayor, director of the United Front Work Department, and secretary of the Shanghai Commission for Discipline Inspection. Yang is currently a Politburo member and chairman of the National Supervision Commission.

The same pattern of privileging individuals with Shanghai connections can be found when looking at the top leadership lineup in 2007, follow-ing the corruption investigations and subsequent purge of Chen Liangyu as Shanghai party secretary.[7] The other highest-ranking leaders in Shanghai—the mayor, deputy party secretaries, and vice mayors—retained their po-sitions following the fall of Chen Liangyu in September 2006. No outsider was transferred into any of these positions in the city. Notably, with the ex-ception of then deputy party secretary Wang Anshun, who was transferred to Shanghai in 2003, all other top leaders in the city had advanced their careers exclusively within Shanghai.

TABLE 6-3. An Overview of the Highest-Ranking Officials in Shanghai, 2001

Name	Current position	Native	Education
Huang Ju	Party secretary	Shanghai	Tsinghua University
Chen Liangyu	Mayor; deputy party secretary	Shanghai	PLA Institute of Engineering
Gong Xueping	Deputy party secretary	Jiangsu	Fudan University (Shanghai)
Liu Yungeng	Deputy party secretary	Shanghai	East China Normal University (Shanghai)
Luo Shiqian	Deputy party secretary	Anhui	China S&T University
Jiang Yiren	Vice mayor	Shanghai	Tsinghua University
Han Zheng	Vice mayor	Shanghai	East China Normal University (Shanghai) (G)
Feng Guoqin	Vice mayor	Shanghai	Central Party School
Zhou Yupeng	Vice mayor, head, Pudong New District	Shanghai	Fudan University (Shanghai) New York Univ. (V)
Zhou Muyao	Vice mayor	Shanghai	Shanghai S&T University (Shanghai)
Yang Xiaodu	Vice mayor	Shanghai	Shanghai Traditional Medical School (Shanghai)
Yan Junqi	Vice mayor	Shanghai	Jiaotong University (Shanghai) and Technical Univ of Denmark (PhD)

Prior position	Chief-of-staff in Shanghai	Exp. other region
Shanghai mayor 1991–95	CCP Com. 1984–85	None
Shanghai executive vice mayor 1998–2001	CCP Com. (deputy) 1992–96	None
Shanghai vice mayor 1993–97	Gov't (deputy) 1992–93	None
Head, Shanghai Public Security Bureau, 1997–99	Gov't (deputy) 1995–97	None
Head, CCP Shanghai Org. Department 1991–2001		None
Head, Shanghai Trade Comm., 1991–1993	Gov't (deputy) 1993	None
Head, Shanghai Planning Comm. 1996–98	Gov't (deputy) 1995–96	None
Chief-of-staff, Shanghai gov't, 1995–96	Gov't, 1995–96	None
Chief-of-staff, Shanghai gov't, 1997–98	CCP Com. 1997–98	None
Chief-of-staff, 1997–98	Gov't, 1997–98	None
Vice governor, Tibet 1998–2001		Tibet
Deputy director, Shanghai IT Office		None

Source: Cheng Li, "Shanghai Gang: Force for Stability or Fuse for Conflict?" *China Leadership Monitor,* no. 2 (Winter 2002): 18, updated by the author.

Note: CCP (Chinese Communist Party), Com. (Committee), Comm. (Commission), G (graduate degree), Gov't (government); IT (information technology), Org. (Organization), PLA (People's Liberation Army), S&T (science and technology), Univ. (University), V (visiting scholar).

Most of the senior leaders (75 percent) in Shanghai listed in table 6-3 previously served as chief of staff for Shanghai's Municipal Party Committee or the municipal government. For example, Chen Liangyu served as the deputy chief of staff for both Wu Bangguo and Huang Ju (each for two years) when Wu and Huang were Shanghai party bosses at different times. Similarly, Han Zheng served as the deputy chief of staff to the mayor between 1995 and 1998, first to Huang Ju and then to Xu Kuangdi. Since the 1980s, if not earlier, serving as a leader's personal assistant (*mishu*) or chief of staff (*mishuzhang*) has been seen as a stepping-stone to further promotion.[8] Probably no patron-protégé relationship is closer than that between a *mishuzhang* and his or her boss. The high percentage of top Shanghai leaders who have served as a *mishuzhang* further illustrates the prevalence of favoritism in elite promotion, as exemplified in the case of the Shanghai Gang. The career advancement of these Shanghai leaders can be directly attributed to help from their patrons in higher places, whose own careers often advanced through Shanghai.

A prime example of Jiang's strong efforts to control his turf was the appointment of Yang Xiong as mayor of Shanghai in 2012. Yang was born in Shanghai in 1953 and is a close friend of Jiang's son, Jiang Mianheng. Yang previously worked as the president of Shanghai Alliance Investment—a large finance, energy, and life sciences company that Jiang Mianheng founded and for which he served as board chairman in the 1990s.[9] With the help of the Jiang family, Yang later became the deputy chief of staff for the Shanghai municipal government in 2001, vice mayor in 2003, and executive vice mayor in 2008. But Jiang's nepotism, as exemplified by the promotion of Yang, sparked a backlash, even among the Shanghai political establishment. In a "more candidates than seats election" for standing committee members of the Shanghai Municipal Party Committee in May 2012, Yang was eliminated. A few months later, Yang was once more eliminated in the election for alternate members of the 18th Central Committee.[10] Despite these embarrassments, Jiang Zemin still insisted that Yang serve as mayor of Shanghai, and he succeeded in making this very unusual appointment. For the first time in thirty years, the mayor of China's largest economic and financial center was not even an alternate member of the CCP Central Committee.

Of the small number of leaders transferred to top municipal positions in Shanghai since the early-1990s, most were confidants of Jiang or Zeng. For example, Xi Jinping and Yu Zhengsheng are not only princelings but also protégés of Jiang. Wang Anshun, who served as the director of the Organization Department and later as deputy party secretary of the Shanghai Municipal Party Committee from 2003 to 2007, had a significant background in the petroleum industry, which had been Zeng's power base. Another example is Li Xi, a protégé of Xi Jinping, who occupied the same positions in Shanghai from 2011 to 2013 that Wang Anshun had held earlier. Shen Deyong, whose legal career began in Jiangxi Province, served as vice president of the Jiangxi Provincial Supreme Court and the deputy party secretary of the Jiangxi Provincial Party Committee. He was then transferred to Shanghai in the wake of the Chen Liangyu corruption case. A trusted political ally of Jiang, Shen served as secretary of the Shanghai Commission for Discipline Inspection from 2006 to 2008 and later as executive vice president of the Supreme People's Court. Wu Zhiming, Jiang's nephew, became the director of the Public Security Bureau of Shanghai between 1999 and 2002, and he later advanced to the post of secretary of the Political and Legal Committee of the Shanghai Municipal Committee—a role in which he supervised the public security affairs of the city for over a decade (2002–2012).

While a majority of senior officials who have held municipal leadership positions in Shanghai since 1990 could be considered members of the Shanghai Gang, exceptions exist. One important exception is former PRC vice president and Politburo member Li Yuanchao. He was born into the family of a high-ranking official—his father was vice mayor of Shanghai in the early 1960s—and he advanced his career in Shanghai, where he served as deputy secretary and secretary of the Shanghai Municipal Youth League Committee in the early 1980s. Li Yuanchao is not usually considered a member of the Shanghai Gang, but rather as the protégé of two leaders with strong Chinese Communist Youth League (CCYL) backgrounds: Chen Pixian (Shanghai party secretary before the Cultural Revolution) and Hu Jintao. The CCYL faction, led by former party secretary Hu Jintao and current premier Li Keqiang, has long been seen as the principal rival faction of the Shanghai Gang.[11] For this reason, the Shanghai Gang has long considered Li to be a threat and has often blocked his promotion.[12] In 2012, the Jiang-Xi camp—particularly members of the Shanghai Gang—successfully prevented Li Yuanchao from obtaining a PSC seat.[13] At the 19th Party Congress in 2017, Li Yuanchao was forced to retire.

JIANG ZEMIN AND ZENG QINGHONG: THE FORMATION OF THE SHANGHAI GANG

Jiang Zemin acts as the godfather of the Shanghai Gang. The formation of the Shanghai Gang was extremely important for Jiang's consolidation of power in the 1990s, first in Shanghai and then in Beijing. In this endeavor, Jiang relied heavily on Zeng Qinghong, a Dick Cheney–like figure in Chinese politics, who was often described as Jiang's "hands, ears, and brain" and later served as the vice president of the PRC. Zeng began working in

Shanghai in late 1984, a few months before Jiang's arrival there. Zeng had strong political connections in the city. His father, Zeng Shan, became vice mayor of Shanghai soon after the Communist victory in 1949. In the early 1980s, three of his father's former junior colleagues—Chen Guodong, Hu Lijiao, and Wang Daohan—held top posts in the city.[14] Soon after Jiang arrived in Shanghai as mayor, Zeng was promoted to the director of the Party Organization Department in the city in charge of personnel affairs. One year later, when Jiang was promoted to party secretary of the city, Zeng became Jiang's chief of staff in the Shanghai Municipal Party Committee, and they began their "long-term mutually beneficial cooperation."[15]

When Jiang was appointed general secretary of the CCP in June 1989 after the Tiananmen incident, he brought Zeng with him to Beijing. This decision was partly motivated by Zeng's deep connections to the power circles in Beijing as he was in Shanghai, largely due to his extremely influential parents.[16] His father had notable leadership experiences in the central government after he moved from Shanghai to Beijing in the early 1950s, serving consecutively as minister of the textile industry, minister of commerce, minister of transportation, and minister of internal affairs. Zeng Qinghong's mother, Deng Liujin, was one of a small number of women who participated in the Long March. After the founding of the PRC, she established a kindergarten exclusively for the children of high-ranking officials or orphans of Communist revolutionary martyrs, creating a broad political network. According to some sources, many of the children who had attended this kindergarten emerged as senior political and military leaders in the early 1990s.[17]

After Jiang and Zeng moved from Shanghai to Beijing in 1989, it has been widely recognized that Zeng helped Jiang defeat his political rivals, including the "generals of the Yang family" (Yang Shangkun and Yang Baibing), Chen Xitong (former party chief in Beijing), and Deng Xiaoping's children.[18] For example, after Deng Xiaoping transferred Jiang to Beijing to serve as the secretary general of the CCP, Chen Xitong was seen as behaving insolently toward Jiang. Understandably, Jiang saw Chen as one of the primary obstacles to forming his own leadership team.[19] In the mid-1990s, Jiang put Chen Xitong in jail on charges of embezzlement, and he relied on Zeng to rally support from senior veteran leaders.[20] The purge of Chen Xitong paved the way for Jiang to wield greater, unrestricted power in the following years. While in Beijing, Zeng served consecutively as director of the General Office of the CCP Central Committee (Jiang's chief of staff), head of the Central Organization Department, executive secretary of the Secretariat of the CCP Central Committee, and president of the Central Party School. These positions are among the most influential in the Chinese political system. More recently, it has been suggested that Zeng may have initiated the move to select Xi as Jiang's heir to power at the 17th Party Congress in 2007.[21]

The relationship between Jiang and Zeng differs profoundly from many other important patron-protégé relationships in CCP history, such as that between Mao and Hua Guofeng, or between Deng and Jiang. Unlike these other relationships, in which the protégés (Hua and Jiang) heavily depended on the patrons (Mao and Deng), Jiang has greatly depended on his protégé Zeng—more specifically, on Zeng's family network, administrative skills, and political wisdom. Zeng has earned Jiang's respect for his contributions to political victories and, more recently, the factional deal making and coalition building they have jointly achieved over the past thirty years.

In addition to Zeng, Jiang also brought two of his most trusted confidants—You Xigui (his bodyguard) and Jia Ting'an (his personal secretary)—to Beijing with him in 1989. Jia Ting'an started as a *mishu* for Jiang when he served as vice minister of the Electronics Industry Ministry in the early 1980s. Jia followed Jiang to Shanghai in 1985 when Jiang was appointed mayor. Three years later, Jia was promoted to deputy director of the General Office of the Shanghai Municipal Party Committee, assisting then Shanghai party secretary Jiang. In June 1989, Jia served as director of Jiang's office while Jiang held the position of CCP general secretary. Five months later, he also took on the role of Jiang's *mishu* in the Office of the Chairman of the Central Military Commission (CMC). It is believed that Jia did not join the PLA until his CMC *mishu* appointment. In 1994, Jia was simultaneously promoted to be deputy director of the General Office of the CMC and director of the Office of the Chairman of the CMC, with the military rank of major general. He was promoted to director of the General Office of the CMC in 2003. One year after Jiang stepped down as CMC chairman, Jia was granted the military rank of lieutenant general in 2005, and he later became full general in 2011. From 2008, Jia served as deputy director of the General Political Department of the PLA before his retirement in 2016.

Jiang's other most trusted confidant, his former bodyguard You Xigui, served as deputy director of the Bodyguard Bureau, which was responsible for Jiang's security when he was appointed as party general secretary in 1989. You was elevated to director of the Bodyguard Bureau in 1994 and deputy director of the General Office of the CCP Central Committee in 1997. He was granted the military rank of major general in 1990, lieutenant general in 1997, and full general in 2004. Zeng, Jia, and You constituted the most important figures in Jiang's inner circle when he oversaw the CCP and CMC.

In 1991, Jiang's successor in Shanghai, Zhu Rongji, was also promoted to positions in Beijing, where he served as both vice premier and a Politburo member. During their time in both Shanghai and Beijing, Jiang and

Zhu maintained a mutually respectful and supportive working relationship. But Zhu's advancement to the national leadership came from Deng Xiaoping's influence rather than that of Jiang Zemin. Although Zhu has generally been considered a member of the Shanghai Gang, there is an important distinction between Jiang's Shanghai Gang and Shanghai leaders promoted by Zhu. Most of the officials that Zhu has promoted have been financial and economic experts. Xu Kuangdi, former mayor of Shanghai, is generally considered to be a protégé of Zhu, not Jiang. Zhu elevated his own associates in the city to central government positions. For example, his personal secretary, Lou Jiwei, followed Zhu to Beijing in 1991 and later served as minister of finance. When Zhu took over the governorship of the People's Bank of China (PBOC) in 1993, he immediately appointed Dai Xianglong, former governor of the Shanghai-based Bank of Communications, to be vice governor of the PBOC.[22] Two years later, in 1995, Zhu passed the bank governorship to Dai. While some tensions may exist between officials who have risen to their posts primarily under Jiang and those who have been appointed by Zhu, there is no evidence of serious friction or animosity between these two groups.

In a general sense, the Shanghai Gang primarily comprises Jiang Zemin's patron-protégé network from when he served as the party boss, first in Shanghai and later for the whole country. Members include Zeng Qinghong, Wu Bangguo, Huang Ju, Chen Liangyu, Meng Jianzhu (who later served as minister of public security and secretary of the Central Political and Legal Committee), Vice Premier Zeng Peiyan, State Councilor Hua Jianmin, and State Councilor Chen Zhili. They all share strong patron-protégé ties with Jiang. For example, Zeng Peiyan was Jiang's junior colleague at the Shanghai Institute of Electrical Science in the early 1960s when they both worked there. Zeng also served as the director of the office of the Electronics Industry Ministry in the early 1980s when Jiang was vice minister there.

In the late 1990s, Jiang promoted three Shanghai-born and Shanghai-educated leaders in their early forties to important national leadership positions. Wang Huning, a political scientist and former dean of the Fudan University Law School, was transferred to the Central Policy Research Center, where he later served as deputy director and director. He is now executive secretary of the Secretariat and a member of the PSC. Wang is one of the principal drafters of the theory of the "three represents" promulgated by Jiang Zemin.[23] Cao Jianming, a law professor and former president of the East China Institute of Politics and Law, was transferred to the Supreme People's Court, where he served as vice president and then executive vice president. Cao also served as procurator general of the highest People's Procuratorate and is now vice chairman of the NPC. Zhou Mingwei, former director of the Foreign Affairs Office, both at Fudan University and the Shanghai municipal government, was appointed to be deputy minister of the Taiwan Affairs Office of the State Council.

All three spent time in the United States as visiting scholars: Wang at the University of California at Berkeley, the University of Michigan, and Iowa State University; Cao at San Francisco State University, after which he gave several lectures to Politburo members about legal issues related to the World Trade Organization;[24] and Zhou at Harvard University, where he was a visiting scholar. Zhou also received a master's of public administration from the University at Albany-SUNY. Their path to preeminence from academia to politics indicates that Jiang was focused on fostering domestic expertise in law, political science, and public policy, which had been disregarded for many years during the pre-reform era. It also reflected Jiang's recognition of the need for new ideology and policy initiatives. Additionally, from Jiang's perspective, the prevalence of policymakers from the Shanghai Gang in the national leadership would allow him greater control over his legacy, as he could play an influential behind-the-scenes role after he stepped down at the 2002 Party Congress.

PERSONALITY, POLITICS, AND POLICY IN SHANGHAI: THE CASE OF CHEN LIANGYU

The enduring power and influence of the Shanghai Gang in present-day China reveals some important characteristics regarding the personality of Shanghai officials, the formation of elite factions, coalition-building and factional compromise, and leaders' interests in developing regionally favorable policies. The dominance of Shanghai in elite promotion and resource allocation has involved vicious factional competition and behind-the-scenes deal making. These dynamics were particularly evident in the purge of former Shanghai party secretary Chen Liangyu for corruption. In 2006, at the outset of the investigation of Chen Liangyu, Hong Kong and nonofficial mainland media widely publicized Jiang Zemin's angry remarks about Chen Liangyu's "bullying behavior" and "rotten lifestyle."[25] Jiang reportedly told others that "Chen deserves to be punished."[26] Nevertheless, Chen's prior ascent to political prominence, including his seat in the 16th Politburo, was largely due to Jiang's patronage. On a number of occasions, Jiang played a crucial role in helping Chen advance his political career.

Like Jiang Zemin, Chen Liangyu spent the majority of his career in Shanghai. Born in 1946, Chen joined the PLA at the age of 17. He was enrolled in the PLA Academy of Logistical Engineering between 1963 and 1968. After serving in the PLA for two more years, Chen was demobilized, and he was sent to work at the Shanghai Pengpu Machine Factory in 1970. Chen worked in that factory for thirteen years, first as a worker, then as an engineer, and eventually becoming the deputy director of the factory. In 1984, Chen served as party secretary of the Shanghai Electrical Appliances Corporation. Both the Pengpu Machine Factory and the Shanghai Electrical Appliances Corporation were affiliated with the First Bureau of Electrical Machinery of the Shanghai municipal government. From the mid-1980s through the 1990s, officials from that bureau formed a powerful network that dominated the top leadership of the Shanghai branch of the CCP and the Shanghai municipal government. The most notable figures in this network included Huang Ju, who served as deputy bureau chief in the early 1980s, and Hua Jianmin, who advanced his career in a research institute that was part of the First Bureau.

Shanghai's First Bureau of Electrical Machinery also fell under the leadership of the Electronic Industry Ministry, which was headed by Jiang Zemin in the early 1980s. It was not a coincidence that officials from that bureau became the main source of elite recruitment during the Jiang era. Soon after Jiang moved to Shanghai to serve as mayor in 1985, Chen was promoted to be director of the Retired Cadre Bureau of the Shanghai municipal government. That appointment was the first important stepping-stone for Chen, who was then only 39 years old. Many influential senior leaders in Shanghai had just retired or retired soon after Jiang's arrival. Jiang needed to ensure that their retirements would be handled smoothly, as these retired leaders still held political influence—their praise and endorsements could be crucial for promotions. In fact, it was the influence of these retirees that later helped elevate Chen Liangyu.

After his service as the head of the Retired Cadre Bureau, Chen was on the fast track for career advancement, serving as deputy party secretary and director of the Huangpu District—one of the most important commercial districts in Shanghai—between 1987 and 1992. He also spent nine months studying public policy at the University of Birmingham in the United Kingdom in 1992. After returning from studying abroad, Chen served briefly as deputy secretary general of the Shanghai municipal committee of the CCP, assisting then party secretary Wu Bangguo (who later became a PSC member and NPC chairman). Chen was then promoted to the post of the deputy party secretary of Shanghai.

The second major career boost that Jiang gave to Chen occurred at the 15th Party Congress in 1997. Jiang planned to have four Shanghai leaders—Party Secretary Huang Ju, Mayor Xu Kuangdi, and Deputy Party Secretaries Chen Liangyu and Meng Jianzhu—occupy full membership seats on the 15th Central Committee. But the delegates rejected this plan. On the 15th Central Committee, all but one of the thirty-one provincial-level administrations already had two full members.[27] The party secretary and governor (or mayor or chairman) usually occupy these two seats.[28] Nevertheless, with the help of Jiang and Zeng Qinghong, Chen obtained an alternate seat on the 15th Central Committee and became one of the youngest members of this powerful organization.[29]

In 2002 Chen Liangyu simultaneously served as party secretary and mayor of Shanghai, and he obtained Politburo membership on the 16th Central Committee. As one of the three youngest members of the Politburo, Chen seemed poised for an even brighter future in the top national leadership. However, the prevalence of the patron-protégé political networking of the Shanghai Gang and the city's construction fever led to serious resistance and constraints when the competing coalition led by Hu Jintao and Wen Jiabao became in charge of Zhongnanhai between 2002 and 2012. In early 2004, Hu and Wen adopted a macroeconomic control policy to limit bank lending, land use, and fixed-asset investment.[30] Their aim was to cool down the construction boom in Shanghai and surrounding areas.

In response, members of the Shanghai Gang and leaders in other coastal cities raised concerns about whether national leaders who had mainly worked in the inland region, like Hu and Wen, could handle tough economic issues in an era of globalization.[31] According to some observers, Chen had expressed interest in taking over Zeng Qinghong's position as the "operator" of the Shanghai Gang. However, Chen did not have the same political savvy and broad factional support as Zeng. Additionally, Chen seemed to underestimate the power and influence of the Hu-Wen administration and the broader geographic support that this rival camp enjoyed at the time.

After Jiang and Zhu ascended to the highest levels of China's national leadership, the uneven regional development and growing economic disparities across China resulted in growing public resentment against Jiang and his Shanghai Gang. Several anecdotes from that period are particularly revealing. For example, at the Ninth Chinese National Games held in Guangzhou in 2001, the audience routinely cheered for whichever team or athlete was competing against those from Shanghai. The Shanghai soccer team often received similar condescension at tournaments in other cities. A joke circulating throughout China in the late 1990s also reflected public resentment of the Shanghai nepotism in elite promotion. Whenever a line formed to get on a train or bus, people often teased: "Let comrades from Shanghai board first" (*rang Shanghai de tongzhi xianshang*).[32] This pervasive public sentiment gave the Hu-Wen administration greater motivation to address the potential property bubble and other socioeconomic problems in Shanghai and the coastal region, which came from the single-minded construction mania in those areas.[33]

In 2004, during a Politburo meeting held that summer, Chen voiced strong opposition to the Hu-Wen administration's macroeconomic control policy.[34] Chen accused then premier Wen of harming the interests of the Yangtze River delta and Shanghai, in particular. Citing statistics to bolster his points, Chen argued that Wen's conservative administrative regulations would not lead to a soft landing, but would instead hamper the country's future economic growth, especially its booming real estate industry.[35] Chen bluntly stated that Wen should take "political responsibility" for the damaging consequences of his economic policy. Chen's real target probably was not Wen, but Hu, whose macroeconomic control policy was part of a much broader plan to regionally balance China's socioeconomic development. Given the importance of these economic policies to his overall vision of China's development, Hu quickly rejected Chen's criticism, noting that the collective leadership of the Politburo had already adopted this macroeconomic policy and that all local governments, including Shanghai, should therefore carry it out.[36]

The political conflict in the Politburo between Hu, Wen, and their supporters on one side and the members of the Shanghai Gang on the other, lasted for two more years. Ultimately, the most outspoken representative of the Shanghai Gang, Chen Liangyu, was purged. In the fall of 2006, Chen was charged with siphoning RMB 3.45 billion (US$439.5 million) from the Shanghai social security pension fund to make illicit loans and investments. In 2008, Chen was sentenced to an eighteen-year jail term. Chen's expulsion was a big victory for the Hu-Wen camp, and it sent an important message to individual leaders and other political factions—including the formidable Shanghai Gang—that they no longer enjoyed absolute power, even on their own turf.

While the fall of Chen Liangyu was a major blow for the Shanghai Gang, this political faction nonetheless survived with almost all of its prominent members retaining positions of power. The top leadership posts of the Shanghai municipal government remained in the control of Jiang and Zeng's confidants.[37] The three subsequent Shanghai party secretaries after Chen's fall—Xi Jinping, Yu Zhengsheng, and Han Zheng—were all protégés of Jiang and Zeng. Their appointments as the party bosses of Jiang's turf, instead of the promotion of Hu Jintao's allies from elsewhere, were likely the result of a political compromise.

The removal of Chen Liangyu also allowed Hu Jintao to consolidate his power in the national leadership, giving him the leverage to push the political establishment to endorse his populist policy agenda. Under the Hu-Wen administration, China's western, northeastern, and central provinces—especially major cities, such as Chongqing and Tianjin—received more financial support and policy incentives from the central government than during the Jiang era. From 2003 to 2008, for example, the central government allocated RMB 280 billion for major construction projects in the western region.[38] The 11th Five-Year Plan (2006–2010) placed Chongqing on the fast track of economic growth. The central government planned to invest RMB 350 billion (US$43.5 billion) in new industrial renovation projects in Chongqing during these five years. In 2010, the total GDP in the greater Chongqing region reached RMB 1.4 trillion (US$173.9 billion)—two times higher than its GDP in 2006.[39] Aided by the central government's favorable policies, Chongqing underwent the most dramatic economic development in its history, and the city even claimed to have more construction cranes than Shanghai.[40] In 2008, Chongqing saw 14.3 percent GDP growth—4 percent higher than the national average.[41]

In 2006, the Hu-Wen administration designated Tianjin's Binhai District as the country's third state-level special economic zone—adding it to the ones already in Shenzhen and Shanghai's Pudong District, and also granting it favorable tariff, income tax, and technological innovation policies. With the completion of major projects, such as the Beijing-Tianjin High-speed rail line and the Airbus 320 assembly line, Tianjin's economic growth skyrocketed. In the first quarter of 2009, Tianjin saw 16 percent GDP growth, the highest in the country.[42] During the same period, the Tianjin municipal government had a total revenue of RMB 36 billion, which was around 12 percent higher than the national growth rate.[43] In contrast, Shanghai's GDP growth in the first quarter of 2009 was only 3.1 percent, the lowest growth rate among China's thirty-one province-level administrative areas and much lower than the national average of 6 percent.[44] In 2008, the GDP growth of Tianjin's Binhai District was 23 percent while that of Shanghai's Pudong District was only 10 percent.[45]

Shanghai's rapid economic slowdown after the fall of Chen Liangyu, however, lasted for only a few years. At the end of 2017, the new Shanghai party secretary Yu Zhengsheng reported in an official meeting that Shanghai had fallen below the national average in eight major economic indexes.[46] Yu called for the structural transformation of Shanghai's economy, with the objective of building new service-centered and advanced manufacturing industries in the city. To achieve these goals, Shanghai needed favorable policies from the central government in the areas of financing, revenue, and taxes. Shanghai leaders, especially then vice mayor Tu Guangshao, lobbied various relevant departments of the central government.[47]

Unsurprisingly, Shanghai's request was endorsed by top leaders in Beijing with strong ties to Shanghai, most notably two former party secretaries of Shanghai—Wu Bangguo and Xi Jinping. In 2008, Wu was chairman of the NPC and Xi was vice president of the PRC. Early that year, Wu reportedly said to his colleagues in Shanghai that "Shanghai should be bold enough to rush" into the new phase of economic development.[48] A few months later, in the spring of 2008, the Policy Research Office of the CCP

Central Committee, headed by Wang Huning, sent a team to Shanghai to evaluate the construction of the Yangshan port and the prospects for Shanghai to become an international shipping center. The team's assessment was very favorable.[49]

As discussed in chapter 5, the establishment of the Yangshan Deepwater Port cemented Shanghai's status as an international shipping hub, serving the interests of the entire Yangtze River delta region. Media reports have shown that, in 2009, then Shanghai party secretary Yu Zhengsheng lobbied aggressively in Beijing to secure Shanghai's status as the dual center of international shipping and finance. Yu made concerted efforts to ask the "State Council and related state offices to give their support."[50] In his brief tenure as Shanghai party secretary, Xi Jinping was also known for his strong advocacy for the city.[51] Current Shanghai party secretary Li Qiang, as a result of his previous leadership experience in Zhejiang and Jiangsu, has been increasingly explicit in his requests for greater resource allocation and preferential policies to promote the development of the Yangtze River delta region.[52] Li claims that during the Xi new era, "the development of regional integration in the Yangtze River Delta has risen to become a national strategy."[53] These economic policies align with the views long held by scholars of Shanghai, who assert that, by the logic of market economics, human and economic resources in China's western region should be "used" by the rich, well-developed eastern regions rather than the poor western region.[54]

THE SHANGHAI GANG'S STATUS, REORGANIZATION, AND PROSPECTS UNDER XI

Xi Jinping's overall approach toward governance and policy suggests that he has a strong understanding of Shanghai's distinct nature and importance. Despite his moves to appoint his own protégés to top positions in Shanghai in recent years, Xi has been noticeably cautious to maintain some semblance of political equilibrium between Jiang's protégés and his own—or in other words, between outsiders and native Shanghainese leaders. Given that Xi's ascendance to the top leadership position was due—at least in part—to the strong support of Jiang Zemin and Zeng Qinghong, the Shanghai Gang has maintained its representation in the national leadership and preferable economic and financial treatment on its home turf.

During the Jiang era, the Shanghai Gang enjoyed tremendous power and influence in the national leadership, as the group served as the main powerbase for Jiang and made up the "core faction" in the Jiang-led political coalition. Under the Xi administration, the Shanghai Gang has remained part of Xi's own political coalition—which largely inherited Jiang's political resources—but it by no means functions as the core faction for Xi.[55] Two unfolding trends—the shifting loyalty of certain heavyweight members of the Shanghai Gang from Jiang to Xi, and the hands-on approach by Xi in appointing his own protégés to top leadership posts in Shanghai—have greatly impacted the future development of this political faction that was once the most powerful in the country.

Under Xi's leadership, members of the Shanghai Gang have remained visible on both the 18th and 19th Central Committees, including the Politburo and the PSC. But the Shanghai Gang's share of seats on the Central Committee (counting both full and alternate memberships) has always been small. For example, their share of seats was only 4.1 percent on the 15th Central Committee and 4.5 percent on the 18th.[56] These numbers suggest that the Shanghai Gang's control over the Central Committee has been very limited, even in the years when Jiang had full influence over the 15th Central Committee. These limitations have restrained the power and influence of the Shanghai Gang, and they have also reinforced the need for coalition-building by both the Jiang Zemin camp and the Xi Jinping camp.

As has been the case since the 1990s, members of the Shanghai Gang have usually been prominently represented in the Politburo and some of the most crucial positions in the national leadership. At the 18th Party Congress, in addition to Xi Jinping, five other Shanghai Gang members—namely Yu Zhengsheng, Meng Jianzhu, Han Zheng, Wang Huning, and Xu Qiliang—served on the Politburo, accounting for 24 percent of the officials in this important leadership body. The Politburo, and especially its PSC, is of course, where the real power lies.

Compared with its representation at the 18th Central Committee, the Shanghai Gang has gained two more seats in the current Politburo and one more seat on the PSC. Table 6-4 lists the thirty members of the Shanghai Gang on the 19th Central Committee. The group includes nineteen full members—three of whom serve as PSC members and six of whom serve as Politburo members—and eleven alternate members. Altogether, they currently account for 43 percent of PSC membership, 36 percent of the Politburo, and 8 percent of the Central Committee. Thirteen of these Shanghai Gang members were born in Shanghai, seven are from the nearby provinces of Jiangsu and Zhejiang, and the remaining ten are from other areas of China. Most of them have held substantial leadership positions in Shanghai. Some have worked as university presidents, senior executives in major Shanghai-based corporations, or chief officers of military bases in Shanghai. During their tenures in their respective positions, they have all developed close political ties with top leaders in the city. Seven currently serve as provincial chiefs outside Shanghai.

It is important to note that the current top two leaders in Shanghai, party

TABLE 6-4. Prominent Members of the Shanghai Gang on the 19th Central Committee, 2020

Name	Year born	Current position	19th CC status
Xi Jinping	1953	Secretary general of the CCP	PSC member
Wang Huning	1955	Executive secretary of the Secretariat	PSC member
Han Zheng	1954	Executive vice-premier of the State Council	PSC member
Ding Xuexiang	1962	Director of the General Office of the CCP Central Com.	Politburo member
Yang Jiechi	1950	Office director of the Foreign Affairs Committee	Politburo member
Yang Xiaodu	1953	Chairman of the National Supervision Commission	Politburo member
Xu Qiliang	1950	Vice-chairman of the Central Military Commission	Politburo member
Li Qiang	1959	Shanghai Party secretary	Politburo member
Li Xi	1956	Guangdong Party secretary	Politburo member
Ying Yong	1957	Hubei Party secretary	Full member
Gong Zheng	1960	Shanghai mayor	Full member
Yang Zhenwu	1955	Secretary general, NPC	Full member
Cao Jianmin	1955	Vice-chairman of the National People's Congress	Full member
Xu Lin	1963	Director of the Information Office of the State Council	Full member
Yu Zhongfu	1956	Political commissar of the Air Force	Full member
Xu Lejiang	1959	Executive dep. director of United Front Work Dep't	Full member
Du Jiahao	1955	Hunan Party secretary	Full member
Chen Hao	1954	Yunnan Party secretary	Full member

Birthplace	Experience in Shanghai
Beijing	Shanghai party secretary (2017)
Shanghai	Dean of Fudan University Law School (1994–95), Chairman of the Department of Int'l Politics (1989–94)
Shanghai	Party secretary (2012–17, 2006–07), mayor (2003–12), vice-mayor (1998–2003)
Jiangsu	Secretary of the Political and Law Commission (2012–13), chief of staff of the Municipal Party Com. (2007–12)
Shanghai	Shanghai native, protégé of Jiang Zemin and Xi Jinping
Shanghai	Sec. of the Discipline Comm. (2012–13), director of United Front Dep't (2006–12), vice-mayor (2001–06)
Shandong	Chief of staff of the Air Force Command in Shanghai (1985–86)
Zhejiang	Shanghai party secretary (2017–date)
Gansu	Shanghai deputy party secretary (2013–14), director of the Organization Department (2011–13)
Zhejiang	Shanghai mayor (2017–2020), executive vice mayor (2016–17), dep. secretary (2014–date), director of the Org. Dep't (2013–14), president of the court (2007–13)
Jiangsu	Mayor (2020–date)
Hebei	Director of Propaganda Department of Shanghai (2009–13)
Shanghai	President of the East China University of Political Science and Law (1997–99)
Shanghai	Director of the Propaganda Dep't (2013–15), party secretary of Pudong District (2008–13)
Shandong	Commissar of the Air Force's Shanghai Command (2008–12)
Shandong	Chairman (2007–16), general manager (2004–07), deputy general manager (1994–2004) of Bao Steel
Shanghai	Deputy chief of staff (2003–04), director of Pudong District (2004–07)
Shanghai	Vice-chairman of MPC (2003–11), dep. chief of staff of the Party Committee (1997–2003)

table continues on next page

Name	Year born	Current position	19th CC status
Shen Xiaoming	1963	Hainan governor	Full member
Tang Dengjie	1964	Deputy minister of NDRC	Alternate member
Wang Wentao	1964	Heilongjiang governor	Alternate member
Yin Hong	1963	Henan governor	Alternate member
Zhou Bo	1962	Deputy party secretary of Liaoning	Alternate member
Shi Xiaolin (f)	1969	Director of the Propaganda Dep't and member of the Standing Committee of Jiangxi	Alternate member
Ma Guoqiang	1963	Former party secretary of Wuhan and Hubei deputy party secretary	Alternate member
Jin Donghan	1961	President of Tianjin University	Alternate member
He Dongfeng	1966	Chairman of COMAC	Alternate member
Tan Zuojun	1968	Party secretary of Dalian	Alternate member
Yu Shaoliang	1964	Director of the Organization Department of Shanghai	Alternate member
Wang Xi	1966	Vice-minister of science and technology	Alternate member

Birthplace	Experience in Shanghai
Zhejiang	Party secretary of Pudong (2013–16), vice-mayor (2008–13), head of the Education Comm. (2006–08)
Shanghai	Vice-mayor (2003–11), director of the Economic Commission (2001–03)
Jiangsu	Party secretary (2008–11), dep. party secretary and director (2007–08) of Huangpu District, dep. director of Songjiang District (2001–04)
Shanghai	Deputy party secretary (2017–19), chief of staff and dep. chief of staff (2008–17) of Municipal Party Com., dir. of Zhabei District (2004–08)
Shanghai	Executive vice mayor (2017–19), vice-mayor (2013–17), dep. chief of staff (2008–13) of the Shanghai Municipal Government
Shanghai	Dir. of the United Front Work Dep't of the Party Com. (2017–18), party sec. of Putuo District (2015–17), dir. of Civil Affairs of the Municipal Gov't (2013–15)
Hebei	Staff and dep. general manager of Bao Steel (1995–08)
Zhejiang	Party secretary and president of Shanghai University (2015–19), staff and director of No. 711 Research Institute (1989–2015)
Heilongjiang	Assistant general manager (2008–09), deputy general manager (2009–12), and general manager (2012–17) of COMAC
Hunan	Chairman of the China Shipbuilding Jiangnan Heavy Industry Co., Ltd. (2005–08), chairman of the Shanghai Waigaoqiao Shipbuilding Co. Ltd. (2002–05)
Hebei	Director of the Organization Department of Shanghai (2018–date)
Shanghai	Dep. director (2004–17) of the Shanghai Institute of Microsystems and Information Technology

Source: Cheng Li's database.

Note: CCP (Chinese Communist Party), Com. (Committee), Comm. (Commission), COMAC (Commercial Aircraft Corporation of China, Ltd.), Dep. (deputy), Dep't (Department), Dir. (director), f (female), Int'l (International), MPC (Municipal People's Congress), NDRC (National Development and Reform Commission), PSC (Politburo Standing Committee).

secretary Li Qiang and mayor Gong Zheng, have advanced from careers in Zhejiang. Li was one of Xi Jinping's protégés during Xi's tenure in Zhejiang. Li and Gong are primarily considered to be members of another political faction, the Zhejiang Gang. Li Qiang worked directly under Xi from 2004 to 2007 as chief of staff for the Zhejiang Provincial Party Committee. Li was born in 1959 in Rui'an County, Zhejiang Province. He has spent his entire career in his native province, serving consecutively as the director of the Industry and Commerce Bureau of Zhejiang Province, party secretary of Wenzhou, and secretary of the Politics and Law Committee of the Zhejiang Provincial Party Committee. In 2016, Li was appointed to serve as party secretary of Jiangsu, and one year later at the 19th Party Congress, he entered the Politburo and was then appointed to be Shanghai party secretary. He is the first leader in PRC history to have served as a provincial or municipal chief in Zhejiang, Jiangsu, and Shanghai. With strong support from his former boss Xi Jinping and his substantial administrative experience in one of the most important regions in the country, Li is expected to enter the PSC at the next Party Congress, and he will be a leading candidate for premiership in the years to come.

Former mayor Ying Yong also spent much of his early career exclusively in Zhejiang, and he worked directly under Xi Jinping as deputy chief of the Public Security Bureau. From 2002 to 2007, he served in Zhejiang as the deputy director of the Commission for Discipline Inspection, director of the Supervision Commission, and president of the province's High Court, and his tenure in these positions coincided with Xi's time as Zhejiang party secretary. Xi transferred Ying to be president of the Shanghai High Court in 2007 and later appointed him to be director of the Organization Department of the Shanghai Municipal Committee (2013–14), Shanghai deputy party secretary (2014–present), executive vice mayor (2016–17), and mayor of Shanghai (2017–2020). Like Li Qiang, Ying is widely considered to be a member of Xi's Zhejiang Gang rather than of the Shanghai Gang.[57] Xi's appointments of Li and Ying in 2017, two of his long-time protégés, to the top leadership positions in Shanghai reflect the enormous importance of Shanghai in Xi's mind.

In February 2020, amid the devastating COVID-19 outbreak and in the face of public outrage over the Hubei leadership's poor response, Xi moved his trusted protégé Ying Yong from Shanghai to Hubei to serve as party boss of this important province. Since Hubei was the initial epicenter of the virus, it was widely believed that the antiepidemic endeavors in Hubei were crucial to Xi's antiepidemic mobilization for the entire country. The lockdown of Wuhan (with a population of over 11 million people) was a difficult and controversial decision in many respects. Nevertheless, Ying proved to be an effective leader in coordinating the battle against COVID-19 in Hubei, which lifted public confidence in party leadership. As might be expected, Ying is now seen as a potential leading candidate for the next Politburo.

Two years earlier, in 2018, Yu Shaoliang, an alternate member of the 19th Central Committee, was transferred from Hubei to Shanghai, where he currently serves as director of the Organization Department of the Shanghai Municipal Party Committee in charge of personnel appointments in the city. Yu's career has largely involved propaganda work. It is believed that Yu became acquainted with Xi in the early 1980s when both worked in Hebei Province, where Yu served as a reporter and official for Xinhua News Agency's Hebei Branch, and Xi was party secretary of Zhengding County. Yu later served as the deputy director and then director of the Xinhua News Agency's Shaanxi branch for a decade (1999–2008), during which he overlapped with then Shaanxi party secretary Zhao Leji, a confidant of Xi and now a member of the PSC.

The four appointments of Li, Gong, Ying, and Yu signal Xi's plans to reorganize Shanghai leadership and consolidate his own power—whether that be in Beijing or in Shanghai. To that end, Xi and the central leadership have also changed the norm established under Jiang that all or most of Shanghai's leaders should be selected from the city. Table 6-5 lists twelve members of the Standing Committee of the Shanghai Municipal Party Committee— the city's highest-ranking officials in 2020. They were all appointed to their current positions within the last three years. Only one of them is a Shanghai native, in sharp contrast to 2001, when ten of the city's twelve highest-ranking officials were born in Shanghai (see table 6-3). Also, only two of the leaders in 2020 have had leadership experience only in Shanghai. However, in 2001 all but one of Shanghai's highest-ranking officials had only had previous leadership experience in the city. Just two current Shanghai leaders received their college or postgraduate degrees from institutions in Shanghai. Executive Vice Mayor Chen Yin studied civil engineering at Shanghai's Tongji University and attended a graduate program in economics at East China Normal University in Shanghai. Vice Mayor Wu Qing graduated from Shanghai University of Finance and Economics. A majority of Shanghai leaders in 2020 received their college education from outside Shanghai, and they were transferred to the city from another province or from the national leadership. These policymakers are thus largely considered to be "outsiders," reflecting the drastic change in elite recruitment and promotion in Shanghai from the Jiang era to the Xi era.

Most of the prominent members of the Shanghai Gang on the 19th Central Committee were born in the 1960s, and thus they are identified as part of the so-called sixth generation. This generational composition suggests that under Xi's leadership, the Shanghai Gang will likely remain an important player in the years to come. Ding Xuexiang (b. 1962) and Li Qiang (b. 1959)

TABLE 6-5. An Overview of the Standing Committee Members of the Shanghai Municipal Party Committee, 2020

Name	Current position	Birth year	Tenure since	Native
Li Qiang	Party secretary	1959	2017	Zhejiang
Gong Zheng	Mayor	1960	2020	Jiangsu
Liao Guoxun	Deputy party secretary	1963	2016	Sichuan
Liu Xuexin	Secretary of the Discipline Comm.	1963	2020	Shandong
Yu Shaoliang	Director of the Organization Dept.	1964	2018	Hebei
Zheng Gangmiao	Director of United Front Work	1963	2018	Shaanxi
Chen Yin	Executive vice mayor	1962	2019	Jiangsu
Weng Zuliang	Party secretary of Pudong	1963	2016	Fujian
Zhou Huilin	Director of the Propaganda Dept.	1962	2018	Shandong
Zhuge Yujie	Chief-of-staff, Municipal Party Committee	1971	2017	Shanghai
Ling Xi	Garrison commissar	1961	2017	Jiangsu
Wu Qing	Vice mayor	1965	2019	Anhui

Education	Prior position	Experience in other region
Zhejiang Agriculture University, CPS, HK S&T University	Jiangsu party secretary	Zhejiang, Jiangsu
University of Int'l Business and Economics, Xiamen University	Shandong governor	Zhejiang, Shandong, Tianjin, Guangdong
Guizhou Normal University, CPS	Director of the Organization Dept., Zhejiang Party Com.	Zhejiang, Guizhou
Economics, Xiamen University	Secretary of the Fujian Discipline Comm.	Guizhou, Tianjin, Fujian
Hebei University	Director of the Organization Dept., Hubei Party Com.	Hubei, Shaanxi, Hebei
Northwestern University of Political Science and Law	Vice president of the Academy of Socialism	Beijing, Sichuan
Shanghai Tongji University, East China Normal University	Shanghai vice mayor	Tibet
Macau S&T University	Deputy chief-of-staff, Shanghai Municipal Gov't	None
Beijing Normal University	Deputy director of the State Administration of Radio and Television	Beijing, Xinjiang
Southwestern University (Nanjing)	Deputy chief-of-staff, Shanghai Municipal Party Committee	None
PLA Military Academy	Deputy director, Political Dept., Eastern Theater	Jiangsu, Fujian
Shanghai University of Finance and Economics	Party secretary of Shanghai Stock Exchange	Beijing

Source: Cheng Li's database.

Note: Com. (Committee), Comm. (Commission), Dept. (Department), CPS (Central Party School), HK (Hong Kong), PLA (People's Liberation Army), S&T (science and technology).

are widely seen as rising stars for the next PSC. Li Xi (b. 1956), although a few years older than most members of the sixth generation, is also a strong candidate for the next PSC. Considering both the importance of their current leadership positions and their strong ties with Xi Jinping, Gong Zheng (b. 1960), Xu Lin (b. 1963), and Yang Zhenwu (b. 1955) are also possible candidates for the next Politburo. Additionally, because of their broad leadership experience and frequent changes in position, three officials are likely to assume more important roles in the near future: Heilongjiang governor Wang Wentao (b. 1964), who previously served as Kunming mayor, Jinan party secretary, and Nanchang party secretary; Dalian party secretary Tan Zuojun (b. 1968), who previously served as general manager of the China State Shipbuilding Corporation and chief-of-staff of the Liaoning Provincial Party Committee; and deputy director of the National Development and Reform Commission Tang Dengjie (b. 1964), who previously served as Shanghai vice mayor, chairman of China Ordnance Equipment Group Corporation, vice minister of Industry and Information Technology, director of the National Space Administration, director of the National Atomic Energy Agency, and the governor of Fujian Province.

Additionally, the political careers of many Shanghai Gang members have benefited from their strong ties to current PSC member Han Zheng and other former top leaders in Shanghai during the Jiang era. Henan governor Yin Hong (b. 1963) and Liaoning deputy party secretary Zhou Bo (b. 1962), who previously served as executive vice-mayor of Shanghai, are both protégés of Han Zheng and are strong candidates for further promotion in the years to come. Zhuge Yujie (b. 1971), who previously served as chief of staff to Party Secretary Han Zheng and now serves in the same role to Party Secretary Li Qiang, is one of the few officials born in the 1970s to reach the vice governor or vice minister level of leadership. Earlier in his career, Zhuge played an important role in the development of the Yangshan Deepwater Port when he served as the general manager of Shanghai Port Engineering Co., Ltd., the general manager of Yangshan Tongsheng Port Construction Co., Ltd., and the president of Shanghai International Port (Group) Co., Ltd. He is expected to ascend to higher positions in the near future.

FINAL THOUGHTS

During the reform era, top leadership positions in China's provinces and major cities have become important stepping-stones to national political office. The advancement of provincial leaders has been influenced by favoritism and political networking, the importance of province-level administrations in the country's economic and sociopolitical development, and the central government's efforts to improve national governance by offering career incentives for capable provincial and municipal leaders. For example, during the Jiang era, Shanghai leaders were usually Shanghai natives or had previously studied and worked in the city for many years. The increased representation of national leaders born in Shanghai or with prior leadership experience in Shanghai has been an enduring pattern, despite the fall of Shanghai party secretary Chen Liangyu more than a decade ago and the significant consolidation of personal power by Xi Jinping in recent years.

Shanghai has long been a key political battleground among various forces. As a Western study of Shanghai in the nineteenth and early twentieth centuries observes, "When Shanghai began to assert its position as China's premier business port and main financial and industrial center, it found itself at the crossroads of numerous political ambitions."[58] Since the mid-1990s, when former Shanghai leaders Jiang Zemin and Zhu Rongji were in charge of the national leadership, Shanghai has vigorously advanced its own interests through rapid urban transformation. However, in recent years Shanghai has also come to represent its neighbors, acting more as a leading member of an emerging coastal coalition rather than an economic center that overshadows China's other cities. Thus Shanghai and its leaders have become more important for regional and national development. As the late distinguished scholar Lucian Pye asserted, Shanghai is "critical in the sense that serious analysis of nearly all of the important aspects of life in China must, eventually, confront Shanghai and its special place in the Chinese scheme of things."[59]

The geographic origins of party and state officials are closely related to the crucial economic and political issues that China faces. These include the growing economic disparities between coastal and inland regions; the need for both regional autonomy and national unity; incentives for power sharing, negotiation, and consensus building pushing against concerns about fragmentation and factional deadlock; and the tension between demand for regional representation and restraints on the rise of localism. The elevation of local interests and the rise of regional political coalitions, as exemplified by political dynamics in Shanghai since the early 1990s, are important trends that reveal the intriguing and important interactions between regional economic growth, elite politics, and public policy.

New developments in elite formation and central-local relations do not change the authoritarian nature of the Chinese one-party system. Nevertheless, they reflect influential dynamics of region-based factional competition and policy choices in a seemingly monolithic political entity. The ramifications of these political trends and tensions are quite significant if they can be linked to broad changes in society, especially in the domains of education and culture—the central areas of inquiry for the chapters that follow.

IV

EDUCATION AND ART IN GLOBAL SHANGHAI: VIEWS, VALUES, AND VOICES

CHAPTER 7

"Sea Turtles"

The Study Abroad Movement and the Tidal Wave of Returnees

Any nation, any country, needs to learn the strengths of other nations, other countries, and to learn the advanced science and technology of others. China has to catch up with the world's advanced level of development. Sending our students to study abroad is a concrete measure.
—DENG XIAOPING

They not only saw the emergence of a "new China"; they prepared the way.
—THOMAS E. LaFARGUE

When Deng Xiaoping and Jimmy Carter launched the first student exchange programs between the People's Republic of China (PRC) and the United States in 1978, they explicitly linked these educational exchanges to a broader aspiration of promoting "many more areas of bilateral cooperation" and contributing to world peace and regional stability.[1] There has been a long-standing premise underlying U.S. policy toward China that the ability of the United States to educate young Chinese elites will allow the country to eventually influence China's political development.[2] Arguably, the objective of American decisionmakers in opening educational exchanges with China of training the future generations of Chinese elites has largely been fulfilled. For instance, the Asia Pacific region has generally remained peaceful since the 1980s. Additionally, Chinese nationals educated abroad, especially those who studied in the United States, have emerged as a distinguished elite group in the PRC.

This phenomenon has resulted in the coining of a new Chinese term to refer to this fast-growing group of Chinese students returning from abroad—"returnees from overseas" (*haigui*) or "sea turtles." In Chinese, the words for "returnee" and "sea turtle" have the same pronunciation, hence the dual translation and meaning of the nickname. When these educational exchanges began, some foreign observers commented that the move was "unprecedented in the Communist world."[3] As a Chinese scholar described, "A whole new generation of China's potential leaders in all fields of learning are being educated in capitalist countries."[4] The depth and breadth of the educational exchanges between these two countries with vastly different political systems and ideologies have been truly remarkable. However, as U.S.-China relations have deteriorated in recent years, and a significant number of Chinese U.S.-educated returnees have developed a critical—or even a hawkish—view of the U.S. government's policy toward China, Washington seems to have become more cynical about the results of bilateral educational exchanges.

From a historical perspective, Deng's 1978 decision to send a large number of Chinese students to study overseas, especially in the United States, was indeed seen at the time as the first astonishing sign of Communist China's opening to the outside world, and the strategic "prelude" (*xumu*) to China's reform and opening-up.[5] On December 26, 1978, the first group of fifty-two Chinese students and scholars traveled to the United States to pursue academic studies.[6] Their arrival in America occurred just a few days after the 3rd Plenary Session of the 11th Party Congress—an important meeting that marked the beginning of China's economic reform and opening up—and a few days before the establishment of diplomatic relations between the United States and the PRC. These vanguards of Sino-U.S. educational exchanges were regarded as "political missionaries" or "goodwill ambassadors," rather than students or academics.[7]

What happened over the following four decades—the sheer number of Chinese nationals who went to study abroad and the tidal wave of Chinese students and scholars who returned home after completing their overseas education—was perhaps beyond anyone's imagination in 1978. In 2018 alone, approximately 662,100 Chinese students studied abroad, including 30,200 who were sponsored by the Chinese government, 35,600 who were sponsored by various institutions, and 596,300 (90 percent) who were self-sponsored.[8] As a result, China was the country that sent the most students to study overseas for ten consecutive years.[9] In the 2017–18 academic year, a total of 363,341 PRC students enrolled in schools in the United States, making China the country that sent the most foreign students to study in American schools for the ninth consecutive year.[10] PRC students accounted for 33 percent of the total number of international students in the United States that year.

Between 1985 and 2005, one-third of Chinese nationals who studied in American institutions returned to China after their educational pursuits, one-third decided to seek employment or otherwise settle down in the United States, and one-third continued their education.[11] Those who obtained doctoral degrees, especially the most accomplished academics, tended to find jobs in American universities and research institutions. According to a study conducted by the U.S. National Science Foundation in 2017, from 2005 to 2015, nearly 90 percent of PRC students who had earned Ph.D. degrees intended to remain in the United States after their degree programs.[12]

According to a recent study, around 320 tenured professors in the eight American Ivy League universities were born in the PRC, and almost all of them attended graduate programs in the United States or other Western countries after their undergraduate education in China.[13] In almost every academic discipline in the natural sciences and engineering (and to a lesser extent in the social sciences and humanities) at leading American universities, one can find PRC-born faculty members. These ethnic Chinese professors usually received their undergraduate degrees in China and earned doctoral degrees in the West.[14] There are twenty-six PRC-born academicians in the prestigious National Academy of Sciences in the United States at present, and most of them have this educational background—an undergraduate degree from China and a graduate degree from the United States.[15] Overall, there are more than 300 PRC-born academicians in the four prestigious academies in the United States (i.e., the National Academy of Sciences, the National Academy of Engineering, the National Academy of Medicine, and the American Academy of Arts and Sciences).[16]

It is expected, however, that the ongoing U.S. "educational decoupling" policy toward China will drastically decrease the number of PRC students and scholars studying in the United States in the years to come. In fact, the number of Chinese student visas for admission to the United States in 2017 dropped 24 percent from that of 2016.[17] The main reason for the anticipated decline of Chinese students in the United States is the new set of regulations adopted by the U.S. government in July 2018, which require that PRC students in the fields of science and technology must undergo additional screening.[18] The number of Chinese tourists to the United States in 2018 dropped by 6 percent as well, falling for the first time in fifteen years.[19] The White House's May 2020 decision to suspend entry of PRC graduate students and researchers believed to have connections to military-civil fusion projects in China affected thousands of Chinese students and researchers in the United States.[20]

In Washington, the overarching view of bilateral educational exchanges is no longer one of hope for positive political change resulting from academic engagement. Instead, politicians are concerned that Chinese scholars and students in American universities will help China become a science and technology superpower at the expense of the United States. Following FBI director Christopher Wray's 2018 remarks about the "China threat by the whole of society" on the educational and cultural exchange front, "U.S. intelligence agencies are encouraging American research universities to develop protocols" for monitoring students and visiting scholars from the PRC.[21] In the words of some influential U.S. political leaders, as quoted in the prologue of this book, China is "weaponizing" the large number of PRC students enrolled in U.S. universities.[22]

Furthermore, PRC-born Chinese scientists (or even U.S.-born Chinese American scientists) are often subject to heightened suspicion. In an August 2018 memo sent to 10,000 research institutions in the United States, the director of the National Institutes of Health, Francis Collins, called for more scrutiny on projects by researchers who have ties to the PRC.[23] Scholarly collaboration in the areas of public health, cancer research, environmental protection, and basic science between "sister institutions" in the United States and China—which was previously encouraged—is now "quasi-criminalized, with FBI agents reading private emails, stopping Chinese scientists at airports, and visiting people's homes to assess their loyalty."[24] As Bloomberg journalist Peter Waldman asserts, the FBI's large-scale investigations have created a "new red scare," frightening researchers within the U.S. scientific communities, such as the National Institutes of Health, and causing a chilling effect among the 130,000 Chinese graduate students and researchers in the United States, who are "targeted for FBI surveillance."[25] In another speech in July 2020, FBI Director Wray stated that "of the nearly 5,000 active FBI counterintelligence cases currently underway across the country, almost half are related to China."[26] Thus "the FBI is opening a new China-related counterintelligence case about every 10 hours."[27]

A few institutions and American university presidents have recently spoken out against the rise of a new McCarthyism in the United States.[28] The Committee of Concerned Scientists, a nonprofit group that advocates for academic freedom, recently alleged that the U.S. government was waging a "campaign of intimidation of ethnic Chinese scientists" and called for the government to "make a public statement assuring them that they will be treated as equally valuable members of the American society."[29] Unless the ongoing anxiety of PRC-born researchers is assuaged—and the widespread suspicion that they are stealing U.S. science and technology on behalf of the Chinese authoritarian regime abates—one can expect that an increasing number of these Chinese researchers, including a number of world-class scientists, will have no choice but to leave the United States. Even before the "new red scare," a majority of Chinese students who studied in the United States have returned home in recent years. By 2018, over 3.6 million Chinese students who studied abroad had returned to China, accounting for 85 percent of those who had completed their programs.[30] In light of the recent moves by the White House to end the Fulbright Program in China and propose an entry ban on over 92 million Chinese Communist Party (CCP) members and their families, it is not inconceivable that the past forty years of educational exchanges between the United States and China may soon come to a complete halt.

Students of China and Sino-U.S. relations and policymakers in Washington must comprehensively evaluate the results of China's study abroad movement and its impact on the bilateral relationship. They need to assess the impact and limitations of international scholarly exchanges, especially the outcomes for Western-educated returnees in China. This chapter has three parts. It begins with a historical review of China's study abroad movements over the last century and their sociopolitical impact on the country's contemporary development, including a discussion of Shanghai's prominence as both the source and the destination for China's study abroad movement and its tidal wave of returnees. The chapter then describes the characteristics of exchange students, including their sponsorships, types and levels of educational attainment, destination countries, and academic disciplines. The third part of the chapter discusses Chinese government policy regarding foreign studies and foreign-educated returnees over the past two decades.

STUDY ABROAD MOVEMENTS AND THEIR SOCIOPOLITICAL IMPACT IN CONTEMPORARY CHINA

In his pioneering study of the history of study abroad movements in contemporary China, distinguished scholar Shu Xincheng described the China before study abroad programs as "no foreign-educated students, no Chinese new culture."[31] China's study abroad movements have always been catalytic forces for educational reform, cultural transformation, and sociopolitical changes in the country. The late Qing government's decision to send a group of school-age children (*youtong*) to study in America—the first study abroad movement in contemporary China—reflected the state's acknowledgment that they need to learn from foreigners for China to "meet her modern problems."[32]

The Chinese study abroad movement was born in 1872, when the Qing government made the landmark decision to send school-age children to study in the United States. Prior to that, only a handful of Chinese had studied abroad, and they were often self-funded or sponsored by Western missionaries.[33] For example, Yung Wing (Rong Hong) went to study in the United States in 1847 with the support of an American missionary. He was the first Chinese person to receive an American college education (Yale College in 1854).

For a significant period of world history, China had vastly superior science and technology compared to other countries. According to the *World Chronology of Major Events of Natural Sciences*, between the sixth century B.C. and eleventh century A.D., China was responsible for 135 (58 percent) of the 231 major innovations and scientific achievements in the world. During the following period from the eleventh century to the sixteenth century, China contributed 38 (57 percent) of the 67 major scientific innovations.[34] During this time, China had no incentive to send students to study in foreign countries. In fact, China attracted foreign students over many years. The Chinese term "foreign-educated students" (*liuxuesheng*), which appeared during the Tang Dynasty, first referred to the large number of Japanese students who studied in the Tang capital, Chang'an.[35]

But by the nineteenth century, China's devastating defeats during the Opium Wars made it clear that China had lost its edge in science and technology. Since then, sending students overseas to acquire advanced knowledge through education has become a recurrent state strategy, although it has occasionally been interrupted by wars, cultural tensions, ideological disputes, and domestic turmoil. Throughout the twentieth century, many Chinese nationals who returned to China after studying abroad have made considerable political, economic, educational, and social impacts on their home country. Therefore, a review of the major study abroad movements throughout contemporary Chinese history can not only help us understand their general trends and impacts but also highlight long-standing issues about foreign-educated elites and their relevance today.

Table 7-1 provides an overview of the main features of the most important Chinese study abroad movements from 1872 to 2020.[36] The 120 children (ranging in age from 10 to 16) sent by the Educational Mission Commission of the Qing government to the United States between 1872 and 1875 made up the first cohort of state-sponsored exchange students.[37] These young children had originally planned to study in the United States for about fifteen years through the end of their college education, but the students, along with Vice Commissioner Yung Wing who administered the program, were all recalled to China in 1881.[38] Only two of them, including Zhan Tianyou (known as "the father of China's railways"), were able to complete their college programs at Yale University prior to their return home. This drastic policy change was partly due to the "anti-Chinese sentiment in the United States" at the time, but it was mainly the result of concerns from conserva-

TABLE 7-1. An Overview of Study-Abroad Movements in Contemporary China, 1872–2020

Period/movement	Year	Total number	Main designated countries	Educational attainment	Prominent political leaders later in their careers
Educational mission students in the U.S.	1872–1881	120	U.S.	Students in schools ranging from elementary to college level	Tang Shaoyi, Liang Tun Yen, Tang Guo'an
"Japan Fever"	1896–1911	22,000	Japan	Students at specialized (technical) schools and colleges	Sun Yat-sen, Chiang Kai-shek, Chen Duxiu
Studying in the U.S. with Boxer Indemnity Funds	1908–1929	1,800	U.S.	Students at universities	Mei Yiqi, Hu Shi, Ma Yinchu
Work-study program in France	1911–1924	1,600	France	Part-time students at language schools	Zhou Enlai, Deng Xiaoping
Political study in the Soviet Union	1921–1930	800	Soviet Union	Ideological (Communist) education	Liu Shaoqi, Chiang Ching-kuo
Post-1949 study in socialist countries	1950–1965	10,000	Soviet Union and other socialist countries	Students and trainees at universities	Jiang Zemin, Li Peng, Luo Gan
The era of reform and opening up	1978–2020	5.9 million	U.S., Europe, Japan, and Australia	Students and visiting scholars at universities	Wang Huning, Liu He, Yang Jiechi

Sources: The Hong Kong Museum of History, comp., *Boundless Learning: Foreign-Educated Students of Modern China* (Hong Kong: The Hong Kong Museum of History, 2003); and Yang Xiaojing and Miao Danguo, "Xin Zhongguo chuguo liuxue jiaoyu zhengce de yanbian guocheng ji duice yanjiu" [The policy changes toward overseas study in the PRC] in *Quanguo chuguo liuxue gongzuo yanjiuhui chengli shizhounian jinian wenji* [The 10th anniversary commemorative collection of the National Research Association of Overseas Study], edited by Min Weifang and Wang Yongda (Beijing: Beijing daxue chubanshe, 2002), 38. "Zhongguo qunian chuguo liuxue renshu shou po 60 wan" [The number of Chinese students studying abroad last year exceeded 600,000], *Renmin ribao* [overseas edition], April 1, 2018, www.gov.cn/xinwen/2018-04/01/content_5278951.htm. "Chuguo liuxue wushi nian shuju huizong" [Summary of 50 years of Chinese students study abroad], Jiemodui website, April 10, 2019, www.jiemodui.com/N/105783.html. Assembled and tabulated by Cheng Li.

tives in the Qing government about the cultural and political alienation of the students in the United States.[39]

Even though their study abroad experiences were cut short, these returnees made great contributions to the development of contemporary China in areas such as mining, railways, telegraphy, and education. Many later worked for the government, including Tang Shaoyi (the first premier of the Republic of China) and Liang Tunyen (minister of foreign affairs prior to the 1911 Revolution). Nineteen served as admirals or naval officers, contributing to the birth of the modern navy in the country. In Sun Yat-sen's temporary cabinet after the 1911 Revolution, a stunning 83 percent of the officials (fifteen of the eighteen ministers and vice ministers) were returnees.[40]

Between 1896 and 1911, China's study abroad movement experienced a "Japan fever," with about 22,000 students traveling to Japan to study.[41] During the first two decades of the twentieth century, those studying in Japan accounted for 90 percent of the Chinese students who studied abroad during that period.[42] This study abroad movement was unusual in that half of the Chinese students in Japan studied political science and law.[43] Some of them studied modern military affairs, and many were actively involved in the 1911 revolution that ended the Qing dynasty. It is not an exaggeration to say that the rush of students studying in Japan during the late Qing period directly contributed to the collapse of imperial China.[44] Among the distinguished political leaders who studied in Japan during this period were Sun Yat-sen, Chiang Kai-shek, Chen Duxiu, and Li Dazhao—the founders of both the Nationalist and Communist parties, which would shape Chinese politics in the decades to come.

Another important Chinese study abroad movement, which occurred between 1908 and 1929, was made possible by the U.S. government through the Boxer Indemnity Funds—the remaining sum of money from the amount paid by the Chinese government for the Boxer Uprising debacle. From 1908 to 1911, the Qing government recruited 183 talented Chinese youth and sponsored their study in the United States using these funds. In 1911, these funds were allocated to students of the Tsinghua School, which was established to select and train students to study in the United States. The first president of the Tsinghua School was Tang Guo'an, one of the 120 school-age children who had previously studied in the United States. When the program ended in 1929, the Tsinghua School had dispatched a total of 1,279 students to America.[45] The Boxer Indemnity Funds also provided support for several hundred Chinese students who studied abroad but did not attend the Tsinghua School. Altogether, some 1,800 Chinese were able to study in the United States using these funds between 1908 and 1929.[46]

A large number of these students received doctorate degrees from prestigious universities. These students majored in a variety of fields, and some became founders of new academic disciplines in China upon their return. They also functioned as leading voices for the renewal of Chinese culture during the May Fourth Movement. Some served as presidents of China's leading universities; for example, Mei Yiqi at Tsinghua University, and Hu Shi and Ma Yinchu at Peking University (Ma also led Zhejiang University). Seventeen presidents of comprehensive universities in China during the 1940s were U.S.-educated returnees who had received Boxer Indemnity scholarships.[47] In general, after their sponsored study in the United States, Chinese students returned to China to provide intellectual leadership for the May Fourth Movement, during which they systemically introduced "science and democracy" to the Middle Kingdom.[48]

Over the course of a little over a century—from 1847, when Yung Wing was enrolled in an American school, to 1949, when the CCP took over power in China—approximately 13,000 Chinese students went to the United States, second only to the total number of students who studied in Japan.[49] The U.S-educated returnees working in the natural sciences constituted a large percentage of China's most prominent scientists. For example, at the founding of the PRC in 1949, the *Who's Who of Chinese Scientists* included 877 distinguished scientists. Among them, 622 (71 percent) were returnees from the United States and other countries. Of the 400 members of the Chinese Academy of Sciences, which was reestablished in 1981, 344 (86 percent) had studied abroad.[50] Of the 801 members of the Academy in 1995, there were 233 (29 percent) who had received a postgraduate degree in the United States, including 179 who held doctorate degrees from American universities.[51]

The Chinese students who participated in the work-study program in France and the political study program in the Soviet Union during the first half of the last century were more engaged in political and ideological activities than academic studies. During their short existence, Sun Yat-sen University and the Communist University for Toilers of the East, both located in Moscow, trained some 800 Chinese "revolutionary comrades," who later became the backbone of both Leninist parties in China (the CCP and the Nationalist Party). In fact, the multitude of Chinese nationals who studied in France and the Soviet Union during the early twentieth century facilitated the birth and growth of the CCP.[52]

Several crucial figures in Chinese politics during the latter half of the last century participated in these two study abroad movements. They include Zhou Enlai, Deng Xiaoping, Liu Shaoqi, and Chiang Ching-kuo. Through their overseas experiences, the first three individuals developed Communist ideas and political skills that they later used to help the CCP seize power and run the most populous country in the world. Chiang later became the president of the Republic of China in Taiwan, and then Deng and Chiang each rose to leadership positions and led the magnificent economic development on both sides of the Taiwan Strait in the late 1970s through the 1980s. As some scholars have observed, without accounting for the impacts of foreign education, "modern China is incomprehensible."[53]

After the 1949 Communist Revolution in China, the Soviet Union became the main destination for Chinese students pursuing education abroad. Between 1950 and 1965, the PRC sent 10,698 students to the Soviet Union, Eastern Europe, North Korea, Cuba, and thirty-nine other countries. Among them, 8,414 (79 percent) were sent to the Soviet Union, and some 1,000 went to other Eastern European socialist countries.[54] During that period, only about 250 (2 percent) of the total number of Chinese nationals who studied abroad went to nonsocialist countries, where they mainly studied foreign languages.[55] Most students studying in the Soviet countries majored in engineering and natural sciences. Technocrats who had studied in the Soviet Union or Eastern European socialist countries in the 1950s dominated the "third generation" of PRC leaders in the reform era. Among their ranks were Jiang Zemin, Li Peng, Luo Gan, Li Lanqing, and Wei Jianxing, all of whom later served on the powerful Politburo Standing Committee. Large-scale educational exchanges between China and the Soviet Union ultimately ended in the early 1960s because of political and ideological disputes between the two countries.

Between 1966 and 1969, China did not send a single state-sponsored student to study abroad.[56] Returnees from previous study abroad movements, especially from the United States and other Western countries, often faced persecution during the Cultural Revolution. When the PRC was founded in 1949, there were about 7,000 Chinese students studying in Western countries and Japan. According to Chinese official sources, approximately 2,500 of them returned to China after 1950.[57] Some returnees from the West were labeled as rightists in political campaigns during the Mao era. During the red terror of the Cultural Revolution, many Western-educated returnees were accused of being "foreign spies."[58]

In 1970, China restarted student exchanges and sent twenty students to France and sixteen students to Great Britain to study French and English, respectively. Yang Jiechi, currently a Politburo member and China's top diplomat, studied in England as part of this initiative. Between 1972 and 1978, China sent a total of 1,977 students to study in thirty-two countries, with a majority of them studying foreign languages.[59] This was largely due to the growing need for interpreters following President Nixon's visit to China in 1972, and the PRC's newly established or resumed diplomatic relations with Japan, Great Britain, and France. Only ninety students (5 percent) studied science and technology.[60]

The history of Chinese study abroad movements highlights the close ties between education and politics—between the destinations of students who studied overseas and China's changing political orientation. This connection can be seen on two levels: the individual and the collective. At the individual level, personal educational experiences had an enduring influence on a number of prominent future leaders (in either the realm of education or politics). It was Yung Wing, the first Chinese person to complete a college education in America, who promoted and administered the Educational Mission Program that brought school-age children to study in America. It was Tang Guo'an, one of the students in the Educational Mission Program, who later served as the first president of the Tsinghua School, the institution responsible for using the Boxer Indemnity Funds to train Chinese students to study in the United States. Mei Yiqi, Hu Shi, and Ma Yinchu all strived to shape Chinese universities in accordance with the American universities that they had attended. Additionally, the representative for the PRC in negotiations with the United States to reestablish educational exchanges during the late 1970s was Zhou Peiyuan, then president of Peking University, who attended the University of Chicago between 1924 and 1926 through the Boxer Indemnity Funds.[61] Similarly, the foreign experiences of political leaders, such as Sun Yat-sen and Chiang Kai-shek, had enduring impacts on their political views and behavior.

At the collective level, both China's educational advancements and political identities have been shaped by the foreign educational and political experiences of elites.[62] As some Chinese scholars have observed, the early Nationalist government was "pro-Japanese," largely because its ruling class was composed of many returnees from Japan. The foreign policy of the Nationalist government later shifted when the number of returnees from the West, especially the United States, rose rapidly into leadership positions. As a result, the government became increasingly pro-American.

A frequently raised question in the study of modern China is why the efforts of Western-educated returnees to promote Western culture and liberal arts education largely failed. While a significant number of political and educational leaders of twentieth-century China gained experience studying abroad, the ruling elite during the first three decades of the PRC consisted mainly of individuals who lacked that experience. In fact, a majority of these leaders were soldiers and farmers without an education beyond the elementary school level.[63] This helps explain why Mao and Maoists were obsessed with the dichotomy of the "reds versus experts," or having "reds" suppress "experts." The "reds" were cadres who had advanced their careers through the strength of their revolutionary pedigree and ideological purity, whereas the "experts" were members of the political or intellectual elite who had distinguished themselves with their educational credentials and technical skills.[64] In the Mao era, especially during the Cultural Revolution, violent social conflict and elite power struggle—at least partially—stemmed from differences in the educational and professional backgrounds of China's leaders.[65]

This historical conflict based on educational background may be of particular relevance today, since China has been witnessing a tidal wave of returnees who have gained growing influence in all walks of life in China, especially in Shanghai, the country's frontier city for international engagement. During the early years of the reform and opening-up era, Shanghai was often called the "cradle" of Chinese foreign studies. According to one study, in 1985 one-fourth of the students in the country who self-sponsored overseas education (mostly to the United States) were from one street neighborhood (*jiedao*)—Yan'an Middle Road in the Jing'an District of Shanghai. This street neighborhood is located in the former French concession and retains a strong foreign influence and overseas connections that originated during the first half of the twentieth century.[66]

China's well-funded universities are disproportionately located in a few coastal cities, as are foreign-educated returnees. In 2003, for example, Shanghai and Beijing collectively hosted approximately 58 percent of the total number of returnees in the country.[67] According to Chinese official media, two quantitative studies conducted in 2009 and 2015 showed that Shanghai was home to one-quarter of the country's foreign-educated returnees and welcomed more returnees than Beijing. This was quite impressive, because the universities and research institutions in Beijing are far more prominent than those in Shanghai.[68] Between 2013 and 2017, approximately 150,000 foreign-educated returnees found employment in Shanghai.[69] Looking at the country overall, the regional gap in human capital is likely to become even larger over time, because foreign-educated returnees who are natives of Shanghai and other coastal cities are often unwilling to work in China's less wealthy inland or western regions.

Foreign-educated returnees in Shanghai have established many clubs and alumni associations in the city, strengthening their ties with one another. The Shanghai Returnees Center (*shanghai haigui zhongxin*), which was established in July 2009, presently has 18,000 registered members.[70] The Center has regularly organized forums and social gatherings, and it shares online essays written by members about economic issues, education, the environment, and entertainment.

To recruit more scientists and other talented professionals to Shanghai, in 2017 the Shanghai municipal government established a high-level scientific and technical expert database—the first of its kind in the country. In 2018, it was reported that the database had gathered information on the professional backgrounds of about 245,000 individuals (including 110,000 foreigners, 40,000 overseas Chinese, 48,000 specialists in Shanghai, and 47,000 specialists in other parts of the country), covering 333 fields in the natural sciences, social sciences, medicine, and more.[71] Just one year before, 215,000 foreigners were working in Shanghai, accounting for about 24 percent of foreigners in the country and ranking Shanghai as first among China's thirty-one province-level entities for the number of foreign professionals.[72] As early as 2004, foreign-educated returnees had established about 3,000 private enterprises in Shanghai.[73] That number has increased to over 5,000 enterprises at present. Additionally, in 2018 Shanghai schools enrolled 61,400 foreign students, second only to Beijing for the number of foreign students hosted.[74] Chapter 8 elaborates on the significant impact of U.S.-China educational exchanges on Shanghai's higher-education sector.

THE LARGEST STUDY ABROAD MOVEMENT IN CHINESE HISTORY

The contemporary Chinese study abroad movement, starting in the early years of the reform era, is undoubtedly the largest in Chinese history in terms of both the number of students and the duration of the period (see table 7-1). From 1978 to 2020, a total of 5,857,100 PRC nationals studied abroad. Among them, over 1.5 million people are still studying and conducting research abroad and over 4.3 million have completed their studies. Of the latter, over 3.6 million have returned to China, accounting for 85 percent of those who completed their foreign study programs.[75] The other 671,800 people (12 percent) have settled down in foreign countries. In recent years, this study abroad movement has rapidly accelerated. Figure 7-1 provides an overview of the annual number of Chinese students and scholars studying abroad and returning from 1978 to 2018, illustrating the exponential increase. In 2000, the total number of PRC nationals that left China to study abroad was 38,989, a number that grew to 662,100 in 2018—a seventeenfold increase in eighteen years.

Participants in the current study abroad movement are more diverse in terms of age and education level, and there is greater diversity in the source of funds used than any in previous study abroad movement in Chinese history. The Chinese government uses the term "foreign-educated personnel" (*liuxue renyuan*) to refer to all PRC citizens who go abroad to study or engage in academic endeavors. This group includes recent high school graduates over 18 years old who go abroad to pursue undergraduate studies, as well as established scholars in their sixties.[76] It also includes candidates for various academic degrees or visiting scholars at foreign universities. A review of the different periods of the study abroad movements during the

FIGURE 7-1. The number of Chinese students and scholars studying abroad and returning, 1978–2018

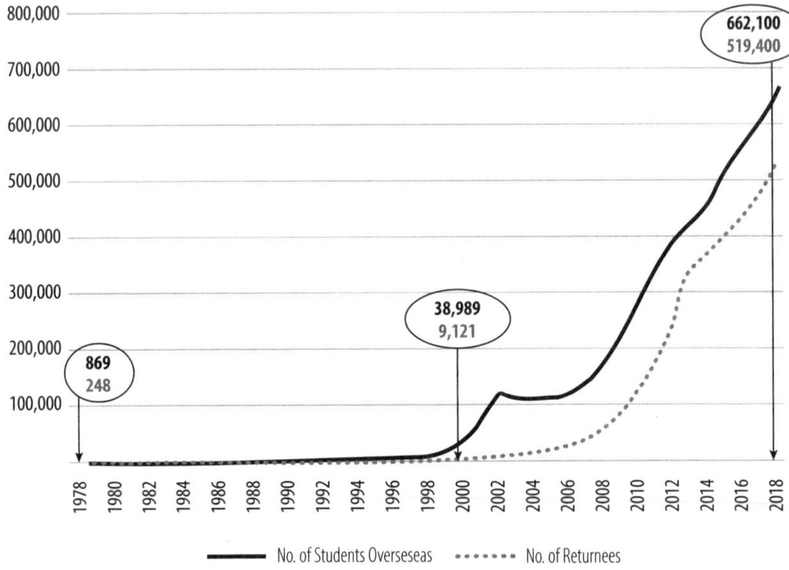

Source: Ministry of Education of the People's Republic of China website, "*2018 Niandu woguo chuguo liuxue renyuan qingkuang tongji*" [Statistics on Chinese students studying abroad in 2018], March 27, 2019, www.moe.gov.cn/jyb_xwfb/gzdt_gzdt/ s5987/201903/t20190327_375704.html; and Jiang Bo, "*Sishinian chuguo liuxue yu gaige kaifang*" [China's forty-year study abroad movement in the era of reform and opening up], a speech delivered at the 2018 Academic Annual Meeting of China Education Development Strategy Society, December 3, 2018. Assembled by Cheng Li.

reform era shows three important trends in sponsorship, type and level of studies, and destination countries.

Sponsorship

In terms of funding, Chinese students and scholars who study abroad are classified into three categories: (1) state-sponsored students and scholars (*guojia gongpai*), referring to those who were selected by the central government to be sent abroad; (2) institution-sponsored students (*danwei gongpai*), referring to those selected by local governments and institutions to be sent abroad; and (3) self-sponsored students and scholars (*zifei*), referring to Chinese nationals who are funded by themselves, relatives, friends, or foreign institutions. Over the past few decades, the study abroad population has gone from being equally distributed between state- or institution-sponsored students and self-sponsored students, to being dominated by self-sponsored students.

At the end of 1978, the first group of Chinese scholars and students in the study abroad movement were entirely state sponsored. After the establishment of diplomatic relations between the PRC and the United States in 1979, the Fulbright program between the two countries was reinstated, and the first group of Fulbright scholars exchanged the following year. Soon afterward, overseas Chinese scientists and scholars Li Zhengdao (Tsung-Dao Lee), Yang Zhenning (Chen-ning Franklin Yang), Wu Rui (Ray Jui Wu), Ding Zhaozhong (Samuel C. C. Ting), Chen Xingshen (Shiing-shen Chern), Zou Zhizhuang (Gregory C. Chow), and Harvard Professor William von Eggers Doering, helped connect Chinese academic institutions with American universities and initiate some educational collaborations. They successively launched the China–United States Physics Examination and Application program, the China–United States Biochemistry Examination and Application program, the Experimental Physics Graduate Program, the Mathematics Graduate Program, the Exchanges in Economics with the PRC Program, and the Chemistry Graduate Program or Doering Program.[77] These U.S.-China exchange programs significantly broadened the channels for Chinese students and scholars to study in the United States, funneling many talented Chinese undergraduates to postgraduate programs at top American universities.

In addition, various U.S.– and Hong Kong–based foundations have also funded important study-abroad programs. Examples include the Ford Foundation–funded economics, law, and international relations exchange programs, and the Pao Yu-Kong and Pao Zhao-Long Scholarship for Chinese Students Studying Abroad. These programs have sent thousands of Chinese students and scholars to the United States for further education. In general, Chinese state-funded programs have usually focused on the natural sciences and engineering, while study abroad programs promoted by the U.S. government and nongovernmental organizations have often emphasized the humanities and social sciences. From 1984 to 1988, the first few years of the study abroad movement in the reform era, there was about an equal share of students—50 percent in each category—who were either state- or institution-sponsored and self-sponsored.[78]

Since the mid-1980s, among the three types of funding for studying abroad, self-sponsorship has increased the most significantly. The total number of self-sponsored students increased from 1,000 in 1983 to 10,000 in 1986, and then to 100,000 in 1987—a 100 percent increase over just a few years.[79] Since the mid-1990s, self-sponsored students have consistently accounted for about 90 percent of the total number of students studying abroad.[80] In 2018, among the 662,100 students and scholars who went overseas, over 30,000 (4.6 percent) were state sponsored, over 35,000 (5.4 percent) were institution sponsored, and over 596,000 (90 percent) were self-sponsored.[81] The prevalence of self-sponsored students over the past three decades is a direct result of the birth and growth of the Chinese middle class, whose members can afford to send their children to study abroad.

Type and Level of Foreign Studies

Between the first decade of the reform era and more recent years, China's study abroad movement has experienced shifts in two primary areas: changing from mostly visiting scholars to mostly degree candidates, and from mostly graduate students to mostly undergraduates. During the initial period of the study abroad movement, a majority of "foreign-educated personnel" were visiting scholars. According to PRC scholar Miao Danguo's study, between 1978 and 1982, of the 9,179 state-sponsored students abroad, 6,843 (75 percent) were visiting scholars, 1,496 (16 percent) were graduate students, and 840 (9 percent) were undergraduates.[82]

The number of students who have gone abroad to enroll in degree programs has increased significantly since the 1990s. This change can be attributed to the uptick in students who passed the national college entrance examination after the Cultural Revolution, completed their undergraduate and master's degree studies in China, and thus were more competitive for postgraduate programs in the West and Japan. According to the PRC Ministry of Education, between 2006 and 2008, approximately 130,000 Chinese citizens left to study abroad each year.[83] During the same period, the State Foreign Studies Fund provided full scholarships to around 5,000 students annually to pursue advanced degrees abroad. In 2009, the Fund provided scholarships for 12,000 students, half of whom were enrolled in graduate programs for master's or doctorate degrees.[84]

The trend toward mostly degree candidates studying abroad is particularly evident in the case of Chinese students in the United States. Among all PRC students studying abroad in the 1988–1989 academic year, the percentage of graduate students reached a high of 93 percent. During the 1996–1997 academic year, 42,503 PRC students were enrolled in degree-granting programs at American universities, while there were only 9,724 PRC visiting scholars in the United States. Among the PRC students in the United States that year, approximately 77 percent were graduate students.[85]

In the past decade, however, the number of Chinese students pursuing an undergraduate degree in the United States has surpassed the number of graduate students studying in the United States. In the 2006–2007 academic year, about 80 percent of Chinese students studying in the United States were graduate students, and the proportion of undergraduates was less than 15 percent. In the past ten years, the percentage of Chinese undergraduates in the U.S. has grown to 40 percent in the 2013–2014 academic year, with the proportion of graduate students dropping during the same period from 71 percent to 42 percent.[86]

Some Ivy League universities have increased their efforts in attracting outstanding students from China. For example, in 2009 Harvard University and the University of Pennsylvania, for the first time, directly admitted 200 students from high schools in China. The number of PRC undergraduates enrolled in U.S. colleges increased from 9,309 in the 2005–2006 school year to 93,768 in the 2012–2013 school year.[87] In the 2014–2015 academic year, the number of Chinese undergraduate students in the United States reached 124,552—an increase of 13 percent over the previous year. Concurrently, the number of Chinese graduate students studying in the United States reached 120,331—an increase of 4 percent over the previous year.[88] Since the 2014–2015 school year, undergraduates make up the majority of participants in China's study abroad movement. According to data released by the U.S. Department of Homeland Security, in 2018, among all PRC students in the United States, 36 percent were pursuing bachelor's degrees, 32 percent master's degrees, 15 percent doctorate degrees, and the remaining 17 percent were in pretertiary studies.[89]

An increasing number of Chinese teenagers have also joined the study abroad movement. According to Chinese official statistics, since 1999 the number of students under the age of 18 studying abroad has grown at a rate of 40 percent per year. In 2000, about 50 percent of the 5,000 to 6,000 self-sponsored students from Guangdong Province were in primary or secondary school.[90] In the 2005–2006 academic year, only 65 Chinese students were enrolled in high schools in the United States. But by the 2012–2013 academic year, that number had skyrocketed to 23,795—a 365-fold increase in only seven years.[91] In 2011, China surpassed South Korea to become the largest source of international high school students in the United States. In 2013, there were more than 30,000 Chinese students enrolled in high schools in the United States, accounting for 46 percent of the total number of foreign high school students in the United States.[92] Again, this phenomenon largely reflects the rapid growth of the Chinese middle class, particularly the enthusiasm of middle-class families for sending their children to study abroad, especially at a young age.

This new wave of younger students studying in the West deserves scholarly attention. Given that these younger students are in their formative years for shaping their worldviews and values, one may argue that young people in Shanghai, Beijing, Shenzhen, and Guangzhou will be more similar to their peers in Taipei, Tokyo, Washington, and New York than to their parents. Despite some cultural differences, these young Chinese students and their international peers share similar lifestyles, cosmopolitan outlooks, and sociopolitical aspirations. These influences could be an important force for profound change in China.

Destination Countries

While Chinese students have made up the largest proportion of international students in the United States in recent years, the number of Chinese students going to the United States has started to decrease significantly. Since the beginning of the study abroad movement in the reform era, the United States has been the most popular destination for Chinese students and scholars. Figure 7-2 provides an overview of the astonishing increase in the number of PRC students and scholars studying in the United States—from 9 in 1978 to 25,170 in 1988, 46,858 in 1998, 81,127 in 2008, and finally to 363,341 in 2018. According to statistics provided by Duke Kunshan University, from 1978 to 2018, more than 1.6 million PRC students studied in the United States.[93] Hundreds of Chinese universities have established joint research initiatives and various exchange programs with American academic institutions. By 2017, over eighty U.S. universities had established joint undergraduate programs, and over thirty schools offered joint graduate degrees with Chinese institutions.[94]

During these four decades, the U.S.-China relationship has experienced crises such as Tiananmen in 1989, the 1996 Taiwan Strait Missile Crisis resulting from Taiwanese president Lee Teng-hui's visit to the United States, the 1999 U.S. bombing of the Chinese Embassy in Yugoslavia, and the 2001 Hainan Island incident. Some of these crises impacted U.S.-China educational exchanges. For example, as shown in figure 7-2, there is a slight decrease in Chinese students in the United States in 1996 around the Taiwan Strait Missile Crisis, and in 2001 when 9/11 occurred, leading the U.S. to issue far fewer visas to international students overall. However, in general, these crises had little to no effect on bilateral educational exchanges.

Figure 7-2 shows that the number of Chinese students coming to the United States grew rapidly following the 2007–2008 academic year, surpassing 100,000 people in the 2009–2010 academic year, 200,000 in the 2012–2013 academic year, and 300,000 in the 2014–2015 academic year. This surge of Chinese students in the United States is attributed to the November 2009 "Sino-U.S. Joint Statement" signed by U.S. president Barack Obama and Chinese president Hu Jintao in Beijing. The U.S. government promised to accept more Chinese students to study in the United States, and it provided a more

FIGURE 7-2. The rapid growth of PRC students studying in the United States, 1977–2018

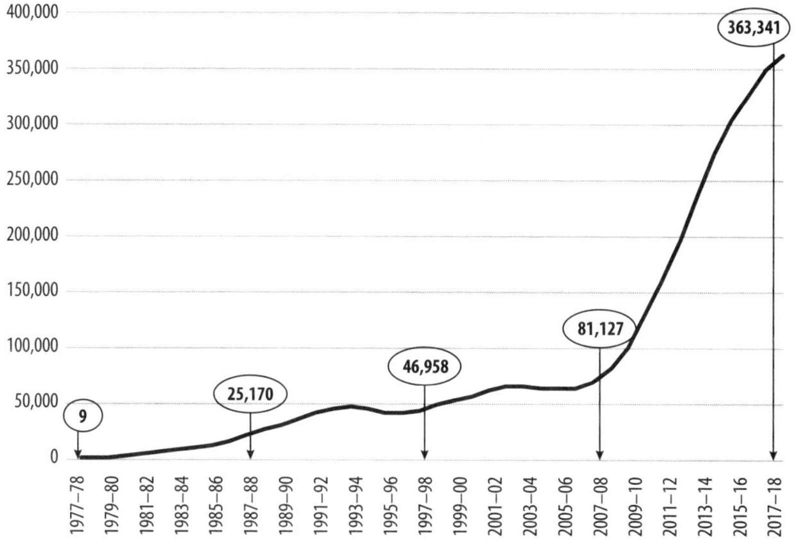

Sources: Institute of International Education, "Fast Facts from 2001 to 2018," Open Doors website, https://opendoorsdata.org/fast_facts/fast-facts-2019; Todd M. Davis, "Open Doors: Report on International Educational Exchange," ResearchGate website, January 2000, www.researchgate.net/publication/234761604_Open_Doors_Report_on_International_Educational_Exchange; and Yuan Qing and Yue Tingting, "*Xin shiqi Zhongguo liumei jiaoyu de fazhan licheng he qushi*" [The history and trends in the development of Chinese student study abroad in the United States in the new era]. *Zhongguo shehui kexue wang* [Chinese social science net], May 6, 2015, http://hprc.cssn.cn/gsyj/whs/jys/201505/t20150506_4111942.html.

Note: These figures include students attending middle/high school, undergraduate, and graduate programs. Assembled by Cheng Li.

convenient visa application process for Chinese applicants. Over the following two years, the approval rate for visas to the United States exceeded 95 percent.[95] For the 2016–2017 academic year, the total number of Chinese students and scholars in the United States surpassed 350,000. The annual growth rate of Chinese students in the U.S. between 2007 and 2009 was around 20 percent, increasing to 30 percent after the 2009–2010 academic year.

Figure 7-3 presents a remarkable increase in both the number and the proportion of Chinese students and scholars in the United States from 1995 to 2018. In the 1988–1989 academic year, out of all countries in the world, China sent the most students to study abroad in the United States for the first time, and it maintained that ranking for six consecutive years. From

FIGURE 7-3. The increase in number and proportion of PRC students studying in the United States, 1995–2018

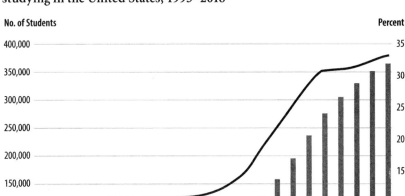

Sources: Institute of International Education, "Fast Facts from 2001 to 2018," Open Doors website, www.iie.org/Research-and-Insights/Open-Doors/Fact-Sheets-and-Info graphics/Fast-Facts; and Todd M. Davis, "Open Doors: Report on International Educational Exchange," Research Gate website, January 2000, www.researchgate.net /publication/234761604_Open_Doors_Report_on_International_Educational_ Exchange. Assembled by Cheng Li.

1994 to 1997, however, Japan took first place, and China moved to second place.[96] Since 2009, China has once again become the country with the largest number of students studying in the United States, overtaking both India and Japan. Figure 7-4 shows that the total number of Chinese students and scholars studying in the United States has significantly outnumbered that of other countries since 2009. For example, in 2017 the number of Chinese students and scholars in the U.S. surpassed 350,000 (363,341 to be exact, or 33 percent of all international students in the United States), whereas India, the number two country on the list, sent fewer than 200,000 students and scholars (196,271; 18 percent) to the United States.[97]

Although the number of PRC students and scholars in American educational institutions has increased significantly (and they are also disproportionately well represented among international students in American

FIGURE 7-4. The top ten countries of origin of students studying in the
United States, 1999–2018

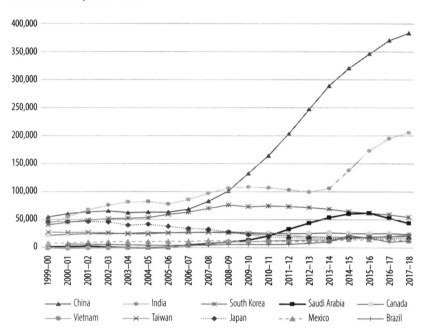

Sources: Institute of International Education, "Fast Facts from 2001 to 2018," Open Doors
website, www.iie.org/Research-and-Insights/Open-Doors/Fact-Sheets-and-Info
graphics/Fast-Facts; and Todd M. Davis, "Open Doors: Report on International Educational Exchange," Research Gate website, January 2000, www.researchgate.net
/publication/234761604_Open_Doors_Report_on_International_Educational_
Exchange. Data on Vietnamese students studying in the United States are from
https://wenr.wes.org/2014/05/higher-education-in-vietnam. Data on Saudi Arabian
students studying in the United States (2004) are from www.wsj.com/articles/SB10
001424052702304830704577492450467667154; and https://files.eric.ed.gov/fulltext
/EJ1161830.pdf. Assembled by Cheng Li.

schools), their proportion among the total number of Chinese students and
scholars studying overseas has seen a relative decline over the past four decades. The trend toward a wider range of country destinations among Chinese students has become more evident in recent years. According to Jiang
Bo of Tongji University, during the reform era, about 90 percent of Chinese
students and scholars went to the following ten countries: the United States,
Australia, Canada, Japan, the United Kingdom, South Korea, France, Germany, New Zealand, and Singapore. Among these students and academics,
about 80 percent went to the English-speaking countries.[98] More recently,
the Chinese government has made a concerted effort to send more stu-

dents and scholars to countries outside those listed above. In 2017, a total of 66,100 Chinese nationals went to study in countries participating in the Belt and Road Initiative, including Russia, which saw a 16 percent increase in Chinese students over the prior year.[99]

Among the 400,000 Chinese students who studied overseas between 1978 and 1999, approximately 165,000 (41 percent) studied in the United States.[100] Adding on the first decade of the twenty-first century (i.e., 1978 to 2008), the total number of Chinese nationals traveling abroad for their education increases to about 1.4 million, with approximately 37 percent going to the United States.[101] In 2000, the number of Chinese students in the United States increased by 54 percent compared to 1998. However, in that same year, the number of Chinese students in the United States accounted for only 27 percent of the total number of Chinese students abroad, a nearly 12 percent decrease from two years prior.

Figure 7-5 shows the distribution of PRC students and scholars by destination country in 2014. The United States had the largest percentage

FIGURE 7-5. Destination countries of Chinese students and scholars studying abroad, 2014

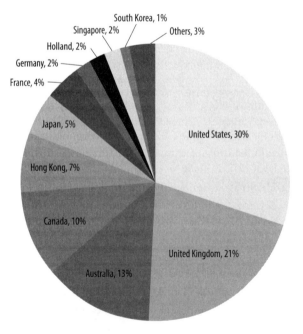

Source: "2014 nian chuguo liuxue qushi baogao" [Report on the status and trends of study abroad in 2014]. *Zhongguo jiaoyu zaixian* [China Education Online], October 12, 2014, www.eol.cn/html/lx/2014baogao/content.html. Assembled by Cheng Li.

(30 percent) of PRC citizens studying abroad, followed by the United Kingdom (21 percent), Australia (13 percent), and Canada (10 percent). These four English-speaking Western countries hosted almost three-quarters of the Chinese students and scholars pursuing foreign studies that year. However, the proportion of Chinese students and scholars in the United States compared to China's total number of overseas students and scholars has gradually—and significantly—decreased since the 1980s. As U.S.-China relations deteriorate, this trend is likely to continue.

In terms of academic fields, over the past decade there have been fewer Chinese students in the U.S. majoring in the natural sciences and engineering—which were popular during the first couple of decades of educational exchange—and more students concentrating in business and management. In the 2013–2014 academic year, for example, the top five majors for Chinese students in the United States were business and management (28 percent), engineering (20 percent), mathematics and computer science (12 percent), physics and life sciences (9 percent), and the social sciences (8 percent).[102]

However, Chinese students at differing levels of their academic careers often elect to study different subjects. In the fall of 2009, for example, 45 percent of Chinese undergraduates chose to study business, which was higher than that of graduate students. Overall, 71 percent of undergraduates concentrated in nonscientific and engineering fields, and the proportion of master's students in business and management was 36 percent, followed by engineering at 17 percent. However, among doctoral candidates from the PRC, 87 percent studied natural sciences and engineering, including mathematics, physical sciences, agriculture, and biological sciences, while only 4 percent studied business and management.[103]

TIDAL WAVES OF "SEA TURTLES" RETURNING HOME

Returnees are, of course, a diverse lot. They vary in terms of foreign experience, professional expertise, political affiliation, and worldview, as well as in the ways they interact with the Chinese party-state system. Most of them work in educational and research institutions or in various industries in the business sector. The official Chinese definition of a returnee (*liuxue huiguo renyuan*) is someone who was born in China, left to study overseas as a student or visiting scholar for over one year, and then returned to China to work on either a temporary or permanent basis. According to this definition, returnees do not include members of the Chinese diaspora—foreign-born ethnic Chinese or Chinese immigrants to foreign countries—who choose to live in China after time overseas.

After Deng's decision to send students and scholars to study in the

West, the Chinese government was concerned about their low return rate to China for many years. In the mid-1980s, Vice Chairman of the State Educational Commission He Dongchang went to Washington to sign a joint statement with his American counterpart, reaffirming that state-sponsored and institution-sponsored students from the PRC have "an obligation to return to their homeland."[104] However, after Tiananmen in 1989 and the U.S. government's issuance of the Chinese Student Protection Act, approximately 50,000 Chinese students and scholars obtained permanent residency in the United States. Similarly, some 10,000 PRC students and scholars in Canada, and over 20,000 in Australia, received permanent residency status, which permitted them to stay and work in those respective countries.[105]

According to official Chinese sources, between 1978 and 1995, a total of 130,000 PRC citizens were sent to study in the United States, and among them, some 20,000 (15 percent) returned.[106] Of approximately 20,000 Chinese students and scholars in Canada during that time period, some 4,000 (20 percent) returned to China. The return rate among those who went to Australia was the lowest—only 2,500 (6 percent) out of 40,000 returned. Compared to visiting scholars, degree candidates were more likely to remain in foreign countries. For example, between 1978 and 1991, among all 54,526 state-sponsored visiting scholars, 35,552 (65 percent) returned to China. By contrast, among 18,898 state-sponsored degree candidates, only 2,671 (14 percent) returned.[107] Since they had no third-party obligations, self-sponsored students had a lower return rate than state-sponsored or institution-sponsored students. Between 1978 and 1989, among the 22,000 self-funded students, less than 1,000 (5 percent) returned.[108]

Despite concern about a "brain drain" (outflow of human capital), Chinese authorities have not closed the door on foreign studies. They cannot afford to lose this important means of improving China's higher-education system and catching up in science and technology. The Chinese government considers the brain drain to be temporary and regards the immigration decisions of individuals to be reversible. Many Chinese scholars cite Taiwan as evidence for these claims, because the island experienced a "brain gain" in the 1980s after three decades of brain drain. They argue that a similar reverse flow of human capital is also likely to happen in mainland China.[109]

While keeping the door to educational exchanges wide open, Deng Xiaoping made an important appeal in 1992, three years after the Tiananmen tragedy, stating that all those who went abroad to study were welcome to return to China, "irrespective of their past political attitudes. Once they return, they will be assigned appropriate work."[110] That same year, the government announced its guiding policy regarding foreign studies, which was based on Deng's comments about the ongoing study abroad movement: "Supporting students who want to go abroad, encouraging them to return, and allowing them to come and go freely." The following year, the government announced "Project 211," which identified 100 institutions of higher education in China that would be improved to meet the "world standard" of quality of education by the beginning of the twenty-first century.[111]

Over the past two decades, Chinese leaders have made a concerted effort to raise human resources in the country. In 1998, Jiang Zemin claimed that "China should establish a few world-class universities."[112] In 2001, Zhu Rongji, then premier of the state council, spoke at the Forum of Chinese Economy, stating that China's emphasis on economic reform would no longer stress attracting capital, but instead concentrate on attracting human resources and technology.[113] At the October 2013 celebration for the 100th anniversary of the founding of the European and American Alumni Association held in Beijing, Xi Jinping used a nationalist appeal to lure Chinese students and scholars overseas to return home to fulfill the "Chinese dream."[114] Xi claimed that in the era of technological revolution, "competition for human resources has become the core of comprehensive national strength competition."[115] Xi's remark that "empty talk harms state affairs, but hard work makes China strong" (*Kongtan wuguo, shigan xing bang*) reflected his expectations for foreign-educated returnees within the tightly controlled political environment of the country.[116]

During the past two decades, the Chinese government has established programs such as the Changjiang Scholar Program, the Chunhui Plan, and the Thousand Talents Plan to recruit distinguished Chinese nationals working or studying overseas.[117] According to Chinese official statistics, among all U.S.-educated returnees from 1979 to 2013, 289 were elected as academicians of the Chinese Academy of Sciences, 68 were elected as academicians of the Chinese Academy of Engineering, 21 were elected as presidents and party secretaries of China's top nine universities, 489 were selected as Changjiang Scholars, and 836 were selected to be part of the Thousand Talents Plan.[118] Additionally, the government initiated Project 985 in 1999. The purpose of this project was to support the country's top nine universities and help them become "world-class" within thirty years.[119] To meet this goal, these elite universities have become more aggressive in recruiting scholars from overseas, including both foreign-educated Chinese nationals and foreign nationals.

Most importantly, during the past decade or so, China has witnessed a tidal wave of returnees, with some 519,400 foreign-educated Chinese citizens returning to the PRC in 2018 alone (see figure 7-1). By comparison, in that year a total of 662,100 Chinese students went abroad to study. Figure 7-1 shows that the increase of returnees between 1978 and 2018 corresponds with the increase in Chinese citizens leaving to study abroad during the same period, and that the return rate was much lower in the earlier years of the reform era study abroad movement. For example, the return rate of Chinese students studying abroad in 1979 was only 10 percent, increasing to about 50 percent in 1992.[120] In 2016, the total number of Chinese students studying abroad was 544,500, and the total number of returnees was 432,500 (79 percent). The previously large gap between the number of students going abroad and the number of students returning in a given year has gradually narrowed. As many Chinese nationals are still pursuing their studies abroad, an even greater number are expected to return to China in the years to come.

FINAL THOUGHTS

The history of contemporary China is also the history of the multifaceted interactions and exchanges between the Chinese people and the outside world. Foreign-educated returnees have often played a crucial role in political change, socioeconomic life, cultural and ideological dissemination, and science and technology development in China. Political leaders like Sun Yat-sen, Chiang Kai-shek, Chen Duxiu, Li Dazhao, Hu Shi, Zhou Enlai, Deng Xiaoping, Chiang Ching-kuo, Jiang Zemin, and Li Peng all studied and worked abroad early in their careers, and they have played outsized roles in shaping the trajectory of contemporary China.

China's study abroad movement in the reform era is highly significant. In Xi Jinping's words, it has been the "largest, most extensive and unprecedentedly wide-ranging study abroad movement" in China's long history.[121] This ongoing movement will likely continue to gain momentum, partly because more of the rapidly emerging Chinese middle class can afford to send their children abroad, and partly because the Chinese government has been steadily increasing funding for postgraduate education overseas with the pronounced goal of making China a global power by the middle of this century.

Policymakers in China and the United States had different agendas when planning these far-reaching educational exchanges four decades ago. For Deng Xiaoping, the primary goal was to "make up for the years lost" during the Cultural Revolution—a decade during which China was almost completely cut off from the international academic community.[122] Today, it is clear that Deng's goal has been met. Yet Chinese authorities have always been concerned about what Deng called the "spiritual pollution" and "bourgeois liberalization" of Chinese students after their exposure to liberal views and values in Western countries, especially because—in the words of Jiang—these students are "too young, too simple, sometimes naïve" (which is similar to his views of Hong Kong journalists). Xi Jinping's tight political control of the media and nongovernmental organizations—and his rejection of universal values—seems to be a manifestation of the CCP leadership's continuing anxiety about and resistance to Western political and ideological influence.

Four decades of U.S. scholars and institutions helping to train China's best and brightest has convincingly demonstrated the generosity, openness, and soft power of American society. Of course, this U.S. open-door policy toward Chinese students and scholars has been partially motivated by self-interest. For American universities, the revenue generated over the most recent decade or so from PRC students paying full U.S. tuition is a significant benefit. Additionally, in terms of U.S. foreign policy, educational exchanges with non-Western countries have long been considered by some decisionmakers to be an excellent form of cultural diplomacy.[123] In the words of U.S. president Dwight D. Eisenhower, "Just as war begins in the minds of men, so does peace."[124] Education, U.S. policymakers believe, may be a vital means for imbuing the future leaders of foreign countries with American values and ideas.[125] However, U.S. policymakers also recognize that PRC students not only encounter liberal ideas on American campuses and in society at large, but also have access to the most advanced science and technology research the United States can offer. Concern and fear over this issue have grown rapidly in recent years, especially because it appears that China's advancement in science and technology has begun to challenge America's long-standing supremacy. For some U.S. policymakers and strategists, the premises on which U.S.-China educational exchanges were founded have failed on all fronts.

Is this U.S. assessment of policy failure premature and shortsighted? How can policymakers develop a more balanced and insightful evaluation of the impact of educational exchanges on today's world? The macrolevel analyses in this chapter have illuminated the broad patterns and trends in educational exchanges. The microlevel examination in chapters 8 and 9 may be particularly valuable for addressing critically important questions, as well as for broadening perspectives during this challenging time for the U.S.-China bilateral relationship.

CHAPTER 8

The Impact of Educational Exchanges

Returnees in Shanghai

We must try to expand the boundaries of human wisdom, empathy and perception, and there is no way of doing that except through education.
—J. WILLIAM FULBRIGHT

It's not that Shanghai people are smart.
It's that smart people come to Shanghai.
—ZHU RONGJI

What do the following people—Chen Danqing, Chen Zhu, Jin Xing, Shen Nanpeng, Xu Kuangdi, Yao Ming, Yuan Yue, Zhang Wenhong, and Zhu Min—have in common? Very little; they differ profoundly from one another in terms of generational attributes, personal characteristics, professional identities, and political views. However, all of them are accomplished celebrities and household names in China, and they are all both Shanghainese *and* returnees. They were either born and raised in Shanghai or spent at least most of their adult life in the city, only to later return from overseas studies.

- Chen Danqing is a graduate of China Central Academy of Fine Arts. He later spent over a decade in New York pursuing a career as an artist, and he is most well known for his "Tibetan paintings." This series embodies Chen's strong critique of both the long-standing, Soviet socialist realism influence on oil painting in China, and the trend of patronizing depictions of Tibetans, which was common at the time. After resigning from his professorship at the Tsinghua Fine Arts School in

2007 in protest of the school's dogmatic admissions policy and lack of academic freedom, Chen has settled down in Shanghai and continuously engaged in artistic creation and political commentary.

- Chen Zhu, a Shanghai native who holds an M.D. from Shanghai Second Medical University and a Ph.D. from Paris Diderot University (Paris 7) in France, is one of the world's leading hematology experts. After his residency at a hospital in Paris, he returned to Shanghai in 1989 and worked as a physician at Ruijin Hospital, first as director of the molecular biology laboratory at the Shanghai Institute of Hematology and then as director of the Institute. As a non–Chinese Communist Party (CCP) member, Chen served as minister of health for six years (2007–2013). Because of his accomplishments in medical research and public health work, Chen has been granted membership in several prestigious academies, including the U.S. National Academy of Medicine, the U.S. National Academy of Sciences, the French Academy of Sciences, the U.K. Academy of Medical Sciences, and the Academy of Sciences for the Developing World.

- Jin Xing is a transgender ballet dancer who studied modern dance in New York and taught dance in Rome in the late 1980s and early 1990s. She returned to Shanghai where she not only founded a contemporary dance company but also became a cultural icon and household name for her televised *Jin Xing Show*. This was the highest-rated late-night show, first in Shanghai and then throughout the entire country, and through it Jin introduced Western middle-class lifestyles and values to Chinese audiences in a thought-provoking manner. In the beginning of 2021, Jin Xing took on a new role running Paramount, a historical nightclub and dance hall in Shanghai, with a commitment to revitalize this cultural hub.

- Shen Nanpeng, a graduate of Shanghai Jiaotong University and Yale University, currently serves as the founder and managing partner of Sequoia Capital China. In this role, he has launched and invested in many successful artificial intelligence firms and e-commerce companies, such as Ctrip.com, Home Inns, the Ant Financial Service Group, and Toutiao. He had previously worked as an investment banker at Deutsche Bank Hong Kong, Chemical Bank, Lehman Brothers, and Citibank. He has been actively engaged in philanthropic work and educational exchanges in both China and the United States, contributing to the establishment of the Yale Beijing Center. In 2020, for the third consecutive year, *Forbes* magazine named him the World's Top Venture Capital Investor.

- Xu Kuangdi, a professor of engineering who taught in Shanghai for a quarter-century earlier in his career, later served as mayor of Shanghai for six years (1995–2001). A returnee from Europe, where he was a visiting professor at Imperial College London and deputy chief engineer at a company in Sweden, Xu's technocratic leadership was instrumental in the urban transformation of Shanghai. After serving as mayor, Xu was president of the Chinese Academy of Engineering for a decade, and he currently serves as a lead consultant for the Beijing-Tianjin-Hebei integration project, including the construction of the Xiong'an New Area.

- Yao Ming, who played for both the Shanghai Sharks and the Houston Rockets and is widely recognized as the most famous Chinese basketball player, returned to his native Shanghai in 2011 after eight seasons with the Rockets in the National Basketball Association (NBA). In addition to serving as chairman of the Chinese Basketball Association, Yao is active in many other causes, including elephant conservation, tobacco control, HIV/AIDS awareness, education for underprivileged children, and the promotion of mutual understanding between China and the United States.

- Yuan Yue is a new Shanghainese (a nonnative Shanghai resident) who founded the Horizon Research Consultancy Group in Shanghai in 1992. He is a returnee from the United States, where he received a master of public administration degree from Harvard Kennedy School in 2001, participated in the Yale World Fellows program in 2007, and took part in the Aspen Scholar program from 2013 to 2015. Yuan's Horizon Research Consultancy Group, the first privately owned, large-scale survey company in China, conducts market research, opinion polls, policy evaluations, and internal management surveys. Over the past two decades, through his frequent media exposure, Yuan has been actively engaged in social issues, such as the protection and promotion of property rights, support of migrant workers, and protection of the rights of underprivileged social groups and persons with disabilities.

- Zhang Wenhong, a medical doctor who became a household name in China during the country's battle over COVID-19, is the head of the Center for Infectious Disease at the Huashan Hospital of Fudan University. Since the outbreak of novel coronavirus, Dr. Zhang has served as head of Shanghai's Anti-COVID-19 clinical expert team of sixty medical specialists. Shanghai had been expected to have a high infection rate and death toll, but by November 2020, it had had only 1,259 cases of infection (including imported cases from abroad) and seven deaths. The low numbers were partly attributed to the outstanding work in prevention and treatment by Dr. Zhang's team. He was particularly praised on Chinese social media for his role in candidly and frequently disseminating useful information and scientific knowledge during a time when people felt in the dark about the coronavirus epidemic. Zhang is a graduate of Shanghai Medical University and has held visiting scholar and postdoctoral fellow positions at Harvard Medical School and Illinois State University at Chicago.

- Zhu Min, a graduate of Fudan, Princeton, and Johns Hopkins, who later served as vice governor of the People's Bank of China and deputy managing director of the International Monetary Fund (IMF), is the first Chinese person to serve in a high office at this important international organization. He played a key role in strengthening the IMF's engagement with Asia and emerging economies, in addition to promoting sustainable growth and financial stability. A frequent speaker at major global economic forums, Zhu remains one of the most articulate and influential economists in the world since he returned to China in 2016 after completing his five-year term at the IMF.

These individuals exemplify the omnipresent and growing influence of returnees in Shanghai. In a way, as many of them have publicly claimed, they represent the interests and concerns of the public, especially the new middle class in the city—whether as part of the system as government officials, outside the system as social and intellectual critics, or as mediators between these two realms. Regardless of their political positions, together they have helped shape socioeconomic life, intellectual discourse, and public opinion in China primarily through their work in Shanghai.

The area most strongly influenced by foreign-educated returnees in China is, unsurprisingly, higher education. Today, an overwhelming majority of professors at leading Chinese universities, as well as most college administrators, have studied in foreign countries, either as degree candidates or as visiting scholars. The strong international ties of these educators have played a vital role in curriculum development, program building, scientific and technological innovation, social science research, policy and scholarly debates, and most importantly, the training of China's future generations of leaders. Chinese who spend time abroad—whether they enroll in self-funded or foreign-funded bachelor's or graduate degree programs, or take long-term teaching roles, or participate in one-year visiting scholar programs—all encounter a wide variety of experiences. However, the concept of the "sea turtle" (returnee), as discussed in chapter 7, is broad enough to reflect both the diversity of the Chinese study abroad movement and its contributions to the development of China's higher education.

This chapter provides a more detailed analysis of the representation of returnees in China's higher education system and the top law firms in Shanghai. The first part offers an overview of the growing representation of foreign-educated returnees in China's universities. By examining comprehensive biographical, personal, professional, and academic background information, this analysis reveals important patterns in both the returnees' foreign studies and distinct characteristics of those who served as senior administrators at Chinese universities in the first decade of this century. The second part focuses on the current, dominant role of Western-educated returnees in higher education in Shanghai. It addresses questions about how returnee administrators today differ from those about a decade ago, and how these differences can shed valuable light on the educational development and political trajectory of the country in the years to come. The third and final part explores the prevalence of returnees in two critically important areas: political leadership at both the national and municipal levels, and senior partnerships in law firms in Shanghai, reflecting the omnipresence of returnees in this pace-setting city.

THE GROWING REPRESENTATION OF RETURNEES IN CHINA'S HIGHER EDUCATION SYSTEM

Sources and Research Methodology

This study is based on three databases constructed by the author starting from 2002. The first database contains the biographical and professional backgrounds of 2,044 returnees who taught at China's top twenty-five universities during the first decade of the twenty-first century. These universities have been identified by selecting from the top twenty institutions from rankings produced by two different Chinese research groups in 2002 and 2003.[1] Due to the overlap between the two lists, there are a total of twenty-five universities featured on one or both of the top-twenty ranking lists.[2]

All institutions that are part of "the top nine universities in 'Project 985' or the 'C9 League'" (*jiuxiao lianmeng*) are included in this study. Project 985 was initiated by the Chinese government in May 1998 with the goal of developing a group of leading universities in the People's Republic of China (PRC) to become "world-class universities" (*shijie zhiming daxue*). The first batch of institutions in Project 985—the nine most prestigious universities in the PRC—were selected in 2003, and they included Peking University, Tsinghua University, Fudan University, Shanghai Jiaotong University, Nanjing University, Zhejiang University, China University of Science and Technology, Harbin Institute of Technology, and Xi'an Jiaotong University. Subsequently, Project 985 has added an additional thirty universities, for a total of thirty-nine universities in the project. According to government plans, the latter thirty universities are also meant to become "world-renowned high-level universities" (*shijie zhiming gao shuiping daxue*). The C9 League universities, or the first batch of Project 985 institutions, account for only 1 percent of the faculty members in China's higher education system, but they receive one-third of the country's research funding.

The biographical information of these 2,044 returnees was collected primarily from university websites. This study includes all returnees for whom biographical data are available on the websites of the top twenty-five universities, so their inclusion in the database is not based on scientific and objective criteria. Nevertheless, their information provides a considerable pool from which to analyze the characteristics of returnees in China's top universities.

The second database contains the biographical and professional information of approximately 936 senior administrators at 134 universities. Senior administrators include presidents, party secretaries, vice presidents, and deputy party secretaries. Chinese universities utilize "administrative systems of dual leaders" (i.e., party secretary and president). Both are considered the most important decisionmakers at a university.[3] Deans of institutions and schools within a university are not included in this database, with the exception of those who concurrently hold senior positions at the university level.

These 134 universities were selected based on the Chinese University Ranking compiled by China's Internet University in 2002.[4] This ranking includes around 1,000 Chinese higher education institutions, and the top forty universities on this list have all been included in this study. All forty top universities belong to "Project 211," which was initiated by the Chinese government in 1995 (even earlier than Project 985) in preparation for the twenty-first century. The Chinese Ministry of Education selected around 100 high-level universities in the country to receive more funding for research and to send more faculty members to study abroad. For example, from 1996 to 2000, approximately $2.2 billion was allocated to Project 211.[5] According to the Chinese official *People's Daily*, by 2008, 116 universities (about 6 percent of the total number of higher education institutions) had been designated Project 211 universities. Altogether, these 116 universities (including the C9 League's top nine universities) were responsible for training four-fifths of doctoral students and two-thirds of master's degree students in China. They oversee 85 percent of the state's key research projects, host 96 percent of China's main research laboratories, and receive 70 percent of the country's scientific research funding.[6]

These forty top universities have official websites that contain information about the current school administrators (*xianren lingdao*). The other ninety-four schools included in the second database were chosen based on two factors. First, only schools with websites that provided biographical information about their current leaders were chosen. Second, in the interest of geographic diversity, the location of a school influenced its inclusion in the database. Therefore, this database is more objective and systematic with respect to the sources from which it draws.

Of course, not all senior administrators from these schools are returnees. In fact, as this study reveals, only 313 (33 percent) of the 936 senior administrators are returnees. This variation allows for a comparison between senior administrators who are returnees and domestically trained senior administrators. According to a 2003 study of faculty profiles conducted by Chinese scholar Chen Xuefei, 102 of 132 (77 percent) top administrators of colleges, departments, research institutes, research centers, and key state labs were returnees.[7] Compared to this study, the percentage of administrators who studied abroad is higher in Chen's research. There are three possible explanations for this difference. First, returnees may have greater representation in China's two "super" universities (i.e., Tsinghua University and Peking University) than in other top schools, and Chen's study has more faculty from these universities in his data set. Second, administrators who were returnees were usually at the department level rather than the university level of leadership at the time, and this study is restricted to the university level. Third, many returnee administrators may serve as assistant presidents, a category often labeled as university-level administrators, but they are not included in this study.

In addition to the information found on school websites, this study makes use of online search engines, both in China and overseas, for additional information about prominent Chinese college administrators.[8] These websites occasionally make available, though often unsystematically, biographical information about college administrators.

This study has also compiled information from other official Chinese sources, for example, the *Yearbook of Who's Who in China*, which provides biographies of newly appointed senior administrators at top Chinese universities.[9] Recently published Chinese books on the achievements of returnees have been particularly helpful in providing detailed information on prominent Chinese educational leaders.[10] The diverse sources of information described here complement one another and allow for cross-verification of data about the educational elites analyzed in this study.

Senior administrators at top universities are considered to be high-ranking officials (usually vice-minister-level) in the country. The position of a senior administrator is often an important stepping-stone for further promotion within the Chinese government. Chen Xi, previously party secretary of Tsinghua University, now serves as director of the CCP Central Organization Department and "personnel chief" for Xi Jinping. He is currently a Politburo member. Former Tsinghua University president Chen Jining currently serves as mayor of Beijing. Another example is Shen Changyu, previously executive vice president of Zhengzhou University, who is now director of the State Intellectual Property Office in the State Council and an alternate member of the Central Committee of the CCP.

The third database focuses exclusively on Shanghai and contains two subsets. The first subset on Shanghai includes 122 top administrators (i.e., presidents, vice presidents, party secretaries, and deputy party secretaries) of the top ten universities in Shanghai. The selection of the top ten universities is based on the 2019 Shanghai University Comprehensive Strength Ranking, including a case study of Fudan University.[11] All data are based on the official websites of these universities and supplemented with information from Baidu biographies and author interviews. The second Shanghai subset focuses on the educational backgrounds of the partners at the top five law firms in Shanghai, a total of 613 partners. The top five law firms were chosen based on the 2018 Shanghai Bar Association annual ranking.[12] These two subsets on Shanghai were assembled between 2017 and 2019 and last updated in July 2020.

The biographical and professional information—including age, gender, birthplace, current positions, academic achievements, administrative experience, political background, educational level, schools attended as a degree candidate, visiting scholar or postdoctoral fellow experience, academic fields of expertise, academic titles, foreign experiences, and duration of foreign studies—of each individual is coded into the database for quantitative analysis. For clarity, the first study pool of returnees is labeled "returnee professors." The second pool of university senior administrators is labeled "senior administrators," and the pool of administrators who studied abroad is labeled "returnee senior administrators" or "returnee administrators." The third pool of Fudan University senior administrators is labeled "Fudan administrators" or "Fudan returnee administrators," and the pool of partners of Shanghai law firms is labeled "Shanghai returnee lawyers."

Findings in 2005 Data

China's returnee professors and senior administrators are predominantly male: 86 percent and 93 percent, respectively. This is striking given that the number of female college students and faculty members has increased during the reform era. The percentage of female college students, for example, increased from 24 percent of the undergraduate student body in 1978 to

34 percent in 1990, 38 percent in 1998, 50 percent in 2010, and 52 percent in 2018.[13] At the postgraduate level, the proportion of women increased from 10 percent in 1980, to 23 percent in 1990, 50 percent in 2010, and 53 percent in 2016.[14] In 2010, female students accounted for 36 percent of the Ph.D. candidates in the country, a figure that increased to 39 percent in 2016.[15]

It remains to be seen whether this marked increase in female students at Chinese universities over the past two decades will affect the extreme gender imbalance at the leadership level of Chinese universities. A comparison between the pool of senior college administrators and the pool of returnee senior administrators in the first decade of this century reveals that there are even fewer female administrators who studied abroad (only 6 percent). As overseas universities tend to admit applicants on a gender-blind basis, a large number of PRC women are now receiving education abroad. According to official Chinese statistics, women accounted for 58 percent of China's foreign-educated returnees in 2013.[16]

An overwhelming proportion of returnee professors and senior administrators (including both domestically trained personnel and returnees) are ethnic Han Chinese. Although China has its own affirmative action policies to promote the recruitment of students and faculty members who are ethnic minorities, only 0.3 percent of returnee professors and 2 percent of both senior administrators and senior returnee administrators at China's top universities are non-Han Chinese. Thus, compared with the ethnic composition of China's population, ethnic minorities are underrepresented among Chinese university faculty and administrators.

The age distribution of returnee professors shows that a majority (52 percent) are in their late thirties and forties. Studies suggest that this group is the most productive age group across multiple countries. The relatively small percentage (22 percent) of returnee professors in their fifties is largely the result of the "Lost Generation phenomenon"—those who were unable to complete their schooling beyond elementary or junior high school due to the turmoil of the Cultural Revolution. Despite the name, this phenomenon does not actually mean that an entire generation of qualified faculty members in Chinese higher education was lost. Some members of the Lost Generation entered college during the late 1970s when Deng reinstituted the university entrance examination, and some were also able to study abroad later. The large number of faculty members with foreign study experience in the West has, in fact, helped to fill the gap created by the Cultural Revolution.

Thus concerns that pre–Cultural Revolution Chinese academic leaders were aging, and that their scheduled retirement at the turn of the century would create a major shortage of qualified faculty members, appear to have been overstated.[17] The tidal wave of returnees from the large-scale study abroad movement in the reform era brought back many new academics ready to step into faculty positions. In the late 1990s and early 2000s, a majority of senior administrators were in their forties and fifties, with about 86 percent of the entire pool of senior administrators and returnee senior administrators falling within this age bracket. As for the returnee professors, about 76 percent were in their fifties or younger. In the future, prospective returnees will likely be even younger given that students who went overseas during the 1990s were on average ten years younger than the students who studied abroad during the 1980s.[18]

Examining the birth provinces of returnee professors and administrators reveals that more than half of them were born in East China. Natives of Jiangsu alone account for 16 percent of returnee professors and 18 percent of returnee senior administrators in this study. This overrepresentation of Eastern China natives aligns with similar trends in studies of political, economic, and military elites in the reform era.[19] For example, there are twenty-four (9 percent) Shanghai natives with experience abroad serving as senior administrators. By comparison, none of the returnee senior administrators in this study were born in Tianjin, one of four municipalities with provincial status in the country.

The uneven geographic distribution of where returnees found careers in China is probably even more significant. In addition to Shanghai, as mentioned earlier in this book, Beijing and Jiangsu are also home to a large number of returnees.[20] By contrast, very few are found at universities in inland China. Because most returnees have settled in coastal regions, Chinese authorities have worked to recruit more of these individuals to China's inland regions in recent years. The Ministry of Education has established an Office of Returnee Affairs, which encourages them to find work in western China. The western provinces also have representatives in Beijing charged with contacting students and scholars abroad.[21]

Among the 2,500 state-sponsored students and scholars sent abroad in 2002, only three were from Qinghai Province in northwest China. At the same time, of the entire population of Qinghai province, only twelve people had doctorate degrees (including both foreign-trained and domestically trained individuals), with eight of them actually working and living in the province. This study of returnee professors and senior administrators reaffirms the geographic imbalance of returnees in coastal regions compared to inland ones. This regional disparity in higher education institutions generally, and foreign-educated instructors in particular, highlights a long-standing problem in the country. The regional gap is likely to become even larger over time, as returnees who are natives of Shanghai, Beijing, and other rich coastal cities will likely remain unwilling to work in China's inland regions.

Table 8-1 shows the educational status of returnee professors and returnee senior administrators when they were abroad. Among 2,044 re-

TABLE 8-1. The Level of Educational Attainment Overseas of Returnee Professors and Senior Administrators, 2005

Educational attainment overseas	Returnee professors		Returnee senior administrators	
	Number	Percentage	Number	Percentage
Degree candidate	602	29.5	76	24.3
Visiting scholar (including postdoctoral fellowship)	1,253	61.3	230	73.5
Both degree candidate and visiting scholar	66	3.2		
Administrative work			7	2.2
Unknown	123	6.0		
Total	2,044	100.0	313	100.0

Source: Cheng Li's research.

turnee professors, a majority (61 percent) were visiting scholars, and almost 30 percent were degree candidates. The data on returnee senior administrators show an even higher percentage (74 percent) of them served as visiting scholars. Among these senior administrators, about 20 percent received doctorate degrees abroad and only 4 percent received master's degrees.

Analyzing the duration of study abroad experiences for professors and senior administrators in the 2005 data shows that most spent only a short time overseas. Among returnee professors and senior administrators for whom information on foreign study duration is available, 61 percent of professors and 65 percent of senior administrators studied abroad between one and two years, most as visiting scholars. Only 4 percent of returnee professors studied and worked overseas for more than ten years, and only one senior administrator, Wang Qinmin, then vice president of Fuzhou University, studied and worked in the United Kingdom for over ten years. He received his Ph.D. degree in engineering from Imperial College London.

In China, a common practice in hiring university faculty members is to recruit from a university's own alumni. This phenomenon, called "inbreeding" (*jinqin fanzhi*) by the Chinese, is often criticized by Chinese scholars for being unconducive to academic development. The new recruitment of returnees for faculty positions at Chinese universities does not seem to have changed this practice. The data from this study show that most returnee professors generally return to teach at the same institution in China from which they graduated. In fact, 63 percent of returnee professors are alumni of the same schools where they serve as faculty members, including 23 percent who received an undergraduate education at their school, 18 percent who received graduate training at their school, and 23 percent who pursued both under-graduate and graduate degrees at their school. Only 37 percent of returnee professors graduated from an institution that differs from where they work.

Notably, senior administrators are also more likely to return to their alma maters for employment. The data reveal that 75 percent of senior administrators who studied abroad and 70 percent of senior administrators overall currently serve at the same institution from which they graduated. This phenomenon may reflect the importance of political networking and patron-client ties in hiring at Chinese higher education institutions. This nepotism may hinder China's drive to build world-class universities, which requires diverse student and faculty academic backgrounds, international inclusiveness, and open competition for faculty and university administrator positions.

Table 8-2 ranks the top ten foreign countries where Chinese returnees studied. The United States ranks first among all three groups: (1) returnee professors (39 percent), (2) returnee professors with foreign doctorate degrees (30 percent), and (3) returnee senior administrators (35 percent). There is a considerable gap between the total number of Chinese students who studied in the United States and the number who studied in Japan, which ranks as the second-most-popular destination among these three pools. In the group of returnee senior administrators with foreign Ph.D. degrees, however, the United States ranks second behind Japan. This is unsurprising because, during the late 1990s, 3,000 Chinese students who received Ph.D. degrees in Japan returned to China—a substantial number.[22] Among the three groups, the proportion of those who studied in Russia was very small, ranging from 2 to 4 percent. But trends suggest that the number of scholars returning from Russia will increase in the near future, given the growing number of Chinese people electing to study in Russia. There were about 10,000 Chinese students in Russia in 2003, most of whom attended top universities in the country.[23] In 2019, that number had grown to 30,000 students.[24]

Table 8-3 shows that 73 percent of returnee professors and 71 percent of returnee professors with a Ph.D. from abroad majored in engineering and the sciences. For senior administrators, however, there is more of a difference between those who received a doctorate degree from overseas and those who did not. Among senior administrators with a foreign Ph.D., a higher percentage (87 percent) majored in the natural sciences and en-gineering, compared to senior administrators overall (64 percent). The predominance of foreign-educated professors in the fields of engineering and the natural sciences in leadership positions in China's higher educa-tion system is further highlighted by the striking contrast between China's

TABLE 8-2. Top Foreign Countries Where Returnees Studied, 2005

Country	Returnee professor (N=2,375)			Returnee professor with foreign Ph.D. (N=370)			Returnee senior administrator (N=392)			Returnee senior administrator with foreign Ph.D. (N=63)		
	Rank	No.	%	Rank	No.	%	Rank	No.	%	Rank	No.	%
USA	1	930	39.0	1	141	30.1	1	138	35.2	2	12	19.0
Japan	2	341	14.3	2	118	25.2	2	61	15.6	1	14	22.2
Germany	3	248	10.4	4	41	8.8	3	45	11.5	3	11	17.5
UK	4	244	10.2	3	43	9.2	4	43	11.0	5	6	9.5
Canada	5	148	6.2	8	12	2.6	5	27	6.9	6	2	3.2
France	6	99	4.1	5	27	5.8	6	17	4.3	4	7	11.1
Australia	7	61	2.6	7	15	3.2	8	10	2.6			
Russia	8	53	2.2	6	17	3.6	7	11	2.8	6	2	3.2
Netherlands	9	39	1.6									
Belgium	10	25	1.0	10	8	1.7	9	4	1.0			
Sweden				8	12	2.6						
Austria										6	2	3.2
Denmark							9	4	1.0	6	2	3.2
Singapore							9	4	1.0			
South Korea							9	4	1.0			
Yugoslavia										6	2	3.2

Source: Cheng Li's research.

prominent natural scientists and social scientists. While 81 percent of the members of the Chinese Academy of Sciences and 54 percent of the members of the Chinese Academy of Engineering were returnees in the early 2000s, only 4 percent of the fellows (*yanjiuyuan*) at the Chinese Academy of Social Sciences were returnees.[25]

Progress and Unresolved Inadequacies in China's Universities

In the spring of 2002, Jiang Zemin made a highly publicized visit to Renmin University in Beijing, during which he called for the promotion of research in the social sciences and philosophy. As Jiang said, "Chinese social scientists should be valued as highly as natural scientists."[26] Yet an analysis

TABLE 8-3. Academic Fields of Returnee Professors and Returnee Senior Administrators, 2005

Academic field	Returnee professors		Returnee professors with foreign Ph.D.		Senior administrators		Senior administrators with foreign Ph.D.	
	No.	%	No.	%	No.	%	No.	%
Engineering and science	1490	72.9	429	71.1	475	64.3	55	87.3
Engineering	517	25.3	163	27.0	199	26.9	25	39.7
Geology	71	3.5	23	3.8	19	2.6		
Agronomy/forestry	27	1.3	18	3.0	32	4.3	3	4.8
Biology	132	6.5	52	8.6	15	2.0	5	7.9
Physics	108	5.3	26	4.3	42	5.7	6	9.5
Chemistry	312	15.3	71	11.8	55	7.4	6	9.5
Computer science	105	5.1	17	2.8	16	2.2	2	3.2
Mathematics and statistics	56	2.7	24	4.0	50	6.8	4	6.3
Psychology	25	1.2	5	0.8	4	0.5		
Architecture	3	0.1	2	0.3	1	0.1		
Medical science	134	6.6	28	4.6	42	5.7	4	6.3
Economics and management	255	12.5	71	11.8	77	10.4	2	3.2
Economics and finance	87	4.3	46	7.6	67	9.1	2	3.2
Management (including MBA)	168	8.2	25	4.1	10	1.4		

Social sciences and law	190	9.3	51	8.5	57	7.7	1	1.6
Politics	28	1.4	15	2.5	30	4.1		
Sociology and anthropology	35	1.7	14	2.3	1	0.1		
Archaeology	2	0.1						
Public administration	24	1.2	1	0.2	1	0.1		
Party history and party affairs	2	0.1						
Journalism and communications	21	1.0	5	0.8				
Law	78	3.8	15	2.5	25	3.4	1	1.6
Asian studies			1	0.2				
Humanities	109	5.3	45	7.5	130	17.6	4	6.3
Art	1	0.0	2	0.3	4	0.5		
History	6	0.3	6	1.0	26	3.5		
Philosophy	27	1.3	12	2.0	32	4.3	1	1.6
Education	6	0.3	2	0.3	12	1.6	1	1.6
Chinese language and literature	11	0.5			42	5.7		
Foreign language and literature	58	2.8	23	3.8	14	1.9	2	3.2
Unknown			7	1.2			1	1.6
Total	2044	100.0	603	100.0	739	100.0	63	100.0

Source: Cheng Li's research.

of China's top universities at the time revealed the inadequacy of faculty resources in the social sciences and humanities, as well as the lack of university administrators in these fields.

The 2005 data on returnee professors and senior returnee administrators at China's top tier universities show unambiguously that Western-educated Chinese scholars dominate leadership positions in the country's higher education institutions. In the early 2000s, they were prevalent among both the faculty and the administration of China's universities. Due to their influence, during the reform era, China's higher education system has come to adopt many educational standards, procedures, and administrative mechanisms from Western countries, especially the United States. Notable examples include the three-level degree system (i.e., bachelor/master/doctorate degrees), the credit system, the establishment of a natural science foundation, and the tenure-track system.

These changes, however, have been constrained by several obstacles, such as the uneven geographic and demographic distributions of returnee professors, the overrepresentation of the natural sciences and engineering at the expense of the social sciences and humanities, the unrestrained nepotism of hiring an institution's own graduates as faculty members, the tight political control over academic and intellectual freedom, and the unmet promises to truly internationalize. All these factors have severely inhibited Chinese universities from fulfilling their core academic missions and objectives. An important question is whether Western-educated returnees can resolve some of these inadequacies in China's higher education system after they become an even greater majority of faculty and administrators. More recent research on returnees at Shanghai's universities may shed valuable light on this inquiry.

RETURNEES IN SHANGHAI'S UNIVERSITIES:
TRENDS AND IMPACTS

Shanghai has long been a hub of China's higher educational institutions. Before the Communist takeover in 1949, there were forty-four higher education institutions in Shanghai, accounting for 25 percent of the entire nation's universities. Among them were several nationally and even internationally renowned universities, such as Jiaotong, Fudan, Tongji, Jinan, Datong, Daxia, Guanghua, Hujiang, Zhendan, and St. John's.[27] In the Mao era, as elsewhere throughout the country, these universities were either merged with one another or downsized, and they were restricted from engaging in any educational exchanges with the West. During that period, Shanghai hardly allowed students and scholars to pursue overseas studies. Between 1958 and 1978, for example, Shanghai issued only about 5,000 private passports. For the entire year of 1968, the city issued only five private passports.[28]

After Deng began reform and opening up in 1978, the number of private passports issued in Shanghai (many of which were for self-sponsored students) increased exponentially—from 10,000 in 1986 to 20,000 in 1987, and to 60,000 in 1988.[29] Also beginning in the mid-1980s, Shanghai's leadership under Jiang Zemin and Zhu Rongji became obsessed with the idea of "connecting with the world." This time-honored motto reflected China's strong desire to be accepted by the "modern world" as part of the process of economic and educational globalization.

In the area of education, higher education in Shanghai has evolved from a system exclusively for elites to one for the masses. From 2011 to 2016, a total of about 185,300 received master's degrees and 28,600 received doctoral degrees. The average years of education for the working-age population in Shanghai was about twelve years, with approximately 35 percent of the working-age population having attained higher education.[30] In 2018, the city had a total of sixty-four colleges and universities, including nineteen private colleges. There were 514,900 college students, nearly ten times more compared to forty years prior.[31] Access to universities increased, as the admission rate of ordinary higher education institutions grew close to 90 percent—22 percent higher than the rate in 2000. There were forty-nine institutions in the city for graduate students, enrolling around 158,500 full-time students in 2018.

Since the early 1990s, several Shanghai universities have established jointly run universities with foreign partners. These include the China Europe International Business School (CEIBS), cofounded by Shanghai Jiaotong University and the European Commission of the European Union in 1994;[32] SHU-UTS SILC Business School, cofounded by Shanghai University and University of Technology Sydney in 1994;[33] the Chinese-German University College, cofounded by Tongji University and the German Academic Exchange Service in 1998;[34] the Joint Institute, cofounded by the University of Michigan and Shanghai Jiaotong University in 2006;[35] and New York University Shanghai, cofounded by New York University (NYU) and East China Normal University in 2011—the first international university jointly established by the PRC and the United States.[36] Two years later in 2013, Duke University and Wuhan University cofounded Duke Kunshan University, another joint international university in Kunshan, near Shanghai.[37] At present, Jeffrey S. Lehman, an American law professor and former president of Cornell University, and Alfred Bloom, an American psychologist and the former president of Swarthmore College, serve as the executive vice chancellors of NYU Shanghai and Duke Kunshan, respectively.

By 2020, there were altogether nine joint venture universities operating in China. Besides NYU Shanghai and Duke Kunshan University, the other seven joint venture universities are University of Nottingham Ningbo in Ningbo (founded in 2004), Beijing Normal University–Hong Kong Baptist

University United International College in Zhuhai (2005), Xi'an Jiaotong–Liverpool University in Suzhou (2006), Wenzhou–Kean University in Wenzhou (2011), the Chinese University of Hong Kong in Shenzhen (2014), Guangdong Technion–Israel Institute of Technology in Shantou (2016), and Shenzhen Moscow State University–Beijing Institute of Technology in Shenzhen (2017). Of these nine joint venture universities, five are in the lower Yangtze River delta, and four are located in the Pearl River delta.[38]

Since 2009, CEIBS has been ranked by the British *Financial Times* as one of the world's top ten business schools and the number one business school in Asia.[39] In 2019, the CEIBS master of business administration program was ranked among the world's top five by the same newspaper.[40] As discussed in chapter 7, Shanghai has played a leading role in the study abroad movement during the reform era. Statistics and case studies may further prove this point. According to a Chinese official report, Shanghai sent about 80,000 students and scholars abroad from 1978 to 2003. About 70 percent of them studied in developed countries, including the United States, Japan, Great Britain, Germany, France, and Australia, and 80 percent received doctorate and master's degrees.[41]

As discussed previously, recent trends in Shanghai reveal that an increasing number of high school graduates have chosen to pursue their undergraduate education abroad rather than in China. Shanghai appears to be leading the nationwide trend of sending teenage students to study abroad. Since the mid-1990s, American Ivy League universities and other prestigious schools have also sent their admissions teams to top high schools in Shanghai to recruit undergraduates.[42]

Over the past couple of decades, the Shanghai municipal government has adopted policies to attract foreign-educated returnees to Shanghai to work. In 2003, Shanghai launched several large-scale professional recruitment projects granting three-year renewable Shanghai residence cards for overseas professionals (mainly returnees).[43] In 2009, Shanghai became the first large city in China to allow cardholders who had stayed in the city for more than seven years to apply for permanent residence (*hukou*).

In 2018, more than 510,000 foreign-educated Chinese students chose to return to their home country, marking a record high. According to research from a Chinese job seeker resource provider, in 2018, more than 36 percent of returnees selected Shanghai and Beijing as their preferred destination, while about 10 percent chose Guangzhou and Shenzhen.[44] In Shanghai, a significant number of returnees teach in the city's universities. In 2003, within the thirty-nine higher education institutions in Shanghai, 80 percent of the presidents, deans, department chairs, and leaders in academic fields were returnees.[45]

Table 8-4 displays the educational backgrounds of the highest-ranking

TABLE 8-4. Representation of Returnees among Top Administrators at the Top Ten Shanghai Universities, 2019

University	President and vice presidents		Party secretary/ deputy secretaries		Total	
	Returnees/ total	% of Returnees	Returnees/ total	% of Returnees	Returnees/ total	% of Returnees
Fudan University	8/8	100.0	5/6	83.3	13/14	92.9
Shanghai Jiaotong University	9/9	100.0	4/5	80.0	13/14	92.9
Tongji University	9/9	100.0	4/6	66.7	13/15	86.7
East China Normal University	7/7	100.0	4/6	66.7	11/13	84.6
East China University of Science and Technology	6/7	85.7	4/5	80.0	10/12	83.3
Shanghai University	6/6	100.0	2/4	50.0	8/10	80.0
Shanghai University of Finance and Economics	4/6	66.7	2/4	50.0	6/10	60.0
Donghua University	6/6	100.0	4/5	80.0	10/11	90.9
University of Shanghai for Science and Technology	4/6	66.7	2/5	40.0	6/11	54.5
Shanghai Normal University	6/7	85.7	2/5	40.0	8/12	66.7
	65/71	91.5	33/51	65.0	98/122	80.3

Sources: The ranking is based on the "2019 nian Shanghai shi daxue zonghe shili paihang bang" [2019 Shanghai University comprehensive strength ranking], Graduate Education website, March 26, 2019, www.yjiedu.com/SHSDXPM/62190.html. All data are based on the official websites of these universities and supplemented with information from Baidu bios and the author's interviews. Individuals are double counted if they serve both as president or vice president and party secretary or deputy party secretary.

administrators at Shanghai's top ten universities in 2019. Among the 122 highest-ranking administrators, 98 (80 percent) are foreign-educated returnees. At Shanghai's two C9 League higher education institutions, Fudan University and Shanghai Jiaotong University, returnees accounted for 93 percent of top administrators, including all seventeen presidents and vice presidents of these two universities.

Most of these returnees pursued their foreign studies in the 1990s. Taking Shanghai Jiaotong University as an example, President Lin Zhongqin, an academician of the Chinese Academy of Engineering and a Changjiang scholar, studied at Sydney University as a visiting scholar from 1994 to 1995. Party Secretary Yang Zhenbin was a visiting scholar at the University of Stuttgart in Germany from 1995 to 1996. Executive Vice President Ding Kuiling, an academician of the Chinese Academy of Science, was a postdoctoral fellow at Ryuku University in Japan during the 1993–1994 academic year and a visiting scholar at Tokyo Institute of Technology from 1997 to 1998. Vice President Huang Zhen pursued his postdoctoral fellowship at Gunma University in Japan from 1991 to 1993. Vice President Mao Junfa pursued his postdoctoral research at the Chinese University of Hong Kong during the 1994–95 academic year, and the University of California, Berkeley from 1995 to 1996.

Vice President Xu Xuemin, daughter of former Shanghai Mayor Xu Kuangdi, received her Ph.D. in Thermal Physics from the University of Illinois at Urbana-Champaign in the early 1990s. She taught in the Department of Mechanical Engineering at the City University of New York and in the Department of Biomedical Engineering at Purdue University for more than ten years. She was a tenured professor at both schools. While in the United States, she also served as cochair of the Biomechanical Heat Transfer Committee of the American Society of Mechanical Engineering. She returned to Shanghai in the early 2000s as a recipient of the Changjiang Project professorship.

Table 8-5 displays the biographical information and educational background of the presidents and party secretaries of Shanghai's top ten universities in 2019. Five were born in the 1950s, eight in the early 1960s, five in the late 1960s, and two in the early 1970s, reflecting the range in ages for holders of these top positions. Both the party secretary of Fudan University and the party secretary of East China University of Science and Technology are women. Table 8-5 also shows that fourteen top administrators (70 percent) in Shanghai attended universities in Shanghai as undergraduates, graduate students, or both. However, only five (25 percent) graduated from the same university where they now serve as top leaders. This percentage is much lower than that of the 2005 study of senior university administrators presented earlier in the chapter.

All except for two of these top administrators (90 percent) have foreign study experience, reaffirming the prevalence of returnees in Shanghai's leading universities. Eleven out of twenty previously studied in the United States, and none studied in Russia. Similar to the early 2000s, most of these returnee administrators held one- to two-year-long stints as visiting scholars at foreign universities. Four received their doctoral degrees at foreign universities, and they all spent over a decade overseas. For example, Xu Ningsheng, president of Fudan, received his bachelor of arts in physics at Sun Yat-sen University in 1982. After teaching at the same school for a year following graduation, he went to Aston University in Great Britain, where he spent three years pursuing a Ph.D. and then conducted research and taught for the succeeding eleven years. Xu returned to his alma mater, Sun Yat-sen University, in 1996. He joined the CCP in 1999, and then he served in a Changjiang Project professorship, as dean of the School of Physical Science and Engineering at Sun Yat-sen University, as director of the State Key Laboratory of Photoelectric Materials and Technology, and as vice president and then president of Sun Yat-sen University. In 2014, he was transferred to Fudan, where he has since served as president.

In contrast to the 2005 analysis of returnee administrators (see table 8-3), in which a large majority (87 percent) studied engineering and natural science, this 2019 study of Shanghai returnee administrators shows that nine out of twenty (45 percent) majored in the humanities and social sciences, including three in philosophy and three in economics or business. Tong Shijun, the party secretary of East China Normal University, was born in Shanghai and received his bachelor's and master's degrees in philosophy at East China Normal University in 1982 and 1984, respectively. After teaching at his alma mater for several years, he went abroad to pursue his doctorate at the University of Bergen, Norway, where he received a Ph.D. in philosophy in 1994. He also visited the University of Marburg in Germany as a guest professor in 1998, and he worked as a Fulbright Scholar in the Department of Philosophy at Columbia University from 2000 to 2001. Tong has published more than ten books and over 100 essays in Chinese, English, and other European languages in his major research areas of epistemology, practical philosophy, and social theory.[46] In particular, Tong has been known for his study of Jürgen Habermas's ideas about civil society, as well as his intellectual passion for dialogues on modernity between the West and China.[47]

Table 8-6 uses the academic administrators (i.e., president and vice presidents) of Fudan University in 2020 as case studies. Most of them are well-accomplished scholars in their fields. Three are academicians of the Chinese Academy of Science. Six out of eight (75 percent) attended the same university—Fudan University and Shanghai Medical College/University,

TABLE 8-5. Educational Backgrounds of Top Administrators at Shanghai's Top Ten Universities, 2019

University	Position	Name	Birth year	Education	Foreign studies	Year	Status	Field
Fudan University	President	Xu Ningsheng	1957	Ph.D. Aston U.; BS, Sun Yat-sen U.	Aston U., UK	1983–86, 1986–96	Ph.D., VS	Physics
	Party secretary	Jiao Yang (f)	1957	MBA, Nanyang Technological U.; BA, Fudan U.	Nanyang Technological U., Singapore	2004–06	Master's degree	Business
Shanghai Jiaotong University	President	Lin Zhongqin	1957	Ph.D., Jiaotong U.	Sydney U.	1994–95	VS	Mechanical engineering
	Party secretary	Jiang Sixian	1954	MS and BS, Jiaotong U.	UBC, Canada; Harvard U.	1993–94	VS	Urban economics
Tongji University	President	Chen Jie	1965	Ph.D., MS and BS, Beijing U. of S&T	UC Berkeley, Tokyo Industrial U	1989–90, 1993, 1996–97	VS	Engineering
	Party secretary	Fang Shouen	1961	Ph.D., MS and BS, Tongji U.	Germany	n.a.	VS	Engineering
East China Normal University	President	Qian Xuhong	1962	Ph.D., MS and BS, East China U. of S&T	Lamar U., US; Humboldt, Germany	1989–90, 1990–91	VS	Chemical engineering
	Party secretary	Tong Shijun	1958	Ph.D. U. of Bergen, Norway; MA and BA, ECNU	U of Bergen, U of Marburg, Germany; Columbia U.	1986–94, 1998, 2000–01	Ph.D., VS	Philosophy
East China University of Science and Technology	President	Qu Jingping	1960	Ph.D., U. of Tokyo	U. of Tokyo	1989–91, 1996–2004	Ph.D., degree	Biochemical engineering
	Party secretary	Du Huifang (f)	1963	Ph.D., Fudan U.	U.S.	n.a.	VS	Environment

Institution	Position	Name	Year	Education	Overseas experience	Year(s)	Type	Field
Shanghai University	President	Liu Changsheng	1967	Ph.D. and MS, East China U. of S&T; BS, Hubei	U. of Pennsylvania	1995	VS	Engineering
	Party secretary	Cheng Danhong	1965	Ph.D., MS and BS, Tianjin U.			VS	Chemical engineering
Shanghai University of Finance and Economics	President	Jiang Chuanhai	1970	Ph.D., Fudan; MS and BS, Anhui U.	Southampton U., UK; U. of Southern Cali.	2002, 2009	VS	Economics
	Party secretary	Xu Tao	1963	Ph.D., Huazhong U. of S&T	Consulate General in Houston and Sydney	n.a.	Work	Education
Donghua University	President	Jiang Changjun	1962	Ph.D., CAS; MS and BS, Shandong U. of S&T	City U. of Hong Kong	1997–98	VS	Computer science
	Party secretary	Liu Chenggong	1968	Ph.D., Fudan U.	Macquarie U. Australia; U. of Valparaiso, U.S.	2003–04	VS	Philosophy
University of Shanghai for Science and Technology	President	Ding Xiaodong	1963	Ph.D., MS Donghua U., BA, Anhui Normal U.	U.S.	n.a.	VS	Engineering
	Party secretary	Wu Jianyong	1970	MA, BA, Fudan U				Law
Shanghai Normal University	President	Zhu Ziqiang	1960	Ph.D., Shizuoka U., Japan; MS and BS, Fudan U.	Heriot-Watt U., UK; UC San Diego	1984–98	Ph.D.	Electronic engineering
	Party secretary	Lin Zaiyong	1965	MA and BA, East China Normal U.	U.S.	n.a.	VS	Philosophy

Sources: The ranking is based on the "2019 nian Shanghai shi daxue zonghe shili paihang bang" [2019 Shanghai University comprehensive strength ranking], Graduate Education website, March 26, 2019, www.yjiedu.com/SHSDXPM/622190.html.

Note: CAS (Chinese Academy of Science), ECNU (East China Normal University), f (female), n.a. (not available), S&T (science and technology), VS (visiting scholar), U. (University).

TABLE 8-6. Foreign Study and Work Experience of the Current President and Vice Presidents of Fudan University, 2020

Name	Position at Fudan	Birth year	Tenure	Prior education background	Foreign experience	Year	Country	Status	Field	Academic titles and awards
Xu Ningsheng	President, Deputy party sec.	1957	2014	BS in Physics, Sun Yat-sen U. (78–82)	Ph.D., Aston U.; taught at Aston U.	83–86, 86–96	UK	Ph.D, Faculty	Physics	Academician of CAS and Academy of Developing Countries
Gui Yonghao	Executive vice president	1958	2017	BS in Medicine, Shanghai Medical C.	VS and MD, U. of Pennsylvania; VS, Osaka U.; VS, Heart Center, Berlin	97–99, 02, 03	USA, Japan, Germany	VS., MD	Medicine	State Council Award
Jin Li	Vice president	1963	2007	BS and MS in genetics, Fudan U. (1981–87)	Ph.D, U. of Texas; taught at Stanford U., U. of Texas and U. of Cincinnati	91–94, 94–05	USA	Ph.D., Faculty	Genetics and biomedical	Academician of CAS
Zhang Zhiyong	Vice president	1961	2015	MD and Ph.D., Shanghai Medical C. (1990–95)	University of Wisconsin–Madison.; UC San Francisco	96–97, 04	USA	VS	Medicine	

Name	Position			Education	VS details	Years	Country		Field	Award
Zhou Yaming	Vice president	1970	2017	BS, MS, and Ph.D. in chemistry, Fudan U. (1988–2003)	VS (details unknown)	n.a.	USA	VS	Chemistry	First Prize, Shanghai S&T Achievement
Chen Zhimin	Vice president	1966	2018	BA, MA, and Ph.D. in world politics, Fudan, (1983–98)	VS, Harvard U., Durham U., Paris U. of Political Science, and Lund U.	96–97, 02–04	USA, UK, France, Sweden	VS	World politics	The Ordre des Palmes Education Award, French Government
Zhang Renhe	Vice president	1962	2018	BA in physics, Lanzhou U., MA and Ph.D. in physics, CAS (1984–91)	VS, Tokyo U. and U. of Maryland	94–96, 98–99	Japan, USA	VS	Atmospheric physics	Academician of CAS
Xu Lei	Vice president	1963	2018	Ph.D. in laser science, Fudan U. (1986–90)	Postdoctoral fellow, Japan Society of Science; VS, UC Berkeley	93–94, 00–01	Japan, USA	VS	Laser science	PRC Ministry of Education Cross-Century Award

Sources: The information is based on the Fudan University website, www.fudan.edu.cn/2016/channels/view/43/, and supplemented with Baidu website biographies.

Note: CAS (Chinese Academy of Science), Med. (medicine), n.a. (not available), PRC (People's Republic of China), S. (school), Sec. (secretary), VS (visiting scholar), U. (University).

which merged into Fudan in 2000. A majority of these returnee administrators (88 percent) previously studied in the United States.

Vice President Jin Li's academic experience is particularly impressive. He was born in Shanghai in 1963, and he received both his bachelor's and master's degrees from Fudan between 1981 and 1987, majoring in genetics. At Fudan, Jin studied under Tan Jiazhen, a Ph.D. from the California Institute of Technology and former vice president of Fudan, who is known as the "founder of modern genetics in China." Soon after receiving his master's degree from Fudan, Jin went to study in the United States and later received his Ph.D. in biomedical science and genetics from the University of Texas–Houston Health Science Center (UTHealth) in 1994. He engaged in postdoctoral research in medical genetics at the Stanford University School of Medicine between 1994 and 1996, and since 1996 he has taught human molecular genetics at the Center for Human Genetics and School of Biomedical Sciences at UTHealth and the Department of Environmental Health at the University of Cincinnati School of Medicine. He was a tenured professor at both universities. Jin was granted a Changjiang Project Professorship in 1999, when he began to teach at Fudan University. He later received additional funding as part of the Thousand Talents Plan. Since 2007, Jin has served as vice president and dean of the graduate school at Fudan. He was elected to be an academician of the Chinese Academy of Science in 2013. Jin Li's case is an example of the Chinese government's efforts to recruit top PRC-born scientists from overseas. Among returnee administrators, many usually received their bachelor's degree (and in some cases also their master's degree) in China and then received their Ph.D. (and in some cases also their postdoctoral fellowship) in the United States. The Chinese official media often claims that these returnee professors and university administrators in China—along with those PRC nationals who still work in U.S. universities and research institutions—are the products of both Chinese and American educations.

Returnee professors in Shanghai universities have often helped develop the social science disciplines in their institutions by introducing Western theories to fields such as sociology, anthropology, psychology, political science, economics, business management, and women and gender studies, among others. For example, they have translated many recent Western scholarly books and published them in Chinese. Professor of political science Lin Gang at Shanghai Jiaotong University (who received a doctoral degree from Pennsylvania State University) and associate professor of political science Lin Xi at Fudan University (who received a doctoral degree from the London School of Economics) translated several volumes of the Series of Contemporary World's Classics in Political Science. This major translation series, initiated by Chinese American political scientist Hua Shiping at the

University of Louisville, has been printed by Renmin University since 2012. The volumes in the series include Robert Dahl's *On Democracy* (2012), Michael Hechter's *Containing Nationalism* (2012), Harold Laski's *The Rise of European Liberalism* (2012), Joseph Nye's *Bound to Lead* (2012), Adam Przeworski's *Capitalism and Social Democracy* (2012), Clyde Wilcox's *The Interest Group Society* (2012), Ian Shapiro's *The State of Democratic Theory* (2013), Samuel P. Huntington's *The Third Wave: Democratization in the Late 20th Century* (2013), Robert D. Putnam's *Making Democracy Work* (2015), Robert Dahl's *Democracy and Its Critics* (2016), Anthony Giddens's *Modernity and Self-Identity* (2016), Bo Rothstein's *Just Institutions Matter* (2017), and Andrew Hurrell's *On Global Order: Power, Values and the Constitution of International Society* (2018).[48] These important Western works have helped inform Chinese political scientists in their teaching and research in this relatively new—and still largely sensitive—academic discipline in China.

REPRESENTATION OF RETURNEES IN SHANGHAI'S POLITICAL LEADERSHIP AND LAW FIRMS

While the predominant role of Western-educated returnees in Shanghai's higher education institutions is most obvious, returnees are omnipresent in all walks of life in the city, including research centers, financial institutions, consulting companies, state and private enterprises, architecture firms, media networks, the entertainment industry, hospitality services, sports clubs, art galleries, hospitals, charitable foundations, churches, and other nongovernmental organizations. Returnees are also prevalent in Shanghai's political leadership and the legal profession, both of which can exert enormous power and influence on the governance of China.

Western-Educated Returnees and the Top Leadership in Shanghai

Under Jiang Zemin's leadership, Chinese authorities made an effort to recruit returnees into the political establishment—first in Shanghai and then for the whole country. In 2000, Jiang's confidant Zeng Qinghong, then the head of the CCP Organization Department, stated that students and scholars returning from abroad were an important source for political recruitment.[49] Zeng also specified that some outstanding returnees should be immediately appointed to leading bureau-level posts (*juzhang*). According to Zeng, these foreign-educated leaders could easily be promoted to even higher posts after serving as bureau heads for just a few years.[50] The events of the following years confirmed Zeng's vision. Western-educated returnees quickly ascended to become ministers in the State Council, as was the case for Chen Zhu (minister of Public Health) and Wan Gang (minister of Science and Technology), both of whom advanced their professional careers in Shanghai.

There are three observations related to Shanghai leaders' strong support for the study abroad movement and the promotion of returnees. First, prominent leaders of the Shanghai Gang all sent their children to study in Western countries, probably earlier than most of their colleagues elsewhere in China. While Jiang Zemin served as a top leader in Shanghai, his two sons were sent abroad to study. The elder son, Jiang Mianheng, left Shanghai for the United States in 1986, and he later received a Ph.D. in electrical engineering from Drexel University in 1991. He is currently president of Shanghai Tech University, where all of the highest-ranking administrators (i.e., party secretary, deputy party secretaries, and vice presidents) are Western-educated returnees. The younger son, Jiang Miankang, is currently the director of the Shanghai Urban Development Information Research Center, and he spent time studying in Germany.

Similarly, Zhu Rongji's son and daughter also enrolled in Western universities. Zhu's son, Zhu Yunlai (Levin Zhu), studied in the United States in the late 1980s and received his Ph.D. in atmospheric physics at the University of Wisconsin–Madison in 1994. Zhu's daughter, Zhu Yanlai, served as a visiting scholar at York University in Canada and received her master's degree in sociology at the University of Regina in Saskatchewan, Canada. Both Zhu Yunlai and Zhu Yanlai returned to China in the 1990s and worked in the financial sector for many years.

The children of two other prominent Shanghai Gang members, former PRC president Zeng Qinghong and former executive vice premier Huang Ju, also pursued foreign studies when their fathers served as senior leaders in Shanghai. Zeng Qinghong's son, Zeng Wei, and Huang Ju's daughter, Huang Fan, went to Australia and the United States, respectively, where they later became naturalized citizens.

The second important observation is that as early as the late 1980s and early 1990s, Jiang Zemin and other top Shanghai leaders were often surrounded by foreign-educated returnees from Shanghai. These included those in their fifties, such as Chen Zhili and Hua Jianmin, both of whom studied in the United States in the early 1980s and later served as state councilor in the State Council, but also younger leaders with foreign experience. As discussed in chapter 6, Jiang and Zeng promoted Wang Huning, Cao Jianming, and Zhou Mingwei—three Shanghai-born and Shanghai-educated leaders in their early forties, whom they had known well in Shanghai—to important national leadership positions in the 1990s. These individuals later ascended to powerful positions in Beijing. Similarly, Jiang played a substantial role in promoting Yang Jiechi, a Shanghai native who studied at the University of Bath and the London School of Economics from 1973 to

1975, to become the vice minister of Foreign Affairs and China's ambassador to the United States.

The third and final observation is that over the past two decades, foreign-educated returnees have often occupied the two top positions in Shanghai, namely party secretary and mayor. Chen Liangyu, who served as mayor between 2002 and 2003 and then party secretary between 2002 and 2006, studied at the School of Public Policy at the University of Birmingham in the United Kingdom for about a year in 1992. Xu Kuangdi, the former mayor of Shanghai between 1995 and 2001, served as a visiting professor at Imperial College London and deputy chief engineer at a company in Sweden for a few years early in his career. The current party secretary Li Qiang received his master of business administration from Hong Kong Polytechnic University Management School, which he attended on a part-time basis between 2003 and 2005.

There are even more Western-educated returnees at the leadership level below these two top positions. Former Shanghai deputy party secretary Yin Hong—who was recently transferred to Henan where he serves as governor—was a visiting scholar at the University of Pennsylvania and Southern Illinois University from 1993 to 1994. Current Shanghai executive vice mayor Chen Yin was a visiting scholar in the United States during the 1996–1997 academic year. Current chair of the Shanghai Municipal People's Congress Yin Yicui also studied in the United States from 1995 to 1996. Current Shanghai vice mayor Chen Qun attended the Tokyo Institute of Technology as a visiting scholar in the 1990–1991 school year.

These returnees also differ from PRC-educated leaders in other ways. For example, returnees generally advance their careers via sectors such as education, policy research, science and technology, economic management and finance, and foreign affairs, but they do not necessarily have strong regional constituencies or governance experience. Only a small number of them have advanced their careers through provincial and municipal leadership posts, which are generally the most likely launching pads to top-echelon positions. The fact that Western-educated returnees have been able to enter the top leadership of Shanghai with little political experience suggests that, barring something entirely unforeseen, the representation of these returnees in the national leadership will likely increase in the years to come.

U.S.-Educated Returnees in Shanghai's Top Law Firms

The Chinese legal tradition has been weak throughout the country's long history. Even Mencius, the most prominent philosopher in the Confucian school of thought who wrote substantially on law, "consistently emphasize[d] filial piety and assign[ed] it a higher value than law."[51] During the first three decades of the PRC, the public's view of Chinese law was characterized by legal nihilism and legal instrumentalism. The government's lack of even a basic legal consciousness accounted for the fact that, from 1949 to 1978, the PRC promulgated only two laws—one being the constitution itself and the other the 1950 New Marriage Law. In Mao's China, law was largely seen as a tool of the ruling class to maintain its power and exercise its dictatorship. As a result, in the late 1950s and early 1960s, it was quite common for officials at various leadership levels to trivialize legal positions and serve concurrently as public security chief, principal prosecutor, and court president.[52]

However, China's painstaking transition toward a market economy since 1978 has required more laws and regulations, without which the economy would have fallen into anarchy. In 1981, the State Council established the Research Center of Economic Laws, which was responsible for drafting large-scale economic legislation. From 1979 to 1993, among the 130 laws approved by the National People's Congress, more than half were in the areas of economic and administrative law.[53] Steadily, reform era China has begun to establish a legal framework. According to official numbers, China has promulgated 239 laws in the reform era. The State Council has issued an additional 690 administrative rules and regulations, and local governments have issued about 8,600 local laws and regulations. Taken together, these developments are a substantial improvement over the legal vacuum of Mao's China.[54] Admittedly, many of these laws either have not been implemented or are insufficiently enforced, but they nonetheless represent an important foundation on which a more effective system can be built over time.

Keeping pace with new developments, a burgeoning legal profession has emerged with this body of laws.[55] In the early years of the PRC, the country had only four colleges that specialized in politics and law.[56] Only a few universities had law departments, and moreover, these departments were all shut down during the Cultural Revolution. In 1983, the first independent law firm in the PRC was established in Shekou, Shenzhen. Notably, in the early 1980s, there were only around 3,000 lawyers in the PRC—a country of approximately 1 billion people—and all of them were allegedly state officials at that time.[57] By the end of 2010, however, that number had expanded sixty-eight-fold to 204,000 licensed lawyers.[58] That year, about 40,000 PRC nationals received licenses to become registered lawyers in the country. In 2011, China's 640 law schools and law departments produced roughly 100,000 law graduates annually.[59] By the end of 2018, China had a total of 423,000 registered lawyers, and the total number of law firms practicing in the country surpassed 30,000.[60]

Meanwhile, the programs in legal studies at Chinese universities—such as jurisprudence, constitutional law, administrative law, criminal law, civil law, procedural law, and environmental law—have become well-established professional subfields over the past two decades. In 1978, there were hardly any textbooks on law, but now law-related books usually constitute a quarter of the books carried in academic bookstores.[61] In 2007, about 400 books and 70,000 scholarly articles on law, including translated works, were published in the country. In 2009, China had over 200 professional journals that focused on law.[62]

All of these new academic subfields, legal programs, and efforts to disseminate knowledge about the rule of law are profoundly shaped and influenced by Western legal doctrines that have made their way to China through international educational exchanges. A good example is the birth and growth of China's legal clinics, which were initiated and sponsored by the Ford Foundation in the United States. On December 6, 1999, the Ford Foundation hosted a seminar on teaching legal clinic courses in Beijing, after which they issued a report on the Foundation's "promotion of the development of legal clinic education courses in the Chinese law schools and law departments." In 2000, the Ford Foundation chose seven Chinese universities (Peking, Tsinghua, Renmin, Wuhan, Central South University of Political Science and Law, East China University of Political Science and Law, and Fudan) as the first institutions to receive legal clinic project assistance.[63] That same year, all seven universities initiated legal clinic education classes.

According to statistics released by the Legal Clinic Education Professional Committee, by the end of 2003, at least thirteen institutions in China had received funding from the Ford Foundation and conducted legal clinic education involving 76 instructors, 38 guest lecturers, and 2,430 students. As real-world engagement was an integral part of the program, they handled 1,136 legal aid cases and provided over 10,000 legal consultations.[64] These legal clinics have addressed issues such as labor rights protection, consumer rights protection, public interest litigation, rights protection of socially vulnerable populations, women's rights protection, civil rights protection, criminal law, environmental law, and legislative matters.

Shanghai has also been at the frontier of the country's legal development in terms of international exchanges, as well as the establishment of law schools and law firms. According to official data released by the PRC Ministry of Justice, in 2018 there were 126 Shanghai-based foreign law firms, accounting for 57 percent of all 223 foreign law firms with branches in China.[65] Many law firms choose to congregate in Shanghai due to the concentration of top legal talent who are trained in the city. East China University of Political Science and Law, Fudan University Law School, the Koguan School of Law at Shanghai Jiaotong University, and the Law School of the Shanghai University of Finance and Economics are among the best law schools in the country. Many universities in Shanghai, including Tongji University, East China Normal University, Shanghai International Studies University, Shanghai University of International Business and Economics, Shanghai University, and East China University of Science and Technology have founded law schools in the past few decades. In 2008, a specialized law school, the School of Law at Shanghai Maritime University, was founded in the city.[66]

Table 8-7 shows the gradual and significant increase in the number of law firms and lawyers in Shanghai over the past decade. The total number of law firms almost doubled in a decade. The number of registered lawyers in Shanghai grew from 16,900 in 2014 to 23,664 in 2018—an increase of 42 percent in five years. Between 2015 and 2018, Shanghai lawyers handled a total of 739,400 cases of various types of litigation, including 107,600 criminal litigation cases, 617,700 civil litigation cases, and 14,000 administrative litigation cases. In addition, they also handled a total of 264,100 nonlitigation cases and more than 5.8 million legal aid cases, providing 274,200 instances of public welfare legal services.[67]

Foreign-educated returnees have played an important role in the growth of the legal profession in Shanghai. Table 8-8 reveals the prevalence of returnees in the top five law firms in the city. This study focuses on senior law-

TABLE 8-7. Number of Law Firms and Lawyers in Shanghai, 2008–2018

Year	Number of law firms	Number of lawyers
2008	889	10,071
2009	976	11,184
2010	1,064	12,298
2011	1,117	13,761
2012	1,158	14,593
2013	1,222	16,692
2014	1,321	16,900
2015	1,409	18,360
2016	1,463	20,319
2017	1,537	21,743
2018	1,602	23,664

Sources: Lin Ge, "10 nian lüshi renshu fan bei" [The number of lawyers doubled in ten years], *Lüshi jie* [Legal community], July 13, 2018, www.zhihedongfang.com/54147. html. Data for 2018 are based on "Shanghai lüshi sishi nian" [40 years of Shanghai lawyers], Douban website, April 13, 2019, www.douban.com/note/714162872/.

TABLE 8-8. The Representation of Returnees in Shanghai's Top Five Law Firms, 2019

Ranking	Law firm name	Year founded	Total number of lawyers	Number of returnee partners	Total number of partners	% of Returnees
1	AllBright Law Offices	1998	1,069	68	215	31.6
2	Dentons Shanghai Office	2001	474	39	157	24.8
3	Yingke Law Firm	2010	672	9	47	19.1
4	Grandall Law Firm	1998	309	29	82	35.3
5	Zhong Lun Law Firm	1993	316	75	112	67.0
	Total			220	613	35.8

Sources: The ranking of the top five law firms is based on the annual ranking of the Shanghai Bar Association in 2018. "2018 Shanghai shi lüshi shiwu suo paiming qian 50 ming" [The 2018 ranking of the top 50 Shanghai law firms], *Mishang faliuwang* [Civil and Commercial Law Network], January 24, 2018, http://m.liuxiaoer.com/shls/7128.html. Data on returnees are based on websites of these law firms. See www.allbrightlaw.com/CN/01.aspx; www.dentons.com/zh/global-presence/china/shanghai; http://shanghaiyingkelawyer.com; www.grandall.com.cn/contact-us/; www.zhonglun.com. Assembled and calculated by Cheng Li.

yers in these firms, including equity partners (*quanyi hehuoren*), nonequity partners (*feiquanyi hehuoren*), and senior advisers. The top law firm, All-Bright Law Offices, was established and headquartered in Shanghai in 1998. The other firms shown are the Shanghai branches of Beijing-headquartered law firms. By 2017, among the 1,537 law firms in Shanghai, only 133 were branches of law firms based in other Chinese cities and provinces, mainly from Beijing (60 percent) and followed by Jiangsu, Guangdong, and Zhejiang provinces.[68] The study looks only at Shanghai-based senior lawyers. Among these 613 partners in Shanghai's top five law firms, 220 (36 percent) are foreign-educated returnees.

In the Zhong Lun Law Firm, 75 of the 112 partners are foreign-educated returnees, accounting for two-thirds of the total. A closer look at the biographical information, especially the educational backgrounds, of returnee partners reveals some interesting patterns. There are 52 males (69 percent) and 23 females (31 percent), which is a slightly smaller proportion of females compared to all registered lawyers in Shanghai in 2018 (40 percent).[69] Additionally, a majority of returnee law partners (48 out of 75, or 64 percent) received their J.D. degrees in the United States, followed by those who received their degrees in the United Kingdom (19 people, or 25 percent).[70] Only a couple of returnee law partners studied in each of the following countries: Australia, Canada, Germany, the Netherlands, Japan, South Korea, and Singapore.

With only one exception, all other 74 returnees (99 percent) received their undergraduate education in China. The exception is Cheng Mingzhi, who attended Yale University between 1978 and 1982 and then attended the J.D. program at the University of California, Berkeley, between 1982 and 1985. A majority attended undergraduate schools in Shanghai (51 partners, 69 percent). Among the total 75 returnee partners at the Zhong Lun Law Firm, 28 (37 percent) attended East China University of Political Science as undergraduates—with some also pursuing graduate degrees there. A significant number of partners were graduates of Fudan University (16 partners, 21 percent). These findings seem to reaffirm the general observation that not only has Shanghai sent a large number of its graduates abroad, but it also attracts many well-accomplished returnees, especially Shanghai natives and school alumni.

Table 8-9 displays the educational pedigrees of twenty-five select U.S.-educated returnees among these seventy-five partners. Women are much better represented among prominent legal professionals than among the returnee senior administrators in higher education, as previously discussed. Some on the list are remarkably young, especially given that they hold the titles of senior legal professionals, such as partner, within these prominent law firms. Chen Chun, Gao Ziyan, Liu Tianshun, and Wang Jianqin, for example, received their bachelor's degrees only twelve years ago. They are most likely still in their thirties. Overall, Chinese lawyers are relatively young. According to a recent study of Shanghai lawyers, 24 percent are under the age of 30, 36 percent are between 31 and 40, and 23 percent are between 41 and 50.[71] Altogether, 83 percent of lawyers in Shanghai are under 50 years old. The relative youth of China's lawyers, an arguably crucial elite group in the country, may be important in China's search for improved governance in a rapidly changing world in the decades to come.

This select sample of U.S. returnee lawyers all went to top American law schools, including Harvard, Stanford, UC Berkeley, and the University of Chicago. A number of them received their J.D. degree from prestigious programs at Columbia University and New York University. Most of them have passed the bar exam in New York so that they can practice as licensed attorneys in that key state for international finance and trade. With an increasingly globalized economy, and with the United States and other Western countries pressuring China to meet international norms and standards—especially in regard to enforcement and compliance with intellectual property rights—these U.S.-educated Chinese lawyers may be instrumental in promoting cooperation and understanding across the Pacific.

FINAL THOUGHTS

In a rapidly emerging power like China, international educational exchange is not just about learning science and technology from Western countries. Rather, it is a complex, multifaceted, and ever-changing process entailing economic reform, cultural regeneration, educational adaptation, and legal and political reconstruction. The growing number of returnees to China—and especially their omnipresence in all walks of life in Shanghai—is a testament to their constructive impact on the city, and a promising sign for the future transformation of the country.

At a time when tensions, prejudices, misunderstandings, and even wars abound in the world—and when policymakers and the general public in the United States are concerned about America's own educational "open-door policy"—we must evaluate whether sweeping away educational and professional exchanges between these two profoundly different countries can truly resolve the issues we face. The enduring dominance of Western-educated returnees in Chinese higher education institutions, the country's pursuit of building world-class universities, the rapid expansion of international, jointly run universities and programs in Shanghai and other Chinese cities, Western-educated Chinese nationals assuming leadership positions in their native land, and the birth and growth of China's legal education and profession primarily from Western influences, all reveal how

TABLE 8-9. The Educational Backgrounds of Selected U.S.-Educated Returnee Partners of the Zhong Lun Law Firms, Shanghai, 2019

Name	Gender	Undergraduate school	Year grad.	Law school in China	Year grad.	Law school in U.S.	Year grad.	Bar exam state in U.S.
Chen Chun	Female	Beijing Foreign Language U.	2009			NYU	2010	New York
Chen Yi	Male	East China U. of Pol. Sci. & Law	1999			UC Berkeley	2014	
Cheng Fang	Female	Lanzhou U.		East China U. of Pol. Sci. & Law		Stanford U.		New York
Cheng Mingzhi	Male	Yale U.	1982			UC Berkeley	1985	California
Fan Xiaojuan	Female	Shanxi U. of Economics		Shanghai Foreign Trade U.		UCLA		New York
Fang Jianwei	Male	East China U. of Pol. Sci. & Law				Columbia U.		New York
Gao Ting	Female	East China U. of Pol. Sci. & Law	2003	East China U. of Pol. Sci. & Law	2006	Chicago U.	2005	New York
Gao Ziyan	Female	East China U. of Pol. Sci. & Law	2008	East China U. of Pol. Sci. & Law	2008	Southern California U.	2009	New York
Gong Lefan	Male	Zhejiang U.		Fudan U.		U. of Michigan		New York
Huang Yilin	Male	East China U. of Pol. Sci. & Law	2006			Chicago U.	2007	New York
Huang Zhigang	Male	East China U. of Pol. Sci. & Law	1995	East China U. of Pol. Sci. & Law	1998	SF State U.	2001	New York

Li Junjie	Male	China U. of S&T	1987			Stanford U.	1994	New York
Liu Tianshun	Male	Nanjing U.	2008			Southern California U.	2009	New York
Ni Yongjun	Male	Fudan U.		Fudan U.		Harvard U.		New York
Si Xiangjun	Male	China U. of Pol. Sci. & Law	2004	China U. of Pol. Sci. & Law	2006	U. of Pennsylvania	2009	New York
Sun Binbin	Female	Shanghai U.		Renmin U.		UC Berkeley		
Wang Jianqin	Female	East China U. of Pol. Sci. & Law	2007			Emory U.	2014	California
Wang Weizhong	Male	Fudan U.		Fudan U.		NYU		New York
Wu Zhongda	Male	Foreign Affairs U.				Columbia U.		New York
Xia He	Female	East China U. of Pol. Sci. & Law		China U. of Pol. Sci. & Law		Columbia U.		
Xia Yan	Female	Fudan U.				Chicago U.		New York
Xu Mo	Male	Shanghai Foreign Trade U.				UC Berkeley		
Yan Jing'an	Female	Fudan U.				Columbia U.		
Zhao Jing	Male	Fudan U.				NYU		New York
Zhou Yun	Male	East China U. of Pol. Sci. & Law	1999			NYU	2001	New York

Source: www.zhonglun.com/Content/2016/08-18/1131484533.html.

Note: Grad. (graduated), NYU (New York University), Pol. Sci. (political science), S&T (science and technology), SF (San Francisco), U. (University).

much China has changed during the reform era, noticeably benefiting from educational exchanges with the West.

As noted at the beginning of this chapter, returnees are a diverse group, and they differ profoundly in terms of their views, values, and visions. As their numbers increase in China, it is not difficult to imagine that they will exert more political influence and demand more power. In a sense, the self-confidence of returnees to help shape their country's future parallels the Chinese public's aspirations for great power status in today's world. Thus it is critical that the Chinese leadership takes the perspective of these return-ees into account when shaping the future of the nation. No country can truly claim that its government includes only the best and brightest, and all nations know that it is important to recruit talented people to work *for* the political establishment rather than *against* it. China's top leaders, from Deng Xiaoping and Jiang Zemin to Hu Jintao and Xi Jinping, have all em-phasized their appreciation for talent and innovation.

However, the government's display of rhetoric and symbolism can go only so far. The CCP leadership's ideological and political control over aca-demic content and intellectual freedom undercuts the country's potential to lead in international higher education. Thus, as for the true impact of edu-cational exchanges on the U.S.-China bilateral relationship, the jury is still out. Time will tell whether the experiences of returnees in America can help reduce misunderstanding and avoid potential major conflicts.

J. William Fulbright's epigraph to this chapter should inspire propo-nents of U.S.-China relations to expand the boundaries of this most conse-quential bilateral relationship of the twenty-first century. After all, if educa-tion cannot bridge minds across the Pacific, what can?

CHAPTER 9

Attitudes and Values

A Longitudinal Survey of Foreign-Educated Elites in Shanghai

Alter ideas and you alter the world.

— H. G. WELLS

I hate American hegemony, and I love NBA games.

— A CHINESE COLLEGE STUDENT

If the success of a country's international educational exchanges were measured by the number of students it sends abroad, reform-era China would undoubtedly be the most successful nation, as it continues to send the most students overseas. The United States, as the host country of most international students, benefits as well. The "soft power" that the United States has accrued by educating students from around the world and disseminating its cultural influence through exchange programs is arguably one of its greatest achievements. However, skeptics and critics take issue with how international educational exchanges impact the collective views and values of students from abroad. Empirical studies can offer essential insight to resolve ongoing intellectual and policy debates regarding these exchanges.

Despite the importance of educational exchanges and their impacts, very few scholars, either in China or abroad, have sufficiently studied this subject, especially the attitudes of foreign-educated returnees in the People's Republic of China (PRC).[1] As a result, broad generalizations about the worldviews of returnees—including that they promote liberal and democratic values and favor friendly, constructive relations with the United States and the West—are anecdotally assumed rather than empirically examined and verified. China studies in general, and scholarly works on educational and cultural exchanges in particular, have failed to adequately investigate this key inquiry.

One of the few research questionnaires of returnees—a 2016 survey of 1,328 returnees conducted by Beijing scholars affiliated with the PRC think tank Center for China and Globalization—presents some interesting findings.[2] In response to the question, "What is the most difficult factor for overseas returnees to adapt to after returning to the home country?" as many as 47 percent of returnee respondents expressed that the most challenging adjustment was the "difference in values" (*jiazhiguan de chayi*), reflecting the variance between Chinese and Western cultures and sociopolitical circumstances. In addition, 29 percent chose "the way of thinking" in the home country as being the most difficult factor, and the choices of "lifestyle" and "Chinese national psychology" accounted for 11 percent and 10 percent of the responses, respectively.[3] The results of this study indicate that Western culture, Western education, and the sociopolitical environment all lead Chinese students in these Western countries to develop certain views and perspectives, which differ markedly from their domestically educated counterparts. The Chinese researchers who led this study note that these changes in perspective led to conflicts in cognition, which caused personal distress and difficulty adapting among returnees.

How do returnees view key issues in China's domestic development, foreign policy, the U.S. hegemonic role in the post–Cold War era, international competition, and common global challenges? In what respects have the views and values of foreign-educated returnees transformed as a result of their overseas experiences? In what respects have their opinions and attitudes remained unchanged? What factors have shaped differences between returnees and their domestically trained counterparts, as well as among the returnees themselves? Do the views and values that returnees develop during their foreign studies endure over time? This chapter aims to shed valuable light on these critically important questions by analyzing surveys of returnees in Shanghai over two different years.

METHODOLOGY AND DATA POOL

Both surveys were conducted by the Horizon Research Consultancy Group, a Shanghai-based public opinion polling firm. The surveys were completed exclusively for this study of Chinese foreign-educated elites, and the findings are presented to the public for the first time through this book. The Horizon Research Consultancy Group was founded by Yuan (Victor) Yue in 1992, and it has collaborated with forty-five countries on academic, policy, and market survey research over the past three decades.[4] Yuan holds an MPA degree from Harvard University's Kennedy School of Government

(2001) and a Ph.D. in sociology from Peking University (2004). Currently, the firm has 250 full-time employees and is one of China's largest research and consultancy companies for professional planning services and public opinion polling.[5]

The data for this analysis come from two waves of survey data. The first survey was conducted in late 2009 (between June 22 and December 7, 2009), and the second survey was carried out in late 2013 (between November 6 and December 17, 2013, with updates completed in early 2014). For the sake of convenience, the first survey is hereafter referred to as "the 2009 survey" and the second as "the 2014 survey." The 2009 survey has 200 respondents, among which 159 responded by email, 33 through face-to-face interviews, 6 by phone call, and 2 by fax. The 2014 survey has 211 respondents, among which 32 responded by email and 179 responded by phone call using computer-assisted telephone interviewing. The lists of survey participants, including their basic biographical and professional information, were provided by the Horizon Research Consultancy Group, but there is no cross-listing of information about any 2014 respondents who may have also participated in the 2009 survey.

The 2009 survey covers 86 questions, and the 2014 survey spans 76 questions. About three-fourths of the questions on the 2014 survey are repeats of those in the 2009 survey, or have only slight wording modifications. The surveys cover important topics, such as China's responsibility regarding climate change, the Chinese government's role in global financial governance, energy security, economic disparities both in China and in the world, the status and future prospects of the Chinese middle class, views of migrant workers and less privileged social groups in the country, assessments of economic growth models for China, food and product safety, social stability, educational development, corruption and governmental accountability, impressions of the United States and American presidents, attitudes toward various countries, evaluation of China's foreign policy, outlook for Cross-Strait relations with Taiwan, views of China's military modernization, perspectives on culture clash and cultural dissemination, and level of nationalism and patriotic sentiment.

This study makes comparisons, whenever necessary, between this research on Shanghai foreign-educated returnees and other surveys on Shanghai residents, various other groups, and the Chinese general public. These comparisons are done using surveys conducted in similar or different time frames (some of which are also conducted by the Horizon Research Consultancy Group).[6] By analyzing responses across various groups, this study elucidates important information about changes in the perspective of Shanghai returnees over time, especially compared to other Chinese citizens.

In both surveys, a majority of participants attended schools in the West (western European countries and the United States). In the 2014 survey, 28 percent studied in Europe, of which the United Kingdom accounted for 17 percent, followed by France and Spain (each of which accounted for 2 percent). Only one student (less than 1 percent) had studied in Russia. A total of 34 students (16 percent) studied in the United States. Among those who studied in Asia (29 percent), Japan accounted for 15 percent, followed by Singapore (9 percent). Those in the "others" category mainly studied in Australia (18 percent), New Zealand (4 percent), and Canada (2 percent). Overall, a total of 77 percent of the 2014 survey participants studied in these eight countries: Australia, United Kingdom, United States, Japan, New Zealand, France, Spain, and Canada. A separate 2009 study conducted by other researchers in Shanghai also shows that returnees in the city had mainly studied in six countries—United Kingdom, Japan, Australia, the United States, France, and Germany—accounting for 68 percent of returnees' study destinations.[7] A total of thirty-seven returnees in this 2009 study went to the United States, accounting for 19 percent of respondents.

Figure 9-1 shows the duration of returnees' foreign education and professional experience, as reported in the 2009 and 2014 surveys conducted for this book. Approximately 55 percent of the 2009 survey respondents and 75 percent of the 2014 survey respondents had studied or worked abroad for three years or longer. This contrasts significantly with earlier studies of returnees, in which a large portion of respondents had only studied abroad for one or two years. For example, a 2005 study of returnee senior administrators and professors in China's top universities shows that in these two groups, those who studied overseas for only a one- to two-year period accounted for the majority—65 percent and 62 percent, respectively.[8]

FIGURE 9-1. Foreign study duration of Shanghai returnees, surveyed in 2009 and 2014

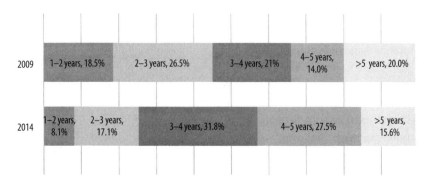

Table 9-1 presents an overview of the demographic and personal information of the participants in the two surveys. A vast majority of returnees in both surveys were in their twenties and thirties. Those younger than 40 years old account for 96 percent and 91 percent of respondents in the 2009 survey and the 2014 survey, respectively. More than half of these returnees (53 percent in the 2009 survey and 52 percent of the 2014 survey) received advanced degrees, mainly master's degrees, and about 3 to 4 percent received doctoral degrees. The 2014 survey shows that a higher percentage of returnees from the United States and Europe are advanced degree holders (62 percent and 73 percent, respectively). This educational attainment pattern is similar to the general trend among Shanghai returnees during the same period. A 2011 large-scale survey of the returnees in Shanghai, for example, also shows that more than half (56 percent) obtained advanced degrees overseas, mainly master's degrees.[9] In recent years, however, the number of returnees with doctoral degrees has significantly increased, especially among those in the 31–40 age cohort in both the city and the country.[10]

Over the past decade, the middle class in Shanghai has grown and the living standards in the city have improved, largely due to the drastic increase in income levels among returnees. In the 2009 survey, 26 percent of returnees had a household monthly income below RMB 10,000. In the 2014 survey, this percentage halved. Meanwhile, the proportion of respondents with a household monthly income above RMB 14,000 increased from 53 percent in the 2009 survey to 61 percent in the 2014 survey. Compared to their counterparts who studied in other countries, the percentage of U.S. returnees in this income group is much higher (76 percent). Given Shanghai's rapid economic development over the past decade, this change in household income should not be a surprise. As discussed early in the book, in 2019 for instance, Shanghai's per capita GDP exceeded USD 20,000.[11]

It may come as somewhat of a surprise, however, to see that percentage of returnees who are religious—especially those who noted that they had converted to Roman Catholicism, Protestantism, or Christianity in these two surveys—is markedly low. None of the returnees from the United States in both surveys had converted to Catholicism, Protestantism, or Christianity, which complicates the argument that foreign exchange programs lead to cultural dissemination and value adoption. The findings on religion from these two surveys contrast with those of a 2018 survey conducted by the Center on Religion and Chinese Society of Purdue University, which focused on the influence of religion on 1,008 Chinese students who had attended a U.S. university in the Midwest.[12] The Purdue University study shows that the number of Chinese students who believe in Catholicism and Taoism doubled from when they first arrived in the United States, and

TABLE 9-1. Demographic and Personal Information of Respondents (N = 200 for the 2009 Survey, N = 2011 for the 2014 Survey) in percentages (%)

		Total		United States	
		2014 Survey	2009 Survey	2014 Survey	2009 Survey
Gender	Male	46.0	53.1	61.1	52.9
	Female	54.0	46.9	38.9	47.1
Age	20 or under	0.5	0.5	0.0	0.0
	21–30	60.0	52.6	56.8	47.0
	31–40	36.0	38.4	43.2	41.2
	41–50	3.0	8.1	0.0	11.8
	51–60	0.5	0.5	0.0	0.0
Education	High school	1.0	0.0	0.0	0.0
	2-Year college	6.0	0.9	10.8	0.0
	Bachelor's	40.0	47.4	32.4	38.2
	Master's	49.5	48.3	56.8	55.9
	Ph.D.	3.5	3.3	0.0	5.9
Marital status	Married	52.3	50.2	62.2	55.9
	Unmarried, living alone	23.1	16.6	18.9	14.7
	Unmarried, living with partner or relative	24.6	32.7	18.9	29.4
Household monthly income	2,000–4,000 yuan	1.7	0.0	0.0	0.0
	4,000–6,000 yuan	3.9	5.2	2.9	0.0
	6,000–8,000 yuan	6.1	1.4	0.0	0.0
	8,000–10,000 yuan	13.9	5.7	5.7	8.8
	10,000–12,000 yuan	17.8	16.1	11.4	11.8
	12,000–14,000 yuan	3.9	9.5	2.9	2.9
	14,000–16,000 yuan	12.8	7.1	17.1	8.8
	Above 16,000 yuan	40.0	54.0	60.0	67.6
Religion	Roman Catholic	0.6	0.5	0.0	0.0
	Protestant/Christian	1.7	1.9	0.0	0.0
	Buddhist	18.3	9.5	21.9	5.9
	No religion	79.4	86.7	78.1	91.2
	No response	0.0	1.4	0.0	2.9
	Total	100.0	100.0	100.0	100.0

Europe		Asia		Other countries*	
2014 Survey	2009 Survey	2014 Survey	2009 Survey	2014 Survey	
43.2	47.5	45.0	54.8	33.3	57.6
56.8	52.5	55.0	45.2	66.7	42.4
0.0	1.7	1.7	0.0	0.0	0.0
63.4	64.4	51.7	50.0	76.2	47.5
31.7	30.5	41.7	38.7	23.8	44.1
3.7	3.4	5.0	9.7	0.0	8.5
1.2	0.0	0.0	1.6	0.0	0.0
0.0	0.0	3.3	0.0	0.0	0.0
2.4	0.0	8.3	3.2	4.8	0.0
29.3	27.1	50.0	59.7	66.7	59.3
61.0	69.5	36.7	35.5	28.6	37.3
7.3	3.4	1.7	1.6	0.0	3.4
48.1	42.4	51.7	46.8	52.4	55.9
25.9	18.6	23.3	14.5	19.0	16.9
25.9	39.0	25.0	38.7	28.6	25.4
1.4	0.0	1.9	0.0	5.6	0.0
1.4	8.5	5.6	6.5	11.1	3.4
12.3	0.0	1.9	1.6	5.6	3.4
13.7	1.7	14.8	6.5	27.8	6.8
17.8	16.9	22.2	12.9	16.7	20.3
1.4	10.2	5.6	9.7	11.1	11.9
11.0	6.8	14.8	8.1	5.6	6.8
41.1	52.5	33.3	54.8	16.7	47.5
0.0	1.7	0.0	0.0	5.0	0.0
1.4	5.1	1.8	1.6	5.0	1.7
11.1	10.2	23.2	12.9	25.0	6.8
87.5	79.7	75.0	85.5	65.0	91.5
0.0	3.3	0.0	0.0	0.0	0.0
100.0	100.0	100.0	100.0	100.0	100.0

*Other countries include primarily Australia, New Zealand, and Canada.

the number of Chinese students who believe in Protestantism quadrupled during the same timeframe.[13] The Purdue University study also reports that about 92 percent of respondents had been subject to proselytization from Protestants, followed by Catholics (35 percent), Falun Gong adherents (32 percent), Mormons (17 percent), Buddhists (8 percent), Muslims (3 percent), and members of other religions (2 percent).[14] The contrasting findings between this study of Shanghai returnees and the Purdue University survey could be explained by other empirical studies, which find that about 80 percent of Chinese students who became Christians in the United States stopped attending services and engaging in religious practices after returning home.[15]

Overall, studies on religion in China generally find that the percentage of religious practitioners among the total PRC population is relatively low. For example, the World Value Survey conducted in China in 2013 found that in response to a question about the importance of religion in life, 1,145 (50 percent) of the 2,300 respondents stated that it was "not important at all" and 682 respondents (30 percent) indicated that it was "not important." Only 60 respondents (3 percent) believed religion to be "very important."[16] However, it is possible that survey respondents in China might be hesitant to truthfully answer this potentially sensitive question. Thus people may underreport religious practices because attending family churches is technically illegal, and they want to avoid legal punishment.

In regard to the occupations of the respondents to the two surveys (Table 9-2), a large number work in business management. Those who work in company middle-level management, or as corporate executives, business owners, and sales managers account for 49 percent of respondents in the 2009 survey and 42 percent in the 2014 survey. Those who work in scientific research, technical fields, and academic realms (e.g., as scientific researchers, engineers, doctors, nurses, public health staff, college professors or school instructors) account for 18 percent of respondents to the 2009 survey and 16 percent to the 2014 survey, respectively. Returnees who work in the financial sector, including bankers, insurance and securities analysts, accountants, statisticians, and auditors, increased from 7 percent to 11 percent between the surveys.

In both the 2009 and 2014 surveys, only about 1 percent of returnees serve as government or state-owned enterprise leaders. Those who work as government civil servants account for only about 3 percent of returnees. A different nationwide survey of returnees conducted in 2016 reports that 32 percent of the returnees had applied (or planned to apply) for civil service exams, of which 14 percent had already taken the exams.[17] Additionally, this study finds that the proportion of returnees who found work as civil servants (2 percent) is slightly higher than that of domestically trained college graduates (1 percent).[18] The same survey also reveals that 21 percent of the returnees who were born in the 1980s and 1990s (27 percent of men and 14 percent of women) were interested in participating in politics and political discourse (*canzheng yizheng*).[19] While this study of Shanghai returnees did not ask participants about their Chinese Communist Party (CCP) membership, another 2010 survey of returnees in Shanghai conducted by the municipal government shows that approximately one-fourth of returnees (24 percent) were CCP members.[20]

MAIN FINDINGS

Both the 2009 and 2014 surveys concentrate on the attitudes of returnees regarding five major issues: (1) climate change and environmental protection, (2) economic outlook, (3) social norms and attitudes, (4) international relations, and (5) impact of cultural assimilation. This section presents the main findings of the surveys in these areas. Graphs have been rescaled to make it easier to compare values across surveys without changing any of the surveys' findings. Due to space limitations, not all questions and responses from the two surveys are presented here. The selected questions and results shown aim to highlight comparisons between the 2009 survey and the 2014 survey, and between Shanghai returnees in this study and other survey studies of Shanghai residents (or the Chinese population in general) as well as various elite groups. Some key findings are illustrated in newly formulated charts, often comparing returnees with nonreturnee groups. Other important findings are summarized briefly in the narrative text. The commissioned study, including the original and much more comprehensive survey results in Chinese, is available upon request.

Views of Climate Change and Environmental Protection

Figure 9-2 presents the degree of concern about climate change among Shanghai returnees in the 2009 and 2014 surveys, and a comparison of these results with three other surveys of the Chinese general public in 2007, 2012, and 2017 on the same question: "How much do you personally worry about climate change?"[21] In the 2009 survey of Shanghai returnees, 83 percent of respondents express worry about climate change. Similarly, 87 percent of Shanghai returnees in the 2014 survey are concerned about climate change, of which 47 percent are "worried a great deal" and 40 percent are "worried a fair amount." These are much higher percentages than those expressing concern in the 2007 survey (69 percent) and in the 2012 survey (62 percent) of the Chinese general public. There is an increase in concern among the Chinese public about climate change in the 2017 national survey (79

TABLE 9-2. Occupational and Professional Information of Respondents (N = 200 for the 2009 Survey, N = 2011 for the 2014 Survey) in percentages (%)

Profession	Total		United States	
	2014 Survey	2009 Survey	2014 Survey	2009 Survey
Company middle-level management	28.6	24.6	18.9	23.5
Corporate executive	11.6	13.7	21.6	29.4
Office nonmanagement staff	10.1	12.3	5.4	14.7
Scientific researcher/engineer	7.0	8.1	8.1	5.9
Banking, insurance, securities analyst	3.0	6.2	8.1	5.9
Accountant, statistician, auditor	3.5	5.2	8.1	2.9
Media/advertising specialist, architect	2.0	3.8	0.0	5.9
Other technical professions	6.5	3.8	10.8	0.0
Lawyer	2.0	3.3	0.0	2.9
Business and service staff	3.0	3.3	0.0	0.0
Government civil servants	3.0	2.8	2.7	0.0
Business owner	3.5	2.4	5.4	0.0
Doctors, nurses, and public health staff	1.5	1.9	5.4	0.0
College professor and school instructor	3.0	1.9	0.0	2.9
Sales manager	5.0	1.4	0.0	2.9
Government and state-owned enterprise official	1.0	0.9	0.0	0.0
Translator	1.0	0.9	0.0	0.0
Salesperson	0.0	0.9	0.0	0.0
Reporter/editor	0.5	0.5	0.0	0.0
Self-employed	0.0	0.5	0.0	0.0
Student	2.5	0.5	0.0	0.0
Retired	1.0	0.5	2.7	0.0
Homemaker (not employed)	0.5	0.5	2.7	2.9
Total	100.0	100.0	100.0	100.0

Europe		Asia		Other countries*	
2014 Survey	2009 Survey	2014 Survey	2009 Survey	2014 Survey	
24.7	30.5	43.3	24.2	19.0	20.3
11.1	8.5	6.7	17.7	9.5	6.8
11.1	13.6	8.3	12.9	19.0	8.5
11.1	8.5	3.3	8.1	0.0	8.5
2.5	11.9	1.7	0.0	0.0	8.5
3.7	3.4	1.7	4.8	0.0	8.5
3.7	1.7		4.8	0.0	3.4
6.2	1.7	5.0	6.5	4.8	5.1
2.5	1.7	3.3	1.6	0.0	6.8
1.2	0.0	5.0	6.5	9.5	5.1
2.5	5.1	5.0	3.2	0.0	1.7
3.5	1.7	1.7	3.2	9.6	3.4
0.0	0.0	1.7	0.0	0.0	6.8
7.4	3.4	0.0	1.6	0.0	0.0
2.5	0.0	10.0	3.2	9.5	0.0
2.5	0.0	0.0	0.0	0.0	3.4
1.2	3.4	1.7	0.0	0.0	0.0
0.0	0.0	0.0	0.0	0.0	3.4
1.2	1.7	0.0	0.0	0.0	0.0
0.0	0.0	0.0	1.6	0.0	0.0
1.2	1.7	1.7	0.0	14.3	0.0
0.0	1.7	0.0	0.0	4.8	0.0
0.0	0.0	0.0	0.0	0.0	0.0
100.0	100.0	100.0	100.0	100.0	100.0

*Other countries include primarily Australia, New Zealand, and Canada.

FIGURE 9-2. A comparison of five surveys on degree of concern toward climate change—"How much do you personally worry about climate change?"

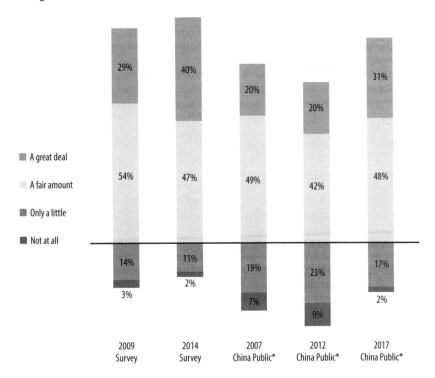

Sources: The "2007 China public" survey refers to the survey conducted by the Committee of 100, *Hope and Fear: American and Chinese Attitudes Toward Each Other—Parallel Survey on Issues Concerning U.S.-China Relations* (New York, Committee of 100 Publication, December 2007), 12. "The 2012 China public" survey refers to the survey conducted by the Committee of 100, *US-China Attitudes toward Each Other* (New York: Committee of 100 Publication, 2012), 53. "The 2017 China public" survey refers to the Committee of 100, *US-China Public Perceptions: Opinion Survey 2017* (New York: Committee of 100 Publication, 2017), 44.

*The 2007 China Public survey, the 2012 China Public survey and the 2017 China Public survey all have respondents who chose "no reply," and thus they do not add up to 100.

percent), but the percentage is still lower than that of Shanghai returnees in the two surveys conducted earlier. Foreign-educated returnees have thus heralded a trend toward greater public concern about climate change and environmental degradation in China.

Figure 9-3 shows that the longer time a respondent spent abroad, the

FIGURE 9-3. Percentage of Shanghai returnees who are "deeply concerned" about climate change, paired with the duration of their foreign stay, surveyed in 2009 and 2014

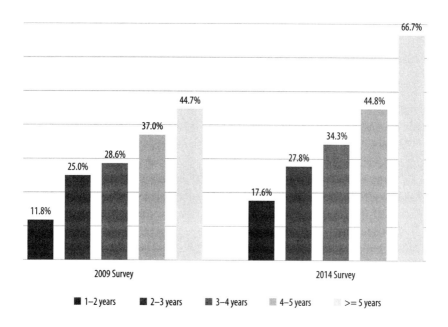

greater their concern regarding climate change. The proportion of Shanghai returnees who express that they are "worried a great deal" about climate change rises as their foreign study time duration increases. In the 2014 survey, 18 percent of those who studied abroad for one to two years are "worried a great deal," while 67 percent of those who studied abroad for more than five years are "worried a great deal"—almost a 50 percent spread. The same pattern can be found in the 2009 survey. These findings indicate that studying abroad may have a strong impact on returnee perceptions of the importance of addressing climate change.

Both the 2009 and 2014 surveys ask respondents for their opinion on whether developed countries or developing countries bear the greatest responsibility for climate change. Forty-four percent of respondents in the 2009 survey and 38 percent in the 2014 survey believe that developed countries should bear greater responsibility. Fourteen percent in the 2009 survey and 22 percent in the 2014 survey believe that developing countries should bear more responsibility, and the remaining 42 percent in the 2009 survey and 37 percent in the 2014 survey believe that both developed and developing countries should bear equal responsibility. Compared to the 2009 re-

FIGURE 9-4. A comparison of five surveys evaluating the Chinese government's performance on environmental governance—"How would you rate the Chinese government's performance in handling environmental issues?"

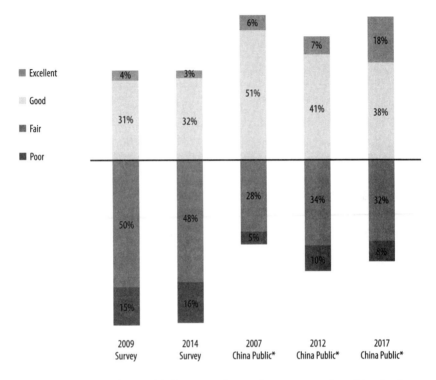

Sources: "The 2007 China public" survey refers to the survey conducted by the Committee of 100, *Hope and Fear: American and Chinese Attitudes toward Each Other—Parallel Survey on Issues Concerning U.S.-China Relations* (New York, Committee of 100 Publication, December 2007), 12. "The 2012 China public" survey refers to the survey conducted by the Committee of 100, *US-China Attitudes toward Each Other* (New York: Committee of 100 Publication, 2012), 53. "The 2017 survey" survey refers to the Committee of 100, *US-China Public Perceptions: Opinion Survey 2017* (New York: Committee of 100 Publication, 2017), 44.

*The 2007 China Public survey, the 2012 China Public survey, and the 2017 China Public survey have respondents who chose "no reply" and thus do not add up to 100.

sults, there was a decline in the proportion of 2014 survey respondents who think developed countries should bear greater responsibility.

Figure 9-4 presents the responses of various surveys to the following question: "How would you rate the Chinese government's performance in handling environmental issues?" In the 2014 survey of Shanghai returnees,

64 percent of the respondents believe that the Chinese government is performing poorly in terms of environmental governance, of which 48 percent think it is "not good" and 16 percent believe it is "not good at all." The responses in the 2009 survey are remarkably similar. Returnees in Shanghai are apparently more aware—and more critical—of the reality that China is one of the world's largest producers of greenhouse gases. In contrast, participants in the three surveys of the Chinese public conducted in 2007, 2012, and 2017 are far less critical of the Chinese government's performance in environmental protection.

Interestingly, only 4 percent of 2009 and 3 percent of 2014 respondents in Shanghai rate the performance of the Chinese government in dealing with environmental challenges as "excellent." The two other national surveys conducted in 2007 and 2012 reveal similar responses among the general public (6 and 7 percent, respectively). The more positive evaluation (18 percent) in the 2017 national survey may be the result of increased efforts to promote "green GDP" by the Xi Jinping administration. After Xi became top leader in 2012, the Chinese leadership has linked performance evaluations of top municipal and provincial leaders to their environmental protection efforts. Xi's appeal for green development is a nod to the widespread public discontent over air, water, and soil pollution, and the environmental degradation that has littered China's path of rapid economic growth.[22]

Although China has continued to face serious environmental issues, the recent efforts of Chinese authorities to shut down a large number of heavily polluting factories and promote clean energy cars seem to have yielded positive results, especially in terms of the pollution levels in China relative to other countries. According to EcoWatch, of the twenty most polluted cities in the world in 2018, fifteen were in India and two were in China.[23] Ten years earlier, in 2008, studies by both the World Bank and the Worldwatch Institute showed that sixteen of the world's twenty most polluted cities were in China.[24]

Economic Outlook

Over the past decade, China has gone through major economic fluctuations and transformations. The 2008 global financial crisis highlighted and accelerated the country's need for fundamental economic structural change, even though China experienced a quick and remarkable V-shaped recovery. While the double-digit growth from the early decades of the reform era has come to the end, the country has emerged as the second-largest economy in the world. China has also begun to change the existing global economic landscape through its Belt and Road Initiative. There has been strong criticism—both in China and abroad—of so-called Chinese state capitalism, which is evident in industrial policy favoring state-owned enterprises and the "Made in China 2025" plan. Both Chinese private firms and foreign companies claim that these policies have enabled increasingly unfair economic competition in recent years.

The 2009 survey of Shanghai returnees was conducted in the middle of the global financial crisis. In that environment, 87 percent of respondents reported that the Chinese government responded well to the financial crisis, including 70 percent expressing that it was handled "reasonably well" and 17 percent "very well." In particular, 24 and 23 percent of returnees studying in Europe and the United States, respectively, thought that the Chinese government performed "very well." These opinions might reflect the substantial economic difficulties in Europe and the United States at the time. Additionally, the level of confidence among Shanghai returnees regarding China's prospects of overcoming the financial crisis was quite high (78 percent). A different 2009 survey of urban residents in China shows 79 percent expressing high confidence in the country's ability to emerge successfully from the financial crisis.[25] Thus, in 2009, both the Shanghai returnees and urban residents in China had similarly high levels of confidence.

The 2014 survey of Shanghai returnees measures participants' confidence in the prospect of economic structural changes in China. Overall, 71 percent have confidence in China's economic restructuring. Of these, 61 percent are "reasonably confident" and 10 percent are "very confident" regarding the country's economic prospects. Respondents who studied in Australia, New Zealand, and Canada express greater confidence in China's economic restructuring, accounting for 81 percent of those who are optimistic about China's economic future. Both the 2009 and 2014 surveys also ask respondents which country will likely be the front runner in the world economy in the next decade or so. Interestingly, the surveys present contrasting results. While the 2009 survey shows 52 percent of respondents ranking China as the front runner and 33 percent ranking the United States as the front runner, the 2014 survey reverses the order with 38 percent ranking the United States at the top and 32 percent favoring China.

Shanghai returnees are more critical of—and concerned about—a regional economic gap and the imbalance between urban and rural areas in China. When asked, "Is China's current economic and social development structure, especially in terms of regional development and urban-rural differentiation, reasonable?" a majority of Shanghai respondents in the 2014 survey (58 percent) express worry about the economic development structure in China, especially the country's regional economic imbalances and urban-rural divides (figure 9-5). Among these concerned respondents, 44 percent think the existing structure is "not reasonable," and 14 percent feel it is "not

FIGURE 9-5. Views of economic development—"Is China's current economic and social development structure, especially in terms of regional development status and urban-rural differentiation, reasonable?"

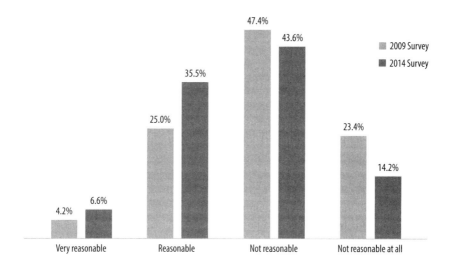

FIGURE 9-6. Views of energy security—"Are you worried about China's energy security in the future?"

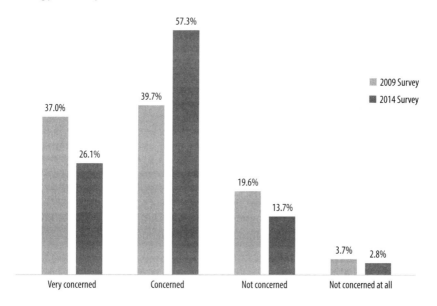

reasonable at all." The proportion of those who believe that it is unreasonable, however, drops from 71 percent in the 2009 survey to 58 percent in the 2014 survey. This decline may reflect the efforts of the Chinese leadership in recent years to promote economic development in inland regions and rural areas.

A large number of Shanghai returnees are also concerned about China's level of economic inequality. In the 2009 survey, 87 percent of respondents think that the current gap between the rich and poor in the country is unreasonable, including 44 percent who think it is "not reasonable" and 43 percent think it is "very unreasonable." Concerns are slightly alleviated but still high in the 2014 survey; 77 percent believe that the gap between the rich and the poor in China is unreasonable, of which 40 percent feel it is "not reasonable" and 37 percent think it is "very unreasonable." In responding to a question about "the extent to which the rights of migrant workers in China have been realized or guaranteed," 66 percent of participants in the 2014 survey think that the rights of migrant workers are basically not guaranteed, including 50 percent stating that migrant worker rights are "not well realized or guaranteed" and 16 percent saying that the protection of rights is "very poor."

Many Shanghai returnees also express apprehension about energy security in the country. In the 2014 survey, as many as 83 percent of respondents expressed concern about energy security challenges, especially given that China's rapid economic development depends on oil and natural gas energy supplies. Among these respondents, 26 percent expressed "serious concern" and 57 percent expressed "concern." Compared with the results of the 2009 survey, the level of concern about energy security has increased (figure 9-6). When looking at the relationship between degree of concern and the geographic location where returnees studied, those from Europe are most concerned about China's future energy security at 88 percent, while 76 percent of returnees who studied in the United States are worried about this issue— the lowest proportion among the different study abroad cohorts.

Social Norms and Attitudes

The two surveys of Shanghai returnees also ask about social norms and attitudes, socioeconomic conditions in China, and issues of governance. They include questions about the role of the middle class, the status of higher education, concerns about food and product safety, economic disparities, migrant worker rights, social stability, corruption and legal development, media supervision, and more.

Figure 9-7 compares the responses to the two surveys of Shanghai returnees against those of three groups—the general public, opinion lead-

FIGURE 9-7. A comparison of five surveys on the importance of the Chinese middle class—"Will the emerging middle class become the most influential force in Chinese society?"

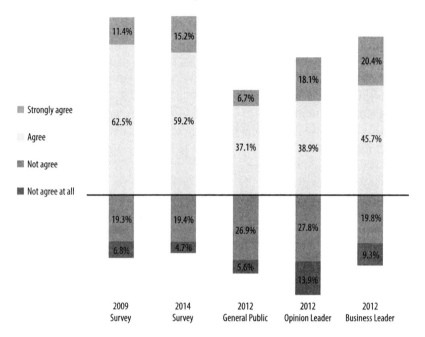

Sources: The "General public 2012" survey, "Opinion Leaders 2012" survey, and "Business Leaders 2012" survey were all based on the degree of agreement with the statement "China's emerging middle class will have great impact on Chinese society and politics" made in the survey conducted by the Committee of 100, *US-China Attitudes toward Each Other* (New York: Committee of 100 Publication, 2012), 97.

ers, and business leaders who were surveyed by the Committee of 100 in 2012—regarding the importance of the Chinese middle class. All these surveys ask the following: "Will the emerging middle class become the most influential force in Chinese society?" Shanghai returnees have a high percentage of positive replies, with 74 percent in both the 2009 survey and the 2014 survey, especially compared to the survey responses of the three other groups—44 percent among the general public, 57 percent among opinion leaders, and 66 percent among business leaders. For returnees in Shanghai, the longer they studied overseas, the more likely they were to report that the middle class plays a crucial role in China. In the 2009 survey, for example, 83 percent of those who studied abroad for four or more years agree with the statement that "the middle class will become the most influential class in Chinese society."

Shanghai returnees have relatively negative opinions about China's higher education system. Three-fourths of respondents (76 percent) to the 2009 survey consider China's higher education to be "poor" or "very poor." In contrast, a 2010 survey of China's urban residents finds that 51 percent have a negative opinion of the country's higher education system.[26] Returnees' view of China's higher education system, however, significantly improves to 52 percent of respondents reporting negative opinions in the 2014 survey. The 2014 survey also shows that returnees from the United States are the most likely (59 percent) to have negative views of China's higher education system.

Figure 9-8 compares the level of concern among Shanghai returnees with that of the Chinese general public regarding food safety and product quality issues. Both the 2009 and 2014 surveys of returnees reveal high levels of worry about food and product safety issues in the country: 86 percent in the 2009 survey express concern, of which 46 percent feel "worried" and 40 percent are "very worried," whereas 82 percent in the 2014 survey express concern, of which 34 percent are "worried" and 48 percent are "very worried." In the 2009 survey, returnees from Asia—primarily Japan and Singapore—expressed the greatest concern about food and product safety (92 percent), and in the 2014 survey, returnees from the United States had the highest concern at 88 percent.

In contrast to returnees, the Chinese general public are far less worried about these safety issues (44 percent in both the 2007 and 2012 surveys, and 46 percent in the 2017 survey). The 2017 survey conducted by the Committee of 100 also asks the same question of three elite groups, and those responding that they are "worried" or "very worried" include 69 percent of business leaders, 63 percent of policy experts, and 67 percent of journalists.[27] While these groups are more concerned about these safety issues than the general public, they are still much less concerned than returnees. Interestingly, in an earlier 2007 survey of Chinese business leaders asking the same question, only 38 percent expressed concerns.[28] According to one Chinese survey conducted in 2009, China's urban residents feel comfortable with food and product safety at 54 points, which is low, but Shanghai returnees are even less sure about food and product safety in China at 25 points.[29]

Compared to the Chinese general public, Shanghai returnees have led the pack in expressing concern about food and product safety issues. Over the decades, partly as a result of numerous high-profile scandals regarding food products and unsafe medicine, the Chinese public has begun to take note and follow Shanghai's lead. In surveys of the Chinese general public, the percentage of respondents saying that food safety is a very big problem rose from 12 percent in 2008 to 38 percent in 2013, and to 40 percent in 2016. Similarly, concerns about medicine safety have grown from 9 percent

FIGURE 9-8. A comparison of five surveys on degree of concern about food and product safety in China—"How much do you personally worry about food and product safety issues in China?"

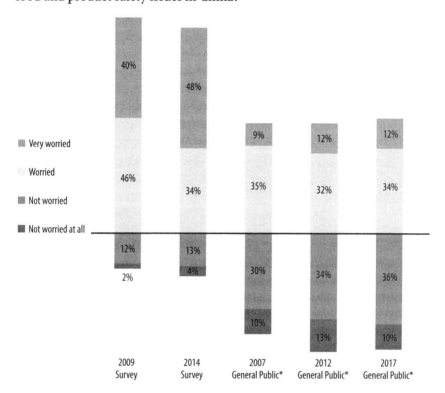

Sources: The "2007 General public" survey refers to the survey conducted by the Committee of 100, *Hope and Fear: American and Chinese Attitudes toward Each Other—Parallel Survey on Issues Concerning U.S.-China Relations* (New York, Committee of 100 Publication, December 2007), 40. "The 2012 General public" survey refers to the survey conducted by the Committee of 100, *US-China Attitudes toward Each Other* (New York: Committee of 100 Publication, 2012), 69. "The 2017 General public" survey refers to the Committee of 100, *US-China Public Perceptions: Opinion Survey 2017* (New York: Committee of 100 Publication, 2017), 71.

*The 2007 General Public survey, the 2012 General Public survey, and the 2017 General Public survey all have respondents who chose "no reply" and thus do not add up to 100. The question for the Committee of 100 surveys is somewhat different: "How do cases of tainted food and unsafe toys in China reduce your confidence in products made in China?"

in 2008 to 27 percent in 2013, and to 42 percent in 2016, according to surveys by the Pew Research Center in China.[30]

In response to a question posed to Shanghai returnees regarding social stability in China: "Are you worried about social stability in China?" 28 percent of respondents expressed worry in the 2009 survey, a percentage that almost doubled (55 percent) in the 2014 survey. Those who studied abroad for four years or more were greatly worried about China's social stability, at 66 percent and 58 percent in 2009 and 2014, respectively. When looking at how this worry varies by study abroad destination, returnees from the United States are the most unconcerned about China's social stability (53 percent). The 2009 survey of Shanghai returnees also shows that when evaluating the severity of governance issues on a four-point scale (with 1 being least severe)—namely legal development, media supervision, and anticorruption—their assessments number 2.42, 2.49, and 1.79, respectively. Converting from a four-point scale system to a 100-point system, Shanghai returnees evaluate China's problem of corruption at just 27 points, which is much lower than the evaluation by urban residents in a nationwide survey (69 points).[31]

Views of International Relations

Over the past two decades, Chinese people have consistently considered the United States to be of great importance to China's economic development and security.[32] Surveys have also revealed the persistent ambivalence of the Chinese public toward the United States. On the one hand, a majority of Chinese citizens hold favorable views of America and support increasing economic interdependence between the United States and China. On the other hand, many Chinese people feel that the U.S. is trying to prevent their country from becoming a great world power.

The spring 2016 Global Attitudes survey conducted by the U.S.-based Pew Research Center, for example, shows that half of Chinese citizens in the survey gave the U.S. a favorable rating. At the same time, 52 percent thought the U.S. was trying to prevent China from becoming an equal power.[33] The survey also shows that a large number of Chinese (75 percent) see China playing a more important role in world affairs compared to a decade ago, which is a much higher percentage than that of respondents in the European Union (EU) (23 percent) and the U.S. (21 percent) when asked about their perceptions of their country or region's role in the world.[34] This 2016 survey also finds that Chinese citizens' confidence about their country's global stature coexists with some degree of anxiety, and an inclination to look more inward than outward. An analysis of the survey results reports that "a majority of Chinese (56 percent) want Beijing to focus on China's problems. Just 22 percent want their government to help other nations."[35]

Similar views are shared among Shanghai returnees, although they also differ from the general public and other elite groups in certain respects. Figure 9-9 presents the results of five different surveys about the overall impression of the United States among Chinese respondents. Shanghai returnees in both the 2009 and 2014 surveys have much more favorable impressions of the United States (90 and 92 percent in the 2009 and 2014 surveys, respectively) than those who took part in three general public surveys (60 percent in 2007, 59 percent in 2012, and 55 percent in 2017). Interestingly, those who returned from studying in the United States report the highest favorability of the United States (100 percent in the 2009 survey and 97 percent in the 2014 survey) compared to those who studied in other countries and regions.

FIGURE 9-9. A comparison of five surveys on overall impression of the United States—"How would you describe your impression of the United States?"

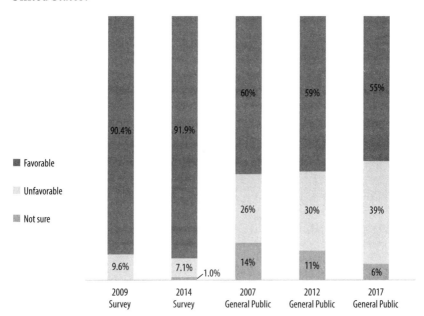

Sources: The "2007 General public" survey refers to the survey conducted by the Committee of 100, *Hope and Fear: American and Chinese Attitudes toward Each Other— Parallel Survey on Issues Concerning U.S.-China Relations* (New York, Committee of 100 Publication, December 2007), 12. "The 2012 General public" survey refers to the survey conducted by the Committee of 100, *US-China Attitudes toward Each Other* (New York: Committee of 100 Publication, 2012), 20. "The 2017 General public" survey refers to the Committee of 100, *US-China Public Perceptions: Opinion Survey 2017* (New York: Committee of 100 Publication, 2017), 16.

In response to the question, "What's your view of U.S. President Obama?" 77 percent of Shanghai returnees in the 2014 survey reported that they like Obama, including 10 percent stating that they "like him very much" and 67 percent just saying that they "like him." The percentage of respondents who expressed favorable views of President Obama in the 2009 survey is even higher: 14 percent "like him very much" and 78 percent "like him." When taking into account the country or region where respondents studied, returnees from the United States expressed the highest favorability of President Obama in both the 2009 and 2014 surveys (94 percent and 88 percent, respectively).

The 2014 survey also asks a few questions concerning Japan and China-Japan relations in light of the tensions between the two countries at the time. In response to a question about overall impressions of Japan, 53 percent of Shanghai returnees said that they have a good overall impression of Japan, including 9 percent rating the country as "excellent" and 44 percent considering it "good." In comparison, the "2012 Survey Report on the Quality of Life of Chinese Residents" shows that China's general public had a less favorable view of Japan, with 87 percent of respondents expressing a negative opinion of Japan.[36] In the 2014 survey, returnees from Asia (predominantly from Japan) reported the highest favorable view of Japan (73 percent). In comparison, only 32 percent of returnees from Australia, New Zealand, and Canada had a favorable view of Japan. As for the Chinese government's handling of Sino-Japan relations, more than half of the returnees believed that the Chinese government did not handle the relationship well (9 percent chose "poorly," and 43 percent chose "not very well"). There is not much variation in opinion based on the country or region where returnees studied.

Figure 9-10 presents the evaluations of Shanghai returnees in the 2014 survey on China's bilateral relationship with selected countries and regions. China's relationships with the United States and Russia were seen as the most important (87 and 86 percent, respectively), followed by the country's relationship with the EU (86 percent). China's relationships with Latin America, North Korea, and Africa were considered the least important. Surprisingly, most respondents viewed China and Russia as having good relations (80 percent), followed by relations with Africa (79 percent) and the EU (74 percent). This result is quite noteworthy given that only 1 percent of returnees in this survey studied in Russia. China's relationships with Japan (50 percent), India (66 percent), and the United States (68 percent) were rated the worst.

In comparison, the 2009 survey of Shanghai returnees ranks the degree of importance of eight countries and regions to China in the following order: the United States, Russia, the EU, Japan, Association of Southeast Asian Nations (ASEAN), India, South Korea, and North Korea. As for rankings of

FIGURE 9-10. Evaluations of China's bilateral relationship with selected countries and regions in terms of "Degree of importance" and "Status of good relations" (surveyed in 2014)

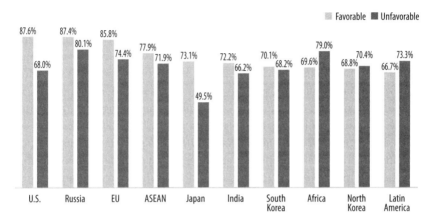

positive relations, Russia is number one, followed by ASEAN, the United States, North Korea, the EU, South Korea, India, and Japan. These results are similar to those of a survey of the Chinese general public conducted during the same year, in which the largest group (64 percent of respondents) considered the United States to be the most important country to China for economic reasons. In response to a question about which country is China's closest ally on the security front, the largest group of respondents (49 percent) considered Russia to be the most important security ally to China.[37]

The 2009 survey of Shanghai returnees also asks about the degree of agreement with China's strategic objective for a "peaceful rise" on the world stage. Ninety-three percent of respondents expressed agreement, including 31 percent in "full agreement" and 62 percent in "agreement." Those who returned from studying in the United States expressed the most agreement (97 percent). For those with an income of over RMB 16,000, 99 percent stated that they agree with China's "peaceful rise" strategic objective. The higher the income of the person, the more likely they were to agree with China's peaceful rise strategy. When it comes to prospects for Cross-Strait relations with Taiwan, 68 percent of returnees believed that Taiwan would maintain the status quo over the next few years, 31 percent believed that Taiwan would move toward unification, and only 2 percent believed Taiwan would move toward independence. The percentage of men who think Taiwan would "maintain the status quo" was at 80 percent, while the percentage of women was at 57 percent. Furthermore, women were more inclined to believe that the two sides of the Taiwan Strait would "move toward unification in the future" (41 percent).

A significant number of returnees believed that the United States uses Taiwan as "an unsinkable aircraft carrier" to contain China. In response to a question regarding the U.S. role in Taiwan, returnees were asked to provide multiple answers. Two-thirds (68 percent) of respondents believed that the United States "really cares about its own interests," 29 percent considered the United States to be a "trouble-maker," 21 percent believed that the United States is "more inclined to promote Taiwan independence," and 20 percent thought that the United States "creates obstacles to Cross-Strait exchanges and integration."

In response to a question about the Chinese government's efforts to pursue military modernization, 90 percent of returnees in the 2014 survey perceived that the Chinese government effectively promotes military modernization, of which 17 percent believed the effort to be "excellent" and 73 percent described it as "good." The positive response in the 2014 survey is slightly higher than that of the 2009 survey (87 percent). In terms of countries and regions in which returnees studied, returnees from Asia had the highest positive assessment of military modernization (97 percent). Returnees from Europe had the lowest assessment among all survey respondents (83 percent).

A longitudinal survey of Beijing residents between 1998 and 2015, consisting of a total of eleven survey waves, reveals similar observations about the strong degree of public support for the efforts of the Chinese government to promote military modernization. In answering the question, "Do you think that the proportion of national defense spending should increase/ maintain/decrease, regarding China's national fiscal expenditure?" over 80 percent of respondents in all eleven surveys believed that China should maintain or increase its national fiscal expenditure.[38] On average, about 65 percent of respondents in all of these surveys believed that China should increase its military expenditure. Interestingly, this longitudinal study also asked the following question seven times (between 2002 and 2015): "Do you agree that the government should reduce defense spending in order to improve social welfare?" With the exception of the 2009 survey, a majority of respondents provided an affirmative answer. In the 2015 survey, for example, about three-fourths of respondents expressed agreement.[39]

Impact of Cultural Assimilation

An overwhelming majority of Shanghai returnees feel that their time abroad had an enormous impact on them in terms of individual development. In the 2009 survey, 94 percent replied positively to the question, "How much did your foreign experience impact your personal growth?" Among them, 39 and 55 percent said they experienced an "enormous" or "significant" impact, respectively (see figure 9-11). The 2014 survey shows an even more significant cultural impact of foreign studies, with 96 percent of respondents stating their overseas experiences had a great impact, including 46 and 50 percent experiencing "enormous" and "significant" impact, respectively.

Both the 2009 survey and the 2014 survey include a question about the patriotism and nationalistic sentiments of Shanghai returnees.[40] Figure 9-12 shows the degree of patriotism in the 2014 survey in relation to the duration of time abroad. While almost all respondents, regardless of how long they spent studying abroad, tend to be highly patriotic (an average of 85 out of 100 points), returnees studying abroad for two to three years express the highest degree of patriotism (87 points). Interestingly, the 2009 survey has the same result, with returnees studying abroad for two to three years expressing the highest degree of patriotism. Both surveys also show that returnees from the United States have the lowest level of patriotism. For example, in the 2014 survey, returnees from the United States have an average patriotism level of 78 points.

The 2009 and 2014 survey results about patriotism and nationalistic sentiments among Shanghai returnees provide valuable insight about the role of higher education in ideological formation, as well as the impact of value dissemination through international educational exchanges. In their comprehensive study of the formation and transformation of political values and views in China, Jennifer Pan and Yiqing Xu, scholars from Stanford and

FIGURE 9-11. The impact of foreign studies on personal development— "How much did your foreign experience impact your personal growth?"

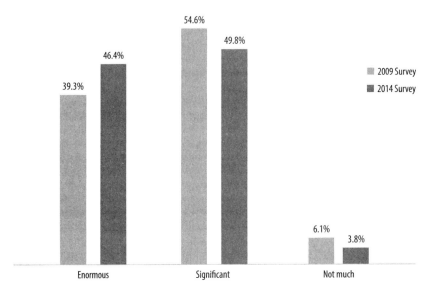

FIGURE 9-12. Degree of patriotism of Shanghai returnees based on the duration of their studies abroad (surveyed in 2014)

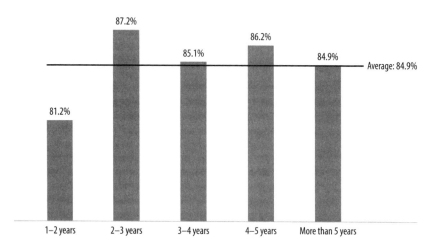

the University of California at Berkeley, respectively, analyze data from an online survey of a large number of Chinese netizens (460,532) collected between January 2012 and December 2014. The survey includes fifty questions across seven categories: (1) political institutions, (2) individual freedom, (3) market economy, (4) capital and labor, (5) economic sovereignty and globalization, (6) nationalism, and (7) traditionalism. They use the questions to search for cleavages delineating "China's ideological spectrum."[41] Based on their analyses, they argue that preferences for liberal, pro-market, nontraditional, and "nonnationalist" values are associated with higher levels of education, income, economic openness, and Western influence, and these values are more common among those who live in well-developed, wealthy regions and cosmopolitan cities, such as Shenzhen, Guangzhou, Shanghai, and Beijing.[42] With regard to nationalism, they divide individuals into two groups: those who endorse patriotism and take a strong stance on defending China's territorial sovereignty while holding an adversarial view of the West (they designate this set of preferences as "nationalist"), and those who oppose such confrontational, "nationalistic" sentiments (they call these "nonnationalist" preferences).[43]

Based on their quantitative analysis, the researchers conclude that "nationalists" differ significantly from "nonnationalists" in a number of respects. Compared to the latter, the former are more likely to support authoritarian rule, to think that the state should be allowed to more actively intervene in the market and the private domain, to believe that China's economic reforms have generated negative impacts in terms of economic disparity and social dislocation, to endorse traditional values such as support for social hierarchy and stances against homosexuality, and to favor nationalistic foreign policy and economic protectionism.[44]

Though the surveys of Shanghai returnees in this study have a much smaller sample size, their findings differ markedly from those of Jennifer Pan and Yiqing Xu. In both the 2009 and 2014 surveys of Shanghai returnees, respondents show strong patriotism and nationalistic sentiments, and their degree of nationalism is by no means lower than that of the Chinese public and other elite groups. In spite of this high degree of "nationalism," as presented earlier, Shanghai returnees' opinions regarding environmental, economic, social, and foreign policy issues, and their views of the Chinese government do not fall neatly into the binary groupings outlined in Pan and Xu's study. Thus a strong sense of national identity and patriotic sentiments are not indicative of an ideologically coherent set of sociopolitical values or foreign policy beliefs. This finding is also echoed by other studies of public opinion surveys conducted in China, as Cornell University political scientist Jessica Chen Weiss recently observed.[45] In her review of five surveys of Chinese citizens, netizens, and elites, Weiss asserts the following:

> While identities play a role in shaping preferences, feelings of national identification are not the same as foreign policy beliefs and attitudes. Identity-based measures of nationalism may not always reflect the pressures that the government grapples with in conducting foreign policy. Preferences may shift with changing external and domestic circumstances even as identities remain the same or change more slowly. One might assume that those who score high on identity-based metrics of nationalism might also express hawkish foreign policy preferences. In some cases, nationalists may support liberal international policies out of deference to the government. Other self-described patriots may prefer that the government focus on domestic priorities and eschew hard-line foreign policies.[46]

The 2009 and 2014 survey results align with this argument—that "hawkish-dovish" policy preferences among Chinese survey respondents are more likely a measure of external cues about Chinese foreign policy that have been internalized by Chinese citizens, rather than Chinese patriotism and perceptions of national identity.[47] Recognizing that there are limits to what generalizations can be made from the small set of data in the 2009 and 2014 surveys, some conclusions can still be derived. Overall, the overseas experiences of Shanghai returnees have had a strong impact on them in terms of cultural assimilation, international perspectives, and certain universal values, but those experiences may not have had a direct effect on their sense of patriotism and perceptions of national identity.

CONCLUSION

For any analysis of the impact of international educational exchanges, it is essential to empirically examine the views and values that students develop through foreign study experiences. This chapter presents the results of two original opinion surveys of foreign-educated returnees in Shanghai—a distinct subset of the city's rapidly growing middle class. The results of these surveys shed light on the attitudes and perspectives of returnees regarding various domestic and international issues. Four key observations can be gleaned from analyzing the responses and participants' demographic and political-economic factors.

First, this study shows the significant impact of foreign studies on returnees' perceptions about the importance of addressing various challenges, such as China's environmental degradation, global climate change, economic disparity, the urban-rural divide, neglect of migrant worker rights, energy security, food and medicine safety, government accountability, rule of law, and governance. Returnees are noticeably more concerned about— and more critical of—virtually all of these issues than the Chinese general public and even some elite groups in China, as other recent surveys reveal. The longer a returnee respondent resides abroad, the more pronounced his or her concerns about these issues often become. Also, on most of these issues, the 2014 survey shows more respondents expressing stronger concerns than were reflected in the 2009 survey. Compared to the Chinese general public, Shanghai returnees have been ahead of their time in expressing critical views and concerns about various challenges that China confronts. In light of growing public awareness of these issues in China over the past decade, it is reasonable to assert that foreign-educated returnees have heralded a trend of increasing public concern and greater pressure on the government to institute policy reforms in these areas.

Second, Shanghai returnees are keenly aware of their middle-class identity and how they have been impacted by their time abroad, and they have strong opinions about China's education system. The longer they studied overseas, the more likely they are to report that the middle class plays a crucial role for China. An overwhelming majority of Shanghai returnees feel that their foreign experiences have had an enormous impact on them in terms of individual development, including both professional growth and cultural assimilation. Shanghai returnees are also much more negative about the status of China's higher education system than China's urban residents. Returnees from the United States, more than those from any other region, are most likely to hold negative views of China's higher education system.

Third, a major finding of this study is that returnees are more likely to have a favorable view of the country where they studied. Those who returned from studying in the United States report the highest favorable impression of the United States compared to those who studied in other countries and regions. Similarly, returnees from Asia (predominantly from Japan in this study) report the highest favorable view of Japan. The degree of favorability a returnee has toward a host country is subject to changing sociopolitical environments at home, in the host country, and in the bilateral relationship. For example, according to a 2018 study of Chinese students in the United States, about 16 percent of respondents indicated that they held a more positive view of America after coming to the United States, while 42 percent of respondents indicated that they developed a more negative view of the United States after their arrival. At the same time, about 46 percent of respondents indicated that they held a better view of China after coming to the United States and 13 percent of respondents indicated that they had a worse view of China. These negative opinions of their host country may be attributed to the deterioration of the Sino-U.S. relationship in recent years, and the new wave of U.S. government accusations about the prevalence of espionage activities among Chinese students in the United States.[48]

Finally, the findings of this study challenge the dichotomies of conservative versus liberal, authoritarian versus democratic, and nationalistic versus nonnationalistic for defining an ideological spectrum split along two clear-cut sets of sociopolitical values or foreign policy beliefs. Shanghai returnees are unique in their high degree of patriotism and nationalistic sentiment, but they are also more globalist cosmopolitans when it comes to certain important issues. They have more favorable views of the United States, but this does not necessarily mean that they are uncritical of U.S. foreign policy, especially of alleged efforts to contain China's rise. A recent study of hundreds of Chinese undergraduates in the United States shows that discrimination on the basis of ethnicity makes students more resistant to democratic values. Although Chinese students who study in the United States are more predisposed to favor liberal democracy than their peers in China, experiencing anti-Chinese discrimination in America significantly increases their support for CCP authoritarian rule.[49]

Like the Chinese public, returnees have ambivalent attitudes toward the United States—they appreciate bilateral cooperation on various fronts but are apprehensive about possible military conflict sparked by Taiwan or other concerns. In that regard, a majority of returnees think the Chinese government is right to promote the country's military modernization. For the same reasons, Shanghai returnees not only rank Russia as having the best relations with China, they also see Russia as China's closest ally on the security front.

To a great degree, Shanghai returnees—and the Chinese middle class in general—have views and values that are both conservative, in that they support the CCP leadership's focus on military modernization and social stability, and progressive, as they also demand government accountability, better legal protections for citizens, restraints on the monopolization of large state-owned enterprises, and greater public participation in the formation of socioeconomic policies. While the Shanghai returnees share many Chinese middle-class characteristics, they are also idiosyncratic, and it is unclear how their opinions, values, and beliefs may continue to evolve over time. Thus it would be ill-advised to extrapolate from this study and declare with certainty the type of political influences and contributions that they will bring to China. As one foreign observer has keenly noted, as far as the political concerns of the middle class go, "the balance of gains and losses keeps changing" depending on ever-changing domestic and international circumstances.[50]

CHAPTER 10

Western Influence and Illusion

Shanghai's Booming Contemporary Art Scene

A masterpiece of art must have multiple interpretations.
—YANG WEI

If a city has a dream, it is to wait for artists. If an artist has a dream,
it is to go to work and live in a city with many artists.
—XUE SONG

In analyzing the relationship between the state and liberal intellectuals in present-day China, the Western scholarly community often commits a mistake by characterizing this relationship in binary terms. Like their international counterparts, Chinese liberal intellectuals and artists are, of course, not fans of the authoritarian political system. By nature, they are inclined to support civil liberties and oppose media censorship. But this does not necessarily mean that they dedicate their work, entirely or primarily, to challenging the Chinese party-state. Without a doubt, some individuals have become internationally renowned for their strong criticism of the communist dictatorship. Prominent examples include the late Nobel Peace Prize laureate Liu Xiaobo, legal scholar and human rights activist Xu Zhiyong, economist Mao Yushi, and artist Ai Weiwei. As a group, however, Chinese liberal scholars and artists exhibit broad and diverse sociopolitical critiques, philosophical concerns, and artistic expressions.

In a recent article titled "Why Westerners Misinterpret Modern Chinese Art," Uli Sigg, a seasoned Swiss art collector, observed that "Western curators have tended to choose items for display according to their own preconceptions about China."[1] In the same article, He Xiangyu (born in 1986), a Chinese avant-garde artist who splits his time between Berlin and Beijing, commented on his own experiences with Western interpretations of his work. He Xiangyu's famous piece, *The Tank Project*, was produced between 2011 and 2013 and is a life-size tank weighing 2 tons and made entirely of Italian leather, which was seen as a political statement referencing the 1989 Tiananmen crackdown.[2] But He has since explained that his artwork was not intended to make such commentary. In his words, references to Chinese political life in his artwork are just "like a piece of vegetable in a burger." It is only one layer in the burger and is an optional ingredient. As He explained: "It's not necessarily important, and there are more levels [layers]."[3]

He Xiangyu's description of the multilayered interpretations and implications of the works of Chinese avant-garde artists reflects some of the crucial issues inherent in China studies, including the intriguing links between art and politics, the complicated and ever-changing relationship between intellectuals and the state, and the connections between avant-garde art and ideological changes in society. Many China scholars are skeptical of the simplistic assumption that art and politics always develop in parallel. Yet few would dispute the idea that cultural trends relate to changes in other spheres of life, including politics. The history of the People's Republic of China (PRC) shows that innovations by cultural elites, especially independent thinkers, often reflect and sometimes herald important social and political changes in the country.[4]

Avant-garde artists are by definition at the forefront. The Chinese terms for avant-garde artists, *qianwei yishujia* and *xianfeng pai*, describe the artists as being ahead of their time. The concerns of avant-garde artists often include some of the most sensitive and forward-looking issues of their time. To a great extent, the current intellectual ferment of Chinese avant-garde artists reflects the rapidly emerging Chinese middle class. As described earlier in this book, some Chinese scholars who study urban middle-class culture claim that if economic growth is the energy of change, culture determines the forward motion of that change.[5] In a sense, avant-garde artists are by-products of the rise of the middle class in the country, and in turn, they have shaped the anxieties, ambitions, and ambivalence of the middle class.

Contemporary Chinese artists assert that part of China's modernization is cultural. Yu Qiuyu, a distinguished scholar of Shanghai studies, was among the first to advocate for this notion of cultural modernization.[6] Some Chinese political leaders have also expressed similar opinions about the role of culture in the economic and social development of the country. Huang Ju, the former executive vice premier who had previously served as the party secretary and mayor of Shanghai, said that if economic infrastructure is the foundation or framework of a given country, then culture is the spirit.[7]

Any comprehensive study of the middle class in reform-era China, therefore, must include an exploration of the artistic community's political pursuits, especially the dynamic role played by avant-garde artists. During the past two decades, the ideas, views, values, and styles that Chinese artists have expressed through their work reflect an important intellectual discourse among cultural elites in this rapidly changing country. Socioeconomic transformation has given rise to a generation of more creative, more critical, more sophisticated, and less dogmatic artists. During this period, avant-garde works have come out from being underground for most of the 1990s to enter the mainstream art scene in the city during the first two decades of the twenty-first century.[8] Their art is often political and global in nature—their objectives and meanings are much broader than some Western commentators have typically understood, and their messages tend to be "multilayered," in the words of the aforementioned avant-garde artist He Xiangyu. This art must be multifaceted in order to be considered as such, as Chinese art critic Zhang Xiaoling observes that he can hardly imagine how a person who lacks opinions about current economic and sociopolitical challenges, as well as demographic and technological changes around the world, could become a real artist.[9] Thus an understanding of the experimental ideas expressed through the works of contemporary Chinese artists can advance our knowledge of new political and global thinking among Chinese intellectuals and other members of the middle class.

This chapter first explores how Chinese contemporary art can help us understand the dynamism and tensions inherent in the country's socioeconomic and cultural transformation during the reform era, and how some avant-garde artwork has been misinterpreted by foreign commentators. The chapter then details the remarkable rise of avant-garde artists and the vibrant art scene in Shanghai, especially as embodied by the city's internationally renowned Biennale. The Shanghai art scene is notable, as it reflects—and has often heralded—some important national trends in the era of globalization. The third part offers a historical account of Shanghai's role as a cradle of Chinese contemporary art, and it includes a review of the growing role of the avant-garde art community since the 1990s. The fourth and final part of the chapter describes how Shanghai's booming art galleries have been shaped by factors such as Western influence, commercialism, the government's objective of building a cosmopolitan cultural hub, substantial financial investment by private entrepreneurs and philanthropists, and enthusiasm from the middle class to develop new public spaces for civil and intellectual discourse.

UNDERSTANDING AND MISUNDERSTANDING
CHINESE AVANT-GARDE ARTISTS

He Xiangyu's remarks discussed at the beginning of the chapter reflect a widely shared sentiment by Chinese avant-garde artists—that the predominant approach of Western commentators is to excessively politicize Chinese avant-garde art as a conflict between art and the state.[10] For instance, in his comparative study of the avant-garde movements in the former Soviet Union and China during the reform era, Ralph Croizier characterizes Chinese avant-garde art as antiestablishment, Western-inspired, and counterculture.[11] To a great extent, these dubious generalizations about Chinese avant-garde artists are common among Western reporters and art critics. Evidence from the works of Shanghai avant-garde artists in this study, however, suggests that these three characterizations are at the very least inadequate and narrow-minded.

First, while few avant-garde artists in present-day China truly believe in communist ideology and Chinese Communist Party propaganda, the relationship between artists and party authorities is complicated. Artists may not necessarily see the Chinese leadership in monolithic and static terms. They often support some government policies and oppose others, depending on the specific issue and circumstance. However, as economic globalization and the single-minded drive for GDP growth under Deng Xiaoping and Jiang Zemin, in particular, have resulted in tremendous income disparities, social dislocation, and environmental degradation, some artists have become increasingly critical of China's transition to capitalism, or what some call "market fundamentalism."

Second, many Chinese avant-garde artists have indeed been inspired by Western political thought, liberal values, and artistic styles. But since the late 1990s, they have also become cynical and resentful of postcolonialism and cultural chauvinism in the West. In the wake of what many Chinese perceive to be a wave of "anti-China rhetoric of political leaders in the West" and efforts toward a "U.S.-led containment against China's rise," especially through the lens of Samuel Huntington's clash of civilizations theory, some avant-garde artists have begun reevaluating the intentions of Western politicians and their efforts to promote democracy and human rights issues in China.

Third, the line between mainstream culture and counterculture—or between conventional and idiosyncratic expressions of art—has become increasingly hazy in recent years. Other previously distinct conceptual boundaries—including those between socialism and capitalism, tradition and modernity, or even between Chinese and foreign—have also become less clear. As a Shanghainese artist asserts, "In an era of globalization, 'western worship' (*chongyang meiwai*) by Chinese intellectuals has become a past tense, and it has no meaning anymore."[12]

Geremie Barmé, a distinguished Australian expert on Chinese culture, observed in 2000 that Chinese avant-garde artists have gained much of their visibility only when set against the gloomy backdrop manufactured by the state.[13] In another article published during the same period, Barmé and Sang Ye maintain that despite substantial economic development and information inflows, China has remained "limited by intellectual narrowness and Sinocentric bias. Pluralism and the open-mindedness that comes with it . . . simply are not present."[14] Feng Jiali, an artist in Chongqing and cofounder of a feminist group called Siren Studio, finds such commentaries on Chinese art to be offensive. Some Western art critics, she writes, "could very well mistake a splendid rainbow for white mist."[15] For some Chinese scholars, the "intellectual narrowness" demonstrated by these Western commentators and their Eurocentric or American-centric bias prevent them from appreciating the richness and diversity of cultural life, intellectual discourse, and artistic experiments in present-day China, which are all the more remarkable given the uphill battles of confronting tight political control by Chinese authorities that artists face. Some of these scholars and artists believe that the binary thinking of Western commentators has overly simplified the sociopolitical realities in China. Zhang Yimou, the internationally renowned film director, argues that "the West has for a long time politicized Chinese films. If they are not anti-government, they are considered just pro-government propaganda."[16]

Zhang Yimou's observation has been echoed by many prominent Chinese art curators and avant-garde artists. For example, Gao Minglu bemoans the fact that virtually all international exhibitions on Chinese contemporary art since the early 1990s have "presented Political Pop and Cynicism as the major non-official, avant-garde movements, and interpreted them ideologically in light of the Tiananmen Incident of 1989."[17] Zhang Huan and Ma Liuming, who are known for their controversial body art and performance art, have told reporters both in China and abroad that their works should not be seen as antigovernment. In their opinion, not many Chinese avant-garde artists share the same views as the famous dissident artist Ai Weiwei. According to Zhang Huan, "Problems in China are so complicated that people want to find answers for themselves from different angles."[18] Ma Liuming says his controversial performance art pieces are not meant to make a political statement but to show the "spiritual universality of sexual ambiguity."[19] For some Chinese avant-garde artists, their dissent can be aimed at cultural hegemonies even greater and more pervasive than the authorities in Beijing.

Of course, not all overseas critics hold the views of Ralph Croizier, Gere-mie Barmé, or Sang Ye, although, to be fair, their opinions have some truth to them. Additionally, as China watchers become more familiar with recent developments in China's avant-garde scene, these assessments may change. Even though some Western critics are well informed about the dynamism and diversity reflected in the works of avant-garde artists in the PRC, artists from Shanghai have found it surprisingly difficult to convey their insights to a Western public, including colleagues living abroad. Karen Smith, an expert on Chinese avant-garde art who has lived in China for most of the past decade, asks pointedly, "How many [people in the West] would believe us, if we said that [we mainly admire] the sheer quality and diversity of the art being produced in China now?"[20]

THE COMING OF AGE OF AVANT-GARDE ARTISTS:
THE SHANGHAI BIENNALE

Since 1996, artists in China and abroad have jointly organized the Shang-hai Biennale (*Shanghai shuangnian zhan*) in an effort to establish more professional ties, both with the outside art world and with audiences in China. Some experts of contemporary Chinese art believe that the estab-lishment of the Shanghai Biennale has heralded a southward shift, and dy-namism in modern Chinese art is moving from Beijing to Shanghai and other southeastern coastal areas.[21] Since launching the event, Shanghai has made a concerted effort to promote contemporary art—especially avant-garde work—to a new level in the public arena. Ji Shaofeng, a Shanghai art critic, has observed that at the time of the Biennale, museums, art galleries, curators, artists, critics, foundations, auction houses, art schools, media, audiences, and websites altogether construct—both consciously and un-consciously—a knowledge production and dissemination system for pro-moting contemporary art.[22]

The Third Shanghai Biennale, held from 2000 to 2001, was recognized by critics in both China and abroad as an occasion marking the reentry of contemporary Chinese art to its homeland. The event featured a plethora of impressive, high-quality artwork and a wide range of international par-ticipants, especially when compared to the two previous Biennales.[23] With sixty-seven artists from eighteen countries in the formal exhibition, the pieces shown at the Biennale ran the gamut of avant-garde approaches, including performance art, installation art, conceptual art, environmen-tal art, Political Pop, cubism, impressionism, abstractionism, surrealism, cynical realism, modernism, and postmodernism. Throughout these ex-hibitions, the variety within the Shanghai art scene was prominently dis-played.[24] Wu Hung, a University of Chicago art historian, writes that the

Shanghai Biennale, along with other Shanghai art shows opening at the same time, represents a breakthrough in contemporary Chinese art. He says the Biennale normalizes experimental art and creates a legitimate exhibition space for controversial art forms—and for works that challenge social and political norms.[25]

The 12th Shanghai Biennale, held from 2018 to 2019, was the first large-scale exhibition of contemporary Latin American art in the history of the event. This Biennale was noted for its ingenious and thought-provoking thematic title, in both English and Chinese. The English title was "Proregress," a word coined by the American poet E. E. Cummings in 1931, which condensed "progress" and "regress."[26] The word reflects the profound contradictions and anxieties that plagued both the imperative for transformation and the barriers of stagnation in the early decades of the twentieth century. This word had almost been forgotten, but the 12th Shanghai Biennale returned it to the public eye. As one of the curators of the Biennale, Cuauhtémoc Medina (a Mexican professor of art history and philosophy who previously served as the associate curator of the Latin American Art Collection at the Tate Modern) describes, this word is keenly appropriate for today's world because we are in a very uncertain global environment. We are unsure whether human society is moving forward or backward, nor can we comprehend how our ideas affect the world.[27]

Wang Weiwei (b. 1983), another curator of the 12th Shanghai Biennale (and a native of Shanghai who received her undergraduate degree from Fudan University) made a similar call for rethinking modernity, Eurocentrism, and non-anthropocentrism. Echoing the themes of "proregress" and political uncertainty, she highlighted some of the contradicting trends in our time: "On the one hand, society has adopted an important agenda in addressing the issues of feminism, homosexuality, and social minorities. On the other hand, social and ethnic conflicts—and nationalism and racism—are rising in various parts of the world."[28]

Interestingly, the Chinese thematic title of the Biennale employed the rarely used term "*yubu*," which refers to the mystical Daoist ritual dance of ancient China, where the dancer appears to be moving forward while simultaneously going backward, or vice versa. This move can be thought of as similar to Michael Jackson's famous moonwalk. The Chinese thematic title for the Biennale was reflected in a particularly striking piece of work on display at the event. The art piece, titled *Enclosure*, was inspired by Chinese ancient military strategist Sun Tzu's classic work *The Art of War*. The piece consists of cardboard waste, forming a text matrix reading "one step going forward, two steps backward; two steps forward, one step backward."[29] This artwork presents the multilayered political symbolism in both the Chinese and the global contexts. Thus, in a highly imaginative way, the English and Chinese titles of the 2018–2019 Shanghai Biennale echo one another, challenging simplistic dichotomies and calling for urgent and necessary out-of-the-box thinking in the ambivalence of our era. Institutional support for, and the growing international reputation of, the Shanghai Biennale reflects the coming of age of Chinese avant-garde artists and their works on the world stage.

CONTEMPORARY SHANGHAI ART: HISTORICAL CONTEXT

Historically, Shanghai has been a cradle for Chinese contemporary art. China's first modern art school (*Shanghai meizhuan*) was established in the city in 1912 by distinguished artists Wu Shiguang, Zhang Yuguang, and Liu Haisu. During the time of the May Fourth Movement, Shanghai had about ten art schools.[30] In the early decades of the twentieth century, the Shanghai fine arts communities began to challenge the dominance of traditional painting and kicked off an era of coexistence between Chinese traditional paintings and Western-style paintings. At the same time, Shanghai's art communities brought about two major changes in the Chinese art scene: they commercialized it, and they began applying Western theories and painting techniques.[31] In a sense, Shanghai's contemporary art communities came to the forefront of China's international outreach efforts with their strong inclination to connect with the outside world.

According to Zhu Qi, a renowned Shanghainese curator, Shanghai, as the birthplace of Chinese modernism, is the only city in China where modernism was not interrupted in the twentieth century.[32] During the first half of the twentieth century, many Shanghainese artists such as Huang Binhong, Pan Tianshou, Zhang Daqian, Lin Fengmian, Liu Haisu, and Zhang Leping stood out among their contemporaries as some of the best artists of their time—not only in China but also worldwide.[33] Lin Fengmian, Wu Dayu, Guan Liang, and Yan Wenliang settled down in Shanghai after the founding of the PRC, where they and their disciples continued to engage in the creation of "underground" modern paintings.

In the 1960s and 1970s, a sparsely populated "underground modernism" group retained a presence in Shanghai.[34] Although Shanghai was by far the most important center of Chinese painting during the first half of the 20th century,[35] its role as a cultural center was repressed after Mao's time, especially during the Cultural Revolution, when a "monochromatic socialist national culture" became the norm. Under these extraordinary political circumstances, artists from Shanghai, like their colleagues in other parts of the country, were cut off from international trends in their respective genres.[36]

Zhu Qi's exhibition, "Avant-Garde Shanghai: Document Exhibition of 30 Years of Shanghai Contemporary Art (1979–2010)," was presented from 2017 to 2018 at the Ming Yuan Art Museum, a corporate-owned gallery in the city. The exhibition displayed three phases of the reform era avant-garde movement in Shanghai, including the first phase, "To Restart Modernism" (1979–1985), the second phase, "To Launch New Avant-garde Wave" (1985–1992), and the third phase, "To Reconstruct Contemporary" (1992–2010). The exhibition provided a comprehensive review of the rebirth and rapid development of avant-garde art in Shanghai—China's most cosmopolitan and forward-looking city—including the works of about 200 artists across five generations.[37]

Not until the second phase, in early 1990, did Shanghai artists begin to stir with more creative experiments following what Michael Sullivan calls "a long sleep."[38] The awakening of Shanghai's artistic community is a testament to the renewed effort within the cosmopolitan city to search for its own identity—one that distinguishes Shanghai from other Chinese cities and regions, and from China as a whole. Shanghai is a particularly appropriate case study for political culture and experimentation, because since the 1990s arguably no other urban center in China or abroad has been subject to more writing about its internal character and external image than Shanghai. This phenomenon may be due to the influence of Jiang Zemin and his core political allies and confidants (that moved to Beijing from Shanghai), who, as discussed in chapter 5, intended to make Shanghai a showcase city for China's reemergence on the world stage and a laboratory for the country's socioeconomic and cultural development.

One factor explaining the dynamism of the Shanghai art scene is the city's prolonged exposure to Western culture. This is not just due to colonial legacy or the influence of the throngs of foreign visitors to the city; it is also related to the large proportion of Chinese students from Shanghai who studied abroad during the reform era, as discussed in chapter 7. Artists from Shanghai were among the first group of Chinese students to study abroad in the 1980s. Among them were (not all avant-garde) artists, such as Chen Danqing, Chen Yifei, Chen Yiming, Gu Wenda, Hu Bing, Xu Jianguo, and Zhang Jianjun, who went to the United States during the 1980s. Other notable artists, such as Chen Zhen, Xu Mangyao, and Yan Peiming, pursued their studies of modern art in Paris.

Since the early 1990s, these now internationally renowned artists have returned to Shanghai or frequently visit their native city. Despite their busy schedules packed with international shows and exhibitions, artists like Chen Yifei, Chen Zhen, and Gu Wenda spent more time in Shanghai than anywhere else in the early 2000s. International experience, along with recent changes in the city, has inspired these Shanghai-born artists to rediscover their roots. Some utilize their sociological imaginations too. Rather than retire like hermits, they work to ensure that their art is relevant to the problems that Chinese people face.

Meanwhile, artists from China's many provinces and cities have also settled in Shanghai. As a metropolis built largely by migrants from adjacent provinces and farther afield, Shanghai has long been known for its diversity and openness. As discussed in chapter 4, Shanghai was the only city in the world during World War II to admit Jewish immigrants without requiring a visa. Some have proudly claimed that "Schindler saved about 1,000 Jews, but we Shanghainese saved 30,000."[39] During the reform era, Shanghai absorbed several million migrants from other regions. In the 1990s, one in every five people in the city was a migrant.[40] Like other immigrant cities, Shanghai welcomes a diversity of lifestyles, artistic pursuits, and social values. Today, migrant artists have enormously contributed to the cultural dynamics of Shanghai.

THE BLOOMING OF ART GALLERIES IN SHANGHAI

At the turn of the century, Shanghai experienced a phenomenal and rapid rise in art galleries. During most of the Maoist era, Shanghai had just a few art vendors (including the renowned Duoyun Xuan Art Studio on Nanjing Road). Chinese contemporary art, or more precisely, Chinese avant-garde art, was not born in Shanghai, but rather in Beijing in 1979, when a small group of artists organized an unofficial exhibition on the park railings directly opposite the National Art Museum of China. Although this avant-garde exhibition lasted only two days before being shut down by Beijing authorities, the Chinese avant-garde movement continued to grow in the capital and eventually settled down in the 798 Art District in northeast Beijing during the early 2000s.[41]

From the Old Warehouse to the West Bund

Around the same time of China's burgeoning avant-garde movement in Beijing at the turn of the century, a group of artists and curators in Shanghai (mainly Chinese but also some foreign) established what some analysts have called "art clusters" or "an arts colony."[42] They did so by taking over the abandoned warehouses of a former textile mill, as well as factories on Moganshan Road and other nearby areas. Taiwanese architect Teng Kun Yan was the first to discover and relocate into this abandoned, old industrial warehouse area at the end of 1998.[43] A couple of years later, Li Liang, an Australian-born Chinese artist moved his Eastlink Gallery from Fuxing

West Road into a warehouse in the area, and Ding Yi established his studio in the same location.

In 2000, Xue Song was the first artist to establish a studio in the now well recognized building at No. 50 Moganshan Road (later known as M50 Creative Park). This area became home not only to Shanghainese artists, such as Zhou Tiehai, Zhang Enli, and Pu Jie, but also to foreign artists, such as Dvir Bar-Gal, an Israeli who owns Artsea; Davide Quadrio, an Italian who founded Bizart; and foreign organizations, such as the British Art Center in Shanghai, which is headed by Simon Kirby, a Cultural Attaché of the British Consulate General.[44] The area has provided an extraordinary shared space for both Chinese and foreign avant-garde artists. As of 2020, there are still over 100 studios and exhibitions by avant-garde artists in this area.

Lorenz Helbling is the Swiss founder of ShanghART, one of the most respected avant-garde galleries in Shanghai and an early resident of the "arts colony." He described "the old days of the mid-1990s" to a *New York Times* reporter: "There weren't many art museums in Shanghai. Nobody came to Shanghai for art."[45] Helbling studied history at Fudan University in the late 1980s, and he founded his studio in 1996 in the Portman Hotel on Nanjing Road, then settled in Fuxing Park, and later moved to Moganshan Road. The establishment of the Moganshan artist area introduced new dynamics into the art communities in Shanghai, and ShanghART in particular has contributed to these dynamics by showing works from the entire Shanghai Delta region.[46] It is not an exaggeration to say that Helbling has launched some Shanghai-based avant-garde artists into the international spotlight.

The lack of art galleries in China's most cosmopolitan city in the early decades of the reform era has gradually been remedied over time. This improvement partially stems from the rapid rise of the private sector and the middle class in the city, but it is primarily the result of official preparations for the 2010 Shanghai World Expo. At the turn of the century, a local Shanghai English-language magazine identified just forty-seven galleries in the city that were reasonably well established.[47] However, by 2019, according to a ranking by the World Cities Culture Forum—an initiative by the mayor of London and an international online media group focused on global leadership on culture in cities—Shanghai was ranked third in the world in terms of total number of art galleries (770), behind only New York (1,475) and Paris (1,142), and ahead of Tokyo (618), London (478), Rome (355), Brussels (313), Los Angeles (279), Singapore (225), Istanbul (199), Amsterdam (196), and Sydney (170).[48]

The Yibo Gallery in Pudong mainly exhibits works by artists who live in Shanghai.[49] This gallery, along with many others in Shanghai, regularly holds exhibitions organized around a theme. For example, in the four years following its founding in the spring of 1998, the Stanney Gallery held over ten exhibitions covering topics such as individuality in a consumer society, the generation gap, and feminism. Although Shanghai's galleries showcase a wide range of styles, the works of avant-garde artists have been the most prominent. In addition to displaying and selling art pieces, some galleries also offer weekly or monthly public lectures about modern art. A study of art exhibition attendees in Shanghai from 2016 to 2017 shows that 20- to 39-year-olds accounted for 62 percent of attendees, while patrons aged 50 or older accounted for 12 percent. In comparison, when looking at exhibitions in Berlin, these two age cohorts account for 33 percent and 43 percent of attendees, respectively. Since art exhibition patrons are much younger in Shanghai, enthusiasm for art in this cosmopolitan hub could outlast that of Berlin or other cities with similar demographics.[50]

In the early 2000s, a few galleries announced plans to move, partially or entirely, from scattered locations around the city to two commercial streets—Shaoxing Road and Taikang Road—in downtown Shanghai. While these two art streets (*yishujie*) were still being established, they already had nicknames: the "Montmartre of China" and the "Soho of Shanghai."[51] At the same time, other older and well-known spots in the city that were being utilized for other purposes—Tianzi Fang in Taikang Road and 1933 Laochang Fang (also known as Old Millfun, which used to be the largest slaughterhouse in Shanghai in the 1930s) in Hongkou District—became the hubs for new art galleries and other cultural activities.[52] Unsurprisingly, a majority of Shanghai art galleries target overseas buyers for their artwork, and as a result, most galleries that have an online presence offer only English versions of their websites. According to Wu Liang (owner of the Attic Gallery in Shanghai) and Zhang Haiteng (owner of the Stanney Gallery), approximately 95 percent of their customers in the early 2000s came from overseas, including Taiwan and Hong Kong.[53]

In 2001, Yu Qiuyu, then president of the Shanghai Institute of Drama and adviser to the Shanghai municipal government, claimed that although Asia has several financial-economic centers, such as Tokyo, Hong Kong, and Singapore, it lacks international centers of culture like Paris or New York. Shanghai, in his view, should fill that void, especially in the area of contemporary art, dance, music, and theater.[54] Yu's idea seems to have gained strong support among Shanghai municipal government officials. In the years prior to the 2010 Expo, billions of dollars were pumped into the West Bund area (later known as *xi'an* in Chinese) to transform the once-gray industrial and shipbuilding zone into a hip arts corridor along the Huangpu River.[55]

In October 2012, Shanghai opened the country's first state-run contemporary art museum, the Power Station of Art (PSA), in the West Bund, which later became the venue for the Shanghai Biennale. Like the Tate Modern in London, the PSA resides in a converted power plant, which explains the name of the museum. Recently, the Shanghai municipal government recognized the museum as a landmark, and it designated the 8.4-mile stretch of land where the museum sits on the Huangpu riverbank as a priority function zone of Shanghai—"Asia's largest art corridor." This West Bund location is a high-quality downtown public space, and it serves as the international technological and cultural corridor of Shanghai. Thus major multinational companies have chosen to locate their offices here, such as The Huawei Technology Company, which established its 5G exhibition center in the West Bund.

The 4-mile-long Longteng Avenue along the West Bund has become home to dozens of museums and professional art galleries. These include large-scale museums such as the West Bund Art Center, the Long Museum West Bund, the Shanghai Center of Photography (SCoP, a premier museum-quality venue dedicated to the art of photography), and some relatively small art galleries, such as the Don Gallery, a branch of the ShanghART Gallery, the Arario Gallery Shanghai, the Xu Zhen Studio, and the nearby PSA. These museums, art centers, and galleries have frequently featured contemporary art from artists living overseas, as well as in Shanghai and other parts of China.

In September 2019, for example, the Long Museum West Bund displayed *Los Angeles*, which consists of many large-scale paintings of "social abstraction" by L.A. artist Mark Bradford. SCoP featured a photo portrait exhibition called *Close* by New York–based German photographer Martin Schoeller. The Arario Gallery also hosted three exhibitions featuring Korean sculpture artist Kim Byoungho's *Seventy Two Silent Propagations*, an avant-garde exhibition entitled *Staging* by Wen Yipei—a native of Hebei who studied at the Pratt Institute in New York—and another interactive art show called *Island of Immorality* by Xu Bacheng, a Jiangsu artist. During the same month, the PSA hosted several exhibitions, including the photography of Jean Baudrillard, *Freeing Architecture* by Japanese architect Junya Ishigami, and *The Return of Guests*, a collection of avant-garde art by both Chinese and foreign artists. These examples demonstrate the dynamic activity fueling the Shanghai art scene, and its development has far-reaching implications for emerging civil discourse in the city. As one Chinese critic has observed: what China lacks is not artists, but the "sort of people who will accept those artists."[56]

The Rise of Large-Scale, Privately Owned Art Museums

Many of these newly built museums and art facilities in the West Bund were privately funded. The Yuz Museum, for example, was founded in 2014 by Chinese-Indonesian entrepreneur, philanthropist, and art collector Budi Tek (Yu Deyao). Tek built a successful business career through his Indonesia-based PT Sierad Produce Tbk, which specializes in poultry distribution and restaurant management. He began collecting artwork in 2004, amassing a collection of over 1,500 art pieces, including those of Western contemporary artists, such as Maurizio Cattelan, Fred Sandback, and Adel Adbessemed, as well as some Chinese "mega art" works, such as Xu Bing's internationally renowned *Tobacco Project*. In 2011, Tek was ranked eighth on *Art & Auction*'s list of the top ten most influential figures in the art world. In 2017, Tek was awarded "the Legion of Honor" by the French government for his efforts to advance the cultural communication and cooperation between France and China.

The Yuz Museum was designed by Japanese Architect Sou Fujimoto, and it was built on the site of an old aircraft hangar at the former Longhua Airport and the old Shanghai Aircraft Manufacturing Factory. The museum boasts a total area of 9,000 square meters—a new landmark for contemporary Chinese art exhibition spaces in China. The museum broadcasts three goals: "drawing the world's attention to Shanghai, advancing the development of contemporary Chinese art, and promoting cultural dialogue between the East and the West."[57]

The billionaire couple Liu Yiqian and Wang Wei founded the Long Museum West Bund, also in 2014, and just two years after establishing the Long Museum Pudong in 2012. At the time of its opening, the Long Museum West Bund was China's largest private museum. Designed by Liu Yichun, a Chinese architect at Atelier Deshaus, the building covers 33,000 square meters and dedicates up to 16,000 square meters for exhibitions. The museum site was previously the terminal for coal shipping along the Huangpu River. Visitors to the museum can still see the view of a coal hopper unloading bridge from atop a retainer column (about 110 meters long, 10 meters wide, and 8 meters high), which was built on the same site during the 1950s.

Both Liu and Wang were born in Shanghai in 1963. Liu is chairman of the Sunline Group, a Shanghai-based investment company. The couple made their fortune by investing in the stock market, real estate, and pharmaceuticals. In 2015, Liu bought Italian painter Amedeo Modigliani's *Nu couché*, a world-renowned painting of a reclining nude woman, for US$170 million—the second-highest price in the world for an artwork at auction at the time. Liu also bought expensive Chinese antique art pieces from the Southern Song and Ming dynasties.

PLATE 1. Huang Yongping, *Bank of Sand, Sand of Bank* (2000), sand, 350 × 600 × 430 cm.

PLATE 2. Xue Song, *New Shanghai* (2002), mixed media on silkscreen, 210 × 320 cm.

PLATE 3. Shi Yong, *First Date* (1997–1998), mixed-media interactive art.

PLATE 4. Shi Yong, *New Image of Shanghai Today* (1998),
performance and multimedia interactive art.

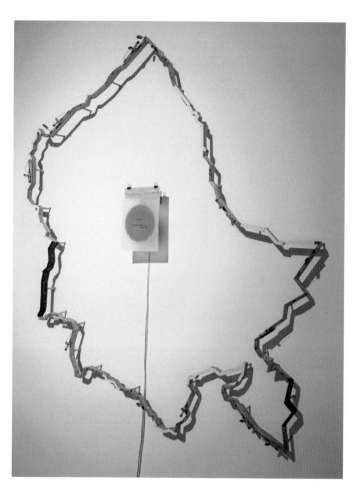

PLATE 5. Shi Yong, *Flickering in Another Sentence—the Gossip Spread Like Wildfire* (2018), wood, paint, stainless steel sheet, sulfuric acid paper, speaker, amplifier, audio player, 180 × 160 × 10 cm.

PLATE 6. Pu Jie, *Internet Time No. 11* (2000), acrylic on canvas.

PLATE 7. Pu Jie, *Oh, Shanghai* (2003), oil on canvas, 185 × 148 cm.

PLATE 8. Pu Jie, *Head Is Her* (2009), oil on acrylic, 20 × 25 cm.

PLATE 9. Zhou Tiehai, *Placebo 4* (1999), acrylic airbrush on canvas, 311 × 250 cm.

PLATE 10. Zhou Tiehai, *Giuliani* (2002), airbrush on canvas, 350 × 250 cm.

PLATE 11. Zhou Tiehai, *Le Juge* (2008), mixed media on paper, 400 × 300 cm.

PLATE 12. Xue Song, *Dialogue with Matisse* (2005), mixed media on canvas, ash, poster, acrylic, 210 × 320 cm.

PLATE 13. Xue Song, *Mali Child* (2002), ad for the exhibition *Ver Da Ga* (No connection at all), mixed media on canvas, 180 × 150 cm.

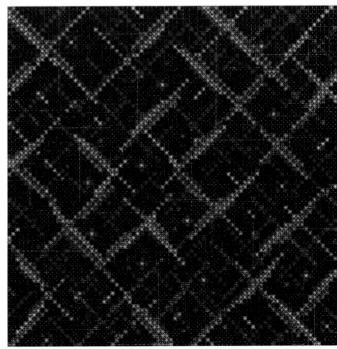

PLATE 14. Ding Yi, *Appearance of Crosses* (2016), basswood panel with engravings, 240 × 240 × 6 cm.

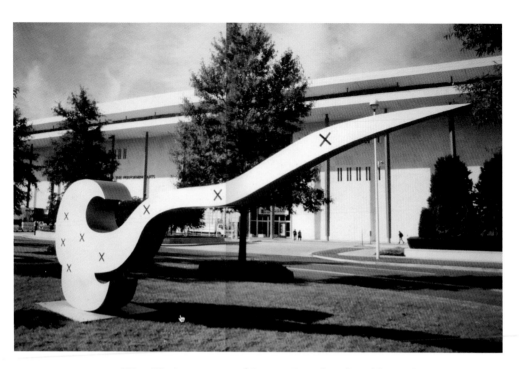

PLATE 15. Ding Yi, *Appearance of Crosses-Ruyi* (2011), public sculpture, stainless steel, automotive metallic paint, 645 × 255 × 55 cm.

PLATE 16. Ding Yi, *Taiji* (Tai Chi) (2012), stainless steel sculpture.

Liu's wife Wang Wei, director of the Long Museum, is more interested in Chinese contemporary art, and she has acquired works by well-known artists, such Li Tiefu, Zhang Daqian, Qi Baishi, Yan Wenliang, Liu Haisu, Lin Fengmian, and Wu Dayu. Wang collects a wide variety of art, ranging from oil and watercolor paintings from the Republic of China and communist revolutionary oil paintings (known as the Chinese realist school) to post–Cultural Revolution avant-garde pieces. Wang seems most interested in collecting art that reflects the far-reaching and multilayered impact of China's rapid economic growth on the Chinese people.[58] The 2014 exhibition, titled *1,199 People Collection from the Long Museum*, showcased Wang Wei's large collection of Chinese contemporary art. These works included masterpieces by the realist artist Luo Zhongli, the portrait series by the late Chen Yifei (e.g., *The Girl in Blue Dress*, *Flutist*, *Lady Playing Guitar*, and *Woman Clarinetist*), the Tibetans series by Chen Danqing, along with world famous post–Cultural Revolution oil paintings (cynical realism and Political Pop) by Wang Guangyi, Fang Lijun, Yue Minjun, Zhang Xiaogang, Zhang Enli, Yu Hong, Zeng Fanzhi, and Zhou Tiehai, as well as avant-garde mixed media works by Yu Youhan and Xue Song.[59]

Wang Wei asserts that broadly speaking, the Long Museum has focused on the "contrastive display and study of art—Western and Eastern, ancient and contemporary," while strengthening its local cultural roots in Shanghai.[60] The museum presents the diversity of visual art from a global perspective by showcasing the prominent works of contemporary Chinese artists, as well as contemporary art and culture from all over the world. Some might say that Liu and Wang have built "China's Solomon Guggenheim Museum."[61] As a demonstration of its remarkable art collection, in 2018, the Long Museum West Bund hosted an exhibition titled *Turning Point: 40 Years of Chinese Contemporary Art*. The exhibition featured the museum's rich collection of representative works from the reform era, which were displayed chronologically and made by ninety-nine prominent Chinese artists.[62]

As Wang Wei has remarked, this exhibition showed the evolutionary changes in the Chinese art scene from the 1980s, when "artists were full of new ideas and idealism," to the 1990s, when "art seemed to have become the subordinate of sociology," to the 2000s, when "artists were seeking cultural identities and self-positioning" in order to find a living space in a rapidly globalizing world, and finally to the 2010s, during which the pursuits of Chinese artists were increasingly "synchronized with the world in terms of concepts and techniques." Regardless of which decade these artists were active, they all distinguished themselves by producing creative pieces that reflected their surroundings at a time of rapid socioeconomic and technological transformation in the country.[63] Thus Wang has proudly claimed that the Long Museum West Bund has never missed any major development in Chinese contemporary art during the reform era. Notably, of the ninety-nine artists whose works were showcased in the exhibition, twenty-nine studied and worked abroad, mainly in Europe, the United States, and Japan.

The Le Freeport, a bonded warehouse built for the storage of artwork, has also found a home in the West Bund. Three relatively small but internationally renowned art galleries—namely MadeIn Gallery, Aike Dellarco, and ShanghART—have also relocated from Shanghai's original art hub, M50 Creative Park, to the West Bund. Lorenz Helbling recently called the West Bund "Shanghai's—if not China's—most exciting up-and-coming art district," saying that his gallery relocated there "to be where the action is."[64] More recently, the Center Pompidou announced its plan to open a Chinese outpost in the David Chipperfield–designed West Bund Art Museum in 2020. Named the Centre Pompidou Shanghai, this new gallery has initiated a long-term cultural cooperation project between France and China that will last until 2025.[65]

When the 2010 World Expo opened, the central government announced that China would build 3,500 new museums across the country within five years. As the British *Economist* magazine observes, this ambitious plan by the Chinese government, which included tax benefits for local governments and developers, actually surpassed that figure three years early in 2012.[66] Without a doubt, the West Bund was one of the most important beneficiaries of this policy. Through the development of its vibrant art scene, Shanghai once more led the way for the country. Some of Shanghai's museums will become—if they are not already—cultural landmarks of Shanghai. In the words of artist Zhou Tiehai, when people think of global megacities, such as New York, Paris, and London, what first comes to mind is likely the Metropolitan Museum and MoMA, the Louvre and Pompidou, the British Museum and Tate Gallery, rather than a restaurant or a shopping mall. For Zhou, these newly founded museums in Shanghai will serve the same role. According to Zhou, "Art space can represent and shape the soul of the city."[67]

In 2017, Shanghai had a total of 124 museums, including 82 high-end art galleries and museums, among which only 18 were state-owned art galleries.[68] More than 80 percent were privately owned. These newly established private art galleries include the Museum of Contemporary Art, the Hao Art Gallery, the Baolong Art Museum, the Suning Art Museum, the Mei Bo Art Museum, the Himalaya Museum, Yoon Arte, Vanguard Gallery, the Shanghai Propaganda Poster Art Center, the Shanghai Duolun Museum of Modern Art, the Shanghai Mingyuan Art Museum, the Pearl Art Museum, and the Yicang Art Museum. In 2012, by comparison, there were 34 high-end art galleries and museums in Shanghai, meaning that the number of these exhibition venues increased by 130 percent over five years. More art galleries and museums are expected to open in the next few years.

In 2017, there were 6.17 million total visitors to art galleries and museums in Shanghai, including 3.96 million visitors to state-owned ones and 2.21 million visitors to private ones.[69] The contributions of these privately owned museums and art galleries—especially the large-scale and well-funded ones like the Yuz Museum and the Long Museum West Bund—have been instrumental to the development of avant-garde art, contributing to a richer artistic atmosphere for the city. Going to a museum is not only a source of entertainment but also "a kind of education, a kind of lifestyle."[70] Attending exhibitions has already become a more popular activity in China. According to one recent study, over the past decade, Shanghai has hosted, on average, 300 international exhibitions every year.[71]

FINAL THOUGHTS

By definition, avant-garde artwork is ahead of its time, and thus often not immediately accepted or understood by the public. In the words of Wu Hung, "When artworks representing new ideas first emerge . . . they are often rejected and excluded by the art mainstream, viewed as outcasts. Only a bold private collector can cast off the fetters of popular tastes and stagnant organizations."[72] According to Wu Hung and Budi Tek, Shanghai "is the only city in China where you're beginning to have this museum culture."[73]

Shanghai avant-garde artists and curators have actively sought out a new and diverse cultural place in the world for the city. Shanghai has now become "a marker of influence in Chinese contemporary art," on par with or even eclipsing Beijing's 798 Art District and the Songzhuang artist community. As Budi Tek recently claimed, "If you really want to see something new, something enchanting, something up to international standards, you have to look to Shanghai."[74]

To a great extent, the art gallery boom in Shanghai reflects the growing demand for cultural experiences by the growing middle class in the city. As art critic Jiang Jun describes,

> When China's emerging middle class has embraced a dynamic and evolving economy, they are no longer interested in a struggle for pluralist political rights, nor a revolution for recognition, but a fusion of cultural life similar to their peers in the West and Japan. They have been in search for an integrated multi-aesthetic consumer choice, and contemporary art is meeting this increasingly urgent need.[75]

Jiang's generalization may be an overstatement, given concerns that some artists and art critics in Shanghai have co-opted contemporary art for commercial reasons. Nevertheless, in contrast to the first half century of the PRC, middle- and upper-class Shanghainese have become increasingly dissatisfied with homogenized products and services, and they are now demanding multiculturalism and pursuing differentiation. Avant-garde art has helped meet these demands, and has also become a symbol of fashion, elitism, individualism, and cosmopolitanism.[76]

Shanghai avant-garde artists are not only products of the city's cultural and sociopolitical environment, reflecting the views and values of middle-class residents, they also serve as agents of the middle class, articulating this group's voice and vision for the future. Chapter 11 examines the critical ideas and intellectual foresight these avant-garde artists have tried to convey through their artwork.

CHAPTER 11

Dialoguing with the West

Critiques of Globalization by Shanghai's Avant-Garde Artists

It is not enough for us to believe that by challenging some social taboos we can somehow free art. . . . To achieve real freedom, first and foremost one must be able to think independently. We cannot view art as simply a struggle over power or ideology.

—HOU HANRU

The value of Chinese contemporary art lies in China, not in art.

—ZHOU TIEHAI

An overarching theme that has emerged within the contemporary Shanghai art scene is that the Chinese intellectual community demands equal dialogue, not just between the state and society but also between China and the West—especially in this era of globalization. Such calls for equal dialogue are by no means unique to China. In many developing countries, nationalist intellectuals aim to end what they consider triumphal postcolonialism. The transition to a consumer-oriented society has created cultural identity issues and given rise to nationalistic sentiments in many nations, and some Chinese critics observe that Western commentators often fail to understand the difficulty of such transitions. Amid these challenges, globalization has spawned a new wave of urbanization and the renewal of intellectual and conceptual searching. The advent of the digital era, along with the rise of popular culture and social media, has further contributed to the development of contemporary art, inextricably linking avant-garde work to society, politics, economy, and ecology.

In a broader context, the vast linkages between avant-garde art and everything else raise additional intriguing questions. In a Chinese political culture that has often been seen as static, conservative, monochromatic, and state centered, how has pluralistic and dynamic avant-garde art so aggressively asserted itself? For what reasons would a communist state—which is thought to maintain strong political control—allow avant-garde artists to flourish and even flood government-sponsored art exhibitions with their works, particularly in Shanghai? What is the most important driver of the avant-garde art gallery boom in Shanghai—an art consumer market built by a large middle class, political incentives on the part of the municipal government (and perhaps by the central government, as well) to make Shanghai a world-class cosmopolitan city, or the desires of rich people and large business firms (both Chinese and foreign) to have an alternate mechanism for allocating their assets? Or a combination of all three? How can two seemingly contradictory observations—that Western-inspired Chinese avant-garde artists have benefited from cultural transnationalism but are becoming increasingly critical of prevailing Western worldviews and globalization—be reconciled? The political and intellectual odyssey of avant-garde artists in Shanghai over the past two decades offers illuminating answers to these questions.

This chapter focuses on the works of five avant-garde artists in Shanghai: Xue Song (b. 1965), Shi Yong (b. 1963), Pu Jie (b. 1959), Zhou Tiehai (b. 1966), and Ding Yi (b. 1962). Other artists and their works are also discussed as comparative references.[1] These five Shanghai artists all belong to the post–Cultural Revolution generation, and their most formative experiences occurred after Deng Xiaoping announced reforms in 1978. Xue Song was born in Anhui and studied fine art at the Shanghai Drama Institute. The latter four were born in Shanghai, where they attended college in the art departments of the Shanghai Light Industrial Institute, the Shanghai School of Arts and Crafts (which later merged into Shanghai University), and Shanghai Normal University, respectively. All five graduated in the late 1980s and currently live and work in Shanghai.

The styles and pursuits of artists are, of course, not regionally bound or determined. Telecommunications and the digital revolution have further blurred the national and regional identities of artists. Yet Shanghai avant-garde artists have some noticeable shared characteristics. This study by no means claims to include all prominent Shanghai avant-garde artists. Some other avant-garde artists, for example, Chen Qiang, Gu Wenda, Hu Jieming, Li Shan, Sun Liang, Yang Fudong, Yu Youhan, and Zhang Enli, have all made important contributions to contemporary Shanghai art. Nevertheless, the five avant-garde artists who are the focus of this chapter represent some of the major artistic and thematic approaches, which can help reveal distinct features of Shanghai avant-garde artists during the reform era.

Since the 1990s, all five of these artists have become widely recognized in art circles and have often exhibited both domestically and abroad. Some, like Zhou Tiehai and Ding Yi, have received awards in prestigious international exhibitions. At present, these five avant-garde artists are among the most active in Shanghai. Each has a distinctive, unique artistic style, but they largely share common social concerns and political critiques, representing new perspectives among this generation of avant-garde artists. This study demonstrates that Shanghai avant-garde art, as represented by the works of these prominent artists, often challenges basic Western perceptions about the political stances and worldviews of Chinese avant-garde artists. Generally speaking, these artists are more anti-Western and antiglobalization, and less opposed to the state, than most Western descriptions of China's intellectual trends would suggest. This does not mean that they are politically conservative, and in regard to many other domestic and global issues, such as media freedom, personality cults and ideological indoctrination, gender equality, gay rights, climate change, and domestic migration and international refugees, they are unquestionably liberal. This observation strongly aligns with the findings from surveys of foreign-educated returnees in Shanghai that were discussed in chapter 10.

Looking more specifically at the attitudes and opinions of Shanghai artists, since the mid-1990s, avant-garde art in the city has mostly not been critical of the Chinese government or socialism. Much of the art denounces the negative effects of economic globalization. American corporate power, political hegemony, perceived hypocrisy, moral superiority, ignorance about and arrogance toward China, and neglect of economic disparities in today's world have all been attacked by these avant-garde artists. Chinese intellectual and college students who do not practice art have articulated similar concerns since the mid-1990s.[2] Nationalistic and anti-American sentiment has grown stronger among Chinese intellectuals and students, who hold a different mindset from the one that prevailed during the days of the Tiananmen Square demonstrations in 1989 and the 9/11 terrorist attacks on the United States. While foreign academic analysts may have varying interpretations of this recent trend, it is critical not to overlook such an important change.

"CHARACTERS ARE DESTINY": SHANGHAI AVANT-GARDE ARTISTS

Britta Erickson, a Stanford-based scholar of Chinese art, compiled biographical data on roughly 1,000 contemporary Chinese artists, including those living in Taiwan, Hong Kong, and overseas, covering everyone who has made prominent contributions to the national or international art world.[3] Among those born in the People's Republic of China, information about birthplace is available for 531 individuals (Table 11-1). Those born in Shanghai (66) are overrepresented in the data set, accounting for 12 percent of the total—ten times more than the city's proportion of the national population. The number of the Shanghai artists in this database is second only to Beijing (14 percent). This is particularly remarkable since Shanghai does not have nearly as many art schools as Beijing. Two other province-level cities, Tianjin and Chongqing, account for only 1.7 percent and 2.3 percent of artists' birthplaces, respectively. Notably, if the artists born in Jiangsu (8 percent) and Zhejiang (6 percent) are added together, the Yangtze River delta accounts for 27 percent of China's prominent artists in the data set.

TABLE 11-1. Distribution of Birthplaces, by Province, of Prominent Contemporary Chinese Artists, 2001

Region/Province	Number	Percentage	Population %
North			
Beijing	72	13.6	1.0
Tianjin	9	1.7	0.7
Hebei	17	3.3	5.3
Shanxi	6	1.1	2.6
Neimenggu	15	2.8	1.9
Subtotal	**119**	**22.4**	**11.5**
Northeast			
Liaoning	23	4.3	3.4
Jilin	8	1.5	2.2
Heilongjiang	26	4.9	3.1
Subtotal	**57**	**10.7**	**8.7**
East			
Shanghai	66	12.4	1.2
Jiangsu	44	8.3	5.9
Shandong	32	6.0	7.2
Zhejiang	31	5.8	3.6
Anhui	4	0.8	5.0
Fujian	15	2.8	2.7
Subtotal	**192**	**36.1**	**25.6**

Region/Province	Number	Percentage	Population %
Central			
Henan	5	0.9	7.5
Hubei	30	5.7	4.8
Hunan	17	3.3	5.3
Jiangxi	3	0.6	3.4
Subtotal	55	10.4	21.0
South			
Guangdong	37	7.0	5.7
Guangxi	0	0	3.8
Hainan	0	0	0.6
Subtotal	37	7.0	10.1
Southwest			
Chongqing	12	2.3	2.5
Sichuan	27	5.1	6.9
Guizhou	6	1.1	2.9
Yunnan	8	1.5	3.3
Xizang (Tibet)	1	0.2	0.2
Subtotal	54	10.2	15.8
Northwest			
Shaanxi	9	1.7	2.9
Gansu	6	1.1	2.0
Qinghai	1	0.2	0.4
Ningxia	0	0	0.4
Xinjiang	1	0.2	1.4
Subtotal	17	3.3	7.1
Total	531	100.0	99.8

Source: Britta Erickson, www.stanford.edu/dept/art/china/ (compiled in 1999 and updated by Erickson in 2001). Population data are calculated from *Zhongguo tongji nianjian*, 1996 [China statistical yearbook, 1996], State Statistical Bureau, comp. (Beijing: Zhongguo tongji chubanshe, 1996), 42–43, and 73; and *Zhongguo tongji nianjian, 1999* [China statistical yearbook, 1999], State Statistical Bureau, comp. (Beijing: Zhongguo tongji chubanshe, 1999). Percentages do not add up to 100 due to rounding. The data were accumulated and tabulated by Cheng Li.

Since the 1990s, most Shanghai avant-garde artists have engaged in cultural negotiation with the authorities rather than political confrontation. Some think that if theatrical gestures are the primary form of so-called democratic revolutions, then they will not benefit the people.[4] For example, many recall an art installation where the artist aimed two gunshots at a mirror in order "to attract public attention," an incident that caused police to close the China Avant-garde Exhibit in Beijing in 1989. Some question whether this artistic act was actually more beneficial than simply just exposing more people to the Exhibit.

Contrasting the Shanghai Avant-Garde with "Shock Art" in Beijing and Other Cities

Shanghai avant-garde artists differ from many of their colleagues in Beijing and Wuhan, who are better known for "shock art" that startles audiences to convey powerful messages. The content of "shock art" is often antiestablishment, and the degree of shock produced is the measure of success.[5] Painting on naked bodies, on animals, and on meat to express radical sentiments has become the standard repertoire of some shock artists. It is hard to imagine any Shanghai artists doing anything akin to Wuhan artist Ma Liuming, whose performance art involves public sex acts, which are illegal even in the most open-minded, liberal cities of the world.[6] This does not mean that Ma's avant-garde pursuits are disregarded as pornography. Artists in Shanghai simply find Ma's approaches too sensational to be effective at conveying certain messages.

No artist is more radical than the eccentric Sheng Qi of Beijing. In an act of agony following the Tiananmen massacre, Sheng cut off the little finger on his left hand. Ten years later, he took a photo of his remaining four fingers, stamped respectively with the numbers "1, 9, 8, 9" and a red ribbon pinned into the flesh of his palm. The title of the photograph, "1989+AIDS," carries an unmistakable political message. Zhou Bin, another artist who lived in an "artist village," Songzhuang, utilizes a similar self-harm approach in his work.[7] Among the Shanghai avant-garde, these types of shock art, either sexual or political, are less common. Some Shanghai avant-garde artists assert that "shock art" can only lead to "shock" and will potentially "kill" art.[8]

Several "artist villages" have emerged in Beijing since the early 1990s. The Yuanming Yuan Artists' Village, for example, became a center for Political Pop and cynical realism. A few years later, a group of performing artists, including Ma Liuming and Zhang Huan, formed the so-called East Village in Beijing's Chaoyang District, which became a hub for experimental performance art. Since the late 1990s, more than 200 artists from various parts of China have settled in the suburban district of Tongzhou.[9] Yang

Wei, a well-known art critic based in Beijing, has profiled forty-one prominent Beijing-based artists and curators of that time, focusing especially on their years in the artist villages of Songzhuang and Tongzhou.[10] These villages have made talented avant-garde artists famous in international circles. The Songzhuang artist communities once claimed to have over 3,000 registered artists.[11] While some of their works are truly innovative, many artists in these villages, in the words of various Western art critics, "are not particularly distinguished."[12] With some notable exceptions, the artists living together in these communities tend to imitate each other, selling rather standard political clichés.[13]

While Beijing-based avant-garde artists form their own villages, their counterparts in Shanghai mostly work in their own separate studios and contract individually with art galleries to exhibit their works. Although some of their galleries and exhibitions are situated in an "art cluster," the residential and social associations among Shanghai artists are far less intimate than those of their peers elsewhere. As Xue Song observes, "Shanghai culture values more independence. Independence requires distance and then distance yields distinctiveness."[14] Another difference between Shanghai artists and their peers in other cities is that during the reform era, Shanghai artists have had little involvement in dissident movements and have been less obviously political.[15]

According to Yang Wei, the aforementioned Beijing art critic, two avant-garde exhibitions held in 1979, the first in Beijing (the *Star Art Exhibition, xingxing huazhan*) and the second in Shanghai (the *12-Person Art Exhibition*), heralded two profoundly different approaches to and emphases on political views and values.[16] The Beijing exhibition was overtly ideological and featured many artists who were born to high-ranking official families. The artworks tended to express strong political views. In contrast, the Shanghai exhibition featured artists from intellectual or humble family backgrounds in the city. Their works often placed great emphasis on artistic self-expression. Yang Wei observed that they represented "two exploration directions of Chinese contemporary art"—Beijing values the sociopolitical criticism function of art, while Shanghai is inclined to deemphasize ideology in abstract art.[17] As a result, Shanghai has become the "capital of contemporary Chinese abstract art" (*chouxiang zhidu*). In 2001, 2002, 2003, and 2005, for example, the Shanghai Art Museum continuously hosted four large-scale abstract art exhibitions under the "metaphysical" theme.[18]

Julia Andrews, a scholar of Chinese art, suggests that some ways to pursue freedom of artistic expression require "work from within the establishment."[19] After all, artists are rarely "free from the pressures of social, political, and economic circumstances."[20] Thus, during the 1990s, independent curators (*duli cezhanren*) began to emerge in Shanghai, playing a professional role in organizing art exhibits. They helped mount both small exhibitions and the large Shanghai Biennales that were neither fully official nor antistate. Additionally, many experimental art shows found ways to "circumvent official channels by exhibiting in private spaces such as galleries, clubs, cafes, and bars."[21] In general, the municipal government has cooperated with groups of artists in the city and publicized the activities of independent art galleries through official media.[22] However, this does not mean there is no tension between avant-garde artists and the authorities, nor does it suggest that avant-garde artists have lost their social and cultural independence. It suggests, instead, that the relationship between art and the state in present-day China is more complicated than Western observers generally realize.

However, by no means do all Chinese art critics have favorable views of the recent developments in Shanghai avant-garde art, as described earlier. For example, in her study of Shanghai contemporary art ecology, Ma Yan has pointed out the problems and deficiencies of contemporary avant-garde art in Shanghai, including the small number of artists, critics, and curators (especially from the younger generation); the absence of specialized academic journals; the insufficient number of popular media outlets focusing on contemporary art; and "strong art galleries but weak art schools."[23] Ma observes that Shanghai's artistic ecological facade gives people a false impression of being lively and flashy, but a closer look at the inner workings of the avant-garde communities in the city shows a lack of oxygen and ecological imbalances. From her perspective, the art institutions in Shanghai are prosperous, but the "production mechanism" of Shanghai artists is thin and frail. The inner paradoxes, contradictions, conflicts, superficialities, and rationalities are always staged in this city.[24]

Ma's sharp criticism enriches the scholarly debate about the status and characteristics of avant-garde art in Shanghai. What may be more important is the trend toward growing diversity in the cultural scenes of Chinese cities, especially the coexistence and competition of two contemporary art centers—Shanghai and Beijing—in recent decades. As some Chinese avant-garde artists have observed, this development itself can be seen as a departure from the centralized, pyramidal power structure in both Chinese tradition and communist authoritarianism.[25]

CONFRONTING COMMERCIAL CULTURE:
ARTISTS AS BOTH BENEFICIARIES AND CRITICS

The rise of commerce is perhaps the most distinct cultural change in China's reform era. Paradoxically, avant-garde artists are both beneficiaries and critics of materialism and capitalism. The seemingly contradictory relationship between Chinese artists and capitalism are understandable, because in the decades prior to reforms, they suffered a sharply repressive environment. China's market transition has brought artists greater political autonomy, economic prosperity, and intellectual freedom (relatively speaking) than anyone could have foreseen just a few years ago. Thus these Chinese artists differ from Western aesthetic modernists, as some members of the latter solely express disgust with materialism, while the former have an uneasy embrace of it. One Chinese critic has chided Western avant-garde artists for this full rejection of capitalism and materialism, suggesting that in doing so, they seek to create a purely aesthetic utopia from aristocratic self-exile in an ivory tower.[26]

This does not mean that Chinese avant-garde artists are just crafty eclectics, immersed in commercial culture and lacking any capacity to censure hegemonistic establishments either in China or abroad.[27] On the contrary, they often challenge both hegemons and each other. They are keenly aware of their awkward role as artists in a country that is quickly commercializing.

This is especially true for avant-garde artists in Shanghai. Many important developments in reform-era China, including the resurgence of a commercial society, the stock market, foreign investment, construction fever, rural-urban migration, and various new forms of capitalist exploitation, began in Shanghai or are prominent there. These profound socioeconomic changes have not occurred in a cultural vacuum. In fact, over the past two decades, existing values and conflicting ideologies—whether they be Maoist or post-Maoist, modernist or postmodernist, Confucian neo-authoritarian or Western postcolonial, nationalist or globalist, multiculturalist or universalist—have been critically reexamined in the city. Works by avant-garde artists in Shanghai illustrate this ongoing, lively political discourse, as well as the awkward positioning of the artists themselves. As early as 1996, Shanghai avant-garde artists Shi Yong, Ding Yi, Zhou Tiehai, and others organized an exhibition in Shanghai titled *Let's Talk About Money*, which conveyed "a kind of warning about the direction that China's art world was taking."[28] In their view, the market had become a new "regulating force of the art system, which changed both the focus and inner dynamics of the field in significant ways."[29]

The Shanghai-educated and Anhui-born artist Xue Song's work, *Jump into the Sea* (*xiahai*), is an example of the tensions in the positioning of Shanghai artists.[30] The title is a reform era slogan for leaving the protection of socialism and going into work or business by oneself. Anybody who lived through the Cultural Revolution, however, immediately recognizes Xue Song's painting as a critical imitation of the well-known propaganda poster of Chairman Mao's Red Guard Jin Xunhua by Chen Yifei and Xu Chunzhong.[31] This Red Guard was a Shanghai youth who was working at a farm in Anhui, where he sacrificed his life to save state property. In contrast to the original poster, the figure in Xue's painting is rough and unclear, without a face, suggesting that the individual's character has been obscured in a money-dominated society. The dark figure's gesturing arms, as drawn by Xue, still look as heroic and eager as the Red Guard's did, but for a different reason: the new figure is surrounded by dollar bills. Juxtaposing the two eras, Xue not only highlights the sharp contrast between the times but also the sense of a repetitive cycle. Xue's piece makes no value judgment, but it prompts its viewers to think critically.

Xue Song's distinctive painting methodology and tactics clearly align with his thematic messages. For over two decades, Xue has integrated various materials into his work. Specifically, he has created his own visual style by using flames, ashes, burned pictures, and print fragments as media, and then applying different approaches, such as baking, pasting, and coloring the images scattered across the canvas.[32] As some critics have observed, "Fire plays a central role in Xue Song's work. It is a form of mourning."[33] For Xue, ash is a reminder of fate and a symbol of rebirth. In his words, "Fire is my creative means."[34] From destruction to rebirth, his works undergo a process of "regeneration," through which they are released from their original meanings and accorded new connotations. Through his artwork, Xue combines historical memory with current reality, traditional culture with modern perspective, and comical imitation with serious criticism, resulting in creative collisions for his viewers. In a sense, he has founded a new vocabulary of collage art from devastating destruction and loss.

Xue Song's artwork on the Shanghai Pudong financial district is constructed from his "signature" materials—a large number of burned pictures and printed fragments of old buildings on the Bund (Plate 2). With paper scraps of pre-1978 or even pre-1949 Shanghai scenes—including symbols of the colonial Bund—pasted on the surface of newly built skyscrapers in Pudong, the piece is like a mirror reflection of both sides of the Huangpu River. The blue sky and white clouds are filled with calendar dates and numerals. They serve as a reminder to people of the waves of turbulent events over the last few centuries, as well as the persistent stock market and real estate bubbles that plague this hub of international engagement. The bottom part of the painting features blurred images of the river's undercurrents, which sharply contrast with the more "glamorous" upper parts. Xue Song uses appropriation, manipulation, and subversion to invoke messages about the loss of historical memories and the irony of a fatalistic cycle.

Shanghai artists use contemporary modes to critique modernity. Their paradoxical attitude toward ongoing global transformation suggests that the role of art has changed. The earlier division between "counterculture" and "mainstream culture" has become increasingly blurred, as counterculture is now fully integrated into the dominant, materialistic mainstream culture.

Artists have been ambivalent toward market transition. They have associated themselves with consumer culture, but they are also sharply uneasy with it. Hou Hanru, a prominent critic of Chinese modern art, observes that despite the "challenges" they pose through social and moral taboos, most avant-garde artists are "in fact in harmony with social reality—their art is about fame, money, consumption, and desire."[35]

The art installations by Shi Yong in the 1990s are known for communicating such paradoxical phenomena and social critiques of them. Although Shi never studied abroad, since the early 1990s his works have been exhibited in Amsterdam, Berlin, Bordeaux, Hamburg, Helsinki, Istanbul, London, Madrid, Mexico City, New York, Rotterdam, Pusan, São Paulo, San Francisco, Seoul, Toronto, Vancouver, Vienna, Venice, and other cities. Shi has adopted a wide range of mediums and produced performance art, installation art, video, and online interactive art. Instead of making direct political statements, Shi Yong seeks a more personal expression by "adopting various media in a surge of creativity and experimentation."[36] Almost all of Shi's works from the 1990s to the early 2000s seek to criticize Shanghai's public image in an increasingly globalized commercial world.

Many of his pieces created during that period involve interactive media, requiring viewer participation to be fully appreciated. In Shi's *First Date*, the background scene is Shanghai's Pudong, including the famous Oriental Pearl Tower—the symbol of China's opening to foreign investment at the time (Plate 3).[37] There is an androgynous figure standing in the piece, and as the title suggests, this person holding a red rose is expecting his or her first date. In his *New Image of Shanghai Today* series, the viewer selects the picture on a computer screen and starts to "communicate" with the figure, who the software then reveals is a man (it is in fact a picture of Shi Yong). The communication includes six parts, each of which requires the viewer to select an answer from multiple choices. The portrait changes based on which option is chosen each time. If the viewer does not like any of the choices provided, he or she can create a new answer. The focus of this interactive art piece is, of course, not merely dating or romance. It is about the relationship between advanced industrial nations and developing nations, about Western and non-Western cultures in a time of globalization, and about the choices that negotiate those norms. Western ideals can determine the public image of Shanghai, Shi suggests. In an online magazine, Shi wrote that so-called multiculturalism is in fact defined by Western power.[38] As a reflection of these remarks, the non-Western character shown on the computer screen directs the "public image" to fall in line with a defined postcolonial standard.

Some pieces in the series, "New Images of Shanghai Today," present an even more sophisticated and multilayered critique of the problems associated with image-making in Shanghai (Plate 4). The art pieces usually include two parts. The first is performance art and the second is interactive multimedia art. As performance art, Shi reveals himself by removing a cloth drape, similar to the unveiling of a statue or plaque at the grand opening of a department store. Before the reveal, which is labeled in English as the *New Image of Shanghai*, the audience can see words on the stand supporting the draped figure: "Made in China." Although the "Image of Shanghai" will be new to the audience once it is unveiled, Shi suggests that this will not change the viewer's existing perceptions. For a Western audience, the words "Made in China" may imply "cheap products," "prison labor in a communist regime," "state capitalism," or the "China threat." The words partly frame and predetermine the way in which the audience will understand the image to be presented later.

In the interactive portion, Shi Yong invites his viewers (netizens from around the world) to participate in designing a more ideal image, the "one most suitable for the rapid modernization of Shanghai." Through an online computer program, audience members can "custom-design" hairstyles and clothes, and then they are invited to vote on the various styles. A computer program tallies the ballots. At first glance, the audience may think that the artist is trying to extol individuality, diversity, and citizen participation in Shanghai. A more important message—and the real theme—of Shi Yong's *New Images of Shanghai Today* is that "society projects its ideas about the good, the beautiful, and the fashionable."[39] Thus Shi Yong presents the argument that it was the "Western client rather than Chinese society that shaped the image of the "spirit of China" during the country's market reforms. In Shi Yong's view, such a process is just like processing an order from a Western client. As Shi characterized it, "So I took the order, processed it in a 'made in China' style, and then produced what the client needs."[40] In other words, Shi Yong was forced to accept a Western perception of China that was "imposed" on his image.

This work by Shi Yong was a response to the changes occurring in Shanghai during the process of becoming a new international city. Chinese contemporary art from the 1990s can be called the export type of contemporary art, or in Shi Yong's words, "biting the bait type" (*yaogou xing*) or "coupling with the West" type, where one created artwork in line with what the Western art system hoped to see in Chinese contemporary art.[41] In Shi's view, "Production on demand is a normal thing in the commercial world, but unbelievable in the art world."[42] A photographic work by Shi, *You Cannot Clone It, But You Can Buy It*," in which his own image is repeated many times, visualizes the overproduction of commercial art in today's world. By confronting these tensions and contradictions, Shi Yong's work radically challenges both the formation of a public image and its interpretation. In an imaginative and thoughtful way, he suggests that the style of a city or the identity of any given place is contextual, multiple, flexible, and often manipulated by economic and political forces.

Shi Yong's work also implies that in a consumer-oriented society, an artist's status cannot depend solely on one masterpiece. In 1980, Luo Zhongli, a brilliant Sichuan artist, gained national recognition with his impressive painting *Father*, a portrait of a weather-beaten Chinese peasant. That single piece catapulted him to stardom in Chinese contemporary art. However, in a fully commercialized and globalized world, no artist could feel secure (or become rich) with just one masterpiece. Instead, it is necessary to produce a large number of similar pieces to occupy a share of the art market. That is one reason why the late Chen Yifei, Shanghai's most famous non-avant-garde artist who was known for his "avant-garde entrepreneurship," often produced his paintings in a series (such as his Jiangnan series or Tibet series). New works in each series sell for ever-higher prices, because earlier works have made them recognizable on the market. His photos of Tibet and Suzhou, combined with his skill as an erstwhile social-realist painter, allowed him to set photographic images to canvas. Through this "modern method," Chen could produce a large number of oil paintings of Tibetan people, plateau landscapes, and scenes of rivers and bridges in southern Jiangsu—and make a significant profit from them. As a matter of fact, each of the five Shanghai avant-garde artists highlighted in this study have produced many art pieces as parts of a series.

Since the early 2000s, Shi Yong's passion for making pieces as part of the "New Images of Shanghai" series has ebbed. His interest in "contemporary Shanghai" has evolved from the individual to the urban dimension. In more recent years, he has produced more abstract installation works, such as the "Illusionary Reality" series and the "Under the Rule" series, which explore issues of technological surveillance, information flow and digital control, as well as privacy and secrecy in the context of globalization.[43] Important events, such as the 2013 Edward Snowden leaking incident, have had a strong impact on intellectual and art communities around the world, including those in China. A significant number of avant-garde artists in Shanghai have been increasingly worried about issues relating to public security and state surveillance, especially in the rapidly evolving digital era.

From Shi Yong's perspective, individuals should be most concerned about the loss of privacy and dignity, the controlling power of machines over humans, and other destructive effects from the current digital revolution. In an article he wrote about his artwork titled "Secret Truth," Shi Yong stated, "In the subconscious, there is always a kind of peeping desire to enjoy the sudden change of affairs under the premise of being in a safe state. Because of this universality, 'secret' is the easiest to constitute subversive energy in reality, and it is often a deadly weapon to control others."[44] Shi Yong's 2018 installation piece, *Flickering in Another Sentence—the Gossip Spread Like Wildfire*, illustrates the anxieties, curiosities, fears, and devastating consequences associated with information dissemination in today's world (Plate 5). This installation is made of various materials such as wood, paint, sheets of stainless steel, sulfuric acid paper, an electronic speaker, an amplifier, and an audio player. The piece also includes a number of devices that look like hidden cameras and monitors. While the circular wire seems to serve as a way to contain the "gossip," as the title of the piece suggests, the wire itself can also be a source for the quick spread of wildfire. Conspicuously, the piece has a shadow, reaffirming Shi Yong's intriguing argument: "What can really manipulate us is not the decorated layer that you see, but the invisible fact that it is unseen and everywhere."[45]

These postmodern—as opposed to antimodern—themes can be amplified by the rapid spread of information through the internet and other social media platforms. Pu Jie is a master of irony in this vein. Many of his works use digital symbols to stress the social dislocations created by the internet. As early as twenty years ago, Pu combined online dating with the "I love you virus," a computer virus that damaged thousands of machines worldwide in 2000, in his artwork *Internet Time No. 11*. In this acrylic painting, a bevy of women extend their hands to a man, who does not even have a head but wears a nice Western suit. The background is filled with numbers in computer programming font, website links, and depictions of the "I love you virus" (Plate 6).

Similar to both Xue Song and Shi Yong, Pu Jie's work often focuses on the urban context in Shanghai, criticizing the blindness and singlemindedness of the city's embrace of globalization. The central message of Pu Jie's 2003 piece *Oh, Shanghai* (Plate 7) is almost identical to that of Shi Yong's *First Date*, although Pu Jie's means of communicating this message is much less tactful. In the piece, Jin Mao Tower, one of the landmark buildings in Pudong and a symbol of foreign commercial power, is painted to look like a penis, which is being approached by a topless Chinese woman.

Pu Jie is known for his "dual overlapping perspectives" (*shuang shijiao*), which reflect "two phenomena" of life experiences among his generation of Chinese artists. Like Xue Song, Pu Jie has often juxtaposed two layers of imagery, two contrasting cultures, two conflicting ideas, two artistic genres, or two different eras by bringing them together in his artwork under a unifying aesthetic expression. Pu Jie's painting *Head Is Her* portrays two eras in opposition to one another. In the art piece, consumption culture is exemplified by the head of an urban woman, who is dressed in lemon yellow with sharp black outlines, accentuating her vitality but also conveying hurriedness, emptiness, and uneasiness. To serve as a point of contrast, there is a portrait of a traditional lady behind her, unruffled and undecorated but more formal and distinguished (Plate 8).

As some viewers of this artwork have insightfully described, "Pu Jie juxtaposes seemingly contrasting narratives and memories as an attempt to show the fragmentary, ever-shifting and therefore incoherent nature of life."[46] For Pu Jie, only this type of comparative imagery enables the viewer to understand the unusual pain that accompanies the transformation of the times and the fracturing of an era. In a broader sense, by demonstrating the efficacy of mutual confrontation, dissolution, and digestion between two opposing forces, Pu Jie tries to balance the dualities of absorption and exclusion in contemporary Chinese life.[47]

Although consumer culture has brought many avant-garde artists both freedom and money, the artists still shine a spotlight on the problems with the cultural changes that have accompanied reforms. The market economy has stimulated a boom in Chinese contemporary art, but it may also become an enemy of art. Art critic Zhang Xiaoling says that "art gains freedom, but it also pays a heavy cost."[48] In the words of other Chinese art critics, "As art has just gotten rid of political chains, it has been caught in economic chains."[49] Given the dramatic and disruptive life experiences of their generation, Pu Jie, Shi Yong, and Xue Song are not naïve about the possibilities of pure artistic and intellectual freedom, which are often advocated by some Western critics. According to Xue, his generation is both lucky and distressed. They transitioned from a contempt of Chinese tradition to blind worship of the West, then slowly and consciously developed their own narrative. In Xue's words, "We don't believe in absolute freedom."[50]

Alienation, artificiality, and absurdity in commercial society are essential themes of avant-garde art everywhere. Satire and self-mockery are among the communication styles most frequently employed. Many works by Shanghai avant-garde artists display a spirit of self-criticism, and arguably no one is more willing to put himself forward as a subject of satire than Zhou Tiehai. In a piece titled *New Listing Zhou Tiehai Rises on Debt before Reaching Fair Value*, Zhou presents himself as a commodity, priced on a stock market. This *New Listing* opens with the caption, "When first offered, July 12, on the Shanghai Stock Exchange, Zhou Tiehai appeared undervalued, rising just slightly in the first few hours of trade." As many social theorists have shown, ethical problems emerge when people enter markets, and Zhou Tiehai highlights these issues with sharp humor.[51] As Zhou's piece alludes to, many contemporary Chinese artists have become commodities themselves, and "the value of any commodity can exist only after it is proven by its price."[52]

Zhou Tiehai has been known for his strong resentment of Western dominance in the era of globalization, whether it be in the domain of the economy, morality, media, or art. In the 1980s, as a young artist who had just graduated with a major in painting and design from the Shanghai College of Fine Arts, Zhou Tiehai believed that art meant "painting as Van Gogh did."[53] But that illusion was soon shattered. In a revelation almost identical to what Xue Song experienced, Zhou came to realize that "the artist is actually never free."[54] As in any postcolonial discourse, artists must struggle for their freedom while simultaneously catering to domineering powers in the art world.

Two meetings he had with Western contacts during his young professional life had profound effects on Zhou. First, when Andrew Solomon, the distinguished American writer and a winner of the National Book Award, arrived in China in 1993 to write a feature story on contemporary Chinese art for the *New York Times Magazine*, he conducted a substantial interview with Zhou Tiehai. However, he ultimately left Zhou out of the article. Zhou was so angered by this encounter that he decided it was time to "get back into art" and tell his story his own way.[55] Second, also in the early 1990s, Zhou came across a list of the best Chinese contemporary artists made by a well-known Western curator. Upon discovering that he and other distinguished artists had been excluded from the list, Zhou decided to directly challenge it.[56] Zhou pointedly asked, "Can a Western curator decide such a list? Can collectors with huge wealth determine the ranking of artists, perhaps by voting with money? Or can the artist, through his or her work, determine his or her reputation and status?" In line with this thinking, Zhou produced fake covers of various world-renowned magazines, such as *Time*, *Newsweek*, the *New York Times Magazine*, *ARTnews*, and *Facts* with his own photos and the headline "Zhou Tiehai," which drew into question the relationship between public attention and art. As some critics observed, by making these self-promotional images, Zhou helped "subvert the establishment notion of how artists should look and behave."[57] As Zhou came to see it, the success of a Chinese avant-garde artist depends entirely on whether the artist can gain Western recognition and acceptance.[58]

The central issue today for Chinese artists in the art world, according to Zhou, is the "right to speak" (*huayuquan*). For Zhou, his artistic pursuit has become an endeavor to gain this "right to speak." In order to obtain it, Zhou believes that he needs to develop "a kind of strategy centering on the triangle relationship between artists, galleries, and museums, or between painter, dealers, curators, and critics."[59] As some Chinese critics have observed, Zhou has become "an artist who has attracted widespread attention with his imaginary strategy." In a broader context, Zhou seems to imply that the contest of strategy between China and the West not only exists in the realms of military might and economic power, it also exists in the arena of cultural and ideological influence, in which art holds significant value.[60]

CALLING FOR EQUAL DIALOGUE IN AN ERA OF GLOBALIZATION

Over the past twenty years, Chinese avant-garde artists have highlighted their reservations about market reform and critiques of the West, which stand in sharp contrast to the intellectual mainstream in China during the 1980s and early 1990s. During the first two decades of the reform era, many avant-garde artists were very enthusiastic about the market economy and were inspired by Western political ideas. Some studied in the United States or other Western countries, as discussed in chapter 10. Some participated in the Tiananmen protests. Today, many Chinese intellectuals and artists have critically observed that market reforms have not brought prosperity to the entire country. Instead, they have led to economic disparity, social dislocation, rampant corruption among officials, and high unemployment rates. Many key events occurring after the 1990s—including Russia's economic shock therapy (which caused more shock than therapy), the 1997 Asian financial crisis, and the 2008 global financial crisis—made many Chinese intellectuals question if Adam Smith might have been as wrong as Karl Marx, even if their errors have led to different consequences.

On the international front, Chinese public intellectuals and college students have become increasingly cynical about the moral superiority of the West, resentful of perceived Western arrogance, and doubtful of whether China can adopt a Western economic and political system. Events such as the Western-led effort to block China's bid to host the Olympics, the perceived demonization of China in the Western media, the 1999 Belgrade bombing incident, the 2001 EP-3 airplane accident, the U.S. missile defense system's targeting of China, the ongoing decoupling movement, the accusations of Western double standards regarding violence in the 2019–2020 Hong Kong protests, and the ongoing tech war against Huawei and TikTok have all fueled Chinese nationalism among public intellectuals and avant-garde artists.

For some artists, personal experiences have laid the groundwork for their resentment of what they see as American arrogance. Artist Feng Jiali, for example, received an invitation from Art Omi in the early years of the reform era to come to the United States as a visiting scholar. She wrote, "Despite the directors of the host organization calling the embassy on several occasions to reassure them that I was indeed a professional artist, my visa was refused. The reason, I was 'unemployed' and a woman."[61] Nonetheless, many other Chinese artists who have recently been critical of the West have still chosen to live there. The late Chen Yifei was often seen as an example of the "American dream," but in his final years he declared to reporters that "I'm a Chinese nationalist."[62] Sun Liang, a Zhejiang-born artist who has worked in Shanghai over the past three decades, even bluntly claimed that "contemporary art was originally a Western scam."[63] He has appealed to his fellow Chinese artists to "challenge the rules of the Western-dominated art world."

Most criticism, however, targets American foreign policy and the perception of a U.S. hegemony in the economic and cultural arenas. In a photograph titled *Press Conference II* (1997), Zhou Tiehai situates himself in front of the national flags of the world and puts forth this claim: "The relationships in the art world are the same as the relationships between states in the post–Cold War era." Zhou's piece echoes a common theme among many avant-garde artists—economic and cultural exchange between the West and China is unequal. In Zhou's view, which is similar to those of other artists, such as the previously mentioned Xue Song, contemporary art does not really enjoy freedom, because it has been controlled globally by Western corporate powers.

For his avant-garde series *Placebo*, Zhou Tiehai reimagined a capitalist yuppie as a camel resembling Joe Camel, who is the iconic image for the American cigarettes that China has imported (Plate 9). For Zhou, "placebo" is the perfect term to reflect the irony of cultural exchanges between East and West. "On the one hand, the East is full of respect for the achievements of Western culture, trying to use Western medicine to save the oriental disease; on the other hand, knowing that the drug has serious side effects."[64] In other words, drugs do not necessarily cure diseases, and their improper use turns them into narcotics.[65]

In a catalog of Zhou's paintings, critic Harald Szeemann interprets Zhou's cool camel as a Godfather figure whose protection is necessary to stay safe. Just as Jupiter controls lightning, so Godfather Camel holds the index of stock market prices in his hand.[66] In some paintings, the camel dresses like a priest and offers religious instruction, advising other people on how to behave themselves. In other pieces, Zhou replaces the heads of figures in paintings from various eras—including the Renaissance (Da Vinci), the Enlightenment (Goya), and contemporary periods (Picasso, Andy Warhol, Jeff Koons, and Richard Prince)—with that of the camel.

Separately, Zhou also draws a Chinese traditional watercolor painting to highlight the contrast between different worldviews—Chinese and American. While Joe Camel wants to dominate the world, the Chinese hermit is more interested in promoting harmony between human and nature. After the September 11 terrorist attacks on the World Trade Center, Zhou's portrayal of Mayor Giuliani (Plate 10) challenges American sentiments in the post-9/11 era, as it mocks the hero worship in the United States.

More recently, Zhou Tiehai has been engaged in a collaboration with a French writer on a new series titled *The Desserts*. This French writer has written stories on the origin and evolution of French desserts, and Zhou has created artwork to utilize connotations of these desserts as sneers directed at Western elite groups, such as diplomats, judges, and ministers. The French writer and Zhou then transformed articles that were collected from the internet, "corresponding to the personages, the allusions, the ingredients that were referenced in the articles." The painting *Le Juge* (Plate 11), for example, consists of 158 pieces of different-sized images as background stories centered around a big piece of dessert made of a biscuit base, a layer of chocolate mousse, and topped by currant jam. In French slang, "biscuit" means "bribe." The currant jam carries the same insinuation, because in old times, the nobility and the bourgeoisie would give expensive currant jam as a gift to the judge when they won a lawsuit.[67]

While it is, of course, debatable whether these feelings of resentment are justified or even representative of all Chinese avant-garde artists, their origins are understandable. These sentiments reflect an intriguing relationship between China and the world today, which is both unprecedented and extremely innovative in terms of how cross-cultural exchanges have facilitated cultural tensions and development. These exchanges have had a complex and unpredictable impact on the restructuring of the global economy and geopolitics.[68] For contemporary Chinese artists, in just one generation, China's art world quickly experienced the evolution that took 150 years for Western art, from realism in the nineteenth century to Political Pop, surrealism, and many other forms of expression today.[69] These dramatic changes have jumbled cultural memories and their interactions and relationships.

In her 1999 book, *Flexible Citizenship: The Cultural Logic of Transnationality*, Singapore scholar Aihwa Ong observes that globalization has induced both national and transnational forms of nationalism that not only reject Western hegemony but seek, in pan-religious civilizational discourse, to promote the ascendancy of the East.[70] The upshot is that an international dialogue has started between Chinese avant-garde artists and their counterparts throughout the world. While some Chinese artists leverage this dialogue to criticize the West, others are more interested in finding ways to transcend old boundaries between the East and the West, as well as tradition and modernity. Art in this fashion doubts the existence of pure culture anywhere. For these artists, tradition and modernity, like the East or the West, need not be major issues for China if they do not necessarily conflict.

DISPUTES AMONG SHANGHAI AVANT-GARDE ARTISTS: CULTURAL CONVERGENCE OR CLASH?

Xu Bing, a Chongqing-born and now New York and Beijing-based artist, received a MacArthur Foundation "Genius Grant" in 1999. He is more interested in transnational creativity than in taking political stands. One of his distinguished artistic pursuits is to create fake Chinese characters that look solemn and exquisite but are devoid of any meaning. These "fake words," as debuted in his internationally famous artwork *A Book from Sky* or *Heavenly Book* (*tianshu*), have no communicatory function at all.[71] Xu believes that artists who have been immersed in culture are now overwhelmed by the impact of cultureless nihilism, or the anticulture movement. Thus one has to call for a historical rethinking of the nature of knowledge. In an interview, Xu said, "My intellectual formation has been the result of four factors: the Marxist ideology I grew up with and the capitalist reality in which I exist today; my extreme Chineseness and my existence as a citizen of the world. I have benefited from experiencing both systems, both cultures. I am interested in fusing global cultures.[72]

Gu Wenda, a Shanghai-born and New York–based artist, has tried for over a decade to transcend old boundaries through his works. He says he wants to transcend the East-West paradigm and find a new way to define the general issues faced by all humanity.[73] Like Xu Bing, Gu has a solid foundation in Chinese landscape painting and calligraphy. He acknowledges being influenced by Western thinkers, such as Nietzsche, Freud, and Wittgenstein, as well as by Chinese eremitism and Zen Buddhism. However, Gu's work does not address any specific political, religious, or sexual issues that these subjects might suggest. "Rather, he explores eternal human verities and the general human condition."[74] Gu also believes that, based on his personal and professional experience, artists should rely on their cultural memory and indigenous experience. At the same time, they should avoid being caught in the traps of either ultranationalism or postcolonialism.

Gu's series *United Nations* was an ambitious ten-year project to create an installation in twenty-five countries at the turn of the twenty-first century.[75] He used human hair, collected from over 300 barber shops around the world, to create multiracial, mixed-hair curtains in various forms. His hair-curtain walls involve "words" in four languages: English, Chinese, Hindi, and Arabic. But the words in all four are fake and meaningless, although those who cannot read these languages (few can read all of them) may not fully comprehend the irony.

Similar to the work of Xu Bing, Gu's installations address problems of (mis)communication between cultures and raise issues of identity, diversity, and modern assimilation. Gu also asks about the formation of knowledge and reveals our limitations in trying to understand the world in which we live. Human beings may experience life through overreliance on language. Gu believes we understand less than we think we do. *United Nations* is a landmark in contemporary art, showing both cultural differences and the common bond of humanity. Apparent in his artwork, Gu believes in—or expresses his hope for—cultural fusion rather than cultural clash in today's world.

Pursuing a similar goal for international dialogue, Xue Song's 2005 piece *Dialogue with Matisse* (Plate 11) pays tribute to the famous Henri Matisse piece *The Dance*, and it is made using Xue's distinctive style of mixed media material on canvas. Xue Song utilizes Matisse's work as the blueprint, which he "dissolves" through his burning method to create fragments, ashes, and paste. The result is a work displaying strange visual effects that also highlight multiple conflicts and transformations between cultures and religions. As in the original work by Matisse, the five individuals may be interpreted as five continents of Earth. But in contrast to the original, Xue Song uses his medium to express his overarching concern about one trend in today's world: different religions have become the causes of conflicts and wars. The fragments Xue pastes together are different religious materials. The scene showing all five individuals holding hands together suggests the world faces a shared destiny—peace or war.[76]

The artwork produced by the five Shanghai artists in this study suggests that the problems of global modernity extend beyond a single country like China. For example, Xue Song's 2002 solo exhibition in the ShanghART Gallery was titled *Ver Da Ga*, a phrase in the Shanghai dialect meaning "no connection at all." The art that was used to advertise this exhibition portrayed a starving Mali child (based on a well-known photo by Brazilian photographer Sebastião Salgado) and a dead tree (Plate 13). Faintly present among the golden background of the painting, however, are symbols of modern luxuries—fancy cars, boats, villas, pets, sunglasses, and the faces of the rich. They live in a completely different world from that of the starving child. The art piece suggests that during globalization, human segregation and economic disparity persist as moral scourges.

In contrast to some of China's avant-garde artists—including the four aforementioned Shanghai artists—who aim to attract attention through their presentations of striking contrasts, paradoxical juxtapositions, political satire, provocative irony, or even palpable anger, Ding Yi employs a different style that evokes philosophical meditation, inner calm, and self-revelation. Born in 1962 in Shanghai, Ding Yi worked at a printing factory for a couple of years before attending the Shanghai School of Arts and Crafts, where he majored in decoration design from 1981 to 1983. He later attended the School of Fine Arts of Shanghai University. In 1988, while still a college student, Ding began a series of painting experiments titled *Appearance of Crosses*, in which he used + and × shapes as a recurring motif with the intention of merging painting and design into a single form of expression. In a way, his art is similar to the Chinese traditional plaid fabric (*gezibu*). Ding's designs have now been adopted by the luxury fashion brand Hermès to create twelve scarves. Thus Ding Yi's signature *Appearance of Crosses* can be seen as an artistic fusion between tradition and modernity, East and West, and abstract and utility.

Ding's search for his distinct artistic style occurred, in his own words, "when Chinese contemporary art was experiencing the strong impact of Western culture and a critical reflection on traditional culture by Chinese artists.... But I want[ed] to go back to the origin of art—the essence of the form of painting."[77] In an imaginative way, Ding intends to "make painting that is not like painting." He explains that the images of + and × are meaningless, and they are simply technical terminologies and symbols in the printing industry. The dense and orderly arrangements of + and ×, however, explore the shallow spatial relationship of the picture in a rational way.

As of today, Ding Yi has painted the *Appearance of Crosses* for over thirty years, continuously and exclusively creating abstract paintings made of small cross shapes (Plate 14). The majority of Ding's work features repetitions of the + and × signs superimposed in different layers, colors, and rotations. At first glance, Ding's *Appearance of Crosses* pieces are deceptively simple and monotonous. But a thorough review of his work reveals rich variations and a profound transformation in Ding's artistic pursuits. As Ding has acknowledged, in the original period of the *Appearance of Crosses* series, the method employed was more or less "a pure abstraction with some kind of avoidance or escape from reality."[78] Gradually, the crosses have become like a style of drawing, or even a philosophical perspective and vision of the world. Feng Boyi, a scholar on Chinese contemporary art, observes that for Ding Yi, his unique style "is not only a form, but also a specific and subtle lived experience and inner feeling, as well as a persistent and paranoid attitude towards art."[79] For Ding, "the essence of art is not to express the symbols that appear in the picture, but to create the overall spiritual power of the times through the brushstrokes of symbolic transformation."[80]

From a broader perspective, Ding's works are not mechanical and artistic symbols, but instead represent two highly integrated cultural and intellectual searches. The first is to develop a distinct visual language—similar to what Zhou Tiehai has described as the "right to speak" through artistic creation—representing Chinese artists in the present-day world. The second is to cultivate a spiritual code for the nation, especially for Shanghai.

For the first, as described by Ding in an interview, "the production of grids of multiple crosses, whose plurality points to the standardization, copying, and repetitive nature of modern industrial civilization," symbolizes seamless production line, commercial products, and mass media advertising. They are all products of a standardized, scaled-up process in our time.[81] Like Zhou Tiehai, Ding Yi believes that Chinese avant-garde artists should develop a sensible strategy to earn their standing in an art world once dominated by the West. Instead of the conventional Chinese painting language that often emphasizes Chinese faces or scenes, Ding strives to create a unique abstract language of + and × shapes to earn a seat in international art circles. Ding's work, resembling magnetic lines of force consisting of + and × symbols, conveys the conciseness of purified language and visual orders, and thus makes him "grasp the right to speak" in his own way.[82] In Ding's view, Chinese artists must first employ language that is understandable to others to engage in a dialogue with the world, and then become better communicators. Through this approach, Chinese artists "can gradually change from being passive to active."[83]

For the second intellectual search, Ding's new abstract language simultaneously serves what Ding Yi calls "a name-card of achievement" for China in general and Shanghai in particular.[84] In this respect, Ding's *Appearance of Crosses* series seems perfectly attuned to the rapid urbanization in the country. The disorder, chaos, and confusion in the process of large-scale demolition and construction of Chinese cities, as exemplified by Shanghai, have left all those who have experienced this transformation with a strong sense of history. In Ding's view, people can easily recognize this period of intensity from the seemingly monotonous and mechanical + and × images in his artwork.

According to Ding Yi, there must be a connection between new city expansion and new forms of art in this era. How does an artist's existence leave a mark of the times on the history of the city? How can artists record the imaginary, chaotic, and fashionable parts of current urban life in a macroscopic and neutral way, while also showing the city's neon lights, flow of people, traffic, advertisements, skyscrapers, stock display screens, and thousands of other scenes that compete for visual attention? Ding Yi poses these questions to other artists and the viewers of his work, and by squeezing these elements onto his palette for the *Appearance of Crosses*, he seems to imply that the aesthetics embodied in his abstract works provide an answer.[85]

In an interview conducted in June 2018, Ding Yi said, "I have a vague idea that I'm looking for a new social spirit, mainly because of the huge transformation that has occurred in society, which offers a more elevated perspective from which to view the world. . . . Chinese culture is still very weak; there is a lack of cultural self-confidence and truly global values that can engender the birth of a new culture."[86] Ding Yi's multifaceted style and seemingly apolitical stance, as some critics describe, are very much in alignment with the distinct cultural expression of Shanghai. His *Appearance of Crosses* series has essentially become the signature, representative avant-garde artwork for Shanghai's character. "In calmness, it also indicates a cultural passion."[87]

While Ding has been consistent in including crosses in almost all of his artwork over the past three decades, he has also tried employing new materials and media, including fluorescent paint, pencil drawing, and spray paint. In addition to producing finished plaids, he has also displayed his crosses on drawing paper, rice paper, corrugated paper, linen, wood, and other materials to readjust the cognitive framework of the subject and "constantly encounter heterogeneity—a new experience from various preset and imagined symbolic orders."[88]

Since the late 1990s, Ding Yi has been trying to extend his unique *Appearance of Crosses* paintings to three-dimensional media, such as installations, sculpture, architecture, lighting, and more. These new art forms have broadened Ding's means of expression, allowing him to more adequately convey his perspectives on cross-cultural dialogue and his critical thinking regarding Chinese outreach in a globalized world. His public sculpture *Appearances of Crosses-Ruyi* is inspired by the Chinese traditional ideograph Ruyi. Originally, Ruyi was a tool used in Chinese folk religion during ancient times as a type of backscratcher. Ruyi also served as a self-defense tool during war. In the contemporary context, Ruyi is widely considered to be auspicious, used in folk communities and mansions alike. When people are preparing to travel, family or friends will send Ruyi as a gift to convey well wishes. Ding Yi's Ruyi sculpture series aims to illustrate that Chinese traditional ideographs and symbols are subject to new interpretations when they are magnified, altered, and re-created, and they might interdict historical experiences and evidence. In 2011, Ding Yi's Ruyi series was exhibited outside the John F. Kennedy Center for the Performing Arts in Washington, D.C. (Plate 15). As Ding pointedly stated, when these small forms of Ruyi are enlarged multiple times, more challenges emerge for cultural memory and semiotic orientation.[89]

Along the same line of thinking, Ding Yi's 2012 sculpture series *Taiji* (Tai Chi) presents a pair of individuals engaged in Chinese traditional boxing (Taijiquan) (Plate 16). In the Chinese conception, Taijiquan is often characterized as gentle, indirect, slow-moving, and relaxed—reflecting the Chinese Taoist worldview of Yin-Yang balance. In the sculpture *Taiji*, however, Ding Yi abstracted the figures engaged in Taijiquan and blended them with his classic *Appearance of Crosses* symbols. As the two characters are repositioned and deformed by Ding Yi, the posture of the Taiji practitioners appears highly rigid, intense, and antagonistic. In a sense, Ding rejects the conventional description of Tai Chi, as he believes the conception must be altered when the circumstances have profoundly changed.

Thus, at a time when China is experiencing a historic rise on the world stage, making cross-cultural communication and international dialogue increasingly important, Ding seems intent on conveying a message to both Beijing and Washington. For Ding, it is not just the West that should develop a more updated and balanced assessment of China's ongoing transformation, which is, of course, needed. Equally important, China also must better understand how its changing status may affect (and be perceived) by the outside world, especially the United States. While the U.S.-China relationship may loosen and tighten, and at times the two countries may seem like Yin-Yang polar opposites, cultural and educational engagement is critical for ensuring a prevailing sense of balance. If that balance is interrupted as cross-cultural misunderstandings arise amid political and economic antagonism, a collapse of the relationship is unavoidable.

FINAL THOUGHTS

The conceptions of Shanghai avant-garde artists of the political realm often extend far beyond the state.[90] Their discourse about cultural identity, individuality, and diversity, as well as economic globalization and geopolitical power relations, is ubiquitous but subtle, as illustrated in the works of all five artists in this study. What has emerged most clearly in the Shanghai avant-garde art scene is an intellectual effort to transcend old boundaries in search of new ways to negotiate cultural changes both at home and abroad. These five artists have overcome initial inclinations to overthrow their own cultural heritage and adopt foreign practices, and they have forged a path that deftly navigates and incorporates both the local and global on their own terms. The call of Chinese avant-garde artists for an equal dialogue with the West is loud and clear. Hence, to a significant degree, the works by the Shanghai avant-gardists featured in this chapter provide evidence of new trends in the political consciousness of the Chinese middle class in general. These avant-garde artworks should be seen not only as efforts to revive China's contemporary morals but also as appeals by these artists to engage in further dialogue about art and politics, nationalism and internationalism, and peace and justice on the world stage.

This dialogue is political, but not just about the particular polity in China. It involves an argument imbued with both subtle anger and humor. It calls for new understandings from both Chinese people and outsiders. Previously binary divisions—between East and West, socialism and capitalism, tradition and modernity—have become blurred in the works of Shanghai avant-garde artists. All of these Shanghai artists have been influenced—at different points in their lives—by the Maoist Cultural Revolution, Western intellectual thought, and market consumerism. The real question is not how much they have been shaped by any of these influences, but rather, whether they still have their own views and voices after experiencing all of these powerful forces, and whether they remain open-minded and forward-looking as their nation and the world meet at a crossroads of uncertainty.

This discussion shows that consumer-oriented middle-class culture and globalization have not resulted in the homogenization or "death" of art. On the contrary, Shanghai's international engagement in the reform era has injected a vitality among the vanguard of artists of this city. In the words of a Shanghainese artist, "It is fortunate that art still exists that embodies the inspiration and adventure in our life, which is not lost by the same standard nor can be made just through mass production."[91]

V

CONCLUSION AND
RECOMMENDATIONS

CHAPTER 12

Toward a Dynamic and Diverse Society

Implications for China and the United States

Human history becomes more and more a race
between education and catastrophe.
—H. G. WELLS

The well-being of the American middle class ought to be
the engine that drives our foreign policy.
—WILLIAM J. BURNS

The tragic loss of Kobe Bryant on January 26, 2020, came as a devastating shock to sports fans around the world, including millions of people on the other side of the Pacific who awoke to this terrible news. The emotional reaction of the Chinese people—and their heartfelt affection and admiration for this legendary basketball player—is particularly notable given that the country was also in the throes of the deadly coronavirus crisis. On January 27, there were more than 1 billion web searches for Bryant's name and the helicopter crash on the Chinese social media site Weibo, more than double the number of searches for coronavirus, the second-most-searched term in China.[1]

Bryant's outsized influence in China reflects his long-standing goodwill toward the Chinese people. He saw himself as more than an athlete, since basketball alone did not define his legacy. After winning his fourth NBA championship in 2009, Bryant established the Kobe Bryant China Fund in partnership with the Soong Ching Ling Foundation, one of China's largest charities.[2] The Fund's first donation was a grant of RMB 5 million aimed at reconstructing areas affected by the 2008 earthquake in Sichuan and promoting sports activities for children. Since then, Bryant had traveled to China more than a dozen times, during which he not only showed his genuine interest in the rapidly changing country but also provided Chinese youth—particularly those from both the middle class and less privileged families—with an opportunity to see themselves in him. His daughter Gianna, who often traveled with him to China, was able to speak, read, and write Mandarin. Even after retiring, Bryant regularly updated his Weibo account with personalized videos and messages to his 10 million Chinese followers.[3]

The admiration of the Chinese people for Kobe Bryant and the widespread mourning throughout the country that followed his tragic passing are telling reminders that U.S.-China relations are not just state-to-state relations—they are also people-to-people relations. Bryant's interactions with the Chinese people on a personal level highlight the important role of sports in public diplomacy, as well as the enduring legacy of cultural exchanges, even at a time when the bilateral relationship has drastically deteriorated. More broadly, Bryant's relationship with and impact on Chinese people reaffirms the overarching thesis of this book—that cultural and educational exchanges between two countries with profoundly different ideologies and political systems can promote mutual understanding and goodwill, diffuse global norms, and thus reduce the likelihood of military conflict.

This revelation is both timely and important, as decoupling has dominated Washington's policy discourse about China. Now, the pervasive view about bilateral educational and cultural exchanges is no longer one of hope for positive change through engagement, but rather one of fear that scholars and students from the People's Republic of China (PRC) attending American educational and research institutions are "weapons" of the Chinese Communist Party (CCP) who will hasten China's ascent to superpower status in science and technology at the expense of the United States. Against the bleak backdrop of the COVID-19 pandemic and this growing mutual suspicion and animosity between China and the United States, the goodwill and empathy between an American icon, Kobe Bryant, and the Chinese people provide a ray of hope.

This glimmer of hope for mutual understanding should inspire policymakers in both Washington and Beijing to look for an off-ramp from the historically dire situation today. To a certain degree, COVID-19 has unfortunately accelerated decoupling and the deterioration of U.S.-China relations, rather than becoming an opportunity for much needed cooperation. While the drastic policy moves to end engagement with China may stem from domestic political factors, the underlying causes of tensions and competition in the bilateral relationship are much deeper and broader. The downward spiral of the relationship seems to have placed the United States and China on a collision course that, if not carefully managed by both countries, could lead to devastating consequences.

Even after the world defeats and emerges from COVID-19, the United States will have to reevaluate its decoupling approach to China and its understanding of the country's emerging middle class, as both will influence the postcoronavirus world order. More urgently, the Biden administration should construct a comprehensive strategy toward China that is guided by a clear-eyed recognition of the capacity and constraints of American power in its future competition and engagement with Beijing. An important component of this strategy should include efforts to explicitly articulate to the Chinese public and elites both the long-standing goodwill that the United States has toward China and America's firm commitment to democracy and diplomacy.

It will also be essential for Beijing to reexamine its own perspectives and behaviors, and it must assume its own responsibility for repairing the bilateral relationship and promoting peace and prosperity in the Asia-Pacific region. In both the United States and China, domestic factors have increasingly shaped their foreign policies and international outreach. Given the great importance of state-society relations in the PRC—which are constantly in flux—and the growing influence of the Chinese middle class, China watchers around the world and Washington policymakers in particular must develop an accurate and balanced assessment of these dynamic new developments.

COVID-19: ACCELERATING ANXIETY AND ANIMOSITY IN U.S.-CHINA RELATIONS

Prior to the outbreak of COVID-19, the mutual mistrust and resentment between Washington and Beijing had already considerably increased. The catastrophic impact of the coronavirus pandemic on the United States—which over ten months (from late February to the end of 2020) resulted in more than twenty million people infected and more than 350,000 killed—touched off anger and anxiety among the American public about the Chinese government's misconduct in the early days of the outbreak. It also provided more ammunition to those calling for decoupling with China.

Like many other countries, the impact of COVID-19 on America was unprecedented in many respects. For the first time in U.S. history, all fifty states issued emergency declarations, and 95 percent of the population was ordered to stay at home.[4] From late March to late April, as many as 27 million people (about 17 percent of the total labor force in the country) lost their jobs.[5] For weeks and even months during the COVID-19 crisis, there were widespread shortages of testing kits, masks, respirators, ventilators, and other personal protective equipment across the country, especially in heavily hit cities like New York, Los Angeles, Miami, and Chicago. As the United States focused inward to address the pandemic, it abandoned its traditional central role on the world stage, leaving China to fill the void. By late May 2020, the Chinese government had provided emergency aid to nearly 150 countries, including airlifting medical supplies to pandemic-ravaged countries and dispatching twenty-six medical expert teams to twenty-four countries.[6] International responses to these actions, however, were a varied mix of praise and appreciation with suspicion and apprehension, especially in the United States.

The American media overflowed with criticism and concern about China during the pandemic as the crisis brought to light important aspects of the U.S.-China relationship, such as America's dependence on China for medicines. As high as 97 percent of antibiotics, 95 percent of ibuprofen, 90 percent of vitamin C, and a large proportion of the basic components of U.S. drugs, known as active pharmaceutical ingredients, come from China. Not surprisingly, as concerns about medicine supplies surfaced during the pandemic, policymakers on Capitol Hill, including both Democrats and Republicans, began calling for a serious examination of U.S. dependence on drugs and pharmaceutical ingredients imported from Chinese manufacturers.[7] Larry Kudlow, then director of the U.S. National Economic Council and President Donald Trump's top economic adviser, urged American companies in China to consider moving back to the United States.[8]

The level of deterioration in the bilateral relationship—and the degree of fear and anger—reached new highs when officials in both the United States and China accused each other of engineering the novel coronavirus to use as a weapon to target the other country.[9] In the United States, a number of senators and representatives, as well as some opinion leaders, demanded that the Chinese government pay the costs incurred by the United States and other countries as a result of the disease.[10] In response, China's Foreign Ministry Spokesperson Geng Shuang claimed that if American politicians made such demands, China—and the international community—could also request that the U.S. provide "compensation for the 2009 H1N1 flu, which was first diagnosed in the United States and then spread to 214 countries and regions, killing nearly 200,000 people."[11] Geng also suggested that the U.S. provide additional compensation for AIDS, which was first reported in the United States in the 1980s.

In this environment of increasingly hostile rhetoric from officials in both Washington and Beijing, nationalist sentiments spiraled out of control in both countries, especially in the months leading up to the U.S. election. In China, both official media and social media were filled with malicious attacks suggesting an American conspiracy to contain China's rise, along with bellicose calls to accelerate the collapse of American hegemony. The tension and mutual hostility were not just limited to what some Chinese analysts referred to as a "scold war."[12] They quickly escalated into the expulsion of journalists from the other country, the closure of the Consulates General in Houston and Chengdu, and the levying of sanctions on senior government officials on both sides.

In this challenging time, there remain, of course, sober, wise, and constructive voices regarding this critical bilateral relationship. Even before the outbreak of coronavirus, in the fall of 2019, former secretary of state Henry Kissinger warned that U.S.-China relations were in the "foothills of a Cold War."[13] In his view, if the troubles in the bilateral relationship were left to run their course, the resulting conflict could be even more serious than the situation prior to World War I. As COVID-19 exploded into a pandemic, Kissinger reiterated his message about the imperative for restraint on both sides, and his conviction that both great powers must embrace their shared interest in managing the crisis. In his words, "failure could set the world on fire."[14] Kissinger called for a "a global collaborative vision and program" in this epochal period.

Along the same lines, Ivo Daalder, president of the Chicago Council on Global Affairs and former U.S. ambassador to NATO, argued that the right approach for Washington policymakers required seeking more, not less, international cooperation. In his words, "Globalization isn't just a policy preference; it is a reality of our world."[15] With the world confronting the common challenge of the novel coronavirus, "there is no national cure for this pandemic. There's only a global cure."[16] In early February 2020, a month before the United States began to contain COVID-19, Joshua Cooper Ramo, a former editor of *Time* magazine and seasoned China expert, warned "decouplers" in the United States that, "As tempting as it is to unplug, to put up walls, to 'decouple' from other nations or whip up old racist tropes, this is exactly what we must not do."[17]

In an article published in *The Atlantic* magazine in March 2020, Peter Beinart, a professor of journalism at the City University of New York, argued that the Trump administration's decoupling policy with China over the past few years very likely contributed to the awful spread of COVID-19. In Beinart's view, if experts from the Centers for Disease Control and Prevention and the National Institutes of Health had maintained close contact with their Chinese counterparts, instead of unfairly and excessively accusing Chinese medical researchers of stealing or spying in U.S. labs, "those informal channels would have given the United States much better information in the virus's early days."[18] This would have allowed U.S. public-health officials and experts to move much faster in a joint effort to stop the virus, as happened with severe acute respiratory syndrome in 2003.

In 2015, prior to Trump's election, Bill Gates insightfully pointed out the misallocation and mismanagement of resources by the U.S. government. He argued that the greatest risk of global catastrophe in today's world was likely a highly infectious virus rather than a nuclear attack.[19] As Gates observed, "We've invested a huge amount in nuclear deterrents. But we've actually invested very little in a system to stop an epidemic."[20] Alarmingly, the attack of *microbes* has increased the likelihood of dangerous *missiles* in today's dire international environment, not least between two of the largest economic and military powers in the world.

COSTS AND RISKS OF ALL-ENCOMPASSING DECOUPLING

To navigate the current perilous and complicated situation, the United States will need to move beyond disputes about COVID-19 and partisan politics with the objective of establishing a long-term, well-grounded strategy toward China. Policymakers in Washington should develop a prudent, comprehensive, and visionary assessment of both China and the United States, as well as the costs and risks involved in an all-encompassing decoupling, if ultimately carried out by America and its allies. Understandably, in the wake of COVID-19, every country will likely reassess their prior embrace of economic globalization as well as the new landscape of major power relations. The United States will surely be determined to maintain its global power and influence. Thus dealing with China will be a key component in U.S. foreign policy going forward. Washington's approach to this rising power should be specific, finite, targeted, and flexible. It should not "inevitably" lead the United States—by design or by default—to a fundamentally antagonistic or adversarial relationship with China that results in a catastrophic war with no winner.

The sensationalism spawned by proponents of decoupling stems from an unbalanced and fatalistic assessment of China's capacity and intentions. The Trump administration's all-encompassing decoupling approach was driven by three misguided (and interconnected) perceptions or strategic propositions: (1) the view that the decades-long engagement policy initiated by Richard Nixon and Henry Kissinger has failed, (2) the idea that a new Cold War with China serves the interests of the United States, and (3) the pronounced goal of pursuing regime change that overthrows the CCP. A critical analysis of these three assumptions is essential before Washington can commit to an all-encompassing decoupling plan. While the decouplers have expressed legitimate concerns about China's destructive impact (either real or potential) on the liberal international order, it is important to set the historical record straight and avoid miscalculations and misperceptions about the most consequential competitor to the United States.

Washington's Legitimate Concerns and Criticisms of China's Rise

Proponents of decoupling in Washington have raised legitimate concerns about Beijing's unfair practices in the economic and technological domains, as well as China's aggressive behavior in the Asia-Pacific region. To a certain extent, decouplers' resentment of China's unfair economic competition should not be a great surprise—the Chinese economic miracle in the reform era has come at the relative expense of America's economic status in the world. As FBI director Christopher Wray described, the global economic landscape change in China's favor "represents one of the largest transfers of wealth in human history."[21] In that regard, former U.S. attorney general William Barr was also right when he said "no one should underestimate the ingenuity and industry of the Chinese people. At the same time, no one should doubt that America made China's meteoric rise possible."[22]

The rapid rise and expansion of the middle class in China documented in this book show this remarkable "transfer of wealth." The middle class in the United States has gradually been shrinking—from 70 percent of the American population in the post–World War years to 61 percent in the early 1970s, to 55 percent in 2000, and to about 50 percent today.[23] According to the statistics provided by the World Inequality Database, between 1980 and 2014, Chinese citizens at every income percentile benefited greatly from economic globalization, and their income grew between 200 percent and 1,500 percent during that period.[24] In contrast, in the United States only the highest (top 20 percent) income percentile group had their income increase by 100 percent to 200 percent, while all other income groups had little to no improvement.[25] America's middle and working classes are now the segments of the socioeconomic spectrum who are most hurt, angry, and disaffected by the economic disparities brought about by financial and economic globalization along with technological revolution.

According to William J. Burns (who does not favor decoupling with China), the United States welcomed China into the World Trade Organization (WTO) with the hope that it would become a "responsible stakeholder," but the WTO "failed to hold [China] to account when it continued to behave irresponsibly, breaking the rules while the American middle class broke its back."[26] China has taken advantage of the openness of the American economy and American universities and research institutions. For critics, China's extensive violations of intellectual property rights, barriers on market access for U.S. companies, state-sponsored economic espionage, mercantilist techniques to gain dominance in new technologies, and global economic and political outreach through state capitalism have unfairly advantaged Chinese economic expansion.

American decouplers claim that some of their current moves to decouple with the PRC are simply counterbalancing responses to Beijing's long-standing practices. China's adoption of a foreign NGO law has greatly restrained the activities of American academic institutions and other organizations in the country. American journalists have confronted many restraints and much obstruction when reporting in China—far more so than their Chinese counterparts in the United States. For the Trump administration's executive orders to restrict Chinese information technology and internet companies (e.g., Wechat, QQ, Weibo, and TikTok) in the U.S. market, decouplers argue that the Chinese government has no grounds for complaint. American firms like Facebook, Google, and Twitter are still shut out of the Chinese market.[27]

The United States is not the sole source of concerns and criticism of Chinese aggression and mercantilist techniques. Chinese "wolf warrior" diplomacy has also elicited strong reactions from China's neighbors. China's ambitious Belt and Road Initiative has greatly undermined the security and economic interests of India, as even some Chinese scholars have pointed out.[28] While China has criticized the United States for ordering U.S. and other countries' companies to stop supplying chips to Huawei and other Chinese firms, Beijing cut exports of rare earth materials to Japan in 2010 after an incident involving disputed islands in the East China Sea. In the words of decouplers, this policy orientation simply reflects "reciprocity."[29]

Despite the validity of some of the concerns and criticism mentioned above, the sensationalism stirred up by decouplers about "China's rise as an existential threat" to world peace, along with America's excessive response to "hold China back through all available means" is overreactive and misguided. In particular, decouplers' assertions that the CCP's "subversive, undeclared, criminal, or coercive attempts" to change the American way of life and to challenge the "free world,"[30] and its ultimate ambition "to raid the United States"[31] are largely exaggerated.

Jeffrey Sachs, a professor at Columbia University and a leading critic of decoupling, observes that it is ironic for Secretary of State Michael Pompeo to claim that the CCP harbors a "decades-long desire for global hegemony."[32] The fact is that only the United States has sought such status for that long, while the Chinese leadership has publicly stated that "China will never follow the beaten track of big powers in seeking hegemony."[33] Sachs explains that the United States has around 800 overseas military bases, while China has just one (a small naval base in Djibouti). The United States has many military bases close to China, which has none anywhere near North America. The United States has 5,800 nuclear warheads, while China has roughly 320. The U.S. Navy has eleven aircraft carriers and the Chinese Navy has only a couple.[34]

How the United States Benefits from Engagement Policy

Although American China watchers have by no means reached a consensus that the United States should no longer engage with China, the prevailing view in Washington is that a new strategy is needed to replace the failed engagement approach. Secretary Pompeo proclaimed a "hard truth," namely that "the old paradigm of blind engagement with China simply won't get it done. We must not continue it and we must not return to it."[35] For Pompeo and other decouplers, the earlier promise that engaging with China would make the country more liberal, more democratic, and more cooperative with the United States has been left unrealized and will never work.

But as many American scholars argue, Pompeo's notion of "blind engagement" and its perceived failure is "a huge distortion of history."[36] They believe that the U.S. opening to China was neither blind engagement nor has it failed. The original, primary objective of the engagement policy was not to transform China internally, but to "use China as a counterweight to the Soviet Union and shape China's foreign policy," as President of the Council on Foreign Relations Richard Haass has pointed out.[37] Nixon-Kissinger's opening to China not only helped end two decades of mutual hostility between China and the United States, it also gave Washington leverage to consolidate a strategic anti-Soviet alliance, which contributed to enhancing the prospects for peace and stability in the world and eventually led to the end of the Cold War. In the words of Haass, these strategic efforts "largely succeeded."[38]

The engagement policy with China has also yielded other important achievements in the interest of the United States. As Jeffrey A. Bader, former senior director for Asia on the National Security Council, has observed, "[East] Asia has avoided major military conflicts since the 1970s. After the United States fought three wars in the preceding four decades originating in East Asia, with a quarter of a million lost American lives, this is no small achievement."[39] This was primarily the result of U.S. engagement with China. Specifically looking at China, despite its military expansion in the South and East China Seas, the country "has not fought a war with another country since its 1979 border conflict with Vietnam. Importantly, China has not used force against Taiwan."[40]

Decouplers often apply a zero-sum game view that China's economic rise has occurred largely at the expense of the United States. But this assumption fails to consider the fact that foreign countries, including the United States, have also benefited from Deng Xiaoping's economic reforms and opening up—through foreign trade, investment, and other economic engagement. Also, American foreign policy has not completely been driven by self-interest. The exceptional humanitarian accomplishments of reform era China, when around 800 million people were lifted out of poverty, should instill pride among not only the Chinese but the entire international community as well. As the Trump White House stated, "[The] American people's generous contributions to China's development are a matter of historical record—just as the Chinese people's remarkable accomplishments in the era of Reform and Opening are undeniable."[41] Additionally, economic engagement with China has enhanced the leverage with which the United States and the international community can push for China's constructive cultivation of global public goods, especially in dealing with climate change.

This book demonstrates that engagement policy with China—especially its components of cultural diplomacy and educational exchange—has also achieved its intended results. The United States has *successfully* trained generations of Chinese elites, and these elites have played crucial roles in all areas of Chinese society, including as leaders in politics and the law. This study has also provided multifaceted evidence of how these cultural and educational exchanges have led to societal transformation in China. These changes have certainly benefited China, but cultural and educational exchanges are not a one-way street; the U.S. has also accrued benefits. Thus the United States has not failed on this front, and only decouplers have failed to recognize some of these achievements.

In addition to training generations of Chinese elites, the United States has also gained many talented Chinese immigrants who have chosen to work in their adopted country. According to one recent study, 27 percent of PRC immigrants to the United States have a master's degree or higher, while only 13 percent of immigrants from other countries and only 12 percent of American natives have a master's degree or higher.[42] Chapter 7 of this book provides detailed documentation of the remarkable impact of educational exchanges on both countries. For example, from 2005 to 2015, nearly 90 percent of PRC students who had earned Ph.D. degrees intended to remain in the United States after their degree programs.[43] The same was true for a large number of undergraduates from China's top schools, such as Tsinghua, Peking, and Fudan universities, who had enrolled in graduate programs in the United States. These PRC-born scholars and students have contributed to academic research in American universities. One recent example is that the COVID-19 dashboard produced by Johns Hopkins University, which has played a leading role for real-time tracking of the pandemic, is run by an American professor and her PRC-born Chinese students.[44]

Danger of Plunging into a New Cold War

The current military and ideological tensions between the United States and China have naturally increased public speculation that a new Cold War is on the horizon. This assumption, however, is dangerous and deceiving. Decouplers acknowledge some of the differences between the Soviet Union then and China now. The Soviet Union was not part of a global economy, but China today is a major player. Former secretary of state Pompeo noted, "[The] USSR was closed off from the free world. Communist China is already within our borders."[45] Decouplers' actions to round up other countries, especially in Europe and Asia, to side with the United States to contain Communist China, only strengthens this adversarial trend. As an American scholar points out, from the perspective of decouplers, the "contest with China is not another Cold War to avoid, but one to fight with confidence and win."[46]

Notably, Pompeo made an explicit comment on the similarities between the former Soviet Union and today's China: "The CCP is repeating some of the same mistakes that the Soviet Union made—alienating potential allies, breaking trust at home and abroad, rejecting property rights and predictable rule of law."[47] While the CCP certainly confronts many challenges both at home and abroad, all of these assumptions made by Pompeo are subject to serious scrutiny. To say the least, China has shown more adaptability than the Soviet Union, in both domestic appeals and international outreach. His suggestion that China has rejected property rights is factually wrong. The rise of the private sector and middle class in the country, as described in this book, is a direct result of the CCP leadership's promotion of property rights in the reform era.

Interestingly, many Chinese scholars are critical of what they call an "outdated Cold War mentality," even though some of their Chinese colleagues may share this same assumption as decouplers in the United States. In an opinion survey of 100 Chinese experts on U.S.-China relations, an overwhelming majority assert that "[the] global environment in which there was a great ideological confrontation between capitalism and socialism no longer exists."[48] The cultural and educational exchanges between China and the United States over the past decades alone highlight the fundamental difference between the historical circumstances of the Cold War and present conditions. Neither the United States nor China has a homogeneous and antagonistic ideology, even among the current leadership circles, and both countries have pluralistic societies.

In contrast to the Soviet Union, which disproportionately invested its resources in military development, China has primarily concentrated on becoming economically competitive in the world. Many countries in East and Southeast Asia have reservations about the PRC's mercantilist techniques and Chinese national chauvinism, but it is still in their best interest to engage with China, at least economically. They often benefit from geoeconomic landscape changes that favor the region as a whole. Over the past three decades, the center of the world economy has begun to move eastward, gradually shifting from Europe and North America to Asia. In 1980, Asia's GDP accounted for 20 percent of the world's total, and in 2019 it reached 36 percent. It is estimated that by 2030, Asia's GDP will account for 40 percent of the world economy.[49]

Economic decoupling with China would likely require a U.S.-led reorganization of the entire East Asian industrial supply chain. The cost for this undertaking would be enormous.[50] Based on a survey carried out by the American Chamber of Commerce in China at the end of 2019, only 9 percent of American businesses planned to relocate manufacturing or sourcing outside China.[51] Similarly, a survey conducted by the European Union Chamber of Commerce in China in February 2020 shows only 11 percent of respondents are considering shifting current or planned investments from China to other markets, which is lower than a year ago.[52]

Just as the United States cannot dictate what its allies do to navigate U.S. competition with China, politics alone cannot determine the behavior of the market economy. As of early 2020, an estimated 70,000 American companies were still doing business in China.[53] Like their business competitors elsewhere, it would not make business sense for these profit-driven American firms or multinational corporations to lose the China market. According to McKinsey's *China Consumer Report 2020* released in December 2019, by 2030 China's consumer market will likely be valued around US$6 trillion, which is equivalent to the total consumption of the United States and western Europe combined, or about twice that of India and all ASEAN countries (Association of Southeast Asian Nations) combined.[54] China's trade exports accounted for 19 percent of the country's GDP in 2007 and amounted to only 5 percent by 2020.[55] China's manufacturing sectors are more comprehensive than those of many other countries, so their supply chain adjustment costs are relatively small compared to those of other countries.

Any workable grand strategy must be backed by financial and economic capacity. Decouplers have yet to publicly release a plan for funding a major war with China. Even before COVID-19, the United States confronted serious budget deficits. According to Yale University economist Stephen Roach, America's public debt-to-GDP ratio, which reached 79 percent in 2019, will almost certainly exceed the 106 percent record set at the end of World War II.[56] Roach believes that the "federal budget deficit is likely to soar to a peacetime record of 18 percent of gross domestic product in 2020."[57] Preparation for a new Cold War will undoubtedly be costly. While the military-industrial complex may be a beneficiary, the American public will bear the burden, just as it did for wars in Afghanistan and Iraq.

Most importantly, given that China's challenge to the United States differs profoundly from that of the Soviet Union, it would be a mistake for American policymakers to assume that the outcome of a new Cold War would be the same. As the prime minister of Singapore Lee Hsien Loong recently wrote in *Foreign Affairs Magazine*, "[Any] confrontation between these two great powers is unlikely to end as the Cold War did, in one country's peaceful collapse."[58] The technological revolution and its implications for asymmetrical warfare has further complicated military competition, making the prevention of hot wars even more difficult.

Loss of U.S. Leverage in Its Pursuit of CCP Regime Change

In official speeches and legislation prior to the 2020 U.S. election, decouplers frequently portrayed the CCP regime as an evil monster. They have drawn a line between the CCP and China and implicitly appeal to the Chinese people to overthrow CCP rule. From decouplers' perspective, this seems logical. Given the U.S.-China conflict is primarily due to communist ideology and Xi Jinping's ambition for China to replace the United States and dominate the world, then the only long-term solution for the United States is to overthrow the CCP regime. When rivals see the nature of the other side as an existential threat in itself, "a struggle to the death becomes the only alternative."[59]

The reach of CCP power within both the Chinese state and society has risen to new levels in recent years, as private companies, foreign firms, and joint ventures have been ordered to establish party branches. Observers both in China and abroad have criticized these developments. Critics of the Chinese party-state system can certainly challenge its authoritarian nature and political legitimacy, given that there are no open and competitive elections in the country. But it is one thing to condemn the omnipresence of the CCP in the country; it is quite another thing to separate, both conceptually and practically, this party-state political structure. The way in which decouplers divide the CCP and China is highly problematic. Richard Haass has insightfully pointed out that "Secretary Pompeo doesn't speak of China but of the Chinese Communist Party as if there were a China apart from the party. This is meant to antagonize and make diplomacy impossible."[60] If the U.S. continues to employ an all-encompassing decoupling approach and uses ideological rhetoric to promote regime change, they will likely negate any influence they could exert on broad constituencies in the PRC.

Several factors can explain this ill-grounded theory underlying decoupling. First, some American politicians have adopted an increasingly shrill tone of cultural supremacy and hypocrisy in blaming China and the Chinese people for the spread of COVID-19 in the United States. They have mobilized other—particularly Western—countries to demand indemnity payments. These rhetoric and actions have spurred strong nationalist sentiments in China. The Chinese media have ceaselessly referenced China's historical humiliation and victimization by "the boxer's Indemnity" and "the new Eight-Power Allied Forces that intend to encircle and suppress China."[61] Such an approach has put pro-U.S., liberal Chinese scholars in the PRC in a terrible situation, and it has also sparked anger toward the United States among the Chinese public.[62] As Daniel Russel has argued, under these circumstances, the practice of separating the CCP from the Chinese people is "primitive and ineffective," causing the undesired effect of helping the hard-liners in the CCP leadership consolidate power.[63]

Second, the decouplers' plan for regime change is based on the assumption that there has been widespread dissatisfaction among the Chinese people with the CCP leadership. Without a doubt, there has been dissatisfaction with, criticism of, and reprehension of CCP authorities within Chinese society. But as this book shows, the state-society relations in present-day China—including the views of the middle class of the CCP—are not predetermined and are subject to changing circumstances, both domestically and internationally. Several recent opinion surveys in China conducted by American scholars all show a high degree of public satisfaction with the Chinese government. A longitudinal survey conducted by scholars at the Harvard Kennedy School found that Chinese citizen satisfaction with government (township, county, provincial, and central) has increased virtually across the board.[64] As a result of policy measures in the areas of economic well-being, anticorruption, poverty reduction, environmental protection, and public health, Chinese citizens rate the government as more capable and effective than ever before. This is particularly evident in public opinion of the central government, where satisfaction has been consistently high: 86 percent in 2003, 81 percent in 2005, 92 percent in 2007, 96 percent in 2009, 92 percent in 2011, and 93 percent in 2015.[65] Another recent opinion survey conducted by scholars of the University of California at San Diego reveals similar findings.[66] A comprehensive and cross-country comparative report written in early 2020 by Andrew Nathan, a renowned China expert, also echoed this observation.[67]

Third, the much-discussed proposal by the Trump administration to ban travel by CCP members and their families has generated much criticism both inside and outside China.[68] This proposed ban, if adopted, would affect 92 million CCP members and over 200 million of their family members. Given the size of China's population, the enforcement of such a ban would be virtually impossible, as there is no way to determine the party membership or political background of Chinese visitors and their families. Ironically, although the decouplers' push for regime change is supposed to win broader public support in China, this proposed move appears to designate 300 million Chinese people as enemies. It may reveal the true intention of some anti-China hawks in Washington: to push back on what they perceive as a "whole-of-society" threat from China. Such a policy would inevitably result in the ethnic profiling of all Chinese citizens as well as some Chinese Americans. One may go so far as to say that this would have potential to become the twenty-first-century version of the notorious Chinese Exclusion Act of 1882.

Additionally, for the first time in U.S. history, the Department of Justice has established an initiative focusing on a particular country (and ethnic group) titled the China Initiative. At the same time, the number of China-related investigations by the FBI has risen from 1,000 in February 2020 to 2,000 in June, and to 2,500 in July, constituting 50 percent of the total cases currently handled by the FBI. Some of the China-related cases are characterized by an odd new term, "academic espionage."[69] Maggie Lewis, a law professor at Seton Hall University, believes that this practice will entail a much higher chance for Chinese Americans to be investigated. In her view, the China Initiative does not align with American values, nor does it reflect American academic norms.[70]

In 2018, the National Institutes of Health and the FBI jointly launched an investigation into the relationship between researchers in the biomedical field and China. A total of 399 people were included on the suspect list, with 251 people being identified as having problems and 72 people still under review. Most of those identified as suspects were ethnically Chinese.[71] Understandably, there have been growing concerns about the emergence of a new form of McCarthyism. The alleged racial profiling in some of these cases has reminded people of what happened to the Japanese during World War II and to Soviet scientists during the Cold War.

While national security and intellectual property rights should be vigorously protected in the United States, the racial profiling of PRC-born scientists or Chinese American researchers will hurt U.S. interests. A 2020 study by the Paulson Institute shows that in the artificial intelligence field, the United States is home to 60 percent of the world's top researchers. This is six times greater than the 10.6 percent of top researchers found in China, which is ranked second. But among the 60 percent of those who work in the United States, native-born American researchers account for 31 percent, whereas PRC-born researchers account for 27 percent.[72] As reporters for the *New York Times* have observed, "If the U.S. no longer welcomed these top researchers, Beijing would welcome them back with open arms."[73]

U.S. decoupling with China likely has little chance of preventing China from becoming a technological superpower. While U.S. supremacy in technological innovation will not be easily surpassed, China has developed its own advantages in the areas of R&D investment, human resources, and innovation, among others. China's share of the world's total spending in R&D grew from 3.4 percent in 2000 to 17.7 percent in 2018.[74] By comparison, R&D investment in the United States accounted for 18.6 percent of global expenditures in 2018. The average annual growth rate of China's R&D expenditures (PPP [purchasing power parity], 2011 international dollar) from 2000 to 2018 was 14.8 percent, which was much faster than the growth rate of the United States (2.3 percent). As discussed in early chapters of this book, about one-fourth of the world's STEM (science, technology, engineering, and math) workers are already in China.

WARNINGS AND SUGGESTIONS FOR BOTH WASHINGTON AND BEIJING

If all-encompassing decoupling with China engenders more harm and risks for the United States, how should the United States handle unbounded competition with China? What are the other possible paths by which the United States can transform the current adversarial relationship and advance its security and prosperity? To what strategic objectives—and policy measures—can American policymakers aspire in the areas of soft power influence? The rapid deterioration of U.S.-China relations over the past few years is largely the result of the action-reaction spiral from both sides; therefore, Beijing should also seriously address these questions about how to correct its own missteps and positively improve the bilateral relationship. The following strategic and policy adjustments—five for each Washington and Beijing—are essential.

Priorities for Washington

1. **Advance American soft power through domestic renewal.** America's strength lies in its democracy, diversity, and openness. The U.S. global leadership is not only based on its military and economic might, but also on its soft power influence. President Trump, however, damaged American democracy with his repeated characterization of the U.S. media as "the enemy of the people," his disrespect for an independent judiciary, his deployment of federal forces to confront protesters, and his frequent use of racist remarks to stoke tension and animosity between ethnic groups in the United States.[75]

Effective foreign policy is supposed to begin at home with a resilient democracy, a strong economy, an inclusive society, and a healthy living environment.[76] The United States should lead by example—unless the country practices at home, it cannot preach abroad. The alleged "no bottom-line suppression on China" tactic employed by Trump's hawkish team has undermined America's image of fairness and goodwill.[77] In international competition, including with China, the United States cannot win by engaging in a competition for who behaves nastier. Rather, the United States should compete to hold higher standards in order to win hearts and minds around the world, including those of the Chinese population.

In contrast to the Trump administration's approach, Antony Blinken has said that the United States needs to be engaged in "a race to the top, not a race to the bottom" with China.[78] The Biden administration presents an opportunity for the United States to rejuvenate its values and regain the moral high ground on human rights. As a promising start, the new president has designated addressing racial inequity as one of his top four priorities. While national security should be vigorously protected, efforts to do so should neither compromise American values nor erode soft power outreach to the Chinese people. In his election victory speech, Joe Biden emphasized that the time has come for America to "lead not by the example of our power, but by the power of our example."[79]

2. **Boost the American middle class.** The shrinking of the middle class in the United States over the past few decades, as discussed earlier in the chapter, must be reversed if the United States hopes to effectively compete with China. The growing economic disparity in the United States reflects inherent structural and distributional problems between capital and society, and it also raises questions about the status of social mobility in the country. This problem cannot be blamed entirely on the Trump administration, although its handling of COVID-19 may aggravate economic disparity. Prior to the Trump presidency, the size of the middle class in the United States decreased by roughly 1 percent each year.[80]

An all-encompassing decoupling with China will delay rather than accelerate the renewal of the American middle class simply because the United States does not have much leverage to pursue such an approach in a globalized economy. Instead, America should prioritize narrowing the income gap and promoting inclusive economic growth at home, with the key objective of expanding the American middle class. On the economic front, policymakers should promote America's own manufacturing sector. At the same time, e-commerce infrastructure—including internet, online payment, and express delivery services, which originated in the United States—should be strengthened. Additionally, the United States should allocate more resources through both federal government spending and corporate investment to modernize infrastructure, promote basic research, more quickly commercialize science and technology breakthroughs, reform the public health system, and attract talented people from around the world. American city leaders may find the story of Shanghai's rejuvenation over the past three decades to be instructive.

3. Don't push the Chinese middle class to oppose the United States. Decoupling with China hurts the Chinese middle class in two critical respects. First, the U.S.-China trade war has directly undermined the economic well-being of small businesses in China. Second, the restrictions imposed by the Trump administration on Chinese students who have been studying or who plan to study in the United States, and especially the proposed travel ban or restrictions on 300 million Chinese citizens, will not inspire them to challenge the authoritarian CCP leadership. Instead, it will alienate them and push them to embrace anti-American sentiment and more intense nationalism.

The racism and McCarthyism directed by some U.S. politicians toward Chinese people, especially young PRC students in the United States, neither serve the interests of the United States nor align with American values. Unfortunately, these extreme U.S. policies have considerably undermined all the positive effects of decades-long cultural and educational exchanges. For policymakers in Washington, cultural and educational engagement with China should not be thrown out the window so easily, and instead should be further promoted, as it remains the most effective way to advance American soft power.

4. "Estimate correctly one's own strength as well as that of one's opponent." One of the problems with the decouplers' ineffective and extreme measures stems from their ill-grounded assessment of both powers. The above aphorism, which is from Sun Tzu's *The Art of War*, should be helpful to policymakers and their strategic advisers in Washington. Decouplers have tended to go to two extremes—either overestimate the capacity of the United States, and thus become too arrogant, or overlook America's strength and advantages, and thus be overly defensive and insecure. Their hysteria about the dominance or threat of the "Chinese hegemony" in economics, science and technology, and ideological and political influence in the world, as discussed earlier in the chapter, reflects a lack of self-confidence on the part of decouplers. They have overlooked the fact that the United States is still the largest economy in the world, backed by the "strongest military, most expansive alliance system, and most potent soft power."[81]

Of course, China may catch up in some or even all these areas in the coming decades. This book also shows that China has benefited greatly from economic globalization along with cultural and educational exchanges, as Chinese people have primarily learned from the West in the reform era. But in contrast, one hardly hears of any political leader or major media outlet in the United States saying Americans should learn from the Chinese. The Trump administration's recent moves to close the PRC Consulate General in Houston, cancel the Peace Corps and Fulbright Programs in the PRC, expel Chinese journalists and foment retaliation against American reporters on the Chinese side, and restrict academic exchanges with China will significantly diminish America's access to China and jeopardize Americans' chances to better understand this complicated country. At a time when the United States urgently and imperatively needs to know more about China, decisionmakers should not cut off channels for access and learning.

5. **Shape China's choices by improving U.S. ties with allies.** The United States would be far more effective in its competition with China if it were to give more consideration to international coalition building. President Trump's "America first" policies have resonated poorly around the world, including with allies of the United States, and thus have often ended up as "America alone." During the COVID-19 pandemic, hardly any country would follow a "global leader" who has been obsessed with "America first."[82] In the case of 5G development, the United States does not have a 5G alternative to compete with that of China; thus it could not persuade many American allies to ban Huawei equipment.[83] Among those countries that have joined the U.S.-led campaign to decouple with Huawei, most do not necessarily support overall economic decoupling with China. In general, other countries, including some American allies, do not want to be forced to choose between the United States and China.

Most American allies are interested in promoting and protecting international public goods by addressing climate change, global health security, the nonproliferation of weapons of mass destruction, and human rights protection of international refugees. But unfortunately, in recent years, the Trump administration has withdrawn from the Trans-Pacific Partnership Agreement, UNESCO, the Global Migration Agreement, the United Nations Human Rights Council, the Iran Nuclear Agreement, the Intermediate-Range Nuclear Forces Treaty, the Paris Climate Agreement, and the World Health Organization. The United States should reverse this isolationist and unilateralist trend. Enhanced collaboration with American allies and the international communities to promote global public goods will not only push China to work on these areas abroad but also shape China's choices, hopefully making it harder for Chinese authorities to challenge the liberal international order.

Priorities for Beijing

1. The key task for China is to do its own job well. In an era with pervasive disrespect and mistrust in the bilateral relationship and tremendous domestic pressures shaping the foreign policy choices of both countries, China should prioritize domestic governance reform and promoting more balanced, inclusive, and environmentally friendly economic development. Despite China's remarkable achievements during the reform era, the country faces a multitude of daunting problems, including economic disparity, the potential bursting of a property bubble, the negative impact of deglobalization on the Chinese middle class, unemployment pressures, the misuse of power by officials, widely perceived moral decay, frequent occurrence of social unrest, environmental degradation, resource scarcity, food safety, and public health security issues.

The Chinese leadership seems to be keenly aware of some or all of these challenges and to understand the imperative to deal with them. President Xi Jinping recently said that "China must be clear-headed about the long-term and complex nature of both domestic and international unfavorable factors. Under such difficult situations, the most important thing for China is to do its own job well."[84] Following the initial failures at the start of the COVID-19 outbreak, China has prioritized the health and safety of the Chinese people, especially through concrete measures to protect the elderly— arguably the most vulnerable group in this pandemic. Having learned a lesson from COVID-19, the Chinese government has now increased its commitment to allocating resources to improve Chinese "soft infrastructure" (i.e., public health projects, nursing homes, low-income housing, education, etc.).

However, the Chinese leadership should realize that government accountability requires, among other things, transparency, the right of the public to access information and protect individual privacy, and media supervision, the absence of which has resulted in strong criticism both at home and abroad. As for human rights, although China has made important progress on poverty alleviation over the past few decades and protecting the elderly population during the pandemic, the CCP's treatment of the rights of minorities, especially Uyghurs and Tibetans, is simply defenseless in the eyes of the international community. Additionally, house churches have been banned in the country. As for the LGBTQ (lesbian, gay, bisexual, transgender, and queer/questioning) population, homosexuality was decriminalized in 1997 and removed from the official list of mental disorders in 2001. In 2008, the Beijing Public Security Bureau issued approval for household registration change after sex-reassignment surgery. But besides these developments, there are few other legal protections for LGBTQ people. China needs to seriously confront these issues as basic elements of domestic governance, especially since failure to address them will only further alienate the domestic constituencies and the international community.

2. Change China's excessive mercantilism. China's economic development model has often been perceived by the outside world as a "new mercantilist approach with Chinese characteristics," or "innovation-mercantilist strategies."[85] This approach relies on government subsidies and industrial policy, promotes foreign trade, maximizes exports, prioritizes technological progress and the commercialization of innovation, and seeks to gain a significant global market share in a wide array of strategically important industries. These measures have contributed to China's remarkable economic growth. As the geo-economic landscape has profoundly changed, some of these measures have created winners and losers, increasingly making China a "dominant player" in the global economy.

From the perspective of many countries, engaging with China is now seen more as a challenge than an opportunity. But China has continued to be obsessed with the same approach. As some Chinese scholars have recognized, China now promotes "free trade" in foreign countries with practices similar to those of the Western mercantilists centuries ago.[86] This also explains the prevalence of economic determinism in China's diplomacy at present. Beijing should change its excessive Chinese mercantilist approach to foreign relations. Moreover, China should not continue to seek the privileges of the developing country status that was granted by the World Trade Organization, as China is no longer a poor and weak country.

3. Don't fall into the trap of nationalism. No country is immune from nationalism, but three situational factors have made the PRC more likely fall into the trap of ultranationalistic sentiment. First, Chinese historical memory of the aforementioned imperial "Eight-Power Allied Forces" has often reinforced the mentality of victimization among the public. When China was a weak country, the employment of a mentality of victimization might have proved politically effective at home and generated sympathy abroad. But China has now become "an elephant in the canoe," and continuing to obsess over its history of victimization will only generate concern on the world stage as to whether the country will pursue "victim's revenge."[87]

Second, although Chinese leaders often claim that China is not interested in challenging the existing world order, the assertive military buildup by this rising power is not usually perceived by others as defensive in nature. Such sentiment is reasonable from the perspective of small and weak countries in the region when China has threatened to "punish" them. In the case of India (though not a weak country), since its defeat in the Sino-Indian border war in 1962, India has maintained strong nationalism by treating China as an adversary, much as China has done with Japan.[88] Unfortunately, with a few exceptions, Chinese discourse on China-India relations has hardly inspired empathy for Indians.[89]

Third, many around the world view China as an emerging superpower, but most Chinese see their country as a divided nation with a runaway Taiwan province. For the CCP leadership, the Taiwan issue involves national sovereignty, territorial integrity, and political legitimacy. Recent legislation in the U.S. Congress regarding Taiwan, high-level official visits between Washington and Taipei, and the calls of some pro-Taiwan political leaders in the United States for establishing diplomatic relations with Taiwan and stationing U.S. troops there "have all crossed the red line," in the eyes of the Chinese authorities, making the Taiwan Strait the most dangerous potential arena for military conflict. Interestingly, sober and rational voices also exist in Beijing. Qiao Liang, former People's Liberation Army major general, argues that it would be a mistake to believe only territorial sovereignty is China's core interest. In his words, "[For] the Chinese nation, there is no greater cause than realizing national rejuvenation. Everything must make way for this great cause, including the settlement of the Taiwan issue."[90] Qiao believes that time is on the side of the Mainland, and the use of force will result in 20 million hostile Taiwanese agitators. Avoiding the trap of nationalism and reducing the exacerbation of the mutually reinforced fear between China and other stakeholders should be a top priority for China.

4. **Adjust to U.S. pressure with empathy.** A lack of empathy by China is arguably most evident in Chinese understanding or misunderstanding of the United States. This chapter primarily addresses the problems arising from misjudgments and misperceptions of China by the United States. But similar problems also exist on the other side of the Pacific. Over the past few years, such a lack of empathy helps explain China's slow comprehension of many factors, including the causes of the Trump administration's prolonged trade war with China, the underlying resentment of Chinese state capitalism by U.S. corporations, displeasure of members of the American middle class as they view the advance of Chinese counterparts at their own expense, fears of the American public about the replacement of U.S. world leadership by China, dependence on Chinese industrial and supply chains, and American concerns about technological surveillance and privacy violations.

In particular, over the past few decades, China has overtaken the United States to become the world leader in automobile assembly, manufacturing, construction of railways and highways, container ports, bank assets, telecommunications, and even e-commerce. Emergent Chinese dominance in these areas is largely the result of the rapid expansion of the Chinese middle class. But noticeably, both the CCP government and the Chinese public still ascribe to the outdated view that China is unfairly treated and criticized by the United States in their economic competition.

Chinese lack of empathy for its principal competitor also reflects its underestimation of the determination of the United States to maintain its global leadership and protect its vital geopolitical and economic interests. In the wake of both the COVID-19 pandemic and the horrific death of George Floyd, Americans have been engaged in the painstaking search for solutions to some of the structural deficiencies and systemic injustices as well as the revitalization of American values in this multiethnic immigrant society. But unfortunately, with some exceptions, the Chinese media have tended to mischaracterize the Black Lives Matter movement as riots and the decisions to remove some statues representing racial segregation as the "American version of the Chinese Cultural Revolution."[91] Without an accurate understanding of the United States—and without a sense of empathy—the Chinese government will not be able to develop the constructive and cooperative relationship that it claims to seek.

5. Emphasize similarities rather than differences between China and the West. Most Chinese leaders have always rejected the notion of universal values. As for their discussion of China and the West, they have tended to emphasize differences rather than similarities. The calls of Washington hawks for regime change in the PRC will only reinvigorate the CCP leadership in resolute defense of its political system. Foreign Minister Wang Yi recently stated: "No one has the right to rebuff the development path of other countries. And no country will remold its own system to the liking of other countries."[92]

The emphasis Chinese leaders place on the coexistence of different political systems and diverse cultures as well as their pride in the long history of the country is understandable. But their ideological claim that attributes China's successes in economic development, political stability, containment of the COVID-19 pandemic, and international outreach to the "advantages of the system and culture" (*zhidu youshi, wenhua youshi*) naturally arouses suspicion and criticism among Western countries. Ironically, it can be reasonably argued, as many Chinese liberal intellectuals have done, that the PRC's reform era achievements have materialized largely as a result of concerted efforts to learn from the West to improve China's governance. Additionally, there is hardly any correlation between long history and modern achievements. As this book shows, Shanghai, the Chinese metropolis with the shortest history in the country, has in fact been the frontier city of China's reemergence on the world stage.

China and the United States have many shared values, especially following the expansion and integration into the globalized world of the Chinese middle class. The overemphasis on mutual differences has contributed to "we-they" binary thinking and enhanced mistrust and opposition. Universal values and cultural pluralism should not be seen as contradictory. The following remarks delivered by Jack Ma in his commencement speech at NYU Shanghai in May 2020 should be illuminating for policymakers in Beijing:[93]

> No people or nation are the same. They are and will continue to be different. Today's global problems are a result of our focus on too many differences. Identifying differences among us is not something to be praised. What is truly praiseworthy is to see through our differences and put faith in our common areas, to have the ability to put aside our differences and walk forward together.

THE CHINESE MIDDLE CLASS: RESHAPING THE LONG-TERM FUTURE

In his insightful essay, "China in the American Imagination," which was published at the turn of the century, distinguished sociologist Richard Madsen of the University of California at San Diego observed that American discourse about the Middle Kingdom "has long been as much about ourselves as about China."[94] Far too often, American analysts evaluate China based on their preconceived notions or the prevailing ideology of what the country is like, rather than paying much attention to the Chinese mentality, sensibility, and reality.

Over the past twenty years, the American imagination has often focused on China's emerging middle class. The long-standing thesis of the "peaceful evolution," as explained in early chapters of the book, has centered on the hope that the Chinese emerging middle class, especially the Western-educated new generation of elites in the country, would be inspired by Western democracy and thus increasingly "look like us." The other group of analysts that predicted revolutionary changes in China also placed much weight on the antiregime role of the middle class. These analysts—from Gordon Chang, who predicted the "coming collapse of China" in 2001, to Minxin Pei, who recently forecasted "China's coming upheaval" in 2020—all believe a "Chinese color revolution" will soon occur in China.[95] Minxin Pei, for example, in the wake of the outbreak of coronavirus in China, argued that "signs of social unrest, such as riots, mass protests, and strikes, will become more common. The deepest threat to the regime's stability will come from the Chinese middle class."[96]

A more influential—and potentially more damaging to American interests—U.S. policy proposition at present is to contain China's rise by treating it as a "whole-of-society threat," which has become the ideological foundation for the all-encompassing decoupling. This new disengagement approach has had a strong negative assessment of the Chinese middle class, as a majority of members have been seen by decouplers as nationalistic, anti-U.S., and pawns of the CCP to undermine American interests in the economic, educational, ideological, technological, and military domains. But, rather than being shaped by wishful thinking and ideological dogmatism, any assessments of the Chinese middle class and China's future trajectory should be well grounded in empirical facts and a solid, balanced understanding of the changing nature of state-society relations in China.

Over the past two decades, especially in recent years, Chinese public intellectuals—an influential group of opinion leaders in the country's middle class—have indeed expressed strong criticism of the United States. They have been influenced by Western political thought, liberal values, and artistic styles (in the case of avant-garde artists), especially in the early decades of reform. Yet they tend to reject ideas of cultural dominance, homogeneity, and uniformity, along with dogmatic and stagnant views pronouncing the "end of history." They have become increasingly cynical and resentful of postcolonialism and chauvinism in the West. Many Chinese scholars, including avant-garde artists, have been engaged in an intellectual effort to transcend old boundaries in search of new ways to negotiate cultural and sociopolitical changes, both at home and abroad. Shanghai has long served as the manifestation of this transcendence with its integration of civilizations. In the recent past, as in the contemporary era, it was Shanghai that introduced the world to China, and it was also Shanghai that projected China into the world. Therefore, these Chinese intellectuals demand a dialogue on equal footing with both Chinese state authority and Western cultural power.

Both the qualitative analysis and survey research in this study show that U.S.-educated Chinese elites have more favorable views of the United States. In general, there is a correlation between the country in which a returnee studied and the likelihood that a returnee has favorable views toward that same country. But this does not necessarily mean that U.S.-educated returnees are uncritical of American foreign policy, especially the Trump administration's policy toward China. A high degree of patriotism and nationalist sentiments exists among foreign-educated returnees, but these views coincide with cosmopolitan perspectives on various important issues.

In light of the drastic changes around the world in recent years, the Chinese intellectual community has also begun rethinking issues regarding domestic governance and political systems. For them, if democracy could lead to social instability, vicious infighting for power among political elites, poor coordination between national and local governments, or even the dissolution of China, there would be no incentive for the Chinese people—including its emerging middle class—to pursue it. In a fundamental way, as some Chinese scholars argue, sociopolitical stability and democracy should be a set of complementary, rather than contradictory, phenomena.[97] One can reasonably assume that opinion leaders and members of the middle class in the United States would express similar concerns and criticism under the same circumstances, which has certainly been the case during the coronavirus crisis. Open, honest, and acute criticism of the flaws of the U.S. political system and the policy mistakes by the leadership is the foundation of American democracy and the beliefs of the Founding Fathers. This ability to criticize certainly should not be limited only to Americans.

China should not be viewed monochromatically, and the Chinese middle class should also not be viewed as a homogeneous subset of Chinese society. At the heart of this study of middle-class Shanghai is the argument that neither Chinese society nor Chinese culture is monolithic. If cultural trends can be instrumental in shaping the sociopolitical trajectory of a given country, competing subcultures—for example, between the Shanghai-style culture (*haipai*) and the Beijing-style culture (*jingpai*), or between coast and inland—may reveal the availability of alternative choices rather than a single and predetermined outcome. As elaborated in the early chapters of the book, China's trend toward cultural pluralism over the past two decades has generated a renewed sense of locality, individuality, and diversity.

In particular, *haipai* has embodied ideas of openness, diversity, entrepreneurship, cosmopolitanism, innovation, and inclusiveness, and it has served to undermine and balance out some of the ultranationalist sentiments expressed in other cities like Beijing. The issues examined in this study—extensive foreign educational exchange, the growing prominence of Western-educated returnees in all walks of life in Shanghai, the development of the legal profession and legal education, the diffusion of international norms and people-to-people friendship through cultural diplomacy, and the increasing pluralism in social values—are very much in accordance with American interests.

Students of Shanghai will likely continue to debate the existence of "Shanghai exceptionalism" and dispute the extent to which the city's present can predict the country's future. There is no controversy, however, that China has emerged as a global economic powerhouse with Shanghai as an impressive exemplar of middle-class development, cultural dynamism, and international engagement. China's economic power will naturally enhance its military might. The People's Liberation Army's intensifying naval activities and other military exercises in the Asia-Pacific region, along with the CCP leadership's ambitious plans for cyber, space, artificial intelligence, biotechnology, and other R&D areas, all constitute a real challenge for the United States. While American policymakers will never allow the United States to lose its military edge, which helps deter hostile actions, they should also continue to leverage the advantages of American soft (and smart) power.

If Washington disengages from China in the areas of economic and financial stability, public health cooperation, environmental protection, energy security, and cultural and educational exchanges, then there is little the United States can do to sway China's middle class—the most dynamic force in Chinese society. The United States should not fall into the trap of adopting a strategy that attempts to isolate China but only further isolates itself.

Most importantly, in this period of uncertainty, and especially in the wake of the "pandemic of the century," the two largest middle-class countries in the world need to find a way to reshape their long-term engagement. The United States and China should strive to have a vision for their shared future, confidence in their collective strengths, and humility and humanity in their beliefs.

NOTES

PROLOGUE

1. The HSBC building was the second-largest bank building in the world at that time. Tess Johnston and Deke Erh, *A Last Look Western Architecture in Old Shanghai* (Hong Kong: Old China Hand Press, 1993), 53.

2. Cited in Lu Daqian, Han Juntian, Fan Yunxing, and Sun Lei, *Shanghai: Guoji lüyou chengshi* [Shanghai: A world-famous tourist city in China] (Beijing: Zhongguo luyou chubanshe, 2003), 52. For a detailed discussion of the design and construction of the building, see Lou Chenghao and Xue Shunsheng, *Laoshanghai jingdian jianzhu* [Old Shanghai: Classic architecture] (Shanghai: Tongji daxue chubanshe, 2000), 20–23.

3. In 1955, HSBC gave the building to the Shanghai municipal government as compensation for the taxes it had owed the city for years. On July 1, 1995, the Shanghai government and Party committee moved to their new office building in People's Square. During the first few years of the Cultural Revolution, the building was occupied by the so-called working class rebels and their revolutionary committee.

4. *Shijie ribao* [World Journal], March 30, 2020, A5.

5. "Education: From Disruption to Recovery," United Nations Educational, Scientific, and Cultural Organization (UNESCO) (website), https://en.unesco.org/covid19/education response.

6. Henry A. Kissinger, "The Coronavirus Pandemic Will Forever Alter the World Order," *Wall Street Journal*, April 3, 2020.

7. Pi Daojian and Lu Hong, *Yishu xin shijie—26 wei zhuming pipingjia tan Zhongguo dangdai meishu de zoushi* [New horizon of art: Comments by twenty-six critics on trends in contemporary Chinese art] (Changsha: Hunan meishu chubanshe, 2003), 89.

8. For a recent critique of the destructive effects of economic and cultural globalization in East Asian cities, including Shanghai, see Tsung-Yi Michelle Huang, *Walking Between Slums and Skyscrapers: Illusions of Open Space in Hong Kong, Tokyo, and Shanghai* (Hong Kong: Hong Kong University Press, 2004).

9. Hou Hanru, "A Naked City: Curatorial Notes around the 2000 Shanghai Biennale," *Art Asia Pacific*, no. 31 (2001), 62.

10. Tu Wei-ming, "Cultural China: The Periphery as the Center," *Daedalus* 120, no. 2 (1991), 25.

11. This echoes a similar critique of the historical determinism of globalization made by many social scientists. Manfred B. Steger, *Globalism: The New Market Ideology* (Lanham, MD: Rowman & Littlefield, 2002), 54. Cited in Chalmers Johnson, *The Sorrows of Empire: Militarism, Secrecy, and the End of the Republic* (New York: Henry Holt and Company, Metropolitan Books, 2004), 260.

12. For the statistics from the Chinese government and foreign multinational corporations, see Niu Qisi, "Zhongguo zhongdeng shouru qunti" [Middle-income group in China], *Zhongguo jingji zhoukan* [China Economic Weekly], April 17, 2018, http://industry.people.com.cn/n1/2018/0417/c413883-29930573.html.

13. Zhongguo renming yinhang diaocha tongji si chengzhen jumin jiating zichan fu-zhai diaocha ketizu [Research Group of Urban Residents' Assets and Liabilities Survey, the Statistics Department of the People's Bank of China], "Chengzhen jumin jiating zichan fu-zhai diaocha" [Urban Household Assets and Liabilities Survey], *Zhongguo jinrong* [China Finance], no. 9 (2020).

14. Chas W. Freeman Jr. "After the Trade War, a Real War with China?" Remarks to the St. Petersburg Conference on World Affairs, St. Petersburg, Florida, February 12, 2019, https://chasfreeman.net/after-the-trade-war-a-real-war-with-china/.

15. Mark Warner, remarks at a public event, "Global China: Assessing China's Growing Role in the World," Brookings Institution, May 9, 2019, www.brookings.edu/events/global-china-assessing-chinas-growing-role-in-the-world/.

16. Fareed Zakaria, "The New China Scare: Why America Shouldn't Panic about Its Latest Challenger," *Foreign Affairs* 99, no. 1 (January–February 2020), 52–69.

CHAPTER 1

1. Many recent public opinion surveys around the world indicate that the U.S. has been increasingly losing its soft power influence in recent years. "U.S. Image Suffers as Publics around World Question Trump's Leadership," Pew Research Center, June 26, 2017, www.pewglobal.org/2017/06/26/u-s-image-suffers-as-publics-around-world-question-trumps-leadership/.

2. Michal Kranz, "The Director of the FBI Says the Whole of Chinese Society Is a Threat to the US—and That Americans Must Step Up to Defend Themselves." *Business Insider*, February 13, 2018, www.businessinsider.com/china-threat-to-america-fbi-director-warns-2018-2.

3. Milton Friedman, *Capitalism and Freedom* (Chicago: University of Chicago Press, 1962); and Seymour Martin Lipset, *Political Man, Where, How and Why Democracy Works in the Modern World* (New York: Doubleday, 1960).

4. Merrit Kennedy, "Costco Opens in Shanghai, Shuts Early Owing to Massive Crowds," NPR, August 28, 2019, www.npr.org/2019/08/28/755038200/costco-opens-in-shanghai-shuts-early-owing-to-massive-crowds.

5. Quoted in *Zhongguo Qingnian Bao* (China Youth Daily), February 11, 2010. Also see Qian Xi, "Zhongchan jieceng de bili bushi you zhuanjia suan chulai de" [The proportion of the middle class is not calculated by experts], *Huaxia jingwei wang* (China Latitude and Longitude Net), February 12, 2010, www.viewcn.com/xw/mttt/2010/02/1756965.html.

6. Jinyuan Investment Group, *2018 China New Middle Class Report*, Shanghai, 2018, http://res.hurun.net/Upload/file/20181123/201811231444279775571.pdf.

7. Ibid.

8. Raksha Arora, "Homeownership Soars in China: Ninety-three Percent Own Their

Homes." Gallup, March 1, 2005, https://news.gallup.com/poll/15082/homeownership -soars-china.aspx.

9. Zhongguo renming yinhang diaocha tongji si chengzhen jumin jiating zichan fuzhai diaocha ketizu [Research Group of Urban Residents' Assets and Liabilities Survey, the Statistics Department of the People's Bank of China], "Chengzhen jumin jiating zichan fuzhai diaocha" [Urban Household Assets and Liabilities Survey], *Zhongguo jinrong* [China Finance], no. 9 (2020).

10. Lu Zhe, "Zai hu guiguo liuxue renyuan zong liang da 7.5 wan ren yue zhan quanguo de ¼" [The total number of returned overseas students in Shanghai reached 75,000, accounting for about a quarter of the country], *Xinmin Wanbao* (Xinmin Evening News), January 28, 2009, www.chinanews.com/edu/cglx/news/2009/01-28/1542594.shtml.

11. Ibid.

12. *Dongfang Zaobao* [Oriental Morning News], February 26, 2009.

13. Yang Dongping, *Chengshi jifeng: Beijing he Shanghai de wenhua jingshen* [City monsoon: The cultural spirit of Beijing and Shanghai], (Beijing: Dongfang Press, 1994).

14. For more discussion of Jin Xing and her show, see Alice Yan, "How Transgender Dancer Jin Xing Conquered Chinese TV," *South China Morning Post*, April 15, 2017, www .scmp.com/news/china/society/article/2087720/how-transgender-dancer-jin-xing-con quered-chinese-tv; Matt Sheehan, "Meet the Badass Transgender Talk Show Host Who Wants to Be China's Most Influential Woman," *Huffington Post*, December 6, 2017, www. huffpost.com/entry/jin-xing-transgender-china_n_7034270; and Seth Faison, *South of the Clouds: Exploring the Hidden Realms of China* (New York: St. Martin's Press, 2004), chapter 14, 199–216.

15. Quoted from Alan Balfour and Zheng Shiling, *World Cities: Shanghai.* (West Sussex, England: Wiley-Academy, 2002), 1.

16. Wen-Hsin Yeh, eds. *In the Shadow of the Rising Sun: Shanghai under Japanese Occupation* (Cambridge: Cambridge University Press, 2004).

17. Stella Dong, *Shanghai: The Rise and Fall of a Decadent City, 1842–1949* (New York: Perennial, 2001), 22.

18. Nicholas R. Clifford, *Spoilt Children of Empire: Westerners in Shanghai and the Chinese Revolution of the 1920s* (Hanover: Middlebury College Press, 1991), 283.

19. Mayfair Mei-hui Yang, "Mass Media and Transnational Subjectivity in Shanghai: Notes on (Re)cosmopolitanism in a Chinese metropolis," in Aihwa Ong and Donald M. Nonini, eds., *Ungrounded Empires: The Cultural Politics of Modern Chinese Transnationalism* (London: Routledge, 1997), 289.

20. Clifford, *Spoilt Children of Empire*, xi.

21. Harriet Sergeant, *Shanghai: Collision Point of Cultures, 1918–1939* (New York: Crown, 1990), 14.

22. Marie-Claire Bergére, " 'The Other China': Shanghai from 1919 to 1949," in Christopher Howe, ed., *Shanghai, Revolution and Development in an Asian Metropolis* (Cambridge: Cambridge University Press, 1981); Linda C. Johnson, *Shanghai: From Market Town to Treaty Port, 1074–1858* (Stanford, CA: Stanford University Press, 1995), 11.

23. Bergére, " 'The Other China,' " 2–3.

24. Carrie Waara, "Invention, Industry, Art: The Commercialization of Culture in Republican Art Magazines," in Sherman Cochran, ed. *Inventing Nanjing Road: Commercial Culture in Shanghai, 1900–1945* (Ithaca, NY: Cornell University Press, 1999), 87.

25. Shanghai zhengda yanjiusuo, *Xin Shanghairen* [New Shanghainese] (Beijing: Dongfang chubanshe, 2002), 11.

26. Yan Yunxiang, "Managed Globalization: State Power and Cultural Transition in China," in Samuel P. Huntington, ed. *Many Globalizations: Cultural Diversity in the Contemporary World.* (New York: Oxford University Press, 2002), 34.

27. Grace C. L. Mak and Leslie N. K. Lo. "Education," in Yeung Yue-man and Sung Yun-

wing, eds. *Shanghai: Transformation and Modernization under China's Open Door Policy* (Hong Kong: Chinese University of Hong Kong Press, 1996), 378.

28. Rhoads Murphey, *Shanghai, Key to Modern China* (Cambridge, MA: Harvard University Press, 1953).

29. Betty Peh-T'I Wei, *Shanghai: Crucible of Modern China* (New York: Oxford: Oxford University Press, 1987), 9.

30. Zhou Wu, "Shanghai xingqi dui xiandai Zhongguo yu shijie de yiyi" [The significance of the rise of Shanghai to modern China and the world], *Pengpai News*, February 10, 2018, www.thepaper.cn/newsDetail_forward_1988313.

31. Xiong Yuezhi and Zhou Wu, *Haina baichuan: Shanghai chengshi jingshen yanjiu* [The sea that embraces thousands of rivers: Study of the Shanghai spirit] (Shanghai: Shanghai renmin chubanshe, 2003), 22.

32. Li Lunxin and Ding Ximan, *Shanghai laowai* [Successful foreigners in Shanghai] (Shanghai: Wenhui chubanshe, 2003), 40.

33. Peter T. Y. Cheung, "The Political Context of Shanghai's Economic Development" in Yeung, Yue-man and Yun-wing Sung, eds. *Shanghai: Transformation and Modernization under China's Open Door Policy* (Hong Kong: Chinese University of Hong Kong, 1996), 56.

34. Quoted from Wei, *Shanghai*, 122.

35. Lu Hanchao, *Beyond the Neon Lights: Everyday Shanghai in the Early Twentieth Century* (Berkeley: University of California Press, 1999), 17–18.

36. Ma Haoge, "Xi Jinping zhuchi zhengzhiju huiyi shenyi changsanjiao yitihua fazhan guihua gangyao" [Xi Jinping chaired the Politburo meeting to deliberate the outline of the Yangtze River Delta integrated development plan]. *Xinjingbao wang* [New Beijing News Net], May 13, 2019, www.bjnews.com.cn/news/2019/05/13/578453.html.

37. Dominic Barton, Yougang Chen, and Amy Jin, "Mapping China's Middle Class," *McKinsey Quarterly*, June 2013, www.mckinsey.com/industries/retail/our-insights/mapping-chinas-middle-class.

38. Ibid.

39. Robert Hormats made these remarks at the roundtable discussion, "The Long-Term Future of U.S.-Chinese Relations: Economic, Political, and Historical Aspects," Kissinger Institute on China and the United States, Woodrow Wilson International Center for Scholars, August 2, 2010.

40. For the summary of the findings of Zhang's survey study, see August 2, 2010, www.c-spanvideo.org/program/294618-1.

41. Shanghai bainian wenhuashi bianzuan weiyuanhui. *Shanghai bainian wenhuashi* [Shanghai cultural history of the twentieth century], vol. 3 (Shanghai: Shanghai kexue jishu wenxian chubanshe, 2002), 1828. For the notion of "post-modern" values and an excellent discussion of diversified cultural values in Latin America, see Ronald F. Inglehart and M. Carballo, "Does Latin America exist? A Global Analysis of Cross-Cultural Differences," *Perfiles Latinoamericanos* 16, no. 31 (2008): 13–38.

42. Bao Zonghao, *Quanqiuhua yu dangdai shehui* [Globalization and contemporary society] (Shanghai: Shanghai sanlian shudian, 2002), 179.

43. The author is grateful to Lynn White, professor emeritus at Princeton University, both for pointing me to Clifford Geertz's groundbreaking work on cultural diversity and for offering intellectual stimulation on this discussion. Clifford Geertz, "Thick Toward an Interpretive Theory of Culture," in Clifford Geertz, ed., *The Interpretation of Culture: Selected Essays by Clifford Geertz* (London: Basic Books, 1973), 3–30.

44. Manfred B. Steger and Paul James, "Ideologies of Globalism," in Paul James and Manfred B. Steger, eds, *Globalization and Culture: Vol. 4, Ideologies of Globalism* (London: Sage, 2010); Jonathan Xavier Inda and Renato Rosaldo, "Introduction: A World in Motion," in Jonathan Xavier Inda and Renato Rosaldo, eds, *The Anthropology of Globalization* (Hoboken, NJ: Wiley-Blackwell, 2002), 1–34.

CHAPTER 2

1. David J. Lynch, "China Has a Big Weapon That It Hasn't Used in the Trade War Yet: Tourists," *Washington Post*, October 31, 2018, www.latimes.com/business/la-fi-china-tourists-20181031-story.html.

2. Xia Lin and Zhang Yichi, "Meiguo qianzheng zhengce zao goubing" [U.S. Visa Policy Criticized], Xinhua News Agency, January 2, 2020, www.xinhuanet.com/world/2020-01/02/c_1125412971.htm.

3. Demetri Sevastopulo and Tom Mitchell, "US Considered Ban on Student Visas for Chinese Nationals." *Financial Times*, October 2, 2018, www.ft.com/content/fc413158-c5f1-11e8-82bf-ab93d0a9b321.

4. Peter Hessler, "The Peace Corps Breaks Ties with China." *New Yorker*, March 16, 2020, www.newyorker.com/magazine/2020/03/16/the-peace-corps-breaks-ties-with-china.

5. Elizabeth Redden, "Trump Targets Fulbright in China, Hong Kong." *Inside Higher Ed*, July 16, 2020, www.insidehighered.com/news/2020/07/16/trump-targets-fulbright-china-hong-kong.

6. The White House, "Proclamation on the Suspension of Entry as Nonimmigrants of Certain Students and Researchers from the People's Republic of China," May 29, 2020, www.whitehouse.gov/presidential-actions/proclamation-suspension-entry-nonimmigrants-certain-students-researchers-peoples-republic-china/.

7. Paul Mozur and Edward Wong, "U.S. Weighs Sweeping Travel Ban on Chinese Communist Party Members," *New York Times*, July 16, 2020, www.nytimes.com/2020/07/15/us/politics/china-travel-ban.html.

8. Chas W. Freeman, Jr. "On Hostile Coexistence with China." Remarks to the Freeman Spogli Institute for International Studies China Program, Stanford University, May 3, 2019, https://chasfreeman.net/on-hostile-coexistence-with-china/.

9. Mary Brown Bullock, "American Exchanges with China, Revisited," in Joyce K. Kallgren and Denis Fred Simon, eds., *Educational Exchanges: Essays on the Sino-American Experience* (Berkeley, CA: Institute of East Asian Studies, 1987), 26.

10. The democratic peace theory posits that liberal democracies are hesitant to engage in war with other identified democracies because of governmental accountability, the role of diplomatic institutions, middle-class interests, and peer identity. Hostile ideologies usually do not exist between two liberal democracies. See Michael Doyle, "Kant, Liberal Legacies, and Foreign Affairs," *Philosophy and Public Affairs* 12, no. 4 (Summer 1983).

11. Philip Coombs, *The Fourth Dimension of Foreign Policy: Educational and Cultural Affairs* (New York: Harper and Row, 1964), 6–7, 17.

12. Ibid., 17.

13. Dwight D. Eisenhower, "Remarks at Ceremony Marking the Tenth Anniversary of the Smith-Mundt Act," January 27, 1958, the American Presidency Project website, www.presidency.ucsb.edu/documents/remarks-ceremony-marking-the-tenth-anniversary-the-smith-mundt-act, accessed on October 31, 2020.

14. Bu Liping, *Making the World Like US: Education, Cultural Expansion, and the American Century* (Westport, CT: Praeger, 2003), 7.

15. Zhang Hongjie, *Jituo de yidai—Qinghuaren he Beidaren liumei koushu gushi* [A Generation of GRE and TOEFL: Oral Accounts of the American-Educated at Qinghua and Beijing Universities]. (Shenyang: Chunfeng wenyi chubanshe, 1999), 3.

16. Jonathan D. Spence, *To Change China: Western Advisers in China, 1620–1960* (Boston: Little, Brown, 1969), 292.

17. Bu, *Making the World Like US*, 86.

18. Bernard Gwertzman, "U.S. and China Sign Agreements; Carter Sees an 'Irreversible' Trend." *New York Times*, February 1, 1979, A16; see also Administration of Jimmy Carter, *Presidential Documents*, Washington, DC, February 2, 1979, 201.

19. Gwertzman, "U.S. and China Sign Agreements," A16.

20. Ministry of Education of the People's Republic of China website, "2018 niandu woguo chuguo liuxue renyuan qingkuang tongji" [Statistics on Chinese students studying abroad in 2018], March 27, 2019, www.moe.gov.cn/jyb_xwfb/gzdt_gzdt/s5987/201903/t20190327_375704.html; and "Zhongguo qunian chuguo liuxue renshu shou po 60 wan" [The number of Chinese students studying abroad last year exceeded 600,000], *Renmin ribao* (overseas edition), April 1, 2018, www.gov.cn/xinwen/2018-04/01/content_5278951.htm.

21. Ministry of Education of the People's Republic of China website, "2019 niandu woguo chuguo liuxue renyuan qingkuang tongji," www.moe.gov.cn/jyb_xwfb/gzdt_gzdt/s5987/202012/t20201214_505447.html

22. "Zhongguo fu mei liuxuesheng renshu diaocha baogao" [Survey Report on the Number of Chinese Students Studying in the United States], ForwardPathway website, July 28, 2019, www.forwardpathway.com/16600. For the original source, see Open Doors website, https://opendoorsdata.org/data/international-students/leading-places-of-origin/, accessed on November 2, 2020. For the previous year, see U.S.-China Press, December 28, 2018, www.uschinapress.com/2018/1228/1152456.shtml.

23. Ministry of Education, "2018 nian laihua liuxue tongji" [Statistics on foreign students studying in China in 2018], PRC Ministry of Education website, April 12, 2019, www.moe.gov.cn/jyb_xwfb/gzdt_gzdt/s5987/201904/t20190412_377692.html.

24. U.S.-China Press, December 28, 2018, www.uschinapress.com/2018/1228/1152456.shtml.

25. A total of 4,323,200 students completed their degrees or programs. Ministry of Education of the People's Republic of China website, "2018 niandu woguo chuguo liuxue renyuan qingkuang tongji."

26. "Zhongguo qunian chuguo liuxue renshu shou po 60 wan."

27. In particular, this was the view shared by John D. Rockefeller, Jr., and his associates, quoted in Bu, *Making the World Like Us*, 85.

28. See Cheng Li, with Zachary Balin and Ryan McElveen, *Xi Jinping's Protégés: Rising Elite Groups in the Chinese Leadership* (Washington, DC: Brookings Institution, forthcoming).

29. Based on Vice President for International Affairs of Nanjing University Wang Zhenlin's remarks at the 2019 Duke International Forum, "A New Age of Sino-US Higher Education Cooperation," held in Kunshan, China, December 16–18, 2019.

30. For the remarks of the vice chairman of the Mainland Affairs Commission in the Republic of China in Taiwan, see Lin Zhongbing, February 19, 2004, news.bbc.com.uk.

31. Cheng Li, ed., *China's Emerging Middle Class: Beyond Economic Transformation* (Washington, DC: Brookings Institution, 2010).

32. David Zweig, Chen Changgui, and Stanley Rosen, *China's Brain Drain to the United States: Views of Overseas Chinese Students and Scholars in the 1990s* (Berkeley, CA: Institute of East Asian Studies, University of California Press, 1995), 7.

33. Wang Fengxian, "Meeting Points of Transcultural Exchange: A Chinese View," in Ruth Hayhoe and Julian Pan, eds., *Knowledge across Cultures: A Contribution to Dialogue among Civilizations* (Hong Kong: Comparative Education Research Centre, University of Hong Kong, 2001), 299.

34. The rankings between 1979 and 1989 are from Zhong Wenhui, "Chinese Scholars and the World Community," in Michael Agelasto and Bob Adamson, eds., *Higher Education in Post-Mao China* (Hong Kong: Hong Kong University Press, 1998), 61; the ranking in 2003 is from the remarks of PRC Minister of Science and Technology Xu Guanhua, February 23, 2004, xinhuanet.com; and the ranking in 2017 is from Science Net, October 11, 2017, http://news.sciencenet.cn/htmlnews/2017/10/392690.shtm.

35. Yu Wingyin, "China's Drive to Attract the Return of Its Expatriate Talents," *EAI Background Brief*, no. 76 (November 27, 2000), ii.

36. Song Xinning, "Building International Relations Theory with Chinese Characteristics," *Journal of Contemporary China* 10, no. 26 (February 2001): 62.

37. Bob Woodward, *Bush at War* (New York: Simon & Schuster, 2002); and Richard A. Clarke, *Against All Enemies: Inside America's War on Terror* (New York: Free Press, 2004).

38. Dulles made three speeches in 1958 and 1959 elaborating on his idea to promote peaceful evolution within the Communist world.

39. Bullock, "American Exchanges with China, Revisited," 26.

40. In his memoir, Bo Yibo, a Communist veteran leader and former member of the Politburo, provides a detailed discussion of Mao's "perception of and reaction to John Foster Dulles's policy toward China." Bo Yibo, *Ruogan zhongda juece yu shijian de huigu* [Recollections of certain major decisions and events], two volumes (Beijing: Zhonggong zhongyang dangxiao chubanshe, 1991, 1993). For the English translation and an excellent review of the memoir's excerpt on Mao's concern over the peaceful evolution, see Qiang Zhai, "Mao Zedong and Dulles's "Peaceful Evolution" Strategy: Revelations from Bo Yibo's Memoirs," October 4, 2004, www.gwu.edu/~nsarchiv/CWIHP/BULLETINS/b6-7a19.htm.

41. Deng's words are quoted from Gang Ding, "Nationalization and Internationalization: Two Turning Points in China's Education in the Twentieth Century," in Glen Peterson, Ruth Hayhoe, and Lu Yongling, eds. *Education, Culture, and Identity in Twentieth-Century China* (Ann Arbor: University of Michigan Press, 2001), 174.

42. Du Ruiqing, *Chinese Higher Education* (New York: St. Martin's Press, 1992), 108.

43. The term first appeared in the mid-1980s but became very popular in the early 1990s. For an insightful discussion of its origin and significance, see Li Tuo, Bao Yaming, Wang Hongtu, and Zhu Shengjian, *Shanghai jiuba—Kongjian, xiaofei yu xiangxiang* [Bars in Shanghai: Space, consumption and imagination] (Nanjing: Jiangsu renmin chubanshe, 2001), 149.

44. Li, Bao, Wang, and Zhu, *Shanghai jiuba*, 149.

45. Yin Jizuo, *Jingji quanqiuhua yu Shanghai wenhua fazhan—2001 nian Shanghai wenhua fazhan lanpishu* [Economic globalization and Shanghai cultural development: A bluebook of social development in Shanghai] (Shanghai: Shanghai shehui kexueyuan chubanshe, 2001), 108, 139.

46. For the complete list of these meetings and their main content, see http://news. xinhuanet.com/zhengfu/2003-08/14/content_1026586.htm.

47. www.xinhuanet.com, July 1, 2004.

48. Tania Branigan, "Wen Jiabao Talks of Democracy and Freedom in CNN Interview," *Guardian*, October 4, 2010.

49. For the Chinese idea of "China's peaceful rise," see Zheng Bijian, *China's Peaceful Rise*. (Washington, DC: Brookings Institution, 2005).

50. George Soros, "Xi Jinping Is the Most Dangerous Enemy," *Financial Review*, January 28, 2019.

51. Curt Milles, "Steve Bannon Declares War on China," *American Conservative*, April 12, 2019.

52. National Security Strategy of the United States of America, December 2017, www. whitehouse.gov/wp-content/uploads/2017/12/NSS-Final-12-18-2017-0905.pdf.

53. Thorsten Benner, Jan Gaspers, Mareike Ohlberg, Lucrezia Poggetti, and Kristin Shi-Kupfer, "Authoritarian Advance: Responding to China's Growing Political Influence in Europe," Global Public Policy Institute, February 5, 2018, www.gppi.net/2018/02/05/ authoritarian-advance-responding-to-chinas-growing-political-influence-in-europe.

54. Fred Lucas, "John Bolton: US Must Curb Chinese, Russian Influence in Africa," *Daily Signal*, December 13, 2018.

55. Tom Phillips, "Xi Jinping Tells Army Not to Fear Death in Show of China's Military Might," *Guardian*, January 4, 2018.

56. Ming-Hsien Wong, "An Analysis of the Taiwan Travel Act and Its Implications for US, China and Taiwan Relations," The Prospect Foundation, April 24, 2018, www.pf.org.tw /article-pfch-2049-5911.

57. "China's Military Rise: The Dragon's New Teeth," *The Economist*, April 7, 2012, SIPRI and IMF estimates, www.economist.com/briefing/2012/04/07/the-dragons-new -teeth. See Brian Wang, "China increases defense spending by 10.7% and is 30 years from catching up the USA," *Next Big Future*, April 3, 2013, www.nextbigfuture.com/2013/04/ china-increases-defense-spending-by-107.html.

58. Kenneth Rapoza, "Senator Rubio: The U.S. Has No Industrial Policy to Counter China Made In 2025," *Forbes*, February 12, 2019.

59. CNN Transcripts, February 13, 2018, http://transcripts.cnn.com/TRANSCRIPTS /1802/13/cnr.04.html.

60. Francis Fukuyama, "China's 'Bad Emperor' Returns," *Washington Post*, March 6, 2018.

61. Han Zhang, "The 'Post-Truth' Publication Where Chinese Students in America Get Their News," *New Yorker*, August 19, 2019.

62. Ibid.

63. Kenneth Rapoza, "Kudlow: 'Pay the Moving Costs' of American Companies Leaving China," *Forbes*, April 10, 2020.

64. Donald J. Trump, National Security Strategy of the United States of America (NSS) (Washington, DC: White House, 2017), www.whitehouse.gov/wp-content/uploads/2017 /12/NSS-Final-12-18-2017-0905.pdf.

65. Ibid.

66. The National Security Strategy report states that "we will consider restrictions on foreign STEM students from designated countries to ensure that intellectual property is not transferred to our competitors."

67. "Meiguo de 'zidan' fei xiangle Huawei" [The US "bullet" flew to Huawei], *Diyi caijing* [China Business News], May 17, 2019, www.sohu.com/a/314704079_114986.

68. Andreas Fulda, "A New Law in China Is Threatening the Work of International NGOs," *The Conversation*, January 6, 2017.

69. Demetri Sevastopulo and Tom Mitchell, "US Considered Ban on Student Visas for Chinese Nationals," *Financial Times*, October 2, 2018.

70. Ibid.

71. National Security Strategy. For Wray's briefings and speeches, see, for example, CNN Transcripts, February 13, 2018, http://transcripts.cnn.com/TRANSCRIPTS/1802/13 /cnr.04.html. Christopher Wray, "The Threat Posed by the Chinese Government and the Chinese Communist Party to the Economic and National Security of the United States," Lecture, Hudson Institute, July 7, 2020, www.fbi.gov/news/speeches/the-threat-posed-by -the-chinese-government-and-the-chinese-communist-party-to-the-economic-and -national-security-of-the-united-states.

72. Bethany Allen-Ebrahimian, "The Chinese Communist Party Is Setting Up Cells at Universities across America," *Foreign Policy*, April 18, 2018.

73. Bethany Allen-Ebrahimian, "China's Long Arm Reaches into American Campuses," *Foreign Policy*, March 7, 2018; see also Stephanie Saul, "On Campuses Far from China, Still Under Beijing's Watchful Eye," *New York Times*, May 4, 2017.

74. Rachelle Peterson, "Outsourced to China," National Association of Scholars, July 12, 2017, https://nas.org/blogs/dicta/outsourced_to_china.

75. Ibid.

76. John Hayward, "Defense Bill Makes Universities Choose Between Pentagon Programs and China's Confucius Institute," *Breitbart*, August 15, 2018, www.breitbart.

com/national-security/2018/08/15/defense-bill-makes-universities-choose-between-pentagon-programs-and-chinas-confucius-institute.

77. "How Many Confucius Institutes Are in the United States?" National Association of Scholars website, July 1, 2020, www.nas.org/blogs/article/how_many_confucius_institutes_are_in_the_united_states.

78. Juan Pablo Cardenal, Jacek Kucharczyk, Grigorij Mesežnikov, and Gabriela Pleschová, "Sharp Power: Rising Authoritarian Influence," The National Endowment for Democracy, December 5, 2017, Washington, DC; and Larry Diamond and Orville Schell, eds., "China's Influence and American Interests: Promoting Constructive Vigilance," Hoover Institution, November 29, 2018, Stanford University, www.hoover.org/research/chinas-influence-american-interests-promoting-constructive-vigilance.

79. U.S. Congress, Senate, Foreign Influence Transparency Act, S. 2583, 115th Cong., introduced on March 21, 2018, www.govinfo.gov/content/pkg/BILLS-115s2583is/pdf/BILLS-115s2583is.pdf.

80. Adam Taylor, "The Worst Justification for Trump's Battle With China? The 'Clash of Civilizations,'" *Washington Post*, May 2, 2019.

81. Ibid.

82. "Susan Thornton on a Crisis in U.S.-China Relations," *ChinaFile*, April 15, 2019, www.chinafile.com/library/china-world-podcast/susan-thornton-crisis-us-china-relations.

83. Richard C. Bush and Ryan Hass, "The China Debate Is Here to Stay," *Order from Chaos* (blog), Brookings Institution, March 4, 2019, www.brookings.edu/blog/order-from-chaos/2019/03/04/the-china-debate-is-here-to-stay.

84. Finbarr Bermingham, "You Can't Contain China: Former US Trade Chief Robert Zoellick Warns Donald Trump," *South China Morning Post*, January 14, 2019.

85. Jeffrey D. Sachs, "Will America Create A Cold War with China?" *Horizons*, no. 13 (Winter 2019), 36.

86. Ibid.

87. Timothy R. Heath, "China's Military Has No Combat Experience: Does It Matter?" *The Rand Blog*, November 27, 2018, www.rand.org/blog/2018/11/chinas-military-has-no-combat-experience-does-it-matter.html.

88. Ibid.

89. Jeffrey Bader, "Changing China Policy: Are We in Search of Enemies?" Brookings John L. Thornton China Center Strategy Paper Series, Volume 1, June 2015, www.brookings.edu/wp-content/uploads/2016/06/Changing-China-policy-Are-we-in-search-of-enemies.pdf.

90. Jhana Gottlieb, "The Beijing Consensus: A Threat of Our Own Creation." April 22, 2017, Center for International Maritime Security, http://cimsec.org/beijing-consensus-threat-creation/32178.

91. Stephen Roach, "Who Wins in the U.S.-China Trade War," *Yale Insights*, December 6, 2018, https://insights.som.yale.edu/insights/three-questions-prof-stephen-roach-on-who-wins-in-the-us-china-trade-war.

92. Ibid.

93. Freeman, Jr. "On Hostile Coexistence with China."

94. Peter Dockrill, "China Just Overtook the US in Scientific Output for the First Time." Science Alert, January 23, 2018, www.sciencealert.com/china-just-overtook-us-in-scientific-output-first-time-published-research.

95. Freeman, Jr. "On Hostile Coexistence with China."

96. Ibid.

97. Rafael Reif, Speech delivered at the MIT China Summit, Beijing, China, November 13, 2018, http://president.mit.edu/speeches-writing/mit-china-summit.

98. David Ho, Keynote Remarks at the SupChina's "Next China Conference," New York, November 21, 2019.

99. Larry Summers, "Can Anything Hold Back China's Economy?" December 5, 2018, http://larrysummers.com/2018/12/05/can-anything-hold-back-chinas-economy.

100. Kai-Fu Lee, *AI Superpowers: China, Silicon Valley, and the New World Order* (New York: Houghton Mifflin Harcourt, 2018).

101. Remco Zwetsloot, Helen Toner, and Jeffrey Ding, "Beyond the AI Arms Race: America, China, and the Dangers of Zero-Sum Thinking," *Foreign Affairs*, November 16, 2018, www.foreignaffairs.com/reviews/review-essay/2018-11-16/beyond-ai-arms-race.

102. Carol Christ, "Reaffirming Our Support for Berkeley's International Community," *Berkeley News*, February 21, 2019, https://news.berkeley.edu/2019/02/21/reaffirming-our -support-for-berkeleys-international-community/?from=timeline&isappinstalled=0.

103. Minnie Chan, "Yale University Chief Stakes Support for International Students Amid China-US Academic Visa Turmoil," *South China Morning Post*, May 25, 2019.

104. Ibid.

105. Peterson, "Outsourced to China."

106. Steven Ward, "Because China Isn't 'Caucasian,' the U.S. Is Planning for a 'Clash of Civilizations.' That Could Be Dangerous," *Washington Post*, May 4, 2019.

107. Samuel P. Huntington, "The Clash of Civilizations?" *Foreign Affairs*, Summer 1993.

108. Gerry Shih, "China's Xi Rallies Asia by Appealing to Shared Culture—with Subtle Dig at U.S.," *Washington Post*, May 15, 2019.

109. "Congressional Statements," APA Justice website, www.apajustice.org/congress ional-statements.html/.

110. "'The Key Problem of Our Time': A Conversation with Henry Kissinger on Sino-U .S. Relations," Wilson Center, September 20, 2018, www.wilsoncenter.org/article/the-key -problem-our-time-conversation-henry-kissinger-sino-us-relations.

111. Cheng Li, "How China's Middle Class Views the Trade War," *Foreign Affairs*, September 10, 2018, www.foreignaffairs.com/articles/china/2018-09-10/how-chinas -middle-class-views-trade-war.

CHAPTER 3

1. The pyramidal structure at the turn of the century is most vividly presented in Lu Xueyi's 2004 study. See Lu Xueyi, *Dangdai Zhongguo shehui liudong* [Social mobility in contemporary China] (Beijing: Shehui kexue wenxian chubanshe, 2004), 14.

2. John King Fairbank, *The United States and China*, 4th ed. (Cambridge, MA: Harvard University Press, 1983), 51.

3. For the early development of the Chinese bourgeoisie, or the middle class, see Marie-Claire Bergère, *The Golden Age of the Chinese Bourgeoisie, 1911–1937*, translated by Janet Lloyd (Cambridge: Cambridge University Press, 1989).

4. *China News Analysis*, no. 1501, January 1, 1994, 2.

5. Ming Yongchang, "Zhongchan jieji zhengzai shixian 'Zhongguomeng'" [The middle class is realizing its "Chinese dream"], *Lianhe zaobao* [United morning news], October 1, 2008, 2.

6. Zhang Wanli, "Zhongguo shehui jieji jieceng yanjiu ershi nian" [Research on classes and social status during the last twenty years in China], *Shehuixue yanjiu* [Sociological research], no. 1 (2000): 24–39; and also Cheng Li, "'Credentialism' versus 'Entrepreneurism': The Interplay and Tensions between Technocrats and Entrepreneurs in the Reform Era," in Chan Kwok Bun, ed., *Chinese Business Networks: State, Economy and Culture* (New York: Prentice Hall, 1999), 86–111.

7. Cheng Li, "Introduction: The Rise of the Middle Class in the Middle Kingdom," in Cheng Li, ed., *China's Emerging Middle Class: Beyond Economic Transformation* (Washington, DC: Brookings Institution Press, 2010), 8.

8. "China Issues 7.83 Billion Bank Cards in Total," Xinhua News Agency, June 23, 2019, http://www.xinhuanet.com/english/2019-06/23/c_138167182.htm.

9. Ibid., and "2020 nian Zhongguo xinyongka de shiyong jiang dadao quanxin gaodu" [Chinese credit card usage will reach new heights in 2020], https://fsight.qq.com/insight/excellentInfo/1001500114fd152e715b2f82a2fdbfa671ad33b5.html.

10. See http://cn.chinagate.cn/chinese/jj/67931.htm (May 16, 2010).

11. The annual growth rate of output and sales is 48 percent and 46 percent, respectively. Quoted from Zhang Xue, "Domestic Auto Sector Undergoes Structural Adjustments," *Economic Daily*, February 9, 2010.

12. Wang Qian, "Woguo jidongche baoyouliang da 3.25 yiliang [China's motor vehicle ownership has reached 325 million], Xinhua Newsnet, December 1, 2018, http://www.xinhuanet.com/legal/2018-12/01/c_1123793884.htm.

13. Ibid.

14. "2018 nian Shanghai shi guomin jingji he shehui fazhan tongji gongbao" [Statistical Communique of Shanghai National Economic and Social Development in 2018]. *Shanghai tongji* [Shanghai Statistics], March 1, 2019, https://web.archive.org/web/20190306052003/http://www.stats-sh.gov.cn/html/sjfb/201903/1003219.html.

15. Lin Jing, "Woguo sijia che baoyou liang shouci tupo 2 yi liang" [China's private car ownership exceeds 200 million for the first time]. *Beijing ribao* [Beijing daily], January 8, 2020.

16. Ibid.

17. Credit Suisse Research Institute, *Quanqiu caifu baogao* [Global wealth report], Hong Kong 2015, quoted from Sun Yang, "Yige jieceng de chenfu—chongxin renshi dalu zhong-chan" [Ups and downs of a class: Re-recognizing the mainland middle class]. *Fenghuang zhoukan* [Phoenix Weekly], no. 561 (November 17, 2015).

18. Dominic Barton, Yougang Chen, and Amy Jin, "Mapping China's Middle Class." McKinsey & Company, June 2013, https://www.mckinsey.com/industries/retail/our-insights/mapping-chinas-middle-class.

19. Li Chunling, "Zhongguo zhongchan jieji yanjiu de dongli yu quxiang" [The motives and trends in the study of China's middle class], in Fang Xiangxin, ed., *Hexie shehui yu shehui jianshe* [Harmonious society and social development] (Beijing: Shehui kexue wenxian chubanshe, 2008).

20. Graham Young, "Mao Zedong and the Class Struggle in Socialist Society." *Australian Journal of Chinese Affairs* 16 (July 1986): 41–80.

21. *Nanfang ribao* [Southern daily], February 26, 2000, 1. For more discussion on the background of Jiang's ideological innovation, the "three represents," see Cheng Li, "China in 2000: A Year of Strategic Rethinking," *Asian Survey* 41, no. 1 (2001): 71–90.

22. Chen Xinnian, *Zhongdeng shouruzhe lun* [Middle-income stratum]. (Beijing: Zhongguo jihua chubanshe, 2005), 1.

23. Liu Xiuhong, "'Sige quanmian' zhongda zhanlue buju" ["Four comprehensives" lay-out major strategic blueprint]. *China Daily*, February 26, 2015.

24. Xi Jinping, "Jixu chaozhe zhonghua minzu weida fuxing mubiao fenyong qianjin" [Continue to march forward toward the goal of the great rejuvenation of the Chinese nation]. The Central People's Government of the PRC website, November 29, 2012, http://www.gov.cn/ldhd/2012-11/29/content_2278733.htm.

25. Ibid.

26. Niu Qisi, "Zhongguo zhongdeng shouru qunti chao 3 yi ren, 2050 nian youwang da 9 yi ren yishang" [China's middle-income group exceeds 300 million people. It is expected to reach more than 900 million people in 2050], *Zhongguo Jingji Zhoukan* (China Economic Weekly), April 17, 2018, http://industry.people.com.cn/n1/2018/0417/c413883-29930573.html.

27. Ibid. Also see Zhao Jianhua, "Maoyi zhan meiyou yingjia" [There is no winner in the trade war]. Zhongguo xinwenwang (China News Net), March 24, 2018, http://www.chinanews.com/gn/2018/03-24/8475281.shtml.

28. Niu, "Zhongguo zhongdeng shouru."

29. Ibid.

30. Li, "Introduction: The Rise of the Middle Class in the Middle Kingdom," 3–30.

31. Notable exceptions include Alastair Iain Johnston, "Chinese Middle Class Attitudes towards International Affairs: Nascent Liberalization?" *China Quarterly* 179 (September 2004), 603–628; David S. G. Goodman, ed., *The New Rich in China: Future Rulers, Present Lives* (New York: Routledge, 2008); and Deborah Davis and Feng Wang, eds., *Creating Wealth and Poverty in Post Socialist China* (Stanford, CA: Stanford University Press, 2008). Even some of these scholars, such as David Goodman, have some reservations when they employ the term "middle class."

32. For example, in David Goodman's view, the argument that members of the Chinese "new rich" are "just like us" can be "very seductive," but it obscures the fact that they represent a minuscule elite that has benefited disproportionately from economic reforms. See Rowan Callick, "Myth of China's New Middle Class," *Australian*, January 14, 2008, 2.

33. Barrington Moore Jr., *The Social Origins of Dictatorship and Democracy: Lord and Peasant in the Making of the Modern World* (Boston: Beacon Press, 1966), 418, 430.

34. Seymour Martin Lipset, "Some Social Requisites of Democracy: Economic Development and Political Legitimacy," *American Political Science Review* 53, no. 1 (1959), 69–105; and Seymour Martin Lipset, *Political Man: The Social Bases of Politics* (Garden City, NJ: Anchor Books, 1963).

35. Margaret M. Pearson, *China's New Business Elite: The Political Consequences of Economic Reform* (University of California Press, 1997); Andrew G. Walder, "Sociological Dimensions of China's Economic Transition: Organization, Stratification, and Social Mobility," Shorenstein Asia/Pacific Research Center, April 2003; Yanjie Bian, "Chinese Social Stratification and Social Mobility," *Annual Review of Sociology* 28, no. 1 (2002), 91–116; and Elizabeth J. Perry, "A New Rights Consciousness?" *Journal of Democracy* 20, no. 3 (2009), 17–20.

36. Li Chunling, "Zhongguo zhongchan jieji yanjiu de lilun quxiang ji guanzhudian de bianhua" [Theoretical orientation and the change of focus in the study of the middle class in China], in Li Chunling, ed., *Bijiao shiyexia de zhongchan jieji xingcheng: guocheng, yingxiang yiji shehui jingji houguo* [Formation of middle class in comparative perspective: Process, influence, and socioeconomic consequences] (Beijing: Shehui kexue wenxian chubanshe, 2009), 47–48.

37. Gary Burtless, "Growing American Inequality: Sources and Remedies," *Brookings Review* (Winter 1999), 31–35.

38. Homi Kharas and Geoffrey Gertz, "The New Global Middle Class: A Crossover from West to East," in Li, ed., *China's Emerging Middle Class*, 32–51.

39. Johnston, "Chinese Middle Class Attitudes towards International Affairs," 607.

40. C. Wright Mills, *White Collar: The American Middle Classes* (Oxford, UK: Oxford University Press), 1951.

41. Wang Jianying and Deborah Davis, "China's New Upper Middle Classes: The Importance of Occupational Disaggregation," in Li, ed., *China's Emerging Middle Class*, 157.

42. See Li Peilin and Zhang Yi, "Zhongguo zhongchan jieji de guimo, rentong, he shehui taidu" [Scale, recognition, and attitudes of China's middle class], in Tang Jin, ed., *Daguoce tongxiang Zhongguo zhilu de Zhongguo minzhu: Zengliang shi minzhu* [Strategy of a great power: Incremental democracy and Chinese-style democracy] (Beijing: Renmin ribao chubanshe, 2009), 188–190.

43. Lu Xueyi, *Dangdai Zhongguo shehui jiegou* [Social structure of contemporary China] (Beijing: Shehui kexue wenxian chubanshe, 2010), 402–406.

44. Lu Xueyi, *"Xianzai shi Zhongguo zhongchan jieceng fazhan de huangjin shiqi"* [Now is the golden age of China's middle-class development], *Zhongguo qingnian bao* (China Youth Daily) February 11, 2010, 10.

45. *Zhongguo xinwen zhoukan* [China newsweek], January 22, 2010.

46. Niu, "Zhongguo zhongdeng shouru."

47. *Zhongguo xinwen zhoukan.*

48. Lu Xueyi, *Dangdai Zhongguo shehuijieceng yanjiu baogao—Zhongguo shehui jieceng yanjiu baogao* [Research report on social strata in contemporary China] (Beijing: Shehui kexue wenxian chubanshe, 2002), 9.

49. This pyramidal structure is most vividly presented in Lu Xueyi's 2004 study. See Lu Xueyi, *Dangdai Zhongguo shehui liudong* [Social mobility in contemporary China] (Beijing: Shehui kexue wenxian chubanshe, 2004), 14.

50. Lu, *Dangdai Zhongguo shehuijieceng yanjiu baogao*, 44.

51. Wu Wei, "Zongli shuo de 6 yi ren yue shouru jin 1000 yuan" [Premier said that the monthly income of 600 million people is only 1,000 yuan], *Xinjing bao* [Beijing News], May 28, 2020, https://www.sohu.com/a/398461294_114988.

52. Liu Xin, "Class Structure and Income Inequality in Transitional China." *Journal of Chinese Sociology* 7, no. 4 (2020): 1–24.

53. Li Lulu and Li Sheng, "Shutu yilei—Dangdai Zhongguo chengzhen zhongchan jieji de leixinghua fenxi" [Different approaches and different types: A typological analysis of the middle class in Chinese cities and towns], *Shehuixue yanjiu* [Sociology studies] 22, no. 6 (2007): 15–37.

54. *Nandu Zhoukan* [Southern Metropolis Weekly], July 14, 2006.

55. Chen Baorong, "Jiushi niandai Shanghai geti siying jingji fazhan yanjiu" [Study of the development of the private economy in Shanghai during the 1990s] (working paper, Shanghai Academy of Social Sciences, 1994); and Zhu Guanglei, *Dangdai zhongguo shehui gejieceng fenxi* [Analysis of social strata in China] (Tianjin: Tianjin renmin chubanshe, 1998), 376.

56. For the original argument, see Talcott Parsons, *The Social System* (New York: Free Press, 1951).

57. He Qinglian, "Zhongchan jieji gaibian Zhongguo zhengjushuo shi huanxiang" [The myth of how the middle class will change Chinese politics] in *Dajiyuan* [Epoch], August 2, 2004, 1; and for Xu Zhiyuan's comments, see Wei Cheng, *Suowei zhongchan* [The so-called middle class] (Guangzhou: Nanfang ribao chubanshe, 2007), 208.

58. Yuan Jian, *Zhongguo: Qiji de huanghun* [China: the dusk of the miracle], online book, 2008, 116.

59. Chen Yiping, *Fenhua yu zuhe: Zhongguo zhongchanjieceng yanjiu* [Separation and coherence: A study of China's middle class] (Guangzhou: Guangdong renmin chubanshe, 2005), 52–53.

60. 2017 nian quanguo jiaoyu shiye fazhan tongji gongbao [2017 National Statistical Report on Education Development]. PRC Minister of Education website, July 19, 2018, http://www.moe.gov.cn/jyb_sjzl/sjzl_fztjgb/201807/t20180719_343508.html.

61. Zhou Xiaohong, *Quanqiu zhongchanjieji baogao* [Report on middle classes in the world] (Beijing: Shehui kexue wenxian chubanshe, 2005), 64, and 118–119.

62. For more discussion of the core values in present-day China, especially among members of the emerging middle class, see Pan Wei and Ma Ya, *Jujiao dangdai Zhongguo jiazhiguan* [Focusing on contemporary Chinese values] (Beijing: Shenghuo dushu xinzhi sanlian shudian, 2008); and Xu Rong, *Zhongguo zhongjian jieceng wenhua pinwei yu diwei konghuang* [Cultural taste and status panic of the Chinese middle class] (Beijing: China Encyclopedia Publishing House, 2007).

63. Wei, *Suowei zhongchan.*

64. Wang Jianping, "Zhongchan jieceng—Shehui hexie de jiji liliang" [Middle stratum:

a positive force for harmonious society], *Tianjin shehui kexue* [Tianjin Social Sciences], no. 4 (2008): 62–65.

65. Zhang Yiwu, "Yeshuo zhongchan jieceng" [Comments on the middle stratum], *Huanqiu* [Globe], April 12, 2010.

66. Chen Xinnian, *Zhongdeng shouruzhe lun* [Middle-income stratum] (Beijing: Zhongguo jihua chubanshe, 2005).

67. Zhou Xiaohong and others, *Zhongguo zhongchan jieji diaocha* [A survey of the Chinese middle class] (Beijing: Shehui kexue wenxian chubanshe, 2005), 47–48; and Wei, *Suowei zhongchan*, 3.

68. Zhou, *Quanqiu zhongchanjieji baogao*, 227.

69. "You hengchan zhe you hengxin," quoted in Jiang Shan, *Zhongchan luxiantu* [A road map to be middle class] (Wuhan: Changjiang Publishing House, 2005), 32.

70. Chen, *Fenhua yu zuhe*, 23.

71. For Tang Jun's view, see *Zhongguo xinwen zhoukan* [China newsweek], January 22, 2010.

72. Wei, *Suowei zhongchan*, 109–110.

73. He Qinglian, "The New Myth in China: China's Rising Middle-Class Will Accelerate Democratization," *Finance and Culture Weekly*, November 8, 2006.

74. Wu Si, *Qian guize* [Hidden rules] (Shanghai: Fudan University Press, 2009).

75. Zhou Xiaohong, "Globalization, Social Transformation, and the Construction of China's Middle Class" in Li, ed., *China's Emerging Middle Class: Beyond Economic Transformation*, 84–103.

76. Li Peilin and others, *Zhongguo shehuihexie wending baogao* [Social harmony and stability in China today] (Beijing: Shehui kexue wenxian chubanshe, 2008), 198.

77. Ibid.

78. Zhang Yi, "Dangdai Zhongguo zhongchan jieceng de zhengzhi taidu" [Political attitudes of the middle stratum in contemporary China], *Zhongguo shehui kexue* [Chinese social sciences] 2 (Summer 2008), 117–118.

79. Mark Tran, "Phenomenal Success for New Film That Criticizes China's Environmental Policy," *Guardian*, March 2, 2015, https://www.theguardian.com/world/2015/mar/02/china-environmental-policy-documentary-under-the-dome-chai-jing-video.

80. Gabriel Wildau and Yizhen Jia, "Collapse of Chinese Peer-to-Peer Lenders Sparks Investor Flight." *Financial Times*, July 22, 2018, https://www.ft.com/content/75e75628-8b27-11e8-bf9e-8771d5404543.

81. "China's Vaccine Scandal: Firm Made 500,000 Substandard Doses, Twice as Many as First Thought, State Media Says." *South China Morning Post*, August 15, 2018, https://www.scmp.com/news/china/policies-politics/article/2159892/chinas-vaccine-scandal-firm-made-500000-substandard.

82. Liu Xin, "Zhongguo chengshi de zhongchan jieceng yu shequ zhili" [Middle classes and community governance in urban China], paper prepared for the conference Middle Class Studies in the Chinese Societies, Changchun, July 22, 2008; and Liu Xin, "Class Structure and Income Inequality in Transitional China," *Journal of Chinese Sociology* 7, no. 4 (2020): 1–24.

83. Li Lulu, "Zhongjian jieceng de shehui gongneng: xin de wenti quxiang he duowei fenxi kuangjia" [The social function of the middle class: The new question-oriented approach and multidimensional analysis framework], *Journal of Renmin University* 4 (April 2008). Also see Li Lulu and Wang Yu, "Dangdai Zhongguo zhongjian jieceng de shehui cunzai: Jieceng renzhi yu zhengzhi yishi" [The social existence of the middle stratum in contemporary China: Strata recognition and political consciousness], *Shehui Kexue Zhanxian* [Social sciences frontline] 10 (2008): 202–215.

84. Samuel P. Huntington, *Political Order of Changing Societies* (New Haven, CT: Yale University Press, 1969).

85. Feng Ting, "Biegei zhongchan jieceng tietaiduojin" [Don't gild the middle stratum], *Renmin luntan* [People's forum], no. 10 (April 2010).

86. Qin Hui, "Zhongchan jieji bingfei minzhu biyao tiaojian" [The middle class is not a necessary condition for democracy], *Lüye* [Green leaf], no. 12 (2009).

87. Hu Lianhe and Hu Angang, "Zhongchan jieceng: Wendingqi haishi xiangfan huo qita" (Middle stratum: A stabilizer, a disrupter, or something else], *Zhengzhixue yanjiu* [Political science studies], no. 2 (May 2008).

88. Yan Yunxiang made this observation. He believes that this is in opposition to most Western discussions that "treat globalization as a postindustrial, postmodern phenomenon." Yan Yunxiang, "Managed Globalization: State Power and Cultural Transition in China," in Samuel P. Huntington, ed. *Many Globalizations: Cultural Diversity in the Contemporary World* (New York: Oxford University Press, 2002), 36.

89. For example, see Li Qiqing and Liu Yuanqi, *Quanqiuhua yu xin ziyouzhuyi* [Globalization and neo-liberalism] (Guilin: Guangxi shifandaxue chubanshe, 2003).

90. Anthony Giddens, *Beyond Left and Right: The Future of Radical Politics* (Palo Alto, CA: Stanford University Press, 1994); and Akira Iriye, *Cultural Internationalism and World Order* (Baltimore: Johns Hopkins University Press, 1997).

91. Iriye, *Cultural Internationalism and World Order*, 3.

92. Akira Iriye, *Power and Culture* (Cambridge, MA: Harvard University Press, 1982), vii.

93. Iriye, *Cultural Internationalism and World Order*, x.

94. Joseph S. Nye, *Soft Power: The Means to Success in World Politics* (New York, NY: Public Affairs, 2004), 11.

95. Li Tuo, Bao Yaming, Wang Hongtu, and Zhu Shengjian, *Shanghai jiuba—Kongjian, xiaofei yu xiangxiang* [Bars in Shanghai: Space, consumption and imagination] (Nanjing: Jiangsu renmin chubanshe, 2001), 86.

96. Ma Qingyu, "Quanqiuhua he dui wenhua xiangduizhuyi de piping" (Globalization and a critique of cultural relativism). *Dangdai Zhongguo yanjiu* (Contemporary China studies), no. 2 (2003).

97. Ye Weili, *Seeking Modernity in China's Name: Chinese Students in the United States, 1900–1927* (Stanford, CA: Stanford University Press, 2001), 7.

98. Shanghai bainian wenhuashi bianzuan weiyuanhui, *Shanghai bainian wenhuashi* [Cultural history of twentieth-century Shanghai], Vol. 1 (Shanghai: Shanghai kexue jishu wenxian chubanshe, 2002), 15.

99. Glen Peterson and Ruth Hayhoe, "Introduction" in Glen Peterson, Ruth Hayhoe, and Lu Yongling, eds. *Education, Culture, and Identity in Twentieth-Century China* (Ann Arbor: University of Michigan Press, 2001), 1.

100. An Yu and Zhou Mian, *Liuxuesheng yu zhongwai wenhua jiaoliu* [Foreign-educated students and China's cultural exchange with the outside world] (Nanjing: Nanjing daxue chubanshe, 2000), 1.

101. This is based on Wang Huiyao's presentation at the 2019 Duke International Forum, "A New Age of Sino-US Highe)r Education Cooperation," held in Kunshan, China on December 16–18, 2019.

102. Wang Ning, *Quanqiuhua yu wenhua: Xifang yu Zhongguo* [Globalization and culture: The West and China] (Beijing: Beijing daxue chubanshe, 2002), 226–227.

103. See http://www.chinesenewsnet.com, January 26, 2004.

104. David Zweig, *Internationalizing China: Domestic Interests and Global Linkages* (Ithaca: NY: Cornell University Press, 2002), 161; and David Zweig, "Leaders, Bureaucrats, and Institutional Culture: The Struggle to Bring Back China's Top Overseas Talent," in Jacques deLisle and Avery Goldstein, eds., *China's Global Engagement: Cooperation, Competition, and Influence in the 21st Century* (Washington, DC: Brookings Institution Press, 2017), 325–358.

105. Li Xiaodong, *Quanqiuhua yu wenhua zhenghe* [Globalization and integration of cultures] (Changsha: Hunan renmin chubanshe, 2003), 35.

106. Wang Ning, *Quanqiuhua yu wenhua: Xifang yu Zhongguo* [Globalization and culture: The West and China] (Beijing: Beijing daxue chubanshe, 2002), 11.

107. For a critique of this view, see Manfred B. Steger, *Globalism: The New Market Ideology* (Lanham, MD: Rowman & Littlefield, 2002), 12–13.

108. Li Huibin, *Quanqiuhua: Zhongguo daolu* [Globalization: China's path] (Beijing: Shehui kexue wenxian chubanshe, 2003), 267.

109. Wang, *Quanqiuhua yu wenhua*, 8.

110. Wang Yizhou, *Quanqiuhua shidai de guoji anquan* [International security in the era of globalization] (Shanghai: Shanghai renmin chubanshe, 1999), 17. For the original concept of the "third culture," see Mike Featherstone, "Introduction," in Mike Featherstone, ed. *Global Culture: Nationalism, Globalization and Modernity* (London: Sage, 1990), 6.

111. Investors in the Xintiandi complex include Jackie Chan, a famous movie star from Hong Kong. Qiu Zhengyi, *Shanghai shishang ditu* [Fashion map of Shanghai] (Shanghai: Hanyu dacidian chubanshe, 2002), 123.

112. Qiu, *Shanghai shishang ditu*, 126–127.

113. The motto is posted in big letters at a prominent site within the Xintiandi complex.

114. Li Tuo, Bao Yaming, Wang Hongtu, and Zhu Shengjian, *Shanghai jiuba* [Bars in Shanghai], 11.

115. Giddens, *Beyond Left and Right*, 4. Cited in Yang Boxu, *Quanqiuhua: qiyuan, fazhan he yingxiang* [Globalization: Its origin, process, and impact] (Beijing: Renmin chubanshe, 2002), 36.

116. Harriet Sergeant, *Shanghai: Collision Point of Cultures, 1918–1939* (New York: Crown Publishers, 1990), 2; quoted from Rhoads Murphey, *Shanghai, Key to Modern China* (Cambridge, MA: Harvard University Press, 1953).

117. Shanghai bainian wenhuashi bianzuan weiyuanhui, *Shanghai bainian wenhuashi* [Cultural history of the twentieth-century Shanghai], Vol. 3 (Shanghai: Shanghai kexue jishu wenxian chubanshe, 2002), 1698.

118. Wang, *Quanqiuhua yu wenhua*, 3.

119. For a review of these schools of thought in international relations, see Henry R. Niu, *Perspectives on International Relations: Power, Institutions, and Ideas* (4th ed.). New York: CQ Press, 2014.

120. For an overview of the realist perspective of this issue, see Robert Gilpin, *The Political Economy of International Relations* (Princeton, NJ: Princeton University Press, 1987).

121. For a critique of both the constructivist paradigm and the thesis of China's peaceful rise under the U.S.-led world order, see John J. Mearsheimer, *The Tragedy of Great Power Politics*, 2nd ed. (New York: W. W. Norton, 2014).

122. Martha Finnemore and Kathryn Sikkink, "International Norm Dynamics and Political Change," *International Organization* 52, no. 4 (Autumn 1998), 888.

123. For a more comprehensive view of constructivists, see Alexander Wendt, *Social Theory of International Politics* (Cambridge: Cambridge University Press, 1999); Ted Hopf, *Social Origins of International Politics: Identities and Construction of Foreign Policies at Home* (Ithaca, NY: Cornell University Press, 2002); and Finnemore and Sikkink, "International Norm Dynamics and Political Change," 887–917.

124. Martha Finnemore, *National Interest in International Society* (Ithaca, NY: Cornell University Press, 1996), 15.

125. Samuel Huntington, "The Clash of Civilizations?" *Foreign Affairs* 72, no. 3 (1993): 49.

126. Finnemore, *National Interest in International Society*, 2. According to Finnemore, foreign policy debates during and after the Cold War showed that "interests are not just 'out there' waiting to be discovered; they are constructed through social interaction."

127. Finnemore, *National Interest in International Society*, 3.

128. Wendt, *Social Theory of International Politics*, 1.

129. For example, Finnemore argues that "tensions and contradictions among normative principles in international life mean that there is no set of ideal political and economic arrangements toward which we are all converging. There is no stable equilibrium, no end of history." Finnemore, *National Interest in International Society*, 135. Fukuyama, "The End of History?" 3–18.

130. Finnemore, *National Interest in International Society*, 15.

131. Ibid.

132. Frank A. Ninkovich, "Introduction," in Frank A. Ninkovich and Liping Bu, eds., *The Cultural Turn: Essays in the History of U.S. Foreign Relations* (Chicago: Imprint Publications, 2001), 1.

133. Ninkovich, "Introduction," 2.

134. Shanghai zhengda yanjiusuo, *Wenhua Shanghai—2010: Ba yige shenmeyang de Shanghai daigei Zhongguo he shijie* [Cultural Shanghai—2010: What kind of Shanghai will be presented to China and the world] (Beijing: Renmin chubanshe, 2003), 5.

135. "Age of anxiety for the Chinese middle class," CGTN, January 2, 2018, https://web .archive.org/web/20190206230816/https://eblnews.com/video/age-anxiety-chinese -middle-class-293588.

136. Jean Louis Rocca, "Zhengzhi jiaocha, shehui bianzheng yu xueshu ganyu: Zhongchan jieji zai Zhongguo de xingcheng" [Political interaction, empirical characterization, and academic intervention: The formation of the middle class in China], in Li, ed., *Bijiao shiyexia de zhongchan jieji xingcheng*, 59–83.

CHAPTER 4

1. Arthur Miller, "In China," *Atlantic Monthly*, March 1979, 90.

2. Václav Havel, "The Post-Communist Nightmare," *New York Review of Books*, May 27, 1993, 8.

3. "Fragmented Fractals: Towards Chinese Culture in the 21st Century." *China News Analysis*, no. 1462, June 15, 1992, 2; and "Cultural Issues." *China News Analysis*, no. 1310, May 15, 1986, 1.

4. Yang Dongping, *Chengshi jifeng: Beijing he Shanghai de wenhua jingshen* [City monsoon: The cultural spirit of Beijing and Shanghai] (Beijing: Dongfang Press, 1994), 12.

5. Xiong Yuezhi and Zhou Wu, *Haina baichuan: Shanghai chengshi jingshen yanjiu* [The sea that embraces thousands of rivers: Study of the Shanghai spirit] (Shanghai: Shanghai renmin chubanshe, 2003), 22.

6. *Beijing Review*, November 25–December 1, 1991, 34.

7. *Beijing Review*, March 19–25, 1990, 46.

8. Xu Jian and G. Thomas Goodnight, "Guoji wenhua da dushi pingjia baogao." [Evaluation report on international cultural metropolis], China Institute for Urban Governance (Shanghai), March 14, 2019, http://ciug.sjtu.edu.cn/Mobile/Show/36?fid=4273.

9. Planet Institute, comp., "Weishenme Shanghai bei cheng wei 'modu?'" [Why is Shanghai called "Magic Capital?"], June 27, 2019, www.zhihu.com/question/63282342

10. Panos Mourdoukoutas, "New Cafes Won't Solve Starbucks China Problem." *Forbes*, February 18, 2019, www.forbes.com/sites/panosmourdoukoutas/2019/02/18/all-day -dining-cafes-wont-solve-starbucks-china-problem/#32526d7e4c2c.

11. Ailin Tang, "The World's Biggest Starbucks Opens in Shanghai. Here's What It Looks Like." *New York Times*, December 6, 2017, www.nytimes.com/2017/12/06/business/ starbucks-shanghai.html.

12. Jürgen Habermas, *The Structural Transformation of the Public Sphere: An Inquiry into a Category of Bourgeois Society* (Cambridge: The MIT Press, 1991).

13. Elizabeth J. Perry, "Partners at Fifty: American China Studies and the PRC," an un-published paper prepared for Conference on Trends in China Watching. Washington, DC: The George Washington University, October 8–9, 1999, 1.

14. For a similar observation, see *Far Eastern Economic Review*, November 26, 1998, 50; and Arif Dirlik and Zhang Xudong, "Postmodernism and China," *Boundary* 2, no. 24 (Fall 1997), 8.

15. Heath B. Chamberlain, "Coming to Terms with Civil Society," *Australian Journal of Chinese Affairs*, no. 30 (January 1994), 116.

16. Yu Jianhua, *Zhongguo huihua shi* [History of Chinese Painting]. Vol. 2 (Shanghai: Shangwu yinshu guan, 1937), 196.

17. Lu Hanchao, *Beyond the Neon Lights: Everyday Shanghai in the Early Twentieth Century*. (Berkeley, CA: University of California Press, 1999), 59.

18. Zheng Shiling, "Architecture before 1949," in Alan Balfour and Zheng Shiling, *World Cities: Shanghai* (West Sussex, England: Wiley-Academy, 2002), 92.

19. Betty Peh-T'i Wei, *Shanghai: Crucible of Modern China* (Oxford: Oxford University Press, 1987), 45; and Stella Dong, *Shanghai: The Rise and Fall of a Decadent City, 1842–1949* (New York: Perennial, 2001), 2.

20. Zheng, "Architecture before 1949," 89.

21. Balfour and Zheng, *World Cities*, 29.

22. Wei, *Shanghai*, 5.

23. Balfour and Zheng, *World Cities*, 32.

24. Lu Daqian, Han Juntian, Fan Yunxing, and Sun Lei. *Shanghai: Guoji lüyou chengshi* [Shanghai: A world-famous tourist city in China] (Beijing: Zhongguo lüyou chubanshe, 2003), 6.

25. Balfour and Zheng, *World Cities*, 34.

26. Lu Hanchao, "'The Seventy-two Tenants': Residence and Commerce in Shanghai's Shikumen Houses, 1872–1951," in Sherman Cochran, ed. *Inventing Nanjing Road: Commercial Culture in Shanghai, 1900–1945* (Ithaca, NY: Cornell University Press, 1999), 182.

27. Bruce Jacobs J., "Shanghai: An Alternative Centre?" in David S.G. Goodman ed. *China's Provinces in Reform: Class, Community and Political Culture* (London: Routledge, 1997), 164.

28. Xiong Yuezhi and others, *Shanghai tong shi* [General history of Shanghai]. Vol. 14 (Shanghai: Shanghai renmin chubanshe, 1999), 2.

29. Zhou Wu, "Shanghai xingqi dui xiandai Zhongguo yu shijie de yiyi" [The significance of the rise of Shanghai to modern China and the world], *Pengpai News*, February 10, 2018, www.thepaper.cn/newsDetail_forward_1988313.

30. Ibid.

31. Xiong Yuezhi, Ma Xueqiang, and Yan Kejia, *Shanghai de waiguoren, 1942–1949* [Foreigners in Shanghai, 1942–1949] (Shanghai: Shanghai guji chubanshe, 2003), 1.

32. Shanghai bainian wenhuashi bianzuan weiyuanhui [Committee of the centennial history of Shanghai]. *Shanghai bainian wenhuashi* [Shanghai cultural history of the twentieth century]. Vol. 3 (Shanghai: Shanghai kexue jishu wenxian chubanshe, 2002), 1665.

33. Ibid., 1661.

34. Xiong and Zhou, *Haina baichuan*, 90.

35. Ibid., 79, 88.

36. Balfour and Zheng, *World Cities*, 89.

37. Lu, *Beyond the Neon Lights*, 322.

38. Miller, G. E. (pseudonym), *Shanghai, The Paradise of Adventurers* (New York: Orsay Publishing House, 1937), 17.

39. Xiong, Ma, and Yan, *Shanghai de waiguoren*, 2.

40. These figures come from Xiong, Ma, and Yan, *Shanghai de waiguoren*, and some data are from Tang Zhenchang and Shen Hengchun, *Shanghai shi* [History of Shanghai] (Shang-

hai: Shanghai renmin chubanshe, 1989), 148; Tang Jiwu and Yu Xingmin, *Fei di* [The land that flies] (Shanghai: Shanghai yuandong chubanshe, 2003), 80; and Jerome Chen, *China and the West: Society and Culture 1815–1937* (London: Hutchinson, 1979), 207.

41. Balfour and Zheng, *World Cities*, 69.

42. Xiong, Ma, and Yan, *Shanghai de waiguoren*, 155.

43. Cai Zheren and Shen Ronghua, *Zouxiang rencai guojihua—Shanghai rencai fazhan yanjiu baogao* [Toward the globalization of human resources: Report on human resources development in Shanghai] (Shanghai: Shanghai shehui kexueyuan chubanshe, 2002), 195–196.

44. Harriet Sergeant, *Shanghai: Collision Point of Cultures, 1918–1939* (New York: Crown Publishers, 1990), 31.

45. Xiong, Ma, and Yan, *Shanghai de waiguoren*, 87. Earlier, the number of American residents in Shanghai rose from 378 in 1865 to 1,608 in 1930, with the largest jump being from 562 to 911 Americans from 1900 to 1905. Wei, *Shanghai*, 105.

46. Xiong and Zhou. *Haina baichuan*, 54.

47. Ibid.

48. Shanghai bainian wenhuashi bianzuan weiyuanhui, *Shanghai bainian wenhuashi*, 1666, 1831.

49. Michael Buckley et al., *China*, 4th ed. (Sydney: Lonely Planet Publications, 1994), 453.

50. Lu, *Beyond the Neon Lights*, 55.

51. Ibid., 57–58.

52. The multiple meanings include (1) "isolation, abandonment, orphan," (2) "an oasis that afforded protection in a realm of violence," and (3) "lone army of resisters." Christian Henriot and Wen-Hsin Yeh, eds. *In the Shadow of the Rising Sun: Shanghai under Japanese Occupation* (Cambridge: Cambridge University Press, 2004), 6.

53. Balfour and Zheng, *World Cities*, 99.

54. Cheng Naishan. *Shanghai Tange* [Shanghai Tango] (Shanghai: Xuelin chubanshe, 2002), 58.

55. "National Archives opens postwar Shanghai visa records." *Times of Israel*, November 23, 2014, www.timesofisrael.com/national-archives-opens-postwar-shanghai-visa-archives/.

56. Xiong, Ma, and Yan, *Shanghai de waiguoren*, 3.

57. Gabe Friedman and Juie Wiener, "From the Archive: Life in the 'Shanghai Ghetto.'" Jewish Telegraphic Agency website, February 8, 2015, www.jta.org/2015/02/08/culture/from-the-archive-the-world-war-ii-jews-of-shanghai; also James R. Ross, *Escape to Shanghai: A Jewish Community in China* (New York: Free Press, 1994).

58. Xiong, Ma, and Yan, *Shanghai de waiguoren*, 3.

59. Wei, *Shanghai*, 15–16.

60. Tang Jiwu and Yu Xingmin, *Feidi* [Foreign enclave] (Shanghai: Shanghai yuandong chubanshe, 2003), 271.

61. Quoting Linda Cooke Johnson, Balfour and Zheng, *World Cities*, 67.

62. Xiong Yuezhi and others, *Shanghai tong shi* [General history of Shanghai]. Vol. 14 (Shanghai: Shanghai renmin chubanshe, 1999), 343. Another study showed that in 1949, Shanghai had 427 churches. Chen, *Shanghai wenhua tongshi*, 303.

63. Tang and Yu. *Fei di*, 293.

64. Xiong Yuezhi and others, *Shanghai tong shi*, 346.

65. Chen, *Shanghai wenhua tongshi*, 851.

66. Ibid., 854–855.

67. Ibid., 450.

68. Ibid., 453.

69. Ibid., 312.

70. Qiu Zhengyi, *Shanghai shishang ditu* [Fashion map of Shanghai] (Shanghai: Hanyu dacidian chubanshe, 2002), 16.

71. Shanghai bainian wenhuashi bianzuan weiyuanhui, *Shanghai bainian wenhuashi*, 15.

72. Shanghai Institute of Educational Research, *Hu feng meiyu bainian chao: Shanghai yu meiguo difang jiaoyu jiaoliu* [A century of educational exchanges between Shanghai and the United States, the volume of local educational exchanges] (Shanghai: Shanghai renmin chubanshe, 2019).

73. Li Kanghua, *Manhua Laoshanghai zhishi jieceng* [Regarding the stratum of intellectuals in old Shanghai] (Shanghai: Shanghai renmin chubanshe, 2003), 36–37.

74. In 1911, Shanghai had 110 newspapers. By comparison, Guangzhou had 99, Hong Kong 30, and Beijing 20. Shanghai bainian wenhuashi bianzuan weiyuanhui. *Shanghai bainian wenhuashi*, 1833.

75. Chen, *Shanghai wenhua tongshi*, 453.

76. Xin Ping, *Cong Shanghai faxian lishi—Xiandaihua jinchengzhong de Shanghairen jiqi shehui shenghuo* [Discovering history from Shanghai: Shanghainese and their social life in the process of modernization] (Shanghai: Shanghai renmin chubanshe, 1996), 211.

77. Chen, *Shanghai wenhua tongshi*, 2144.

78. Xin, *Cong Shanghai faxian lishi*, 213.

79. Tang and Shen, *Shanghai shi*, 11.

80. Chen, *Shanghai wenhua tongshi*, 1251–1252.

81. Shanghai bainian wenhuashi bianzuan weiyuanhui. *Shanghai bainian wenhuashi*, 1833.

82. Ibid., 457.

83. Shanghai bainian wenhuashi bianzuan weiyuanhui. *Shanghai bainian wenhuashi*, 1847.

84. Ibid., 1838. Another study reported that John Fryer translated a total of 129 books into Chinese, but this figure might include all the translation projects in which he participated. Tang and Shen, *Shanghai shi*, 303–304.

85. Tang and Shen, *Shanghai shi*, 296.

86. Shanghai bainian wenhuashi bianzuan weiyuanhui. *Shanghai bainian wenhuashi*, 1862.

87. Quoted in Zhou, "Shanghai xingqi dui xiandai Zhongguo yu shijie de yiyi."

88. Chen Bohai, *Shanghai wenhua tongshi* [History of Shanghai culture], Vols. 1 and 2 (Shanghai: Shanghai wenyi chubanshe, 2001).

89. Xin, *Cong Shanghai faxian lishi*, 212–213.

90. Jiang Di and Chen Kongguo. *Yu Qiuyu—Xunzhao wenhua de zunyan* [Yu Qiuyu: Search for cultural dignity] (Changsha: Hunan daxue chubanshe, 2001), 32.

91. Meng Yankun, *Xin Shanghai nüren* [The new Shanghai women] (Shanghai:Shanghai renmin chubanshe, 2003), 26.

92. Chen, *Shanghai wenhua tongshi*, 1303.

93. Grace C. L. Mak and Leslie N. K. Lo. "Education," in Yeung Yue-man and Sung Yun-wing, eds. *Shanghai: Transformation and Modernization under China's Open Door Policy* (Hong Kong: Chinese University of Hong Kong Press, 1996), 377.

94. Zhou, "Shanghai xingqi dui xiandai Zhongguo yu shijie de yiyi."

95. Tang and Yu, *Feidi*, and Sergeant, *Shanghai*, 24.

96. Lucian W. Pye, "Foreword," in Christopher Howe, ed. *Shanghai, Revolution and Development in an Asian Metropolis* (Cambridge: Cambridge University Press, 1981), xv.

97. Tang and Shen, *Shanghai shi*, 372–373.

98. Shanghai bainian wenhuashi bianzhui weiyuanhui, *Shanghai bainian wenhuashi*, 1901.

99. Xiong and Zhou, *Haina baichuan*, 52.

100. Chen, *Shanghai wenhua tongshi*, 1970.

101. Xiong and others. *Shanghai tong shi*, 3.

102. Zhou, "Shanghai xingqi dui xiandai Zhongguo yu shijie de yiyi."

103. Zhou, "Shanghai xingqi dui xiandai Zhongguo yu shijie de yiyi."

104. Parks M. Coble, *The Shanghai Capitalists and the Nationalist Government, 1927–1937* (Cambridge, MA: Harvard University Press, 1980), 1–2.

105. Zhao Xiaoguang and Liu Jie, "Deng Xiaoping wannian yihan houhui gao jingji tequ mei jia Shanghai" [Deng Xiaoping regretted in his final years that he had not added Shanghai as a special economic zone], Xinhua, March 24, 2014, http://history.people.com.cn/n/2014/0324/c372327-24719902-2.html.

106. Clifford Geertz, "Thick toward an Interpretative Theory of Culture," in Clifford Geertz, ed., *The Interpretation of Culture: Selected Essays by Clifford Geertz* (London: Basic Books, 1973), 30.

107. Lynn White and Cheng Li, "China Coast Identities: Regional, National, and Global," in Samuel Kim and Lowell Dittmer, eds. *China's Quest for National Identities* (Ithaca, NY: Cornell University Press, 1993), 154–193.

108. Mayfair Mei-hui Yang, "Mass Media and Transnational Subjectivity in Shanghai: Notes on (Re)cosmopolitanism in a Chinese Metropolis," in Aihwa Ong and Donald M. Nonini, eds., *Ungrounded Empires: The Cultural Politics of Modern Chinese Transnationalism* (London: Routledge, 1997), 289.

109. Wang Gungwu, "The Study of Chinese Identities in Southeast Asia," in Jennifer Cushman and Wang Gunwu, eds., *The Changing Identities of Chinese in Southeast Asia* (Hong Kong: Hong Kong University Press, 1988), 17.

110. Lu, Han, Fan, and Sun, *Shanghai: Guoji lüyou chengshi*, 56.

111. Lu Hanchao, "'The Seventy-two Tenants,'" 181.

112. Ibid., 183.

113. Gandelsonas Mario, Ackbar Abbas, M. Christine Boyer, and M. A. Abbas, eds. *Shanghai Reflections: Architecture, Urbanism, and the Search for an Alternative Modernity* (Princeton, NJ: Princeton Architectural Press, 2002), 21.

114. Kevin Platt, "'Titanic' Cultural Invasion Hits China." *Christian Science Monitor*, April 20, 1998, www.csmonitor.com/1998/0420/042098.intl.intl.2.html.

115. "*Zong shuji miaoyu lianzhu Guangdong tuan*" [General Secretary Jiang makes wonderful remarks], *Yangcheng wanbao* [Guangzhou evening news], March 10, 1998, 1.

116. "Pavarotti duets with Chinese president." BBC News, June 26, 2001, http://news.bbc.co.uk/2/hi/entertainment/1408455.stm.

117. Steven Mufson, "China's Musical Leader Sings in Many Keys." *Washington Post*, February 23, 1997, www.washingtonpost.com/archive/politics/1997/02/23/chinas-musical-leader-sings-in-many-keys/9d305ded-12a6-47cc-b25c-afef5e265396/?noredirect=on#comments.

118. Ibid.

119. Ma Jifen, "Chen Yun zai haipai wenhua (pingtan) fazhan yu yanjiu zhong de lishi gongxian" [Chen Yun's historical contributions in the development and research of *haipai* culture (*pingtan*)] in Li Lunxin, Fang Minglun, Li Youmei, and Ding Ximan, eds., *Haipai wenhua yu chengshi chuangxin* [Shanghai culture and urban innovation] (Shanghai: Wenhui chubanshe, 2010), 15.

120. Ibid.

121. Yan Yunxiang, "Managed Globalization: State Power and Cultural Transition in China," in Samuel P. Huntington, ed. *Many Globalizations: Cultural Diversity in the Contemporary World* (New York: Oxford University Press, 2002), 33.

122. Ibid., 34.

123. Cheng Li, "Rediscovering Urban Subcultures: Contrast between Shanghai and Beijing," *The China Journal*, no. 36 (July, 1996), 139–153.

124. Robert Redfield and Milton Singer, "The Cultural Role of Cities," in Richard Sennett, ed., *Classic Essays on the Culture of Cities* (New York: Meredith Corporation, 1969), 210–211.

125. Zhou, "Shanghai xingqi dui xiandai Zhongguo yu shijie de yiyi."

126. Li, "Rediscovering Urban Subcultures," 145.

127. Yu Qiuyu, *Wenhua kulü* [The bitterness of cultural travels] (Shanghai: Zhishi Press, 1992), 261.

128. Yu Tianbai, *Shanghai: Xingge ji mingyun* [Shanghai: Her character is her destiny] (Shanghai: Wenyi Press, 1992), 235.

129. Geremie Barmé, "TV Requiem for the Myths of the Middle Kingdom," *Far Eastern Economic Review*, September 1, 1988, 40–43. For the debate over *River Elegy*, see Staley Rosen and Gary Zou, "The Chinese Television Documentary 'River Elegy,'" *Chinese Sociology and Anthropology* 24, no. 2 (Winter 1991–1992), 24, no. 4 (Summer 1992), and 25, no. 1 (Fall 1992).

130. Ibid.; and "Chinese Culture: Of Tradition and Symbols." *China News Analysis*, no. 1376, January 1, 1989.

131. Yu, *Shanghai*.

132. Luo Shuang and others, eds., "'Pipan Beijingren?!" [A critique of the Beijingers?!] (Beijing: Zhongguo shehui chubanshe, 1994).

133. Ibid., 27, 33.

134. Ibid., 291.

135. Yang, *Chengshi jifeng*.

136. Ibid. 483.

137. Ibid.

138. Ibid. 349.

139. Ibid. 510.

140. Ibid. 457–481. Interestingly, in the mid-1960s, a Western scholar made similar observations about stereotypes of China's regional cultures as Yang did on Shanghai in his list. See Wolfram Eberhard, "Chinese Regional Stereotypes," *Asian Survey* 5, no. 12 (December 1965): 596–608.

141. Liu Mingming, "Jianxi haipai wenhua zhong de Zhou Libo yu Han Han xianxiang" [A brief analysis of Zhou Libo and Han Han phenomena in the Shanghai culture] in Li, Fang, Li, and Ding, eds., *Haipai wenhua yu chengshi chuangxin*, 293–296.

142. Qin Yaqing and Guo Shuyong, "Beijing xuepai VS Shanghai xuepai: Quanqiu shiyexia de Zhongguo xuepai." [Beijing school verses Shanghai school: Chinese schools of international relations from a global perspective]. Soho Net, February 11, 2018, www.sohu.com/a/222311899_99906585.

143. Liu Siyue and Niu Ning, "Xi Jinping lian shuole 5 nian de 'Shanghai jingshen' shi shenme." [What did Xi Jinping mean by "Shanghai spirit," which he has referenced for five years?]. Overseas Net, June 6, 2018, http://opinion.haiwainet.cn/n/2018/0606/c456318-31329161.html.

144. Ibid.

145. Balfour and Zheng, *World Cities*, 116.

CHAPTER 5

1. Shōfu Muramatsu (Muramatsu Giichi), *Modu* [Magic Capital], originally published in Japanese as *Mato* (also translated as *Demon City*), 1924, translated by Xu Jingbo (Shanghai: Shanghai renmin chubanshe, 2018).

2. Seiji Lippet, *Topographies of Japanese Modernism* (New York: Columbia University Press, 2002); and Xu Jingbo, "Translator's prequel," in Muramatsu, *Modu*.

3. Ibid.

4. For example, Ge Jianxiong, *Shanghai jijianshi* [Minimalist Shanghai history] (Shanghai: Shanghai renmin chubanshe, 2019); and Luo Jun, ed. *Modu manbu* [Walk in magic capital Shanghai] (Shanghai: Shanghai renmin chubanshe, 2018).

5. Yan Weiqi, Xu Danlu, Shang Jie, and Cao Jijun, "Yizuo chengshi de shidai zuobiao—tuidong gaozhiliang fazhan de Shanghai lujing" [A pioneering city in the new era: The Shanghai path to promote high quality development], *Guangming Daily*, April 21, 2019, https://news.gmw.cn/2019-04/21/content_32760564.htm.

6. Planet Institute, comp., "Weishenme Shanghai bei cheng wei 'modu?'" [Why is Shanghai called "Magic Capital?"], June 27, 2019, www.zhihu.com/question/63282342.

7. Zhou Wu, "Xin wenhua yundong shi jing hu gong mou de jieguo" [The New Culture Movement is the result of the collusion between Beijing and Shanghai], Shanghai Federation of Literary and Art Circles, May 6, 2019, www.shwenyi.com.cn/renda/2012shwl/n/zt/u1ai6239931.html.

8. Ding Jun, Zhan Jiwei, Fan Ziheng, and Yang Meng, "Renkou huiliu Shanghai" [Population returning to Shanghai], 21 Shiji caijing [twenty-first-century finance], March 2, 2019, https://m.21jingji.com/article/20190302/herald/39e8a9724358267c16a004e82b963da2.html.

9. Will Harris, "'Magic City': Shanghai's Spellbinding Nickname," *Cultural Trip*, March 19, 2019, https://theculturetrip.com/asia/china/articles/shanghai-magic-city/.

10. Ibid., 13.

11. Qianjiang wanbao xinminsheng, *Changsanjiao—xiayige taojindi* [The Yangtze River delta: The next frontier for a gold rush] (Hangzhou: Zhejiang renmin chubanshe, 2003), 67.

12. Yue Qintao, *Yi Shanghai wei zhongxin: huning, huhangyong tielu yu jindai changjiang sanjiaozhou diqu shehui bianqian* [Taking Shanghai as the center: Shanghai-Nanjing, Shanghai-Hangzhou-Ningbo Railway and the social changes in the modern Yangtze River delta] (Beijing: Zhongguo shehuikexue chubanshe, 2016).

13. Yan Weiqi et al., "Yizuo chengshi de shidai zuobiao."

14. Jia Yuankun and Zhou Lin, "Daxiang Shanghai 'Jinzi zhaopai'" [Launching Shanghai's "golden signboard"], *Liaowang xinwen zhoukan* [Outlook News Weekly], August 7, 2018, http://sh.xinhuanet.com/2018-08/07/c_137371550.htm.

15. Tan Yan and Meng Qunshu, "Li Qiang huijian masike dui tesila chun diandong che xiangmu zhengshi qianyue biaoshi zhuhe" [Li Qiang meets with Musk to convey congratulations on the official signing of the Tesla Pure Electric Vehicle Project]. *Jiefang ribao* [Liberation Daily], July 11, 2018, 1.

16. "Elon Musk Heads to Shanghai to Deliver His First Made-in-China Teslas," Bloomberg, January 6, 2020, https://fortune.com/2020/01/06/elon-musk-shanghai-first-made-in-china-tesla/.

17. "Tesla's market value eclipses GM and Ford combined," Reuters, January 8, 2020. www.autoblog.com/2020/01/08/tesla-stock-market-value-ford-gm/.

18. Russ Mitchell, "Tesla's Insane Stock Price Makes Sense in a Market Gone Mad," *Los Angeles Times*, July 22, 2020. www.latimes.com/business/story/2020-07-22/why-the-stock-market-is-so-high-and-tesla-even-higher.

19. Wang Zhan, Weng Shilie, Yang Shengli and Wang Zhen. *Zhuanxing shengji de xinzhanlue yu xinduice* [New strategy and new measures for transformation and upgrading] (Shanghai: Shanghai shehui kexueyuan chubanshe, 2015), 4.

20. Rong Yueming and Zheng Chongxuan, *Shanghai wenhua fazhan baogao 2017* [Annual report on cultural development of Shanghai 2017] (Beijing: Social Science Academic Press, 2017), 39.

21. Ibid., 179.

22. Xie Liping, ed. *Shanghai gaige kaifang shihua* [History of Shanghai's reform and opening up] (Shanghai: Shanghai renmin chubanshe, 2018), 184.

23. Alan Balfour, "Introduction," in Alan Balfour and Zheng Shiling, eds, *World Cities: Shanghai* (West Sussex, England: Wiley-Academy, 2002), 9.

24. Planet Institute, "Weisheme Shanghai bei chengwei 'modu?'"

25. Lu Shuping, *Shanghai niaokan* [Bird's eye views of Shanghai] (Shanghai: Shanghai renmin meishu chubanshe, 2017), 67.

26. Tsung-Yi Michelle Huang, *Walking between Slums and Skyscrapers: Illusions of Open Space in Hong Kong, Tokyo and Shanghai* (Hong Kong: Hong Kong University Press, 2004), 103.

27. "APEC 2001 in China," China Internet Information Center, October 21, 2001, www.china.org.cn/english/12585.htm.

28. The numbers are based on *Jiefang ribao* [Liberation Daily], March 26, 2009, http://jfdaily.eastday.com/j/20090326/u1a552585.html.

29. Balfour and Zheng, *World Cities*, 110.

30. Quoted from www.justholiday.com/china/shanghai/pudong.html, August 25, 2004.

31. Huang, *Walking between Slums and Skyscrapers*, 7.

32. Planet Institute, "Weishenme Shanghai bei chengwei 'modu?'"

33. Pamela Yatsko, *New Shanghai: The Rocky Rebirth of China's Legendary City* (New York: John Wiley & Sons, 2000), 26.

34. Huang, *Walking between Slums and Skyscrapers*, 7. Also see Joe Gamble, *Shanghai in Transition: Changing Perspectives and Social Contours of a Chinese Metropolis* (London: Routledge Curzon, 2003), x.

35. James P. Sterba, "A Great Leap Where?" *Wall Street Journal*, December 10, 1993, sec. R, 9.

36. Huang Ju and others, eds., *Maixiang 21 shiji de Shanghai* [Shanghai: Toward the twenty-first century] (Shanghai: Shanghai renmin chubanshe, 1995); and Gamble, *Shanghai in Transition*, xi.

37. Xie, *Shanghai gaige kaifang shihua*, 110.

38. Balfour and Zheng, *World Cities*, 66.

39. Lou Chenghao and Xue Shunsheng, *Laoshanghai jingdian jianzhu* [Old Shanghai: Classic architecture] (Shanghai: Tongji daxue chubanshe, 2000), 1. According to a study conducted in the early 1990s, "Shanghai has the largest array of Art Deco edifices of any city in the world," Tess Johnston and Deke Erh, *A Last Look: Western Architecture in Old Shanghai* (Hong Kong: Old China Hand Press, 1993), 70.

40. Cheng Naishan, *Shanghai Tange* [Shanghai Tango] (Shanghai: Xuelin chubanshe, 2002), 201.

41. Zhang Wei, *Hudu jiuying* [Reviewing snapshots of old Shanghai] (Shanghai: Shanghai cishu chubanshe, 2002), 299.

42. Ibid., 301.

43. Ibid.

44. Also see Xiong Yuezhi and Zhou Wu, *Haina baichuan: Shanghai chengshi jingshen yanjiu* [The sea that embraces thousands of rivers: Study of the Shanghai spirit] (Shanghai: Shanghai renmin chubanshe, 2003), 51.

45. For more comprehensive information about skyscrapers in Shanghai and elsewhere, see www.emporis.com/en/wm/bu/?id=103803.

46. "Shanghai Sprawling: The Chinese Mega-city's Best Architecture and Design," Wallpapers online, March 22, 2018, www.wallpaper.com/gallery/architecture/shanghai-architecture-and-design-to-visit.

47. Ren Lizhi, Chen Jiliang, and Liu Qi, "*Shanghai zhongxin dasha de chengshi xing shijian*" [Urban Experiment of the Shanghai Center Building], *Jianzhu xuebao* [Architectural Journal] 606, no. 3 (2019): 35–40.

48. Zheng Shiling, "Challenge and Potential," in Alan and Zheng, eds., *World Cities: Shanghai*, 135.

49. For a list of international bids for buildings in Shanghai, see Zheng Shiling, "Contemporary Architecture Urbanism" in Alan Balfour and Zheng Shiling, eds., *World Cities: Shanghai* (West Sussex, England: Wiley-Academy, 2002), 121.

50. Zheng, "Contemporary Architecture and Urbanism," 120.

51. *Shanghai Art Museum Magazine*, no. 1 (2003), 15.

52. *Shanghai yishujia* [Shanghai Artists], nos. 4–5 (2003): 159.

53. *Shanghai Art Museum Magazine*, no. 1 (2003): 9.

54. Emily Dixon, "Shanghai Opens World's Longest 3D-printed Concrete Bridge," CNN, January 24, 2019, www.cnn.com/style/article/shanghai-3d-printed-bridge-scli-intl/index.html.

55. Yin Luobi, a Ph.D. student at Shanghai Normal University, wrote, "The sturdy skyscrapers recently built in Shanghai symbolize the human being's dream to conquer the heights. But the September 11 terrorist attack to the World Trade Center revealed the paradox of skyscrapers: its endeavor to overcome the globe's gravity is parallel to its enormous power for collapse." *Shanghai yishujia* [Shanghai Artists], nos. 5–6 (2002): 126.

56. Shang Jie, Yan Weiqi, and Xu Danlu, "*Yizuo chengshi de kaifang pinge—tuidong gao zhiliang fazhan de Shanghai lujing*" [The open character of a city: Shanghai's path to promote high-quality development], Guangming website, April 22, 2019, www.ahnews.com.cn/zhuanti/pc/con/1284_109256.html.

57. Zhang Yuan, "*Lianxu 5 nian! Xi Jinping zai Shanghai tuan, dou yao ti zhe 6 ge zi*" [For 5 consecutive years! Xi Jinping's speech at the Shanghai delegation always includes these words], CCTV Network, March 6, 2017, http://m.news.cctv.com/2017/03/06/ARTI Een0shlvUBvsHcMkSYjv170306.shtml.

58. Yang Dongping, *Chengshi jifeng: Beijing he Shanghai de wenhua jingshen* [City monsoon: The cultural spirit of Beijing and Shanghai] (Beijing: Dongfang Press, 1994), 313–314.

59. Yang Zukun and Zeng Hua, *Binfen Shanghai* [Colorful Shanghai] (Shanghai: Fudan daxue chubanshe, 2003), 72.

60. Shi Lei, Qi Ge, and Yuan Min, *Xiang Shanghai xuexi* [Learn from Shanghai] (Shanghai: Shijiezhishi chubanshe, 2003), 6.

61. J. Bruce Jacobs, "Shanghai: An Alternative Centre?" in David S.G. Goodman, ed. *China's Provinces in Reform: Class, Community and Political Culture* (London: Routledge, 1997), 169.

62. Chen Bohai, *Shanghai wenhua tongshi* [History of Shanghai culture] Vol. 1 (Shanghai: Shanghai wenyi chubanshe, 2001), 63; and Zheng Shiling, "Architecture before 1949," in Balfour and Zheng, *World Cities*, 95.

63. James Fallows, "Shanghai Surprise." *Atlantic Monthly*, July 1988, 76.

64. Xie, *Shanghai gaige kaifang shihua*, 34.

65. Cheng Li, *Rediscovering China: Dynamics and Dilemmas of Reform* (Lanham, MD: Rowman & Littlefield Publishers, 1997), 19.

66. State Statistical Bureau of the People's Republic of China, Comp, *China Statistical Yearbook, 1999* (Beijing: Zhongguo tongji chubanshe, 1999), 186.

67. Kang Yan, *Jiedu Shanghai* [Understanding Shanghai] (Shanghai: Shanghai renmin chubanshe, 2001), 387.

68. Li, *Rediscovering China*, 19.

69. According to a recent study, some 78 companies, including the United Parcel Service (UPS) and Honeywell International, have already established regional or Chinese headquarters in Shanghai. Michael S. Chase, Kevin L. Pollpeter, and James C. Mulvenon, *Shanghaied? The Economic and Political Implications of the Flow of Information Technology and Investment across the Taiwan Strait* (Arlington, VA: The Rand National Defense Research Institute, 2004), 79.

70. Shanghai shi tongji ju guojia tongji ju Shanghai diaocha zongdui [Shanghai Statistical Bureau and National Statistical Bureau Shanghai Survey Group], *2018 nian*

Shanghai shi guomin jingji he shehui fazhan tongji gongbao [2018 Shanghai National Economic and Social Development Statistical Report]; and He Wei, "Shanghai sets priorities for attracting investment," *China Daily*, April 22, 2019, www.chinadaily.com.cn /a/201904/22/WS5cbcf7f8a3104842260b7642.html.

71. Liu Yuanyuan, Wang Chun, and Tan Ling, "Chuangxin, rongzhu gao zhiliang fazhan bu jie dongli" [Innovation: Melting a high quality and sustainable development], China IPR, website, June 5, 2019 www.iprchn.com/cipnews/news_content.aspx?newsId =116467.

72. The Shanghai Municipal Government Office, *Shanghai, China* (Shanghai: City Government Publication, 2004), 1.

73. Shi, Qi, and Yuan, *Xiang Shanghai xuexi*, 13.

74. Xie, *Shanghai gaige kaifang shihua*, 103–104, 116.

75. Raksha Arora, "Homeownership Soars in China," March 1, 2005, Gallup Polls, www .gallup.com/poll/15082/Homeownership-Soars-China.aspx.

76. Xie, *Shanghai gaige kaifang shihua*, 120.

77. Lu, *Shanghai niaokan*, 97.

78. Luo Jun, ed. *Modu manbu* [Walk in the magic capital Shanghai] (Shanghai: Shanghai renmin chubanshe, 2018), 196.

79. Xie, *Shanghai gaige kaifang shihua*, 116–119.

80. Zhang Minyan, *"Zhe xiang 'xin shishang' gongzuo, Xi Jinping feichang kanzhong"* [Xi Jinping very much values this "new fashion" work], Xinhua News Agency Net, June 6, 2019, www.xinhuanet.com/politics/xxjxs/2019-06/04/c_1124581549.htm.

81. Dai Lili and Li Yibo, "Waimai, zhengzai huimie women de xia yidai?" [Food delivery is destroying our next generation?], *Liaowang zhiku* [Outlook Think Tank], September 18, 2017, https://web.archive.org/web/20170919050759/https://wemedia.ifeng.com/30193920/ wemedia.shtml.

82. Chen Yani, *Shanghai 15 nian* [Fifteen years in Shanghai] (Beijing: Xinhua chubanshe, 2003), 168.

83. Daniel Ren, "London-Shanghai Stock Connect Goes Live, Allowing Foreign Firms to List Their Shares in Mainland China for the First Time," *South China Morning Post*, June 17, 2019, www.scmp.com/business/companies/article/3014809/london-shanghai -stock-connect-goes-live-allowing-foreign-firms.

84. Hu Min, "New foreign investment law takes effect," Shine website, January 1, 2020, www.shine.cn/biz/economy/2001019012/.

85. Amanda Lee, "Xi Jinping's market opening pledges fail to impress European firms who have 'heard it all before,'" *South China Morning Post*, November 6, 2019, www.scmp .com/economy/china-economy/article/2171931/xi-jinpings-market-opening-pledges-fail -impress-european-firms.

86. Bob Davis, "When the World Opened the Gates of China," *Wall Street Journal*, July 27, 2018, www.wsj.com/articles/when-the-world-opened-the-gates-of-china-1532701482.

87. Gabriel Wildau, "Shanghai Free-trade Zone Struggles for Relevance," *Financial Times*, September 26, 2015, www.ft.com/content/8cec0faa-6364-11e5-9846-de406ccb37f2.

88. Lee, "Xi Jinping's Market Opening Pledges Fail."

89. Pamela Yatsko, *New Shanghai: The Rocky Rebirth of China's Legendary City* (New York: John Wiley & Sons, 2000), 213.

90. Liu Yuanyuan, Tan Lin, and Wang Chun, "Gao zhiliang fazhan" [High Quality Development], *Keji ribao* [Science and Technology Daily], April 10, 2019, www.stdaily.com /zhuanti01/kjrbzl/2019-04/10/content_759944.shtml.

91. *Meiri toutiao* [Daily Headline News], September 25, 2018, https://kknews.cc/zh-my/ news/o293ja6.html.

92. Gao Qian and Wu Yebai, "Shanghai gaozhiliang fazhan zhanlue lujing yanjiu" [Research on the path of Shanghai's high-quality development strategy], Shanghai shi

renmin zhengfu fazhan yanjiu zhongxin Website [The Development Research Center of Shanghai Municipal People's Government Website], April 15, 2019, http://fzzx.sh.gov.cn/LT/KDUCO9973.html.

93. Xie, *Shanghai gaige kaifang shihua*, 77.

94. Liu, Tan, and Wang, "Gao zhiliang fazhan."

95. Shang, Yan, and Xu, *"Yizuo chengshi de kaifang pinge."*

96. Meiri Jingji Xinwen net [Daily Economic News Net], July 19, 2019, https://ishare.ifeng.com/mediaShare/home/373005/media.

97. The Planet Institute, "Weishenme Shanghai bei chengwei 'modu?' "

98. Ibid.

99. Xu Xiaoqing, Pan Qing, and Zhou Rui, " 'Kaifang 100 tiao': Goule weilai luxian tu" ["Open 100" outlines the future roadmap], *Liaowang xinwen zhoukan* [Outlook News Weekly], August 7, 2018, http://sh.xinhuanet.com/2018-08/07/c_137371546.htm.

100. Wang Hongyi, "Shanghai to Develop as an International Trade Center," *China Daily*, November 11, 2016, www.chinadaily.com.cn/cndy/2016-11/11/content_27342165.htm.

101. Xie, *Shanghai gaige kaifang shihua*, 66–67.

102. Shang, Yan, and Xu, "Yizuo chengshi de kaifang pinge."

103. Xie, *Shanghai gaige kaifang shihua*, 77.

104. *Dongfang Zaobao* [Oriental Morning News], March 26, 2009.

105. Duan Siyu, "Dui biao niuyue lundun–Shanghai guoji jinrong zhongxin jianshe jinrr chongci jieduan" [Targeting New York and London: Shanghai International Financial Center construction into the sprint stage]. *Diyi caijing* [China Business News], March 15, 2019, www.yicai.com/news/100139640.html.

106. Cheng Li, "Reclaiming the 'Head of the Dragon': Shanghai as China's Center for International Finance and Shipping," *China Leadership Monitor* 28 (Spring 2009): 8; and Duan, "Dui biao niuyue lundun."

107. Xie, *Shanghai gaige kaifang shihua*, 82.

108. Shanghai Stock Exchange website, www.sse.com.cn/aboutus/sseintroduction/introduction/.

109. Duan, "Dui biao niuyue lundun."

110. Ji Shuoming and Liu Ying, "Zhongguo tiaozhan meiyuan baquan" [China challenges U.S. dollar hegemony], *Yazhou zhoukan* [Asia Weekly], April 2, 2009, https://web.archive.org/web/20090405033312/http://www.dwnews.com/gb/MainNews/Forums/BackStage/2009_4_2_4_12_17_308.html.

111. Xuan Zhaoqiang, "Shanghai: Chutai 'kuoda kaifang 100 tiao' dazao quanmian kaifang xin gaodi" [Shanghai: Introduced "enlarged and open 100" to create a new open highland], Renmin Net, July 12, 2018, http://sh.people.com.cn/n2/2018/0712/c134768-31804687.html.

112. Daniel Ren, "China Has Six of the World's 10 Busiest Container Ports, Spurred by Booming Trade and a State Coffer That Invests in Public Works," *South China Morning Post*, April 13, 2019, www.scmp.com/business/companies/article/3005945/china-has-six-worlds-10-busiest-container-ports-spurred-booming.

113. The Planet Institute, "Weishenme Shanghai bei cheng wei 'modu?' "

114. *Dongfang Zaobao* [Oriental Morning News], March 26, 2009.

115. http://info.cncshipping.com/i/20090325/12379395719335.shtml.

116. http://tech.it168.com/erp/2008-01-16/200801162026125.shtml.

117. *Dongfang Zaobao* [Oriental Morning News], March 26, 2009.

118. In 2008, the world's ten busiest container ports were Singapore, Shanghai, Hong Kong, Shenzhen, Pusan, Dubai, Guangzhou, Ningbo, Zhoushan, and Qingdao.

119. For a more detailed discussion of the Yangtze Strategy, see www.chinanews.com.cn//news/2005/2005-12-12/8/663857.shtml.

120. Ibid.

121. Xuan Zhaoqiang, "Shanghai yang shan gang daidong quyu tengfei" [Shanghai Yangshan Port drives regional take-off]. Jiangsu Net, July 11, 2006, web.archive.org/web /20080414192758/http://www.jschina.com.cn/gb/jschina/news/zt200602/node21263/ node21276/userobject1ai1293825.html.

122. Ren, "China Has Six of the World's 10 Busiest Container Ports."

123. Liu, Wang, and Tan, "Chuangxin, rongzhu gao zhiliang fazhan bu jie dongli."

124. Ibid.

125. Wang Zhan, Weng Shilie, Yang Shengli, and Wang Zhen, *Zhuanxing shengji de xinzhanlue yu xinduice* [New strategy and new measures for transformation and upgrading] (Shanghai: Shanghai shehui kexueyuan chubanshe, 2015), 26–27.

126. Ibid., 154.

127. Ibid.

128. Ibid., 156.

129. Ibid., 12.

130. Ibid., 29.

131. Gao and Wu, "Shanghai gao zhiliang fazhan zhanlue lujing yanjiu."

132. Wang Zhan, Weng Shilie, Yang Shengli, and Wang Zhen. *Zhuanxing shengji de xinzhanlue yu xinduice*, 1.

133. Wang Chun, Tan Lin, and Liu Yuanyuan, "Rencai, jihuo gao zhiliang fazhan di yi ziyuan" [High quality human resources should be seen as the top resources], Keji ribao [Science and Technology Daily], April 23, 2019, www.stdaily.com/zhuanti01/kjrbzl/2019 -04/23/content_762038.shtml.

134. Lu Dong, "Ke chuang ban zhengshi kai ban! Zhongguo ziben shichang ying lai lishi xing shike" [The science and technology stock board officially opened! China's capital market ushers in a historic moment], *Guancha zhe* [Observer], June 13, 2019, www. guancha.cn/economy/2019_06_13_505437.shtml.

135. Lin Zehong, "Zhi hua 22 tian Shanghai kechuangban kaiban." [It takes only 22 days for the Shanghai Sci-Tech Innovation Board to open], *Shijie ribao* [World Journal], June 14, 2019.

136. Wang Zhen and Li Kaisheng, eds., *Tanxun guoji hezuo xinjiyu: shoujie "yidaiyilu" Shanghai luntan lunji* [Exploring New Opportunities for International Cooperation: The First Shanghai Forum on the "Belt and Road Initiative"] (Shanghai: Shanghai shehui kexueyuan chubanshe, 2018), 133–164.

137. Ibid., 159.

CHAPTER 6

1. Cheng Li, *Chinese Politics in the Xi Era: Reassessing Collective Leadership* (Washington, DC: Brookings Institution, 2016), 111–114.

2. Ibid., 113.

3. For a detailed discussion of the growing importance of provincial leaders in the reform era, see Cheng Li, "After Hu, Who? Provincial Leaders Await Promotion," *China Leadership Monitor*, no. 1 (Winter 2002).

4. Cheng Li, "Shanghai Gang: Force for Stability or Fuse for Conflict?" *China Leadership Monitor*, no. 2 (Winter 2002): 1–18.

5. Gao Xin, "Xi Jinping yu Zeng Qinghong de guanxi shi xue nong yu shui" [The relationship between Xi Jinping and Zeng Qinghong is blood thicker than water], *Ziyou yazhou diantai* [Radio Free Asia Website], June 21, 2016, www.rfa.org/mandarin/zhuanlan /yehuazhongnanhai/gx-06212016102229.html.

6. Li, *Chinese Politics in the Xi Era*, 93–94.

7. Cheng Li, "Was the Shanghai Gang Shanghaied? The Fall of Chen Liangyu and the Survival of Jiang Zemin's Faction," *China Leadership Monitor*, no. 20 (Winter 2007): 12–13.

8. For a detailed analysis of *mishu* and *mishuzhang*, see Li Wei and Lucian Pye, "The Ubiquitous Role of the *Mishu* in Chinese Politics," *China Quarterly* 132 (December 1992): 913–936; and Cheng Li, *China's Leaders: The New Generation* (Lanham, MD: Rowman & Littlefield Publishers, 2001), 127–174.

9. Liu Dong, "Xi Jiang zhenying 'zuoyou fenming'" [The Xi-Jiang camp: The division between "the left and the right"], *Mingjing yuekan* [Mirror Monthly], October 2014.

10. Li, *Chinese Politics in the Xi Era*, 262–263.

11. Ibid., 249–300.

12. Cheng Li, "China's Two Li's: Frontrunners in the Race to Succeed Hu Jintao," *China Leadership Monitor*, no. 22 (Fall 2007); also see Shi Guangjian, "Dixi Yang Weize luoma, Li Yuanchao kaishi mafan" [The fall of Protégé Yang Weize begins to cause trouble for Li Yuanchao], *Mingjing News* [Mirror News], January 4, 2015, www.mirrorbooks.com/MIB/magazine/news.aspx?ID=M000002407.

13. Yi He, "Tuanpai laojiang Li Yuanchao de chulu" [The future of *tuanpai* veteran leader Li Yuanchao], *Kaifang Net* [Open Net], March 9, 2013, www.open.com.hk/content.php?id=1199#.X6ZIVYhKg2w.

14. Chen was the first party secretary of Shanghai, Hu was chairman of the Shanghai Municipal People's Congress, and Wang was mayor.

15. Xiao Chong, *Zhonggong disidai mengren* [The Fourth Generation of Leaders of the Chinese Communist Party] (Hong Kong: Xiafeier guoji chubangongsi, 1998), 23; and Li, *China's Leaders*, 161–162.

16. For a more detailed discussion of Zeng's political connections in Beijing, see Li, *China's Leaders*, 160–161.

17. Xiao, *Zhonggong disidai mengren*, 18.

18. For more on the power struggle between Jiang and his rivals, see Cheng Li and Lynn White, "The Fifteenth Central Committee of the Chinese Communist Party: Full-Fledged Technocratic Leadership with Partial Control by Jiang Zemin," *Asian Survey* 38, no. 3 (March 1998): 236–239.

19. Chen Xitong served as a top leader in Beijing for twelve years, first as mayor and then party secretary. Reportedly, Chen and Jiang Zemin competed for the position of general secretary after Zhao Ziyang's ousting in the wake of the Tiananmen incident in 1989. Chen resented the fact that the post went to Jiang, who was then party secretary of Shanghai. Seth Faison, "Ex-Party Chief in Beijing Gets 16 Years in Prison," *New York Times*, July 31, 1998, 3.

20. When he was the man with final say over land leasing during the construction fever in the early 1990s in Beijing, Chen Xitong amassed RMB 24 million for his own use. Chen was sentenced to serve a sixteen-year term in jail.

21. "Zeng Qinghong de dali jingangzhang, ba Xi Jinping tuishang dawei" [Zeng Qinghong pushes for granting important position to Xi Jinping], *Da Shijian* [Major Event], December 2, 2014; also see https://boxun.com/news/gb/china/2014/12/201412021542.shtml.

22. See John P. Burns, "Strengthening Central CCP Control of Leadership Selection," *China Quarterly* 138 (June 1994): 472.

23. In an important speech delivered at the 80th anniversary of the founding of the CCP in 2001, Jiang claimed that the party should be representative of three components of society: advanced social productive forces, advanced culture, and the interests of the overwhelming majority, known as the "theory of the three represents."

24. *Shijie ribao* [World Journal], November 1, 1999, A8.

25. "Jiang Zemin ren Chen Liangyu 'zuofeng badao, shenghuo milan' tongyi yanban"

[Jiang Zemin recognizes Chen Liangy's "domineering style and eroded life" and agrees to strictly handle this case], *Yazhou zhoukan* [Asia Weekly], September 28, 2006, www.wen xuecity.com/news/2006/09/28/314844.html.

26. *Pingguo ribao* [Apple daily], December 7, 2006, 1.

27. The exception is Yunnan, which had only one seat.

28. See Cheng Li and Lynn White, "The Fifteenth Central Committee of the Chinese Communist Party: Full-Fledged Technocratic Leadership with Partial Control by Jiang Zemin," *Asian Survey*, 38, no. 3 (March 1998): 247.

29. Li, "Was the Shanghai Gang Shanghaied?" 5.

30. For a detailed discussion of the impact of macroeconomic control measures on Shanghai and elite politics related to the policy initiatives, see Cheng Li, "Cooling Shanghai Fever: Macroeconomic Control and Its Geopolitical Implications," *China Leadership Monitor*, no. 12 (Fall 2004).

31. Li, "Was the Shanghai Gang Shanghaied?"

32. Cheng Li, "Shanghai Gang: Force for Stability or Fuse for Conflict?" *China Leadership Monitor*, no. 2 (Winter 2002): 3.

33. Li, "Cooling Shanghai Fever," 12.

34. *Straits Times* (Singapore), July 10, 2004.

35. *Shijie ribao* [World Journal], July 11, 2004, A1.

36. See www.chinesenewsnet.com, July 28, 2004; also see Cheng Li, "Cooling Shanghai Fever."

37. Li, "Was the Shanghai Gang Shanghaied?"

38. Cheng Li, "Reclaiming the "Head of the Dragon": Shanghai as China's Center for International Finance and Shipping." *China Leadership Monitor*, no. 28 (Spring 2009).

39. *Diyi caijing ribao* [China Business News], February 6, 2006, 2.

40. For a detailed discussion of the economic and physical landscape changes in Chongqing, see Howard W. French, "Big, Gritty Chongqing, City of 12 Million, Is China's Model for Future," *New York Times*, June 1, 2007, A15.

41. *Duowei yuekan* [Chinese News Monthly], March 2009.

42. For the data on other provinces and cities, see http://economy.enorth.com.cn/system /2009/04/24/003980260.shtml.

43. *Meiri xinbao* [Everyday News], April 22, 2009.

44. http://economy.enorth.com.cn/system/2009/04/24/003980260.shtml; Li Zhongyuan, "Shanghai GDP zengsu weihe daoshu diyi" [Why Shanghai's GDP growth rate is the lowest in China], Dajiang wang [Jiangxi News Net], May 4, 2009, www.jxnews. com.cn/jxcomment/system/2009/05/04/011095702.shtml.

45. Ma Hui, "Binhai zhuigan pudong" [Binhai District is catching up with Pudong District], Xinlang shangpin [Xinlang Style], January 1, 2009, http://style.sina.com.cn/news /2009-01-13/082631317.shtml.

46. Tan Jialong, "Shanghai jian guoji jinrong zhongxin yu hangyun zhongxin yijian chutai shimo" [The insider's story of the approval for the proposal of building Shanghai into a center of an international finance and shipping], *Zhongguo jingji zhoukan* [China's economic weekly], April 20, 2009.

47. Ibid.

48. Ibid.

49. Ibid.

50. Yu Zhengsheng, "Shanghai jinrong zhongxin jianshe mianlin xin de lishi jiyu" [Shanghai's financial center construction is facing new historical opportunities], Wangyi caijing [NetEase Finance], May 15, 2009, http://money.163.com/09/0515/09/59BIDQSG00 253CDO.html.

51. Xi Jinping, "Shanghai si ge zhongxin jianshe bixu qude tupo" [Shanghai's four

centers must make breakthroughs], *Diyi caijing ribao* [China Business News], May 25, 2017, http://news.sina.com.cn/c/2007-05-25/035813070154.shtml.

52. Li Qiang, "Hu su zhe jiaojie chu jiang sheli chang sanjiao yiti hua shifan qu," *Soho Net*, March 6, 2019, www.sohu.com/a/299471416_222256.

53. Ibid.

54. Shanghai zhengda yanjiusuo, *Changjiangbian de Zhongguo—Dashanghai guoji dushiquan jianshe yu guojia fazhan zhanlue* [China on the Yangtze River: Construction of Greater Shanghai and the National Development Strategy] (Shanghai: Xuelin chubanshe, 2003), 237.

55. For more discussion of this topic, see Cheng Li with Ryan McElveen and Zachary Balin, *Xi Jinping's Protégés: Rising Elite Groups in the Chinese Leadership* (Washington, DC: Brookings Institution, forthcoming).

56. Li, "The 'Shanghai Gang,'" 6, and Li, *Chinese Politics in the Xi Era*, 263.

57. For more detailed discussion of Xi's Zhejiang Gang, see Li, *Chinese Politics in the Xi Era*, 343–345.

58. Betty Peh-T'I Wei, *Shanghai: Crucible of Modern China* (Oxford: Oxford University Press, 1987), 50.

59. Lucian W. Pye, "Foreword," in Christopher Howe, ed. *Shanghai, Revolution and Development in an Asian Metropolis* (Cambridge: Cambridge University Press, 1981), xi.

CHAPTER 7

1. Bernard Gwertzman, "U.S. and China Sign Agreements: Carter Sees an 'Irreversible' Trend," *New York Times*, February 1, 1979, A16.

2. Jonathan D. Spence, *To Change China: Western Advisers in China, 1620–1960* (Boston, MA: Little, Brown Publishers, 1969), 292.

3. *Beijing Review* 42, no. 5 (February 1–7, 1999): 17.

4. Du Ruiqing, *Chinese Higher Education* (New York: St. Martin's Press, 1992), 101.

5. See, for example, Patrick Tyler, *A Great Wall: Six Presidents and China* (New York: Public Affairs, 2000); David M. Lampton, Joyce A. Madancy, and Kristen M. Williams, *A Relationship Restored: Trends in U.S.-China Educational Exchanges, 1978–1984* (Washington, DC: National Academy Press, 1986).

6. These 52 students and scholars were middle-aged, with the oldest being 49 and the youngest being 36. They completed their undergraduate education before the start of the Cultural Revolution. They came from twenty-two educational and research institutions across China. In the United States, they first studied conversational English at American University and Georgetown University in Washington, DC, for a few months and then dispersed to the University of California at Berkeley, Massachusetts Institute of Technology, Columbia University, the University of Wisconsin, Princeton University, and other institutions to complete postgraduate study and research in the natural sciences and engineering. See Karl Li and Richard Elwell, "Chatting with the Chinese," *American Education* (May 1979): 17–19; and *Beijing Review* 42, no. 5 (February 1–7, 1999): 17.

7. *Beijing Review* 32, no. 5 (January 30, 1989): 39.

8. Ministry of Education of the People's Republic of China website, "2018 niandu woguo chuguo liuxue renyuan qingkuang tongji."

9. Ibid.

10. "All Places of Origin," Open Doors website, https://opendoorsdata.org/data/international-students/all-places-of-origin/.

11. Li Cheng, ed., *Bridging Minds across the Pacific: U.S.-China Educational Exchanges 1978–2003* (Lanham, MD: Lexington Books, 2005), 1–24, 69–109.

12. Alexandra Yoon-Hendricks, "Visa Restrictions for Chinese Students Alarm

Academia," *New York Times*, July 27, 2018, https://cn.nytimes.com/usa/20180727/visa-restrictions-chinese-students/dual/.

13. De Xiansheng, "550 wan huaren zai mei rencai xianzhuang" [Current situation of human resources among 5.5 million Chinese in the United States], *Zhihu* [Know how], June 16, 2020, https://zhuanlan.zhihu.com/p/148860475.

14. Cheng Li's database. Also, Li, *Bridging Minds across the Pacific*, 69–109.

15. Huang Yasheng, "Zhishi yu guojia anquan, meiguo huaren xuezhe de shengcun weiji," [Knowledge and national security: The survival crisis of Chinese American scholars], *Zhongmei Yinxiang* website [U.S.-China Perception Monitor], May 29, 2019, www.uscnpm.com/model_item.html?action=view&table=article&id=18662.

16. De, "550 wan huaren zai mei rencai xianzhuang."

17. "Meiguo gei Zhongguo xuesheng de qianzheng zhou jian" [The United States drastically reduces visas for Chinese students], Sina website, May 7, 2018, http://edu.sina.com.cn/a/2018-05-07/doc-ifzfkmth9996575.shtml.

18. Emily Feng, "FBI Urges Universities to Monitor Some Chinese Students and Scholars in the U.S.," NPR, June 28, 2019, www.npr.org/2019/06/28/728659124/fbi-urges-universities-to-monitor-some-chinese-students-and-scholars-in-the-u-s.

19. Yang Ming, "Zhongguo fu mei youke renshu 15 nianlai shouci xiajiang" [The number of Chinese tourists to the United States has fallen for the first time in 15 years], Voice of America, May 28, 2019, www.voachinese.com/a/Chinese-Tourism-To-US-Drops-For-First-Time-In-15-Years-20190528/4935327.html.

20. "Proclamation on the Suspension of Entry as Nonimmigrants of Certain Students and Researchers from the People's Republic of China," The White House, May 29, 2020, www.whitehouse.gov/presidential-actions/proclamation-suspension-entry-nonimmigrants-certain-students-researchers-peoples-republic-china/.

21. CNN Transcripts, February 13, 2018, http://transcripts.cnn.com/TRANSCRIPTS/1802/13/cnr.04.html; and Feng, "FBI Urges Universities."

22. Mark Warner, "Global China: Assessing China's Growing Role in the World," remarks at public event, Brookings Institution, May, 9, 2019, www.brookings.edu/events/global-china-assessing-chinas-growing-role-in-the-world/.

23. Feng, "FBI Urges Universities."

24. Peter Waldman, "The U.S. Is Purging Chinese Cancer Researchers from Top Institutions," *Bloomberg Businessweek*, June 13, 2019, www.bloomberg.com/news/features/2019-06-13/the-u-s-is-purging-chinese-americans-from-top-cancer-research.

25. Ibid.

26. Christopher Wray, "China's Attempt to Influence U.S. Institutions" (Speech at the Hudson Institute, Washington, DC, July 7, 2020), FBI, www.fbi.gov/news/speeches/the-threat-posed-by-the-chinese-government-and-the-chinese-communist-party-to-the-economic-and-national-security-of-the-united-states.

27. Ibid.

28. See, for example, L. Rafael Reif, "Letter to the MIT Community: Immigration Is a Kind of Oxygen," *MIT News*, June 25, 2019, http://news.mit.edu/2019/letter-community-immigration-is-oxygen-0625http://news.mit.edu/2019/letter-community-immigration-is-oxygen-0625.

29. Timothy Puko and Kate O'Keeffe, "U.S. Targets Efforts by China, Others to Recruit Government Scientists," *Wall Street Journal*, June 10, 2019, www.wsj.com/articles/energy-department-bans-personnel-from-foreign-talent-recruitment-programs-11560182546.

30. A total of 4,323,200 students completed their degrees or programs. Ministry of Education of the People's Republic of China website, "2018 niandu woguo chuguo liuxue renyuan qingkuang tongji."

31. Shu Xincheng, *Jin dai Zhongguo liu xue shi* [History of study abroad in contempo-

rary China], (Shanghai: Shanghai wenhua chubanshe, 1989), 1. The first edition was published in 1927.

32. Teng Ssu-yu and John Fairbank. *China's Response to the West: A Documentary Survey.* (Cambridge, MA: Harvard University Press, 1954), 276.

33. Wang Qisheng, "Foreign-Educated Chinese," in Hong Kong Museum of History, comp., *Boundless Learning: Foreign-Educated Students of Modern China* (Hong Kong: The Hong Kong Museum of History, 2003), 14.

34. Quoted from An Yu and Zhou Mian. *Liuxuesheng yu zhongwai wenhua jiaoliu* [Foreign-educated students and China's cultural exchange with the outside world] (Nanjing: Nanjing daxue chubanshe, 2000), 4.

35. Hong Kong Museum of History, *Boundless Learning*, 17.

36. For the various ways to divide the periods of China's study abroad movements, see Zhang Ning, "Zhongguo liuxue yanjiu wenti ji sikao" [Research issues and thinking about Chinese overseas study] in Min Weifang and Wang Yongda, eds., *Quanguo chuguo liuxue gongzuo yanjiuhui chengli shizhounian jinian wenji* [The 10th anniversary commemorative collection of the National Research Association of Overseas Study] (Beijing: Beijing daxue chubanshe, 2002), 104; and Wang Y. C., *Chinese Intellectuals and the West: 1872–1949* (Chapel Hill: University of North Carolina Press, 1966), 42.

37. Wang, "Foreign-Educated Chinese," 10.

38. Two students, however, refused to return. They were Tan Yaoxun and Yung Kwai, the nephew of Yung Wing. Both later graduated from Yale and worked at the Chinese embassy. www.chinesenewsnet.com, April 23, 2004. However, nongovernment-sponsored Chinese were still able to study in the United States during this period.

39. Thomas E. LaFargue, *China's First Hundred: Educational Mission Students in the United States, 1872–1881* (Seattle, WA: Washington State University Press, 1987), 53–66.

40. *Nanfang Zhoumo* [Southern Weekend], April 15, 2005.

41. An and Zhou, *Liuxuesheng yu zhongwai wenhua jiaoliu*, 47.

42. Wang, "Foreign-Educated Chinese," 13.

43. Li Xisuo and Liu Jilin. *Jindai Zhongguo de liumei jiaoyu* [U.S.-educated Chinese and contemporary China] (Tianjin: Tianjin guji chubanshe, 2000), 366.

44. Huang Fu-ch'ing, *Chinese Students in Japan in the Late Ch'ing Period*, translated by Katherine P. K. Whitaker (Tokyo: The Centre for East Asian Cultural Studies, 1982).

45. Zhongguo kexueyuan chuguo liuxue gongzuo yanjiuhui, "Zhongguo jinxiandai liuxue jiaoyu shishu" [A history of overseas study in contemporary China] in Min Weifang and Wang Yongda, eds., *Quanguo chuguo liuxue gongzuo yanjiuhui chengli shizhounian jinian wenji* [The 10th Anniversary Commemorative Collection of the National Studying Abroad Work Research Association] (Beijing: Beijing daxue chubanshe, 2002), 447.

46. The Hong Kong Museum of History, *Boundless Learning*, 111.

47. Zhang Yufa, "Returned Chinese Students from America and the Chinese Leadership, 1846–1949)." *Chinese Studies in History* 35, no. 3, (Spring 2002): 53.

48. Li and Liu, *Jindai Zhongguo de liumei jiaoyu*, 64–114.

49. Li and Liu, *Jindai Zhongguo de liumei jiaoyu*, 1.

50. Tang Quanqi and Wang Huilan, "21 shiji Zhongguo liuxue jiaoyu quxiang fenxi" [An analysis of the trends in China's overseas education in the twenty-first century], *Chuguo liuxue gongzuo yanjiu* [Research on studies overseas], no. 3 (1998): 4.

51. Cao Cong, "Modernizing Science through Educating the Elite," in Michael Agelasto and Bob Adamson, eds., *Higher Education in Post-Mao China* (Hong Kong: Hong Kong University Press, 1998), 107.

52. Zhang, "Zhongguo liuxue yanjiu wenti ji sikao," 101–106.

53. G. Martin Wilbur, "Foreword," in *Chinese Intellectuals and the West: 1872–1949*, v.

54. Yang Xiaojing and Miao Danguo, "Xin Zhongguo chuguo liuxue jiaoyu zhengce de

yanbian guocheng ji duice yanjiu" [Research on the Evolvement Process and Countermeasures of China's Educational Policy for Studying Abroad], *Xin jiaoyu shidai* [New Education Era], October 2015, 2–3.

55. Wei Nengtao. "Xin shiqi chuguo liuxue jiaoyu niaokan" [An overview of overseas study in the new era], in Min and Wang, eds., *Quanguo chuguo liuxue gongzuo yanjiuhui chengli shizhounian jinian wenji*, 435. From 1956 to 1957, China sent fifty students to study languages in capitalist countries. From 1957 to 1965, China sent about 200 students to study in Italy, Belgium, Switzerland, Sweden, Norway, Denmark, and other countries. Most studied languages; only 21 studied natural sciences. Zhongguo kexueyuan chuguo liuxue gongzuo yanjiuhui. "Zhongguo jinxiandai liuxue jiaoyu shishu" [A history of overseas study in contemporary China], in Min and Wang, eds., *Quanguo chuguo liuxue gongzuo yanjiuhui chengli shizhounian jinian wenji*, 449.

56. Zhongguo kexueyuan chuguo liuxue gongzuo yanjiuhui, "*Zhongguo jinxiandai liuxue jiaoyu shishu*," 450.

57. Ibid.

58. For more discussion about the difficult experiences of returnees from the West during the Mao era, see Ye Weili, *Seeking Modernity in China's Name: Chinese Students in the United States, 1900–1927* (Stanford, CA: Stanford University Press 2001).

59. Zhongguo kexueyuan chuguo liuxue gongzuo yanjiuhui. "*Zhongguo jinxiandai liuxue jiaoyu shishu*," 450.

60. Ibid.

61. For further discussion about Zhou's role in the reestablishment of educational exchanges between the United States and China and the "success of long-standing American cultural and scientific policies toward China," see Mary Brown Bullock, "American Science and Chinese Nationalism: Reflections on the Career of Zhou Peiyuan," in Gail Hershatter et al., eds., *Remapping China: Fissures in Historical Terrain* (Stanford, CA: Stanford University Press, 1999), 210.

62. Y. C. Wang observed that from 1906, Japanese-trained men began to influence educational policy in China, and they "introduced a number of changes along Japanese lines." But as more American-trained students returned and grew in influence, "a complete overhaul of the educational system took place in 1922." Wang, *Chinese Intellectuals and the West: 1872–1949*, 362.

63. Li, *China's Leaders*, 33–34.

64. Li, *Chinese Politics in the Xi Era*, 121.

65. Hong Yung Lee, *The Politics of the Chinese Cultural Revolution: A Case Study* (Berkeley, CA: University of California Press, 1978); Susan L. Shirk, "Educational Reform and Political Backlash: Recent Changes in Chinese Educational Policy," *Comparative Education Review* 23, no. 2 (June 1979): 185; and Anita Chen, "Dispelling Misconceptions about the Red Guard Movement: The Necessity of Re-Examining Cultural Revolution Factionalism and Periodization," *Journal of Contemporary China* 1 (September 1992): 62–85.

66. Liu Xiaodong and Tian Jun, *Zhongguo liuxuesheng de sishinian 1978–2018* [Studying Abroad: A forty-year history, 1978–2018] (Hong Kong: China Tourism Press, 2019), 76.

67. *Beijing qingnian bao* [Beijing youth daily], December 12, 2003, 1.

68. "*Shanghai 'haigui' renshu quanguo ju shou zhan zongshu si fen zhi yi*" [Shanghai's "foreign-educated returnees" rank first in the country, accounting for a quarter of the total], *Xinmin Wanbao* [Xinmin evening news], January 31, 2009.

69. Han Chunli, "Zuixin zuiquan Shanghai luohu banfa" [The latest and most complete channels to settle down in Shanghai]. *Laodong bao* [Labor daily], May 20, 2018, www.sohu .com/a/232260298_467882.

70. "Huanying jiaru Shanghai haigui zhongxin huiyuan julebu" [Welcome to Shanghai

Haigui Center Member Club]. Shanghai Returnee Center website, March 31, 2019, www.sohu.com/a/305043384_653397.

71. Han, "Zuixin zui quan Shanghai luohu banfa."

72. Ibid.

73. *Jiefang ribao* [Liberation daily], January 1, 2005, 1.

74. "2018 nian laihua liuxue tongji" [Statistics on foreign students in China in 2018]. Ministry of Education of the PRC website, April 12, 2019, www.moe.gov.cn/jyb_xwfb/gzdt _gzdt/s5987/201904/t20190412_377692.html.

75. "Chuguo liuxue wushi nian shuju huizong" [Fifty years of study abroad data summary], Meiri toutiao [Daily Headlines], April 10, 2019, https://kknews.cc/education/ kvrjoxp.html.

76. Individuals under the age of 18 who go abroad to attend high school are called "*xiao liuxue sheng.*" According to China's Ministry of Education, these "*xiao liuxue sheng*" are not considered to be *liuxue renyuan.* "Chuguo liuxue gongzuo qingkuang fabuhui" [Press conference on the work of studying abroad], Ministry of Education of the PRC website, February 16, 2004, http://jsj.moe.gov.cn/news/1/263.shtml.

77. Zengyi Chang, "The CUSBEA Program: Twenty Years After." *IUBMB Life* 61, no. 6 (June 2009): 555–565; and Yuan Qing and Yue Tingting, "Xin shiqi Zhongguo liumei jiaoyu de fazhan licheng he qushi" [The development history and trends of Chinese foreign students studying in the United States in the new era], *Zhongguo shehui kexue wang* [Chinese social science net], May 6, 2015, http://hprc.cssn.cn/gsyj/whs/jys/201505/ t20150506_4111942.html.

78. Li, *Bridging Minds across the Pacific*, 77.

79. "Chuguo liuxue wushi nian shuju huizong."

80. Ibid.

81. Ibid.

82. Miao Danguo, *Chuguo liuxue liushi nian* [Sixty years of studying abroad] (Beijing: Zhongyang wenxian chubanshe, 2010).

83. Ministry of Education of the PRC, "Ge lei liuxue renyuan qingkuang tongji jieguo" [Statistics of various types of overseas students], Ministry of Education of the PRC website, www.moe.gov.cn/s78/A20/gjs_left/moe_851/201006/t20100628_90108.html.

84. Ibid.

85. Wei, "Xin shiqi chuguo liuxue jiaoyu niaokan," 442.

86. Yuan and Yue, "Xin shiqi Zhongguo liumei jiaoyu de fazhan licheng he qushi."

87. Chen Zhu, "2014 nian chuguo liuxue qushi baogao" [Report on the status and trends of study abroad in 2014], *Zhongguo qingnian bao* [China Youth Daily], March 24, 2014, http://edu.people.com.cn/n/2014/0324/c1053-24714300.html.

88. "Chuguo liuxue wushi nian shuju huizong."

89. Youyou Zhou, "The Impact of Chinese Students in the US, Charted and Mapped." *Quartz*, October 2, 2018, https://qz.com/1410768/the-number-of-chinese-students-in-the -us-charted-and-mapped/.

90. Ibid.

91. Wang Shi, "2014 Zhongguo chuguo liuxuerenyuan zaizeng" [Continuing increase in Chinese students and scholars studying abroad]; and *Shijie ribao* [World Journal], March 25, 2014, A12.

92. Yuan and Yue, "Xin shiqi Zhongguo liumei jiaoyu de fazhan licheng he qushi."

93. "A New Age of Sino-U.S. Higher Education Cooperation," A 2019 Duke International Forum held at the Duke Kunshan University in Kunshan, China, December 16–18, 2019.

94. Ibid.

95. Yuan and Yue, "Xin shiqi Zhongguo liumei jiaoyu de fazhan licheng he qushi."
96. Ibid.
97. "Chuguo liuxue wushi nian shuju huizong."
98. Jiang Bo, "Sishinian chuguo liuxue yu gaige kaifang" [China's forty-year study abroad movement in the era of reform andopening up], a speech delivered at the 2018 Academic Annual Meeting of China Education Development Strategy Society, December 3, 2018.
99. Zhang Shuo, "Zhang Shuo: Zhongguo qunian chuguo liuxue renyuan shou po 60 wan" [China's overseas students last year broke 600,000], *Renmin ribao* website, April 1, 2018, www.gov.cn/xinwen/2018-04/01/content_5278951.htm.
100. Jiaoyubu guojisi chuguoliuxue gongzuochu, Shanghaishi jiaoyukexue yanjiuyuan zhili kaifa yanjiusuo. "Liuxue renyuan huiguo chuangye xianzhuang ji zhengce yanjiu" [Work status of returnees and an analysis of policy], *Chuguo liuxue gongzuo yanjiu* [Research on studies overseas], no. 2 (2000): 1.
101. "Zhongguo liuxue renyuan gaikuang" [Overview of Chinese Study Abroad], Xinhua net, January 3, 2009, http://news.xinhuanet.com/newscenter/2009-01/03/content _10596719.htm. The total number of Chinese students and scholars who have studied in the United States is based on a speech delivered by China's ambassador to the United States, Zhou Wenzhong, in Seattle on June 1, 2005. See www.chinesenewsnet.com.
102. Ibid.
103. Ibid.
104. Robert L. Jacobson, "China and U.S. Express Concerns over Return of Exchange Students," *The Chronicle of Higher Education*, June 17, 1987, 32.
105. David Zweig, "To Return or Not to Return? Politics vs. Economics in China's Brain Drain," *Studies in Comparative International Development* 32, no. 1 (Spring 1997): 92–125.
106. Wei, "Xin shiqi chuguo liuxue jiaoyu niaokan," 314.
107. Tang and Wang, "21 shiji Zhongguo liuxue jiaoyu quxiang fenxi," 4.
108. Wei, "Xin shiqi chuguo liuxue jiaoyu niaokan," 438.
109. Du, *Chinese Higher Education*, 103.
110. Xin Fuliang. "The Basic Line of Thinking in Shanghai's Efforts to Attract Overseas Chinese Intellect," *Chinese Education and Society* 34, no. 3 (May/June 2001): 65–77.
111. Cheng Kai-ming. "Reforms in the Administration and Financing of Higher Education," in Agelasto and Adamson, eds., *Higher Education in Post-Mao China*, 23.
112. Quoted from Pei Zhaohong, "Miaozhun shijie yiliu, gouzhu rencai gaodi" [Aiming to become a world-class university and building talented human resources], *Shenzhou xueren*, no. 1 (2003): 34. Jiang made these remarks at the centennial anniversary meeting of the founding of Peking University in May 1998. *Xinwen zhoukan* [Newsweek], no. 26 (July 2003).
113. *Shenzhou xueren*, July 2003; and www.chisa.edu.cn. July 27, 2003.
114. Xi Jinping, "Zai oumei tongxue hui chengli 100 zhounian qingzhu dahui shang de jianghua" [Speech at the celebration of the 100th anniversary of the establishment of the European and American Alumni Association]. *Renmin* net, October 21, 2015, http://cpc. people.com.cn/n/2013/1021/c64094-23277634.html.
115. Ibid.
116. Ibid.
117. Funding for the Changjiang Scholar Program came from Li Ka-shing and his Hong Kong–based Changjiang Group, Inc. During the first phase of the Changjiang Plan with a total of 60 million Hong Kong dollars, the Ministry of Education established 300–500 Changjiang Special Professor appointments beginning in 1998 (see www.sino -education.org). By 2003, among 445 Changjiang Scholars, 410 (92 percent) were returnees. "The Chunhui Plan" offers short-term (6–12 months) support for those Chinese nationals with Ph.D. degrees to work at educational institutions overseas. They receive a

salary, free housing, round trip airfare, and insurance during their short-term work period. According to China's Ministry of Education, since its establishment in 1996, some 7,000 scholars have already received grants from the "Chunhui Plan" (http://moe .edu.cn), August 17, 2003.

118. Yuan and Yue, "Xin shiqi Zhongguo liumei jiaoyu de fazhan licheng he qushi."

119. *Lianhe zaobao* (United morning news), April 11, 2003. These nine top elite schools are: Peking University, Tsinghua University, Fudan University, Shanghai Jiaotong University, Nanjing University, Zhejiang University, Xi'an Jiaotong University, University of Science & Technology of China, and the Harbin Institute of Technology.

120. "Chuguo liuxue wushi nian shuju huizong."

121. Xi, "Zai oumei tongxue hui chengli 100 zhounian qingzhu dahui shang de jianghua."

122. David Zweig, Chen Changgui, and Stanley Rosen, *China's Brain Drain to the United States: Views of Overseas Chinese Students and Scholars in the 1990s*, China Research Monograph no. 47 (Berkeley, CA: Institute of East Asian Studies, University of California, 1995), 7.

123. Philip Coombs, *The Fourth Dimension of Foreign Policy: Educational and Cultural Affairs* (New York: Harper and Row, 1964), 6–7, 17.

124. Dwight D. Eisenhower, Remarks at a ceremony marking the tenth anniversary of the Smith-Mundt Act (speech, Washington, DC, January 27, 1958).

125. Bu Liping, *Making the World Like Us: Education, Cultural Expansion, and the American Century* (Westport, CT: Praeger, 2003), 7.

CHAPTER 8

1. These are (1) the 2002 rankings of China's top 100 universities conducted by the Institute of Guangdong Management Science, and (2) the 2003 Chinese University Ranking made by China's Internet University. For more information about the methodology of their rankings, see www.edu.cn and web.archive.org/web/20130513221544/http://rank 2003.netbig.com/cn/rnk_0_0_3.htm.

2. These top twenty-five universities are (in alphabetical order): Beijing Aeronautical & Aerospace University, Beijing Normal University, Central China University of Science and Technology, Chongqing University, Dalian University of Science and Technology, Fudan University, Harbin Institute of Technology, Jilin University, Nanjing University, Nankai University, Peking University, Renmin University, Shandong University, Shanghai Jiaotong University, Sichuan University, South China University of Science and Technology, Southeastern University, Sun Yat-sen University, Tongjin University, Tsinghua University, the University of Science and Technology of China, Wuhan University, Xi'an Jiaotong University, Zhejiang University, and Zhongnan University.

3. Chen Wenshen. *Gonggong zuzhi de renshi juece* [Personnel decisions in public organizations: policy choices and personnel reform in Chinese universities] (Zhengzhou: Henan renmin chubanshe, 2002), 176–177.

4. "Zhongguo gaoxiao paiming bang" [China University Rankings], Renmin website, http://edu.people.com.cn/GB/8216/9320/index.html.

5. *Li Lixu, "China's Higher Education Reform 1998–2003: A Summary," Asia Pacific Education Review 5, no. 1 (2004): 14–22.*

6. "Over 10 Billion Yuan to Be Invested in "211 Project," *People's Daily* online, March 26, 2008, http://en.people.cn/90001/6381319.html.

7. Chen Xuefei, "Rencai liudong yu liuxue zhi pingshuo" [The mobility of human resources and an assessment of the effects of study abroad], *Shenzhou xueren*, July 2003.

8. They include baidu.com, sohu.com, sina.com, xinhuanet.com, chinesenewsnet.com, google.com, bing.com, and yahoo.com.

9. Zhongguo wenxueyishujie lianhehui, *Zhongguo renwu nianjian* [Yearbook of Who's Who in China] (Beijing: Zhongguo renwu nianjianshe, 2001 and 2002).

10. For example, see Wang Dahang and Ye Duzheng, eds. *Wo de shiye zai Zhongguo— Liuxue yu fengxian* [My career in China: Study abroad and contributions back home] (Shanghai: Shanghai jiaoyu chubanshe, 1999).

11. "2019 nian Shanghai shi daxue zonghe shili paihang bang" [2019 Shanghai University Comprehensive Strength Ranking], Graduate Education website, March 26, 2019, www.yjiedu.com/SHSDXPM/622190.html.

12. "2018 Shanghai shi lüshi shiwu suo paiming qian 50 ming" [2018 Rankings of Shanghai's Top 50 Law Firms], *Minhang falüwang* [Civil and Commercial Law Network], January 24, 2018, http://m.liuxiaoer.com/shls/7128.html.

13. Xu Meide (Ruth Hayhoe), *Zhongguo daxue 1895–1995: Yi ge wenhua chongtu de shiji* [China's universities, 1895–1995: A century of cultural conflict], translated by Xu Jieying(Beijing: Jiaoyu kexue chubanshe, 2000), 165; National Bureau of Statistics, comp. *China Statistical Yearbook, 1999* (Beijing: China Statistics Press, 1999), 651; "Zhongguo gaoxiao nüsheng bili buduan shangsheng" [The proportion of female students in Chinese colleges and universities keeps increasing], Science Net, October 25, 2012, http://news.sciencenet.cn/htmlnews/2012/10/270876.shtm, and "2018 jie daxuesheng xingbie bili baogao" [2018 report on the gender ratio of college students], Sohu Net, April 5, 2018, www.sohu.com/a/227342403_391394.

14. "Zhongguo yanjiusheng nannü bili nüxing nixi" [Gender ratio of Chinese graduate students, women have surpassed men], Xinhua, March 26, 2014; and Fang Linlin, "Zhongguo kexue jie: Nuxing cheng qi banbiantian renzhongdaoyuan" [The Chinese scientific community: The prospect of women holding up half the sky still has a long way to go], Xinhua Net, May 8, 2018, www.xinhuanet.com/tech/2018-05/08/c_1122797300.htm.

15. "Zhongguo gaoxiao nüsheng bili buduan shangsheng" [The proportion of female students in Chinese colleges and universities keeps increasing], Science Net, October 25, 2012, http://news.sciencenet.cn/htmlnews/2012/10/270876.shtm, and Fang, "Zhongguo kexue jie: Nüxing cheng qi banbiantian renzhongdaoyuan."

16. *Shijie ribao* [World Journal], August 3, 2013, A12.

17. For example, according to a study conducted by Zhang Yandong at Syracuse University in the late 1990s, only 5 percent of the 3,700 department head positions in Chinese universities were held by people under the age of 50. For more information about Zhang's study, see *Sanlian zhoukan* [United Weekly], November 1997.

18. www.chinesenewsnet.com (January 2, 2004). A recent survey of young students who went overseas to study shows that the majority (two-thirds) of them planned to return to China after completing their studies. The proportion of parents who hoped their children would come back to China was less than the proportion of students wishing to do so. Yi Songguo, "Why do College and Middle School Students Want to Go Abroad?" *Chinese Education and Society* 34, no. 3 (May/June 2001): 48–56.

19. See Cheng Li, "Analysis of Current Provincial Leaders." *China Leadership Monitor*, no. 7 (Summer 2003): 1-13. and Li Cheng and Lynn White, "The Army in the Succession to Deng Xiaoping: Familiar Fealties and Technocratic Trends," *Asian Survey* vol. 33, no. 8 (August 1993): 757–786.

20. The Jiangsu provincial government plans to have educational expenditures account for 6 percent of its total GDP by 2010. Much of the funding will be used for human resource development. www.chinatalents.gov.cn (July 27, 2003).

21. www.taisha.org (July 27, 2003).

22. Cheng Li, ed., *Bridging Minds across the Pacific: U.S.-China Educational Exchanges 1978-2003*. (Lanham, Maryland: Lexington Books, 2005), 96.

23. http://news.chinastar.com (July 27, 2003).

24. Wu Yan, "Russian official: Exchange students between China and Russia reach 85,000." CGTN Website, June 4, 2019. https://news.cgtn.com/news/3d3d514e3467444d354 57a6333566d54/index.html.

25. Huang Ping, former director of international cooperation at CASS, said that an inconsistency in the definition of returnees may explain this huge gap. However, he acknowledged that the statistics reveal an enormous disparity between the promotion of education for natural scientists and social scientists abroad. See www.xinhuanet.com (March 4, 2004).

26. Lei Shishan and Liao Heping, "Shi lun Jiang Zemin zhishi fenzi sixiang de fazhan guiji" [On the Development Track of Jiang Zemin's Intellectual Thought]. *Zhongguo shehui kexue wang* [China Social Sciences Net]. September 3, 2009, www.cssn.cn/ddzg/ddzg_ldjs/ rwyj/200909/t20090903_806431.shtml.

27. Xiong Yuezhi and others, *Shanghai tong shi* [General history of Shanghai], Vol. 14 (Shanghai: Shanghai renmin chubanshe, 1999), 1–2.

28. Chen Qiang, ed. *Hai shang chaoyong: jinian Shanghai gaige kaifang 40 zhounian* [Commemorating the 40th anniversary of reform and opening up] (Shanghai: Shanghai daxue chubanshe, 2018), 264, 271.

29. Ibid.

30. Ibid.

31. Shanghai shi tongji ju he guojia tongji ju, Shanghai diaocha zongdui [Shanghai Municipal Bureau of Statistics and Shanghai Bureau of Statistics, National Bureau of Statistics]. "2018 nian Shanghai shi guomin jingji he shehui fazhan tongji gongbao" [Statistical Communique of Shanghai National Economic and Social Development in 2018], Shanghai tongji wang [Shanghai Statistics website], November 15, 2019, http://tjj.sh .gov.cn/tjgb/20191115/0014-1003219.html.

32. See website: www.ceibs.edu.

33. See website: https://shusilc.shu.edu.cn/About_SILC/SILC_History.htm.

34. See website: http://cdhk.tongji.edu.cn/zh-hans/.

35. See website: http://umji.sjtu.edu.cn/about/.

36. See website: https://shanghai.nyu.edu.

37. See website: https://dukekunshan.edu.cn/zh.

38. Denis Simon, "Starting a New University from Scratch in China: The Case of Duke Kunshan University," A presentation at the 2019 Duke International Forum "A New Age of Sino-US Higher Education Cooperation" held in Kunshan, China on December 16–18, 2019.

39. "Zhong'ou guoji gongshang xueyuan" [China Europe International Business School], *Fenghuang wang* [Phoenix Network], October 9, 2012, http://qd.ifeng.com/ jiaoyuliuxue/shangxueyuan/detail_2012_10/09/369332_0.shtml.

40. "2019 nian FT quanqiu MBA paihang bang chulu" [2019 FT Global MBA Rankings Released], *Mei ri jingji xinwen* [Daily economic news], January 28, 2019, www.nbd.com.cn /articles/2019-01-28/1295631.html.

41. http://chinatalents.gov.cn (June 2, 2003).

42. Yale, Duke, the University of Chicago, and Dartmouth jointly formed a team to travel to Shanghai, recruiting high school students in the city. These four schools had joint recruitment efforts overseas for over ten years.

43. "City residence for Chinese returnees," Shanghai Municipal Government website, January 6, 2011, www.shanghai.gov.cn/shanghai/node27118/node27818/u22ai42033.html.

44. "More than 510,000 overseas students returned," *Asia Times*, April 11, 2019, www. asiatimes.com/2019/04/article/more-than-510000-overseas-students-returned/.

45. Li, *Bridging Minds across the Pacific*, 96.

46. See, for example, Tong Shijun, *Lun guize* [On the rule], 2nd edition (Shanghai:

Shanghai renmin chubanshe, 2019); and Tong Shijun, *Dangdai Zhongguo de jingshen tiaozhan* [The spiritual challenge of contemporary China] (Shanghai: Shanghai renmin chubanshe, 2017).

47. For Tong's English bio, see www.english.ecnu.edu.cn/_t89/1724/list.htm.

48. For example, Andrew Hurrell, *Quanqiu zhixu yu quanqiu zhili* (On global order: Power, values and the constitution of international society). Translated by Lin Xi (Beijing: Zhongguo renmindaxue chubanshe, 2018).

49. Cheng Li, *Chinese Politics in the Xi Era: Reassessing Collective Leadership.* (Washington, DC: Brookings Institution Press, 2016), 148.

50. Cheng Li, "The Status and Characteristics of Foreign-Educated Returnees in the Chinese Leadership," *China Leadership Monitor*, no. 16 (Fall 2005): 2.

51. He Weifang, *In the Name of Justice: Striving for the Rule of Law in China* (Washington, DC: Brookings Institution, 2012), 58.

52. Chen Su, *Dangdai Zhongguo faxue yanjiu (1949–2009)* [Research on law in contemporary China, 1949–2009] (Beijing: Zhongguo shehui kexue chubanshe, 2009), 26.

53. Cai Dingjian, "Yifa zhili" [Rule of law], in Yu Keping, ed., *Zhongguo zhili bianqian sanshi nian: 1978–2008* [China's political reform toward good governance: 1978–2008] (Beijing: Shehui kexue wenxian chubanshe, 2008), 142.

54. Ren Miao, "Falü wenben chengxing, fazhi rentong shangyuan" [The law texts are all available, but the rule of law is still far off], *Duowei Times,* March 18, 2011, 17.

55. For discussion of a more optimistic view of China's legal development in terms of professional expansion, see Cheng Li and Jordan Lee, "China's Legal System," *China Review*, no. 48 (Autumn 2009): 1–3.

56. Chen, *Dangdai Zhongguo faxue yanjiu*, 13.

57. Gu Xin, "Revitalizing Chinese Society: Institutional Transformation and Social Change," in Wang Gungwu and John Wong, ed., *China: Two Decades of Reform and Change* (Singapore: Singapore University Press and World Scientific Press, 1999), 80.

58. See "Woguo lüshi renshu yi chao ershiwan" [The number of China's lawyers surpasses 200,000], China Lawyers' Network, January 10, 2011, www.zgdls.com/2011/lvjieneican_0110/114973.html.

59. Ren, "Falü wenben chengxing, fazhi rentong shangyuan."

60. "Quanguo lüshi yi da 42.3 wan" [Lawyers in the country have reached 423,000], *Meiri tou tiao* [Everyday's headlines], March 27, 2019, https://kknews.cc/news/9g286nq.html.

61. He Weifang, He Qinhua, and Tian Tao, eds., *Falü wenhua sanrentan* [A tripartite discussion of legal culture] (Beijing: Beijing daxue chubanshe, 2010), 87.

62. Chen, *Dangdai Zhongguo faxue yanjiu*, 238.

63. Zhang Lei and Chen Zanqiang, "Falü lilun jiaoxue yu shijian de jiehe—Falü zhensuo jiaoyu" [The combination of legal theory in teaching and practice: Legal clinic education], *Zhongguo daxue jiaoxue* [Chinese university education], no. 11 (2006), also www.readers365.com/zgdxjy/dxjx2006/dxjx20061117.html.

64. Ibid.

65. Lin Ge, "10 nian lüshi renshu fan bei" [The number of lawyers doubled in ten years]. *Lushi jie* [Legal community], July 13, 2018, www.zhihedongfang.com/54147.html.

66. For more discussion of Shanghai's law schools and universities, see Nick William, "Faxueyuan fengyun zhi Shanghai tan" [Rapid development of Law Schools in Shanghai], LawSchool website, September 18, 2017, www.zhihedongfang.com/42565.html.

67. Zhou Zheng and Dong Yuzhou, "Cong shuzi kan Shanghai lüshi hangye 4 nian fazhan" [Statistic-based evaluation of the four-year development of the legal profession in Shanghai], Tencent website, April 2, 2019, https://new.qq.com/omn/20190402/20190402A04ATI.html.

68. Lin, "10 nian lüshi renshu fan bei".

69. "Shanghai lüshi sishi nian" [40 years of Shanghai Lawyers], Douban Wesbsite, April 13, 2019, www.douban.com/note/714162872/.

70. Anyone who studied in two countries is counted twice, once for each country.

71. Zhou and Dong, "Cong shuzi kan Shanghai lüshi hangye 4 nian fazhan."

CHAPTER 9

1. A notable exception is David Zweig and Feng Yang, "Overseas Students, Returnees, and the Diffusion of International Norms into Post-Mao China," *International Studies Review* 16, no. 2 (June 2014): 252–263.

2. Miao Lü, Zheng Jinlian, and Wang Jianfang, "2016 nian Zhongguo liuxue huiguo renyuan fazhan qingkuang diaoyan baogao" [2016 Survey Report of the Status of Chinese Returnees of Foreign Studies], in Wang Huiyao and Miao Lü, eds., *Zhongguo liuxue fazhan baogao* [China Study Abroad Development Report], no. 6. (Beijing: Shehui kexue wenxian chubanshe, 2016), 56–85.

3. Ibid., 82.

4. Victor Yuan also served as a Yale World Fellow in 2007 and an Aspen Scholar in 2013–2015, and he has taught at Tsinghua University and Zhejiang University, among a few other Chinese universities.

5. The Horizon Research Consultancy Group has four subsidiaries: Horizon Research (market research), founded in 1992; Progress Strategy (strategic consulting), founded in 2000; Horizonkey.com (online studies), founded in 1999; and Vision Investment (investment consulting), founded in 2002. As exclusive representatives of ESOMAR (the European Society for Opinion and Marketing Research) and AMCF (Association of Management Consulting Firms) in China, Horizon Group has established four global research consultancy networks. For the website of the Horizon Research Consultancy Group, see http://horizon.3see.com/member/company.php?show=1.

6. This study includes many comparisons between this survey research and other surveys that I have conducted for different projects. For one example, see Committee of 100, *Hope and Fear: American and Chinese Attitudes toward Each Other—Parallel Survey on Issues Concerning U.S.-China Relations.* New York, Committee of 100 Publication, December 2007. The author served as a cochair for this Committee of 100 survey.

7. Huang Ying, "Shanghai shi haigui qunti fazhan zhuangkuang diaocha" [Investigation on the status of Shanghai returnees], *Zhongguo rencai* [China's talent] (December 2009): 20.

8. Cheng Li, "Coming Home to Teach: Status and Mobility of Returnees in China's Higher Education," in Cheng Li, ed., *Bridging Minds across the Pacific: U.S.-China Educational Exchanges 1978–2003* (Lanham, MD: Lexington Books, 2005), 92–93.

9. Shanghai Municipal Government Overseas Chinese Affairs Office and the Municipal Overseas Chinese Federation, "Shanghai shi jiben qiao qing" [Basic Conditions of Overseas Chinese and Returnees in Shanghai], Shanghai difangzhi bangongshi [Shanghai Local History Office] website, February 4, 2013, www.shtong.gov.cn/Newsite/node2/node19828/node83911/node83971/node83988/userobject1ai122993.html.

10. Jiaoyu bu liuxue fuwu zhongxin [Overseas Education Service Center of the Ministry of Education], *Zhongguo jiaoyu baogao: fazhan yu zhiliang—Zhongguo liuxue huiguo jiuye lanpishu 2016* [China Education Report on Development and Quality: Blue Book on Employment for Chinese Students Returning from Overseas Studies 2016] (Beijing, Renmin jiaoyu chubanshe, 2017).

11. Luo Peipeng, "Shanghai renjun GDP tupo 2 wan meiyuan" [Shanghai's per capita GDP exceeds 20,000 USD], *Jiefang ribao* [Liberation Daily], March 2, 2019.

12. The Center on Religion and Chinese Society of Purdue University, *2018 niandu zai mei Zhongguo liuxuesheng yu fangwen xuezhe diaocha baogao* [Survey Report on Chinese Students and Visiting Scholars in the United States in 2018], October 17, 2018.

13. Ibid., 6.

14. Ibid., 26.

15. Feng Shaoqiu, "Zhonggong qianghua liuxuesheng zongjiao xinyang guanli" [CCP strengthens religious belief management for Chinese students who pursued foreign studies], Duowei News, October 14, 2018, www.dwnews.com.

16. "World Value Survey Wave 6: 2010–2014," www.worldvaluessurvey.org/WVSOnline .jsp.

17. Miao, Zheng, and Wang, "2016 nian Zhongguo liuxue huiguo renyuan fazhan qingkuang diaoyan baogao," 77.

18. Ibid.

19. Ibid.

20. Shanghai shi oumei tongxue hui ketizu [Shanghai European and American Students Association], "Liuxue huiguo renyuan zai hu gongzuo qingkuang de diaocha yu sikao" [Investigation and Reflection on the Work Situation of Returned Overseas Chinese Students in Shanghai], *Haigui xueren* [Returnees], no. 10, April 7, 2010.

21. "The 2007 China public" survey refers to the survey conducted by the Committee of 100, *Hope and Fear: American and Chinese Attitudes toward Each Other*, 12. "The 2012 China public" survey refers to the survey conducted by the Committee of 100, "US-China Attitudes toward Each Other" (New York: Committee of 100 Publication, 2012), 53. "The 2017 survey" refers to the Committee of 100, "US-China Public Perceptions: Opinion Survey 2017" (New York: Committee of 100 Publication, 2017), 44.

22. Cheng Li, "Xi Jinping's 'Proregress': Domestic Moves toward a Global China," Washington, DC, Brookings Institution, September 2019, www.brookings.edu/research/xi -jinpings-proregress-domestic-moves-toward-a-global-china/.

23. Olivia Rosane, "The World's 20 Most Polluted Cities in 2018," *EcoWatch*, March 6, 2019, www.ecowatch.com/worlds-most-polluted-cities-2630812632.html.

24. "The World's 10 Worst Cities," Popular Science, June 23, 2008, www.popsci.com/ environment/article/2008-06/worlds-10-dirtiest-cities/; "16 of World's 20 Most-Polluted Cities in China," Voice of America, October 31, 2009, www.voanews.com/archive/ worldwatch-institute-16-worlds-20-most-polluted-cities-china.

25. The 2009 survey on the overall confidence level of urban residents in China was also conducted by the Horizon Research Consultancy Group. See "The 2009 Urban Life Survey Report" released in June 2009. The survey used targeted interception access methods. The survey was conducted from May 4 to May 10, 2009 in Beijing, Shanghai, Guangzhou, Harbin, Qingdao, Dalian, Wuhan, Nanjing, Chengdu, and Shenzhen. There were 3,295 valid samples obtained from these ten cities, and the respondents were aged 24 to 45.

26. The Horizon Research Consultancy Group and the Sohu News Center, "2010 Survey on Hot Topics in the Two Sessions of the Chinese Government's Annual Meeting." The report was published by the Horizon Research Consultancy Group, January 2010.

27. The Committee of 100, "US-China Public Perceptions: Opinion Survey 2017," 71.

28. The Committee of 100, *Hope and Fear*, 40.

29. The Horizon Research Consultancy Group, "China Public Service Public Evaluation Index Report 2009." The survey used a multistage random sampling method in seven cities (Beijing, Shanghai, Guangzhou, Wuhan, Chengdu, Shenyang, and Xi'an) to conduct home visit surveys of residents aged 18 to 60. The results have been weighted according to the actual population size of each place. The margin of error is ± 0.92 percentage points.

30. Richard Wike and Bruce Stokes, "Chinese Public Sees More Powerful Role in World, Names U.S. as Top Threat." Pew Research Center web page, October 5, 2016, www.

pewresearch.org/global/2016/10/05/chinese-public-sees-more-powerful-role-in-world
-names-u-s-as-top-threat/.

31. The Horizon Research Consultancy Group, "The Quality of Life Index Survey 2009." The survey adopted a multistage random sampling method for seven cities (Beijing, Shanghai, Guangzhou, Wuhan, Chengdu, Shenyang, and Xi'an) and seven towns (Zhuji, Shaoxing, Zhejiang; Changle, Fuzhou, Fujian; Beining, Jinzhou, Liaoning; Xinji, Shiji-azhuang, Hebei; Linxiang, Yueyang, Hunan; Pengzhou, Chengdu, Sichuan; and Xingping, Xianyang, Shaanxi). It surveyed residents aged 16 to 60 and visited the towns. The results have been weighted according to the actual population size of each place, and the sampling error of this survey is ± 0.91 percent with 95 percent confidence.

32. For example, Committee of 100, *Hope and Fear.*

33. Wike and Stokes, "Chinese Public Sees More Powerful Role in World."

34. Ibid.

35. Ibid.

36. The Horizon Research Consultancy Group, "The 2012 Survey Report on the Quality of Life of Chinese Residents."

37. The Horizon Research Consultancy Group, "The Relationship Evaluation between China and Other Countries by Chinese urban residents" in "the 2009 World in the Eyes of Chinese People survey." The survey uses a multistage random sampling method to target 3,000 people in ten cities, including Beijing, Shanghai, and Guangzhou, above the age of 18. The sampling error for this survey is ± 1.06% with a 95% confidence level.

38. Jessica Chen Weiss, "How Hawkish Is the Chinese Public? Another Look at 'Rising Nationalism' and Chinese Foreign Policy," *Journal of Contemporary China*, 28, no. 119 (March 2019): 689.

39. Ibid.

40. The measure of patriotism and nationalism in this study is largely in line with Wenfang Tang's groundbreaking method adopted in his 2008 China Survey to estimate Chinese nationalism. Tang's survey asks respondents whether they agreed or disagreed with four statements capturing "sentiment toward my country (China)": (1) "I would rather be a citizen of my country than of any other country." (2) "The world would be a better place if people from other countries were more like people from my country." (3) "My country is a better country than most other countries." And (4) "It makes me proud when my country does well in international sports." For a detailed discussion of Tang's measurement, see Wenfang Tang, *Populist Authoritarianism: Chinese Political Culture and Regime Sustainability* (Oxford: Oxford University Press, 2016), 46.

41. Jennifer Pan and Yiqing Xu, "China's Ideological Spectrum," *Journal of Politics*, 80, no. 1 (January 2018): 258–260.

42. Ibid., 271.

43. Ibid., 255.

44. Ibid., 255, 262.

45. Weiss, "How Hawkish Is the Chinese Public?" 679–680.

46. Ibid., 680.

47. Ibid., 692.

48. The Center on Religion and Chinese Society of Purdue University, *2018 niandu zai mei Zhongguo liuxuesheng yu fangwen xuezhe diaocha baogao*, 5.

49. Fan Yingjie, Pan Jennifer, Shao Zijie, and Xu Yiqing, "How Discrimination Increases Chinese Overseas Students' Support for Authoritarian Rule." 21st Century China Center Research Paper, June 29, 2020, https://ssrn.com/abstract=3637710.

50. An Chen, "Capitalist Development, Entrepreneurial Class, and Democratization in China," *Political Science Quarterly* 117, no. 3 (2002): 422.

CHAPTER 10

1. Peter Neville-Hadley, "Why Westerners Misinterpret Modern Chinese Art—and How Perceptions Can Be Changed." *South China Morning Post*, April 7, 2019, www.scmp .com/magazines/style/news-trends/article/3004346/why-do-westerners-misinterpret -modern-chinese-art.

2. "Leather tank at Christie's auction preview, Hong Kong, China, May 23, 2019." Shutterstock, www.shutterstock.com/editorial/image-editorial/leather-tank-at-christies -auction-preview-hong-kong-china-23-may-2019-10245472a.

3. Neville-Hadley, "Why Westerners Misinterpret Modern Chinese Art."

4. For evidence from the early period of China's reform that supports this argument, see Lynn T. White III, *Unstately Power*, vol. 2. *Local Causes of China's Intellectual, Legal and Government Reforms* (Armonk, NY: M. E. Sharpe, 1999), 141–160.

5. Shi Xuanqing, "Xinshiqi Shanghai meishu chuangzuo gaikuang" [Survey of Shanghai art in the new era], *Shanghai yishu jia* [Shanghai Artists], 2 (1999): 12; and Zhongguo wen- hua shuyuan jiangyanlu bianweihui [Editing Committee of Lecture Records of Chinese Culture Academy], *Zhongwai wenhua bijiao yanjiu* [Comparative studies of Chinese and foreign cultures] (Beijing: Sanlian Press, 1989).

6. Kang Yan, *Jiedu Shanghai* [Understanding Shanghai] (Shanghai: Shanghai renmin chubanshe, 2001), 351.

7. Quoted in Yin Jizuo, *Shanghai wenhua fazhan lanpishu* [Blue book of cultural devel- opment in Shanghai, 2000] (Shanghai: Shanghai shehui kexueyuan chubanshe, 2000), 3.

8. Shanghai avant-garde artist Shi Yong described the art scene in the city in the early 1990s as follows: "'Underground! Underground!' This word is used by many and is always associated with resistance, a backbone to stand for strong arguments. But, in actual fact, most of the time it was only because we didn't have a choice! During that time, the main- stream art scene saw the art we made as rubbish (and people who hold this point of view still exist, although they no longer have a monopoly on what is said about art)." Quote from Biljana Ciric, "Hank Bull, Shen Fan, Zhou Tiehai, Shi Yong, and Ding Yi—*Let's Talk about Money*: Shanghai First International Fax Art Exhibition," *Yishu: Journal of Contemporary Chinese Art* 18, no. 2 (March/April 2019): 9.

9. Zhang Xiaoling, *Guannian yishu jiegou yu chongjian de shixue* [Conceptual arts: The rhyme of deconstruction and reconstruction] (Changchun: Jilin meishu chubanshe, 1999), 86.

10. Part of this chapter first appeared in Cheng Li and Lynn White III, "Dialogue with the West: A Political Message from Avant-Garde Artist in Shanghai," *Critical Asian Stud- ies* 35, no. 1 (March 2003): 59–98.

11. Ralph Croizier, "The Avant-garde and the Democracy Movement: Reflections on Late Communism in the USSR and China," *Europe-Asia Studies* 51, no. 3 (May 1999): 483–513.

12. Liu Chun, *Xue Song Fangtanlu* [Interview with Xue Song] (Taiyuan: Shanxi chuban chuanmei jituan, 2015), 48.

13. Geremie R. Barmé, "Artful Marketing: Who Buys It? Contemporary Chinese Art at Home and Abroad," *Persimmon* 1, no. 1 (Spring 2000): 23.

14. Geremie Barmé and Sang Ye, "The Great Firewall of China," *Wired*, June 1997, 11.

15. Feng Jiali, "Limitless Difference: On Being a Chinese Woman Artist," *Art Asia Pa- cific*, 31 (2001): 68.

16. Maggie Farley, "One Less Movie at Cannes," *Los Angeles Times*, May 7, 1999, F1.

17. Gao Minglu, ed., *Inside Out: New Chinese Art* (Berkeley and Los Angeles: University of California Press, 1998), 29.

18. Qian Zhijian, "Performing Bodies: Zhang Huan, Ma Liuming, and Performance Art in China," *Art Journal* 58, no. 2 (Summer 1999): 70.

19. Ibid., 78.

20. Karen Smith, "China's Avant-garde," August 20, 2001, www.china-avantgarde.com/. For similar arguments, see Gao Minglu, *Total Modernity and the Avant-Garde in Twentieth -Century Chinese Art* (Cambridge, MA: The MIT Press, 2011).

21. Karen Smith, "The Spirit of Shanghai," August 20, 2001, www.china-avantgarde. com/; and Ji Shaofeng, "Dangdai yishu bantu zhong de Shanghai" [Shanghai in the contemporary art map] in Ma Qinzhong, ed., *Xiangjie: Shanghai dangdai yishujia xunli* [Image boundary: Shanghai contemporary artists overview] (Shanghai: Xuelin chubanshe, 2015), 11.

22. Ji, "Dangdai yishu bantu zhong de Shanghai,"12.

23. Smith, "The Spirit of Shanghai."

24. For detailed information about the Third Shanghai Biennale, see the catalog of the Shanghai Biennale (Shanghai: Shanghai Shuangnian Zhan, 2000).

25. Wu Hung, "The 2000 Shanghai Biennale: The Making of a Historical Event," *Art Asia Pacific*, 31 (2001): 47.

26. For more detailed information about the 12th Shanghai Biennale, see its official website, www.shanghaibiennale.org/cn/.

27. Cuauhtémoc Medina, "Theme of the 12th Shanghai Biennale: Proregress: Art in an Age of Historical Ambivalence," 12th Shanghai Biennale website, www.shanghaibiennale .org/en/page/detail/308cw.html.

28. Quoted in Qian Xueer, "Di 12 jie Shanghai shuang nian zhan kaimu: Jintui zhi jian, wu xu huo maodun" [The opening ceremony of the 12th Shanghai Biennale: Between advance and retreat, disorder or contradiction], *Pengpai xinwen* [The Paper], November 10, 2018, www.thepaper.cn/newsDetail_forward_2619003.

29. For the art piece, see www.shanghaibiennale.org/en/artist/detail/437/95.html.

30. After the nationwide educational restructuring during the early 1950s, many of these schools were closed. Some moved to Hangzhou and became part of the Zhejiang Academy of Fine Arts. Shanghai did not have any art schools for several decades. See Yu Ding, *Xingudian feng yishu –shijimo de huisheng* [Neoclassical Art: The Echo of the End of the Century] (Changchun: Jilin meishu chubanshe, 1999), 23.

31. Shanghai bainian wenhuashi bianzuan weiyuanhui, *Shanghai bainian wenhuashi* [Shanghai cultural history of the 20th century], 1. (Shanghai: Shanghai kexue jishu wenxian chubanshe, 2002), 35.

32. Zhu Qi, "Bannian duo, san zhanlan, wudai ren, Shanghai dangdai yishu sanshi nian" [More than half a year, three exhibitions, five generations, 30 years of Shanghai contemporary art] Overseas Group website, http://zazhi.qunba.com/wenzhang/1058135.

33. This assessment is based on criticisms expressed in China and abroad. See Shi Xuanqing, "Xinshiqi Shanghai meishu chuangzuo gaikuang" [Survey of Shanghai arts in the new era], *Shanghaiyishujia* [Shanghai Artists], 2 (1999): 12–23; and Benoit Vermander, "The Future of Chinese Painting," *China News Analysis*, 1601 (January 1, 1998): 1–10.

34. Zhu, "Bannian duo, san zhanlan, wudai ren, Shanghai dangdai yishu sanshi nian."

35. White, *Unstately Power*, vol. 2, 144. Johnson Chang, a well-known dealer in Chinese contemporary art says, "In different eras, different provinces have shone. In the eighteenth century, it was Yangzhou; in the nineteenth, Shanghai. Today it is Shanghai, Beijing and Sichuan." From *Art Newspaper*, 77 (January 1998): 23.

36. Richard Kraus and Richard P. Suttmeier, "Reconstituting the Arts and Sciences," in Edwin A. Winckler, ed., *Transition from Communism in China: Institutional and Comparative Analyses* (Boulder, CO: Lynne Rienner, 1999), 212.

37. For the exhibition's official website that presents the art works, see http:// mingyuanartmuseum.com/zlhg/html/?153.html.

38. Michael Sullivan, *Art and Artists of Twentieth-Century China* (Berkeley and Los Angeles: University of California Press, 1996), 272. However, some peripheral forms of art

in Shanghai, such as graphic stories (*lianhuan hua*) and peasant painting (*nongmin hua*), developed quickly, even during the 1960s and 1970s, and they had a high aesthetic quality. See White, *Unstately Power*, 2, 144.

39. Quoted from Jiang Zuxuan, ed., *Shenhua Chen Yifei* [The fairy tale about Chen Yifei] (Changsha: Hunan meishu chubanshe, 1999), 225.

40. Kang, *Jiedu Shanghai*, 334; also, Dorothy J. Solinger, *Contesting Citizenship in Urban China* (Berkeley and Los Angeles: University of California Press, 1999).

41. "Shanghai is racing to become China's cultural capital," *The Economist*, November 24, 2016, www.economist.com/books-and-arts/2016/11/24/shanghai-is-racing-to-become -chinas-cultural-capital.

42. Gu Xin: "The Art of Re-industrialisation in Shanghai," in Johan Fornäs, Martin Fredriksson, and Jenny Johannisson, eds., *Shanghai Modern: The Future in Microcosm?* Vol. 4, in the series *Culture Unbound* (Linköping, Sweden: Linköping University Electronic Press, 2012), 193–211; and Justin Bergman, "An Arts Explosion Takes Shanghai," *New York Times,* November 8, 2015, www.nytimes.com/2015/11/08/travel/shanghai-west-bund -museums.html.

43. Han Yuqi and Zhang Song, *Dongfang de Saina zuoan: Suzhouhe yanan de yishu cangku* [Left bank of the Seine of the East: The art warehouses of Suzhou Greek] (Shanghai: Shanghai guji chubanshe, 2004), 28–29.

44. Ibid., 71.

45. Bergman, "An Arts Explosion Takes Shanghai."

46. For its well-administered website, see www.shanghartgallery.com.

47. *That's Shanghai*, June 2001, 36–38.

48. "Global Leadership on Culture in Cities," World Cities Culture Forum, www. worldcitiescultureforum.com/data/art-galleries.

49. Yibo Gallery has a Chinese-language website: www.yibo-art.com/.

50. Rong Yueming and Hua Jian, *Shanghai wenhua chanye fazhan baogao 2018* [Annual report on cultural industry development of Shanghai 2018] (Shanghai: Shanghai renmin chubanshe, and Shanghai shudian chubanshe, 2018), 200.

51. For more information about these two art streets in Shanghai, see Iris Zheng, "Painting by the Street Numbers: The Creation of a New Art District on Shao Xing Lu," *That's Shanghai*, May 2001, 37; and *Shijie ribao*, August 11, 2001, A8.

52. Li Lunxin, Fang Minglun, Li Youmei, and Ding Ximan, eds. *Haipai wenhua yu chengshi chuangxin* [Shanghai culture and urban innovation] (Shanghai: Wenhui chubanshe, 2010), 11.

53. *Shijie ribao*, June 3, 2001, A4; also based on Cheng Li's interview with Zhang Haiteng in Shanghai during the summer of 2001. This pattern will probably change as the Chinese middle class grows. Some observers say that foreigners' share of the art market has been slowly diminishing since the early 2000s. According to Benoit Vermander, a Taipei-based expert on contemporary Chinese art, approximately 30 percent of Chinese artwork purchases in the early 2000s came from Taiwan. Residents of Hong Kong and Southeast Asia accounted for another 5 percent each. Vermander, "The Future of Chinese Painting," 8.

54. Quoted in Kang, *Jiedu Shanghai*, 370.

55. Helmi Yusof, "Shanghai's Bid to Be an Arts Capital." *Business Times* (Singapore), December 16, 2016, www.businesstimes.com.sg/lifestyle/arts/shanghais-bid-to-be-an-arts -capital.

56. Xue Hongyan. *Shanghai, 9+1!—Zoujin Suzhouhe yishujia* [Shanghai, 9+1!: Getting to know Suzhou creek artists] (Shanghai: Shanghai renmin chubanshe, 2005), 4.

57. "Myth/History II: Shanghai galaxy." *YUZM Magazine*, May 2015, 6.

58. Xu Zhen, *1199 ge ren: Long meishuguan shoucangzhan* [1199 people: Collection from the Long Museum] (Shanghai: Gezhi chubanshe, Shanghai renmin chubanshe, 2019).

59. For the collection, see Xu, *1199 ge ren: Long meishuguan shoucangzhan.*

60. Wang Wei, "A Message from the Director," *Long yishu* [Long art magazine], 4 (2019): 2.

61. Ibid.

62. Wang Wei, Zhang Qingjie, and Xu Zihan, eds, *Zhuanzhedian: Zhongguo dangdai yishu sishi nian* [Turning point: 40 years of Chinese contemporary art] (Shanghai: Shanghai wenhua chubanshe, 2018).

63. Ibid., 6–7.

64. Yusof, "Shanghai's Bid to Be an Arts Capital."

65. Ali Morris, "Centre Pompidou to open Shanghai outpost in David Chipperfield's West Bund Art Museum," Dezeen website, August 8, 2017, www.dezeen.com/2017/08/08/centre-pompidou-shanghai-david-chipperfield-west-bund-art-museum-shanghai-china/.

66. "Shanghai is racing to become China's cultural capital," *The Economist*, November 24, 2016, www.economist.com/books-and-arts/2016/11/24/shanghai-is-racing-to-become-chinas-cultural-capital.

67. Zhou Tiehai, "Hao de yishu kongjian keyi daibiao chengshi de linghun" [A good art space can represent the soul of the city], *Yishu guoji* [Art International], November 5, 2014.

68. Rong Yueming and Zheng Chongxuan, *Shanghai wenhua fazhan baogao 2017* [Annual report on cultural development of Shanghai 2017] (Beijing: Shehui kexue wenxian chubanshe, 2017), 5; and also Jiang Jun, "Ruhe lijie 'jintian' Shanghai dangdai yishu de fanrong." [How to understand the prosperity of "today's" Shanghai contemporary art], *Fenghuang yishu* [Phoenix Art], November 19, 2018, news.artron.net/20181119/n1033290.html.

69. Jiang Jun, "Ruhe lijie 'jintian' Shanghai dangdai yishu de fanrong."

70. Ibid., 125.

71. Planet Institute,"*Weishenme Shanghai bei cheng wei 'modu'?*" [Why is Shanghai called "Magic Capital"?], June 27, 2019, www.zhihu.com/question/63282342.

72. Wu Hung, "Why China Needs Private Contemporary Art Museums (Preface)," in Wu Hung, ed. *Shoucangjia yu meishuguan: Shanghai Yu Deyao meishuguan choubei zhuanji* [Collectors and art museums: special issue on the planning and opening of the Yuz Museum, Shanghai] (Guangzhou: Lingnan meishu chubanshe, 2013), 5.

73. Wu Hung, ed., *Dangdai yishu de Shijian: meishuguan shoucan yu yanjiu* [Practices in contemporary art: Museum, collections and research] (Guangzhou: Lingnan meishu chubanshe, 2014), 89.

74. Quoted in Wu, *Shoucangjia yu meishuguan*, 64.

75. Jiang Jun, "Ruhe lijie 'jintian' Shanghai dangdai yishu de fanrong."

76. Ibid.

CHAPTER 11

1. All five of these artists have works exhibited in the ShanghART Gallery in Shanghai, accessible through www.shanghart.com. Cheng Li is grateful to Lorenz Helbling of the ShanghART Gallery for his assistance regarding 1990s works by these artists. Cheng Li also conducted research on their post-1990s works through his visits to other art galleries in Shanghai and elsewhere between 2017 and 2019. Part of this chapter was first published with Lynn White as "Dialogue with the West: A Political Message from Avant-Garde Artists in Shanghai," *Critical Asian Studies* 35, no. 1 (March 2003): 59–98.

2. For a detailed discussion of the criticism of U.S. foreign policy by Chinese public intellectuals and college students, see Song Qiang, Zhang Zangzang, and Qiao Bian, *Zhongguo keyi shuobu* [China can say no] (Beijing: Zhonghua gongshang lianhe chubanshe, 1996); and Fang Ning, Wang Bingquan, and Ma Lijun, *Chengzhang de Zhongguo: Dangdai zhongguo qingnian de guojia minzu yishi yanjiu* [Growing China: A study of nation-state consciousness among contemporary Chinese youth] (Beijing: Renmin chubanshe, 2002).

3. See the website of Britta Erickson, www.stanford.edu/dept/art/china/. Compiled in 1999 and updated in January 2001.

4. For a parallel view from a Western scholar, see Elizabeth J. Perry, "Casting a Chinese 'Democracy' Movement: The Roles of Students, Workers, and Entrepreneurs," in Jeffrey Wasserstrom and Elizabeth Perry, eds., *Popular Protest and Political Culture in Modern China* (Boulder, CO: Westview, 1994), 74–92.

5. Hou Hanru, "A Naked City: Curatorial Notes around the 2000 Shanghai Biennale," *Art Asia Pacific*, 31 (2001): 61.

6. In one of Ma Liuming's performance art pieces, Ma is completely naked, masturbates before the audience, and "then mixes his semen with water and drinks it." This performance art aims to shock the audience into seeing the futility and circularity in human life. See Maranatha Ivanova, "Ambiguity, Absurdity, and Self-Creation in the Art of Ma Liuming," *East Asia Culture Critique* 7, no. 1 (Spring 1999): 208.

7. Yang Wei, *Sishiyi ge ren* [Forty-one people] (Changsha: Hunan meishu chubanshe, 2012), 31–35.

8. For a discussion of the shock art in Beijing and other cities, see John Pomfret, "Shock Artists Take Freedom to New Lows," *Washington Post*, July 31, 2001, C01.

9. For more discussion of these artist villages in Beijing, see Yang Yingshi, "The Tongzhou Artists Community," *Art Asia Pacific*, 31 (2001): 72–75.

10. Yang, *Sishiyi ge ren*, 31.

11. Ma Yan, "Meishuguan shidai xia de Shanghai dangdai yishu shengtai" [Shanghai Contemporary Art Ecology in the Era of Rapid Expansion of Art Museums], *Yishu guoji* [Art International], February 12, 2013.

12. Yang, *Sishiyi ge ren*, 31.

13. Lynn T. White, *Unstately Power: Local Causes of China's Intellectual, Legal and Governmental Reforms*, Vol. 2 (Armonk, NY: M. E. Sharpe, 1999), 156.

14. Quoted in Liu Chun, *Xue Song fangtanlu* [Interview with Xue Song] (Taiyuan: Sanjin chubanshe, 2015), 232.

15. Michael Sullivan, *Art and Artists of Twentieth-Century China* (Berkeley: University of California Press, 1996), 272.

16. Yang Wei, "Yiban haishui yiban huoyan: luetan Beijing yu Shanghai yishu shengtai de chayi" [Half of the sea and half of the flame: A brief discussion about the difference between Beijing and Shanghai art ecology] in Ma Qinzhong, ed., *Xiangjie: Shanghai dangdai yishujia xunli* [Image boundary: An overview of Shanghai contemporary artists] (Shanghai: Xuelin chubanshe, 2015), 16.

17. Ibid.

18. Li Xu, "Shanghai chouxiang—Zhongguo dangdai yishu de zhongyao fanben" [Shanghai Abstract Art: An Important Model of Chinese Contemporary Art], *Yishujie* [Art World], February 1, 2012.

19. Quoted from Ralph Croizier, "The Avant-garde and the Democracy Movement: Reflections on Late Communism in the USSR and China," *Europe-Asia Studies*, 51, no. 3 (May 1999): 498.

20. Julia F. Andrews, *Painters and Politics in the People's Republic of China, 1949–1979* (Berkeley: University of California Press, 1994), 400.

21. Kris Imants Ercums, "Cancelled!" *Art Asia Pacific*, 31 (2001): 37.

22. Yin Jizuo, *Shanghai wenhua fazhan lanpishu* [Blue Book of Cultural Development in Shanghai 2000] (Shanghai: Shanghai shehui kexueyuan chubanshe, 2000), 105.

23. Ma Yan, "Biaopi yu neili—Shanghai dangdai yishu shengtai baogao." [Surface and Inner: Shanghai Contemporary Art Ecological Report], *Dongfang yishu dajia* [Oriental Art Overview], 12 (2012): 130–139; also Ma, "Meishuguan shidai xia de Shanghai dangdai yishu shengtai."

24. Ma, "Biaopi yu neili."

25. Yang, "Yiban haishui yiban huoyan," 15.

26. Minglu Gao, *Inside Out: New Chinese Art* (Berkeley: University of California Press, 1998), 31.

27. See the classic Marxist analysis of cultural hegemony by Antonio Gramsci, *Selections from the Prison Notebooks* (New York: International Publishers, 1971).

28. Biljana Ciric, "Hank Bull, Shen Fan, Zhou Tiehai, Shi Yong, and Ding Yi—Let's Talk about Money: Shanghai First International Fax Art Exhibition," *Yishu: Journal of Contemporary Chinese Art* 18, no. 2 (March/April 2019): 17.

29. Ibid.

30. For Xue Song's piece "Xiahai," see www.christies.com/lotfinder/lot_details.aspx ?from=salesummery&intobjectid=5936726&sid=b41ff24e-e10d-49c8-a115-3172daf259b 6&lid=4.

31. Li and White, "Dialogue with the West," 69–70, 83–84.

32. Liu, *Xue Song Fangtanlu*, 86.

33. ShanghART, https://shanghartgallery.com/galleryarchive/artist.htm?artistId=35.

34. Xue Song, "Wo de chuangzuoguan" [My artistic view] in Ma, *Xiangjie*, 170.

35. Hou, "A Naked City," 61.

36. Gao Minglu uses this description to refer to a shift in the Chinese avant-garde artist movement in general. Gao, *Inside Out*, 8.

37. See www.shanghart.com/texts/shiyong1tm.htm.

38. Ibid.

39. Hou, "A Naked City," 61.

40. Art and Collection Group, *Shi Yong, 1993–2014* (Shanghai: ShanghaiART Gallery, 2018), 65.

41. Ibid., 40–41.

42. See www.shanghart.com/texts/shiyong1tm.htm. Similarly, Ren Jian, an artist in Wuhan, proclaimed that contemporary art had been transformed into product art, similar to fast food, ready to serve people. This is what some critics call the "McDonaldization of art." Quoted from Gao, *Inside Out*, 28.

43. Art and Collection Group, *Shi Yong*, 86.

44. Shi Yong, "*Mimi de zhenxiang*" [Secret truth] in Ma, *Xiangjie*, 142.

45. Art and Collection Group, *Shi Yong*, 214.

46. ShanghART, www.shanghartgallery.com/galleryarchive/artists/name/pujie.

47. Sine Bepler, "Pu Jie de eryuan shijiao" [Pu Jie's dual perspective], Art Link Art, 2007, www.artlinkart.com/cn/article/overview/bb7iyBt/about_by2/P/37.

48. Zhang Xiaoling, *Guannian yishu jiegou yu chongjian de shixue* [Conceptual arts: The rhyme of deconstruction and reconstruction] (Changchun: Jilin meishu chubanshe, 1999), 27.

49. Huang Danhui and Hu Rong, *Xin biaoxian yishu qinggan de qijudi* [New performance art: The habitat of sentiments] (Changchun: Jilin meishu chubanshe, 1999), 7.

50. Ibid., 48.

51. Karl Polanyi, *The Great Transformation* (New York: Reinhardt, 1944).

52. Zhang, *Guannian yishu jiegou yu chongjian de shixue*, 27. Zhang is a scholar from the Academy of Chinese Art in Beijing.

53. Pi Li, "Zhou Tiehai: The Strategy of Contemporary Art," in Hou Hanru, *Zhou Tiehai* (Shanghai: ShanghART Gallery Publication, 2003), 4.

54. Ibid.

55. Jon Burris, "Zhou Tiehai: It Is Not Difficult to Make Art," *China Daily*, November 7, 2014, www.chinatoday.com.cn/english/culture/2014-11/07/content_650662.htm.

56. Zhou Tiehai, "Hao de yishu kongjian keyi daibiao chengshi de linghun" [Good art spaces can represent the soul of the city], *Yishu guoji* [Artintern.net], November 5, 2014, http://art.ifeng.com/2015/0810/2465900.shtml.

57. ShanghART online, www.shanghartgallery.com/galleryarchive/artists/name/zhou tiehai.

58. Xue, *Shanghai, 9+1!,* 183.

59. Pi, "Zhou Tiehai."

60. Xue, *Shanghai, 9+1!,* 87.

61. Feng Jiali, "Limitless Difference: On Being a Chinese Woman Artist," *Art Asia Pacific,* 31 (2001): 68.

62. Jiang Zuxuan, ed., *Shenhua Chen Yifei* [The fairy tale about Chen Yifei] (Changsha: Hunan meishu chubanshe, 1999), 154.

63. Sun Liang, "Tan Zhongguo dangdai yishu zhi shang" [Discussion on the loss of Chinese Contemporary Art], *Dongfang zaobao* [Oriental Morning Post], April 1, 2011.

64. Xue, *Shanghai, 9+1!,* 86.

65. Pi, "Zhou Tiehai," 5.

66. Zhou Tiehai (Catalog), Shanghai, ShanghART, 2000.

67. ShanghART online, www.shanghartgallery.com/galleryarchive/artist.htm?artistId=42&section=key.

68. Hou Hanru, "On Zhou Tiehai's Work: Mr. Camel, the Most Faithful Portrait of Shanghai Today," ShanghART, September 11, 2006, www.shanghartgallery.com/galleryarchive/texts/id/440.

69. Sun Jin, *Bopu yishu duanceng yu mianyan* [Pop art: Disconnection and continuity] (Changchun: Jilin meishu chubanshe, 1999), 21–22.

70. Aihwa Ong, *Flexible Citizenship: The Cultural Logic of Transnationality* (Durham, NC: Duke University Press, 1999), 18.

71. Wang Changhao, "Xishijian–tianshu" [An analysis of the world book: Heavenly book] in Jin Mengmeng, Wang Qingyun, and Hao He, comp., *Weida de zuopin, weida de licheng 1978–2018* [Outstanding work, great journey 1978–2018] (Beijing: Renmin meishu chubanshe, 2018), 40.

72. Quoted in Simon Leung and Janet A. Kaplan, "Pseudo-Languages: A Conversation with Wenda Gu, Xu Bing, and Jonathan Hay," *Art Journal* 58, no. 3 (Fall 1999): 87–99.

73. Quoted from Gao, *Inside Out,* 35.

74. Ibid.

75. For Gu Wenda's "United Nations Series—China Monument: Temple of Heaven," see Google Arts & Culture, https://artsandculture.google.com/asset/united-nations-series-china-monument-temple-of-heaven-gu-wenda/qAEKdGptiiRNJw.

76. Xue Song, "Interview," *Meishu wenxian* [Art Literature], July 15, 2014.

77. Ding, "Xingshi ji jingshen" [Form is the spirit], in Ma, *Xiangjie,* 88.

78. Lu Shiwei, "Ding Yi: Chengshi de yishu wenmai" [Ding Yi: City's artistic context] *Shichang zhoukan* [Market weekly] (October 2013): 78–79.

79. Artspy.cn website, May 5, 2019, www.artspy.cn/activity/view/10691.

80. Ding, "Xingshi ji jingshen," 92.

81. Feng Boyi, ed., *Shi x sanshi: Ding Yi zuopin* [+ x 30 years: Ding Yi's works] (Shanghai: Shanghai renmin meishu chubanshe, 2018), 54.

82. Shen Jialu, "Ding Yi de mima" [Ding Yi's password], *Xinmin zhoukan* [Xinmin weekly] (December 14, 2011), 60.

83. Xue, *Shanghai, 9+1!,* 5.

84. Shen, "Ding Yi de mima," 58.

85. Ding, "Xingshi ji jingshen," 92.

86. Feng, *Shi x sanshi,* 29.

87. Ji Shaofeng, "Dangdai yishu bantu zhong de Shanghai" [Shanghai in the contemporary art map], in Ma, *Xiangjie,* 15.

88. Bao Dong, "Ding Yi 'shi shi': Cong jingshen qimeng dao guannian zixing" [Ding Yi's "Appearance of Crosses": From Spiritual Enlightenment to Conceptual Introspection],

Zhongguo Yishu [Chinese Art], May 18, 2016, www.rbz1672.com/article/?act=article_info
&cate_id=27&article_id=4667&nav_type=3.

89. Feng, *Shi x sanshi*, 251.

90. For a comparison between the reality of politics outside government and in business, see E. E. Schattschneider, *The Semi-Sovereign People* (New York: Dreyden, 1960).

91. Wang Yuan, "Yige 'tuxiang' zhizaozhe de ziyu" [The self-conversation of a "painting
maker"], in Ma, *Xiangjie*, 176.

CHAPTER 12

1. Jonathan White, "Kobe Bryant: China's Tributes Led by Ex-Lakers Teammates as
China Mourns NBA Star," *South China Morning Post*, January 27, 2020, www.scmp.com/
sport/china/article/3047737/kobe-bryant-chinas-tributes-led-ex-lakers-teammates.

2. Cheng Li and Qiuyang Wang, "Kobe Bryant and His Enduring Impact on the Sino
-American Friendship," *China-U.S. Focus*, March 4, 2020, www.chinausfocus.com/society
-culture/kobe-bryant-and-his-enduring-impact-on-the-sino-american-friendship.

3. For Kobe Bryant's Weibo account, see www.weibo.com/kobebryantmamba.

4. Justine Coleman, "All 50 States Under Disaster Declaration for First Time in US
History," *The Hill*, April 12, 2020, https://thehill.com/policy/healthcare/public-global
-health/492433-all-50-states-under-disaster-declaration-for-first; and Holly Secon and
Aylin Woodward, "About 95% of Americans Have Been Ordered to Stay at Home. This
Map Shows Which Cities and States are Under Lockdown," *Business Insider*, April 7, 2020,
www.businessinsider.com/us-map-stay-at-home-orders-lockdowns-2020-3.

5. Dominic Rushe and Amanda Holpuch, "Hit by a Hurricane: 22m Out of Work in US
as Coronavirus Takes Heavy Economic Toll," *The Guardian*, April 16, 2020, www.
theguardian.com/business/2020/apr/16/us-unemployment-coronavirus-economic-toll
-jobless.

6. Wang Yi, "Zhongguo yi xiang jin 150 ge guojia he 4 ge guoji zuzhi tigong jinji
yuanzhu" [China has provided emergency assistance to nearly 150 countries and 4
international organizations], Sina website, May 24, 2020, https://tech.sina.com.cn/roll
/2020-05-24/doc-iirczymk3301545.shtml.

7. Yanzhong Huang, "The Coronavirus Outbreak Could Disrupt the U.S. Drug Supply."
Council on Foreign Relations, March 5, 2020; www.cfr.org/in-brief/coronavirus-disrupt
-us-drug-supply-shortages-fda, and Doug Palmer and Finbarr Bermingham, "U.S.
Policymakers Worry about China 'Weaponizing' Drug Exports," Politico, April 20, 2020,
www.politico.com/news/2019/12/20/policymakers-worry-china-drug-exports-088126.

8. Josh Wingrove, "Kudlow Says U.S. Should Allow Firms '100% Immediate Expensing,'"
Bloomberg, April 9, 2020, www.bloomberg.com/news/articles/2020-04-09/kudlow-says-u
-s-should-allow-firms-100-immediate-expensing.

9. Jane Li, "The US and China Are in an Increasingly Nasty War of Words over the Coronavirus," *Quartz*, March 17, 2020, https://qz.com/1819704/us-and-china-in-a-nasty-war
-of-words-over-coronavirus/.

10. For example, see Joshua Nelson, "Tom Cotton Touts Bill to Make China Pay for
Unleashing Pandemic on the World," *Fox News Flash*, April 20, 2020, www.foxnews.com/
media/tom-cotton-bill-china-pay-coronavirus-pandemic.

11. "Foreign Ministry Spokesperson Geng Shuang's Regular Press Conference on April
20, 2020," Ministry of Foreign Affairs of the People's Republic of China, April 20, 2020,
www.fmprc.gov.cn/mfa_eng/xwfw_665399/s2510_665401/2511_665403/t1771576.shtml.

12. "China Can Deal with the US: Scholars," *Global Times*, July 7, 2020, www.globaltimes
.cn/content/1193707.shtml.

13. John Bowden, "Kissinger Warns China, US Are in 'Foothills of a Cold War,'" *The*

Hill, November 21, 2019, https://thehill.com/blogs/blog-briefing-room/news/471460 -kissinger-warns-china-us-are-in-foothills-of-a-cold-war.

14. Henry A. Kissinger, "The Coronavirus Pandemic Will Forever Alter the World Order," *Wall Street Journal*, April 3, 2020.

15. Ivo Daalder, "Amid the Pandemic, a Sobering Lesson. More, Not Less, International Cooperation Needed," *Chicago Tribune*, April 9, 2020, www.chicagotribune.com/opinion/ commentary/ct-opinion-coronavirus-globalization-america-superpower-daalder -20200409-kvhof5y5nnayjljxn3byvbbuli-story.html.

16. Ibid.

17. Joshua Cooper Ramo, "I Had a Ringside Seat For the SARS Virus in 2003. Here's How This Coronavirus Is Different," *Los Angeles Times*, February 11, 2020, www.latimes .com/opinion/story/2020-02-11/how-this-coronavirus-is-different-from-sars.

18. Peter Beinart, "Trump's Break with China Has Deadly Consequences," *The Atlantic*, March 28, 2020, www.theatlantic.com/ideas/archive/2020/03/breaking-china-exactly -wrong-answer/608911/.

19. Bill Gates, "The Next Outbreak? We're Not Ready," TED Talks, April 3, 2015, www .ted.com/talks/bill_gates_the_next_outbreak_we_re_not_ready?language=en.

20. Ibid.

21. Christopher Wray, "The Threat Posed by the Chinese Government and the Chinese Communist Party to the Economic and National Security of the United States" (speech, Hudson Institute, Washington, DC, July 7, 2020), www.fbi.gov/news/speeches/the-threat -posed-by-the-chinese-government-and-the-chinese-communist-party-to-the-economic -and-national-security-of-the-united-states.

22. William Barr, "Remarks on China Policy at the Gerald R. Ford Presidential Museum," (speech, Grand Rapids, MI, July 16, 2020), U.S. Department of Justice, www. justice.gov/opa/speech/attorney-general-william-p-barr-delivers-remarks-china-policy -gerald-r-ford-presidential.

23. "America's Shrinking Middle Class: A Close Look at Changes within Metropolitan Areas," Pew Research Center, May 11, 2016, www.pewsocialtrends.org/2016/05/11/ americas-shrinking-middle-class-a-close-look-at-changes-within-metropolitan-areas/.

24. The World Inequality Database, "Income Growth 1980–2014," Global Strategies, November 20, 2018, https://daveporter.typepad.com/global_strategies/2018/11/from-the -ny-times-series-china-rules-here.html.

25. Ibid.

26. William J. Burns, "The United States Needs a New Foreign Policy," *The Atlantic*, July 14, 2020, www.theatlantic.com/ideas/archive/2020/07/united-states-needs-new-foreign -policy/614110/.

27. Barr, "Remarks on China Policy."

28. Zheng Yongnian, "Bianjing shi nao dale, jue buneng zai digu Zhongyin guanxi" [The border incidents have become serious, and Sino-Indian relations must not be underestimated], *Wenhua zongheng* [Cultural aspect], June 16, 2020, https://user.guancha .cn/main/content?id=329494.

29. Barr, "Remarks on China Policy."

30. Wray, "The Threat Posed by the Chinese Government."

31. Barr, "Remarks on China Policy."

32. Jeffrey D. Sachs, "America's Unholy Crusade against China," *Project Syndicate*, August 5, 2020. www.project-syndicate.org/commentary/america-evangelical-crusade -against-china-by-jeffrey-d-sachs-2020-08.

33. The State Council of the People's Republic of China, "The White Paper: China's National Defense in the New Era," July 24, 2019, http://english.www.gov.cn/archive/ whitepaper/201907/24/content_WS5d3941ddc6d08408f502283d.html.

34. Sachs, "America's Unholy Crusade against China."

35. Michael R. Pompeo, "Communist China and the Free World's Future," Yorba Linda, California, The Richard Nixon Presidential Library and Museum, July 23, 2020, www.state .gov/communist-china-and-the-free-worlds-future/.

36. Michael D. Swaine, "Wo xiwang Meiguo zhengfu buyao chun dao zai zhexie lingyu tiaoxin Zhongguo" [I hope the U.S. government will not be stupid enough to provoke China in these areas], Global Times website, August 5, 2020, https://m.k.sohu.com/d /471632691?channelId=1&page=1.

37. Richard Haass, "What Mike Pompeo Doesn't Understand about China, Richard Nixon and U.S. Foreign Policy," *Washington Post*, July 25, 2020, www.washingtonpost.com /opinions/2020/07/25/what-mike-pompeo-doesnt-understand-about-china-richard-nixon -us-foreign-policy/.

38. Ibid.

39. Jeffrey A. Bader, "Changing China policy: Are We in Search of Enemies?" Brookings China Strategy Paper Series, No. 1, June 2015, www.brookings.edu/blog/up-front/2015/06 /22/changing-china-policy-are-we-in-search-of-enemies/.

40. Haass, "What Mike Pompeo Doesn't Understand about China."

41. "United States Strategic Approach to the People's Republic of China," The White House, May 20, 2020, www.whitehouse.gov/wp-content/uploads/2020/05/U.S.-Strategic -Approach-to-The-Peoples-Republic-of-China-Report-5.20.20.pdf.

42. De Xiansheng, "550 wan huaren zai mei rencai xianzhuang" [Current situation of human resources among 5.5 million Chinese in the United States], *Zhihu* [Know how], June 16, 2020, https://zhuanlan.zhihu.com/p/148860475.

43. Alexandra Yoon-Hendricks, "Visa Restrictions for Chinese Students Alarm Academia," *New York Times*, July 27, 2018, https://cn.nytimes.com/usa/20180727/visa -restrictions-chinese-students/dual/.

44. Jon Hilsenrath and Jon Kamp, "How a Johns Hopkins Professor and Her Chinese Students Tracked Coronavirus," *Wall Street Journal*, May 9, 2020, https://www.wsj.com/ articles/how-a-johns-hopkins-professor-and-her-chinese-students-tracked-coronavirus -11589016603.

45. Pompeo, "Communist China and the Free World's Future."

46. Burns, "The United States Needs a New Foreign Policy."

47. Pompeo, "Communist China and the Free World's Future."

48. "China Can Deal with the US."

49. Huang Qifan, "Zhong Mei guanxi ji weilai 10 nian shijie wuda qushi" [China-US relations and the world's five major trends in the next 10 year], Speech delivered at the Forum of Forty People in China Finance, June 9, 2020, https://www.chainnews.com/ articles/964056363606.htm.

50. Zheng Yongnian, "Meiguo yu Zhongguo tuogou, yiweizhe yu zhengge Dongya chanye lian chongzu, chengben tai da" [The decoupling of the United States from China means the reorganization of the entire East Asian industrial chain, which is too costly], June 2, 2020. https://finance.sina.com.cn/china/gncj/2020-06-02/doc-iircuyvi6341663. shtml.

51. Scott Kennedy and Shining Tan, "Decoupling between Washington and Western Industry," CSIS website, June 10, 2020, https://www.csis.org/blogs/trustee-china-hand/ decoupling-between-washington-and-western-industry.

52. Ibid.

53. Evan Osnos, "Fight Fight, Talk Talk: The Future of America's Contest with China," *New Yorker*, January 13, 2020, 35.

54. James Manyika, Anu Madgavkar, Susan Lund, and Andrey Mironenko, *Zhongguo yu shijie: lijie bianhua zhong de jingji lianxi* [China and the world: Understand the changing economic links], McKinsey Global Institute Publication, July 2019, 17.

55. Lev Borodovsky, "The Daily Shot: Is U.S. Consumer Sentiment Bottoming?" *Wall*

Street Journal, April 20, 2020, https://blogs.wsj.com/dailyshot/2020/04/20/the-daily-shot -is-u-s-consumer-sentiment-bottoming/.

56. Stephen Roach, "The End of the US-China Relationship," *China-US Focus*, May 3, 2020, https://www.chinausfocus.com/foreign-policy/the-end-of-the-us-china-relation ship.

57. Stephen Roach, "A Crash in the Dollar Is Coming," *Bloomberg*, June 8, 2020, https:// www.bloomberg.com/opinion/articles/2020-06-08/a-crash-in-the-dollar-is-coming.

58. Lee Hsien Loong, "The Endangered Asian Century America, China, and the Perils of Confrontation," *Foreign Affairs*, July/August 2020. https://www.foreignaffairs.com/ articles/asia/2020-06-04/lee-hsien-loong-endangered-asian-century.

59. Stephen Walt, "Everyone Misunderstands the Reason for the U.S.-China Cold War," *Foreign Policy*, June 30, 2020, https://foreignpolicy.com/2020/06/30/china-united-states -new-cold-war-foreign-policy/.

60. See the Q&A session in Pompeo, "Communist China and the Free World's Future."

61. Wang Yiwei, "Xifang de 'shuangchong biaozhun': Genyuan yu genzhi" ["Double standards" in the West: Roots and cure], *Pengpai xinwen* [The Paper], May 5, 2020, https:// www.thepaper.cn/newsDetail_forward_7267860.

62. Yu Donghui, "Xie Shuli da zhongping: Lengzhan yanxing ling mei shiqu Zhongguo pengyou" [Interview with Susan Shirk: The Cold War rhetoric and deeds caused the United States to lose Chinese friends], *Zhongguo pinglun xinwen wang* [China Review News] July 26, 2020, http://hk.crntt.com/doc/1058/3/4/7/105834725.html?coluid=7&kindid=0&docid =105834725.

63. Quoted in Yen Nee Lee, "Pompeo's Speech Slamming China Will Have the 'Opposite Effect,' Says Former U.S. Diplomat." CNBC website, July24, 2020, https://www.cnbc.com /2020/07/24/pompeo-speech-will-have-the-opposite-effect-in-china-says-former-us -diplomat.html.

64. Edward Cunningham, Tony Saich, and Jessie Turiel, "Understanding CCP Resilience: Surveying Chinese Public Opinion through Time," Ash Center for Democratic Governance and Innovation, Harvard Kennedy School, July 2020, https://ash.harvard.edu /publications/understanding-ccp-resilience-surveying-chinese-public-opinion-through -time.

65. Cunningham, Saich, and Turiel, "Understanding CCP Resilience."

66. Lei Guang, Margaret Roberts, Yiqing Xu, and Jiannan Zhao, "Pandemic Sees Increase in Chinese Support for Regime, Decrease in Views towards the U.S." China Data Lab at University of California at San Diego, June 30, 2020, http://chinadatalab.ucsd.edu/ viz-blog/pandemic-sees-increase-in-chinese-support-for-regime-decrease-in-views -towards-us/.

67. Andrew J. Nathan, "The Puzzle of Authoritarian Legitimacy," *Journal of Democracy* 31, no. 1 (January 2020): 158–168.

68. "China Says a US Travel Ban on Communist Party Members Would Be 'Pathetic'" BBC, July 16, 2020, https://www.bbc.com/news/world-asia-china-53427782.

69. Maggie Lewis, "Criminalizing China," *Journal of Criminal Law and Criminology* 111, no. 1 (June 2020); and also Chen Yuxuan and Zhang Juan, "Maggie Lewis: Meiguo sifabu de 'Zhongguo xingdong" you bei yu Meiguo de jiazhiguan [Maggie Lewis: The "China Initiative" of the U.S. Department of Justice is contrary to American values], *Zhong Mei yinxiang* [U.S-China Perception Monitor], July 25, 2020, www.uscnpm.com/model_ item.html?action=view&table=article&id=22477.

70. Lewis, "Criminalizing China."

71. Huang Rong, "Mei FBI gu huaren jubao huayi kexuejia" [The FBI hired Chinese to report Chinese scientists], *Zhong Mei yinxiang* [US-China Perception Monitor], June 19, 2020, www.uscnpm.com/model_item.html?action=view&table=article&id=22095.

72. Paul Mozur and Cade Metz, "A U.S. Secret Weapon in A.I.: Chinese Talent," *New*

York Times, June 9, 2020, https://www.nytimes.com/2020/06/09/technology/china-ai -research-education.html. See also Marco Polo, "The Global AI Talent Tracker," Paulson Institute, https://macropolo.org/digital-projects/the-global-ai-talent-tracker/.

73. Ibid.

74. "Research and Development Expenditure (% of GDP)—World, United States, China," UNESCO Institute for Statistics, https://data.worldbank.org/indicator/GB.XPD .RSDV.GD.ZS?end=2018&locations=1W-US-CN&start=1990&view=chart.

75. Haass, "What Mike Pompeo Doesn't Understand about China."

76. Burns, "The United States Needs a New Foreign Policy."

77. Liang Jianzhang, "Kaifang guoji hulianwang, keyi chedi da sui Meiguo fengsuo Tiktok de zhengdang xing" [Opening up the internet can completely smash the legitimacy of the US blockade of TikTok], Sino Website, August 2, 2020, https://info.williamlong.info /2020/08/tiktok.html.

78. Deputy Secretary of State Antony Blinken, United States Ambassador to China Max Baucus, press roundtable, Lost Heaven Restaurant, Beijing, China, October 8, 2015, U.S. Embassy and Consulates website, https://china.usembassy-china.org.cn/deputy-secretary -state-antony-blinken-united-states-ambassador-china-max-baucus-press-roundtable -lost-heaven-restaurant-beijing-china/.

79. Alex Ward, "Joe Biden in Victory Speech: 'Let This Grim Era of Demonization in America Begin to End.'" Vox, November 7, 2020, https://www.vox.com/2020/11/7 /21554701/joe-biden-acceptance-speech-2020-election.

80. Zheng Yongnian, "Zhongmei zhizheng" [The Sino-American Controversy]. *Hua Erjie wenzhai* [Wall Street Digest], July 8, 2020, https://wsdigest.com/article?artid=6995.

81. Burns, "The United States Needs a New Foreign Policy."

82. Yuval Noah Harari, "The World after Coronavirus," *Financial Times*, March 20, 2020, www.ft.com/content/19d90308-6858-11ea-a3c9-1fe6fedcca75.

83. Osnos, "Fight Fight, Talk Talk," 38.

84. Xi Jinping, "Guanche xin fazhan linian tuidong gao zhiliang fazhan" [Implement new development concepts to promote high-quality development]. Xinhua News Agency website, May 22, 2019, www.xinhuanet.com/politics/leaders/2019-05/22/c_1124529225. htm.

85. Robert D. Atkinson and Nigel Cory, "Stopping China's Mercantilism: A Doctrine of Constructive, Alliance-Backed Confrontation." *SSRN Electronic Journal*, January 2017, www.researchgate.net/publication/321232169_Stopping_China%27s_Mercantilism_A_ Doctrine_of_Constructive_Alliance-Backed_Confrontation.

86. Zheng, "Bianjing shi nao dale, jue buneng zai digu Zhongyin guanxi."

87. Liang Jianzhang, "Shuli qiangguo xintai, suzao youhao xingxiang" [Establish a strong nation mentality and build a friendly image], *Jingji xue zatan* [Economics Miscellaneous], June 21, 2020, www.cnpop.org/column/ljz/202006/00006958.html.

88. Zheng, "Bianjing shi nao dale, jue buneng zai digu Zhongyin guanxi."

89. Ibid.

90. Qiao Liang, "Taiwan wenti you guan guoyun buke qingshuai jijin" [The Taiwan issue is at stake], *Zhongmei yinxiang* [U.S.-China Perception Monitor], May 4, 2020, www .uscnpm.com/model_item.html?action=view&table=article&id=21580.

91. Hao Zhidong, a scholar at the Macao University, reviewed some of the Chinese characterization (and misinterpretations in his view) of the Black Lives Matter movement. See Hao Zhidong, "Te lang pu hua" de Zhongguo zhishi fenzi yu tamen yanzhong de "bai zuo" ["Trumplized" Chinese intellectuals and the "White Left" in their eyes], *FT Zhongwen wang* [*Financial Times* Chinese version website], July 1, 2020, www.ftchinese.com/story /001088366?full=y&archive.

92. Wang Yi, "Stay on the Right Track and Keep Pace with the Times to Ensure the Right Direction for China-US Relations." Remarks by State Councilor and Foreign

Minister Wang Yi at the China-US Think Tanks Media Forum, July 9, 2020, https://language.chinadaily.com.cn/a/202007/10/WS5f07d402a3108348172588a9.html.

93. Jack Ma, Remarks at NYU Shanghai Commencement (speech, Shanghai, May 29, 2020), https://shanghai.nyu.edu/news/jack-ma-at-commencement-2020.

94. Richard Madsen, "China in the American Imagination," *Dissent* (Winter 1998): 54.

95. Gordan G. Chang, *The Coming Collapse of China* (New York: Random House, 2001); and Minxin Pei, "China's Coming Upheaval: Competition, the Coronavirus, and the Weakness of Xi Jinping," *Foreign Affairs*, April 3, 2020, www.foreignaffairs.com/articles/united-states/2020-04-03/chinas-coming-upheaval.

96. Pei, "China's Coming Upheaval."

97. Yu Keping, *Democracy Is a Good Thing: Essays on Politics, Society and Culture in Contemporary China* (Washington DC: Brookings Institution Press, 2009).

BIBLIOGRAPHY

ENGLISH

Andrews, Julia F., and Gao Minglu. "The Avant-Garde's Challenge to Official Art," in Deborah S. Davis, Richard Kraus, Barry Naughton and Elizabeth J. Perry, eds., *Urban Spaces in Contemporary China: The Potential for Autonomy and Community in Post-Mao China*. Cambridge: Cambridge University Press, 1995, pp. 221–278.

———. *Fragmented Memory: The Chinese Avant-Garde, in Exile*. Columbus: Wexner Center for the Arts, Ohio State University, 1993.

Art and Collection Group, *Shi Yong, 1993–2014*. Shanghai: ShanghaiART Gallery, 2018.

Balfour, Alan, and Zheng Shiling. *World Cities: Shanghai*. West Sussex, England: Wiley-Academy, 2002.

Barber, Noel. *The Fall of Shanghai*. New York: Coward, McCann, and Geoghegan, 1979.

Barme, Geremie. *In the Red: On Contemporary Chinese Culture*. New York: Columbia University Press, 1999.

Bergére, Marie-Claire. *The Golden Age of the Chinese Bourgeoisie, 1911–1937*. Translated by Janet Lloyd. Cambridge: Cambridge University Press, 1989.

———. "'The Other China': Shanghai from 1919 to 1949," in Christopher Howe, ed., *Shanghai, Revolution and Development in an Asian Metropolis*. Cambridge: Cambridge University Press, 1981, pp. 1–34.

Bickers, Robert A. *Changing Shanghai's "Mind": Publicity, Reform, and the British in Shanghai, 1927–1931*. London: China Society, 1992.

———. *Empire Made Me: An Englishman Adrift in Shanghai*. New York: Columbia University Press, 2003.

Bieler, Stancy. *"Patriots" or "Traitors"? A History of American-Educated Chinese Students*. Armonk, NY: M.E. Sharpe, 2003.

Bonnell, Victoria E., and Lynn Hunt, eds. *Beyond the Cultural Turn: New Directions in the Study of Society and Culture*. Berkeley, CA: University of California Press, 1999.

Bu Liping. "Cultural Understanding and World Peace: The Role of Private Institutions in the Interwar Years." *Peace and Change* 24, no. 2 (April 1999): 148–171.

——. "Educational Exchange and Cultural Diplomacy in the Cold War." *Journal of American Studies* 33, no. 3 (December 1999): 393–415.

——. *Making the World Like US: Education, Cultural Expansion, and the American Century.* Westport, CT: Praeger, 2003.

Buckley, Christopher. "How a Revolution Becomes a Dinner Party: Stratification, Mobility and the New Rich in Urban China," in M. Pinches, ed., *Culture and Privilege in Capitalist Asia.* London: Routledge, 1999, pp. 208–229.

Burns, William J. *The Back Channel: A Memoir of American Diplomacy and the Case for Its Renewal.* New York: Random House, 2019.

Cao Cong. "The Changing Dynamic between Science and Politics: Evolution of the Highest Academic Honor in China, 1949–1998." *Isis* 90, no. 2 (June 1999): 298–324.

——. "Modernizing Science through Educating the Elite," in Michael Agelasto and Bob Adamson, eds. *Higher Education in Post-Mao China.* Hong Kong: Hong Kong University Press, 1998, pp. 99–119.

Chamberlain, Heath B. "On the Search for Civil Society in China." *Modern China* 19, no. 2 (1993): 199–215.

Chan Kam Wing. *Cities with Invisible Walls: Reinterpreting Urbanization in Post-1949 China.* New York: Oxford University Press, 1994.

Chan, Ming K., and Arif Dirlik. *Schools into Fields and Factories: Anarchists, the Guomindang, and the National Labor University in Shanghai, 1927–1932.* Durham, NC: Duke University Press, 1991.

Chang, Parris, and Zhiduan Deng. "The Chinese Brain Drain and Policy Options." *Studies in Comparative International Development* 27, no. 1 (Spring 1992): 44–60.

Chang Sen-dou. "The Morphology of Walled Capitals," in G. W. Skinner, ed., *The City in Late Imperial China.* Stanford, CA: Stanford University Press, 1977, pp. 75–100.

Chao, Linda, and Ramon H. Myers. "China's Consumer Revolution: The 1990s and Beyond." *Journal of Contemporary China* 7, no. 18 (1998): 351–368.

Chase, Michael S., Kevin L. Pollpeter, and James C. Mulvenon. *Shanghaied? The Economic and Political Implications of the Flow of Information Technology and Investment across the Taiwan Strait.* Arlington, VA.: The Rand National Defense Research Institute, 2004.

Chen, Jerome. *China and the West: Society and Culture 1815–1937.* London: Hutchinson, 1979.

Chen Jian. "Sino-American Relations Studies in China," in Warren I. Cohen, ed. *Pacific Passage: The Study of American-East Asian Relations on the Eve of the Twenty-First Century.* New York, NY: Columbia University Press, 1996, pp. 3–35.

Chen Jie and Chunlong Lu. "Democratization and the Middle Class in China: The Middle Class's Attitudes toward Democracy." *Political Research Quarterly* 64, no. 3 (September 2011): 705–719.

Cheung, Peter T. Y. "The Political Context of Shanghai's Economic Development" in Yueman Yeung and Yun-wing Sung, eds. *Shanghai: Transformation and Modernization under China's Open Door Policy.* Hong Kong: Chinese University of Hong Kong, 1996, pp. 49–92.

Ciric, Biljana. "Hank Bull, Shen Fan, Zhou Tiehai, Shi Yong, and Ding Yi—Let's Talk about Money: Shanghai First International Fax Art Exhibition." *Yishu: Journal of Contemporary Chinese Art* 18, no. 2 (March/April 2019): 8–18.

Clifford. Nicholas R. *Spoilt Children of Empire: Westerners in Shanghai and the Chinese Revolution of the 1920s.* Hanover, NH: Middlebury College Press, 1991.

Coble, Parks M. *The Shanghai Capitalists and the Nationalist Government, 1927–1937.* Cambridge, MA: Harvard University Press, 1980.

Cochran, Sherman, ed. *Inventing Nanjing Road: Commercial Culture in Shanghai, 1900–1945*. Ithaca, NY: Cornell University Press, 1999.

Cohen, Myron L. "Being Chinese: The Peripheralization of Traditional Identity." *Daedalus* 120, no. 2 (1991): 113–134.

Cohen, Warren I., ed. *Pacific Passage: The Study of American-East Asian Relations on the Eve of the Twenty-First Century*. New York, NY: Columbia University Press, 1996.

Coombs, Philip. *The Fourth Dimension of Foreign Policy: Educational and Cultural Affairs*. New York: Harper and Row, 1964.

Davis, Deborah, Richard Kraus, Barry Naughton, and Elizabeth J. Perry, eds. *Urban Spaces in Contemporary China: The Potential for Autonomy and Community in Post-Mao China*. Cambridge: Cambridge University Press, 1995.

Dong, Stella. *Shanghai: The Rise and Fall of a Decadent City, 1842–1949*. New York: Perennial, 2001.

Elvin, Mark. "The Administration of Shanghai, 1905–1914," in Mark Elvin and G. W. Skinner, eds., *The Chinese City between Two Worlds*. Stanford, CA: Stanford University Press, 1974, pp. 239–262.

Erickson, Britta. *The Art of Xu Bing: Words without Meaning, Meaning without Words*. Washington, DC, and Seattle: Arthur M. Sackler Gallery and University of Washington Press, 2001.

Fairbank, John King. *Trade and Diplomacy on the China Coast: The Opening of the Treaty Ports 1842–1854*. Cambridge, MA: Harvard University Press, 1953.

Fargue, Thomas E. *China's First Hundred: Educational Mission Students in the United States, 1872–1881*. Seattle, WA: Washington State University Press, 1987.

Farrer, James. *Opening Up: Youth Sex Culture and Market Reform in Shanghai*. Chicago: University of Chicago Press, 2002.

Featherstone, Mike, ed. *Global Culture: Nationalism, Globalization and Modernity*. London: Sage, 1990.

Fewsmith, Joseph. *Party, State and Local Elites in Republican China: Merchant Organizations and Politics in Shanghai, 1890–1930*. Honolulu: University of Hawaii Press, 1985.

Finnemore, Martha. "International Organizations as Teachers of Norms: The United Nations Educational, Scientific and Cultural Organization and Science Policy." *International Organization* 47, no. 4 (Autumn 1993): 565–597.

———. *National Interest in International Society*. Ithaca, NY: Cornell University Press, 1996.

———. "Norms, Culture, and World Politics: Insights from Sociology's Institutionalism. *International Organization* 50, no. 2 (1996): 327–347.

Fiske, J. *Understanding Popular Culture*. London: Routledge, 1989.

Friedman, Milton. *Capitalism and Freedom*. Chicago: University of Chicago Press, 1962.

———, and Rose Friedman. *Free to Choose: A Personal Statement*. New York: Penguin Books, 1980.

Fu, Poshek. *Passivity, Resistance, and Collaboration: Intellectual Choices in Occupied Shanghai, 1937–1945*. Stanford, CA: Stanford University Press, 1993.

Fung Ka-iu. "The Spatial Development of Shanghai," in C. Howe, ed., *Shanghai, Revolution and Development in an Asian Metropolis*. Cambridge: Cambridge University Press, 1981.

Gamble, Jos. *Shanghai in Transition: Changing Perspectives and Social Contours of a Chinese Metropolis*. London: RoutledgeCurzon, 2003.

Gandelsonas, Mario, Ackbar Abbas, M. Christine Boyer, and M. A. Abbas, eds. *Shanghai Reflections: Architecture, Urbanism, and the Search for an Alternative Modernity*. Princeton, NJ: Princeton Architectural Press, 2002.

Gao Minglu. *Total Modernity and the Avant-Garde in Twentieth-Century Chinese Art*. Cambridge, MA: The MIT Press, 2011.

Gaubatz, Piper. "China's Urban Transformation: Patterns and Processes of Morphological Change in Beijing, Shanghai and Guangzhou." *Urban Studies* 36, no. 9 (August 1999): 1495–1521.

Geertz, Clifford. "Thick toward an Interpretative Theory of Culture," in Clifford Geertz, ed., *The Interpretation of Culture: Selected Essays by Clifford Geertz*. London: Basic Books, 1973, pp. 3–30.

Geithner, Peter F. "Ford Foundation Support for International Relations in China," in Ford Foundation's Beijing Office, *International Relations Studies in China: A Review of Ford Foundation Past Grantmaking and Future Choices*. Beijing: Ford Foundation's Beijing Office, 2003, pp. 89–103.

Giddens. Anthony. *The Consequences of Modernity*. Stanford, CA: Stanford University Press, 1990.

———. *Modernity and Self-Identity: Self and Society in the Late Modern Age*. Cambridge: Polity Press, 1991.

Gladston, Paul. *"Avant-garde" Art Groups in China, 1979–1989*. Bristol, UK: Intellect Ltd., 2013.

———. *Contemporary Art in Shanghai: Conversations with Seven Chinese Artists* [Yu Youhan, Liang Shaoji, Ding Yi, Yang Fudong, Song Tao, Ji Weiyu and Zhang Ding.]. Hong Kong: Blue Kingfisher, 2012.

Gold, Thomas B. "Go with Your Feelings, Hong Kong and Taiwan Popular Culture in Greater China." *China Quarterly* 136 (1993): 907–925.

Goodman, Bryna. *Native Place, City, and Nation: Regional Networks and Identities in Shanghai, 1853–1937*. Berkeley: University of California Press, 1995.

Goodman, David S. G. "The Politics of Regionalism: Economic Development, Conflict and Negotiation," in D.S.G. Goodman and G. Segal, eds., *China Deconstructs: Politics, Trade and Regionalism*. London: Routledge, 1994, pp. 1–20.

———. "Locating China's Middle Classes: Social Intermediaries and the Party-State." *Journal of Contemporary China* 25, no. 97 (September 2015): 1–13.

Green, Q. M. *The Foreigner in China*. London: Hutchinson, 1942.

Gu Xin. "The Art of Re-Industrialisation in Shanghai." *Culture Unbound* 4 (2012): 193–211.

Guo Shaohua. "Acting through the Camera Lens: The Global Imaginary and Middle Class Aspirations in Chinese Urban Cinema." *Journal of Contemporary China* 26, no. 104 (2017): 311–324.

Gupta, Akhil, and James Ferguson. "Beyond 'Culture': Space, Identity and the Politics of Difference." *Cultural Anthropology* 7, no. l (1992): 6–23.

Hall, Stuart. "The Local and the Global: Globalization and Ethnicity," in A. K. King, ed., *Culture Globalization and the World System: Contemporary Conditions for the Representation of Identity*. London: Macnillan, 1991.

Hannerz, Ulf. *Transnational Connections: Culture, People, Places*. London: Routledge, 1996.

Harvey, David. *The Condition of Postmodernity: An Enquiry into the Origins of Cultural Change*. Cambridge: Blackwell, 1990.

———. *Spaces of Hope*. Berkeley: University of California Press, 2000.

Hayhoe, Ruth. *China's Universities and the Open Door*. Armonk, NY: M.E. Sharpe, 1989.

———. "Shanghai as a Mediator of the Educational Open Door." *Pacific Affairs* 61, no. 2 (Summer 1988): 253–284.

———, and Julian Pan, eds. *Knowledge Across Cultures: A Contribution to Dialogue among Civilizations*. Hong Kong: Comparative Education Research Centre, University of Hong Kong, 2001.

Henriot, Christian. *Shanghai, 1927–1937: Municipal Power, Locality, and Modernization*. Translated by Noel Castelino. Berkeley: University of California Press, 1993.

———, and Wen-Hsin Yeh, eds. *In the Shadow of the Rising Sun: Shanghai under Japanese Occupation*. Cambridge: Cambridge University Press, 2004.

Heppner, Ernest G. *Shanghai Refuge: A Memoir of the World War II Jewish Ghetto*. Lincoln: University of Nebraska Press, 1994.

Hershatter, Gail. *Dangerous Pleasures: Prostitution and Modernity in Twentieth-Century Shanghai*. Berkeley: University of California Press, 1997.

The Hong Kong Museum of History, comp. *Boundless Learning: Foreign-Educated Students of Modern China*. Hong Kong: The Hong Kong Museum of History, 2003.

Honig, Emily. *Creating Chinese Ethnicity: Subei People in Shanghai, 1850–1980*. New Haven, CT: Yale University Press, 1992.

———. *Sisters and Strangers: Women in the Shanghai Cotton Mills, 1919–1949*. Stanford, CA: Stanford University Press, 1986.

Hook, Brian, ed. *Shanghai and the Yangtze Delta: A City Reborn*. Cambridge, England: Oxford University Press, 1998.

Hopf, Ted. *Social Origins of International Politics: Identities and Construction of Foreign Policies at Home*. Ithaca: NY: Cornell University Press, 2002.

Howe, Christopher, ed. *Shanghai, Revolution and Development in an Asian Metropolis*. Cambridge: Cambridge University Press, 1981.

Huang Fu-ch'ing. *Chinese Students in Japan in the Late Ch'ing Period*. Translated by Katherine P. K. Whitaker. Tokyo: The Centre for East Asian Cultural Studies, 1982.

Huang Jianyi. *Chinese Students and Scholars in American Higher Education*. Westport, CT: Praeger, 1997.

Huang, Tsung-Yi Michelle. *Walking between Slums and Skyscrapers: Illusions of Open Space in Hong Kong, Tokyo and Shanghai*. Hong Kong: Hong Kong University Press, 2004.

Huang Ying-Fen. "Spectacular Post-Colonial Cities: Markets, Ideology and Globalization in the Making of Shanghai and Hong Kong." Simon Fraser University. Doctoral Thesis. Summer 2008.

Hunter, Neale. *Shanghai Journal: An Eyewitness Account of the Cultural Revolution*. New York, NY: Praeger, 1969.

Huntington, Samuel. "The Clash of Civilizations?" *Foreign Affairs* 72, no. 3 (1993).

Inglehart, Ronald F., and M. Carballo. 2008. "Does Latin America Exist? A Global Analysis of Cross-Cultural Differences." *Perfiles Latinoamericanos* 16, no. 31 (2008): 13–38.

Iriye, Akira. *Cultural Internationalism and World Order*. Baltimore: The Johns Hopkins University Press, 1997.

———. *Power and Culture*. Cambridge, MA: Harvard University Press, 1982.

Israel, John. *Lianda: A Chinese University in War and Revolution*. Stanford, CA: Stanford University Press, 1998.

Jacobs, J. Bruce. "Shanghai: An Alternative Centre?" in David S.G. Goodman ed. *China's Provinces in Reform: Class, Community and Political Culture*. London: Routledge, 1997, pp. 163–193.

———, and Hong Lijian. "Shanghai and the Lower Yangzi Valley," in D.S.G. Goodman and G. Segal, eds., *China Deconstructs: Politics, Trade and Regionalism*. London: Routledge, 1994, pp. 224–252.

Jardine, Lisa, and Jerry Brotton. *Global Interests: Renaissance Art between East and West*. London: Reaktion Books, 2000.

Jaros, Kyle A. *China's Urban Champions: The Politics of Spatial Development*. Princeton, NJ.: Princeton University Press, 2019.

Ji Zhaojin. *A History of Modern Shanghai Banking: The Rise and Decline of China's Finance Capitalism*. Armonk, NY: M.E. Sharpe, 2003.

Johnson, Chalmers. *The Sorrows of Empire: Militarism, Secrecy, and the End of the Republic*. New York: Henry Holt and Company, Metropolitan Books, 2004.

Johnson, Linda C., ed. *Cities of Jiangnan in Late Imperial China*. New York: State University of New York Press, 1993.

———. *Shanghai: From Market Town to Treaty Port, 1074–1858*. Stanford, CA: Stanford University Press, 1995.

Johnston, Alastair Iain. "The State of International Relations Research in China: Considerations for the Ford Foundation," in Ford Foundation's Beijing Office, *International Relations Studies in China: A Review of Ford Foundation Past Grantmaking and Future Choices*. Beijing: Ford Foundation's Beijing Office, 2003, pp. 131–184.

Johnston, Tess, and Deke Erh. *A Last Look: Western Architecture in Old Shanghai*. Hong Kong: Old China Hand Press, 1993.

Jones, Susan M. "The Ningpo Pang and Financial Power at Shanghai," in M. Elvin and G. W. Skinner, eds., *The Chinese City between Two Worlds*. Stanford, CA: Stanford University Press, 1974, pp. 73–96.

Kallgren, Joyce K., and Denis Fred Simon, eds. *Educational Exchanges: Essays on the Sino-American Experience*. Berkeley, CA: Institute of East Asian Studies, 1987.

Katzenstein, Peter, ed. *Cultural Norms and National Security: Police and Military in Postwar Japan*. Ithaca, NY: Cornell University Press, 1996.

———. *The Culture of National Security: Norms and Identity in World Politics*. New York: Columbia University Press, 1996.

Kellner, Douglas. "Popular Culture and the Construction of Postmodern Identities," in S. Lash and J. Friedman, eds., *Modernity and Identity*. Oxford: Blackwell, 1992, pp. 141–177.

Kim, Samuel, ed. *Globalization and East Asia*. Lanham, MD: Rowman and Littlefield Publishers, 2000.

King, Anthony D. *Global Cities: Post-Imperialism and the Internationalization of London*. New York: Routledge, 1990.

Koehn, Peter H., and Yin Xiao-huang, eds. *The Expanding Roles of Chinese Americans in U.S.-China Relations: Transnational Networks and Trans-Pacific Interactions*. Armonk, NY: M.E. Sharpe, 2002.

Krasno, Rena. *Strangers Always: A Jewish Family in Wartime Shanghai*. Berkeley, CA: Pacific View Press, 1992.

Kraus, Richard C. "China's Artists between Plan and Market," in Deborah S. Davis, Richard Kraus, Barry Naughton, and Elizebeth J. Perry, eds., *Urban Spaces in Contemporary China: The Potential for Autonomy and Community in Post-Mao China*. Cambridge: Cambridge University Press, 1995, pp. 173–192.

———. *The Party and the Arty in China: The New Politics of Culture*. Lanham, MD: Rowman and Littlefield Publishers, 2004.

LaFargue, Thomas E. *China's First Hundred: Educational Mission Students in the United States, 1872–1881*. Seattle: Washington State University Press, 1987.

Lampton, David M., Joyce A. Madancy, and Kristen M. Williams. *A Relationship Restored: Trends in U.S.-China Educational Exchanges, 1978–1984*. Washington, DC: National Academy Press, 1986.

Law, Wing-Wah, and Ho Ming Ng. "Globalization and Multileveled Citizenship Education: A Tale of Two Chinese Cities, Hong Kong and Shanghai." *Teachers College Record* 111, no. 4 (April 2009): 851–892.

Lee, Leo Ou-fan. *Shanghai Modern: The Flowering of a New Urban Culture in China: 1930–1945*. Cambridge, MA: Harvard University Press, 1999.

Lee, Tahirih V. "Introduction to Coping with Shanghai: Means of Survival and Success in the Early Twentieth Century—a Symposium." *Journal of Asian Studies* 54, no. 1 (February 1995): 3–18.

Leibo, Steven. *Transferring Technology to China, Prosper Giquel and the Self-Strengthening Movement*. Berkeley: University of California Press, 1985.

Li Cheng, ed. *Bridging Minds across the Pacific: U.S.-China Educational Exchanges 1978–2003*. Lanham, MD: Lexington Books, 2005.

———. *China's Leaders: The New Generation.* Lanham, MD: Rowman & Littlefield Publishers, 2001.

———. "Diversification of Chinese Entrepreneurs and Cultural Pluralism in the Reform Era," in Shiping Hua, ed., *Chinese Political Culture 1989-2000.* Armonk, NY: M.E. Sharpe, 2001, pp. 219-245.

———. *Rediscovering China: Dynamics and Dilemmas of Reform.* Lanham, MD: Rowman & Littlefield Publishers, 1997.

———. "Rediscovering Urban Subcultures: Contrast between Shanghai and Beijing," *China Journal* 36 (July 1996): 139-153.

———, and Lynn White. "China's Technocratic Movement and the World Economic Herald," *Modern China* 17, no. 3 (July 1991): 342-388.

Li Hongshan. *U.S.-China Educational Exchange: State, Society, and Intercultural Relations, 1905-1950.* New Brunswick, NJ: Rutgers University Press, 2008.

Li Zhang. *In Search of Paradise: Middle-Class Living in a Chinese Metropolis.* Ithaca, NY: Cornell University Press, 2012.

Liang, Ellen Johnston. *The Winking Owl: Art in the People's Republic of China.* Berkeley: University of California Press, 1989.

Ling Pan. *Old Shanghai: Gangsters in Paradise.* Hong Kong: Heinemann, 1984.

Link, Perry E. *Mandarin Ducks and Butterflies: Popular Fiction in Twentieth Century Chinese Cities.* Berkeley: University of California Press, 1981.

Lipset, Seymour Martin. *Political Man, Where, How and Why Democracy Works in the Modern World.* New York: Doubleday, 1960.

Liu Xin. "Class Structure and Income Inequality in Transitional China." *Journal of Chinese Sociology* 7, no. 4 (2020): 1-24.

Liu Xun. "Space, Mobility, and Flexibility: Chinese Villagers and Scholars Negotiate Power at Home and Abroad," in Aihwa Ong and Donald M. Nonini, eds., *Ungrounded Empires: The Cultural Politics of Modern Chinese Transnationalism.* London: Routledge, 1997, pp. 91-114.

Lu Hanchao. *Beyond the Neon Lights: Everyday Shanghai in the Early Twentieth Century.* Berkeley: University of California Press, 1999.

———. "'The Seventy-two Tenants': Residence and Commerce in Shanghai's *Shikumen* Houses, 1872-1951," in Sherman Cochran, ed. *Inventing Nanjing Road: Commercial Culture in Shanghai, 1900-1945.* Ithaca, NY: Cornell University Press, 1999, pp. 133-184.

MacPherson, Kerrie. *A Wilderness of Marshes: The Origins of Public Health in Shanghai, 1843-1893.* Oxford: Oxford University Press, 1987.

Mak, Grace C. L. and Leslie N. K. Lo. "Education," in Yeung Yue-man and Sung Yun-wing, eds. *Shanghai: Transformation and Modernization under China's Open Door Policy.* Hong Kong: Chinese University of Hong Kong Press, 1996, pp. 375-398.

Martin, Brian G. *The Shanghai Green Gang: Politics and Organized Crime, 1919-1937.* Berkeley: University of California Press, 1996.

Metzgar, Emily T. "Institutions of Higher Education as Public Diplomacy Tools: China-Based University Programs for the 21st Century." *Journal of Studies in International Education* 20, no. 3 (July 2016): 223-241.

Miao Ying. *Being Middle Class in China.* London: Routledge, 2016.

———. "The Paradox of Middle-Class Attitudes in China: Democracy, Social Stability, and Reform." *Journal of Current Chinese Affairs* 45, no. 1 (2016): 169-190.

Miller, G. E. *Shanghai, the Paradise of Adventurers.* New York: Orsay Publishing House, 1937.

Mittler, Barbara. *A Newspaper for China? Power, Identity, and Change in Shanghai's New Media, 1872-1912.* Cambridge, MA: Harvard University Press, 2004.

Morreale, J. C., Anna Shostya, and Mariana Villada. "China's Rising Middle Class: A Case

Study of Shanghai College Students." *Journal of International Studies* 11, no. 2 (2018): 9–22.

Murphey, Rhoads. *The Outsiders.* Ann Arbor: University of Michigan Press, 1970.

———. *Shanghai, Key to Modern China.* Cambridge, MA: Harvard Univ. Press, 1953.

———. "The Treaty Ports and China's Modernization," in M. Elvin and G. W. Skinner, eds., *The Chinese City between Two Worlds.* Stanford, CA: Stanford University Press, 1974, pp. 17–71.

Nathan, Andrew J. "The Puzzle of the Chinese Middle Class." *Journal of Democracy* 27, no. 27 (April 2016): 5–19.

Ni Ting. *The Cultural Experiences of Chinese Students Who Studied in the United States during the 1930s–1940s.* Lewiston, NY: Edwin Mellen Press, 2002.

Ninkovich, Frank A., and Bu Liping, eds. *The Cultural Turn: Essays in the History of U.S. Foreign Relations.* Chicago, IL: Imprint Publications, 2001.

Nye, Joseph S. *Soft Power: The Means to Success in World Politics.* New York, NY: Public Affairs, 2004.

Olds, Kris. "Globalization and the Production of New Urban Spaces: Pacific Rim Megaprojects in the Late 20th Century." *Environment and Planning* A 27 (1995): 1713–1743.

———. "Globalizing Shanghai: The 'Global Intelligence Corps' and the Building of Pudong." *Cities* 14, no. 2 (1997): 109–123.

Ong, Aihwa. *Flexible Citizenship: The Cultural Logics of Transnationality.* Durham, NC: Duke University Press, 1999.

———, and Donald M. Nonini, eds., *Ungrounded Empires: The Cultural Politics of Modern Chinese Transnationalism.* London: Routledge, 1997.

Osnos, Evan. "Fight Fight, Talk Talk: The Future of America's Context with China." *New Yorker,* January 13, 2020, 32–45.

Orleans, Leo S. *Chinese Students in America: Policies, Issues and Numbers.* Washington, DC: National Academy Press, 1988.

Pan, Jennifer, and Yiqing Xu. "China's Ideological Spectrum." *Journal of Politics* 80, no. 1 (January 2018): 254–273.

Pan Lu. "Nostalgia as Resistance: Memory, Space and the Competing Modernities in Berlin and Shanghai." *European Journal of East Asia Studies* 12, no. 1 (2013): 135–160.

Pan, Lynn. *Shanghai: A Century of Change in Photographs.* Hong Kong: Haifeng Press, 1993.

Pellow, D. "No Place to Live, No Place to Love: Coping in Shanghai," in G. E Guldin and A. Southall, eds., *Urban Anthropology in China.* Leiden: E.J. Brill, 1993, pp. 396–424.

Perry, Elizabeth J. "Introduction: Chinese Political Culture Revisited," in J. N. Wasserstrom and E. J. Perry, eds., *Popular Protest and Political Culture in Modern China: Learning from 1989.* Boulder, CO: Westview Press, 1992, pp. 1–13.

———. *Shanghai on Strike: The Politics of Chinese Labor.* Stanford, CA: Stanford University Press, 1993.

———. "State and Society in Contemporary China." *World Politics* 41, no. 4 (1989): 579–591.

———, and Li Xun. *Proletarian Power: Shanghai in the Cultural Revolution.* Boulder, CO: Westview Press, 1997.

Peterson, Glen, Ruth Hayhoe, and Lu Yongling, eds. *Education, Culture, and Identity in Twentieth-Century China.* Ann Arbor: University of Michigan Press, 2001.

Pun, Ngai, and Kim-ming Lee. "Locating Globalization: The Changing Role of the City-State in Post-handover Hong Kong." *China Review* 2, no. 1 (Spring 2002): 1–28.

Pye, Lucian W. "Foreword," in Christopher Howe, ed. *Shanghai, Revolution and Development in an Asian Metropolis.* Cambridge: Cambridge University Press, 1981, pp. xi–xvi.

———. "How China's Nationalism Was Shanghaied." *Australian Journal of Chinese Affairs,* no. 29 (January 1993): 107–133.

Qian Ning. *Chinese Students Encounter America.* Translated by T. K. Chu. Seattle: University of Washington Press, 2002.

Redfield, Robert, and Milton Singer. "The Cultural Role of Cities," in Richard Sennett, ed. *Classic Essays on the Culture of Cities*. Englewood Cliffs, NJ: Prentice-Hall, 1969, pp. 206–220.

Ren Xuefei. *Urban China*. Cambridge: Polity Press, 2013.

Robertson, Roland. *Globalization: Social Theory and Global Culture*. London: Sage, 1992.

———, and H. H. Khondker. "Discourses of Globalization: Preliminary Considerations." *International Sociology* 13, no. 1 (1998): 25–40.

Rosen, Stanley. "Chinese Media and Youth: Attitudes toward Nationalism and Internationalism," in Lee Chin-Chuan, ed. *National and Global: Chinese Media Discourses*. London and New York: Routledge Curzon, 2003, pp. 97–118.

———. "Brain Drain and Brain Gain." *Chinese Education and Society* 36, no. 2 (March–April 2003): 6–11.

Ross, James R. *Escape to Shanghai: A Jewish Community in China*. New York: Free Press, 1994.

Rothkopf, David. "In Praise of Cultural Imperialism." *Foreign Policy*, no. 107 (Summer 1997).

Said, Edward. *Cultural and Imperialism*. New York, NY: Alfred A Knopf, 1993.

———. *Orientalism*. New York: Random House, 1978.

Sassen, Saskia. *The Global City: New York, London, Tokyo*. Princeton, NJ: Princeton University Press, 1991.

———. Globalization and Its Discontents: Essays on the New Mobility of People and Money. New York: New Press, 1998.

Scott, Peter, ed. *The Globalization of Higher Education*. Buckingham, England: Open University Press, 1998.

Sergeant, Harriet. *Shanghai: Collision Point of Cultures, 1918–1939*. New York: Crown Publishers, 1990.

Shen Wei. "Chinese Student Circular Migration and Global City Formation: A Relational Case Study of Shanghai and Paris." Loughborough University Institutional Repository. Doctoral Thesis. October 1, 2009.

Shen Yicheng. *Shanghai: Approaching China*. Shanghai: Shanghai People's Fine Arts Publishing House, 2005.

Skinner, G. William, ed., *The City in Late Imperial China*. Stanford, CA: Stanford University Press, 1977.

Solinger, Dorothy J. "Urban Entrepreneurs and the State: The Merger of State and Society," in A. L. Rosenbaum, ed., *State and Society in China: The Consequences of Reform*. Boulder, CO: Westview Press, 1992, pp. 121–141.

Spence, Jonathan D. *To Change China: Western Advisers in China, 1620–1960*. Boston: Little, Brown, 1969.

Steinberg, James, and Michael E. O'Hanlon. *Strategic Reassurance and Resolve: U.S.-China Relations in the Twenty-First Century*. Princeton, NJ.: Princeton University Press, 2015.

Stephens, Thomas B. *Order and Discipline in China: The Shanghai Mixed Court, 1911–27*. Seattle: University of Washington Press, 1992.

Sutherland, Christopher F. *Urban Change in Revolutionary China: Shanghai 1949–1982*. Ann Arbor, MI: University Microfilms International, 1985.

Tang Wenfang. *Populist Authoritarianism: Chinese Political Culture and Regime Sustainability*. Oxford: Oxford University Press, 2016.

Teng Ssu-yu, and John Fairbank. *China's Response to the West: A Documentary Survey*. Cambridge, MA: Harvard University Press, 1954.

Thompson, John B. *Ideology and Modern Culture: Critical Social Theory in the Era of Mass Communication*. Stanford, CA: Stanford University Press, 1990.

Tinsman, Marilyn Williams. *China and the Returned Overseas Chinese Students*. New York: Columbia University Teachers College, 1983.

Tomlinson, John. *Globalization and Culture*. Chicago: University of Chicago Press, 2000.

Trumbull, Randolph. *Shanghai Modernists*. Ph.D. Dissertation. Stanford University. 1989.

Tu Wei-ming. "Cultural China: The Periphery as the Center," *Daedalus* 120, no. 2 (1991): 1–32.

Waara, Carrie. "Invention, Industry, Art: The Commercialization of Culture in Republican Art Magazines," in Sherman Cochran, ed. *Inventing Nanjing Road: Commercial Culture in Shanghai, 1900–1945*. Ithaca, NY: Cornell University Press, 1999, pp. 61–89.

Wakeman, Carolyn, and Ken Light, eds. *Assignment: Shanghai. Photographs on the Eve of Revolution*. Berkeley: University of California Press, 2003.

Wakeman, Frederic Jr. *Policing Shanghai, 1927–1937*. Berkeley: University of California Press, 1995.

———, and Yeh Wen-hsin, eds. *Shanghai Sojourners*. Berkeley: University of California, Berkeley, Institute of East Asian Studies, 1992.

Wang Jisi. "International Relations Studies in China Today: Achievements, Trends, and Conditions," in Ford Foundation's Beijing Office, *International Relations Studies in China: A Review of Ford Foundation Past Grantmaking and Future Choices*. Beijing: Ford Foundation's Beijing Office, 2003, pp. 105–129.

Wang Xin. "Divergent Identities, Convergent Interests: The Rising Middle-Income Stratum in China and Its Civic Awareness." *Journal of Contemporary China* 17, no. 54 (February 2018): 53–69.

Wang Y. C. *Chinese Intellectuals and the West: 1872–1949*. Chapel Hill: University of North Carolina Press, 1966.

Wasserstrom, Jeffrey N. *Global Shanghai, 1850–2010: A History in Fragments*. London: Routledge, 2008.

———. *Student Protests in Twentieth-Century China: The View from Shanghai*. Stanford, CA: Stanford University Press, 1991.

Watson, James L, ed. *Golden Arches East: McDonald's in East Asia*. Stanford, CA: Stanford University Press, 1997.

———. "Transnationalism, Localization, and Fast Foods in East Asia," in J. L. Watson, ed., *Golden Arches East: McDonald's in East Asia*. Stanford, CA: Stanford University Press, 1997, pp. 1–38.

Wei, Betty Peh-T'i. *Shanghai: Crucible of Modern China*. Oxford: Oxford University Press, 1987.

Weiner, Rebecca. *Culture Shock! Shanghai at Your Door*. New York: Graphic Arts Center Publishing, 2003.

Weiss, Jessica Chen. "How Hawkish Is the Chinese Public? Another Look at 'Rising Nationalism' and Chinese Foreign Policy." *Journal of Contemporary China* 28, no. 119 (March 2019): 679–695.

Wendt, Alexander. *Social Theory of International Politics*. Cambridge, England: Cambridge University Press, 1999.

West, Philip. *Yenching University and Sino-Western Relations, 1916–1952*. Cambridge, MA: Harvard University Press, 1976.

White, Donald W. *The American Century: The Rise and Decline of the United States as a World Power*. New Haven, CT: Yale University Press, 1996.

White, Lynn T III. *Policies of Chaos: The Organizational Causes of Violence in China's Cultural Revolution*. Princeton, NJ: Princeton University Press, 1989.

———. *Shanghai Shanghaied?: Uneven Taxes in Reform China*. Hong Kong: Centre of Asian Studies, University of Hong Kong Press, 1991.

———. *Unstately Power: Vol. 1 Local Causes of China's Economic Reforms*. Armonk, NY: M.E. Sharpe, 1998.

———. *Unstately Power: Vol. 2 Local Causes of China's Intellectuals, Legal and Governmental Reforms*. Armonk, NY: M.E. Sharpe, 1999.

———, and Li Cheng. "Politics and Government," in Brian Hook, ed. *Shanghai and the Yangtze Delta: A City Reborn.* Cambridge, England: Oxford University Press, 1998, pp. 30–73.

———. "China Coast Identities: Regional, National, and Global," in Samuel Kim and Lowell Dittmer, eds. *China's Quest for National Identities.* Ithaca, NY: Cornell University Press, 1993, pp. 154–193.

Whyte, Martin K. "Urban China: A Civil Society in the Making?" in Arthur Lewis Rosenbaum, ed., *State and Society in China: The Consequences of Reform.* Boulder: Westview Press, 1992, pp. 77–101.

Wiseman, Mary Bittner. "Subversive Strategies in Chinese Avant-Garde Art." *Journal of Aesthetics and Art Criticism* 65, no. 1, Special Issue: Global Theories of the Arts and Aesthetics (Winter 2007): 109–119.

Wong, Linda, Lynn T. White, and Gui Shixun, eds. *Social Policy Reform in Hong Kong and Shanghai: A Tale of Two Cities.* Armonk, NY: M.E. Sharpe, 2004.

Wong Siu-Lun. *Emigrant Entrepreneurs: Shanghai Industrialists in Hong Kong.* Oxford: Oxford University Press, 1988.

Wong Wang-Chi. *Politics and Literature in Shanghai: The Chinese League of Left-Wing Writers, 1930–36.* Manchester, England: Manchester University Press, 1991.

Wu Fulong. "The Global and Local Dimensions of Place-Making: Remaking Shanghai as a World City." *Urban Studies* 37 no. 8 (2000): 1359–1377.

———. *Globalization and the Chinese City.* London: Routledge, 2005.

Xin, Fuliang. "The Basic Line of Thinking in Shanghai's Efforts to Attract Overseas Chinese Intellect." *Chinese Education and Society* 34, no. 3 (May/June 2001): 65–77.

Xu Xiaoqun. *State and Society in Republican China: The Rise of Shanghai Professional Associations, 1912–1937.* Ph.D. Dissertation. Columbia University. 1993.

Yan Yunxiang. "Managed Globalization: State Power and Cultural Transition in China," in Samuel P. Huntington, ed. *Many Globalizations: Cultural Diversity in the Contemporary World.* New York: Oxford University Press, 2002, pp. 19–47.

———. "McDonald's in Beijing: The Localization of Americana," in James L. Watson, ed., *Golden Arches East: McDonald's in East Asia.* Stanford, CA: Stanford University Press, 1997, pp. 39– 76.

Yan Zhongmin. "Shanghai: The Growth and Shifting Emphasis of China's Largest City," in V.F.S. Sit, ed., *Chinese Cities: The Growth of the Metropolis Since 1949.* Hong Kong: Oxford University Press, 1985, pp. 94–127.

Yang, Mayfair Mei-hui. "Mass Media and Transnational Subjectivity in Shanghai: Notes on (Re)cosmopolitanism in a Chinese Metropolis," in Aihwa Ong and Donald M. Nonini, eds., *Ungrounded Empires: The Cultural Politics of Modern Chinese Transnationalism.* London: Routledge, 1997, pp. 287–319.

Yatsko, Pamela. *New Shanghai: The Rocky Rebirth of China's Legendary City.* New York: John Wiley & Sons, 2000.

Ye Weili. *Seeking Modernity in China's Name: Chinese Students in the United States, 1900– 1927.* Stanford, CA: Stanford University Press, 2001.

Ye Xiaoqing. *The Dianshizhai Pictorial: Shanghai Urban Life, 1884–1898.* Ann Arbor: The University of Michigan Press, 2003.

Yeh Wen-Hsing. *The Alienated Academy: Higher Education in Republican China.* Ph.D. dissertation. University of California Berkeley. 1984.

Yeung Yue-man. *Globalization and Networked Societies: Urban-Regional Change in Pacific Asia.* Honolulu: University of Hawaii Press, 2000.

———, and Sung Yun-wing, eds. *Shanghai: Transformation and Modernization under China's Open Door Policy.* Hong Kong: Chinese University of Hong Kong, 1996.

Yue, Meng. "Chinese Cosmopolitanism Repositioned," in *Shanghai and the Edges of Empire.* Minneapolis: University of Minnesota, 2006, pp. 210–232.

Yung Wing (Rong Hong). *My Life in China and America*. New York: Henry Holt and Company, 1909.

Zakaria, Fareed. "The New China Scare: Why America Shouldn't Panic about Its Latest Challenger." *Foreign Affairs* 99, no. 1 (January–February 2020): 52–69.

Zhang Yingjin, ed. *Cinema and Urban Culture in Shanghai, 1922–1943*. Stanford, CA: Stanford University Press, 1999.

———. *Configurations of Space, Time, and Gender*. Stanford, CA: Stanford University Press, 1996.

Zhang Yufa. "Returned Chinese Students from America and the Chinese Leadership (1846–1949)." *Chinese Studies in History* 35, no. 3 (Spring 2002): 52–86.

Zhao Bin. "Consumerism, Confucianism. Communism: Making Sense of China Today," *New Left Review* 222 (1997): 43–59.

Zheng Yongnian. *Discovering Chinese Nationalism in China: Modernization Identity, and International Relations*. Cambridge, England: Cambridge University Press, 1999.

Zhong Wenhui. "Chinese Scholars and the World Community," in Michael Agelasto and Bob Adamson, eds. *Higher Education in Post-Mao China*. Hong Kong: Hong Kong University Press, 1998, pp. 59–77.

Zukin, Sharon, Philip Kasinitz, and Xiangming Chen. *Global Cities, Local Streets: Everyday Diversity from New York to Shanghai*. London: Routledge, 2015.

Zweig, David. *Internationalizing China: Domestic Interests and Global Linkages*. Ithaca: NY: Cornell University Press, 2002.

———. "Leaders, Bureaucrats, and Institutional Culture: The Struggle to Bring Back China's Top Overseas Talent," in Jacques deLisle and Avery Goldstein, eds., *China's Global Engagement: Cooperation, Competition, and Influence in the 21st Century*. Washington, DC: Brookings Institution Press, 2017.

———. and Feng Yang, "Overseas Students, Returnees, and the Diffusion of International Norms into Post-Mao China." *International Studies Review* 16, no. 2 (June 2014): 252–263.

CHINESE

An Yu and Zhou Mian. *Liuxuesheng yu zhongwai wenhua jiaoliu* [Foreign-educated students and China's cultural exchange with the outside world]. Nanjing: Nanjing daxue chubanshe, 2000.

Bao Zonghao. *Wangluo yu dangdai shehui wenhua* [Internet and contemporary culture and society]. Shanghai: Shanghai sanlian shudian, 2001.

———. *Quanqiuhua yu dangdai shehui* [Globalization and contemporary society]. Shanghai: Shanghai sanlian shudian, 2002.

——— and Hu Yishen. *Wenhua: guoji dadushi de linghun* [Culture: The spirit of metropolis]. Shanghai: Shanghai shehui kexueyuan chubanshe, 2004.

Beijing daxue liuxue guiguo renyuan danren lingdaozhiwu wenti yanjiu ketizu. "Beijing daxue liuxue guiguo renyuan danren lingdaozhiwu wenti yanjiu" [A study of returnees who hold administrative posts at Peking University]. *Chuguo liuxue gongzuo yanjiu* [Research on studies overseas] no. 3 (2002): 7–22.

Brown, Kerry. Shanghai 2020: Xifang xuezhe guanzhao zhong de Shanghai yu Zhongguo [Shanghai 2020: Shanghai and China in the eyes of a Western scholar]. Translated by He Fang and Jiang Xiaoning. Beijing: Foreign Languages Press, 2013.

Cai Zheren and Shen Ronghua. *Zouxiang rencai guojihua—Shanghai rencai fazhan yanjiu baogao* [Toward globalization of human resources: Report on human resources development in Shanghai]. Shanghai: Shanghai shehui kexueyuan chubanshe, 2002.

Cao Shichao. *Diyi jingzhengli—Chengjiu shijie yiliu de wenhua zhanlue* [The first competitive power: Strategy in achieving a world-class culture]. Shanghai: Shanghai wenhua chubanshe, 2003.

Chen Bohai. *Shanghai wenhua tongshi* [History of Shanghai culture]. 2 volumes. Shanghai: Shanghai wenyi chubanshe, 2001.

Chen Changgui. *Rencai wailiu yu huigui* [Brain drain and return of talented students]. Wuhan: Hubei jiaoyu chubanshe, 1996.

Chen Danyan. *Shanghai de fenghua xueyue* [Shanghai memorabilia]. Beijing: Zuojia chubanshe, 1998.

Chen Guanzhong, Liao Weitang, and Yan Jun. *Boximiya Zhongguo* [Bohemian China]. Guilin: Guangxi shifan daxue chubanshe, 2004.

Chen Peiqin, Guo Ke, and Wu Ying. *Shanghai wenhua huodong guoji yingxiangli baogao* [Report on international influences of cultural events in Shanghai]. Shanghai: Shehui kexue wenxian chubanshe, 2017.

Chen Qiang, ed. *Hai shang chaoyong: jinian Shanghai gaige kaifang 40 zhounian* [Commemorating the 40th anniversary of the reform and opening up]. Shanghai: Shanghai daxue chubanshe, 2018.

Chen Shui. *Weilai zhi lu: Zhongguo shehui de duowei kongjian toushi* [The road ahead: An analysis of multi-dimensions of Chinese society]. Beijing: Shehui kexue wenxian chubanshe, 2004.

———. *Wenhua Zhongguo: Jubian Beijing xia de Zhongguo qianyan lunbian* [A cultural China: Debates on frontier issues in a rapid-changing era]. Beijing: Shehui kexue wenxian chubanshe, 2004.

Chen Wenshen. *Gonggong zuzhi de renshi juece* [Personnel decisions in public organizations: Policy choices and personnel reform in Chinese universities]. Zhengzhou: Henan renmin chubanshe, 2002.

Chen Yani. *Shanghai 15 nian* [Fifteen years in Shanghai]. Beijing: Xinhua chubanshe, 2003.

Chen Yanni. *Meiguo zhihou—wushi wei lümei renshi de guiguo zhilu* [Interviews of those who studied in the United States]. Beijing: Zuojia chubanshe, 2000.

Chen Yingfang. *Yimin Shanghai—52 ren de koushu shilu* [The Migrants' Shanghai: Oral Accounts of Fifty-Two People]. Shanghai: Xuelin chubanshe, 2003.

Cheng Naishan. *Shanghai Tange* [Shanghai Tango]. Shanghai: Xuelin chubanshe, 2002.

Dai Jinhua. *Shuxie wenhua yingxiong shiji zhijiao de wenhua yanjiu* [On cultural heroes: Cultural research on the eve of the new century]. Nanjing: Jiangsu renmin chubanshe, 2000.

Diao Pengfei. *Zhongchan jieji de shehui zhichiwang,* [Middle class social support network]. Beijing: Shehui kexue wenxian chubanshe, 2010.

Ding Gang. *Chuangxin: Xinshiji de jiaoyu shiming* [Innovation: The mission of education]. Beijing: Jiaoyu kexue chubanshe, 2000.

Ding Xiaohe and Wan Xian. *Zhongguo bainian liuxue quanjilu* [The entire account of foreign education of Chinese students in the century]. Zhuhai: Zhuhai chubanshe, 1998.

Ding Xilin, Su Qingxian, Cao Zhiyuan, and Wang Jie. *Shanghai siren hualang* [Shanghai's private galleries]. Shanghai: Shanghai kexuejishu wenxian chubanshe, 2002.

Dongfang Zaobao. *Shanghai zhongchan quanjing baogao* [Shanghai middle class landscape report]. Shanghai: Shanghai shehui kexue chubanshe, 2004.

Duan Ruopeng, Zhong Sheng, Wang Xinfu, and Li Tuo. *Zhongguo xiandaihua jinchengzhong de jieceng jiegou biandong yanjiu* [Study of social mobility in China's modernization process]. Beijing: Renmin chubanshe, 2002.

Fan Lizhu, ed. *Quanqiuhua xia de shehuibianqian yu fei zhengfuzuzhi (NGO)* [Social transformation and the NGOs in the age of globalization]. Shanghai: Shanghai renmin chubanshe, 2003.

Fan Wenbing. *Shanghai lilong de baohu yu gengxin* [The conservation and renewal of Lilong housing in Shanghai]. Shanghai: Shanghai kexue jishu chubanshe, 2004.

Fang Minglun, Li Lunxin, and Ding Ximan. *Haipai wenhua fazhan chuangxin de dongli he huoli* [Shanghai culture: Dynamism and vitality of innovation]. Shanghai: Shanghai daxue chubanshe, 2004.

Fang Ning, Wang Bingquan, and Ma Lijun. *Chengzhang de Zhongguo—Dangdai Zhongguo qingnian de guojia minzu yishi yanjiu* [Growing China: A study of Chinese youths' consciousness of state and nation]. Beijing: Renmin chubanshe, 2002.

Fang Ning, Wang Xiaodong, and Song Qiang. *Quanqiuhua yinyingxia de Zhongguo zhilu* [China's road in the shadow of globalization]. Beijing: Zhongguo shehui kexue chubanshe, 1999.

Fang Zengxian and Xu Jiang. *2004 Shanghai shuangnianzhan yingxiang shengcun* [2004 Shanghai biennale techniques of the visible guide]. Shanghai: Shanghai shuhua chubanshe, 2004

Feng Boyi, ed, *Shi x sanshi: Ding Yi zuopin* [+ x 30 years: Ding Yi's works]. Shanghai: Shanghai renmin meishu chubanshe, 2018.

Forbes China. *2018 Zhongguo xinxing zhongchanjieceng caifu baipishu* [White paper on wealth of Chinese emerging middle class]. Shanghai: Forbes China, 2018.

Fu Yinying and Zhu Hehuan. "Lun xinhaipai piping liupai de xingcheng yu tese" [On the formation and characteristics of the literature critics of the new Shanghai School]. *Shehui kexue* [Social Sciences], no. 5 (2002): 77–80.

Gan Yang and Li Meng. *Zhongguo daxue gaige zhi dao* [The road of reform for China's universities]. Shanghai: Shanghai renmin chubanshe, 2003.

Gao Minglu. *Zhongguo jiduozhuyi* [Chinese maximalism]. Chongqing: Chongqing chubanshe, 2003.

Gao Ruxi and Zhang Jianhua. *Lun da Shanghai dushiquan* [On clusters of cities around metropolitan Shanghai]. Shanghai: Shanghai shehui kexueyuan chubanshe, 2004.

Gaoshi Xiongdi (Gao brothers). *Zhongguo qianweiyishu zhuangkuang—Guanyu Zhongguo qianweiyishu de fangtan* [Status of China's avant-garde art: Talks related to China's avant-garde art]. Nanjing: Jiangsu renmin chubanshe, 2002.

Ge Fengzhang. *Da Shanghai Taishang chuanqi* [Legendary stories of Taiwanese entrepreneurs in Greater Shanghai]. Beijing: Jiuzhou chubanshe, 2003.

Ge Hongbing. *Chengshi piping Shanghai juan* [Urban critique, volume of Shanghai]. Beijing: Wenhua yishu chubanshe, 2002.

———. *Weinasi de chouti—Wenxue shiye zhong de Zhongguo xianfeng yishu* [China's avant-garde arts from the perspective of literature]. Wuhan: Hubei meishu chubanshe, 2003.

Ge Jianxiong. *Shanghai jijianshi* [Minimalist Shanghai history]. Shanghai: Shanghai renmin chubanshe, 2019.

Gong Yang. *Sichao—Zhongguo "xinzuopai" jiqi yingxiang* [Ideological trend: China's "new left" and its influence]. Beijing: Zhongguo shehui kexue chubanshe, 2003.

Gong Yunbiao. *Shanghai chouxiang* [Shanghai abstract art]. Shanghai: Shanghai shudian chubanshe, 2004.

Gu Chengfeng. *Guannian yishu de Zhongguo fangshi* [Chinese style of conceptual art]. Changsha: Hunan meishu chubanshe, 2002.

Gu Chengfeng and He Wanli. *Zhuangzhi yishu* [Installation arts]. Changsha: Hunan meishu chubanshe, 2003.

Gui Shixun and Huang Li Ruolian. *Shanghai yu Xianggang—Shehui zhengce bijiao yanjiu* [Shanghai and Hong Kong: A comparative study of social policy]. Shanghai: Huadong shifan daxue chubanshe, 2002.

Guo Qingsong. "Kuawenhua guanli: ershiyi shiji Shanghai fazhande xin mingti" [Cross-cultural management: A new topic in the cultural development of Shanghai in the 21st century]. *Shehui kexue* [Social Sciences], no. 10 (2002): 22–25.

Guowuyuan fazhan yanjiu zhongxin guoji jishu jingji yanjiusuo [International Institute of Technology and Economy in the Development Research Center of the State Council], *Rengong zhineng quanqiu geju: Weilai qushi yu Zhongguo weishi* [Global landscape of artificial intelligence: Future trends and China's position]. Beijing: Zhongguo renmin daxue chubanshe, 2019.

Han Deqiang. *Pengzhuang—Quanqiuhua xianjing yu Zhongguo xianshi xuanze* [Collision: The pitfalls of globalization and real choices for China]. Beijing: Jingji guanli chuban-she, 2000.

Han Yuqi and Zhang Song. *Dongfang de Saina zuoan: Suzhouhe yanan de yishu cangku* [Left bank of the Seine of the East: The art warehouses of Suzhou Greek]. Shanghai: Shanghai guji chubanshe, 2004.

Hauser, Ernest O. *Chumai Shanghaitan* [Shanghai: City for sale]. Translated by Zhou Yumin. Shanghai: Shanghai shudian chubanshe, 2019.

He Zhifan. *Shanghai jiqi zhoubian diqu jingdian daoyou yu lüyou wenhua zhishi* [Scenic highlights of Shanghai and its neighboring areas with insight into tourism culture]. Shanghai: Shanghai jiaotong daxue chubanshe, 2001.

Hoogewerf, Rupert, and Lu Zhaoqing, *2018 Zhongguo xinzhongchan quanceng baipishu,* [China new middle-class report 2018]. Shanghai: Jinyuan Investment Group and Hurun Report, 2018.

Hou Hanru. *Zhou Tiehai*. Shanghai: ShanghArt Gallery Publication, 2002.

Hu Angang. *Quanqiuhua tiaozhan Zhongguo* [Globalization challenges China]. Beijing: Beijing daxue chubanshe, 2002.

Hu Angang and Zhou Shaojie. *Zhongguo kuayue zhongdeng shouru xianjing* [China: Surpassing the middle-income trap]. Hangzhou: Zhejiang renmin chubanshe, 2018.

Hua Tianxue, Ai Weiwei, and Feng Boyi. *Bu hezuo fangshi* [Fuck off]. Shanghai: East Link Gallery Shang Hai, 2000.

Huang Beiyan. *Chuangshi fengbao: yintewang xijuan quanqiu* [The storm of innovation: Globalization of the Internet]. Shanghai: Shanghai yuandong chubanshe, 2000.

Huang Danhui and Hu Rong. *Xin biaoxian yishu qinggan de qijudi* [New performance art: The habitat of sentiments]. Changchun: Jilin meishu chubanshe, 1999.

Huang Guoxin, ed. *Kuashiji de Shanghai xinjianzhu* [New and trans-century architecture in Shanghai], vol. 3. Shanghai: Tongji daxue chubanshe, 2000.

Huang Ke. *Shanghai meishushi zhaji* [History of Shanghai fine art]. Shanghai: Shanghai renmin meishu chubanshe, 2000.

Huang Ping and Cui Zhiyuan, eds. *Zhongguo yu quanqiuhua: Huashengdun gongshi haishi Beijing gongshi* [China and globalization: The Washington consensus, the Beijing consensus, or what?]. Beijing: Shehui kexue wenxian chubanshe, 2005.

Huang Wenzhong. *Shanghai weixingcheng yu Zhongguo chengshihua daolu* [Shanghai's satellite cities and the road to China's urbanization]. Shanghai: Shanghai renmin chubanshe, 2003.

Jia Fangzhou. *Piping de shidai: ershi shiji mo Zhongguo meishu piping wencui* [Era of criticism: Selected works of Chinese art critics in the end of 20th century]. Nanning: Guangxi meishu chubanshe, 2003.

Jia Hao. "Dui dangqian woguo liuxue renyuan zhuangkuang de fenxi he jidian jianyi" [Analysis of current Chinese study abroad situation and some recommendations]. *Shehui kexue* [Social science], no. 6 (1997): 58–62.

Jia Kailin, Zhang Qiuping, and others. *Jianguo chuqi liuxuesheng guiguo jishi* [Accounts of returnees in the early years of the People's Republic of China]. Beijing: Zhongguo wenshi chubanshe, 1999.

Jiang Wenjun. *Dushi shehui de xingqi: jindai Shanghai de zhongchan jieceng yu zhiye tuanti,* [The rise of civil society: The middle class and professional groups in modern Shanghai]. Shanghai: Shanghai cishu chubanshe, 2017.

Jiang Xiyuan and Xia Liping. *Zhongguo heping jueqi* [Peaceful rise of China]. Beijing: Zhongguo Shehui kexue chubanshe, 2004.

Jiang Yuzhen. *Shanghai shi yige hai* [Shanghai is a sea]. Shanghai: Shanghai huabao chubanshe, 2002.

Jiao Yang and Wu Jinlan, eds. *Huazhong Shanghai: shijie huajia kan Shanghai* [Shanghai in paintings: Shanghai in the eyes of world artists]. Beijing: China Intercontinental Press, 2003.

Jin Mengmeng, Wang Qingyun, and Hao He, comp., *Weida de zuopin, weida de licheng 1978-2018* [Outstanding work, great journey 1978-2018]. Beijing: Renmin meishu chubanshe, 2018.

Jin Minqing. *Wenhua quanqiuhua yu Zhongguo dazhong wenhua* [Cultural globalization and popular culture in China]. Beijing: Renmin chubanshe, 2004.

Kang Yan. *Jiedu Shanghai* [Understanding Shanghai]. Shanghai: Shanghai renmin chubanshe, 2001.

Le Shan. *Qian liu: dui xiaai minzuzhuyi de pipan yu fansi* [Undercurrent: Critique and reflection of narrow-minded nationalism]. Shanghai: Huadong shifan daxue chubanshe, 2004.

Li Chuansong and Xu Baofa. *Yu zuguo fengyutongzhou: dangdai Zhongguo liuxue renyuan chuangye jianshi* [Standing with the motherland in both good times and bad times: A brief history of returnees from foreign study in contemporary China]. Shanghai: Shanghai waiyu jiaoyu chubanshe, 2001.

Li Chunling. *Bijiao shiyexia de zhongchan jieji xingcheng: guocheng, yingxiang yiji shehui jingji houguo,* [Formation of middle class in comparative perspective: Process, impact and socioeconomic outcome]. Beijing: Shehui kexue wenxian chubanshe, 2009.

———. *Duanlie yu suipian—Dangdai Zhongguo shehuijieceng fenhua shizheng fenxi* [Cleavage and fragment: An empirical analysis of the social stratification in contemporary China]. Beijing: Shehui kexue wenxian chubanshe, 2005.

Li Huibin. *Quanqiuhua: Zhongguo daolu* [Globalization: China's path]. Beijing: Shehui kexuewenxian chubanshe, 2003.

Li Jian. *Shehui bianqian, chengxiang liudong yu zuzhi zhuanxing* [Social change, urban-rural mobility and organizational transformation]. Shanghai: Shanghai daxue chubanshe, 2016.

Li Kanghua. *Manhua Laoshanghai zhishi jieceng* [Regarding the stratum of intellectuals in old Shanghai]. Shanghai: Shanghai renmin chubanshe, 2003.

Li Lunxin and Ding Ximan. *Shanghai laowai* [Successful foreigners in Shanghai]. Shanghai: Wenhui chubanshe, 2003.

Li Lunxin, Fang Minglun, Li Youmei, and Ding Ximan, eds. *Haipai wenhua yu chengshi chuangxin* [Shanghai culture and urban innovation]. Shanghai: Wenhui chubanshe, 2010.

Li Peilin. *Ling yizhi kanbujian de shou—Shehui jiegou zhuanxing* [Another invisible hand: The transformation of social structure]. Beijing: Shehui kexue wenxian chubanshe, 2005.

———, Li Qiang, and Sun Liping. *Zhongguo shehui fenceng* [Social stratification in China today]. Beijing: Shehui kexue wenxian chubanshe, 2004.

Li Peilin, Zhang Yi, Zhao Yandong, and Liang Dong. *Shehui chongtu yu jieji yishi—dangdai Zhongguo shehui maodun wenti yanjiu* [Social conflicts and class consciousness in China today]. Beijing: Shehui kexue wenxian chubanshe, 2005.

Li Qi and Chen Qixing. *Xinshiji Zhongguo teda chengshi gonggong xingzheng guanli—Yi Shanghai wei gean de fazhan zhanlue yanjiu* [The new century and urban public administration in Chinese metropolitan cities: The case of Shanghai]. Shanghai: Wenhui chubanshe, 2003.

Li Qiang. *Zhuanxing shiqi Zhongguo shehui fenceng* [Chinese social stratification in the transition period]. Shenyang: Liaoning jiaoyu chubanshe, 2004.

Li Qiqing and Liu Yuanqi. *Quanqiuhua yu xin ziyouzhuyi* [Globalization and neoliberalism]. Guilin: Guangxi shifandaxue chubanshe, 2003.

Li Shitao, ed. *Zhishifenzi lichang: ziyouzhuyi zhizheng yu Zhongguo sixiangjie de fenhua* [From the standpoint of intellectuals: The debate over liberalism and the split among Chinese intellectuals]. Changchun: Shidai wenyi chubanshe, 2000.

Li Tao, ed. *Zhonghua liuxue jiaoyu shilu* [A history of Chinese study abroad]. Beijing: Higher Education Press, 2003.

Li Xuanhai and Feng Xiaomin. *Shanghai jiaoyu gaige yu chuangxin* [Educational reform and innovation of Shanghai]. Shanghai: Shanghai renmin chubanshe, 2004.

Li Xiaodong. *Quanqiuhua yu wenhua zhenghe* [Globalization and integration of cultures]. Changsha: Hunan renmin chubanshe, 2003.

Li Xisuo. *Zhongguo jindai shehui yu wenhuayanjiu* [A study of society and culture in contemporary China]. Beijing: Renmin chubanshe, 2003.

—— and Liu Jilin. *Jindai Zhongguo de liumei jiaoyu* [U.S.-educated Chinese and contemporary China]. Tianjin: Tianjin guji chubanshe, 2000.

Li Yining, ed. *Zhongguo daolu yu lanling zhongchan jieji chengzhang* [China's path for development and the growth of blue-collar middle class]. Beijing: Shangwu yinshuguan, 2015.

Li Youmei, Weng Dingjun, Zhang Wenhong, and Zhang Haidong. *Shanghai diaocha: Xin bailing shengcun zhuangkuang yu shehui xinxin* [Shanghai survey: The living conditions and social confidence of new white-collar]. Beijing: Shehui kexue wenxian chubanshe, 2013.

Li Zhi. *Quanqiuhua shidai de guoji sichao* [International schools of thought in the era of globalization]. Beijing: Xinhua chubanshe, 2003.

Liao Wen. *Nüxing yishu: nüxingzhuyi zuowei fangshi* [Characteristics of feminism: Feminist art]. Changchun: Jilin meishu chubanshe, 1999.

Lin Shangli. *Shanghai zhengzhi wenming fazhan zhanlue yanjiu* [Studies of development strategy of political civilization in Shanghai]. Shanghai: Shanghai renmin chubanshe, 2004.

Lin Xi, *Ciqidian li de xiongmao: Zhishi shehuixue shiyexia de Zhongguo* [Panda in a porcelain shop; China in the perspective of sociology of knowledge]. Shanghai: Fudan daxue chubanshe, 2019.

Liu Chun, *Xue Song fangtanlu* [Interview with Xue Song]. Taiyuan: Sanjin chubanshe, 2015.

Liu Haiping. *Shijizhijiao de Zhongguo yu Meiguo* [China and the U.S. at a new millennium]. Shanghai: Shanghai waiyujiaoyu chubanshe, 2000.

Liu Ming. *Meishu wenxian* [Fine arts literature]. Wuhan: Hubei meishu chubanshe, 2004.

Liu Xiao. *Tingjin meilijian—ershi shiji liumei jingyingpu* [Chinese elites who studied in the U.S. in the 20th century: Their exploration of and success in a new world]. Baoding: Hebei daxue chubanshe, 2000.

Liu Yexiong. *Ala Shanghairen* [We Shanghainese]. Shanghai: Shanghai renmin chubanshe, 2002.

Liu Yungeng. *Xiandaihua yu fazhihua—Shanghai chengshi fazhihua yanjiu* [Modernization and legalization: Study of legal development in Shanghai]. Shanghai: Shanghai renmin chubanshe, 2004.

Lou Chenghao and Xue Shunsheng. *Laoshanghai jingdian jianzhu* [Old Shanghai: Classic architecture]. Shanghai: Tongji daxue chubanshe, 2000.

Lu Chunlong. *Zhongguo xinxing zhongchan jieji de zhengzhi taidu yu xingwei qingxiang,* [Political attitudes and behavioral tendencies of China's emerging middle class]. Beijing: Zhishi chanquan chubanshe, 2011.

Lu Daqian, Han Juntian, Fan Yunxing, and Sun Lei. *Shanghai: Guoji lüyou chengshi* [Shanghai: A world-famous tourist city in China]. Beijing: Zhongguo lüyou chubanshe, 2003.

Lu Hanlong, Yang Xiong, and Zhou Haiwang. *Shanghai shehui fazhan baogao 2019* [Annual report of social development of Shanghai 2019]. Beijing: Shehui kexue wenxian chubanshe, 2019.

——. *Shanghai shehui fazhan baogao 2017* [Annual report of social development of Shanghai 2017]. Beijing: Shehui kexue wenxian chubanshe, 2017.

Lu Peng. *1990–1999 Zhongguo dangdai yishushi* [1990s Art China]. Changsha: Hunan meishu chubanshe, 2000.

Lü Pintian. *Manyou de cunzai xinshengdai yishu* [Wandering existence: The art of the new generation]. Changchun: Jilin meishu chubanshe, 1999.

Lü Shiping. *Shanghai niaokan* [Bird's eye views of Shanghai]. Shanghai: Shanghai renmin meishu chubanshe, 2017.

Lu Xueyi. *Dangdai Zhongguo shehui liudong* [Social mobility in contemporary China]. Beijing: Shehui kexue wenxian chubanshe, 2004.

———. *Dangdai Zhongguo shehuijieceng yanjiu baogao* [Research report on social strata in contemporary China]. Beijing: Shehui kexue wenxian chubanshe, 2002.

LuLe Zheng. *Jindai Shanghai ren shehui xintai, 1860–1910* [Collective mentality of contemporary Shanghainese, 1860–1910]. Shanghai: Shanghai renmin chubanshe, 1992.

Luo Jun, ed. *Modu manbu* [Walk in the magic capital Shanghai]. Shanghai: Shanghai renmin chubanshe, 2018.

Luo Shuang and others. *Pouxi Shanghairen* [Analyzing Shanghainese]. Beijing: Zhongguo shehui chubanshe, 1995.

Luo Xiaowei and Wu Jiang. *Shanghai Longtang* [Shanghai alley]. Shanghai: Shanghai renmin meishu chubanshe, 1997.

Ma Changlin, ed. *Zujie li de Shanghai* [Shanghai in foreign concessions]. Shanghai: Shanghai shehui kexueyuan chubanshe, 2003.

Ma Dandan. *Zai lixing yu huanxiang zhijian: Zhongguo zhongchan jieji xingqi de zhidu he huayu kaocha* [Between rationality and fantasy: An institutional and discourse investigation of the rise of the Chinese middle class]. Beijing: Zhongguo shehui kexue chubanshe, 2016.

Ma Qingyu. "Quanqiuhua he dui wenhua xiangduizhuyi de piping" [Globalization and critique of cultural relativism]. *Dangdai Zhongguo yanjiu* [Contemporary China studies], no. 2 (2003).

Ma Qinzhong. *Katong yidai yu xiaofei wenhua* [The cartoon generation and consumption culture]. Changsha: Hunan meishu chubanshe, 2002.

———, ed. *Xiangjie: Shanghai dangdai yishujia xunli* [Image boundary: Shanghai contemporary artists overview]. Shanghai: Xuelin chubanshe, 2015.

———. *Zhongguo Shanghai 2000 nian shuangnianzhan ji waiweizhan wenxian* [Collected works of the Shanghai 2000 Biennale and other exhibitions]. Wuhan: Hubei meishu chabanshe, 2002.

Ma Shanglong, *Weishenme shi Shanghai* [Why Shanghai]. Shanghai: Shanghai shudian chubanshe, 2014.

Ma Xuexin and Chen Jianglan. *Dangdai Shanghai chengshi fazhan yanjiu* [Studies of the urban development of contemporary Shanghai]. Shanghai: Shanghai renmin chubanshe, 2008.

———. *Ershiyi shiji Shanghai jishi: 2001–2003* [The chronicle of Shanghai in the 21st century, 2001–2003]. Shanghai: Shanghai renmin chubanshe, 2004.

Ma Yan. "*Meishuguan shidai xia de Shanghai dangdai yishu shengtai*" [Shanghai contemporary art ecology in the era of rapid expansion of art museums]. *Yishu guoji* [Art International], February 12, 2013.

Medina, Cuauhtemoc, ed. *Yubu: Di shierjie Shanghai shuangnian zhan* [Proregress: The 12th Shanghai Biennale]. Shanghai: Shanghai wenhua chubanshe, 2018.

———, and the Power Station of Art, ed. *Di shierjie Shanghai shuangnian zhan* [12th Shanghai biennale]. Shanghai: Shanghai wenhua chubanshe, 2018.

Meng Fanhua. *Zhongshen kuanghuan dangdai Zhongguo de wenhua chongtu wenti* [The carnival of the Gods: Issues on the cultural clash in contemporary China]. Beijing: Jinri Zhongguo chubanshe, 1997.

Meng Yankun. *Xin Shanghai nüren* [The new Shanghai women]. Shanghai: Shanghai renmin chubanshe, 2003.

Ouyang Guangming. *Xinshiqi de dushi renwen suyang* [Urban citizenship development in the new era. A survey and research based on Shanghai humanities and social sciences knowledge]. Shanghai: Shanghai daxue chubanshe, 2015.

Ouyang Guangming and Si Saisai. *Chengshi wenhua rentong yu renwen suyang jianxingli fazhan* [The development of urban cultural identity and humanistic literacy practice: A comparative study based on the investigation of the cultural development of Shanghainese]. Shanghai: Shanghai daxue chubanshe, 2018.

Pan Chenguang and Wang Li. *Zhongguo rencai fazhan baogao* [The report on the development of Chinese talents]. Blue book of Chinese talents. No. 1. Beijing: Shehui kexue wenxian chubanshe, 2004.

Pan Wei and Ma Ya. *Jujiao dangdai Zhongguo jiazhiguan* [Focusing on contemporary Chinese values]. Beijing: Shenghuo dushu xinzhi sanlian shudian, 2008.

Pang Zhongying. *Quanqiuhua, fan quanqiuhua yu Zhongguo* [Globalization, anti-globalization, and China]. Shanghai: Renmin chubanshe, 2002.

Pei Changhong and Liu Yingqiu. *Ershiyi shiji zhongguo renwen shehui kexue zhanwang* [Prospects of humanities and social sciences in China in the 21st Century]. Beijing: Zhongguo shehui kexue chubanshe, 2001.

Peng Peng. *Heping jueqilun: Zhongguo chongsu daguo zhi lu* [Peaceful rising theory: The path of China in becoming a great power]. Guangzhou: Guangdong renmin chubanshe, 2005.

Pi Daojian and Lu Hong. *Yishu xin shijie—26 wei zhuming pipingjia tan Zhongguo dangdai meishu de zoushi* [New horizon of art: Twenty-six critics' comments on the trend of contemporary Chinese art]. Changsha: Hunan meishu chubanshe, 2003.

Qian Liqun and Gao Yuandong. *Zhongguo daxue de wenti yu gaige* [Problems and reform of Chinese universities]. Tianjin: Tianjin renmin chubanshe, 2003.

Qian Ning. *Liuxue Meiguo—Yige shidai de gushi* [Studying in the USA]. Nanjing: Jiangsu wenyi chubanshe, 1997.

Qianjiang wanbao xinminsheng. *Changsanjiao—xiayige taojindi* [The Yangtze River delta: The next frontier for a gold rush]. Hangzhou: Zhejiang renmin chubanshe, 2003.

Qiu Qintao. *Yi Shanghai wei zhongxin: huning, huhangyong tielu yu jindai changjiang sanjiaozhou diqu shehui bianqian* [Taking Shanghai as the center: Shanghai-Nanjing, Shanghai-Hangzhou-Ningbo Railway and the social changes in the modern Yangtze River delta]. Beijing: Zhongguo shehui kexue chubanshe, 2016.

Qiu Zhengyi. *Shanghai shishang ditu* [Fashion Map of Shanghai]. Shanghai: Hanyu dacidian chubanshe, 2002.

Ren Ping. *Shishang yu chongtu: Chengshi wenhua jiegou yu gongneng xinlun* [Fashion and clash: New theories on urban cultural structures and functions]. Nanjing: Dongnan daxue chubanshe, 2000.

Rong Yueming and Hua Jian. *Shanghai wenhua chanye fazhan baogao 2018* [Annual report on cultural industry development of Shanghai 2018]. Shanghai: Shanghai renmin chubanshe, and Shanghai shudian chubanshe, 2018.

Rong Yueming and Zheng Chongxuan. *Shanghai wenhua fazhan baogao 2017* [Annual report on cultural development of Shanghai 2017]. Beijing: Social Science Academic Press, 2017.

Ru Xin. *Xinshiqi Zhongguo zhengzhixue fazhan ershinian 1980–2000* [Development of political science in China from 1980 to 2000]. Beijing: Zhongguo shehui kexue chubanshe, 2001.

Ru Xin, Lu Xueyi, and Li Peilin. *2005 nian: Zhongguo shehui xingshi fenxi yu yuce* [Analysis and forecast on China's social development, 2005]. Blue book of China's society. Beijing: Shehui kexue wenxian chubanshe, 2004.

———. *2009 nian Zhongguo shehui xingshi fenxi yu yuce* [Society of China: Analysis and forecast of 2009]. Beijing: Shehui kexue wenxian chubanshe, 2008.

Shanghai bainian wenhuashi bianzuan weiyuanhui. *Shanghai bainian wenhuashi* [Shanghai cultural history of the 20th century]. Shanghai: Shanghai kexue jishu wenxian chubanshe, 2002.

Shanghai shehui kexueyuan qingnian xueshu jiaoliu zhongxin. *Shanghai de xiandaihua moshi: Zhidu jiangou yu chuangxin zhi lu* [The Shanghai model of modernization: The road of institutional construction and innovation]. Shanghai: Shanghai shehui kexueyuan chubanshe, 2004.

Shanghai zhengda yanjiusuo. *Changjiangbian de Zhongguo—Dashanghai guoji dushiquan jianshe yu guojia fazhan zhanlue* [China on the Yangtze River: Construction of Greater Shanghai and the National Development Strategy]. Shanghai: Xuelin chubanshe, 2003.

———. *Wenhua Shanghai—2010: Ba yige shenmeyang de Shanghai daigei Zhongguo he shijie* [Cultural Shanghai: 2010 what kind of Shanghai will be presented to China and the world]. Beijing: Renmin chubanshe, 2003.

———. *Xin Shanghairen* [New Shanghainese]. Beijing: Dongfang chubanshe, 2002.

Shanghaishi jiaoyu kexue yanjiuyuan [Shanghai Research Institute of Education]. *Hufeng meiyu bainianchao: Shanghai yu Meiguo difang jiaoyu jiaoliu* [A century of educational exchanges between Shanghai and the United States]. Shanghai: Shanghai jiaotong daxue chubanshe, 2017.

Shanghaishi renmin zhengfu fazhan yanjiu zhongxin [The Development and Research Center of the Shanghai Municipal Government], comp. *Jianshe zhuoyue de quanqiu chengshi: 2017/2018 Shanghai fazhan baogao* [Building an Excellent Global City: 2017–2018 Shanghai development report]. Shanghai: Gezhi chubanshe and Shanghai renmin chubanshe, 2018.

Shanghaishi shehui kexuejie lianhehui. *Feng cong haishang lai: Jindai Shanghai jingji de jueqi zhi lu* [The wind comes from the sea: The rise of modern Shanghai economy]. Shanghai: Shanghai renmin chubanshe, 2018.

Shanghaishi tongjiju. *Shanghai tongji nianjian—2004* [Shanghai statistical yearbook 2004]. Beijing: Zhongguo tongji chubanshe, 2004.

Shen Chunyao, Xu Anbiao, Zang Tiewei, and Liu Yunlong, ed, *Dazhi lifa: Xin Zhongguo chengli qishinian lifa licheng* [Supreme wisdom makes law-builders: 70 Years of legislative history of the People's Republic China]. Beijing: Law Press, 2019.

Shen Fuxi and Huang Guoxin. *Jianzhu yishu fengge jianshang—Shanghai jindai jianzhu saomiao* [Appreciation of architectural art: A glance at Shanghai's modern architecture]. Shanghai: Tongji daxue chubanshe, 2003.

Shen Kaiyan, Tu Qiyu, and Yang Yaqin. *Jujiao dadushi—Shanghai chengshi zonghe jingzhengli de guoji bijiao* [Focusing on cosmopolitan cities: Comprehensive comparison of competitiveness in the international arena]. Shanghai: Shanghai shehui kexueyuan chubanshe, 2001.

Shen Weibing and Jiang Ming. *Ala Shanghairen* [We are Shanghainese]. Shanghai: Fudan daxue chubanshe, 1993.

Shi Bi, *Shanghaibang de huanghun* [The dusk of the Shanghai Gang]. Hong Kong: Wenhua yishu chubanshe, 2003.

Shi Lei, Qi Ge, and Yuan Min. *Shanghairen de xingfu shenghuo* [Happy lives in Shanghai]. Shanghai: Shanghai shehui kexueyuan chubanshe, 2003.

———. *Xiang Shanghai xuexi* [Learn from Shanghai]. Shanghai: Shijiezhishi chubanshe, 2003.

Shu Kewen. *Xiangxin yishu haishi xiangxin yishujia* [To follow the arts or to follow the artists]. Beijing: Zhongguo renmin daxue chubanshe, 2003.

Shu Xincheng. *Jin dai Zhongguo liu xue shi* [History of study abroad in contemporary

China]. New edition. Shanghai: Shanghai wenhua chubanshe, 1989. The first edition was published in 1927.

Shu Fen and Zhang Xichang. *Shanghai chihewanle—Dadushi li de xiuxian shenghuo* [Eat, drink, travel and play in Shanghai: Leisure time in this metropolitan city]. Shanghai: Xuelin chubanshe, 2004.

Su Zhiliang, ed. *Shanghai: chengshi bianqian, wenming yanjin yu xiandaixing* [Shanghai: Urban change, civilization evolution and modernity]. Shanghai: Shanghai renmin chubanshe, 2011.

Sun Ganlu. *Shanghai de shijian wanou* ["Time dolls" in Shanghai]. Shanghai: Xuelin chubanshe, 2003.

Sun Jin. *Bopu yishu duanceng yu mianyan* [Pop art: Disconnection and continuity]. Changchun: Jilin meishu chubanshe, 1999.

Sun Liping. *Zhuanxing yu duanlie: Gaige yilai Zhongguo shehui jiegou de bianqian* [Transition and abruption: Changes of China's social structure in the reform era]. Beijing: Qinghua daxue chubanshe, 2004.

Sun Luyi. *Rencai zhanlue yu xiandaihua guoji dadushi* [Strategy for human resources and a modern metropolis]. Shanghai: Shanghai renmin chubanshe, 2002.

Sun Xue and Li Min, eds. *Zhongguo meng: quanqiu zuida de zhongchan jieji de jueqi jiqi yingxiang* [The Chinese Dream: The rise of the world's largest middle class and its impact]. Shanghai: Wenhui chubanshe, 2011.

Sun Zhenhua. *Zai yishu de beihou* [Inside art]. Changsha: Hunan meishu chubanshe, 2003.

Tang Jiwu and Yu Xingmin. *Fei di* [The land that flies]. Shanghai: Shanghai yuandong chubanshe, 2003.

Tang Ping. *Dushi yujing xia de Zhongguo dangdai youhua* [Chinese contemporary oil painting in urban context]. Beijing: Wenwu chubanshe, 2017.

Tang Qiancao. *Chengshi zhongchan jieceng de zhuzhai fuli yu jieceng rentong* [Residential welfare and class identity of the urban middle class]. Shanghai: Shanghai jiaotong daxue chubanshe, 2016.

Tang Yulan, *Tuozhan yu shengji—Zhongguo (Shanghai) ziyou maoyi shiyan qu jianshe jincheng yu zhanwang* [Development and upgrade: Construction process and prospects of the China (Shanghai) Pilot Free Trade Zone]. Shanghai: Shanghai renmin chubanshe, 2019.

Tang Zhenchang and Shen Hengchun. *Shanghai shi* [History of Shanghai]. Shanghai: Shanghai renmin chubanshe, 1989.

Tian Zhengping. *Liuxuesheng yu Zhongguo jiaoyu xiandaihua* [Foreign educated students and contemporary Chinese education]. Guangzhou: Guangdong jiaoyu chubanshe, 1996.

Wan Fei and Wang Qiangbin. *Zhongguo gaoxiao fenbu yu gaikuang* [A survey of the distribution of China's higher educational institutions]. Guangzhou: Guangdongsheng ditu chubanshe, 2003.

Wang Anyi. *Xunzhao Shanghai* [Searching for Shanghai]. Shanghai: Xuelin chubanshe, 2001.

Wang Depei, *Zhongguo jingji 2020: Bainian yiyu zhi dabianju* [China's Economy 2020: The transformation that occurs once in a century]. Beijing: Zhonggo youyi chuban gongsi, 2020.

Wang Jianping, Gu Chengwei, and Yang Yaowu. *Shanghai keji rencai fazhan yanjiu baogao 2017* [Research report on the development of Shanghai human resources in science and technology 2017]. Shanghai: Shanghai renmin chubanshe, 2016.

Wang Licheng. *Meiguo wenhuashentou yu jindai Zhongguo jiaoyu—Hujiang daxue de lishi* [American cultural penetration and the modern education of China: A history of the University of Shanghai]. Shanghai: Fudan daxue chubanshe, 2001.

Wang Ming, Liu Guohan, and He Jianyu. *Zhongguo shetuan gaige—Cong zhengfu xuanze dao shehui xuanze* [Reform of social organizations in China: From government choices to social choices]. Beijing: Shehui kexue wenxian chubanshe, 2001.

Wang Ning, ed. *Quanqiuhua yu wenhua: Xifang yu Zhongguo* [Globalization and culture: The West and China]. Beijing: Beijing daxue chubanshe, 2002.

Wang Qian. *Biena Shanghairen shuo shier* [Don't take the Shanghainese too seriously]. Beijing: Zhongguo youyi chuban gongsi, 2003.

Wang Qisheng. *Zhongguo liuxuesheng de lishi guiji, 1872–1947* [Historical track of foreign-educated students in China]. Wuhan: Hubei jiaoyu chubanshe, 1992.

Wang Wei, Zhang Qingjie, and Xu Zihan, eds, *Zhuanzhedian: Zhongguo dangdai yishu sishi nian* [Turning point: 40 years of Chinese contemporary art]. Shanghai: Shanghai wenhua chubanshe, 2018.

Wang Yaohua. *Zhexienian, wo jingli de Shanghai shuzhan* [Shanghai Book Fairs that I have experienced in these years]. Shanghai: Shanghai shudian chubanshe, 2016.

Wang Yuechuan. "90 niandai Zhongguo xianfeng yishu de tuozhan yu kunjing." [The expansion and dilemma of Chinese avant-garde art in the 1990s]. *Wenyi yanjiu* [Literature and Art Studies], no. 5 (1999): 4–18.

Wei Daozhi and Zhang Jie. *Zhongwai jiaoyu jiaoliushi* [A Chinese-foreign exchange history of education]. Changsha: Hunan jiaoyu chubanshe, 1998.

Wu Chenrong. *Wuwei xianfeng—Shanghai xinshengdai feizhuliu meishu xianxiang wenhua toushi* [The fearless vanguard: A cultural perspective on the new generation of non-mainstream artists in Shanghai]. Shanghai: Shanghai shudian chubanshe, 2003.

Wu Daqi. *2016 nian Shanghai guoji jinrong zhongxin jianshe lanpishu* [Blue book on building the Shanghai international finance center 2016]. Shanghai: Shanghai renmin chubanshe, 2016.

Wu Hung, ed. *Dangdai yishu de shijian: meishuguan shoucang yu yanjiu* [Practices in contemporary art: Museum, collections and research]. Guangzhou: Lingnan meishu chubanshe, 2014.

———, ed. *Shoucangjia yu meishuguan: Shanghai Yu Deyao meishuguan choubei zhuanji* [Collectors and art museums: Special issue on the planning and opening of the Yuz Museum, Shanghai]. Guangzhou: Lingnan meishu chubanshe, 2013.

Wu Jing. *Shanghai weixingcheng guihua* [Shanghai satellite city planning.]. Shanghai: Shanghai daxue chubanshe, 2016.

Xiao Lin. *Shanghai 2050 quanqiu chengshi chuangxin yu sheji: Lianheguo dierjie shijie chengshiri quanqiu chengshi luntan shilu* [Shanghai 2050 innovation and design of global city: The record of global city forum on the second UN world cities day]. Shanghai: Gezhi chubanshe, and Shangahi renmin chubanshe, 2016.

Xiao Rikui. *Jieceng de wenhua weidu: wenhua ziben yu zhongchan jieji yanjiu—jiyu woguo Shanghai he Taiwan diqu de diaocha shuju* [Cultural dimension of class: A study of cultural capital and middle class basing on survey data in Shanghai and Taiwan]. Beijing: Jingji guanli chubanshe, 2018.

Xie Liping. ed. *Shanghai gaige kaifang shihua* [History of Shanghai's reform and opening up]. Shanghai: Shanghai renmin chubanshe, 2018.

Xie Liping, Huang Jian and Sun Baoxi, *Shanghai wenhua jianshe sanshi nian* [The 30-year cultural development of Shanghai]. Shanghai: Shanghai renmin chubanshe, 2008.

Xin Ping. *Cong Shanghai faxian lishi—Xiandaihua jinchengzhong de Shanghairen jiqi shehui shenghuo* [Discovering history from Shanghai: Shanghainese and their social life in the process of modernization]. Shanghai: Shanghai renmin chubanshe, 1996.

Xiong Yuezhi. *Xixue dongjian yu wan Qing shehui* [The dissemination of Western learning and the late Qing society]. Shanghai: Shanghai renmin chubanshe, 1994.

———, Ma Xueqiang, and Yan Kejia. *Shanghai de waiguoren, 1942–1949* [Foreigners in Shanghai 1942–1949]. Shanghai: Shanghai guji chubanshe, 2003.

Xiong Yuezhi and Gaogang Bowen. *Toushi lao Shanghai* [An analysis of Old Shanghai]. Shanghai: Shanghai shehui kexueyuan chubanshe, 2004.

Xiong Yuezhi and Zhou Wu. *Haina baichuan: Shanghai chengshi jingshen yanjiu* [The sea that embraces thousands of rivers: Study of the Shanghai spirit]. Shanghai: Shanghai renmin chubanshe, 2003.

———. *Haiwai Shanghaixue* [Shanghai studies in the world]. Shanghai: Shanghai guji chubanshe, 2004.

Xiong Yuezhi and others. *Shanghai tong shi* [General history of Shanghai]. Volume 14. Shanghai: Shanghai renmin chubanshe, 1999.

Xu Deming, ed. *Shanghai fazhan zhi hun—Shanghai chengshi jingshen wencui* [The spirit of Shanghai's development]. Shanghai: Wenhui chubanshe, 2004.

Xu Deming, Chen Zhenmin, and He Jiliang. *Shanghai fazhan zhi hun: Shanghai chengshi jingshen wencui* [The spirit of urban development in Shanghai]. Shanghai: Wenhui chubanshe, 2004.

Xu Jiang and Li Xiangyang. *Dushi yingzao—2002 Shanghai shuangnian zhan* [Urban creation: The 2002 Shanghai Biennial Guide]. Shanghai: Shanghai Museum of Art, 2002.

Xu Jiangang, Yan Aiyun, and Guo Ji. *Shanghai gaige kaifang sanshi nian* [The 30-year reform and opening of Shanghai]. Shanghai: Shanghai renmin chubanshe, 2008.

Xu Meifang. *Quanqiu jingzheng geju xia de guoji jinrong zhongxin jianshe: Shanghai tansuo yu shijian* [International Financial Center construction under the global competitive situation: Shanghai exploration and practicee]. Shanghai: Shanghai renmin chubanshe, 2019.

Xu Xixian and Xu Jianrong. *Baibian Shanghai* [A changing Shanghai]. Shanghai: Shanghai people's fine art publishing house, 2004.

Xu Zhen. *1199 ge ren: Long meishuguan shoucangzhan* [1199 people: Collection from the Long Museum]. Shanghai: Gezhi chubanshe, Shanghai renmin chubanshe, 2019.

Xue Hongyan. *Shanghai, 9+1!—Zoujin Suzhouhe yishujia* [Shanghai, 9+1!: Getting to know Suzhou creek artists]. Shanghai: Shanghai renmin chubanshe, 2005.

Yan Ming. *Yimen xueke yu yige shidai—Shehuixue zai Zhongguo* [An academic field and an era: Sociology in China]. Beijing: Qinghua daxue chubanshe, 2004.

Yang Dongping. *Chengshi jifeng: Beijing he Shanghai de wenhua jingshen* [City monsoon: The cultural spirit of Beijing and Shanghai]. Beijing: Dongfang Press, 1994.

Yang Liuxin. *Renli ziben yu Zhongguo xiandaihua: Zhongguo renli ziben chengzhang moshi yanjiu* [Human resources and China's modernization: Studies of the growth model of China's human resources]. Jinan: Shandong University Press, 2003.

Yang Wei. *Sishiyi ge ren* [Forty-one people]. Changsha: Hunan meishu chubanshe, 2012.

Yang Xiong and Tao Xidong. *Shanghai minsheng minyi baogao* 2017 [2017 survey of livelihood of Shanghai residents]. Shanghai: Shanghai renmin chubanshe, 2017.

Yang Xiong and Zhou Haiwang. *Shanghai lanpishu: Shanghai shehui fazhan baogao* [Blue book of Shanghai: Annual report on social development of Shanghai 2019]. Shanghai: Shanghai shudian chubanshe & Shanghai renmin chubanshe, 2019.

Yang Zhijiang and Qi Kang. *Dangdai yishu shiyezhong de jianzhu* [Architecture seen through the lens of contemporary art]. Nanjing: Dongnan daxue chubanshe, 2003.

Yang Zukun and Zeng Hua. *Binfen Shanghai* [Colorful Shanghai]. Shanghai: Fudan daxue chubanshe, 2003.

Ye Juelin. *Shanghai siren hualang* [Shanghai's private galleries]. Vol. 2. Shanghai: Shanghai kexuejishu wenxian chubanshe, 2002.

Ye Qing and Shi Jiansan. *Shanghai fazhi fazhan baogao 2015* [Annual report on development of rule of law in Shanghai 2015]. Beijing: Shehui kexue wenxian chubanshe, 2015.

Ye Xin. *Shanghai zhuan* [The biography of Shanghai]. Beijing: Xinxing chubanshe, 2018.

Yin Jizuo. *2002 nian Shanghai shehui baogaoshu* [Report on Shanghai society in 2002]. Shanghai: Shanghai shehui kexueyuan chubanshe, 2002.

———. *2003 nian Shanghai fazhan lanpishu—Wenhua fazhan yu guoji dadushi jianshe* [A cultural development bluebook of Shanghai, 2003—cultural development and construction of an international metropolis]. Shanghai: Shanghai shehui kexueyuan chubanshe, 2002.

Yu Keming. *Xiandai Shanghai yanjiu luncong* [The series on studies of contemporary Shanghai]. Vol. 6. Shanghai: Shanghai shudian chubanshe, 2008.

Yu Keping. *Quanqiuhua yu zhengzhi fazhan* [Globalization and political development]. Beijing: Shehui kexue wenxian chubanshe, 2003.

———. *Zhongguo gongminshehui de xingqi yu zhili de bianqian* [The emerging of civil society and its significance for governance in reform China]. Beijing: Shehui kexuewenxian chubanshe, 2002.

Yu Qiuyu. *Wenhua kulü* [The bitter travel of culture]. Shanghai: Zhishi Press, 1992.

Yu Tianbai. *Shanghai: xingge ji mingyun* [Shanghai: Her character is her destiny]. Shanghai: Wenyi Press, 1992.

Yu Zhi. *Modeng Shanghai* [Modern Shanghai]. Shanghai: Shanghai shudian chubanshe, 2003.

Yuan Zhiping, Cui Guiling, and Guo Ji. *Shanghai shehui fazhan sanshi nian* [The 30-year social development in Shanghai]. Shanghai: Shanghai renmin chubanshe, 2008.

Zeng Jianjun. *Sansetu—Lümei zhiqing de gushi* [The land with three colors: Stories of the "sent-down youths" who currently study in the United States]. Shanghai: Wenhui chubanshe, 2001.

Zhai Mo. *Rongchuang shidai: Dangdai yishu shouji* [The era of convergence and innovation: The chronicle of contemporary art]. Beijing: Renmin meishu chubanshe, 2002.

Zhang Shuanggu, Deng Guangdong, Guan Xiaoqun, and Zhu Guoliang. *Zhongguo bainian liuxue jingyingzhuan* [Biographies of foreign-educated Chinese elites for the past 100 years]. Vol. 6. Nanchang: Baihuazhou wenyi chubanshe, 2002.

Zhang Shuanggu and Jiang Bo. *Chuguo liuxue gongzuo 20 nian* [A review of foreign studies over the past 20 years]. Beijing: Gaodeng jiaoyu chubanshe, 1999.

Zhang Yongbin, Nian Shiping, Jia Yan, Sun Baoxi, and Cui Guilin, *Shanghai kejiao fazhan sanshi nian* [The 30-science and technology development in Shanghai]. Shanghai: Shanghai renmin chubanshe, 2008.

Zhang Wei. *Chongtu yu bianshu—Zhongguo shehui zhongjian jieceng zhengzhi fenxi* [Conflict and uncertainty: Political analysis of middle stratum in Chinese society]. Beijing: Shehui kexue wenxian chubanshe, 2005.

Zhang Weitian. *Guigu taojin—Zhongguo liuxuesheng de chuangye gushi* [Gold rush in the Silicon Valley: Adventures of Chinese students]. Shanghai: Shanghai renmin chubanshe, 2001.

Zhang Xiaochun. *Xingzou Shanghai* [Discovering Shanghai]. Shanghai: Shanghai wenhua chubanshe, 2002.

Zhang Xiaoling. *Guannian yishu jiegou yu chongjian de shixue* [Conceptual arts: The rhyme of deconstruction and reconstruction]. Changchun: Jilin meishu chubanshe, 1999.

Zhang Xiaoming. *Hou Jiang Zemin shidai de Zhongguo xinzheng zhinang* [Think tanks for China's new deal in the the post-Jiang Zemin era]. Hong Kong: Gonghe chuban, 2004.

Zhang Yu and Shen Min. *Shufa zhuyi* [Calligraphism]. Changsha: Hunan meishu chubanshe, 2003.

Zheng Yongnian, *Da qushi: Zhongguo xiayibu* [Mega trends: China's next move]. Beijing: Dongfang chubanshe, 2019.

Zhongguo jingji xinxishe, and Xinhua tongxunshe Shanghai fenshe. *Haipai jiangxin: duihua guoqi lingdao* [Haipai spirit: Dialoguing with leaders of state-owned enterprises]. Shanghai: Shanghai renmin chubanshe, 2017.

Zhou Weizhong and Sun Hongkang. *Shanghai gaige kaifang 40 nian: naxienian, women de gushi* [Our stories in the 40 years of reform and opening up in Shanghai]. Shanghai: Shanghai renmin chubanshe, 2018.

Zhou Wu, ed, *Shijie de Zhongguo: Haiwai Zhongguoxue yanjiu huiwang yu qianzhan* [China in the eyes of the world: A retrospective and reflection on the future of overseas Chinese studies]. Shanghai: Shanghai shehui kexueyuan chubanshe, 2019.

Zhou Xiaohong and others. *Zhongguo zhongchan jieji diaocha* [A survey of the Chinese middle class]. Beijing: Shehui kexue wenxian chubanshe, 2005.

Zhou Yaohong. *Zhongguo shehui zhongjie zuzhi* [The intermediary organizations of the Chinese society]. Shanghai: Shanghai jiaotong daxue chubanshe, 2008.

Zhou Zhenhua, Chen Xiangming, and Huang Jianfu, eds. *Shijie chengshi yu Shanghai fazhan* [World city: International experiences and Shanghai's development]. Shanghai: Shanghai shehui kexueyuan chubanshe, 2004.

Zhu Hua. *Shanghai yibai nian* [One hundred years of Shanghai's history]. Shanghai: Shanghai renmin chubanshe, 1999.

Zhu Qi. *1990 nian yilai de Zhongguo xianfeng sheying* [Chinese avant-garde photography since 1990]. Changsha: Hunan meishu chubanshe, 2004.

INDEX